"Rilke goes on speaking to us, for us, and for his own rare self. Polikoff's generous journey through a life's work demonstrates the poet's ultimate affirmation and may transform your sense of what it means to fully honor the soul."

JOHN FELSTINER, author of *Translating Neruda: The Way to Macchu Picchu, Paul Celan: Poet, Survivor, Jew,* and *Can Poetry Save the Earth? A Field Guide to Nature Poems*

"The best study on Rilke I have read in English. . . . A superb piece of academic scholarship and much more. . . . This book offers an education not only in Rilke and Hillman, but also in what soul-making means in a person's life."

LUDWIG FISCHER, Wilamette University, producer of *In the Temple of Listening: The Poetic Vision of Rainer Maria Rilke*

"This book is a masterpiece that will change your vision of Rilke's poetry and inner journey forever. Rilke is the Rumi of western civilization, an indispensable guide to the deepest mysteries of inner transformation. It is the peculiar greatness of this book to offer us at last a luminous and comprehensive map of Rilke's life and work, and to provide us with readings of his poems that lift us into the atmosphere of their majesty and truth."

ANDREW HARVEY, author of *Song of the Sun: The Life, Poetry & Teachings of Rumi* and *The Hope: A Guide to Sacred Activism*

Also by Daniel Joseph Polikoff

POETRY

Dragon Ship

The Hands of Stars

TRANSLATION

Parzival/Gawain: Two Plays
an edited translation of *Der Gral* by A. M. Miller

In the Image of Orpheus

RILKE

A Soul History

Daniel Joseph Polikoff

Chiron Publications | 2011

2011
Chiron Publications
P.O. Box 68, Wilmette, Illinois 60091
www.chironpublications.com

Book and cover design: William Jens Jensen
Cover image: Copyright © Swiss National Library (used by permission)
Excerpts used by permission: see page 739 for souces.

Library of Congress Cataloging-in-Publication Data

Polikoff, Daniel J. (Daniel Joseph)
In the image of Orpheus : Rilke : a soul history / Daniel Joseph Polikoff.
p. cm.
Includes index.
ISBN 978-1-888602-52-4
1. Rilke, Rainer Maria, 1875–1926—Criticism and interpretation.
2. Rilke, Rainer Maria, 1875–1926—Spiritualistic interpretations.
3. Spirituality in literature. 4. Jung, C. G. (Carl Gustav), 1875–1961.
I. Title.
PT2635.I65P65 2011
831'.912—dc22

2010052650

CONTENTS

BOOK TWO LOVE'S LABORS: Paris to Muzot

ACKNOWLEDGMENTS

The seed of this book may be found in a talk I gave at the Festival of Archetypal Psychology at the University of Notre Dame in 1992, but the extended series of Rilke workshops I offered in Marin County beginning in 2003 provided the impetus for its writing. I am unendingly grateful to Rose Black for suggesting and organizing the sessions that nourished the soul of this work. Likewise, my heartfelt thanks go to Richard Brown for hosting so many of those gatherings at his beautiful Kentfield home, and indeed to all the many participants (including Margaret Kaufman, who graciously hosted the series' launch) over the years who contributed so much thought and heart to our shared engagement with Rilke.

Andrew Harvey was the first to read the whole text—or rather, what was the whole text before he gently bullied me into "beefing up" the section on Rilke's *Elegies*. As Andrew predicted, the new chapters that resulted greatly strengthened the book. Thereafter, Andrew helped find this book's publisher. I remain deeply indebted to his brilliant intelligence and contagious passion.

Let me extend my deep thanks as well to the vanguard of dedicated readers who, following in Andrew's footsteps, lent precious time and attention to this literary project—most especially David St. John, John Felstiner, Richard Tarnas, and Ludwig Fischer. Their informed and critical encouragement proved invaluable to the book's nascent career.

It is my pleasure, too, to tender many, many heartfelt thanks to Curdin Ebneter, director of the Fondation Rilke in Sierre, Switzerland, for all his multifaceted and invaluable assistance: supplying crucial photographs; tirelessly sharing his encyclopedic knowledge of Rilke to identify various source references; and making available Erich Unglaub's valuable Petrarch essay at the eleventh hour.

The images used in the book derive from multiple sources, and I would like to extend special thanks to Beata C. Arnold at the Barkenhoff Stiftung

/ Heinrich Vogeler Museum for her generous aid in securing Worpswede-related images; Ephraim Rosenstein of the Ludwig von Hofmann Nachlass for his kind help with the Hofmann images; and Tanja Fengler-Weit at the German Literary Archive in Marbach as well as the staff at the Swiss National Library for their help in supplying the photographs that grace the book, inside and out.

It was, however, Dr. Renata Scharffenberg who helped me (among other things) avoid the egregious error of using "Rilke's death mask" as a cover image. (She informed me that—whoever may be depicted in the death mask photo once found in the Insel archive—it is not Rilke!) Thanks to Dr. Klaus Bohnenkamp for his help in identifying the source of the Hofmannnsthal citation that furnishes my first chapter's first sentence.

I would like to extend my gratitude as well to James Hillman, the man as well as the brilliant intellectual pioneer. My profound debt to him is inscribed in every sentence of this book. Ralph Freedman's fine biography provided a foundation for my own work, and neither this book nor my Rilke workshops could have moved confidently forward without Edward Snow's epic labors as a translator. Thanks also to Anita Barrows and Joanna Macy for providing a *Book of Hours* that so powerfully translates Rilke's seminal vision into a modern idiom, and to Laura Kramer for graciously granting permission to cite her father's translation of Rilke's *Visions of Christ.*

Nathan Schwarz-Salant at Chiron welcomed the book, and provided unfailing support and kind guidance through the long publication process. Sarah Gallogly performed her Herculean editing tasks with indefatigable commitment and sterling skill; Jens Jensen provided expert work on the book's design with friendly conscientiousness. I would also like to thank Richard Grossinger at North Atlantic Books for his valuable encouragement and understanding.

Lastly, I wish to thank my family for their unfailing support over the years: my author-parents (Alexander and Barbara Polikoff), who inaugurated my own soul history and are still there every step of the way; my sisters, nephews, and in-laws of various sorts for their interest as well as all the Rilke books sent from abroad; and, lastly, my wife, Monika, and my children, Allason and Hyden, for honoring the untold hours the project required. It is their love and forbearance that buoys this book, belying Rilke's own fears concerning the incompatibility of Life and Art.

FOR MONIKA

partner in translation

The soul: what dubious questions concerning it admit of solution, or where we must abide our doubt—with, at least, the gain of recognizing the problem that confronts us—this is matter well worth attention. On what subject can we more reasonably expend the time required by minute discussion and investigation?

—Plotinus, *The Enneads*
(trans. Stephen MacKenna)

INTRODUCTION

Rainer Maria Rilke has long been considered a poet of singular significance, and (if the steady stream of new translations and commentaries proves any indication) critical interest in his life and work appears at a high-water mark today. Yet it is not only the professional literati who read Rilke. Since the publication of his *Das Stunden-Buch* (*The Book of Hours*) just over one hundred years ago, the poet has commanded a wide popular audience, and today one frequently finds multiple copies of this same work in an attractive new translation[1] on the bookstore shelf. People have long hungered for Rilke's words, and the appetite remains keen. What may be the reason for Rilke's compelling and durable appeal?

No good one, some would claim, for the poet, now as always, does have his detractors. A brief essay by J. D. McClatchy in *Poetry* magazine begins with a sardonic nod to Rilke's unique stature among poets:

> Every trade has its patron saint, and if butchers and silversmiths, why not poets? Since I can remember, poetry's patron saint—revered and invoked—has been Rainer Maria Rilke.[2]

. . . before listing the lamentable affectations and pretensions that fit Rilke out to be "the favorite of fledglings." McClatchy's caricature of Rilke's aesthetic and moral foibles includes his "being passionate about 'spirituality,'" and when, at the end of his brief essay, McClatchy queries the reason for Rilke's high repute, he returns to this theme:

> Part of the problem, I suspect, is marketing. Rilke is now sold as "wisdom literature." It is hardly surprising that one of Rilke's most prominent recent translators, Stephen Mitchell, went on to offer versions of mystical poetry, along with the Tao.[3]

His evident scorn notwithstanding, McClatchy has, I think, hit upon a crucial point. While McClatchy, the urbane humanist, may be thoroughly cynical about Rilke's "spirituality," I would propose that it is precisely this—in conjunction with Rilke's lyric genius—that draws readers to him like a magnet.

Of course, to attribute Rilke's appeal to his peculiar "spirituality" says very little. The meaning of the word itself remains, at best, somewhat mysterious; at worst (as McClatchy's scare quotes imply), it is a portentous cipher signifying nothing. Fortunately, others have ventured out upon these troubled waters and speculated upon the content of the spirit in specific relation to art. In a 1999 address in Berkeley ("Raiding the Inarticulate: A Talk on Poetry and Spirituality"), Robert Hass explored the "connections between poetry and spiritual life," and I will take his provocative remarks as a point of departure for my own.

Religion and its institutions provide an official place, an established cultural domain, for pursuit of the spiritual life and so frequently condition our sense of the nature of spirituality. Yet Hass (who was raised Catholic but later became estranged from the church) declares that, in his own experience, "spirituality was in some ways the opposite of everything that got cultivated by being a member of a religious community." Understanding religion as "communal worship, a community gathered around commonly held symbols of the sacred," Hass foregrounds the social conformity—the prescription of belief and behavior—that such worship characteristically demands, and states:

> For me, the content of spirituality was almost always everything in me that rebelled against whatever the pattern of being a socially approved and good person was.... And...what drew me to poetry—the way in which I could say to myself it was spiritual—was that it was connected to that sense of rebellion and wonder.
>
> I found myself thinking...spirituality is the private relationship to the mystery of being alive, which for me was so much connected with rebellion...with suffering...with resistance to the public self.[4]

Further on, Hass tries to elaborate more fully and concretely his sense of the spiritual:

> The term that came to me for spirituality...is that certain kinds of experience are "numinous." And I liked that word because it has philosophical echoes to do with feeling like you're in the presence of the thing itself, which cannot be named, and also because it's

> connected to "luminous," that there's a quality of light about that kind of experience.
>
> And numinosity can be connected, on the one hand, to erotic passion; on the other hand, to intense grief; it can be connected to the presence of a liberating and terrifying ignorance, and helplessness. And it's often accompanied in the spiritual traditions that interest me by an awakened sense of absence.[5]

Experiences of light and the presence of the thing itself are quintessentially *objective* characteristics, inherently distinct from (even while perhaps "connected to") powerful personal emotion. Not so all Hass describes in that second paragraph: erotic passion, grief, and terrifying helplessness are, on the contrary, epitomes of intensely subjective experience. That Hass can—in one train of thought—associate spirituality with *both* a heightened sense of "presence" *and* "an awakened sense of absence" reveals the deeply paradoxical ground upon which his sense of spirituality rests.

Such contradiction hardly invalidates Hass's line of thought, but it does plead for further and more detailed elucidation of the differences internal to his experience of spirituality. What is the nature of that all-important "connection" between (on the one hand) numinosity, luminosity, and objective presence and (on the other) passion, grief, terror, ignorance, liberation, helplessness, and absence? And can all this really be usefully ranged under the single rubric of "the spiritual"?

These questions are material not only to Hass's spirituality but to Rilke's as well, for even the casual reader of Rilke will realize that most of Hass's terms prove potently relevant to that subject. What are the famous *Dinggedichte* of the *New Poems* but poetic attempts to register the presence of "the thing itself"? What poet has drawn more deeply from the fathomless wells of grief ("Far too much you belong to grief") and erotic love ("when the longing comes over you, sing the great lovers"); which more powerfully evoked the sense of the human being's terrifying helplessness in the face of a numinous truth?

> Who, if I cried out, would hear me among the angelic
> orders? And even if one of them
> suddenly took me to heart: I'd be destroyed
> by his more powerful being....[6]

Finally, who has felt more deeply that "awakened sense of absence" than the poet who, by his own account, stopped writing in German because the language offered no word which conveyed the meaning of the French term *absence* "in the great *positive* sense that Valéry has stamped upon it"?[7]

Still—*can* all that Hass describes as characteristic of or connected to the "numinous" be *unambiguously* signified by the term "spiritual"? Another writer—the one who will be our chief guide as we plumb the labyrinthine complexities of Rilke's life and work—would probably answer in the negative. In fact, James Hillman, founder of the school of archetypal psychology, would likely see the tensions inherent in Hass's formulation as symptomatic of a fundamental confusion that has conditioned the ground of western culture for a thousand years or more, a confusion originally born not of ignorance, but of conscious and determined ideology. For what is missing in Hass's discussion of spirituality is the term Hillman places at the center of his psychology, his broad-ranging revisioning of the aims and means of western culture, namely, *soul*—especially in the sense in which this term must be comprehended as specifically *distinct* from spirit.

For some background on Hillman's position, let us turn to the opening of his landmark essay "Peaks and Vales: The Soul/Spirit Distinction as Basis for the Differences between Psychotherapy and Spiritual Discipline," initially delivered as a talk in San Francisco thirty years ago.

> Long ago and far away..., there took place in Byzantium, in the city of Constantinople, in the year 869, a Council of the Principals of the Holy Catholic Church, and because of their session then and another one of their sessions a hundred years prior (Nicaea, 787), we are all in this room tonight.
>
> Because at that Council in Constantinople the soul lost its dominion. Our anthropology, our idea of human nature, devolved from a tripartite cosmos of spirit, soul, and body (or matter), to a dualism of spirit (or mind) and body (or matter). And this because at that other Council, the one in Nicaea in 787, images were deprived of their inherent authenticity.
>
> We are in this room this evening because we are moderns in search of a soul, as Jung once put it. We are still in search of reconstituting that third place, that intermediate realm of psyche—from which we were exiled by theological, spiritual men more than a

> thousand years ago: long before Descartes and the dichotomies attributed to him, long before the Enlightenment and modern positivism and scientism. These ancient historical events are responsible for the malnourished root of our psychological culture and of the culture of each of our souls.
>
> What the Constantinople Council did to soul only culminated a long process beginning with Paul, the Saint, of substituting and disguising, and forever after confusing, soul with spirit.[8]

Hillman's words offer a means of parsing the contradictions implicit in Hass's discourse. Even as Hass resolutely distances himself from the dictates of any church council by iconoclastically construing "spirituality" in opposition to religious worship, his language and thought remain molded by the fiat of Constantinople and its historical consequences. Firstly, because the term that represents the human search for true value—that stands *against* materialism and all its ethical concomitants, and appears conjoined with "poetry" in Hass's title—is taken directly and exclusively from the realm of spirit. We have no term that signifies the dominion of "soul" (what Hillman would call our "psychological culture") the way "spirituality" signifies the dominion of spirit. Our language and culture is so shaped that any word we might suggest ("soulfulness," for instance) rings quaint and even trivial. Furthermore, once Hass takes "spirituality" as his explicit subject, it is the qualities of spirit—the "numinous," the "luminous," and "presence"—that naturally define the center of his attention even while all the manifold manifestations of soul that underlie the spiritual experience—grief, erotic passion, terror, helplessness, loss—are subordinated, named as various subjective qualities "connected to" spiritual experience, but not the thing itself.

To be sure, the dynamics of soul and spirit incessantly *interweave.* Nonetheless, the general tenor of Hass's argument as well as its crucial moments of critical obscurity[9] reveal his discourse to be implicated in the cultural habit Hillman so vigorously prosecutes, that inveterate practice—promoted if not inaugurated by the Bible—of "substituting and disguising, and forever after confusing, soul with spirit."

This suppression, while it impinges upon and shapes most every aspect of western civilization, naturally nests most securely in the religious culture that worded it—the dominant theology that shapes the terms of the spiritual lives of even those who (like Hass) define themselves in opposition to its established institutions. In fact, Hillman sees religion itself, as we know and experience it in the West, to be founded upon this rock:

> Religion in our culture derives from the spirit rather than from soul, and so our culture does not have a religion that reflects psychology or is mainly concerned with soul-making. Instead we have a psychology that reflects religion.[10]

Is it not possible that what someone like Hass (whose "spiritual" terms are so closely "connected to" and indeed ultimately dependent upon qualities of soul) is really looking for outside the church is in fact a "spirituality" that more fully honors the soul?—a spirituality, that is, which might work to transform the manifold moral, psychological, and practical effects that flow from its historic subordination?

Rilke, like Hass, was raised Catholic. His mother's fervent piety proved one of the most powerful forces shaping Rilke's personality and poetic disposition. Rilke's own spirituality—again, like Hass's—developed in good measure in the form of a rebellion against his inherited (and initially willingly absorbed) Catholicism. Just how vital this wrestling with the angels and devils of Christianity was to Rilke is not always fully appreciated. In many ways, the twenty-one-year-old poet's *Visions of Christ* initiated his original poetic career (even as it proved a means of introduction to the woman—Lou Andreas-Salomé—who would change his life), and the same astonishing burst of inspiration that crowned it with his famous *Elegies* and *Sonnets* produced, simultaneously, another intensely antagonistic dialogue with Christianity. In "The Young Workman's Letter," Rilke—in the persona of the young workman—inveighs against the social norms of Christian culture in terms that parallel Hass's:

> They have made a métier out of Christian living, a bourgeois occupation.... Everything that they do of themselves, in harmony with their insuppressible nature (in so far as they are still alive), is a contradiction of this strange situation.[11]

He then proceeds to provide an impassioned indictment of the general cultural effect of the spirit-matter dualism that structures conventional Christian belief:

> In their zeal, they do not hesitate to make this life, which should be an object of desire and trust for us, bad and worthless—and so

> they hand over the earth more and more to those who are ready to gain at least temporary and quickly won profit from it, vain and suspect as it is, and no good for anything better. This increasing exploitation of life, is it not a result of the century-old denial of the worth of this world? What folly to direct our thoughts to a Beyond, when we are surrounded here by tasks and expectations and future prospects! What deceit to misappropriate pictures of present delight in order to sell them behind our backs to heaven! Oh! the impoverished earth ought long ago to have called in all these loans which have been drawn on its happiness so that the Hereafter might be adorned with them.[12]

"The Young Workman's Letter" is not merely a polemic against inherited forms of belief; it seeks, too, to sketch valuative alternatives. While still indentured to the dualistic cosmology it laments, the letter's language depends not merely upon reversing the values traditionally accorded to our *spiritual* heaven and *material* earth, but to figures, images, and arguments that result from the intervention of that third, mediating term—the soul.[13] This contributes essentially to the special power of not only the "The Young Workman's Letter," but also the *Elegies* and *Sonnets* and, in fact, all Rilke's major work. Indeed, it is my hypothesis that the extraordinary depth and breadth of interest in Rilke flows from just this source; that so many moderns in search of a soul hunger for Rilke because this writer's poetic vision engages the leviathan force of our dominant religious tradition but effectively transforms it into what might be understood as a soul-based spirituality, something akin to Hillman's vision of "a religion that reflects psychology or is mainly concerned with soul-making." That, at any rate, is the argument of this book, and to substantiate and elaborate it I endeavor to read Rilke—the lines of his life and, more consistently, his poetic oeuvre—through the critical lens of Hillman's archetypal psychology.

From a theoretical standpoint alone, there is good reason to presume a fertile confluence between Rilke's life work and the thought-stream that feeds archetypal psychology, for poetry and psychology spring from and return to one and the same source: that historically excluded "third term," *soul*. Archetypal psychology, by definition, takes the soul as its central subject as well as the ultimate author of its insight. Moreover, the soul is—according to Hillman at least—inherently and essentially poetic.

Hillman uses the term "soul" more or less synonymously with the Greek term "psyche" and understands the intermediary realm of soul or psyche to be the realm of *image*—that liminal realm between spirit and body, universal idea and material particular, supersensible and sensible form. Hillman founds his psychology—his attempt to articulate the logic, or logos, of the soul—upon the primacy of the image. This is why, in his mind, the Nicaean Council's radical restriction of the power of image inevitably prepared and predicted the later Council's epochal metaphysical erasure. Hillman, moreover, construes the archetypal idea of image to be intrinsically poetic in nature:

> I am working toward a psychology of soul that is based in a psychology of image. Here I am suggesting both a poetic basis of mind and a psychology that starts ... in the processes of the imagination.[14]

In this, Hillman deliberately follows C. G. Jung, who states: "Every psychic process is an image and an imaging," and explicitly clarifies that his term "image" does not connote the reflection of an object but is drawn "from poetic usage, namely a figure of fancy or fantasy image."[15]

Granted these poetic premises, it is logical that the vocabulary of archetypal psychology might help illuminate the poetic art of such a consummate image-maker as Rilke, whose muse, more and more, came to dwell in that double, in-between realm—that *metaxy* that is the abode of image and imagining—until the Orphic voice of the *Sonnets* declares:

> Even when the reflecting pool
> blurs, and is dumb:
> know the image.
>
> Only in the realm of the dual
> do voices first become
> mild, eternal.[16]

The presumption of a deep link between Rilke's art and the fount of psychology can draw upon biographical as well as theoretical and textual evidence. Rilke's life and work were, from the beginning, ineluctably entwined with intellectual historical developments that signaled the surfacing of psyche, the (re)emerging of the soul to consciousness. Rilke was born in the same year (1875) as the great godfather of archetypal psychology, C. G. Jung, and his formative years coincided with those of the professional field of psychology itself. When he met Lou Andreas-Salomé (who was later to become a colleague and confidante of Freud's) in 1897, he encountered, through her, ideas about psychology, religion, and art that revolutionized his thinking.

Nor did the relevant intersection end there, though Rilke did not always maintain so positive a relation to the representatives of psychology's spreading influence. It may well be that the poet's difficult decision *not* to enter psychoanalysis in January 1912 played a role in triggering the conception of his *Duino Elegies*, which were begun just days after that decision was reached. Scarcely less than his instructive letters to Lou, the *Elegies*—especially the Third—reveal Rilke wrestling with the tenets of psychoanalysis. That he did, ultimately, reject orthodox Freudian analysis because he thought it might usurp the function of his art supplies one hint why we will be turning, not to Freud, but to (early) Andreas-Salomé and to Hillman to draw out the deep psychological resonances of Rilke's work as we explore the poetic twists and turns of the poet's own soul-making, which—notwithstanding his quintessentially lyric genius—ultimately assumes epic proportions.

The engine of Rilke's art, in all its multifarious transformations, is the drive to realize the soul's intrinsic nature; to unfold the acorn of its being into the risen tree.

That acorn/oak metaphor is taken from Hillman,[17] but the theory of organic form it implies derives from thoroughly Romantic premises. Nor is it any accident that Hillman borrows the key term of his psychology—"soul-making"—from a Romantic poet. Soul-making—or some similar notion of a spiritual entity gradually *becoming* what it, in essence, *is*—counts as one of Romanticism's halcyon themes. Like Rilke, many of the great Romantic poets and philosophers eschewed the orthodoxies of traditional faith and sought a new, more vital relation to spirit in the ground of the human being and the dynamic movements of its intrinsic creativity.

For some, such as Wordsworth, this exploration took an autobiographical form which understood the soul's spiritual prerogatives to be founded in its own beginning. Romantically speaking, *childhood* figures a stage of true imagination, an origin wherein the spark of divine spirit—not yet dimmed or clouded by worldly traffic—burns brightly in the soul. Even so, childhood, in its innocence and unconsciousness, is doomed to fade—a dimming famously recorded, for instance, in Wordsworth's "Ode on the Intimations of Immortality." Consequently, the aim of the soul's development becomes conscious recovery of the unity and authenticity of imaginative being represented by childhood, one that includes in its dynamic compass those forces of destruction—death, illness, reflective consciousness itself—responsible for childhood's inevitable passing.

Though his childhood was not, like Wordsworth's, particularly happy, no poet honors the archetype of childhood more than Rilke, or more persistently aims at achieving the consciousness it symbolizes. In this, Rilke remains profoundly indebted to Romantic currents; his religious instinct is formed along the lines of the essentially Romantic project of unfolding the spiritual nature immanent within the soul's own dynamic development. M. H. Abrams calls a related dynamic "the internalization of divinity."[18] James Hillman, following Keats, calls it "soul-making."[19]

While Rilke inherits much from the great Romantic tradition, his life and work remain, in many signal respects, distinctively modern—or, more precisely, twentieth century. We do not, for instance, find a poetic epic that could be subtitled "The Growth of a Poet's Mind" or anything like a classic *Bildungsroman* among Rilke's works. In place of a *Wilhelm Meister's Apprenticeship* or *Heinrich von Ofterdingen*,[20] we have Rilke's highly original *The Notebooks of Malte Laurids Brigge*—a fractured, collage-like account of what is not so much the growth and development as the disintegration of a mind. Moreover, whereas Wordsworth's *Prelude* or Hegel's *Phenomenology of Spirit* figure as *the* central testaments of their authors, *Malte*, as crucial as it is, figures as just one of a host of highly diverse major works. Does the notion of continuous development potentially implicit in the idea of "soul-making" risk distorting the signal heterogeneity of Rilke's oeuvre?

It is true that Rilke's works are notably diverse—Stefan Zweig marveled at how Rilke reinvented his style anew with each major work.[21] Nonetheless, it is also true that Rilke's poetic oeuvre does in fact evince profound continuities; that the dramatic transformations of style do not belie the underlying unity. Commenting upon the consistencies that bind Rilke's earliest and latest work together, Frank Wood writes:

> The youthful poetry of most major writers is usually demarcated from their mature work by abrupt transitions; the art of Rilke from

> beginning to end evolves almost foetus-like, with almost biological consistency, from original cell to mature organism.[22]

Still more persuasively, Rilke, in a letter written roughly a year before his death, bears eloquent testimony to the thread connecting his major works:

> I regard [the *Duino Elegies*] as a further elaboration of those essential premises that were already given in the *Book of Hours*, that in the two parts of the *New Poems* tentatively played with the image of the world and that then in the *Malte*, contracted in conflict, strike back into life and there almost lead to the proof that this life so suspended in the bottomless is impossible. In the *Elegies*, starting from the same postulates, life becomes possible again, indeed, it experiences here that ultimate affirmation to which young Malte, though on the difficult right path "des longues études," was as yet unable to conduct it.... I am amazed that the *Sonnets to Orpheus*... filled with the same essence, are not more helpful to you in the understanding of the *Elegies*.[23]

Those "premises" are the seed-thoughts underlying, if you will, Rilke's "religion of soul-making." Yet it is no simple matter to extract those formative ideas from the dynamic weave of his life work. The archetypal psychology at work in Rilke cannot be grasped merely by analyzing his most obviously psychological work (*Malte*); still less can the wisdom embodied in his opus be garnered by distilling the metaphysics implicit in his *Elegies*. Such unpoetic critical method belies the essence of the poetry and betrays its informing soul. We will pursue another approach and attempt to comprehend Rilke by tracing the path of the poet's soul-making as it weaves the fabric of his poetic text from its earliest, most imperfect expression through to the *Elegies* and *Sonnets*. If we are fortunate, the "essential premises" of Rilke's unique spirituality will reveal themselves, in the making, along the way.

A greybeard
can give you nothing, youth.
What I know
is all that I possess.
Let that burden rest
in my hands.
You, whose world it is—
sing!
You are the child of things,
I am their guest.

Rilke
Alongside the Pictures

Opposite: "Parzival II," Ludwig von Hofmann

BOOK I

ETERNAL YOUTH

Prague to Paris

"The Savior," Andrei Rublev

PART I

REALISM IN RELIGION

CHAPTER 1

BOHEMIAN MELODIES

"How far one can grow beyond such beginnings!"[24] Hugo von Hofmannsthal—himself a literary prodigy—once glossed the poetic career of his friend and compatriot, Rainer Maria Rilke, with this pointed exclamation. To be sure, Rilke's first, most puerile publications hardly bear the stamp of poetic genius. In his later years, the poet himself often disparaged his early work, and modern critics have tended to give Rilke's juvenilia particularly short shrift. In his long essay "Looking for Rilke," Robert Hass declares *Tales of God* and *The Book of Hours* Rilke's "first readable work," passing without mention over the substantial volume of poems, plays, and prose that predated Rilke's trip to Russia in 1899, the twenty-fourth year of the poet's life.[25]

From a purely aesthetic perspective, such neglect may be largely justified. Most of Rilke's early texts (including the lyric volumes *Advent* and *In My Honor*) remain, at best, only very partially translated, and the English-speaking world has not felt the loss too keenly. Even so, given the aim of the present project, we cannot altogether emulate Hass's benign neglect. Rilke's early works play a significant role in the first phase of his inner development, and the topics, concerns, and tensions that shaped and reshaped his mature oeuvre over the course of his decades-long literary career reveal themselves—albeit in nascent form—in his early literary efforts. This work, in turn, remains umbilically attached to the *life* that generated it. In particular, key issues revolving around the interface of religion and psychology find dramatic inscription in the initial phase of Rilke's biography as well as in his early writings. Let us begin, then, at the less than glorious beginning—or rather, just *before* it—and endeavor to trace the opening scenes of Rilke's soul history.

Christened René Karl Wilhelm Johann Josef Maria, Rilke was born on December 4, 1875, in Prague to Sophie (Phia) and Josef Rilke. In a recollection written on the occasion of the poet's forty-seventh birthday, Phia Rilke remembered the circumstances of her son's birth:

> It was a holiday season bright with memories, ushered in on the 3rd of December. The snow was terribly deep, but at five we ventured out, visited grandmamma...and then your good papa joyfully agreed to my suggestion to buy our baby a tiny gold cross at Rummel's, even though we weren't expecting it until February. But it cheered us having such a treasure on hand as a first little present. At around eight o'clock I suddenly felt so unwell that we asked the indispensable madame to make an evening call....Around midnight, the very hour at which our Savior was born...and as it was going on Saturday, suddenly there you were, a child of Mary!—consecrated to our oh! so gracious Lady. Papa and I blessed you and kissed you as we happily sent our prayers of gratitude to Jesus and Mary. Our sweet little boy-child was tiny and delicate, but splendidly formed. And the next morning, when he lay in his little crib, he was given the tiny cross so that "Jesus" was his very first gift.[26]

From the outset, Rilke's life proved a study in contrast. His place of birth was a divided city, one linguistically, culturally, and economically split between the dominant German-speaking minority (to which the Rilkes belonged) and a Czech majority just beginning to assert its native prerogatives. Closer to home, the growing child experienced two dramatically different economic and social environments within his own family circle. The rented flat where he lived with his mother and father on Heinrichsgasse (now Jindřišská) was set in a distinctly modest, lower-middle-class neighborhood; yet when René visited the well-appointed mansion of his maternal grandparents in the nearby Herrengasse (now Panská), he entered the world of an entirely different class—a pattern repeated in later years, when the poet-wanderer familiar with conditions of near-abject poverty found himself moving among—and even into—some of the richest and most aristocratic houses (and castles!) in old Europe.

Perhaps the most significant polarity, however, played itself out in the clashing personalities of young René's own parents. Despite the pleasant picture painted in Phia's reminiscence, her marriage to Josef Rilke did not thrive. As a young man, Josef looked forward to a promising military career; bedeviled by illness, however, he repeatedly failed to obtain desired commissions and finally left the service altogether. At the time of his marriage in 1873, he worked as a minor railroad official living off a modest salary. Sophie Entz—a woman of wealth, class, and persistent social ambition—found herself attracted by Josef's personal magnetism and the not yet wholly faded aura of his military bearing. Mistakenly, she hoped for social advancement from the liason. Josef's brother, Jaroslav, had been awarded a noble rank, and Phia dreamt of a similar boon for Josef. When no such glittering destiny materialized, Phia found herself trapped in rather poor and limited circles and, over time, grew bitter about what she came to consider a most misguided marriage.

Social circumstances aside, however, Josef and Phia's personal dispositions were, in most ways, diametric opposites, diverging along typical—indeed, almost stereotypical—gender lines.

Josef Rilke—though often wearing the appearance of a gallant cavalier—proved a formal and emotionally controlled man. His military mien displayed the decidedly masculine bent of his personality, one reflected in everything from his attitudes about what kind of playthings (soldiers, dumbbells) were appropriate for a growing boy to opinions as to the kind of work that might qualify as a respectable and responsible profession (poetry certainly did not qualify). Phia, on the other hand—by far the more emotionally expressive of the two—did nothing to disguise her natural preference for things feminine in her dealings with René—an inclination accentuated by the fact that she had lost an infant daughter the year before René was born. Not only did her boy-child have names that can be heard as feminine (René, Maria), Phia dressed him in girl's clothing until he was seven and would often have him play at being a girl-child—her "little Sophie." Such escapades left an indelible impression upon the young child, and the mature poet later recorded his own version of them in his quasi-autobiographical *Malte*.

Phia Rilke herself entertained modest literary aspirations and, in her later life, published a little book of aphorisms titled *Ephemerides*. When her young son revealed a rather precocious interest in verse, Phia conscientiously fostered it, reading poetry (including Schiller ballads) with him and encouraging him to copy out poems. Eight-year-old René wrote a poem celebrating his parents' wedding anniversary in May 1884. Tragically, within a year, his parents separated, but little René

Rilke in 1884, 1887, c.1891, and 1897

(living now with Phia) continued his poetic pursuits. Vacationing with his mother in Italy, he wrote to his father that he was "diligently practicing his poetry" and would "be decked with laurels" upon his return to Prague.[27] From the first, Rilke's involvement with poetry inhabited the space between the masculine and feminine, trying to span a widening, even unbridgeable gap.

If Phia's interest in poetry appeared largely beneficial to her son, her fervid religiosity proved a far more complicated and vexed legacy for the child. Phia Rilke's Catholic piety was, by all accounts, excessive. While there may well have been elements of true devotion in her, it seems clear that her marital and social disappointment fueled her religious passion in a less than entirely sincere way. Dressed, most always, in black, Phia wore her suffering as a mantle, not insensible to the dark glamour of the pose. The element of vanity, however, only seemed to increase the intensity of her piety. Remarking the extremity of her behavior, Pater writes, "Religious observance and the ritual of the Catholic Church occupied her to the point of bigotry, and in later life almost of mania."[28]

Nor did Phia spare her child her enthusiasms. At every church visit, René was required to kiss the wounds of Jesus on the crucifix. Later in life, Phia recalled an early occasion of religious "instruction": "Once I taught René how one must pray—he was three years old—and that great suffering came from the Savior and that therefore we must never complain when we suffer."[29]

Phia's doings and sayings molded her child's nascent spiritual life. René grew up sharing his mother's overweening piety. On one occasion, Phia recalled, she hurried to little René's bedside where her distraught child exclaimed: "But mama, how can I fall asleep, I haven't yet given the dear God a kiss," before she calmed him with a crucifix.[30]

At the age of ten, Rilke went off to military school at St. Polten. Young René did so at his father's urging, but the aspiring cadet took his own version of his mother's religion—most signally, a tendency towards martyrdom—with him. Predictably, sensitive René proved ill equipped to handle the physical and psychological rigors of St. Pölten and soon became something of a whipping boy at the school (which he later famously depicted as a veritable hell on earth). In order to negotiate the ordeal of school, young René typically employed two lines of defense—illness, and a religious stance of quasi-heroic suffering.

> Following the example of Phia's impetuous religiosity, the child believed that his capacity for patient suffering resembled Christ's, a notion he articulated to his torturers. When a classmate hit him in the face so violently that his knees buckled, he responded in a quiet voice: "I suffer as Christ suffered, quietly and without complaint, and as you hit me I pray to our dear Lord that He will forgive you."[31]

Dumbstruck, at first, by this proclamation, René's assailant recovered quickly, and broadcast the matter across the schoolyard. Naturally, more derision—and more abuse—followed. His first gift, that tiny gold cross, was slowly becoming an albatross around the young boy's neck.

Somehow, he survived. René Rilke finally graduated St. Pölten in 1890. He was even intact enough to enter a military high school in Weisskirchen in order continue his military training. Soon enough, however, persistent illness—born of psychological as well as physical causes—forced Rilke's departure from Weisskirchen, and the misguided fantasy of a military career was forever abandoned. With his exit from Weisskirchen, a new phase in Rilke's life began, one marked by the youth's first romantic episodes, by long stretches of serious academic study, and a fundamental revision of his religious attitude. All of these went hand in hand with a growing commitment to art, to the poetic vocation that would ultimately command Rilke's most genuine and lasting devotion.

After his stint at Weisskirchen, Rilke enrolled in a commercial school in Austrian Linz in the fall of 1891. The idea, ostensibly, was to learn a trade that would allow the young man to make a respectable living. Even as a young man, however, Rilke—already working assiduously at his writing—could not tolerate such narrow goals for long. The proud author of a long history, *The Thirty Years War* (a topic borrowed from Schiller), as well as numerous verses, he published his first poem by winning a contest offered by a Viennese journal and reported to his mother that he had become "ganz Literat," a man of letters.[32]

It was not, however, literary ambition that summarily derailed René's budding business career, but his first erotic escapade. René became infatuated with a young townswoman named Olga Blumauer and, after courting her intensely in the spring of 1892, finally ran off with her in May. René's concerned landlady contacted Rilke's parents, who notified the police, and after three days the young couple was finally found in an obscure hotel in Vienna. The affair ended there, but so did Rilke's term in Linz: the young gallant found himself immediately expelled from school.

That, in itself, may not have been such an unhappy consequence for René. Though ending in fiasco, the episode revealed just how loath the young man was to subjugate himself to conventional and familial aims and expectations and disclosed the vein of passionate rebellion hidden in his character. As a mature artist, the prodigal son was one of Rilke's favorite motifs—in part because had already begun to live the archetype in his youth.

At this critical juncture, Rilke's uncle Jaroslav—by far the more successful brother—intervened in a manner most helpful to René. Despite René's repeated failures, Jaroslav saw promise in the boy, and—partly in the hope that he would some day work in and inherit Jaroslav's own legal firm—decided to make it possible for René to complete the European equivalent of his high school education, a necessary prerequisite to the study of law. To that end Jaroslav supplied René with a monthly stipend, arranged for him to live with the boy's Aunt Gabriele in a building in Prague owned by Jaroslav, and provided for a rigorous course of private tutoring. Finally, René applied himself conscientiously to the task at hand. In the summer of 1892, he began a fairly intensive course of study that ultimately culminated in his successful graduation in July of 1895.

By the time of his graduation, however, much had changed. Uncle Jaroslav died unexpectedly in 1892. Contrary to Rilke's initial fears, the death did not adversely affect his financial support: Jaroslav had expressed the wish that René receive his monthly stipend so long as he continued his education, and the relatives who disposed of his estate respected that wish. His uncle's death did, however, relieve Rilke of the responsibility to study law, and so left him with a greater degree of intellectual and emotional freedom. In fact, Rilke had already begun to exercise that freedom to significant effect. By the end of 1895, René had experienced his first serious love affair: indeed, he had already been engaged, and broken off that engagement. He had also—with the indispensable emotional and financial aid of his erstwhile fiancée—published his first book of poems.

Rilke's *Life and Songs*, published in November of 1894, contains work dating as far back as Rilke's time in Linz in 1891–92. A significant number postdate Rilke's meeting with Valerie David-Rhonfeld in 1893 in Prague. "Vally" was an artistic and well-connected young woman who offered René both emotional communion and a window to wealthier circles beyond the purview of Aunt Gabriele's dark apartment (as Freedman notes, it was Heinrichgasse and Herrengasse all over again). Meanwhile, Vally found herself powerfully attracted by the young René's sensibility and, above all, his poetic pretensions. Rilke and Vally became engaged not long after their initial meeting, and remained in intimate connection for over two years. For that period, Vally served as the aspiring young poet's muse and, as well, his patroness: it was Vally's financial support that made possible the publication of *Life and Songs*.

Life and Songs can hardly be considered a promising literary debut. The title—generic and entirely undistinguished—sets the tone for the whole book, which is chiefly interesting insofar as it provides a yardstick by which to measure the poet's future progress. In the book, the young Rilke tried his hand at a variety of themes and forms: love poems, descriptive landscapes, verse narratives with domestic or military themes, social satires. While the young poet wrestled honestly with his poetic matter, on the whole the fare remains remarkably poor.

Leppman has remarked that, in many ways, Rilke's personal origins were inhospitable to the culture of art: the tearing insecurities of his childhood; the cultural isolation of the German-speaking minority in his native Prague and the brittle poverty of the language he therefore inherited; the largely moribund literary traditions (neo-romanticism, naturalism) available to him—all militated against a brilliant beginning. Vaguely Romantic in drift, the poems in *Life and Songs*—while exhibiting a gift for verse and a wide-ranging albeit undeveloped technical facility—are nonetheless consistently marred by superficial sentiment and cliché. Above all, a peculiar vacuity—the absence of anything truly individual—hollows these poems. The more narrative pieces prove the most interesting (in general, Rilke's creative prose matured well before his verse) while the book's weakness stands out most glaringly when the poet treats the kind of inner psychological and spiritual content that would, in time, become the trademark of his maturity. Take, for instance, the following—the first section of the last poem in the book.

ALOFT

I

Sometimes exhausted from running after joy
I yearn once again for blessed blindness,
call up the cozy days of childhood
call the days of innocence back.

Where with cheerful hope I still carried
childish faith in a dawning heart
and where, to heal the smallest hurt,
a toy, a pretty one, was still enough.

Where I knew nothing of the rush of the world,
as yet perceived nothing of error and of guilt,
where I saw truth in every single soul,
and loyalty in each and every breast.

Where, deep within, I believed I heard
teachings of the divine Word, where peace
cradled me when at evening I pressed,
wearily, my curly head into the pillows.

And then also dreams gently embraced me,
bore me on shimmering arms away from there
far into the world and wove and stretched
a golden veil around the happy child.[33]

"How far one can grow," indeed! In these stanzas from "Aloft," language as well as feeling remains within the realm of the wholly general; no single realized image conveys original insight or memorable perception. The poem mentions matters of the utmost import, yet these references remain peculiarly empty. "What is the child hoping for? What kind of truth is found in the soul? How does one 'hear' a doctrine within?" complains Rolleston.[34] It is precisely such profound spiritual questions that Rilke will ultimately make his own, but here, at the outset of his career, René has precious little to say about them. The emotion the poem records—recognizable enough, to be sure—is worth next to nothing as it has not yet been worked upon, deepened, or enlivened by imagination. Accordingly, Rolleston goes so far as to deny the name of poetry to such lines, calling them (and indeed the whole of *Life and Songs*) mere "versifying" instead.

In his biography of Rilke, Leppmann criticizes the poems of *Life and Songs* along similar lines, declaring that "they reveal no particular conviction; nowhere can one discern the poet's own point of view or even any immediate experience." Leppman ventures a kind of psychobiographical explanation as to why these juvenile poems ring so hollow:

> It is as if the young poet, feeling rooted neither in his family nor in a sustaining faith, neither in the city of his birth nor among the Volk of the countryside, were attempting to cover up for his inner emptiness by adopting the widest variety of masks.[35]

This perceptive remark must be carefully read, lest it mislead. For the lacks Leppmann mentions here become, in time, the ground of Rilke's unique character, the conditions and terms of the poet's spiritual, psychological, and poetic development. It is as if Rilke's mature individuality—his decidedly solitary character; his intense yet wholly unorthodox spirituality; the peripatetic cosmopolitanism which was always, too, a species of homelessness—grew to fill in the (empty) soul-space Leppman quickly sketches here. For the topoi Leppmann lists are not so much real voids as psychic arenas full of material crying for transformation. The long-drawn-out deed of enacting that transformation supplies the stuff of Rilke's poetry and the making of his soul.

Ironically, the publication of the book that had, in a sense, been their deepest bond augured the end of the relationship between René and Vally. With the book finished and his studies completed in July of 1895, René's need and love for Vally faded. Looking forward to new horizons, he began to experience his commitment as unduly limiting. Vally recognized his need for freedom, and they separated at the end of the summer. It was to be the first of many painful partings, for Rilke would never really outgrow the need to fall in and out of love. Again and again, Rilke would find himself in the position of the mythical Eros, winging away from the feminine psyche that wished to hold him fast.

Free from school and, for a time, from love, Rilke turned concerted and energetic attention toward the forging of a literary career. "The year spent in Prague before he moved to Munich in September 1896 represents Rilke's emergence as a writer," writes Freedman.[36] The young poet immersed himself in the literary and cultural life of his native city, frequenting cafés, joining literary societies, and forging personal associations with a wide range of relatively influential artists and intellectuals, such as the German literature professor August Sauer, the linguist Fritz Mauthner, the poets Emil Faktor and Detlev von Liliencron, the painter Emil Orlik, and the playwrights Max Halbe and Rudolf Christof Jenny.

Halbe and Jenny, in particular, encouraged Rilke's theatrical ambitions. René had not yet recognized lyric poetry as his true forte, and the young writer, dreaming of being a man of the theatre, worked assiduously towards this end. Beginning with *Hoar Frost* and the one-act *Now and in the Hour of Our Dying Away*—both completed in Prague—Rilke averaged roughly a play a year over the next six years. None, however proved very successful, artistically or commercially. His early efforts, in particular, mire in a melodramatic naturalism. *Hoar Frost* revolves around a sordid plot of crime and sexual blackmail; *Now and in the Hour* "explores every aspect of social and spiritual misery."[37] In his drama, young René Rilke did begin to confront weighty matters of personal and social psychology, but did so with a painfully heavy hand. Though his relation to theatre remained important to him (Rilke's theoretical engagement with Maeterlinck's drama proved especially stimulating), theatre would, slowly but surely, move to the periphery of the poet's literary vision.

Another one of René's attempts to make his mark on his Prague world proved still more anomalous. Toward the end of 1895, Rilke—in a rare display of social activism—founded his own populist literary journal (*Wegwarten*), which he himself distributed free of cost. The effort represents Rilke's laudable—though rather ill-conceived and largely ineffectual—attempt to reach out from the enclave of his primarily German-speaking literary world to embrace the wider Czech population. After just three issues (containing almost exclusively work by Rilke, including *Now and in the Hour*) *Wegwarten* expired, a testament of the young poet's outsized ambitions more than of his true talent.

Still another poetic project rooted in his Czech locale proved more successful and, too, more organically related to the poet's vocation. Rilke had already long been wrestling with faith and (as his dramas show) familial psychology, but was only beginning to negotiate that difficult terrain poetically. Seeking material for his lyric work, Rilke—ensconced, for the time being, in Prague—turned to the world around him and trained his poetic attention upon the sights, sounds, and history of his native city, especially the manifestations of the folk-soul embodied in its native Czech heritage. Though Rilke's literary romance with his native Bohemia proved short-lived, his attempt to ground his art in a reality outside of himself did bear abundant—albeit motley—fruit.

Rilke wrote most of the eighty-some-odd poems comprising *Larenopfer*, or *Offering to the Lares*, in the fall of 1895. The resonant specificity of the title—which refers to the deities who watched over Roman households to ensure their well-being—figures a marked advance beyond the pallid *Life and Songs*. The volume contains a mélange of poems on a wide variety of subjects, but the largest number are primarily descriptive in character, poeticizing specific sites (churches, streets, hills and parks and rivers) in and around Prague. Rilke's poetic evocations often remain stilted and egregiously sentimental, especially when the young poet takes a slice of human life as his subject. Nonetheless, many of the poems manifest the poet's growing imaginative power, and their publication in December of 1895 effectively marked the beginning of Rilke's literary career.

A number of the best pieces offer concretely realized images of objects or places; several of Rilke's scene-paintings foreshadow the poet's lifelong preoccupation with death. As Demetz drolly comments: "René's favorite landscapes are cemeteries, tombs, and dark cloisters.... it often seems as though he sees Prague through the gloomy gaze of one possessed by death."[38] One of Rilke's best "touring" poems, however, looks at the city from a higher vantage-point:

FROM THE LOOKOUT

(On Laurenzi Hill)

I see towers, roundly domed like acorns
and some thinning to a point like pears.
There lies the city; nestling gently against
her thousand brows, Evening already nears.

She stretches her dark body far. But look—
back there! St. Mary's twin spires gleam up high.
As if through those two points of feeling
she were sucking in the violet ink of sky.[39]

Not all the poems in the volume fit this generic mold; indeed, the range of subject and style in *Offering to the Lares* remains impressive. In "The Dreamer," Rilke touches upon the kind of subjective terrain he is soon to make his own in language original enough to be recognizably Rilkean: "Träume scheinen mir wie Orchideen." ("Dreams seem to me to be like orchids"). In marked contrast, a more strong-willed poem honors the Czech religious revolutionary Jan Hus, convicted of heresy and burned at the stake in 1415:

Superavit

Never does the heroic deed
go up in smoke. The funeral pyre
taught this to Constance—
from the hot baptismal fire
a noble spirit rose still higher.

There looms yet large in our own day
the Reformer Hus.
Awed by fiery intellect,
we bow still in deep respect
before his genius.

He, whom the council condemned,
was, at heart, deep and pure,
persuaded of his office.
The glowing stake wrote his name
in the illumined book of fame.[40]

"Superavit" foreshadows elements of the heretical spiritual heroism we will soon encounter in Rilke's own career and qualifies as one of the volume's more significant poems.

Still, the dominant feeling-tone of the book finds truer expression in its best-known lyric:

Folk Melodies

Bohemian melodies
move me so deeply,

stealing into the heart,
making it heavy.

When a child weeding potatoes
sings softly in the fields,
her tune haunts the dreams
the dark night yields.

And though you may travel far
year after year,
you will hear it again and again
as if it were near.[41]

This poem (deservedly the most famous of the book) conceals the profound irony at its emotional center. While the poem evokes a sense of an individual deeply and enduringly rooted in the soul of his native land, that is precisely what the young Rilke was not. While one can admire the youthful poet's generous honoring of Czech heritage, his attempt to find or create a poetic homeland in Prague and its environs could not wholly succeed; that domain was not ultimately capacious enough to house his restless spirit. In fact, René Rilke—keenly aware of the cultural limitations of the place—would soon leave his native city. Though he made a literary return to Prague in two novellas begun in 1897 and published in 1899,[42] Prague and its Slavic ancestry would ultimately prove most important to him as a stepping stone on his way toward the far broader intellectual and spiritual horizons of Mother Russia.

In the last poem in *Offering to the Lares*, "Das Heimatlied" ("Native Song"), a traveler, the speaker of the poem, hears strains of a song wafting over the fields through which he is walking. He bids its source, a farmer girl, to come and sing for him. She sets down her sickle and sings "Kde domov můj"—the song that was to become the Czech national anthem after 1918. To inscribe the singing and the hearing of this song as the closing gesture of *Offering to the Lares* evokes the irony that informs the whole volume, for its title asks the poignant question: "Where is my homeland?" It was a song one can imagine Rilke, who was to live a virtually nomadic existence, singing all of his adult life.

In a sense, Rilke left Prague even before his physical departure for Munich in October of 1896. Most of the poems comprising *Offering to the Lares* were written in the latter part of 1895; during the next year, Rilke wrote many poems of a markedly different character, and it is these, together with a handful written after his arrival in Munich, that make up his next volume of lyrics.

Traumgekrönt or *Dreamcrowned* marked a new departure for the young poet. Leaving all traces of geography and history behind, Rilke here enters into intensely subjective terrain, a lyric atmosphere in which outward phenomena function merely as signifiers of the inner moods and feelings that comprise the true subject of the poems. In the first, the poet lays claim to his domain:

King's Song

If you dare bear life with dignity,
only the petty will it demean;
beggars may call you brother,
yet you still may be a king.

Though no circlet of red gold
break the divine silence of your brow,
blissful dreamers will gaze at you in wonder,
and children—bow.

Days weave your purple and your ermine
out of the sun's soft shimmer of light;
nights will kneel before you,
hands full of woe and deep delight.[43]

This poem sets forth the essential premise of the whole. The poet lays claim to a species of royal authority that flows, not from external sources, but from an inward dignity recognized and confirmed both by the ambassadors of the world of imagination (children and dreamers) and the primordial forces of the cosmos (day and night). "King's Song" qualifies as a kind of title poem for the book; if the poet bears his mission with the honor of which it is worthy, he will truly be "crowned with dreams."

The history of psychology bears witness to the preeminent importance of dream in defining the field of soul. One might contend that modern psychology effectively commenced with the publication of Freud's *The Interpretation of Dreams*, deliberately published in the pivotal year 1900. In his own synopsis and historical review of archetypal psychology, Hillman writes:

> Soul-making does imply a metaphysical fantasy, and the implied metaphysics of archetypal psychology are best found in *The Dream and the Underworld* (1979).... There the dream is taken as the paradigm of the psyche.[44]

The signal importance of *Dreamcrowned* in Rilke's oeuvre derives from its status as a transitional work; it ushers in an important phase of lyric work continued and completed by Rilke's two subsequent volumes of verse, *Advent* (1897) and *In My Honor* (1897). These texts are sometimes decried for the excessive subjectivity they exhibit. Fuerst, for instance, writes:

> *Dreamcrowned* and *Advent*... embroider a thin experience with heavily fragrant flowers of mood and atmosphere. On the whole, *Offering to the Lares* is superior to the immediately following collections by virtue of its topographic value.... His next collections were overflowingly subjective, evaporatingly vague.[45]

While not without merit, Fuerst's critique misses a crucial point. For all its poetic limitations, *Dreamcrowned* registers a vital turn toward recognizing the autonomy of psyche. If *Offering to the Lares* represents Rilke's first noteworthy addressing of the objective world (an initiative that will ultimately yield the *Dinggedichte* characteristic of his famous *New Poems*), *Dreamcrowned* marks Rilke's deliberate incursion into the distinctly interior world of the soul. Rilke's long career will unfold as a development of these two complementary initiatives until culminating in a masterpiece (*Sonnets to Orpheus*) that finally achieves their most integral fusion.

After the "King's Song," *Dreamcrowned* offers fifty poems in two (separately titled) parts. The name of the first part of the book indicates that we are to read or understand the individual (numbered, but unnamed) poems as, in fact, "Dreams." Against the background of the young Rilke's spiritual struggles, it is noteworthy that the very first such dream/poem deals with the theme of religious worship:

I

My heart resembles a forgotten chapel;
on the altar, there swaggers a wild May.
The storm, a rollicking companion,
long ago broke in two the little windows;
he now sneaks up to the sacristy
and there tugs at the altar chimes.

The shrill bell's quivering cry of longing
calls the utterly astounded distant God
to the long-abandoned place of sacrifice.
The wind laughs and hops through the window
and, raging, lays hold of the waves of sound
and smashes them in two upon the floor.

And poor wishes kneel in a long row
before the door, and beg on the mossy threshold.
Yet, for a long time, no one praying has passed by.[46]

Here, the inner picture reveals itself clearly enough. The chapel, place of established worship, has long been abandoned and unvisited by prayer, but the wild wind wakes the soul from a spiritual sleep, evoking a "cry of longing" (*Sehnsuchtsschrei*) that surprises the distant, long-absent God. The poem implies formal worship to be a thing of the past; even so, the very process of translating the scene of devotion from an outward to an inner place—the dream of the heart—reawakens the soul's own longing and spiritual initiative. Not the church, but the dream itself qualifies as the house of prayer; or, rather, of the wishes that express the psyche's innermost longings, long locked out of the sanctuary.

This first poem is followed by several more that play on the motif of the house:

II

I imagine:

A small village in peaceful splendor, and in it
a rooster crow;

and this village gradually lost
in flower blossom snow.
And in the village, looking like Sunday,
a neat little house;
and from behind the lace curtain, a blond head
secretly peeking out.
The door opens quickly, and the hinges
hoarsely call for help,—
and then, in the room, a soft, soft
lavender scent.[47]

True, this is not great poetry. The highly idealized images border on stylized cliché, and the introductory "I imagine" (a device Rilke employs in many poems in the book) emphasizes their distance from any particular objective reality. Such a poem may indeed seem a poetic regression from the concrete imagery characterizing the more successful descriptive poems in *Offering to the Lares*. Nonetheless, the move away from naturalism toward dream or fantasy image accords with the young poet's nascent exploration of the soul's own more subjective domain.

For Hillman (again following Jung), fantasy figures as the constitutive act of the psyche, and the soul cannot truly come into its own unless, at some point, "fantasy" claims an authority usually reserved for "reality," revaluing the very notions of "fantasy" and "reality" in the process:

> For archetypal psychology, "fantasy" and "reality" change places and values. First, they are no longer opposed. Second, fantasy is never merely mentally subjective but is always being enacted and embodied. Third, whatever is physically or literally "real" is always also a fantasy image. Thus the world of so-called hard factual reality is always also the display of a specifically shaped fantasy, as if to say, along with Wallace Stevens...there is always "a poem at the heart of things."[48]

In the *New Poems*, Rilke would write poems that expressed both the "heart of things" and the core of his own poetic personality, but he had not yet reached that point in *Offering to the Lares*. While it is true that the descriptive poems in *Offering to the Lares* boast more successful rendering of outward things than those in *Dreamcrowned*, they do not express a developed inner life or original subjective perspective; hence the awful cloying of the poems that deal head-on with domestic relations and other matters of the heart. While such deficiencies are no means erased in *Dreamcrowned*, this volume carries forward Rilke's inner, subjective development: to realize the third phase Hillman speaks of above, one must first go through—and not superficially—the prior phases. *Dreamcrowned* enacts understanding of the crucial psychological truth that "fantasy is never merely mentally subjective." It augurs, too, Rilke's imminent involvement with the kindred aesthetics of the Jugendstil movement—an involvement that helped lend imaginal form and substance to the young poet's dream world.

Nor are all the poems in *Dreamcrowned* quite so nebulous as they may appear at first. Some do speak the language of the soul with a degree of eloquence:

XV

In the womb of a silvery snow-night
all things slumber, far and wide,
except an endless wild woe awakes
loneliness in a single soul.

You ask why the soul holds silent,
why she does not pour it forth
into the night?—She knows, if it left her
the flood would put out all the stars.[49]

In this poem, once again, phenomena (e.g., a snowy night) appear generic rather than particular and are important not as actual things but as conveyors of the embracing mood that ultimately envelopes them. Yet the "overflowing" subjectivity Fuerst alludes to is not merely gratuitous. As this small poem displays, that which spills over all objective boundary is actually the feeling substance of the soul itself—most particularly, the inveterate *longing* that issues forth from the emptiness or lack inherent in it.

If soul itself qualifies as the true subject of these poems, longing is its calling card. (In his workshops, James Hillman was fond of quoting the German romantic maxim: "Tell me what you long for, and I will tell you who you are.") In another poem in *Dreamcrowned*, the poet explicitly takes a personified figure of Longing as surrogate mother and spiritual guide:

VI

We sat by one another in the twilight.
"Mother," I pleaded, "Please be fair—
tell once more the beautiful story
of the princess with the golden hair."

Since Mother died, Longing, the pale lady,
now leads me towards the coming night,
and like Mother, she can tell the story
of the beautiful princess just right.[50]

The beautiful princess figures as an archetypal fairy-tale image of the anima or soul. Guided no more by the touristic charms of his native city, by strains of native folk songs, or by the examples of heroic social or religious reformers, this poem dramatizes the poet's turning to his own experience of Longing as a means of listening in to the soul, hearing the unfolding of the psyche's fairy tale, the inner story the poet himself will tell over the course of the next three decades.

As the first poem in *Dreamcrowned* implies, while Rilke himself survived his military schooling, his childhood faith did not. More and more, he experienced the trappings of religion as ineffectual and hollow, and even began to associate the forced exercise of prayer with military-style compulsion. When it was time to go to sleep at St. Pölten, an officer would stride down the row of beds "as if he were in the service of silence and darkness," Right-side turn, 'heavenly Father' pray; go to sleep!"[51] Finally, as Rilke recalled many years later: "After long fearful battles, I abandoned the violent Catholic piety of childhood, made myself free of it in order to be even more, even more comfortlessly alone..."[52]

In Prague, the young man's broadening intellectual and emotional horizons distanced him still further from his childish piety. In a poem called "Confession of Faith," written in April, 1893, the eighteen-year-old Rilke aggressively assumes an atheistical stance reviling the shallow pretenses of believers who, like dumb sheep, mindlessly follow the precepts of the church:

You pious-lipped Christians
call me the Atheist,
and run away from me,
because I do not, like you,
foolishly fall into the traps
set by Christianity.

I know it, all your teachings—
they know how to convert,
they make one pious and—dumb....[53]

Rilke's relationship to religion, however, was far too deep and complex to rest with wholesale rejection. Another poem written later that same year, "Christ on the Cross," is far less polemical and much more interesting, for it adumbrates the maturing Rilke's deeply considered conception of the Christ figure. Out on a dawn walk in the countryside, the poem's speaker witnesses an impoverished woman and her two children praying before a poor and gaudily painted wooden crucifix. He notes their dire poverty and is moved to tears to see how their heartfelt prayer ("Give us this day...our daily bread") seems to give them desperately needed strength and hope. Almost envious of their belief, the speaker wonders why he too cannot pray; why he sees but painted wood when he looks upon the figure on the cross. Then he understands:

He was, like me, a person,—but he trusted
far more upon his powers than he should...
That he was great was proved by his devotion
to noble aims. But one thing made him small...

Not worship as a man did he desire,—
no, he would rather suffer and expire,
die on the cross—but die with a God's name.
It's clear to me now why I neither can
love and adore him, nor unto him call:
he would have stayed so godlike as a man;
as god he seems so human now, so small![54]

This view of Christ as a classically tragic figure—a human being ultimately undone by hubris—is one Rilke was soon to elaborate more fully. It figures as the guiding premise of the pivotal yet little-known work that Rilke commenced shortly after his arrival in Munich in the fall of 1896. As is only fitting for a poet who received "Jesus" as his "very first gift," it was Rilke's *Visions of Christ* that truly launched his original poetic career.

CHAPTER 2

ETERNAL ILLUSION

> In the life of every great artist is a watershed where creative energies are channeled away from the juvenile and begin to flow in mature directions. Often the period of emancipation and the efforts to achieve an autonomy of personality and spirit are painful; but when an artist's early upbringing is saturated with piety...his complicated personal experience must find an outlet, if not resolution, in his writings.[55]

So begins Siegfried Mandel's commentary on Rilke's *Visions of Christ*. Neither youthful proclamations nor adolescent polemics could adequately interrogate Rilke's formative relationship with Christianity. That task required far more in-depth treatment, and only in performing it did the young Rilke establish a point of departure for his own maturity.[56]

Anxious to escape the provincialism of his native city, Rilke moved to Munich in the fall of 1896. Already dedicated to his literary vocation, he hoped to break new ground in his novel surroundings. Quickly establishing himself in the fashionably artistic district of Schwabing, the young poet established friendships with many other young artists. One of these, the novelist Jakob Wasserman, introduced Rilke to Turgenev and other icons of Russian literature and to the Danish writer Jens Peter Jacobsen. Jacobsen's *Niels Lyhne* narrates the life of a sensitive artist who, racked by the deaths of loved ones, rejects God and resorts to a tragically heroic brand of atheism. The book—which transparently reflects Rilke's own struggles with art, psychology, and religion—enormously influenced the author's developing sense of the nature and destiny of the artist and furnished a kind of prototype for his later novel *The Notebooks of Malte Laurids Brigge*.

The visual art scene in Munich proved important to Rilke as well. Rilke attended a major exhibit of Jugendstil art in Munich's Glaspalast and so made his first formal connection with the movement. Jugendstil aesthetics harmonized well with Rilke's "dreamcrowned" world:

> The world, as it was portrayed in the art of the [Jugendstil] movement, is a subjective one based on fantasy, dream, or fairy tale, and populated by innocent, dancing maidens, dashing young knights, or mysterious water sprites. It is an artistic realm where a quiet and delicate beauty reigns, where the harsh and blunt realities of "secular" life find no place...there is inherent in all these works an underlying tension created by the polarities and dichotomies of life which these artists acutely felt within themselves and within their age.[57]

Such "dichotomies" may be readily conjured by comparing the harsh social and psychological realities of Rilke's naturalist drama with the neo-romantic idealism permeating *Dreamcrowned*. Rilke wrote enthusiastically about Jugendstil art after visiting the exhibit, and its emergent influence on his work would reach its peak only later, in conjunction with his friendship with Heinrich Vogeler and his sojourn at the artist colony Worpswede (see Part II).

That time, however, was not now. In Munich, meanwhile, the outward change of scene and new social and literary contacts could not in and of themselves transform Rilke's inner landscape and so point the way from the young poet's past towards his future. Nor could formative influences represented by the likes of Jacobsen, the Russians, and Jugendstil truly ripen until Rilke had accomplished the inner work carried through in the *Visions*, a text which directly confronts the spiritual underpinnings of his soul embodied in the image of Christ and the religious universe that revolves around the world of the Son.

The work consists of eleven poems or "Visions"; the eight composing the "First Series" were written in Munich between October 1896 and late summer 1897, and the final three ("Second Series") in Zoppot in July of 1898. The first Visions, then, follow close upon the heels of the poems composing *Dreamcrowned*; indeed, a very few of the latter postdate the first Visions. Rilke in fact initially intended to include the *Visions* as a section of *Dreamcrowned*, a historical detail of interest primarily on account of the light it sheds upon the poetic mode characterizing the *Visions*.

It is no easy matter to identify the genre of Rilke's *Visions of Christ.* Each of the eleven poems narrates, in verse, Christ's appearance in one or another scene and, in often dramatically rendered dialogues, shares his charged encounters with various figures (a child, a prostitute, a painter). Many of the settings—a Prague graveyard, the Munich fairgrounds, a tavern—are recognizably drawn from real scenes in modern life. At the same time, the appearance of the Christ figure often transports the action into a different dimension in which ordinary time and space are effectually suspended—the almost surreal domain of "the vision" itself, closely akin to dream.

Rilke himself, in fact, once called these Visions *Traumepen*, or "dream epics"; he also called them *episch-lyrische Phantasien*, "epic-lyric fantasies."[58] Given what we have already said about dream and fantasy, this should be enough to indicate that Rilke's Christ Visions manifest his attempt to translate his understanding of the West's central religious figure into the imaginative language of the soul; to construe the nature and import of the Christian legacy from the perspective of the psyche. Against the background of our prior discussion, we may even imagine Rilke's *Visions* as an instance of the soul rising up and calling the spirit of Constantinople to account. Indeed, step by step, dream-vision by dream-vision, Rilke's series of poems effectively search and destroy many of the pillars of conventional Christian belief.

The first Vision, "The Orphan," transports us to a graveyard. There, we find ourselves in the company of an impoverished and grief-stricken little girl who has just witnessed her own mother's cheap and dreary funeral. Those in attendance, including the priest, apparently have done nothing more than bury her and utter Christian platitudes ("Today they all said: Thank God—she's free") before leaving the child alone. The poem proceeds to use the child's angle of vision to draw, in the sharpest possible contours, the starkly dualistic outlines of the Christian universe:

> Yes, and what now? They've put her in the ground.
> Dear God in Heaven, why should this damp mound
> of rubbish and of rubble press so hard?...
> Why bury someone in the dank, black loam
> who, high in heaven, has a radiant home?
> Heaven! That fairy-tale town, where every dome

> is made of gold, and every street is white;
> nothing is there but lots of love and light—
> and no one's gloomy and forsaken there,
> and blissful singing is the whole affair.
> A star, there, is a toy—like the white sheep
> with which the little girl once loved to leap;
> and were she truly good, she'd be allowed
> to cradle in the moon's own silver beam,
> burrowing deep inside a downy cloud.
> That must be quite a sleep—and quite a dream![59]

Looking up from her musings, the child finds herself cheered by the spring flowers and the sheen of gold on the church house steeple—for a moment, the earth itself is bathed in the fairy-tale light of heaven. Yet it is just in this moment of gladness that a nearby figure arrests her attention:

> But look: stock-still against the churchyard wall,
> a man who seems to have no strength at all
> is leaning; in his great, dark eyes are fed
> the fires of grief, like candles for the dead.
> Rustic his clothing, of a coarse grey thread;
> he claws his wild hair with a wandering hand
> and stares, quite lost, toward the mountain's rand
> as if with pinions quietly outspread
> his soul readies for that other land.

The man is Jesus; this is Rilke's first, highly unorthodox vision of Christ. The poet portrays him as a wanderer lost between worlds, an almost derelict vagrant consumed by an overwhelming sorrow and sense of emptiness. Most striking, perhaps, is the way the poet likens Christ's eyes (traditionally, the windows of the soul) to mourning candles and so allies the aura emanating from him—not with life and light—but with a disturbing sense of death. Though the depictions of Christ vary somewhat in the course of the whole cycle of poems, this initial one remains typical, accurately establishing the tone of the whole.

The little girl finds herself attracted to the strange figure; his sorrow draws her like a magnet. She approaches him, asks why he is so sad, and inquires if his mother, too, has died. Distracted, at first he does not hear her and tells her to leave him be. When she persists, and he finally understands that she has just buried her mother, he lays his hand upon her head and says, "Lightly upon your mother lie the sod."

Yet here Christ's touch is no blessing, but more like the transmission of a plague. Instead of comforting the child, it reawakens all the profound fears and doubts she had managed, for a moment, to put aside:

> A savage grief gnaws at her heart once more;
> she sidles closer to the man in gray;
> "Isn't it so—the priest says she and I—
> you know it too—will meet in heaven some day?"
> Her words drift off; there comes a cricket cry;
> she harks; a white butterfly flutters by;
> she harks; a shudder of smoke ascends the sky
> from distant huts. . . . The man makes no reply.

Thus ends the first Vision. By refusing to answer in the affirmative—an implicit denial—Jesus casts a terrible shadow of doubt into the heart of the small child's vulnerable belief. In that moment of deafening silence, we hear the impending collapse of the structures of consolation upon which rest the whole cosmos of popular Christianity; its fairy-tale heaven and inherently desolate earth.

Before reading further, it is worth noting the psychopoetic strategy Rilke's employs in his *Visions*. To be sure, fundamental spiritual and metaphysical issues are put in play (the traditional twofold division of the universe and the values attached to heaven and to earth), yet Rilke addresses these matters—not in any theological idiom—but in the imaginative language of the soul. He does so, in part, via personifying—a poetic technique that (as we shall discuss at length in chapter 11) Hillman identifies as one of the primary means of soul-making. In "The Orphan" (which sets the pattern for all the Visions) Rilke lends spiritual matters emotional immediacy and imaginative depth by embodying them in the persons of the orphan girl, Christ, and their dramatic interaction. Nor do the Visions seem less "real" on account of the aura of dream that invests them; on the contrary, the image-characters speak directly to and of the soul.

If "The Orphan" features the figure of Christ himself implicitly stripping away the veil of illusion shrouding conventional images of Christian heaven and earth, in the poet's second Vision, Rilke—and Christ—take the logical next step, questioning the existence of the one who creates and upholds this universe. The scene takes place at the grave of Rabbi Löw, a sixteenth-century figure legendary for the spiritual wisdom flowing from his profound devotion to God, and, too, his occult knowledge of the spirit realm.[60]

Set in an old Jewish graveyard in Prague, "Jewish Cemetery" effectively picks up where "The Orphan" leaves off. Jesus (described—as in the first Vision—as "the poor Jew, not the redeemer... / Within his eyes...a thousand nights of rue") appears at Löw's graveside to settle an old score with God. His harangue is remarkably direct:

> "How badly I've been treated, Lord, by you!
> Here where he rests, your most devoted slave,
> here, graybeard God, we'll settle scores, we two.
> For I have come to fight you here. Who gave
> everything that is yours to boast of, who?—
> Many a bloody mark the foeman drew
> upon your creed with swords that slashed and slew,—
> but then I brought my faith, my daring too,
> and let your godhood glory forth anew,
> and gave it a new face, sublime and true.
> And when mankind in frenzied mobs would rave,
> your name—the great 'He'—unto them I threw.
> And then my soul, heavy with human care,
> took wing, and up to highest heaven it flew;
> and my soul froze, because the place was bare.
> So you had never been—or were no more
> when I, poor wretch, set foot upon this shore.
> Why should the grief of men be my affair,
> when you, the great God, summon them before
> your throne no longer? when their pious prayer
> is only madness—since you'll not reveal
> your face, because you're not."

This powerful monologue captures the heart of Rilke's Christ. In certain respects, he is a classically tragic figure: a human being who aspired to divinity so intensely as to identify himself wholly with it. In classical tragedy, however, such hubris ultimately results in the hero's fall, a calamity generally attributed to the wrath and power of some offended deity. Rilke's Jesus is fallen, to be sure, but has been cast down not by the vengeful power of God *but by the devastating revelation of his absence*, the nonexistence of the deity. In general, Kramer does an excellent job translating the difficult text, but here the English cannot capture the force of Rilke's language and rhymes. The original—from "And when mankind"—reads thus:

> "Und in der Menschen irres Wahngewimmel
> warf deinen Namen ich—das grosse 'Er.'
> Und dann von tausend Erdensorgen schwer
> stieg meine Seele in den hohen Himmel,
> und meine Seele fror; denn er war leer.
> So warst du niemals—oder warst nicht mehr."

Rilke rhymes and so links *Er* (He) with *leer* (empty, or bare), *both* in his end rhyme and—doubling the effect—internally ("denn *er* war *leer*"), thus hammering home the annihilating effect of "his"—God's—absence. If "The Orphan" ends by calling into question the existence of our Father in Heaven, "Jewish Cemetery" begins with a resounding, and resoundingly negative, answer: "He" is not—at least, not for Jesus, or (as we shall see, this is a crucial qualification) for one whose image of God depends on Jesus and his intercession.

Crucial moments of this monologue undoubtedly look back to earlier days when the child or young boy sent fervent prayers to a God who would not answer. At the same time, parts of the monologue look forward as well. Rhetorically and thematically, the latter half of the vision prefigures "The Olive Garden," a "new poem" written ten years later in Paris. Indeed, the end of the monologue segues directly into the setting of the later piece:

> There came to me
> a dream one day, that I was born to be
> the voice of your idea, your sign and seal.
> My one wish, Father, was closeness unto thee,
> Terrible one, and since you were not real,
> it was my love, it was my agony
> that gave you being at Gethsemane.

Yet it is more than the topos of "The Olive Garden" that is anticipated here. The idea Jesus expresses—that although God may not objectively exist, the passion and imagination stirred by a human being's belief in him may, after all, lend him spiritual and psychic reality—anticipates theories of the psychology of religion Rilke will soon encounter in the person and writings of Lou Andreas-Salomé. A passage such as this reveals that—even before his meeting with Lou—Rilke was groping toward the understanding that the heart and living force of religion lie not solely in the transcendent spirit of the human being, but in the fabricative power of the aspiring soul and its capacity to create God-images. As we shall soon see, what Lou calls "God-creation" and what Hillman calls "soul-making" go hand in hand.

Back in the cemetery, however, Jesus' bitterness remains unrelieved, and (in a spirit quite contrary to the forgiving mercy generally associated with Christ) the stricken Christ seeks revenge. Turning to the Rabbi's tomb, Jesus addresses Löw as a kind of partner in crime. Acknowledging Löw's famous occult powers, Jesus then asks him for a kind of curse that will tear the veil of Christian illusion and consume the universe in fire:

> Out with it now! Is there no malediction
> so sharp that I can shear each lying section—
> aye, cut to shreds heaven's blue cloth of fiction?

Driven by his unending pain, Christ does not stop there, but asks for a curse of fire that would "lick without remorse / the utmost hinges of the universe," then—all violent antidotes to his own vain gospel—for a plague of hate and lust that might lay waste the world.

The rant is shocking—one we might expect to pour forth from the mouth of the Beast, the Antichrist, rather than from Jesus himself. It recalls somewhat a short story Rilke had composed earlier in 1896, "The Apostle," which likewise vehemently repudiates the gospel of love and charity in a kind of Nietzschean fury. The story has proved anathema to many critics, some of whom have been understandably loath to acknowledge it as relevant to Rilke's œuvre.[61]

Christ's ravings in "Jewish Cemetery" and "The Apostle" do, however, indicate the depth of Rilke's revulsion at the controlling clichés of popular Christian culture. Mandel comments:

> What Rilke scores in both "The Apostle" and the *Visions* is the enervating effect of pity and charity as against the strength of the solitary with his individualistic convictions. "The Apostle" can be read as a hymn of hate both against humanity and Christ but this would be putting the accent in the wrong places. The emphasis should be on Rilke's insurrection against charity and pity as reflections of ostentatious self-satisfying impulses of the giver, though well-meaning in the case of Christ. What man needs is self-reliance.[62]

The reference to Emerson here (as Mandel himself notes) is highly relevant. At around this time in his life, Rilke was reading (in translation) the American philosopher as well as Nietzsche. Both undoubtedly helped Rilke formulate his convictions about the centrality of the individual and the necessity of freedom from conventional (and specifically Christian) norms. Emerson himself, originally a minister, famously left the church to preach "the infinitude of the private individual."

At the same time, it is important to observe that Ralph Waldo Emerson was, above all, a Transcendentalist, a spokesman for the Spirit: one whose work attains great *height* or spiritual elevation, but tends to shy away from the archetypally psychological *depths* of soul that ultimately become Rilke's métier. Correspondingly, unlike the mature Emerson (who so often projected an air of invulnerability), Rilke himself—despite a core of strength—proved profoundly susceptible to psychic and bodily distress and (for a good deal of his life) feelings of inferiority. It was common for him to swing from assertions of self-reliant strength and even pride to confessions of incorrigible weakness and incapacity, a dialectic of self-assertion and self-abasement closely related to one Lou Andreas-Salomé would recognize as fundamental to the religious sentiment.

As we read to the end of Rilke's second Vision, it is consequently important to recognize a similar dynamic at work in Christ himself: a psychic volatility that ultimately deepens the difficult humanity of the figure. The bitter rage that consumes Rilke's Christ should be construed within the context of the whole psychology of the figure and the full weight of the almost unimaginable betrayal he feels he has suffered. At the end of "The Orphan," Christ denies reply to the little girl and his silence fills the air with an ominous foreboding. In "Jewish Cemetery," it is the spirit, or body, of Rabbi Löw who answers Christ's diatribe with silence, leaving the sound of Christ's own sobbing to resonate in the void of his torn universe.

His laugh is scorn. And where the mute stones lie,
it pierces like a wounded deer's death cry.
A hoarfrost shrouds the May night by degrees.
A black butterfly flutters by, and sees
Christ weeping there alone upon his knees.

Rilke sets his third Vision, "The Fair," in a scene borrowed from his own immediate surroundings, Munich's famous Oktoberfest:

It was at the October festival
in Munich, when Theresa field is pressed
by onlookers, a screaming, heaving swell.
Provincial folk, whose pleasure is to tell
of making cattle plump, converse and jest.
The little girls, who've somehow fled the nest,
flit boldly through the raucous day in pairs...

Rilke deftly paints the buoyant throngs in colorful word-pictures. Significantly enough, in this pivotal Vision, the poem's narrator appears as a chief character for the first and only time in the cycle:

I, too, went wandering where my footstep fell,
and idly blinked against the blinding light...

Amidst all the good-natured hubbub, this fairgoer finds himself inexplicably drawn to something of an anomaly: a modest booth whose makeshift sign announces "The story of Christ Jesus and His passion." Inside, he finds himself separated from the crowd, alone in a waxwork exhibit that displays signal scenes of Jesus' life: the nativity, the flight to Egypt, the young Jesus' teaching in the temple, his entrance into Jerusalem, his trial and crucifixion. Despite the cheap gaudiness of it all, the simple wax scenes exercise a hypnotic effect on the narrator and assume a compelling aura of reality. In the judgment scene before the Roman pontiff, Jesus—"regal in a thorny wreath" and "woe-resplendent"—appears tragically noble. Finally, Pilate declares, "Ecce homo," before the relentlessly vengeful crowd insists, "To the cross with him."

As the narrator gazes upon Jesus on the cross, the entrancing vision usurps his senses altogether. The wax figure seems to open its "gulf-deep, death-dark" eyes, and breathes: "My God, my God, why hast thou forsaken me?" before addressing his visitor thus:

> This is my curse. Since my disciples, led
> to folly by vainglorious boasts of faith,
> plundered my body from the pit of death,
> there's been no place where I could lay my head.
> As long as stars will find their brightness pearled
> in every brook, as long as sunlight calls
> the spring to come back with its bacchanals,
> so long must I keep wandering through the world.
> From rood to rood I travel, penance-bound:
> each time men drive a cross into the ground,
> once more—in bloody sandals—I seek that mound;
> the agony of old returns to hound
> and humble me; a nail grows from each wound;
> the minutes fasten me unto the rood.
> Thus, ever dying, endlessly renewed,
> I live: each day another cross to bear;
> impaled here in the chill of churches, there
> in the profane booth of a gaudy fair;
> powerless today, yet plied by sickening prayer;
> powerless tomorrow, mocked at everywhere;
> powerless forever in the morning gold
> of crossroads just as in the chapel's cold.
> I drive, a dying leaf, the wide world through.
> You know the myth of the Eternal Jew?
> I am myself that Ahasueras old
> who dies each day, that each day he may live;
> a dark, wide sea's my yearning; I can give
> no coin to comfort it, nor a tomorrow.
> Thus they avenge themselves, who came to sorrow
> through what I told them. Martyred for my sake,
> an endless legion follows in my wake.
> Listen, their tread!—the clamor that they make!

This passage counts as central to the whole cycle of Rilke's *Visions.* In it, Rilke carries the logic developed in the first two Visions a crucial step further. If the first casts doubt on Christian eschatological cosmology and the second confirms the absence of God the Father, this Vision conjures the awful consequences that flow from the spread of Christ's false teaching—consequences which afflict, reciprocally, both the world at large and Christ himself.

Rilke brilliantly crystallizes the essence of Christ's agonizing and unending death sentence by his dramatic inversion of the myth of the wandering (or eternal) Jew. According to legend, Ahasuerus was a Jew (in some versions of the legend, a shoemaker; in others, a porter in Pilate's service) who scorned and insulted Christ as he was carrying the cross on the way to Golgotha. As punishment, he is condemned to a dubious species of immortality: incapable of death, he must do eternal penance, wandering the world forever (or at least until the Last Judgment) repenting his deed, his symbolic repudiation of the Christ. The legend took on such reality in medieval Europe that, for centuries, there were regular reports of sightings of the wandering Jew.

In Rilke's mind, however, the Jew was correct—not in insulting Christ, but in denying his godhood. In fact, it is Christ, and still more his disciples, who are guilty of an irrevocable wrong: namely, the spread of false teachings founded, above all, on the claim of Christ's divinity. Effectively denied true mortality by the misguided zeal of his proselytizing disciples, Rilke's Christ finds himself condemned to relive, indefinitely, the horror of his own crucifixion. In a grotesque inversion of the motif of the resurrection—which subsumes bodily death into eternal spiritual life—Christ wanders from one cross to another, suffering eternal death, any ongoing spiritual life he might possess transformed into an endless, senseless repetition of the torturous moment of physical demise.

The mythic picture Rilke boldly paints is no mere phantasm, but a powerful portrayal of a pyschospiritual reality, the poetic image of a truth inscribed in the soul history of humankind. Rilke's image of Christ qua Ahasuerus reflects the chronic fixation on the literal truth of the crucifixion (spectacularly manifested once more in Mel Gibson's 2004 film *The Passion of the Christ*) that qualifies as one prominent feature of the popular reception of the Christ-image. The crucifixion represents—at least in part—the overwhelming pain, suffering, and death inherent in earthly or bodily existence. According to Christian doctrine, redemption from that state is effected in and through the Resurrection, which sublimates earthly and physical existence (represented by the body of Christ) into a blessed spiritual or divine state (initially, the "resurrection body" recognized by Magdalene; later, Christ's estate in heaven). Sign and signature of Christ's divinity, the Resurrection supplies (as Paul famously pronounced) the indispensable foundation for Christian faith, guaranteeing the ultimate efficacy of its promise of salvation.

Once again, the dualism of spirit and matter controls the popular reception of Christianity. The spiritual initiative of the individual soul is accorded terribly restricted agency in the conventional redemptive scheme. According to the more narrow-minded version of official—and popular evangelical—tenet, it is only "belief" in Christ—belief in the literal truth of his divine nature, his resurrection, and his ascent to heaven after his death—that can redeem the human being from the fallenness and sin manifested in the very fact of his or her physical body and mortality.

In Rilke's vision, it is this structure of belief that Christ's disciples promulgate and that untold individuals—"an endless legion"—have accepted. Rilke, however, regarding Christ as purely human, rejects the whole package as false and delusional dogma. Consequently, Rilke's Vision pictures those who have lived (and died) by it as victims of false martyrdom who after the fact discover they have been duped. This discovery, of course, does require imaging some kind of soul or spiritual life after death (Rilke's denial of Christ's divinity never translates into scientific materialism or the rejection of all forms of spiritual existence), and the passage ends in a hellish, Dantesque vision of legions of souls—the ghosts of believers—decrying the fraud that denied them authentic being and clamoring for retribution.

Misery loves company, and the tortured souls are satisfied in their desire, not by any "external" punishment visited upon Christ, but by the internal logic and dynamic of this structure of belief itself—its effective elision of any true imagination of the autonomous spiritual agency of the individual soul. So long as canons of literal belief supersede and impede understanding of the *symbolic* meaning of the crucifixion; so long as individual human beings do not translate the meaning of the event into the imaginative terms constitutive of the psyche or soul's own inner life; the import of the crucifixion remains effectively external to the soul and its creative life. As such, the image of the crucifixion cannot itself be transformed or function transformatively for the human being, but instead remains inscribed in the (individual and collective) psyche as an unprocessed image charged with all kinds of unconscious meanings and energic effects. The inherent urge for resolution—constantly renewed and constantly frustrated—then dictates that the image be obsessively, compulsively repeated *ad infinitum.* In psychological terms, this is the essence of trauma.

Rilke's portrayal of Christ as Ahasuerus, doomed to die again and again and again on the cross, thus offers a precise imaginative picture of a profound trauma afflicting human consciousness across vast stretches of space and time. Certain fundamental(ist) strains of church doctrine—its inherent metaphysical dualism, insistence on specific literal beliefs, and policing of the acceptable forms of representing those beliefs (recall the 787 Council of Nicaea)—can proscribe or depotentiate the individual soul's own original imagination of the events of Christ's life, at one and the same time promoting fixation on the fact of the crucifixion and inhibiting elaboration and transformation of the archetypal image contained in it. In Rilke's Vision, then, it is not merely Rilke's "Christ" who suffers this awful fate, but we ourselves: all those who have created and—by force of deep unconscious cultural habit—continue to recreate him in this image. Rilke's Ahasuerus figure becomes the archetype of that aspect of human consciousness that scorns the true Christ by *merely* believing in him rather than seeking to understand him in a more psychologically awakened fashion: for instance, recognizing the crucifixion as a symbol of the tearing tension of opposites inherent in human soul life (and too the psychological death, or *nigredo*, ultimately consequent upon that tearing tension) and working creatively to transform those energies in the soul itself.[63]

Rilke's Vision holds Christ to some degree responsible for his own fate, insofar as he (or, at his cue, his disciples) laid claim to a unique divinity that set him apart from Everyman—from the archetypal truth inherent in each and every human soul. Needless to say, however, this Ahasuerus lives in us all, including, naturally, Rilke himself, who could never wholly escape the influence of his intensely Catholic childhood. In writing this, and indeed all his Visions, Rilke thus attempts an act of personal as well as cultural exorcism and therapeutic transformation. Rilke's Visions endeavor to redress the trauma induced by an overly pietistic and dogmatic faith in a manner closely akin to traditional psychotherapeutic praxis: revisiting significant events, elaborating their symbolic import through imaginative analysis and dramatic recreation, and, ultimately, freeing the compulsion lodged in the latent image by way of its imaginative transformation.

Consequently, in writing "The Fair," Rilke is actually striving to make it possible for Christ—and us—to escape the curse of Ahasuerus and climb down from the cross, or, better, *up* the tree it may become through imaginative, metaphorical transformation. Note the passage from Rilke's "Young Workman's Letter," written over twenty years later:

> I cannot conceive that the cross should remain, which was, after all, only a cross-roads. It certainly should not be stamped on us on all occasions like a brandmark. For is the situation not this: he intended simply to provide the loftier tree, on which we could ripen better. He, on the cross, is this new tree in God, and we were to be warm, happy fruit at the top of it.
>
> We should not always talk of what was formerly, but the afterwards should have begun. This tree, it seems to me, should have become so one with us, or we with it, and by it, that we should not need to occupy ourselves continually with it, but simply and quietly with God, for his aim was to lift us up and into God more purely.[64]

We have cited repeatedly the inherent connection between the soul and dream. It is no accident that the mode of Rilke's Visions (closely connected, we should recall, with his lyrical efforts in *Dreamcrowned*) remains so close to that of dream work. The art of the Visions begin to reveal the archetypally psychological power of poetry to effect imaginative transformation and, in so doing, (re)make soul.

Finally, a crowd comes into the booth and breaks the narrator's trance. The image of Christ that had assumed such compelling force becomes, once more, a mere waxen figure.

> A crowd came in and stood, with noisy tongue,
> near that first group of figures, and before me
> the body of the Crucified now hung
> sallow and still; no more did he relax
> the pose of wax.

And yet the Vision lingers. The day after he wrote "The Fair," Rilke composed one of the last poems included in *Dreamcrowned*:

XXI

There are such wonderfully white nights
in which all things silver are,
and the clear star-shine so mild
it seems bent on bringing shepherds
to a new Jesus-child.

As if strewn with diamond-dust
heaven's roof and floor spread far,
and in hearts steeped in dream,
rises a faith that knows no chapel,
sewing its miracles silently
into the world's seam.[65]

Rilke wrote the first three Visions one after another in the course of just four days from October 5 through October 9, 1896. Closely related in theme as well as tonal character, it is these Visions that most directly and deeply engage Rilke's fundamental religious and theological concerns: the existence of the Christian God ("our Father in Heaven"), the authenticity of Christian cosmology and its scheme of salvation, the divinity of the Christ himself, and the truth and value of his gospel and personal example. While Rilke does entertain radical views on these subjects, his fundamental positions were by no means unprecedented. Mandel points out that, for half a century at least, numerous European intellectuals (including theologians, especially practitioners of the new "higher criticism," who encouraged more liberal and less literal-minded readings of the Bible) had been actively criticizing the founding tenets of the popular Christian faith. He mentions David Friedrich Strauss's 1835/36 *Das Leben Jesu*, "viewing Jesus as a human about whose life myths were woven"; Feuerbach's 1851 *Das Wesen der Religion* (The Essence of Religion), "suggesting that the hereafter is nothing but the present idealized, that theology is the product of the human spirit, and that the concept of God is an ideal rationalized and projected from the best instincts of man"; Renan's sober *La Vie de Jésus* (1863) and Seeley's *Ecce Homo* (1865), both consciously unromantic portrayals of a very human Jesus.[66] Then, of course, there were the likes of Darwin,

Nietzsche, and Emerson. Rilke hardly lacked intellectual ammunition for the sorts of views inscribed in the *Visions*. Even so, the work's peculiar strength inheres in the combination of the almost psychoanalytic precision and emotional force marshaled by its poetic imaginations—the way Rilke speaks of and to the soul in its native idiom of dream, image, and inner vision.

Rilke wrote the fourth and fifth Visions later in that same year (1896) in Munich. These poems do not deal so directly with theological issues, but further deepen Rilke's probe of the soul of his very human—and yet not human enough—Christ. Both visions portray Jesus as a man whose own humanity—especially his capacity for (human) love—has suffered egregiously on account of his past, unwarranted spiritual presumption.

"The Loon" opens upon a scene of children streaming out of a schoolhouse at noon, frolicking happily about in sunny summer weather. Soon, however, one little girl, Anna, shrieks an alarm, for she has spied a figure whose disordered appearance has, evidently, frightened the children before. The cry "The loon!" goes up. The children scatter and run, but the strange, ominous man pursues them, intent—for his own reasons—upon one little girl:

> His great height,
> his death-white cheeks,
> follow their flight,
> pursue their shrieks...
>
> Around his thighs
> the cloak is flapping,
> its coarse wool trapping
> him, as he flies.
> Death in his cheeks,
> he stands and seeks.

Finally, even as the rest of the children escape and disappear, the "loon" or "fool" (*der Narr*) catches Anna. At first, she is absolutely terrified, but as she looks up at the stranger, a peculiar transformation takes place: "the eyes of the stranger cease to be strange" and a deep trust, even love, springs up in the child's wildly beating heart as the man holds her gently and touches her hair. Then he speaks, softly:

"Is Magdalene your mother's name?"
"Yes."
And the words on his lips are warm as flame:
"Is she in great distress?"
"Yes."
And the words on his lips ring out like chimes:
"Has she much sorrow?"
"Yes.
I have seen her sit up many times
crying from midnight until tomorrow."
"Do you know how to pray?"
"Yes."
"For your papa—have you prayers to say?"
"Yes."
"Do."
"But where's my papa? I don't know...Do you?"
At this he lifts her high as he can.
Like a choir of birds is the voice of the man,
birds lost deep in a blossoming glen
of jasmine: "Give me that word again!"
"What?"
"That."
"Papa?"
"Yes."

And that Yes is a victory chant, a hurrah.
Long do his lips her forehead press;
he drinks her bright eyes with a kiss;
that kiss is love, is gratefulness.

Read in relation to "Jewish Cemetery," there is certainly some irony in Christ's bidding the child—his child—to pray for him. (Within a few years, Rilke will be writing his own *Prayers* in intimate dialogue with God, but those will be his prayers, and his God, not Christ's.) Most noteworthy here, though, is the poignancy of the love between this human father and his child; most wrenching, his incapacity to fulfill or live that love:

And he sets her down tenderly, murmuring;
"I cannot give you anything—"
Only a smile: lips wearily curl:
"I am much poorer than you are, girl..."
Under the words there sounds a sob.
And lightly he motions once more with his hand,
and goes. He goes through the torrid land
like a beggar in his slovenly garb
and yet like a king, so proud and tall.

In what sense is Jesus "poorer" than the child? Materially, perhaps, but not only that. Unable to shed the skin of the savior, his *soul* has evidently been emotionally crippled by his *spiritual* pretension and become incapable, really, of giving love—even to his own child. "The Loon" repeats the structure of the absent father central to "Jewish Cemetery," but on another level—as if the absence of Christ's own divine father has been transferred (in a stepped-down version) to Jesus himself. This Vision portrays Christ as one who has invested his spiritual capital in his (failed) divine mission and gone humanly bankrupt in the process.

Once again, the truth of Rilke's Vision transcends the particulars of this dramatic setting and expresses real archetypal psychological insight. In this case, moreover, the picture he paints has a potent application to his own life, for Rilke's own psychology bears definite resemblances to that of the Christ portrayed in this vision. Recall, for instance, the lead poem in *Dreamcrowned*, "King's Song":

If you dare bear life with dignity
only the petty will it demean.
Beggars may call you brother
yet you still may be a king.

In certain crucial regards, the psychological portrait painted in this poem matches that of the proud beggar-king of "The Loon." Rilke himself—though rejecting worship of the Christ—did not fail to imitate his example, at least in part. In his own unique fashion, the poet found himself inspired by a sense of a sacred mission and dedicated his life uncompromisingly to his art. It is no secret that such an unequivocal commitment to spiritual goals—whether it be in the name of religious worship or at the altar of art—can exact human costs, and the scene painted in "The Loon" proves all the more wrenching for the way it foreshadows Rilke's own abandonment—not long after her birth—of his daughter, his own future performance of the role of the absent father. It is not surprising that in imaginatively (re)creating his human Christ, Rilke was not only transforming the religious legacy of his childhood, but—in so plumbing the depths of his soul—foretelling his future in ways he could hardly have guessed.

In Rilke's fifth Vision, "The Night," we once more encounter Jesus engaged in a very human relationship, but this time the kind of love involved is not parental, but sexual. Throughout Rilke's creative career—from his first book to his last masterpieces—erotic love played a central role in his life and art. One cannot begin to imagine Rilke—man or poet—minus his relationships with Vally, Lou Andreas-Salomé, Paula Becker, Clara Westhoff, Mimi Romanelli, Lou Albert-Lasard, Magdalena von Hattingberg, Baladine Klossowska, and many other women friends or lovers, actual or (Louise Labé, Gaspara Stampa) literary. In one of his letters to young Franz Kappus, Rilke likens the act of poetic creation to the sexual act itself:

> And in fact the artist's experience lies so unbelievably close to the sexual, to its pain and its pleasure, that the two phenomena are really just different forms of one and the same longing and bliss. And if instead of "heat" one could say "sex"—sex in the great pure sense of the word, free of any sin attached to it by the Church...[67]

Given his reverence for the miracle of erotic communion, it is not surprising that Rilke should fault Christian mores for associating sex with sin—an attitude that flows, once more, from a poorly mediated dualism of spirit and body (since these two are split, and sex is manifestly of the body, it must be—according to this blunt logic—inherently anti-spiritual and sinful). Toward the end of "The Young Workman's Letter," Rilke takes Christianity to task for poisoning the well of human being by stigmatizing sexuality:

> And here, in the love which, with an intolerable mixture of contempt, desire, and curiosity, they call "sensual", here indeed are to be found the worst results of that vilification of earthly life which Christianity has felt obliged to engage in. Here everything

> is distorted and disowned, although it is from this deepest of all events that we come forth, and have ourselves the centre of our ecstasies in it. It seems to me . . . more and more incomprehensible that a doctrine which puts us in the wrong in that matter, where the whole creation enjoys its most blissful right, should be able . . . to assert itself over a wide area.[68]

Whatever speculation there may be about Jesus' relationship with Mary Magdalene, he is (unlike numerous deities in other tradition) never represented as a sexual being in the Gospels. Yet in "The Night," we find Rilke's pale and woebegone wanderer playing a lead role in a scene of sexual temptation.

> It's after twelve. Along the row of houses
> dark hours coax home the last of the carousers.
> But in the smoke-filled "Angel Room" a pair
> still lean back in the frayed old velvet chair.
> He and a woman. And a sallow waiter
> reminds them rudely that it's getting later.

The woman is of ill repute, and the name of their place of converse sharply ironic—the first of a whole series of perversely profane caricatures of sacred matters. A cold, reticent, depressed and repressed Jesus at first insists on drinking nothing but water, but she will have none of it and, with a commanding summons to the waiter, turns water into wine—or, as it turns out, champagne—and praises the miraculously foaming fluid as "the incense of our cathedrals." Jesus remains sullen, unmoved, but she persists, downs the champagne, lets her silken clothes slip seductively down her shoulder, leans over, and solicits him with a classic *carpe diem*:

> "Will you forever dawdle?" she demands
> lispingly; "Come!" and closer to him bends,
> with hot words. "You're a young man yet; get wise!
> "Come, I know better than to dream away
> a life: life should be lived! Now take your prize!"

And, at long last, the dam breaks:

> Then the cold, joyless one's caught in the fray;
> his cravings, that so long were held at bay,
> now burst their bonds within his soul, and rise!

He clasps the woman with a madman's cries;
his fingers clutch and claw the folds till they
ecstatically rip her silk array.
Heavy as lead, his wild hands stray
over her body, as if he wanted to mold that clay
into a divine image, worthy of his own.

...and so it goes. Yet, after a pause in the action, Jesus stirs from lethargy, and with whispered urgency, shares with her a faded but haunting memory:

"You, there's something I must say.
They came to arraign me in the court one day.
The judge cried out. His question was so odd:
I hear it still: Are you the son of God?
No longer am I sure of what it meant,
but at the time I let them lash and chide;
and, stirred up by their scorn, I thought my pride
would reach the top star in the firmament.
What do you want? Yes, I am he, I cried.
My throne is stationed at my sire's right side.
—Why are you laughing? So, spit in my face;
I know it, woman; I deserve your sneer
and my remorse. No, I am not—that's clear—
I'm not a god!"

And then follows the crowning comedown:

"You can't take much, I fear.
Such funny talk! Before one glass can race
out of your stomach to the heart and brain
your words become unreal and half-insane.
No, no, you are not God, that's very plain..."

And so: a brothel called the "Angel Room"; Jesus' first miracle—the turning of water into wine at the wedding in Cana—parodied in the form of a whore's peremptory order to a waiter; a sex-starved man's lust-driven groping compared to God's fashioning of Eve—what is the logic informing this series of satiric figures? Perhaps one more example—the framing of Jesus' memory of his appearance before Pilate as a laughable hallucination attributable to the effects of alcohol—may cue us in. This instance figures things spiritual as an epiphenomenal effect or symptom of a bodily condition; indicates, parodically, that the true cause of any recollection of divine character must be a hallucination based in bodily disorder. The realm of spirit is thus denied any authentic reality; is revealed to be, ultimately, a sort of delusion. This represents a satiric reversal of traditional Christian and Platonic metaphysics wherein material or bodily reality is supposed to be a distorted and fallen image or effect of spirit. For the strict Platonist, the world of appearance manifests as the deceptive shadow-image of the realm of authentic existences (divine ideas); for the conventional Christian, physical existence begins as a fall from grace, and salvation entails its transcendence or erasure.

Very well, but what is the point of this table-turning? Once more, Rilke puts poetic figure in the service of archetypal psychological truth. For if body and soul are so thoroughly repressed as to be denied authentic existence and value, then any claims of spiritual worth and character are, precisely, delusional. Why? Because body and soul do in fact exist, and the enormous instinctual and astral forces inherent in them, if not consciously recognized and embraced, operate unconsciously and uncontrollably, determining and distorting everything. In this case, anything presented as "spiritual" inevitably appears as nothing other than the outward face of one or another sort of dirty desire—the lust for sex, money, power. This psychodynamic infests our own contemporary culture: we have a largely puritanical society obsessed with sex and violence; a clergy repeatedly racked by sexual scandals; holier-than-thou evangelists steeped in corruption and greed; and even reports of terrorists who kill imagining they are fighting a holy war, expecting to be rewarded for their atrocities by the attention of hosts of virgins in heaven.

In this Vision, Rilke calls Christianity's historic repression of sexuality to account. He represents the Christian exemplar, Jesus himself, suffering from intense, centuries-long suppression of desire—a symbolic picture, once more, of the suffering of the human soul, the historical psyche, under the thumb of a religious ideology that so strongly identifies sex with sin. It is quite natural and inevitable that—if the curtain on sex were finally lifted—such a one would find himself in a brothel; for is that not how sexuality necessarily appears to the puritanical, eternally virginal attitude? And yet, at the same time, precisely because it has been the forbidden fruit, the sphere of the sensual and sexual inevitably becomes charged with numinosity: on a deep psychic level, the value withheld from that sphere will—when the taboo is momentarily lifted—be transferred to it wholesale, with an indiscriminate rush, so that the crudest expressions of sensual and sexual desire taken on quasi-divine features. In such a dream-vision, then, whores may appear ministering angels, champagne a miracle, and the rabid caress of long-held lust the magical conjuring of a helpmeet that is "bone of my bone, flesh of my flesh." For a moment, for a night, libidinal release must feel like salvation, paradise regained:

> Wildly he draws the curtain; and the air
> holds nothing but the sweet laments, that chime
> like jubilation echoed from a time
> before the human race, grown modest, chose
> to bind the power of its limbs in clothes,
> and every wish was yet a thing to dare.

Such ecstasy may even—as we have seen—be enough, for a moment, to raise the faded memory of that time, long ago, when one felt like a God.

Yet there is another person in the picture—the experienced one for whom sexuality is no mystery, and who is decidedly not duped. For the woman, here, is in something of the opposite psychological circumstance with regard to sex. For her, it is all too familiar, and she knows naked sensuality for what it is; knows the short term of its crowning bliss. She lets him know it, too, in yet one more fine satiric gesture:

> "No, no you are not God, that's very plain;
> nor shall you be accused of such a thing.
> But wait, you pale one! till tomorrow's sun,
> you shall be somewhat of a king.
> That suits you? . . . "
> And dexterously now her fingers braid
> rose unto rose until the wreath is made,
> including leaves that have begun to fade.
> She sets it on his head which, never moving,
> looks empty-eyed upon her all the while;
> then, laughing, she applauds, her nod approving;
> "Bravissimo, the true imperial style!"

The original crown of thorns is itself an ironic object. It satirizes Christ's royal claim, and yet—in the same gesture—recognizes it;

acknowledges the suffering intrinsic to the human state, and concedes, too, that it is the bearing of this suffering that lends man true stature. Here, though, we are not witnessing Christ before Pilate, but Christ with a prostitute, "king" for a night. So the crown of thorns is replaced by a wreath of roses: roses already crushed by the weight of sensual passion (Jesus has rolled over on them in bed), already withering, dying—and so a crown symbolizing the state of purely sensual man, the evanescence of his reign, passion's transient luster. For no sooner is it begun than night is over, and lances of light announce the crucifying morn:

> But dawn takes aim against the panes, and leaves
> his first shafts in the boards: bright shafts that fall
> through the pale widow, and are fixed in the wall.

The woman "yawns herself awake" and shakes Jesus, who sleeps with the crown still upon his head. When she chides that he's crazy enough to walk around wearing it in broad daylight, he looks at her, uncomprehendingly, until:

> With a frown
> she brushes the dead autumn wreath he wore
> from his black hair. He stares at her once more,
> and weeps, as the last withered leaves disperse
> and the last faded rose falls to the floor...
> "We are this world's eternal inbred curse:
> I, the eternal illusion—and you, the eternal whore."—

The Vision ends with these words, Jesus' last judgment. His sentence aptly sums the moral of the scene. In a world in which spirit and body are radically sundered, we are once more in a kind of no-win situation: affirmation of spirit entails the impossible negation of body and so itself recedes into illusion; affirmation of body, as such is constitutionally alien to spirit, results in mere sensual indulgence that lacks any moral or spiritual component—the whoring of the body. In the absence of any real mediation between spirit and body, spirituality amounts to illusion, and sensuality, prostitution.

We might venture to say that what is missing in this scheme and in this scene is, once again, the third term—the soul that moves between spirit and body, connecting these otherwise irreconcilable poles of the universe. And yet soul is not entirely absent—it manifests, for instance, in Jesus' incorrigible sorrow—nor is it soul alone that is capable of playing that central, mediating role. It does so, in fact, only in conjunction with a spiritual character whose very absence defines the whoredom Jesus so keenly feels and laments. It does not take a psychologist or a literary critic to know that what is really missing in Jesus' intercourse with the woman is the source of true joy in the soul: love.

The relationship of the soul to love—mythically figured as the relationship between Psyche and Eros—beats at the heart of James Hillman's archetypal psychology. In his foundational work *The Myth of Analysis*, Hillman suggests that the insights achieved via any psychological theory are largely determined by the underlying myth which, consciously or not, supplies the imaginative ground of that theory. Freudian psychoanalysis, explicitly founded upon Oedipus' story, provides the classic instance. The Oedipus myth, argues Hillman, has bequeathed a tragic legacy:

> The story [Freud] chose to tell us has left behind cursed issues: father-murder, wars of generations, unsolved incest longings and incestuous entanglements in both relationships and ideas, the distortion of the feminine into the Jocasta mold, the anima as an intellectual riddle with a monster's body, and destruction everywhere—suicide, blight and sterility, hanging, blinding—descending to future generations. Is this our myth?[69]

No, contends Hillman. In its place, he would install another story, and proposes the tale first told in the eleventh century by Apuleius—the fable of Amor and Psyche, as "the myth of analysis."

Hillman chooses this story because, like his psychology, it "places soul at the center." The myth stands as the only one in which the soul itself—in the person of its namesake, Psyche—figures as the main character. Equally central, the myth sets Psyche in primary relation to Eros: as the plot unfolds, the myth provides an imaginative model for essential stages and processes of the soul's own development, driven by the soul's relationship to Eros. The soul-making psychology developed along the lines of this myth thus unfolds under the signal auspices of Love and the sacred union—*hieros gamos*—of Psyche and Eros that supplies the climax of the story.

Hillman decries a culture that represses soul and one-sidedly worships spirit—but recognizes, too, that any psychology worthy of the name must imagine soul *in relation to* spirit. If such imagination suffers undue neglect, the art of psychology degenerates into the workaday ministrations of uninspired professional methodology. The question remains, however, what form of spirit (for there are many) may be imagined as the spiritual source of both the logos and mythos of the soul? Hillman's answer is unambiguous: "Eros is the God of psychic reality, the true lord of the psyche...the creative principle which engenders soul and is the patron of the field of psychology."[70]

Eros plays this role because it is Eros, in connection with Psyche, that opens the region between spirit and matter that defines the native domain of soul and, in so doing, connects the otherwise irreconcilably divided poles of the universe. At the same time, Eros holds the key to the spiritual life of the soul, plays the numinous agency that can lend it divine guidance:

> Eros connects the personal to something beyond and brings the beyond into personal experience. It leads (psychopompos) the soul to the Gods and brings some glimmer and sublime horror of the divine into the soul—for we are at our best and worst in love. This *metaxy,* this intermediary region, would best be described today as the *realm of psychic reality*...extending at the one end to the cosmogonic spiritual eros and at the other to the physical and phallic.[71]

Finally, it may be worth making explicit what may already be obvious. Mythically speaking, while the soul is archetypally feminine in gender, Psyche's spiritual partner, Eros, embodies a masculine force:

> The phallic aspect of eros points to its male essence....Whether as grace of spirit descending, as Platonic yearning upward, or as Aristotelian principle of universal motion, love summons, starts, quickens, creates into life... Moreover, his wings...[72]

> And how might Love have come to you?
> Did it come like sun, a blossom-snow,
> or did it come like a prayer?—Tell:
>
> A joy loosed itself, luminous, from the heavens
> and hung with huge, well-folded wings
> upon my blooming soul...[73]

The relation of the soul to love, and love to the soul, supplies the archetypal point of departure for Rilke's poetry, inspiring and centering the poet's creative career no less than it does the praxis of archetypal psychology. We have already mentioned the ubiquity of love in Rilke's life and art; the primacy of the relationship between the soul and love, psyche and eros, weaves the fabric of his poetic oeuvre, manifesting both in fine detail (as in the lines above) and broad outline. Love figures as a principal theme in all of Rilke's well-known major works, from *The Book of Hours* through *Malte* to the *Elegies* and *Sonnets*. His lesser-known early work, too, abounds with love poetry; though much may be eminently forgettable, the seminal importance of the relation between the soul and love can hardly be disputed. We have already discussed *Dreamcrowned* and stressed the significance of the titling of its initial part ("Dreams") but failed to mention the equally significant second part—a series of love poems titled (with equal simplicity) "Loves." It is the first poem of this section that appears above.

The archetypal influence of the Psyche-Eros myth manifests clearly in Rilke's life as well as his art. We have already mentioned Rilke's signature connection with soul as it manifests in the formative influence of feminine figures in his life and hinted at the central role played by the anima archetype in the poet's psychology. We will explore these issues further throughout this book—most especially, in Part II (Death and the Maiden). For now, however, we may merely note that the very premise of this book—the gold chain linking Rilke's life and work, his poetry and his psychobiography; and, too, the mysterious fascination attached to the very subject of Rilke—hinges upon his intimate involvement with psyche qua anima:

> Now the main thing about the anima is just what has always been said about the psyche; it is unfathomable, ungraspable. For the anima, "the archetype of life," as Jung called her, is that function of the psyche which is its actual life, the present mess it is in, its discontent, dishonesties, and thrilling illusions.... The issues she presents are as endless as the soul is deep, and perhaps these very endless labyrinthine "problems" are its depth.[74]

There is, however, another, equally compelling side to this story, and to see it most clearly we need understand something of Eros' own archetypal manifestations.

In *Peaks and Vales*, Hillman makes clear the spiritual character of Eros, and identifies the *puer aeternus*—the eternal youth—as one psychological type closely identified with the transcendent aims of that fiery spirit:

> Or is the one ascending the spiritual impetus of the *puer aeternus*, the winged godlike imago in us each, the beautiful boy of the spirit—Icarus on the way to the sun, then plummeting with waxen wings; Phaëthon driving the sun's chariot out of control, burning up the world; Bellerophon, ascending on his white winged horse, then falling onto the plains of wandering, limping ever after? These are the *puer* high climbers, the heaven stormers, whose eros reflects the torch and ladder of Eros and his searching arrow, a longing for higher and further and more and purer and better. Without this archetypal component affecting our lives, there would be no spiritual drive, no new sparks, no going beyond the given, no grandeur and sense of personal destiny.[75]

And, correlatively:

> The concept puer aeternus refers to that archetypal dominant which personifies or is in special relation with the transcendent spiritual powers of the collective unconscious. Puer figures can be regarded as avatars of the Self's spiritual aspect.[76]

While the anima exerted great sway over Rilke's psychology, his identification with the puer archetype and its inveterate desire for the pure, perfect, immortal spirit proved no less powerful and indeed may well be considered the prevailing influence in the earliest portion of Rilke's career. In the continuation of the just-quoted passage, Hillman notes that, when parental influence proves especially strong, "puer attitudes and impulses will show personal taints of the mother's boy or *fils du papa*, the perennial adolescence of the provisional life"—perspectives hardly irrelevant to Rilke the man or the child René. Another passage proves still more revealing of the syndrome underlying the style of René Rilke's youthful life and art and indeed points toward the underlying reason for the deficiencies marring Rilke's earliest work:

> The puer spirit is the least psychological, has the least soul. Its "sensitive soulfulness" is rather pseudo-psychological. . . . It can search

> and risk; it has insight, aesthetic intuition, spiritual ambition—all, but not psychology, for psychology requires time, femininity of soul, and the entanglement of relationships. Instead of psychology, the puer attitude displays an aesthetic point of view: the world as beautiful images. . . . Life becomes literature.[77]

This passage not only paints a virtual portrait of Rilke in his guise as youthful aesthete, but indicates, too, how radically his poetic growth depended upon a long course of soul work deepening and maturing his (psychologically uninformed) puer origins—soul work this book parses as Rilke's own living of the Psyche-Eros myth. The puer influence—while most dominant in Rilke's adolescence—remains clearly evident in the poet's later life as well, especially (as could be expected) in his love life. Again and again, Rilke would fall in love but fly away when the all-too-human realities of the relationship threatened his idealizations of love. It manifests, too, in his crucial, nearly lifelong fascination with what he called "the early-departed"—souls who did not tarnish their perfection by too long a term on earth before their return to the spiritual sphere. All these expressions are important, yet what remains most crucial is the signal spiritual source behind them; for erotic puer energy, while debilitating in its negative aspect, remains vital and indispensable in the constructive elements of its influence. Sometimes in subtle, sometimes in obvious form, the God Eros acts as the impetus driving Rilke's creative poetic career, lending ideal direction and creative force to the concerns of soul that compose its chief subject. At the same time, the poet's constant preoccupation with anima—so much more pronounced than in, for instance, Emerson—keeps the maturing Rilke's spiritual inclinations intimately involved in the myriad foibles and weaknesses of the human psyche, an involvement that, far from thinning his work, lends it emotional immediacy, depth, and the sense of interiority so remarkable in Rilke's accomplished work.

Hillman elaborates the essential dynamic of the puer-psyche marriage—the reciprocal transformations of spirit and psyche at the heart of soul-making—in a passage resonant with overtones from Rilke's life and the interiority peculiar to his art. Hillman begins by elucidating what soul (psyche) lends to spirit (eros):

> The puer-psyche marriage results first of all in increased interiority. It constructs a walled space, the thalamus or bridal chamber,

> neither peak nor vale, but rather a place where both can be looked at through glass windows or be closed off with doors. This increased interiority means that each new puer inspiration, each hot idea, at whatever time of life... be given psychization. It will first be drawn through the labyrinthine ways of the soul, which wind it and slow it and nourish it from many sides...[78]

before elaborating what the erotic spirit offers to the soul:

> Likewise, for soul: the bridal chamber intensifies the brooding, gives it heat and pressure, building soul from amorphous clouds into driving needs. And these, by benefit of puer, become formulated into language. There is a sense of process, direction, continuity within one's interior life of dreams and wishes. Suffering begins to make sense. Instead of the repetitious and usual youth-nymph pairings of virginal innocence coupled with seed spilled everywhere foolishly, psychic conception takes place and the opus of one's life begins to form.[79]

"And the opus of one's life begins to form." What, then, of the role of the *Visions* in that opus? Have we lost track of the pivotal character of this work in this long excursion on love and the myth of Psyche and Eros? Hardly, for it was the function of Rilke's imaginative *Visions* to deconstruct a system of spiritual belief—deeply rooted in his own psyche—that left insufficient room for the archetypal impetus of his individual creativity, the divinity of love and the passion of the soul that dreamed of union with primordial Eros. Since the conventional myths of Christianity exercise their stranglehold in good measure through popularized images of Christ that sell Christian doctrine to the soul, Rilke, in imaginatively transforming the Christ and elaborating his own original vision of the peculiar deficiencies and strengths of the figure, truly initiated "the opus of his life"; began creating an inner place where his own "religion of soul-making" might unfold under the aegis of Love.

To be sure, the lyrics of a work like *Dreamcrowned* began more directly embodying a poetic vision founded upon the Psyche-Eros mytheme (though at this immature stage, most incompletely so), but the fantasy at play in his early lyrics could not build or deepen without the critical and destructive purgation effected by the *Visions*. Indeed, as Rilke himself noted, the early lyrics may appear "monotonously timid" in comparison with the *Visions*, "the other side of my lyricism," which took

Christian myth and ideology by the horns. Yet, as Rilke's turn of phrase implies, the *Visions* and *Dreamcrowned* are two sides of the same coin. As Hillman mentions, the liberation of psychic energy from the bonds of spiritual system of the kind achieved by the *Visions* itself figures as one of the primary effects of mobilizing the archetypal energies figured in the Psyche-Eros myth:

> The puer psyche marriage finally implies taking our complexes both out of the world and out of the realm of spiritual systems. It means that the search and questing go through a psychological search and questing, and exploration of soul by spirit for psychic fecundation. The messianic, liberating, transcending movement connects first with soul and is concerned first with its movement: not "what does this mean?"—the question asked of spirit by spirit—but "what does this move in my soul?"—the interiorization of the question.[80]

The *Visions*, moreover, were very soon to lead directly to the event that entirely revolutionized Rilke's life and his work. And surely, his meeting with Lou Andreas-Salomé took place under the aegis of the God whom Rilke, in this late poem, celebrates as the spiritual inspiration for the inner religion he was to make his soul's own.

Eros

Masks! Masks! In order to blind Eros.
Who can endure his radiant countenance
when he, like summer's bright solstice,
interrupts spring's slow overture?

How—while conversing—indiscernibly,
it changes; turns serious.... Something cried...
And he throws the nameless shudder like a temple
garment over you, except—inside.

Oh lost, suddenly, oh lost!
Quickly, the Gods lay hold of everything.
Life alters. Fate has been begot.
And deep within you—weeps a spring.[81]

Chapter 3

LAID IN THE HANDS OF LOU

As if the young poet were deliberately striving to attain maturity before the advent of the new century, the years 1897 to 1899 proved pivotal in Rilke's life and work. It was in these years that the author—wrestling ever more intensely with questions revolving around art, religion, and the nature and destiny of the individual soul—first formulated the essential philosophic and religious premises that grounded his conscious sense of artistic vocation. As Rilke's late letter to his Polish translator Hulewicz indicates,[82] these premises would be elaborated in the course of the poet's future development but never fundamentally contradicted or overthrown. Those postulates may be regarded as the founding tenets of a world view that—like Hillman's archetypal psychology—"puts soul at the center."

The *Weltanschauung* Rilke evolved in these years emerged as an organic development of his prior spiritual and artistic initiatives. Literarily speaking, he continued to experiment in drama and in prose, but it was in his poetry that Rilke achieved his most marked advance—one furthered by his ability to incorporate dramatic and narrative elements into his poems. Indeed, in the course of these years, Rilke ultimately managed to fuse the two previously distinct streams of his poetry, wedding the intellectual depth and probity of his *Visions of Christ* with the fount of his own lyric inspiration. Consequently, his relation to religion could become primarily creative rather than critical, and his lyric work—losing its relative timidity—evolved into a vessel capable of containing his most demanding ideation. The transformation thus achieved culminated, in 1899, in the earliest of Rilke's widely known and well-regarded works—the first part of *The Book of Hours*, which greets the momentous turn of the century in these words:

Lou Andreas-Salome, 1897

I live just as the century goes by.
One feels the wind from the great page
where God and you and I have inscribed our age
and which strange hands turn over in the sky.

One feels the glow of a brand new leaf
upon which all may still take place.
Quiet powers draw arrows from a sheaf
and look each other darkly in the face.[83]

Rilke did not undertake the voyage of self-discovery that culminated in *The Book of Hours* alone. The profound developments that marked these formative years (and which give us the first "Rilke" recognized by the world) were triggered by Rilke's meeting with a most remarkable woman, one who was to become the single most important person in the poet's life.

Upon reading the *Visions of Christ* manuscript, a journal editor named Michael Conrad suggested that Rilke might be interested in an article titled "Jesus the Jew," recently published in *Die Freie Bühne*, which expressed views akin to Rilke's own. Rilke did read the article, and, profoundly impressed by it, determined to meet its author. A mutual friend soon made this possible. On the evening of May 12, 1897, in Munich the twenty-two-year-old René Rilke met Lou Andreas-Salomé and—like a true vassal of Eros—immediately fell in love.

Lou Salomé, of German ancestry with an admixture of French blood, grew up in a German-speaking military enclave in St. Petersburg where her father served as a general. At the time of their initial meeting, Lou—fourteen years older than René—was far more accomplished than her youthful admirer. Well known amongst the European intelligentsia for her writings (most especially her books on Ibsen and Nietzsche), she was perhaps still more (in)famous for the unusually free manner in which she conducted her personal relationships. Her friendships with the philosophers Paul Rée and Friedrich Nietzsche had been exceptionally close; nor did her marriage to the scholar Friedrich Carl Andreas conform to expected social norms. Though deeply committed, the marriage was—at Lou's insistence—Platonic, and, by the time of her acquaintance with Rilke, not one which necessarily excluded intimate relations with other men. Indeed, within a month of their first meeting, Lou and Rilke became lovers, and commenced a period of especially intense physical, emotional, and intellectual involvement that lasted (with some interruption) for over three years—years that saw the ambitious young René transform into the poet Rainer Maria Rilke.

The fact that Lou literally gave Rilke his name (René seemed foreign and effeminate to her, and at her suggestion he adopted "the plain, fine, German [Rainer]"[84]) symbolizes the singularly important role Lou played in Rilke's life. While their friendship lasted (though once again, not without interruption) for the rest of Rilke's life, Lou's shaping influence proved most decisive during their initial years together. Meeting Lou, becoming lovers, the summer in the rural retreat of Wolfratshausen and the study of Renaissance art pursued together there; Rilke's subsequent move to Berlin—Lou's place of residence—and their endless walks and talks; the "Italian Journey" prescribed by Lou and the accompanying diary written expressly for her; the two trips to Lou's native country, Russia, which quickly became Rilke's own adopted spiritual homeland and catalyzed the poetic breakthrough of *The Book of Hours*—it was in all that flowed from his relationship with Lou that the poet Rainer Maria Rilke first achieved recognizable identity. A beloved who could inspire and sustain the young poet's idealizations, Lou was, simultaneously, an indubitably *real* human partner; at one and the same time Rilke's Sophie von Kühn and his Charlotte von Stein.[85]

The incalculable importance of Lou's presence in Rilke's life raises interesting questions in connection with the poet's notorious reputation as a sage of solitude or—in W. H. Auden's wry description—"the Santa Claus of loneliness." The contradiction latent in the image of a man who preached his own gospel of self-reliance while relying so deeply on various forms of communion with others throughout his life is no superficial matter, but touches on the very essence of soul itself. Before exploring particulars of Lou and Rainer's relationship, it behooves us to pay some attention to this more general issue, for we will find it illuminates (from yet another perspective) the archetypally *psychological* character of Rilke's life-work.

In the long essay on "Psychological Creativity" that opens his *Myth of Analysis*, James Hillman asserts that the intrinsic character of soul is not so much purely *subjective* as *intersubjective*—dependent upon the continual and constitutive interrelation of souls. Coincidently, Hillman suggests that the impulse towards solitude so often linked with one or

Rilke (seated) and Lou (second from right) in Wolfratshausen

another form of transcendent aim (the quest proceeding "from the alone to the alone," in Plotinus' poetic words) manifests a distinctly *spiritual* calling—a calling to and from the spirit—which exists in tension with the soul's own more inclusive aims:

> Where the spirit lifts, aiming for detachment and transcendence, concern with soul immerses us in immanence: God in the soul or the soul in God, the soul in the body, the soul in the world, souls in each other or in the world-soul. Owing to this immanence, dialogue is not a bridge constructed between isolated skin-encased subjects and objects, I's and Thou's, but is intrinsic, an internal relationship, a condition of the soul's immanence.... Whether we like it or not, whether spirit pulls away and above, we are involved as a psychic necessity.[86]

Hillman continues to explain that such involvement "becomes the first condition for admission to the psychic realm" and hence the prerequisite for what Hillman calls "psychological creativity," the creative work entailed in our commerce with other human souls.

Insofar as Rilke figures as a preeminent poet of soul, it is crucial to recognize the degree to which the lines of his *artistic* and his *psychological* creativity braid inextricably. Rilke's ability to engender significant poetry depended, more or less constantly, upon his capacity to enter into significant relation with other human souls. To be sure, Rilke's own species of psychological creativity ran up against strict bounds in certain directions, but the fact that he was unable or unwilling to sustain a marriage or truly embrace fatherhood should not blind us to the myriad of significant others central to his life and work: family, friends (including fellow artists), lovers, patrons, teachers, even caregivers and adopted charges. Indeed, the genesis of most all of Rilke's major works can be linked to one or more significant human connections: the *New Poems* to Rodin's tutelage; *Malte* to (among others) members of his family; the *Duino Elegies* to Marie von Turn und Taxis-Hohenlohe and Baladine Klossowska; the *Sonnets to Orpheus* to Vera Ouckama Knoop, and *The Book of Hours*, of course, to Lou. Rilke frequently acknowledged his debt to others in a book's dedication, and *The Book of Hours* (indeed dedicated to Lou) represents a signal case in point.

None of this belies the indubitable pull of the spirit. Just as it is misguided to image Rilke too one-sidedly as a lonely seer, it is foolish to deny his genuinely hermetic inclinations. Rilke's work owes much of its richness and value not to one side or the other of the soul-spirit equation, but to the constant and creative tension between the desire for human intercourse and the solitude required to hear and respond to the call of the spirit. Rilke often spoke of this tension in terms of the conflict between "Life" and "Art"; in later life, especially, the demands of his vocation often seemed to him markedly at odds with all forms of social obligation. Yet the truth of the matter was never so simple, and it is both ironic and deeply revealing that the poet who so often bewailed this antagonism was one whose art was so constantly and intimately bound to biographical and psychological development. Mandel states the matter most succintly and unequivocally: "the link between Rilke's biography and poetry is absolute." One can, moreover, point to phases of Rilke's development in which soul and spirit, life and art, did not so much polarize as flow together in reciprocally nourishing—if never perfectly harmonious—union. Rilke's first years with Lou figure as the outstanding example of just such a confluence.

The initial love relationship to Lou derived its special power from its uniquely creative and compelling archetypal basis. In her memoirs, Lou herself provides an unusually unguarded and revealing view of the deep ground of the couple's love:

> If I was your wife for years, it was because you were the first truly real person in my life, body and man indivisibly one, unquestionably a fact of life itself. I could have confessed to you word for word what you said in declaring your love: "You alone are real." Thus we were a couple even before we had become friends, and becoming friends wasn't so much a matter of choice as it was the fulfillment of that underlying marriage. We were not two halves seeking the other: we were a whole which confronted that inconceivable wholeness with a shiver of surprised recognition. We were thus siblings—but from a time before incest had become sacrilege.[87]

The brother-sister pairing Lou alludes to here maintains a singularly close connection to the archetypal energies constellated in the eros-psyche bond. Hillman writes:

> To recreate family in our generation, eros and psyche must have the possibility of meeting in the home; this would favor soul-making and give an altogether different perspective to family relationships. This perspective looks less to the hierarchical connections of parent-child...and more to the soul connection, as between brother and sister....where concern for soul is paramount, a relationship takes on more the nature of the brother-sister pair. Compare the *soror* in alchemy and the appellations of "Brother" and "Sister" in religious societies....Kinship libido, which, as Jung points out, is behind incest phenomena, would flow on the brother-sister model into the mutuality of soul-making rather than regressively toward the parents.[88]

Lou, then, could prove so vital to the making of the young Rilke's soul—and so stimulating to his creativity—because, in its initial phase, *their relationship constellated archetypal energies paradigmatic of the creative act of soul-making itself.* Indeed, one could imagine that their romantic partnership flagged when the parental dynamics of the relationship (Lou as mother, Rainer as son) came to outweigh and invalidate the archetypal brother-sister love. Their term as lovers did, finally, come to an end in 1901, but not before their love had vouchsafed Rilke—not only his true name and a whole new *niveau* of emotional maturity—but, as well, the intellectual foundation of his poetic vocation and his own nascent "religion of soul-making."

It is one of the chief defects of the canon of Rilke criticism that—while virtually all informed readers acknowledge the enormous role Lou Andreas-Salomé played in the poet's human development—none adequately interrogate the substance of her intellectual contribution to his art. Lou's influence flowed in part from her role as a conduit of Nietzsche's ideas, yet her own original theorizing proved still more crucial. The 1890s were especially fertile years for Lou: in the course of this, her fourth decade, she published six books and over thirty articles, roughly half of all the work published in her lifetime. Rilke undoubtedly read many of these, most especially the journal essays dealing with art, religion, psychology, and Russian culture. Even more importantly, perhaps, Rilke and Lou's conversation supplied a rich channel of ongoing intellectual exchange. Rilke's was a highly absorptive nature, and his own thinking and writing during the formative years of their acquaintance bear the unmistakable mark of Lou's creative ideation. Even so, Rilke very rarely merely parroted Lou's insights, but rather assimilated them into the stream of his own reflection, transforming their content into his own forms and idioms. In so doing, Rilke, emerged out of his chrysalis of dream, redefining his vocation and himself.

At the time of their initial meeting, the Rilkean lyric still belonged largely to the twin worlds of dream and longing. At the same time, Rilke was very much involved in writing his *Visions of Christ.*[89] As we have seen, his critical confrontation with his religious heritage encouraged intellectual depth. It triggered a head-on confrontation with fundamental psychological and spiritual issues less evident in his purely lyric output which—despite its inaugurating affirmation of subjective fantasy and Jugendstil idyll-ism—simultaneously tended towards puer escapism. The problem facing Rilke was how to incorporate the spiritual force of his dialogue with religion into the lyrical forms that embodied the more purely creative and constructive movement of his soul; how to further articulate his own original religiosity in and through his art.

As the very name of his 1896–97 poem collection implies, many of the poems in *Advent* (which volume followed immediately upon *Dream-crowned*) anticipate some such spiritual development. Many do so with a receptive gesture, as in these closing lines from the title poem:

> [The pines] stretch their limbs
> over the white paths—ready,
> and deflect the wind, and grow towards
> the single night of splendor.[90]

while others assume a more aggressive tone:

> Do you call that Soul, that chirps and trembles
> in you . . .
> and finally dies a poor death poorly
> in the incense-laden evening of a gothic chapel—
> do you call that Soul?[91]

Neither poem, however, goes very far towards solving the problem of an original relation to religion. The title poem draws upon the resonance of the Advent season in a manner that leaves its traditional valence largely intact, while the second—bristling with spiritual impatience—mires in critical polemic. The author of *Advent* did not yet really know how to wrest the fruit of his religious nature from moribund convention so that it might infuse his soul's art with new spiritual substance, though the strongest poems in the book do make strides in that direction. After the title poem, the first poem in the first section (called "Gifts") confidently proclaims the poet's soul-centered mission even if its formulation remains, still, tinged by youthful escapism:

> That is my fight:
> to roam through all days
> dedicated to longing.
> Then—strong and wide-spreading—
> to reach with a thousand roots
> deep into life—
> and, through sorrow,
> grow far out of life,
> far out of time![92]

The young Rilke's religious renovation inevitably proved strenuous, for it necessarily entailed some kind of overcoming of tradition. Rilke took a huge step in that direction through the writing of his *Visions* (the first of which was written just after the above poem), a step that took him, too, into the congruent intellectual world of the author of "Jesus the Jew." It was largely the fertile effect of Lou's ideas that enabled him to proceed still further along that path and—after three years of what Freedman freely calls "discipleship"—accomplish his own unique marriage of religion and art in the first part of *The Book of Hours*. Intellectually considered, Lou's great contribution to Rilke's development consisted primarily in providing theoretical weight and, crucially, *deep psychological ground* to Rilke's meditations on art, religion, and the spiritual significance of the individual human being. She played the role of a psychologist who took on as her principal subject, not one or another patient, but human culture; an essayistic analyst who helped Rilke to understand the common root of both art and religion in the logos of the soul.

The evolution Rilke underwent in the years 1897–1900 may be divided into two dialectically related phases. The first revolves around his voyage to Florence in the spring of 1898, and the second around the two trips to Russia taken in 1899 and 1900. In both cases, the intense study undertaken in preparation for the voyage, as well as the reflection upon it afterward, proved integral to the experience itself. In both cases, the journeys were orchestrated by Lou, and Rilke's spiritual and artistic transformations were ignited and informed by continual conversation with her and her ideas.

The first of these stages of Rilke's evolution naturally assumes the character of the historical period that helped catalyze it. The Italian Renaissance represents a period of marked intellectual, spiritual, and artistic expansion of the human self's prerogatives. The truths of science—most especially, the epochal Copernican revolution—challenged the established world order sanctioned by the church. In the artistic sphere, titans like Michelangelo—freed from the narrower strictures of medieval mentality—exercised a kind of Promethean force. As symbolized by Michelangelo's famous Sistine Chapel, Renaissance Man received transmission of the primal creative power from God, and effectively became his rival. So it was, too, in Rilke's own version of the Renaissance, a phase which saw him pay unprecedented homage to the conscious will, creative power, and spiritual centrality of the individual Self.

Rilke arrived in Florence during the first week of April 1898 and stayed for roughly a month and a half. The journey was no pleasure trip but—in classic Goethean style—the customary pilgrimage of a German poet to his privileged southern neighbor. This poet, however, was not self-directed, but acting on assignment. Lou, knowing she was going to be in Russia for an extended period that spring and summer, suggested the voyage, planned it with Rilke, and urged him to keep a diary as a record of his experience—a journal he might afterwards submit to her review.

Rilke undertook the task willingly, but the "diary" he ultimately produced bears little resemblance to more usual examples of the genre. Only sporadically taken up, it provides scant record of Rilke's actual experiences. It consists of a page of introductory epigraphs including (significantly) two from Emerson, one from Lou, and three poetic snippets from Rilke himself; a handful of initial poems written near the beginning of the journey; a few lengthy prose descriptions; and—by far the greatest part—many pages of quasi-aphoristic, largely theoretical reflections on selfhood, art, religion, and culture. It is a motley assemblage, yet one eminently revealing of Rilke's prevailing concerns.

The six poems placed at the beginning of the diary all show Rilke—albeit rather tentatively—moving away from his own established tonalities towards a new order of things. The first piece in the body of the text is a kind of dedicatory verse to Lou (dated April 15), which begins with a figure that says a great deal about the way in which Rilke regarded his Italian sojourn: "From our winter-shaped terrain / I've been cast far out, into spring. . . . "[93] In the body of the diary as well as numerous statements thereafter, Rilke repeatedly characterized both the Italian Renaissance itself and his own experience of it as a spring. By his own admission, the Italian Renaissance—true to its name—signified a personal as well as a historical rebirth.

The subsequent poems provide further clues about the character and kind of that new beginning.

Florence, 16 April 1898

Here is life's quiet altar.
Here day is still deep. Here night builds
up around dreams like a baptistery.

Here life nursed the brilliance of the heart
and here all things seemed to tell
of its power: the festiveness of women, the splendor
of princes, Madonnas who invented gratitude,
and the shiver of a monk in his cell...[94]

In many respects, this poem (which follows immediately upon the initial one to Lou) appears barely distinguishable from most of Rilke's earlier lyric work. Still, one can sense slight but significant tonal differences. The repeated "Here" insists upon a kind of immediacy, a present reality incongruent with, for instance, the string of "Mir ist" ("It seems to me," or "I imagine") poems in *Dreamcrowned*. Although we do have a consecration of dream, the poem hinges as well upon intuitive *power* or *strength* ("und hier war Alles Ahnen seiner *Macht*")—implying an active will-force foreign to the prevailing sensibility of his dreamy lyricisim. The next poem—the first of two named "Renaissance"—stresses these elements even more:

Florence, 17 April 1898

RENAISSANCE I

A hush enveloped the man of thorns,
the sound of his suffering faded away
and the folk were freed to live in joy.
Iron-willed solitaries raised the red
banners of strength high on the gray
turrets of time.

Clad in white raiment, all journey
farther into life, finding the land
aglow with the sense of what may emerge.
The only one already weary
—the Madonna—pauses and rests on the verge.[95]

The fourth and fifth lines of the poem pick up the note sounded in the prior one, celebrating active, masculine strength and conscious willpower as signatures of the Renaissance achievement. The feminine element brought in at the end is, by contrast, "already weary." Equally interesting, this poem converses—not so much with Rilke's dream lyrics, but with the other prong of his poetic production (his *Visions of Christ*)—and in this regard the distancing from the prior work catalyzed by Rilke's "Renaissance moment" proves still more pronounced. The poet clearly identifies with the folk no longer psychically dominated by the image of Christ's painful martydom, and we can almost feel the hold the traditional Jesus figure exercised on Rilke's imagination loosening as he—like them—begins to feel "freed to live in joy."

The last of the six poems included in the diary (all presented consecutively at the beginning) does still more work in moving Rilke towards a new vision and idiom:

Renaissance II

Then faith was not the sort of timid dreaming
that led all to fold their fingers out of fear,—
but was a listening, love engendering
the praying of pictures and the building of prayers.

And when one found something in him growing
he'd climb down into that deep knowing
and joyfully find the god prepared;
out of his doubt, he'd raise the hidden being
and lift him trembling into the splendor that they shared.[96]

The first two lines of this poem tend toward identifying dreaminess with spiritual timidity and submission to convention in a manner incommensurate with the tone of most of Rilke's early lyrics. Moreover, the image of Renaissance personalities "praying pictures" and "building prayers" prefigures the kind of original and creative fusion of art and religion that will mark the greatest accomplishment of these crucial years. In these lines—though Russia is as yet far off—we are already gaining definite glimpses of the vision that informs *The Book of Monastic Life*.

The poems in the Florence diary do register a change, a shift in sensibility, and reveal Rilke employing the Renaissance as both a lever which might help loose him from earlier restrictions and a springboard that might propel him towards new realities. The prose aphorisms that comprise the bulk of the text display that change even more clearly and dramatically. In writing echoing Nietzsche and Emerson in both content and style, Rilke trumpets insights revolving around his novel esteem of self. To be sure, similar self-assertion manifests already in a poem such as "King's Song," but Rilke's diary writings intensify and empower it to a new degree. In fact, Rilke freely confesses that his concern with self (most especially his own) wholly subsumed his experience of the historical Renaissance:

> Behold: I had expected to bring home a revelation about Botticelli or Michelangelo. And all I bring back is tidings—about myself, and the news is good.

and, furthermore, makes this prevailing self-concern into a religious principle:

> And if ten thousand times they made Madonnas and saints, and if some of them painted in a monk's habit on their knees, and if their Madonnas perform miracles into these days: they all had but one faith, and but one religion was the fire of their inspiration: the longing for oneself. Their highest ecstasies were the discoveries they made into their own depths. With trembling hands they lifted them into the light. And since the light then was full of God, He accepted their gifts.[97]

It is critical to remark that—even while proclaiming the centrality of the self—Rilke does not indicate that authentic selfhood (unity with the source of one's own true being) is given *a priori*, as immediately present or available; on the contrary, it must be actively sought and unfolded. Again and again, Rilke reiterates the theme of the above passage, speaking with utmost urgency of his deep *longing for himself*:

> Often I have such a great longing for myself. I know that the path ahead still stretches far; but in my best dreams I see the day when I shall stand and greet myself.[98]

We saw in the last chapter that *the soul's longing* had already emerged as the leading motif of Rilke's poetry. What is novel here, however, is the principal *object* of that longing. No longer "the stars," or "eternity," the poet quite frankly identifies that object with the Self. Heerikhuizen aptly speaks of "an intensely romantic feeling of self-awareness"[99] in connection with this phase of Rilke's development. Self-consciousness has often been understood as the signature of the romantics, and when we read Rilke's comment on the unlimited creative purview of that self ("Each person creates the world anew with his own birth; for each person is the world"[100]) we can readily assent to Heerikhuizen's related remark about Rilke's "newly discovered romantic pride."

Rilke's preoccupation with self-discovery at this time engendered a twin: an equally urgent concern with artistic vocation. In fact, these two—the quest for self-realization, and poetic vocation—fused in Rilke's mind as he came to understand art chiefly as *the means by which the self seeks to realize its own nature.* There are so many statements to this effect in the Florence diary that it is difficult to choose between them. Rilke directly links the motif of longing with art:

> Tired of art, one seeks the artist, and in each work looks for the deed that elevated the man, the triumph over something within him, and the longing for himself.

...states the main point flat out:

> Know then that art is: the means by which singular, solitary individuals fulfill themselves.

...and, in a passage that revises the penultimate line of the April 16 poem, combines and amplifies the prior two quotations:

> Suddenly we stand face-to-face with the person who, with rapid or with tenderly hesitant hands, gave form to a piece of his faith and his longing in the enduring work. Suddenly we feel that these Madonnas are not monuments of a quiet gratefulness, that they are only markstones of a dark and somber path to the sun, and we know that the degree of their beauty will be the sign of how near or far they are from this goal. *For beauty is the involuntary gesture in which a personality distills itself.* It becomes more perfect, the more hate and fear fall away from it, the more confident the artist grows on the path that lead to his most sacred fulfillment.[101]

It is sometimes said that Rilke made a religion of art. That notion can be well justified so long as the basis of Rilke's conception of art is correctly understood. Despite Rilke's boundless esteem for art, any idea of "art for art's sake" was entirely foreign to him. As the above passages make clear, Rilke's theory of art rested upon a thoroughly *psychological* foundation: art was nothing other than the expressive vehicle of the soul's own search for itself, its quest for its spiritual origins and ends. Because that search itself effects its end, the soul manifests and indeed (re)creates itself in that process. The gist of art is a self-fashioning, a *soul-making.*

Rilke had already begun formulating ideas about art akin to those expressed in his Florence diary before his Italian voyage. In March of 1898—a month before his departure for Florence, though well after he had begun intense preparation for it—Rilke gave voice to similar (and similarly psychological) reflections in a lengthy lecture on "Modern Lyric" delivered in Prague. Note that the following introductory passage employs the terms "advent," "Renaissance," and "New Life" in a single sentence:

> Look: since the first attempt on the part of the individual *to find himself* amidst the flood of transient experience, since the first striving, amidst the noise of the day, to listen into the deepest solitudes of one's own being—since then, is there *Modern Lyric.* And that is—please do not be shocked—since around the year 1292. This is the year, coincident with the advent of the great Renaissance, in which Dante related the simple story of his first, youthful love in the *Vita Nuova.*[102]

Rilke's lecture continues to emphasize the exclusively psychological ground of the modern lyric. Dismissing formal education, external sensations, and technical facility as inessential, he affirms, "it is only when the individual...reaches down through to the deepest ground-tone of his being, that he steps into a close inner relation to art: *becomes an artist.*" Rather uncharacteristically borrowing the language of philosophy and science, he describes how modern art began "to speak with things, rather than of things; therefore: became 'subjective,'" and declares: "One learned to observe one's own soul, as earlier the external environment; one became here, too, a Realist and Naturalist of one's intimate, inner sensation as before one had with respect to *outer* events...." Finally, expressing the unlimited sense of self-expansion so prevalent in the Florence diary, Rilke celebrates "the sensation of fallen barriers" as

> the ground tone of all creative work....Then subjectivism reached its highest form, because each felt himself one with all appearances

> of the world... became the sole existing one, the solitary... cosmic hermit who perceived what no one had before.[103]

These ideas are characteristically Rilkean, yet the poet elaborated the theoretical gist of these aesthetic matters in the course of ongoing dialogue with Lou. That same year, Lou published an article entitled "The Basic Forms of Art: A Psychological Study." Rilke's lecture and Lou's essay echo each other not only in fundamental outlook, but in many particulars as well. For instance, in a passage near the beginning of the essay, Lou, like Rilke, specifically denies both technical facility and external sensation an essential role in the creation. She continues, in accord with her frank subtitle, to articulate the psychological ground of her aesthetics:

> These secret mysteries in the soul of the artist are so inexpressible because they lead a wholly embryonic life before Art brings them to the light of day—because they represent feelings which are either in the stage of darkest initially unclear germination, or in the darkness of sunken elements of feeling which work into the present in a shadowy, reminiscent-rich way, or finally because they arise out of the broad surging mass of general feelings which do not permit themselves to be grasped purely individually, but nonetheless excite emotion as they flood through the Individual. The artist is fundamentally distinguished from the non-artist in that his sensation-embryos, so to speak, do not grow to completion or come to clarity... under the practical stimulus of personal everyday life, but enter into relation to fantasy in order to form a new world—one's own world—from out of the most subtle personal initiatives.[104]

Characteristically, Lou's psychological terms are more theoretically specific than Rilke's. Indeed, I cite this particular passage in part because—well before the blossoming of Jung's career, let alone Hillman's—it adumbrates (albeit in a rather turgid and murky manner) the founding principles of archetypal psychology: the idea of the archetype itself as such is rooted in some collective unconscious, and the primacy of the connection of the soul with fantasy (Lou's word is *Phantasie*). All this, it should be remembered, in connection with the origin of art.

Ralph Freedman, in his indispensable biography of Rilke, freely affirms the critical influence of Lou's essay on the poet's own theorizing:

> Lou's disciple, scribbling hastily, had gained much of his theory about the lyric from her essay "Basic Forms of Art," especially his comparisons between painting and poetry. Her argument that the artist's vision combines sensation drawn from the outside with unconscious fantasies within provided the background for Rilke's own statement about these two art forms.... The product of his and Lou's close intellectual cooperation, these ideas formed the basis of Rilke's personal view of the lyrical poet.[105]

If Lou's psychological aesthetics helped Rilke articulate the soul-spiritual ground of his artistic vocation, her psychology of religion proved still more vital to the poet's development. As we have seen, religion represented the more vexed and problematic terrain for the poet, and it was especially in this arena that Lou's concentrated, learned, self-searching, and—once more—quintessentially *psychological* inquiry helped the poet open inner doors.

During the relatively brief period of their friendship, Nietzsche had encouraged Lou to write on the subject of religion, and in the years 1891–98 she did so extensively, composing eleven substantial essays squarely on the topic as well as many more that touched upon it less centrally. Lou's essays exhibit a great breadth of interest; her topics range from the early totemic forms of religious belief to the origin and essence of Christianity, from Judaism and Islam to contemporary debates about the Apostolic Creed. Whatever the ostensible subject, however, her perspective remains persistently psychological, aimed at exploring what she calls "the essence of the religious affect" as such is grounded in "the whole reality of the soul."[106]

Both personal and intellectual history fundamentally conditioned Lou's own approach to religion. Her parents were quite religious: after marriage, both had converted to a pietist form of Protestantism which combined cultivation of feeling with strict observance. They naturally expected Lou to follow suit, and (outwardly, at least) she did so for years, but when the time for her confirmation came round she unexpectedly refused the rite and broke from the church. This action naturally caused some grief and upheaval in the close-knit family, but was not, in fact, the most decisive event in Lou's early spiritual development. That had taken place many years earlier when she had still been a small girl.

In her memoirs, Lou recalls how, as a young child, she enjoyed a wholly private, thoroughly imaginative, and deeply satisfying relation to God. She would tell endless stories to this benevolent, grandfatherly figure, most always beginning with "As you know,"—God was, after all, presumed to be all-knowing. Yet when a servant in the household told her about two mysterious callers at her small garden house in the country and—despite her inward plea—God was unexpectedly unable to solve the simple riddle of their identities (they had actually been a snowman and -woman), this seemingly innocuous failing abruptly and irrevocably tore the fabric of the child's naïve faith. God disappeared from her world virtually overnight. Nor could she ever call him back in any like form. It was never possible to resuscitate the intuitive feeling trust of her childhood imagination of God, yet no God-concept borrowed from an established faith or constructed by the rational mind seemed anything other than an idol to Lou. "God," in the form of any already given objective existent, had vanished—permanently—from Lou's world.

One or another form of such an objectively existent godhead (or many such, in polytheism) generally stands as the spiritual foundation of religion. What is most instructive and compelling in Lou's case is that her loss of belief in any such God did not lead her to *reject* religion or its value, but rather moved her to *redefine religion as **a function of the soul** and its native, irrepressible spiritual aspirations.* For Lou, the reality of those aspirations was not contravened by the mere fact that their *end* might be unknown. "God," after all, does not stand as the sole signifier of such ideal ends—"Truth," or "the fullness of Life itself," or other more open terms may also serve to fuel and orient the soul's spiritual drive. It was in her capacity as an explorer in and of the world of soul—one instinctively critical of any spiritual goal not anchored in the soul's own seeking—that Lou Andreas-Salomé may be said to have pioneered the psychology of religion.

Though Lou's own inner experience always lies at the core of her work, her essays reflect, as well, her immersion in prevailing intellectual historical currents. She had been a serious student of philosophy[107] well before her enriching liaison with Nietzsche, who, of course, famously proclaimed the death of God. She was also versed in various social scientific fields (such as psychology and comparative religion) and not disinclined to view herself, in part, as working out of the spirit of modern science. To some degree, the critical perspective toward religion assumed by science supported her own, yet the reach of her own soul-centered psychology left the more purely rationalist strains of both science and philosophy behind.

Lou set forth many of her fundamental insights on religion in her first long, foundational essay on the subject, "Realism in Religion," published in 1891. The essay's point of departure tellingly echoes themes enunciated in the introduction of this book: the irrevocable sterility of the spirit-matter dualism and the consequent urgent need for a reclamation of the soul. Lou recounts how, until roughly the middle of the century, many books dealing with religious questions had appeared every year, for "the old metaphysic had not yet died out.... One imagined it possible to build a philosophical bridge between the contraries of knowledge and belief, between the world of sensible perception and the world of supersensible hope." Realizing the futility of all such attempts, the contemporary spirit had—in her view—turned decisively away from them, and become primarily critical in approach. ("More and more, the philosophy of religion has turned into the science of comparative religion.") Nonetheless, still more recently, another shift had transpired. Once again, numerous books on religious topics were appearing; these books, however, were written

> in an entirely different spirit than before. They no more believe it is possible to mediate the old contraries in a purely theoretical fashion...they ask less about the general validity or intellectual self-consistency of a religious life-view than about its practical worth and inner necessity...whether it offers a filling out of thought satisfying to the feeling soul [*das Gemüt*].[108]

Lou continues to further distinguish two distinct kinds of such books. The first are those which proceed primarily didactically and evangelically (*belehrend und bekehrend*), aiming to "present the spiritual blessing and practical utility that flow from religion in actual life"; the second those that

> ...for the most part, consist of confessions, and are created out of the struggles and doubts of one's own aroused spirit, investigations undertaken upon one's own inner life,—and so, contain a piece of the psychology of religion [*ein Stück Religions-psychologie*].[109]

It is this second sort alone that Lou believes may advance the cause of the "science of religion," shedding light upon the dark, still by no means sufficiently explored world of the religious soul-life [*religiösen*

Seelenlebens]...the finely branched complex of moods and urges of which it consists, its connection with the whole rest of life, its originating causes and peculiarities.[110] Lou clearly considers such work to be of the utmost importance, for she does not count herself among those who feel religion to be an antiquated matter superseded by the advances of modern science—on the contrary.

The bulk of "Realism in Religion" unfolds in the form of a commentary upon and critical review of one of these more valued kinds of books. As befits her psychological outlook, moreover, Lou shows herself much less interested in the *conclusions* reached by her author than in the detailed account of all the phases of his inner development; concerns herself not so much with his spiritual *end* as with his *path*, the story he tells of *the making of his soul.*

> Instead of—as is unfortunately so often the case—laying out before us the result of his religious research in more or less systematic fashion, he simply recounts for us the whole course of his development; he guides us through his life, depicting for us every turning point.[111]

The heart of Lou's theorizing—in this and all her essays on the general topic of the psychology of religion—centers upon how the very idea of God (and so of religion) is engendered in and through the soul, and—still more crucially—the unfolding of the ongoing dynamic relationship between this soul-engendered (idea of) God and the soul itself. Often, anthropological science provides her heuristic point of departure: "the scientific attitude has long since sought to explain how, in primitive religions, the Gods arise through human beings themselves." For Lou, however, the origin of (the idea of) God in the human imagination does not negate the authenticity of religion; nor does it—paradoxical though this may initially seem—*ultimately* belie the *objective* existence of some form of godhead. As a true psychologist, Lou does not reserve the notion of objectivity for purely empirical or purely spiritual entities, but understands that the independent motion of the soul generates psychic realities or facts which thereby attain a correspondent species of objectivity. The reality of the soul's imaginative motion as well as that of its resultant lasting *effects* constitute, for Lou, "the essence of that which the modern science of religion must take as its foundation: the essence of the religious affect."[112] Lou names those who follow this course of thought "religious realists," linking them with the similarly named medieval philosophers who resisted the "scholastic petrification" of nominalism.

Early on in "Realism and Religion," Lou introduces a distinction fundamental to her attempt to identify the essence of the religious sentiment:

> One must, in the "history of God,"—this still by no means completed history of the becoming, passing away, and continual revivification of God...distinguish between the religion-forming impulses and (in the narrow sense) religious sensibilities per se. The first are those which originally created gods and religions, but need not necessarily be accompanied by the feelings we generally identify as religious—contemplative remembrance, enthusiasm, inner devotion to something higher, etc. [113]

Lou continues to explain that the gods were most likely first created out of need (the need for physical protection, for personal and social power and the like) and that their splendid powers and attributes spring from that more or less utilitarian source—the more powerful the god, the more powerful the aid or prestige it might provide one under its protection. Still, she argues, once such wonderful supersensible beings are created, they work back upon the soul and the imagination of human beings and so in time can engender authentic religious sentiments of wonder and devotion. "So might, at last, the humanly created God breed a truly God-created humanity, in which the intrinsic need for God arises, in the course of its development, as a purely ideal or spiritual need."[114] This defines the famous concept of the "back-effect" which Kerényi singled out as the insight that founds the psychology of religion:

> The authentic religious phenomenon in fact first arises out of the *back-effect* [*Rückwirking*] of a godhead—no matter how it arose—upon the person who believes in that godhead.[115]

Lou recognizes that habits of mind and soul bred of the first, need-based phase tend to be intransigent and only gradually transformed into authentically religious sentiments in the course of a long development. At the same time, such evolution is never simple or unidirectional, but typically includes frequent reversals and backsliding. The religions of highly developed civilizations are not, therefore, necessarily less based on need or greed than so-called primitive civilizations. Moreover—despite her sometimes seemingly unequivocal language—Lou makes clear that one cannot too rigidly identify "the authentic religious phenomenon" with the second phase alone. In reality, the two phases are dialectically related in a complex ongoing dynamic, continually and intimately intertwined with one another in the course of spiritual evolution:

> The impulses which originally fashion gods, and those which derive from already established gods, and which gradually arise in the course of religious development, must be considered, logically and historically, as two entirely distinct feeling-complexes.... On the other hand, psychologically considered, they naturally interweave in every single case in the whole history of religion and in the soul life of the human being.[116]

Accordingly, Lou relates how, when established religious beliefs petrify and hollow, true religiosity may reassert itself in imaginative acts which are *at one and the same time creative and authentically religious*. Indeed, the spiritual life of the modern human being—already the effect of a long spiritual evolution—depends utterly upon the perpetual renewal of such imaginative possibility:

> Produced by God, he produces God once more, ceaselessly striving to comprehend God in an image that comports with his current stage of intellectual development. The most serious and interesting question in this matter is in principle only this: whether the old inherited customs have rooted so strongly that the religiosity inherent in the profundity of each and every normal human existence may manifest in many necessarily individual stems which—in healthy circumstances—will also blossom forth; or whether the religiosity of the free-thinker is in fact nothing more than a broken-off, though still living, branch of the great decaying trunk of the old inherited forms of belief. Only in the first case is it possible that the strength and elevation of humankind may ever again enable it to fashion its own God, a God that owes its being not merely to the insufficiency of the intellect, but to the religious productivity born of the lofty striving of the whole human being.[117]

In "Realism and Religion," Lou rehearses her author's confessional account of the many stages of his own spiritual development, a trajectory which includes a pious childhood; disenchantment bred of intellectual development as well as the moral failings of the ostensibly religious; an attempt to replace the meaning lent by religious belief with an aestheticism which proves barren; and a recommitment to engage the fullness of life fired by the moral and practical enthusiasm of an idealistic friend. Finally, as a result of publishing a highly controversial book in his field (historical research into the revolutionary period), the author's professional career is threatened, and his own moral integrity put to a severe test. Consequently, he is led to reexamine the "personal ideals of purely subjective truth" he had come to live by, and to question whether they supplied inner strength and refuge adequate to serve his spiritual needs; whether, that is, they indeed served as viable substitutes for the more formal God-concept he had previously abandoned. The story climaxes when, in the spiritual crisis precipitated by these inward as well as outward developments, the author's

> religious feeling had powerfully intensified and the desire to feel an inward connection with that which stood, for him, as the highest, manifested with unprecedented force—then his subjective ideal suddenly seemed to have to transform itself into a kind of objective godhead. It seemed necessary that a twofoldness [*Zweiheit*] be there, so that a strong relationship might come to consciousness, one that might appease that compelling inner longing. "In this need, I folded my hands to pray."[118]

The spontaneous gesture of prayer climaxes and transforms the author's inner journey. The subsequent chapter of his book focuses on the act of prayer, and it is this chapter that is the central one for Lou; in her mind, it is his interpretation of prayer that enables the author "to display the entire self-submission and self-elevation proper to religion. Insofar as he analyses the essence of prayer . . . the essence of the religious affect opens to him as well."

Or, shall we say, to *her*, for it is not so much the author's interpretation we are given, but Lou's own, illustrated by means of the living example of her author's inner story. The conflict and cooperation between her author's self-conscious sense of his own integrity and capacity on the one hand, and his own spiritual inadequacy on the other, leads Lou to her definitive statement of "the essence of the religious affect."

> In the foregoing portrayal, the two features which constitute the ground and essence of religious culture clearly reveal themselves; those which, through a peculiar form of blending with each other,

> allow themselves to be felt as a single affect. These two features are the deeply felt sensation of one's own insufficiency on the one hand and, simultaneously, the most sharply heightened consciousness of self and feeling of one's own egoity or selfhood [*Ichgefühl*: literally, I-feeling] on the other. Neither the sincerest humility and self-abasement before an ideal experienced as divine, nor the fullest and most satisfying living out of all the faculties of selfhood for their own sakes suffice to release the religious affect. First both together in their riddling self-contradiction produce the friction out of which, hot and vivid, the flame leaps forth.[119]

Lou finds this "inseparable mixture of humility and pride" intrinsic to human nature: "half-creatures" as we are, we are habitually aware of a kind of native helplessness vis-à-vis the world, and, at one and the same time, conscious of a sense of an almost godlike superiority vis-à-vis natural creation.

While never essentially compromising the balance of her religious equation, Lou takes special pains to emphasize its self-affirming side—not because it is more important than the other, but because traditional and institutional forms of religion tend to depreciate if not deny it, at least with respect to the ordinary individual. "It is incorrect," writes Lou, "to seek the origin of worship in our weakness and helplessness only, and to extrapolate the other from that." She claims that, even in primitive forms of prayer in which the human being appears to issue helpless pleas to God, an abiding knowledge of his deep kinship with God—an intimation that the human being and God are somehow of one essence—contributes an underlying tone of the human being's "immeasurable pride." Nor is such self-conscious pride by any means lacking in the religious heroes of later civilizations; it is, after all, the cornerstone of Jesus' unique power that he refused to deny himself or—what amounted to the same thing—his unity with his divine source. Concomitantly, such pride may tend towards what the modern psychologist would call "inflation." Lou's comment to that effect readily calls to mind Rilke's *Visions*, especially the closing line of "The Night":

> The distance between Man and God necessarily lessens with the increasing internalization and spiritualization of God that transpires in the course of religious development until there, where God is already passed over into the form of a process of

> personal ideal-formation, the greatest danger of grand illusion finally manifests.[120]

Such danger notwithstanding, virtually illimitable respect for the prerogatives of the self (what Emerson calls "self-reliance") remains, for Lou, a vital element of true religiosity—not, to be sure, in the form of some merely static pride, but as a driving impetus toward self-realization. This leads to another of her foundational definitions:

> The religious affect is thus also the characteristic sign of all great Egoists—if we understand greatness here in the sense of a force, not merely a selfish direction of one's being.[121]

This rather striking formulation has a less sensational, but perhaps still more vital correlate: namely: *authentic religiosity is necessarily and intrinsically highly individual.* So much so, indeed, that the degree of individuality achieved figures as a measure of religious capacity.

> The more decided and peculiarly self-determined [*eigenartig*—literally, of a kind proper to itself] his Ego, the more he possesses a true individuality, the more certainly he will come to know those hours of despair and blessedness in which, behind the barriers of his Self, a God appears to reveal himself. It is therefore a fine remark, once made by a preacher, that the most religious word which exists is not the word "God," but rather the words, "My God."[122]

From beginning to end, the locus of Lou's understanding of religion remains the individual soul; it remains psychological through and through. Both motor and function of a highly personal process of inner development, religion counts not only as individual, but (to employ the Jungian term) *individuating*. It is nothing other than the ongoing soul-making engendered by the soul's own inherent spiritual aspirations—first and foremost, the drive toward self-realization. Lou, then, reveals herself as one of the first and most articulate proponents of "a religion of soul-making." In her exemplary case, that notion clearly implies evolving the spirit of religion out of the psychological dynamics inherent to the soul, *not* vice versa.

Lou's psychology of religion clearly connects to—and sheds further light upon—many of the basic issues already discussed in this book. Thinking back, for instance, to the terms of Robert Hass's distinction between religion and spirituality, one could well understand Lou's thinking as an attempt to redefine the essence of religion so as to purify it of inauthentic "unspiritual" elements. What Lou understands as genuine religiosity bears very little relation to what is popularly recognized as "religion," but reveals itself to be very close to Hass's "spirituality." Yet while Hass tends to construe the (e)motions of soul in a manner largely dictated by the logic of spirit and its language of numinosity and presence, Lou Andreas-Salomé is careful not to allow the discourse of spirit to dominate or obfuscate her inquiry into the psychological grounds of human spirituality. Recognizing that *it is always in and through soul that the spiritual life of the human being unfolds*, Lou interprets spiritual matters in a mode and idiom proper to soul, rather than vice versa. Hers is a thoroughly soul-based spirituality, yet one no less intense or engaged for all that. In the aftermath of Nietzsche's famous declaration and in the midst of the late-nineteenth-century spiritual crisis precipitated by "the death of God," Lou undertook the revivification of "religion"—the *authentic* spiritual life of the human being—by way of a concerted reclamation of the province and prerogatives of the individual soul.

It is, above all, this agenda—not precisely articulated as such, but by no means entirely unspoken, either—that Lou Andreas-Salomé shared with Rilke. Though we cannot go deeply into all the specifics of the article that initially brought them together, much of "Jesus the Jew" unfolds as a further elaboration of the basic principles articulated in "Realism in Religion," applying them to the exemplary case of Jesus. One can readily understand that the author of the *Visions of Christ* would respond to Lou's portrayal of Jesus as one whose sublime yet ultimately overweening spiritual pride ultimately led to tragic downfall. Still more, perhaps, would he find affirmation in her thesis that the dualistic Christian cosmo-theology built upon Jesus' life, death, and resurrection (which Lou views as an amalgam of Jewish messianic tradition and pagan yearnings for a doctrine of the afterlife) has little or nothing to do with the essence of Jesus' own lived religious experience. The conclusion of Lou's essay resonates with echoes of Rilke's *Visions*, especially "Jewish Cemetery":

> Thus is the image of Jesus on the cross retained in this triumphant Christian world of belief, reminding us that it is only the individual, the great individual, who reaches the peak of religion in its true blessedness and full tragedy. What he lives there above, the mass below do not experience; his tragic end, his tragic knowledge

remain as secret and individual as were his blessedness and inner union with God, escaping history altogether. In the triumphant cry of the compact and useful belief, made to order for all, rings always softly—very softly and painfully, religion's last word, reserved only here and there for the poor solitary who has drunk too deeply from that well: "Eli! Eli! lama sabachthani."[123]

"Jesus the Jew" displays religion in a peculiarly tragic light. We must remember, however, that—according to Lou's analysis—the tragic conclusion to Jesus' life flows in part from the Jewish messianic tradition's insistence that God tangibly manifest himself in the political and material world. While Lou's intrinsically contradictory construction of religion does possess inherent tragic potential, she did not consistently construe religious intensity as inevitably tending toward tragedy, nor did she typically frame her own religious outlook and experience in tragic terms. When she takes herself (rather than Jesus) as her own point of departure, her treatment of religion most frequently strikes an open and optimistic tone, accenting the exhilarating freedom and creativity which accompany true—and truly individual—religiosity.

In good romantic fashion, Lou—persistently disassociating true religion from those moral conventions that so stubbornly adhere to institutionalized forms—finds the archetype for authentic belief in the child whose spiritual imagination remains (ideally) untainted by the adult world's derivate rationalism. Rational understanding tends to drive a wedge between the worlds of spirit and matter, leaving culture with an intellectually disingenuous faith (religion) on the one hand, and a spiritually deficient knowledge (science) on the other. The child's imagination, however, acts as ambassador of the mediatrix soul; its efficacy inheres in its natural blending of (or ready passage between) the supersensible and visible worlds. In her largely autobiographical essay "God-creation," Lou images for us her own childhood God—an abiding presence wrapped, as it were, in a *Tarnkappe*, an invisible cloak—and elaborates why such a God seems to her one that fosters the ongoing imaginative activity essential to a living human spirituality:

> It is not a lack of intellectual development alone which—in the domain of belief—enables such a personal, inner, and wholly irreplaceable relationship with "the God in the magic cloak," despite

> the fact that he does not allow himself to be seen or grasped. It is, above all, the play room [*Spielraum*] that only such a supersensible and invisible being offers all the free-ranging self-creative powers of the soul, allowing them full and unbridled expression. In the Being of that which no earthly eyes can see, one can all the more readily look into that which fills and fulfills the human being himself, and see what moves him in his depths. The more theoretically indeterminate the individual features of God, the better position he is in to conceal within himself the most practically determinate, the most individually unique qualities without losing shape and form—as under a huge mantle, which covers him entirely, and hides a thousand folds and pockets.[124]

Does not such a passage adumbrate the God of *The Book of Hours*? And does not the inflection of Lou's theorizing about the child's spirituality foreshadow, as well, the gesture that engendered *The Book of Hours*' companion prose volume, *Geschichte der Lieben Gott* (*Tales of God*)? In that collection, Rilke deliberately repudiated adult forms of spiritual construction, attempting rather to mythologize and theologize out of the naïveté of the child's imagination:

> These youthful fantasies were almost entirely improvised out of an instinct which, if I were to specify it more particularly, I might describe as busied with transferring God from the sphere of rumor into the realm of direct and daily experiencing; the recommending by every means a naïve and lively taking-into-use of God with which I seemed to have been charged since childhood.[125]

It was thus not only Lou's psychological deconstruction of the bases of organized religion, but (far more, perhaps) her positive view of religiosity as a domain open to—indeed, really only opened by—the individual's own creative imagination, which profoundly touched Rilke. To be sure, the critical and creative strains of both Lou's and Rilke's thought braid closely; one can only attain the new after moving through and transfiguring the old. Yet if Lou's analysis of the double tragedy of the Christian religion (Jesus' own, and the tragedy of the belief system constructed upon it) belonged to the world of Rilke's *Visions of Christ*, that world was fast becoming part of his spiritual and poetic past. The more positive strains of Lou's psychology of religion, on the other hand, pointed towards the poet's rapidly evolving future.

When—upon assignment, remember, from Lou—Rilke began articulating the framework of his own spiritual universe in concerted dialogue with the Italian Renaissance, his thinking about art, religion, and the destiny of the individual was saturated with the substance of all he learned from Lou's psychology of religion. Not that Rilke was incapable of thinking on his own. He had, after all, not waited to read "Jesus the Jew" before writing his *Visions of Christ*; a fact which confirms that the dynamic of their intellectual intercourse was always more one of confluence than influence. Nonetheless, at the time of their meeting, Lou was by far the more intellectually mature, learned, disciplined, and accomplished of the two. *The fundamental tenets of her psychology of religion became, in relatively short order, the intellectual foundation of Rilke's own evolving world view.* He could absorb it so readily not only because he received it in person as well as on the page, but also because it was already so much his own.

When he first read "Jesus the Jew," Rilke wrote Lou that it seemed to stand as reality to his dream; so, more generally, Lou's thinking helped bring consciousness to the intellectual presuppositions underlying Rilke's own vector of artistic and spiritual development. That is not to say that he assimilated her ideas purely intellectually or employed them as the building blocks of some theoretical system. Rather, her ideas conferred an ideational force that helped nourish and free his soul's imagination. Lou's critical and historically learned deconstruction of the theological structure of major religions—above all, Christianity; her lucid formulation of the creative religious potential of the individual soul's own longing; her teaching that (the human being's image of) "God" was in fact a product of the individual's own creative imagination, and that the truth and efficacy of that "God" depended upon the soul's ongoing realization of its own quintessentially individual nature; the (complementary) doctrine of the "back-effect" that taught the objective psychic reality of an (originally subjectively generated) godhead and the spiritually fructifying effects of a dialogic relation with that godhead; the ground of "the religious affect" in a paradoxical blend of *both* self-assertion and self-effacement; the unique religious authority of a naïve, nonrational and childlike imagination of God—these essential premises, and more, wove themselves into the very fabric of Rilke's soul. Nor should we neglect the overriding importance of the *cumulative* effect of such thoughts. Lou's own urgently psychological exploration of religion gave Rilke the courage to imagine that he might engage this domain creatively as well as critically and guided him toward the next stage of his artistic evolution: a wedding of his lyric genius with the intellectual force he was able to marshal when—as in the *Visions*—he dared confront religion head-on.

Rilke's Florence diary includes many aphorisms which concern themselves explicitly with God and religion. Most all reflect the influence of Lou's thought, more or less directly. There is, for instance, this amalgam of Rilke's own notion of individuation and the thesis Lou elaborates in "Jesus the Jew":

> Each person grows from the many toward himself. If once upon a time someone found himself and greeted himself, perhaps he could return to the many and be their savior; they would crucify him or burn him to death. And out of what remained of him afterward, well, they would make themselves a religion.[126]

There are recognitions, too, of the post-Nietzschean situation of religion:

> As the expressions of every language rest upon communal agreement, so also with the word "God." It was meant to include everything one sees at work but can't otherwise name or grasp. Therefore: when man was very poor and knew very little, God was very great. With every experience some little piece fell out of his circle of power, and when at last he scarcely had anything left, Church and State collected for him charitable qualities, which now no one is allowed to touch.
>
> ...As long as this god is alive, we are all children and dependents. We must sooner or later let him die. For we want to become fathers ourselves.
>
> But he *is* dead; the old story of Kara Mustafa. The viziers of the empire must keep silent about his dying so that the janissaries will not rebel and will continue fighting.[127]

Most important, the diary includes a whole series that reflect Lou's theories of "God-creation," childhood's religious authority, the "back-effect," and the inherently individualistic character of religion:

> If only the nations had been creative in the first fearfulness of their childhood: then they would have made a *real* God.

> When all peoples were still like one person, they shaped God out of their longing. God will perform a miracle: each person will become like a people.
>
> Everyone comes away from the deathbed of his childhood god dressed in mourning; but as he walks with increasing confidence and festiveness, God's resurrection takes place *inside him.*

Insofar as the "Florence phase" of Rilke's spiritual development revolves around "romantic pride" and affirmation of the prerogatives of selfhood, his diary emphasizes the correspondingly "egoistical" pole of Lou's dialectical understanding of the religious effect. Florence, however—while an essential step on Rilke's path—was not alone sufficient fuel to fire his religious imagination; nor did it directly issue in any major poetic work. This necessitated another inner and outer journey, one that—*counterbalancing* the Italian experience—might enable plumbing in depth the other, self-effacing pole of "the religious affect." In order to fill out of the range of his spiritual sensibility, Rilke—guided once more (indeed still more strongly!) by Lou's steady hand—needed to travel to a land that harked back to his Slavic roots and revive his own inveterate yearnings for a land he might—spiritually speaking—call his own.

Before, however, our poet might embark upon that journey, he had to endure the disappointing end of his Italian journey and complete some unfinished literary business. Rilke concluded the early phase of his poetic career by tying a knot at the end of its two strands: his early lyric production, and his *Visions of Christ.*

When Rilke and Lou met in the Baltic town of Zoppot after his Italian sojourn in July 1898, theirs was not a particularly happy reunion. For one thing, Lou did not very much like Rilke's Florentine diary. Perhaps she found too much of herself in it (or, more likely, too much of Nietzsche). Nor did their personal relationship thrive. In fact, Lou soon left again for Russia, leaving Rilke to his own devices. Despite initially intense disappointment, Rilke managed to revive himself and put his own time in Zoppot to good use, writing the three Visions of Christ which composed the "second series," and so concluding the whole cycle.

In the closing poems (and in Visions 6, 7, and 8, which we have passed over), aggressive confrontation with the figure of Christ and his legacy—so ferociously intense in the first five—mutes markedly, as if already beginning to fade from consciousness. As Mandel says, these final poems "exhibit no fierceness and no stridency"[128]—not, to be sure, on account of any fundamental reconsideration, but rather, one must suppose, because the psychic struggle had been—to some degree—fought and won. They were written, after all, after meeting Lou as well as after the Italy voyage and its associated self-affirming spiritual and intellectual developments.

Most noteworthy, indeed, in the last Visions is that—in the course of the three poems—the Christ figure gradually disappears altogether. In the first, "The Church in Nago," he is present, but in an attenuated, epigonal form; in the second, "The Blind Boy," he is present only in the surrogate form of a blind boy who, with his mother, wanders singing songs of sorrow from door to door; in the last, "The Nun," the Christ figure is absent altogether and the action revolves around conflicts between spirituality and sensuality personified by two nuns. In this final poem, Rilke returns to the intersection of erotic and spiritual concern central to the fifth Vision, "The Night." Nor has the essential message in this, or any of these final poems changed: Christianity, at least in its popular, otherworldly tendencies, has little spiritual sustenance to offer. Mandel: "In the Visions, the hands of Christ, those of the nun, the Church of Nago, and the heavens are symbolically empty."[129]

After finishing the *Visions*, Rilke was ready to move on. So, apparently, was Lou. They returned to Berlin in late summer of 1898; Rilke took up a new residence in Lou's neighborhood, and they recommenced another long period of close commerce. For Rilke, the time was not yet ripe for major poetic work, but he actively continued the trains of thought which ran through his Florence diary. Despite Lou's indifferent reaction to that work, Rilke continued journaling. He would do so for another two years, producing in turn his "Schmargendorf" (Berlin) and "Worpswede" diaries. More pointedly, he picked up the themes of his Prague lecture on "Modern Lyric" and wrote and published a new essay, "On Art," in the fall and winter of 1898–99. In a passage that alludes to the Emerson citation included as one of his Florence diary epigraphs ("I simply experiment, an endless seeker with no past at my back"), Rilke—still in fine egoistical (and, one must add here, distinctly Emersonian) style—trumpets his doctrine of the artist's essentially religious vocation:

> Therefore is he who makes [Art] into his life-view the Artist, the man of ultimate ends, who goes young through the centuries, with

> no past behind him. Others come and go, he endures. Others have God behind them like a remembrance. For the creator, God is the last and deepest fulfillment. And when the pious say: "He is," and the sorrowful feel: "He was," then the Artist smiles and says: "He will be." And his belief is more than belief; because he himself works and builds upon this God. With every look, with every moment of knowing, in every one of his quiet joys, he adds to him a power and a name...so that God will finally be completed, adorned with all powers and all names. That is the duty of the Artist.[130]

Around the same time, Rilke put the final touches on the lyric volume which succeeded *Advent*. Most of this new book was written in late 1897 and early 1898, though it did include a fair number of poems from his time in Italy as well. Dating from the onset of Rilke's dawning self-consciousness (so pronounced in the above passage), the volume's title—*In My Honor* (*Mir zu Feier*)—could serve as an apt caption for that phase of his development. Representing the culmination of Rilke's early lyric output, the poems are generally tauter and more firmly controlled—both stylistically and emotionally—than in Rilke's earlier work. Even so—as the volume's first poem shows—their tone and mode do remain largely continuous with that of *Dreamcrowned* and (especially) *Advent*:

> That is longing: to live in waves
> and have no home in time.
> And those are wishes: ordinary days'
> soft dialogues with eternity.
>
> And that is life. Until, out of yesteryear,
> the loneliest of all hours arises
> and—speaking differently from her sisters—
> catches eternity's ear.[131]

Despite the obvious continuity with prior work, the shift registered by the title of the new volume reveals itself in numerous subtle ways. In a series of beautiful angel poems, for instance, the speaker—cognizant of his own growth in stature and consciousness—frees his guardian angel to return to heaven and assumes sovereignty over his own life on earth. Still, it is only in the very last poem (written in late 1898 or early 1899) that one can readily recognize the author of "On Art."

You need not wait, until God comes to you
 and says: I am.
A God who must confess his strength,
 makes no sense.
For you must know, that God has worked in you
 from the beginning,
and when your heart glows and betrays nothing,
 he creates therein.[132]

This poem (like the previously cited passage from "On Art," an essay that takes form as a disputation with Tolstoy) clearly looks forward to *The Book of Hours*. Lou, after all, was fresh back from Russia, and had already hatched a plan to return there with Rainer the following spring. Indeed, serious mental preparation for the journey was already under way; at Lou's urging, Rilke had begun studying Russian in the early fall of 1898. Russia, and the climax of Rilke's first great artistic-religious awakening, were right around the corner.

After months of intense intellectual preparation, Lou and Rainer—traveling in the company of Lou's husband, Friedrich Carl Andreas—departed for Russia on April 24, 1899. Arriving just in time for the Russian Easter, Rilke and Lou visited Leo Tolstoy on Good Friday and, on Saturday evening, joined throngs of worshippers listening to the great Easter Bells of the Kremlin ring sonorously all through the night. The memory of this event remained perhaps the most important of all Rilke's Russian remembrances, one he referred to again and again throughout his life.

After a week in Moscow, and roughly five in St. Petersburg (which Rilke spent primarily visiting churches, museums, private collections, and theatres), the threesome returned home to Berlin on June 18. There the "journey" continued as Rilke and Lou immersed themselves in the study of Russian language, literature, history, and art, and began preparations for another, longer voyage the following year. In the midst of these studies, Rilke, in the course of three weeks in the fall of 1899, wrote the sixty-seven poems that compose the first part of *The Book of Hours*, *The Book of Monastic Life*.

Since Rilke began *The Book of Hours* soon after his first Russian journey, and the framing topoi of the poem (notably the icon-painting monk who is its speaker and center) are dressed in Russian garb, one might imagine the work to be the creative fruit of Russia alone. Yet Rilke's Russia would have been unthinkable without the backdrop of his Italian experience; the second phase of this initiatory period remains premised upon—even while, in some ways, contesting—the first. Rilke himself often figured his Russian experience as a completion of his Italian journey: "I perceive my stay in Russia as a strange completion of that Florentine spring, whose influence and success I told you about.... Florence seems to me now a kind of advance training and preparation for Moscow."[133] More pointedly, Graff remarks:

> Italy and Russia, the West and the East, are the two branches of the broad stream of the poet's creative consciousness which issues into the *Book of Hours*.... It is a mistaken view which proclaims that the *Book of Hours*, even the first one, was inspired by Russia alone or that it reflects the Russian experience purely.[134]

That much said, Russia did represent a profound—and profoundly transformative—experience for Rilke, one that, like the guide that led him there, stayed with him his entire life, becoming not so much a person or place as a stratum of his being. In 1902, two years after his second and last Russian journey, Rilke wrote to Tolstoy: "It is becoming clearer and clearer to me that Russia is my homeland, and everything else—is alien."[135] Almost twenty years later—and only six years before his death—Rilke wrote to another correspondent: "What do I owe Russia—it made me what I am. I emerge internally from there, the whole homeland of my instinct, all my inner resources are there!"[136] Clearly, the second and concluding phase of the inner evolution Rilke moved through just before the turn of the century proved decisive.

One does not have to look far to find compelling reasons for Rilke's fascination with Russia. Child of a Slavic land, he had (as *Offering to the Lares* demonstrates) always harbored deep sympathies with the native strains of Slavic culture. Indeed, throughout his life, Rilke maintained that he had Slavic blood. Prague, however, had proved too provincial; nor could Rilke—who was, of course, not Czech after all—ultimately identify with the more narrowly political and nationalistic ambitions informing Czech populism. Russia, however, figured as a Slavic land which offered an infinitely broader canvas for Rilke's cultural imagination, and one with a far more distinguished literary heritage.

Chief among the Czech literary heroes Rilke honored in *Offering to the Lares* was Julius Zeyer, Valerie David-Rhonfeld's uncle, whom Rilke knew personally. Zeyer himself had lived in Russia and (to the chagrin of some Czech intellectuals) revered Russia and its heritage for aesthetic and religious reasons. His study, adorned with Russian things, impressed Rilke at a young age, as did his works, many of which revolved around Russian motifs and exercised a formative influence on Rilke's literary engagement with Russia.[137] While Zeyer himself was Czech, his work pointed beyond Prague, and it is no accident of timing that Rilke wrote his autobiographical novella *Ewald Tragy*—which tells the story of a young man's departure from that city—in the latter half of 1898. The trajectory of Rilke's romance with the Slavic soul was clear: Prague lay in the past while the path to the future ran through Russia.

Still, Rilke's most compelling personal connection with Russia lay in the person of Lou herself. The emergence of Lou's own interest in her Russian heritage coincided with the period of her first acquaintance with Rainer:

> Lou Andreas-Salomé took up Russian studies in the year she met Rilke, sixteen years after her emigration from Russia. She had grown up in Russia, spoke Russian, had "Excellency" in her passport thanks to her belonging to the Russian nobility, and in Germany carried with her an exotic quality—often she was referred to as "the Russian." In taking up these studies she was thus going back, at once visitor and native, to the place where everything had begun for her.[138]

Lou's "Russian studies" naturally blent with her ongoing inquiry into art, religion, and culture and were correspondingly intense and productive. In 1897–98 Lou wrote five long articles on Russia and spent many weeks there. The first two foundational essays ("Russian Literature and Culture" and "Three Stories" in fall 1897) stem from her close collaboration with the Russian critic Akim Volynsky during Rilke and Lou's summer in Wolfratshausen. Two others ("Russian Philosophy and the Semitic Spirit" and "The Russian Holy Image and its Poet") followed soon after in early 1898, and the last ("Leo Tolstoy, our Contemporary") appeared not long before Lou and Rilke's first joint Russian voyage. Clearly, Rilke's formative years with Lou were saturated with Russian matters from the outset. Nor had Rilke's direct involvement waited until preparation for their first joint journey. Called upon to copy out the drafts of the essays Lou worked on with Volynsky in Wolfratshausen, Rilke literally had his hand in from the first. Nonetheless, here—still more clearly than in the case of Italy—Lou took the lead, and Rilke's own "Russian experience" bears the unmistakable imprint of her guiding hand.

As *fin-de-siècle* intellectuals in Europe, Lou and Rilke were hardly alone in their preoccupation with Russia. Historical as well as personal currents led to their involvement with that land. As Brodsky[139] documents, a wave of interest in Russia followed upon the "discovery" of Russian literature, in the 1880s, by German naturalist writers who regarded Tolstoy, Dostoevsky, and others as spokesmen of a vitally new, open-hearted vision of humanity. Vogüé's highly influential *Le roman russe* (1886) "propounded a vision of Russia as the cradle of future humanity" and Nina Hoffmann's equally important biographical study *Dostojewsky* "helped create the myth of a 'Russian soul' which was broad, humane, simple, and thirsting for God." Neo-romantic writers (and Rilke himself had ties to both naturalist and neo-romantic literary schools) contributed to the burgeoning infatuation with an idealized Russia. "Suddenly the German reading public was faced almost daily with new translations, book reviews, editorials, and essays dealing with Russian subjects. The era of Russomania had arrived..."

The phenomenon of Russomania grounded itself in a specific cultural historic logic. The European drawn to Russia (Lou and Rilke included) tended to regard the West's highly sophisticated culture as overintellectualized and on the verge of spiritual exhaustion. In "Russian Literature and Culture," Lou—in a tone far more reasoned and less damning than some kindred remarks by other critics—articulates the logic underlying this judgment.

> The older and more advanced a culture becomes, the more its dark interior clarifies itself in order to flow out into always more complete and fully accomplished forms in which, finally, it petrifies, the more surely the time nears when it begins to look back and yearn for that which, in the course of so long a development, necessarily has gone lost: yearns for what is simple, original, naïve, and—as yet unexhausted—still holds and conceals mysteries.[140]

Russia offered itself as antidote to the West's malaise; Russia—a land far enough East to be other than Western, and yet not so far East as to be

Rilke and the Russian peasant-poet Drozhin

positively Oriental and so ineradicably foreign. Russia, in this romantic conception, had been largely bypassed by the hasty march of western culture, the soul of its people simple, unspoiled, youthful, denizens of a land "which had no past but only a future."[141] A positively messianic force, Russia's national destiny was to unfold *gradually* ("This people... experiencing slowly its process of development, stands today in childhood and is ambling toward middle age"[142]) as the fruit of a cooperation between literate and literary Russia and the all-important reservoir of human nature, the Russian "folk" which "demands from its poets above all, collaboration in its difficult process of becoming." First and foremost, the Russian people were—in the view promoted by Dostoyevsky, but echoed by his influential biographer and many others—*religious*. Revealing "a capacity for suffering and sympathy... the humility of the Russian... is bound up with a profound religiousness."

First Lou, and then (under her auspices) Rilke drank deeply from this well of ideas. The foundation (and much of the brickwork, too) for their individual constructions of Russia may be found in the writing of Vogüé,

Hoffmann (whom Rilke, by his own admission, read "with great inner success"[143]), and others. Even so, both Lou and Rilke did make original and creative use of this cultural myth. That it was indeed a myth—in both the most positive and the negative sense of the term—goes without saying; the underlying realities (psychological, historical, and political) it repressed manifested spectacularly in 1905. Nonetheless, it did prove a tremendously persuasive form of mythologizing for some—like Lou and Rilke—who adopted and embellished it in their own inimitable fashion.

Predictably, the terms of Lou's own peculiar interpretation of Russia flowed from the tenets that grounded her general theories of art and religion. Most fundamentally, she found in Russia a confirmation of her own psychological understanding of the essence of both art and religion. It was, first and last, human soul qualities that shone forth in both Russian art and its natural religiosity and constituted its peculiar excellence.

Lou's first major article, "Russian Literature and Culture," takes the premise of the West's cultural exhaustion as a point of departure and proceeds to incorporate the psychological aesthetics elaborated in her "Basic Forms of Art" into a cultural-historical argument. If the artist is one who taps "the secret mysteries in the soul" ("Basic Forms"), the land which preserves those mysteries naturally proves fertile ground for a vital and spiritually revivifying literature. Citing "Slavic sensitivity and melancholy" as one of the peculiar attributes of Russian literature, Lou offers this portrait of the common Russian's endearing, intrinsicially poetic, features:

> a sense for music and poetry in the people, for simple, melancholy tunes, a tender feeling for nature... a childlike immediacy between persons, and a great deal of simple goodness with respect to all things human,—the goodness that allows the Russians to call a "criminal" an "unfortunate," and idiots and imbeciles those "afflicted by God."[144]

The beginning of this litany cannot help but recall the note Rilke himself struck, so poignantly, in that most famous of his early poems, "Folk Melodies." "Scratch a Russian, and you'll find a poet," writes Lou, and, in her estimation, the leading Russian writers are those who resist undue foreign influence and draw the substance of their art from native depths of soul. Anticipating Rilke's own "Russian" poetics, she proclaims the Russian writer's "peculiar ability to experience life in its innermost depths" and so "by way of aesthetic observation lead us into the last depth of things."[145]

Lou expresses little interest in modernist forms of European aesthetics—symbolist and so-called "decadent" art—that finds itself forced to replace genuine soul-content with what she considers hollow aesthetic play. Naturally, she holds such art to be entirely foreign to Russia ("nothing lies further from the Russian poetic sensibility than 'l'art pour l'art'"[146]), and her opinion that Russian art begins and ends with the life of the human soul finds spectacular—if highly problematic—confirmation in the exemplary case of the titanic figure of Tolstoy, who late in life rejected art altogether in favor of more direct practical, social, moral, and religious initiatives. While repudiating Tolstoy's extreme position (set forth in his famous essay "On Art"), she nonetheless honors the incontrovertible impulse underlying his storied conversion from artist to populist sage:

> The force that has almost brutally split apart every existing vessel of art is here the power of humanity itself...in the long run the energy for everything, including art, comes from it alone....What constitutes morality and religion for him or for the Russian peasantry is not relevant to us: what concerns us is the true fact that all these words are merely meant to point the way to the depths of life and the soul.[147]

If Lou found Tolstoy's versions of morality and religion irrelevant it was hardly because she was uninterested in those topics, but rather on account of her persistently individualistic perspective. Tolstoy wrongly confused his personal codes with universally binding truths and—correcting his error—the conclusion of Lou's essay gestures toward reclaiming Tolstoy for art and the more inclusive godhead it serves:

> We are justly terrified at the rigidly fixed forms that morality and religion assume in Tolstoy's mind. After all, we stride towards our own life goals in clothes quite different from those he wants to throw over our souls in his lordly fashion. He could never recognize us completely, he could never understand us fully when we wanted to reveal through our most personal art and our most private longings the deepest religiosity of our way of living....An

> artist by grace of God even if he wanted to be a thinker, he remains a priest of the unnamed God whom we all serve.[148]

Lou's individual religiosity was not, however, so pure as to prevent her from imagining the general type of religiosity truly characteristic of the Russian soul. Unsurprisingly, she did not find the essence of Russian religiosity necessarily Christian. In fact, in her essay "Russian Philosophy and the Semitic Spirit"[149] she posits a special affinity between the Russian and the Jewish mentality—a position consistent with her notion that Jesus' own authentic religiosity was, after all, not Christian but Jewish. Yet the essay in which she delves most directly into her idea of Russian spirituality is another piece published, like "Russian Philosophy," in January 1898.

"The Russian Holy Image and its Poet"[150] centers upon the life and work of the relatively little known (in the West, at least) writer Nikolai Leskov, whom Lou regards—perhaps still more than Tolstoy—as representative of the Russian people's inherent religiosity. Once again, Lou claims that religion to be Christian in appearance only, finding its human essence largely detached from—if not antithetical to—the traditions of the church. "Leskov's whole greatness consists in the fact that he was the folk poet of the Russian God-image without placing that on the ground of church tradition." In the case of Leskov, her contention runs contrary to that author's own beliefs. Indeed, the main gist of Lou's article revolves around her attempt to demonstrate that the symbolic heart of Leskov's art belies his professed theological commitments. Judging from the evidence she supplies, her case is a strong one, and her rehearsal and analysis of Leskov's story "At the Edge of the World" provides a telling glimpse into her understanding of the archetypally Russian image of God.

The story is so important to Lou that she provides another summary of it in her later piece on Tolstoy, and we can do no better than to supply Lou's sense of the gist of the story in her own words.

> The story is about a highly educated bishop who travels to the north of Siberia to convert the local pagan tribes to Christianity. He and his pagan coachman lose their way. At the point of starving and freezing to death, the coachman saves the bishop by making his way on snowshoes with great effort to an empty bear's lair with a dead bear in it, and bringing a piece of his booty to

> his master. Even though the lair is empty, the pagan coachman disregards the danger of freezing and leaves his fur hat to the bear as compensation for the stolen portion. "God watches him" and does not want him to harm a man, he explains. This experience convinces the bishop that even without scripture a Russian person is "close to God."[151]

The anti-ecclesiastical tenor of the story's symbolism does seem evident. In the face of death, it is the pagan who saves the Christian—spiritually as well as physically—not vice versa. For Lou, Leskov's stories provide the best evidence of "how indeed the Russian feels childishly confident of being 'close to God.' The Russian God is by himself nothing but Goodness and Simplicity, and not an exceptionally mighty ruler."

God's gentle ubiquity reveals itself, too, in the person of Father Cyriac—another priest in this same story who (being deeply religious in the true Russian sense) naturally refuses to do the bishop's evangelical bidding. Father Cyriac himself (and this is important to Lou) found God, not in youth or adult life, but in childhood when, distressed at some misdeed, he prayed for forgiveness, and God "stirred in his heart like a warm dove." Lou writes:

> Thus God shows himself to the Russian's folk's understanding—not in dazzling miracles, which controvert nature's laws, but in tender sympathy with childhood grief: he does not comprehend all and much escapes his notice, but "when a child is sunk in sorrow, he creeps to him in a fresh breeze and stays under his left armpit." Leskov adds, "Then great miracles happen. All blessedness flows from there."[152]

It is hardly an accident that this God so near as to be "under the armpit"—called up not by bishops, but by pagan and child-like purity of heart—is close kin to the famous "Neighbor God" of Rilke's *Book of Hours.*

Despite his upbringing in Prague, despite the historical phenomenon of Russomania, despite, even, his intimacy with Lou, Rilke would not have taken so passionate an interest in Russia if the land and its people did not somehow answer a profound internal necessity. We have already provided the framework which clarifies the internal logic that drove

Rilke's preoccupation with Russia. His encounters with Lou, Emerson, and, above all, the Italian Renaissance kindled the first, self-affirmative phase of his spiritual awakening: "the most full and satisfying enjoyment of all self-assertive powers for themselves alone," as Lou describes it in her psychological definition of "the religious affect." In order to progress further, the *second* phase of the dialectic required its due, a phase embodying (again in Lou's words) "the sincerest humility and self-prostration before an ideal conceived as divine." Heerikhuizen writes:

> As the Renaissance had appealed to his sense of beauty and his individualistic pride, so Russia appealed to his feeling for the dark, mystical unity of things, to his wish to relinquish himself to something greater than himself in a zealous humility, and to his feeling of brotherly kinship with all men. The influence of Russia...was diametrically opposed to that of Italy, yet he felt them both as mutually complementary.[153]

Exhilarating at first, the light-filled lineaments of Renaissance humanity and the self-conscious focus on individual creativity Rilke brought to it ultimately seemed limiting and partial. Rilke's religious imagination required still more room, more dark mystery, more depth of soul. Not Italy's negation, but—as Rilke himself stated—its dialectical completion, Rilke's "Russian myth" became the cradle of his poetic maturity.

Rilke's Russian myth consisted of a whole set of distinct yet mutually interdependent motifs woven together to form the magic tapestry of the land and its people. Russia was infinitely spacious, a land full of immense distance—a land of darkness and, so, deep solitude and mystery that bred a profound self-effacing religiosity in its people. The land, the people, and their God were as yet at the beginning of things—still in childhood, and so near the origin of a long, slow, gradual *becoming* born with suffering, joy, and above all patience; a land and a people, therefore, not of the past, but of the future. Grounded in their essential humanity, the common people, the Russian folk, shared a destiny. Deep in themselves, they were nonetheless bound together in brotherhood. Steeped in the elemental nature of the soul, they were, too, inherently artistic.

In developing this image of Russia, Rilke drew very heavily on Nina Hoffmann, Lou, and others. The whole outline of his picture of Russia as well as many of its specific details derive directly from these sources.

Nonetheless, Rilke never functioned as a mere sycophant and brought his own inimitable poetic stamp to most everything he thought, felt, and wrote on the subject.

After beginning with a paean to the country's natural landscape ("It is not possible to report upon any event in the area of Russian art without first saying something of the land itself"), Rilke's chief article on the topic of Russia—"Russian Art"—offers his own version of the historical logic that grants Russia its unique privilege.

> Next to the feverish development of neighboring cultures... its development goes forward in slow, ever hesitating strides. In the Renaissance, in the Reformation, in revolutions and kingdoms, the West unfolded, as it were, in a moment, and in the twilight of its transitions shot off the fast fireworks of its beauty—and has centuries behind it, while, next to it, in the realm of the Ruriks, the first day still lasted, the day of God, the day of creation.[154]

Rilke's interest in Russia coincided with the pressing necessity of giving voice to his deeply religious nature in a manner authentic to his own intensely individual character. His explicit concern with religion at this time developed in part as a inherent aspect of his own spiritual development and in part as a direct effect of Lou's intellectual influence. Though religion per se remained a concern for Rilke throughout his life, never again did explicitly religious topoi—God, prayer, the icon—play such a dominant role in his life and work as in the years of his closest association with Lou and Russian things. Russian spirituality (or his imagination of it) allowed Rilke to rescue the devotional side of his nature—so fundamental a dimension of his character, and yet one so tainted by his mother's unhappy example—by providing a mythical context within which his religiosity could *participate in human community and tradition* and, at one and the same time, be inimitably *his own creation.*

Accenting the self-effacing side of Lou's religious equation with a vengeance, Rilke could scarcely write about Russia without mentioning its peculiar religiosity and the exceptional humility that characterized it.

> They throw themselves down before [both God and the Czar], feel the ground with their brows, weep and say "I am sinful, forgive me, Father." The Germans who see this maintain: a quite unworthy slavery. I have a different opinion about it. What is this kneeling supposed to mean? It is supposed to express: I am respectful. For

> that it's enough to bow one's head, thinks the German. Well, yes, the greeting, the bow, to a certain extent they too are expressions of this abbreviation which arose in countries where there wasn't so much space that each man could lie down on the earth.[155]

In Rilke's view, the land itself bred Russia's religious character, a religiosity characterized not only by the humility of the folk, but—and this is crucial—by the immanence rather than transcendence of God. Instead of the strong duality of heaven and earth characteristic of popular Christianity (and displayed so wrenchingly in the first of Rilke's *Visions of Christ*), in Russia, heaven—its expansiveness, its limitlessness—was present on and to earth. Unity, rather than duality, prevailed. So Rilke called Russia "the broad land in the East, the only one through which God maintains his connection with the earth."[156]

The "broad land," moreover, was not only the ground of the people's religiosity, but of their historical destiny as well:

> Russia became for me reality, and at the same time the profound daily insight: that reality is something distant, which comes with inexpressible slowness to him who has patience. Russia—that is the land where people are lonely, each with a world with him, each full of darkness, like a mountain; each deep in his humility without fear of humbling himself, and therefore pious. People full of distance, uncertainty, and hopes: people who are *becoming*.[157]

That destiny, like the Russian character, was inherently artistic:

> Like the childhood of an artist is this Russia.... If one speaks of peoples as one speaks of men whose development one grasps, so one can say: this people wants to become a soldier, another a merchant, a third, a scholar; so the Russian folk wants to become an artist, and it is because of this that the best of its creative artists feel themselves called to be its educators.[158]

For Rilke, what was finally most crucial was the *fusion* of the religious and the artistic in the Russian character and destiny. It was this that provided so appropriate a vessel for Rilke's own spiritual and poetic development, his own individuation. Moreover, in order to realize, concretely, the inner fusion of the soul-essence of art and religion, this fusion needed to manifest in outward forms of expression. Rilke, following Lou and Russian tradition, had no trouble identifying the archetypal form of religious expression—prayer—as well as the form of Russian art traditionally identified with it: the icon.

> Whereas elsewhere [in the West] a determined artistic idea seeks to embody itself in ever more mature forms, here [in Russia] there is a dance of thought through an enduring form. For the people, this is the gesture of prayer, which it fills with the content of its entire life and experience; for the artist, the ancient, holy image, the icon.[159]

In order to bring his own development and his experience of Russia to creative fruition, Rilke needed to avail himself of those forms and gestures that, archetypally, traditionally, embodied the essence of Russia's religious art. In a passage that transparently reflects his personal assimilation of Russia and the gist of his own spiritual poetics, Rilke explains how the traditional forms may, paradoxically, grant the innovative artist maximum creative freedom.

> It can well be that, for centuries, both forms, that of the gesture of prayer and that of the image, may be mechanically repeated, empty, senseless, or weighted down with false content—but they will be transmitted further with painful exactitude, and then comes once more a contemplative or an artist, full of genuine worth, and finds the beautiful simple vessel ready to receive his wealth; a vessel large enough to hold everything, even the overflow. Quiet consciousness of the always available form helps sustain the peculiar breadth of the Russian character, this unworried surrender to all life's experiences, even the strangest; this ever-growing *Weltanschauung* of solitary individuals which stretches itself between one contrary and the other, encompassing all powers and opinions, and always finding something deep and full of background even in those fateful events that cover up the heavens.[160]

Alongside this discussion of *icon form*, we can place the following kindred comment on the essence of *prayer* from Lou's "Realism in Religion." Hardly less than Rilke's own, it captures the essential gesture of Rilke's own religious art. Lou begins by citing Strindberg:

> "The weaker an individual is, the lower he stands, the more powerful he is in prayer"—far more, on the contrary, the more he has

> become an individuality, the more capable will he be to worship that in which he believes; to possess what is, to him, most holy and most his own, the innermost ground in which he is rooted, the highest goal toward which he strives. Much more than a mere plea to a supersensible helpmeet-God, for him, prayer has become a remembrance in spirit and in heart in which he measures his momentary and real capability against the living ideal and sacred life-element of the same—his God.[161]

And so it was that when Rilke finally gave his Russian—and Italian!—experiences definitive poetic form in the first part of *The Book of Hours*, *The Book of Monastic Life*, he did so in the persona of a figure who was simultaneously a religious hermit and an artist: an icon-painting monk whose prayers were poems and pictures, and vice versa. Appropriately enough, the collection was originally titled simply *Gebete* (*Prayers*). Appropriately, enough, the dedication of the final version reads: "Laid in the hands of Lou."

Chapter 4

ON A BACKGROUND OF GOLD

One of Rilke's earliest biographers, E. M. Butler, complained that the faith expressed in *The Book of Hours* does not accord with any established system of belief.[162] That, of course, is precisely the point; the unique product of Rilke's singular soul-making, the work culminates the initial phase of the poet's individual spiritual career. Rilke's lyrical imagination, his ongoing confrontation with Christianity, his initiatory experience of Lou, Italy, Russia—all these elements finally blend and attain integral creative expression in the book Rilke himself regarded as his first enduring (and so "undatable") work; the first that articulates those "basic postulates" which underlie the Rilkean opus as a whole.

But *The Book of Hours* is a profoundly religious text. The work unabashedly confronts fundamental spiritual issues: the nature of God, the human being, and the creation. While Rilke's construction of these mysteries remains rooted in the Judeo-Christian ground of his culture, his interpretations of them diverge dramatically from those that define traditional exoteric religion in the west. *The Book of Hours*, in fact, enacts a thoroughgoing revisioning of religion, transfiguring the essence of what we usually understand by the term. Insofar as the spirituality embodied in *The Book of Hours* distills the substance of the soul-developments that birthed it, it is hardly surprising that—*à la* Lou Andreas-Salomé—it does not construe "religion" as the assimilation of any doctrinal content, but as authentic *spirituality in the making*, as *poetry of soul.*

First and foremost, it must be recognized that *The Book of Hours*—even while continually addressing itself to God—does not express "belief" as that notion is customarily understood. This is not to say that Rilke's monk questions the reality of his God (quite the contrary); rather, it is to insist that the posture most clearly inscribed in the rhetorical form of the creed ("I believe in God the Father...") is profoundly alien—even antithetical—to the thrust and meaning of his prayers. *The Book of Hours* does not posit belief in an objective godhead whose reality and power are consistently presumed to be essentially independent of the human psyche. Rilke's monk repeatedly makes abundantly clear that his God depends as much upon him as vice versa. The poems, in fact, revolve primarily neither around God nor around the speaker's soul in and for itself, but rather around the relationship between them, as this relationship—*mediated by the (world of) creation*—defines the monk's consciousness and unfolds within the life of his soul. The principal focus throughout is not so much God or the divine attributes—though these do play an important role—as it is the speaker's own spiritual activity, at once devotional and creative, religious and artistic in all its multiple forms.

Butler, then, is only half right. While *The Book of Hours* may not mirror any familiar theology, it does faithfully reflect—and, still more, embody—one extant theory of spirit: namely, Lou Andreas-Salomé's psychology of art and religion. While Lou's essays perform her theory in their own more intellectual idiom, Rilke's poems do so far more immediately and palpably because he employs religion's own archetypal form (prayer) to give tangible expression to his soul's innermost feelings. Through the mask of his monk, Rilke lends voice, not only to religious ideas, but to heartfelt confessions which double as art and religious praxis.[163]

As we have seen, Lou's psychology of religion recognizes both the constitutive role of the human imagination in the creation of God (or God-images) and, reciprocally (in accordance with the logic of the "back-effect"), the real power of a God so formed to work back upon human consciousness, culturing the sentiments most familiarly associated with religion (devotion, contemplative remembrance, and enthusiasm). Both moments find constant expression in *The Book of Monastic Life*. Above all, it is their ongoing intricate, dialectical, and mutually transformative weave that engenders new senses of God, humanity, and creation.

> I believe in all that is as yet unspoken.
> I wish to free my most pious feelings.
> What no one yet has dared to say
> will one day come naturally to me...
>
> And if that is arrogant, then let me be arrogant
> for the sake of my prayer,

which stands so serious and so alone
before your cloud-strewn brow.[164]

One might marvel at the nerve and verve of the twenty-three-year-old poet who attempted so much. It is, after all, far more difficult to rejuvenate religion—to speak afresh in its own hallowed idiom of prayer—than it is to repudiate it. In doing so, Rilke dons the prophet's mantle, an act which requires an extraordinary quotient of self-reliance. Yet that, too, is a soul-component of authentic religiosity in Lou's understanding—so long, of course, as it is balanced by an equal portion of self-surrender and devotion. On this score, too, *The Book of Hours* exemplifies Lou's theory, displaying it in poetic action. The two contrary poles definitive of Lou's understanding of "the essence of the religious affect" are both transparently manifest in the monk's prayers, as is—most crucially—the paradoxical fusion which alone renders them spiritually effective. Self-assertive pride and humility blend in the inner life of the monk just as poem and prayer meld in its outward expression. And behind it all—the monk's self-image, and his image of God; his vision of history, nature, and all things that comprise the world of creation—lies Italy, Russia, and Lou.

Lou's psychology of religion and aesthetics provides the immediate backdrop of Rilke's own conscious sense of spirituality. Even so, to comprehend the outline of Rilke's emerging world view more fully, we require a still wider perspective; one that can place both Lou and Rilke's spiritual initiatives in broader historical context.

In his recent book *Cosmos and Psyche*, Richard Tarnas delineates the foundations of what he calls "the modern world view"—the construction of Man, God, and Universe that has risen to dominance since the Copernican revolution. Tarnas understands this world view to be defined, above all, by what he—following Weber—calls "the disenchantment" (*Entzauberung*) of the world: the modern mind's peculiar tendency to regard the universe as purely material and therefore void of intrinsic meaning, purpose, intelligence, subjectivity, or soul. The modern mentality reserves all such spiritual characteristics for the human being alone:

> [T]he modern mind experiences a fundamental division between a subjective human self and an objective external world.... Whatever beauty and value that human beings may perceive in the universe,

> that universe is in itself mere matter in motion, mechanistic and purposeless...[it] lacks conscious intelligence, it lacks interiority, and it lacks intrinsic meaning and purpose. For these are human realities....For the modern mind, the only source of meaning in the universe is human consciousness.[165]

Tarnas emphasizes the twin effects of this development: on the one hand, the increasing *empowerment* and *autonomy* of the human subject vis-à-vis any external reality, and—concomitantly—the fundamental *alienation* attendant upon that process and the accompanying tendency to experience the human self as an inconsequential mote in an enormous spiritual void.

None of this is unfamiliar territory: indeed, it is all too familiar. Not only because it describes (in admittedly the broadest of terms) the historical horizon within which we live, but also because we have already encountered kindred versions of the dualistic structure depicted here as an effect of the banishment of that "third" term which mediates spirit and matter: the soul. Tarnas, in fact, defines the modern world view against the background of the "primal world view" out of which it arose—a world view characterized by the omnipresence of soul and the human being's participation in a cosmos instinct with order and purpose; a world not of dead matter, but living meaning; an ensouled world, an *anima mundi.*

> The primal world is ensouled....Primal experience takes place, as it were, within a world soul, an *anima mundi,* a living matrix of embodied meaning. The human psyche is embedded within a world psyche in which it complexly participates and by which it is continuously defined....The many particulars of the empirical world are all endowed with symbolic, archetypal significance, and that significance flows between inner and outer, between self and world....this *participation mystique* involves a complex sense of direct inner participation not only of human beings in the world but also of human beings in the divine powers, through ritual, and of divine powers in the world, by virtue of their immanent and transformative presence.[166]

This passage says much, and implies still more. In particular, I would suggest that *the denial of soul to the world* Tarnas associates with the contrary *modern* world view ultimately imperils, too, *the archetypal soul-quality of the human being*, so that the *exile of (the human) soul* formalized by the Council of Constantinople and the *disenchantment of the world* are linked developments, each, to some degree, cause and effect of the other. The connection between these reciprocal developments emerges most clearly in the light of another, crucial element of Tarnas's discussion—the role played by monotheistic religion in the evolution of modernity.

In Tarnas' view, the quintessentially modern mind is secular: in the inexorable march to full autonomy, the human being denies God as well as the universe any inherent spiritual reality. Logically, Nietzsche figures as Tarnas's emblematic modern—Nietzsche, the thinker whose doctrine of *der Übermensch* (the over- or super-man who generates all meaning out of himself) followed upon his most famous proclamation of the death of God. Yet how did humankind move from a state in which the *universe itself* was regarded as an abode of divine presences (the "primal world view") to one in which things themselves were no longer symbols of an ensouled order and nature no longer alive with indwelling significance?

In Tarnas's analysis, monotheism played a crucial role in this process. Influential forms of monotheist belief posited a God transcendent to—and so, in some decisive way, separate from—the world of creation. Human spirituality, rather than focusing upon an ensouled world inherently revelatory of divine principles, entered into a direct and privileged relationship with a divinity not essentially of this world. "In the monotheistic revelation, a self-subsistent divine Subject created the world as Object, within which the special human subject and its divinely ordained history unfolds."[167] Once spiritual allegiance was decisively transferred to such a God, a decisive step had been taken towards the desacralization of the cosmos, emptying the world itself of indwelling significance, denying it soul. Tarnas writes:

> [W]hat eventually becomes the modern self receives its unique ontological status from its privileged association with the transcendent divine reality that stands above an empirical cosmos that has been increasingly emptied of all inherent significance and value apart from the human.[168]

When, in the course of time, the authority and reality of the transcendent God himself is shaken, the stage is set for modern man's ascension to a position of unprecedented spiritual autonomy—*and* isolation. Tarnas gives a thumbnail sketch of the most relevant cultural history:

> This epochal transformation of the triadic relationship between divinity, humanity, and the world was already set in motion with the emergence of the great world religions and philosophies of transcendence during that period of the first millennium BCE named by Karl Jaspers the Axial Age. The differentiation between self, world, and God was given special force and new definition with the unfolding of the biblical tradition from the later Hebrew prophets through early Christianity to Saint Augustine and the medieval era. It was decisively forwarded, and in a sense absolutized, by the Reformation's militant desacralizing of the world in service of the human being's exclusive allegiance to the sovereign majesty of the Creator. Finally, in the wake of the Scientific Revolution and Enlightenment, this privileged position of the human vis-à-vis the rest of creation was assumed and expanded in entirely secular terms—here too, partly as a result of forces set in motion by the Western religious legacy—as the modern self progressed in its unprecedented development of autonomy and self-definition.[169]

The latter half of the nineteenth century figures as a crucial terminus of the evolutionary process Tarnas describes here. In the long wake of the scientific revolution and—most proximately—the publication of Darwin's *On the Origin of Species* in 1859—science and its materialistic effect had indeed largely "dis-godded"[170] the universe *and* dealt God himself a terrible blow. Consequently (even as Darwinism undermined the human being's own divine pedigree), the human being did indeed accede to a new degree of spiritual autonomy. Nietzsche and his "superman" represent the acme of this trajectory; but reveal, too, the ultimately insupportable strain it placed upon a human consciousness left without mooring in any larger order of things. Heerikhuizen[171] notes the rise of pessimistic philosophies (Schopenhauer, Von Hartmann) in the nineteenth century, just one of many signs that—even as his technological and industrial capacities virtually exploded—man was already beginning to feel lost in space and time, adrift in an existentially indeterminate universe. On a less purely negative note (though Freud could hardly be considered a congenital optimist!), the advent of the field of psychology in the latter half of the century reveals the introspective turn incumbent upon the human being's increasing spiritual isolation. That isolation, while intensely problematic, also invited the mining of as yet undiscovered spiritual resources in the recesses of the human soul.

Lou and Rilke, living and working on the cusp of the new century, inherited this challenging predicament. In certain respects—notably, the assertion of the individual's spiritual autonomy and the inward, psychological inflection of their thought—they bear the logic of modernization dramatically forward. In other crucial regards, however, Lou and Rilke threw the whole weight of their formidable souls *against* modernity's seemingly unstoppable tide. Most signally, the religious character of their personalities led them to resist the secularization of consciousness.

As we have seen, Lou and Rilke sought a revivification of spirituality sourced in the human soul itself. They did *not* do so, however, in the form of any full-blown existentialism that could accept the human individual's alienation from God and Nature as the inescapable ground of its being. Rather, Lou, and most especially Rilke, sought to redeem the failing human spirit by renovating its damaged relationship with both God (or, more generally, divinity) *and* the world of creation. Needless to say, this was no small task, but it defines, in broad terms, the fundamental intention of Rilke's oeuvre, and underlies those "essential premises" first formulated in *The Book of Hours*.

In Rilke's *Book of Hours*, this spiritual project took on a concrete poetic form. Against the background of Tarnas's analysis, the specific intellectual historical logic by which Rilke's text sets about its revisionary aims reveals itself quite clearly: *the poem sets in motion a precise* ***reversal*** *of the evolutionary process Tarnas associates with the rise of monotheistic religion.* Feeling and thinking within a monotheistic frame of reference, Rilke nonetheless moves to *reinvest* the spiritual currency born by the name of God *back* into the world of creation, thereby re- (instead of de-) sacralizing that world. *On account of God's degraded value, however, this move required a vital correlative: namely, the creative self's resuscitation of God himself.*

We have seen how Lou's psychology of religion provided—theoretically, at least—the operative dialectic for this aspect of Rilke's project. We will have more to say about its poetic modus operandi in *The Book of Hours* later in this (and the next) chapter. For now, though, we need note only this: the traditional transcendent image of the godhead could by no means survive Rilke's drastic reversals intact; the Judeo-Christian God himself undergoes a radical revision in the process of Rilke's poem. The weave of the interrelated transformations undergone by Self, God, and the World form the complex subject of Rilke's *Book of Hours*, defining the young poet's unique (anti-) modernity at the dawn of the new century.

The hour bows down and touches me
with its clear metallic ring:
my senses shiver. I feel: I can
grasp the day as a malleable thing.

Nothing was whole before I beheld it;
all becoming stands still.
My glances are ripe, and like a bride,
to each comes the thing that it wills.

Nothing is too small for me to love
and paint great on a background of gold.
I hold it high, and know not whose
soul it will break from the mold.[172]

The Book of Monastic Life begins in a moment of inspiration. The monastery bell rings, and the monk is touched by a creative power. He registers the sensation not so much in his mind as in his bodily senses, the corporeal organs of his soul—and then, too, immediately, his feeling and will are awakened. The book's founding moment is thus one of *conception*, but not in an intellectual sense. It is a moment of spiritual transmission or insemination: Rilke refigures the Annunciation with him—or his monk—in the place of Mary. His fertility, though, takes a different form than hers. He bears the power to take hold of the world—which becomes "plastic" in hands—and refashion and reshape it at will. The monk's principal identity is thus established: the call to prayer is, simultaneously, painterly and poetic vocation. He is an artist.

The book thus takes the creative self as its point of departure. In this first poem, God is not present—or is so only in the emissary form of "the hour" which bows down and touches the monk, just as the angel Gabriel bows to Mary. That bow recognizes the absolute centrality of the human vessel which—in both the Christian context and Rilke's transfiguration of it—is destined to bear God anew—not in heaven, but on earth, in the midst of the world of becoming. In Rilke's poem, all creation literally waits upon the gaze of the artist-monk. Things become what they are only when beheld by his eyes, transfigured by his palette and brush.

Asserting the limitless prerogative of the artist-monk's creative power, this first poem veritably bursts at the seams with the self-affirmation characterizing so much of Rilke's Florence diary, the sentiment Heerikhuizen calls "Romantic pride." Yet this "pride" is really nothing other than a full honoring of the role of the creative imagination, the exercise of which—as that most metaphysical of the English Romantics knew—establishes human being in its divine lineaments: "The primary IMAGINATION," wrote Coleridge, "I hold to be the living Power and prime Agent of all human Perception, and as a repetition in the finite mind of the eternal act of creation in the infinite I AM."[173]

Yet the Self is not the only term dignified in the poem; nor can its imaginative power function in a vacuum. From the first the monk establishes his (imaginative) identity in vital connection to—not only some unmanifest spiritual source—but, as well, the world of creation. Indeed, his intercourse with the world is so intimate as to be figured in marital terms. It is, in fact, in *The Book of Hours* that Rilke first begins using the word "thing" (or "things," *Ding* or *Dinge*) with extraordinary frequency, styling this seemingly abstract term as a veritable insignia of the creation itself. The prominence of the term—which finally reaches its zenith in its guise as the name of a whole new genre of poetry, the *Dinggedichte* or "thing-poems" Rilke essays in his later *New Poems*—indicates the poet's progressive movement away from the extreme subjectivism characteristic of most of his early lyrics. It is a sign that henceforth his poetic soul-making will proceed in ever more intimate converse with the objective world—that same "external world" which modernity tends to present as dead, merely material, and thoroughly "disenchanted."

It is, moreover, by no means for himself alone that the monk paints; the free creative spirit incarnated in his pictures is intended to transmit the like effect to others, grant the gift of spiritual freedom to other receptive souls. Nor does this truly catholic monk discriminate against any aspect of the creation: all things—not merely Madonnas and saints—are worthy of love, fit subjects for his iconic art. All things of the world are, in the monk's religious eyes, holy images, and so the world itself—the whole of it—becomes for him the fittest image of the divine, and love of the world, the way to God.

I live my life in widening circles
that reach out across all things, high and low.
The last one, I may never complete
but will attempt it, even so.

I circle around God, the primordial tower,
circle thousands of years long;
and still don't know: am I falcon, a storm, or am I
a great song.[174]

First, a moment of creative inspiration; then, the soul's unceasing activity, an endless expansion recalling the leitmotif of Rilke's favorite Emerson essay, "Circles." The soul set free at the end of the initial poem is, in the first place, the monk's own: no longer confined within the cell of his monastery or his physical body, it lifts and soars, reaching out across the world (literally, again, *die Dinge*, "things") in an endless attempt to compass the whole. Though elevated, the soul's circular motion emphasizes breadth rather than height, inclusiveness rather than transcendence Indeed (in marked contrast to Charles Wright's "Indian Summer II," analyzed in Appendix I), the poem does not so much figure the soul leaving the body in an errant search for transcendence as much as it "signs" the soul expanding beyond the limits of the monk's own body to encompass the body of the world. No "wandering, moral drug" (Wright) lost in the void between spirit and matter, the poetic speaker's soul-life claims the space between as its own transitional sphere of being.

The second stanza of the poem reveals that this sphere is not merely transitional but transformational as well. It is in this stanza that God puts in his first appearance. That He himself does so in the form of a particular incarnate thing (the first of innumerable such that will bear his name) manifests the soul's signature imaginative power. The age-old tower may be enduring—a long-abiding presence—but is also somewhat antiquated, and certainly immobile. Active power inheres in the ever-expanding life of the soul and it is that life, concerning itself *both* with God and with the things of the world, that relates these terms, seeing each in the other by virtue of its symbolic power.

In the next poem, the monk's discourse takes a critical turn as he begins to interrogate specific historic styles of religious imagination:

I have many brothers in the South
who move, handsome in their vestments,
through cloister gardens.
The Madonnas they make are so human,
and I dream often of their Titians,
where God becomes an ardent flame.

But when I lean over the chasm of myself—
it seems
my God is dark
and like a web: a hundred roots
silently drinking.

This is the ferment I grow out of.

More I don't know, because my branches
rest in deep silence, stirred only by the wind.[175]

"I live my life" gives us our first figure of God, but only in this third poem does the monk directly broach the issue of God's essential nature and—coincidently—the crucial correlative question: *how may God may be imaged or represented?* Like Rilke himself, Rilke's monk takes Italy as his point of departure, but commences his own effort to picture God by deliberately distancing himself from the Italian style, which, while appealing, remains too attached to visible boundaries of human form and, indeed, all that can be *seen*: filled with and revealed by light. Before, however, conjuring the monk's radically different God-concept, we must take note of how he comes to it, for, as always, the nature of his God is one with the manner of his seeking.

The monk introduces his own God-image with the enigmatic line "Doch wie ich mich auch in mich selber neige." The verb *sich neigen* literally means to bend, lean, or incline. The line thus implies an act of psychological introspection—looking into oneself—but doing so with a peculiarly active, almost physical gesture. Bly translates it: "Yet no matter how deeply I go down into myself."[176] The line conveys the element of subjectivity inherent in the very constitution of the monk's God. On one level, it implies that God is found—even engendered—in the depths of the self, in the soil of the soul.

The character of the monk's God is commensurate with that origin. Looking into himself, the monk realizes that his unique religiosity, his own *individual* God-image (Rilke's own emphasis, "*my* God," recalls Lou's citation of this "most religious" expression) premises itself upon a highly unorthodox ground: the dark, unillumined, web-like roots of all things.

Rilke's God cuts a very different figure from the conventional "Father in heaven." Indeed, the image of God he introduces here represents a striking inversion of western religion and philosophy's dominant God-image. Rilke's location of God in the dark, invisible, densely material underground of the earth; his likening of God, not to a single centralized source, but to a spreading network of roots; his emphasis on God's silence (as opposed to his association with speech, logos): all of this controverts both conventional Christianity and the Platonic metaphysics which often (in Renaissance Italy, for instance) supports and blends with it. Platonic philosophy (as in the classic parable of the cave) associates divinity with the sun which—as logos (source of reason, speech, and light)—doubles as the very "idea of the Good." Christian theology's deification of *the son* speaks a kindred spiritual language. The province of darkness underground, on the other hand, may well be regarded as most distant from this divine source and accordingly construed as the domain of increasing unreality, illusion, and nascent evil. No wonder, then, that Butler protests that Rilke's "dark God" does not participate in any familiar—or at least generally acknowledged—religious tradition.

Rilke's move may well be radical, but from a contemporary perspective it is hardly unrecognizable. Insofar as the biases Hillman confronts in "Peaks and Vales" are inscribed in our religion and (somewhat less rigidly perhaps) our philosophy, the principal images of God and of the Good handed down to us are, predominantly, images of transcendent spirit. Rilke's, however, isn't: not perched upon transcendent peaks or towers, neither in heaven nor a self-radiant Divine Mind, his divinity abides down below, at the bottom of everything. Though Rilke's God momentarily reaches into airy heights in the form of "the age-old tower," the poem foregrounds his more characteristic—and quintessentially *psychological*—dimension: *depth*. Immanent in the ground out of which the poetic self rises like a tree, Rilke's image of God is in and of the soul, more kin to what Tarnas speaks of as "a world soul, an anima mundi, a living matrix of embodied meanings" than any purely transcendent sovereign.

At play here, in part, are the Russian roots of Rilke's spirituality, the mystery of an immanent godhead which—while ubiquitous—cannot be revealed by the light of reason, remaining the dark, hidden ground of being. Several poems in *The Book of Monastic Life* explicitly connect Russian imagery with the motif of darkness as (or closely associated with) spiritual source. One poem, based upon Rilke's experience in the Uspensky Sobor, the Cathedral of the Assumption (an important church in the Kremlin illumined solely by two narrow rows of windows), opens "Seldom is there sunlight in Sobor." The potent vision vouchsafed him there (of iconic figures, including Mary and the Christ) effectively originates in what is, at best, a half-light. That God's emergence into the world is veiled—indeed marked—by darkness is still more powerfully figured in the subsequent poem. The poetic speaker enters the church as a pilgrim and, in the traditional act of devotion, places seven candles around "your dark being" and "saw in every image / your dark birthmark." Focusing not on the traditional religious iconography everywhere about him but upon a peasant in the church, the speaker sees

> how he became dark,
> like to all others around,
> and I felt You more than ever before
> mild and silently manifest
> in all and in him.[177]

Indeed, in a poem that appears towards the end of the book, Rilke's monk more or less explicitly identifies his God with the (only peripherally Christian) "dark" land of Russia:

> I was there with the first mythmakers and monks
> who made up your stories, traced your runes.
>
> But now I see you:
> wind, woods, and water,
> roaring at the rim of Christendom—
>
> you, land,
> to be left in darkness.[178]

Evidently, Rilke's relation with "Mother Russia" helped inspire a spiritual vision that—in contrast to the generally more dominant masculine images of deity—manifests unmistakably feminine and maternal overtones. The principal locus or source of creation appears more kin to the earthy darkness of the womb than to the light of heaven above.

In the fourth poem of the cycle, Rilke's monk confronts the problem of imaging God—whose infinitude naturally resists all representation—still more directly. Here, however, alluding to the conservative tenets of traditional Russian icon-painting, he addresses not some foreign heritage, but his own:

> We may not paint you after our own fashion,
> you dawn, out of whom the morning rises.
> We fetch from the old paint pans
> the same strokes and the same colors
> devoted masters have long used to wrap you in stillness.
>
> We build up images before you like screens
> so that soon a thousand walls stand around you.
> For our pious hands cloak you in darkness
> As often as our hearts open to you.[179]

Rilke was well aware of historic controversy within the Russian tradition of iconic representation and—in accord with the attitudes expressed in "On Russian Art"—was inclined to approve the rather strict roles regulating legitimate iconic representation, *at least theoretically*. In the original draft of *The Book of Monastic Life*, the speaker—a monk named Apostol—clearly takes a highly orthodox position;[180] as late as 1922—Rilke (in a letter to Margot Sizzo) once more cast the traditional rules of iconic representation as a salutary means of avoiding overly personalized or individualistic representation. "We may not paint you" evidently intends a similar endorsement, construing the cloaking or veiling act of the icon painter (the German word is *verhüllen*) as a laudable *preserving* of the dark ground of divine existence, a concealing that nonetheless indirectly fosters invisible re(ve)lations.

Even so, Rilke's language remains rife with ambiguity. Indeed, Barrows and Macy's translation of the poem casts the monk, not as a defender of iconic tradition, but as one who repudiates it. *This* monk experiences that tradition as an outworn set of conventions that tend—in a purely negative wise—to occlude or block the individual soul's heartfelt access to God:

> We must not portray you in king's robes
> you drifting mist that brought forth the morning.

Once again from the old paintboxes
we take the same gold for scepter and crown
that has disguised you through the ages.

Piously we produce our images of you
till they stand around you like a thousand walls.
And when our hearts would simply open,
our fervent hands hide you.[181]

Given the evidence provided by the early draft of *The Book of Monastic Life* as well as Rilke's other statements on the subject, it would be possible simply to reject this version as a strong mistranslation. The next two poems in the cycle, however, rather spectacularly support, if not Barrows and Macy's translation of this particular poem, the meaning they find in it. The fifth poem (which we will look at more closely in the next chapter) champions, *not* the legitimacy of tradition, but the access to the timeless ground of being (commensurate, clearly, with the dark God of the third poem) opened in and through the multiple strata of *the individual psyche*.

I love the dark hours of my being
wherein my mind deepens...

From them comes the knowing: within me
there's room for another life that's wide and timeless.[182]

Subsequently, the sixth poem—revisiting the imagery evoked in the third poem—passionately and unambiguously does cast "the wall of images" as—*not* a holy veil—but an unwanted barrier or grate that extinguishes authentic connection with God.

Only a thin wall stands—
by chance—
between us; any moment, a cry
from your mouth or
from mine—
and it will fall without a sound.

It is built of your images.

And your images stand before you like names.
And then when the light inside me

through which I know you
in my being's depths
burns,

the brilliant glow is wasted
on your frames

and my senses, quickly
crippled, are
homeless

and far from you.[183]

If it is not illegitimate to read these meanings back into the fourth poem, we can understand at least an undercurrent of that poem to imply that traditional modes of picturing God obstruct what is, after all, the ground of authentic religiosity: the receptivity of the individual soul seated, not in the intellect or will, but in the soul's own signature organ, *the heart.*

Even so, Rilke's poetic persona—despite his resolute individuality—cannot stand wholly outside the stream of Christian tradition. As monk and icon painter, he necessarily participates in Christian topoi even as he critiques them. Indeed, the very sense of soul or notion of selfhood that functions as the agent of Rilke's re-visioning of religion owes a huge (albeit double-edged) debt to a particular strand of Christian thought, one that predates the Renaissance and Romanticism and modern psychology by more than a thousand years *and figures, to no small degree, as the historical condition of those later developments.* In order to elaborate further the lineaments of Rilke's complex transformation of religious tradition, we will turn our attention to this crucial topos.

The Heart of Augustine

In the thumbnail cultural history cited earlier, Tarnas speaks of many grand movements that contribute (directly or indirectly) to the legacy of monotheistic thought in the West: the biblical tradition, the medieval era, the scientific revolution, the Reformation, and the Enlightenment. That St. Augustine stands as the lone *individual* named in Tarnas's historical sweep bears witness to his signal importance. Adolf von Harnack—a prominent Protestant theologian of the day who figures as the subject of one of Lou Andreas-Salomé's essays—addressed Augustine's significance more directly: "Where in all the history of the Western Church do we encounter a man whose influence is comparable to the influence of St. Augustine?"[184] The closing image of "We may not paint you" can cue us into the reason for Augustine's importance and the nature of Rilke's indebtedness to him. Both inhere in Augustine's revolutionary interpretation of the human heart.

In his *The Thought of the Heart and the Soul of the World,* James Hillman sketches three different understandings of the human being's central organ. Touching first upon the "*coeur de lion*" (the daring, sunlike, often unthinking "heart of the lion" that projects itself in heroic deeds), Hillman proceeds to discuss "the heart of Harvey" (the mechanical pump and circulatory center, brainchild of modern science) before finally evoking a vision of the heart defined neither by the will nor by the intellect, but by *feeling.* Hillman calls this "the heart of Augustine." Quoting the author of the *Confessions*, Hillman writes:

> "Whose heart is seen into? What he is engaged on, what he is inwardly capable of, what he is inwardly doing or purposing, what he is inwardly wishing to happen, or not to happen, who shall comprehend?"... Already, a psychoanalysis of feelings.... Feelings are a way of knowing this heart, and confession brings it to expression. The thought of the heart is feeling.[185]

Much hinges upon these matters. If Aristotle said "The definition of man is the definition of his soul" (the sentence that serves as the motto for Hillman's *The Myth of Analysis*), *The Thought of the Heart and the Soul of the World* implies that both of those definitions depend, in turn, upon that of the heart. Hillman, in fact, credits Augustine—author of the feeling heart—with developing a new, distinctly *psychological* concept of human *personality,* one pioneered in the saint's classic autobiographical text.

> Augustine's thought of the heart begins with his *Confessions.* This book is a testament of interior experience, the first book of psychology developing an idea of person as experiencing subject. "Person" is a word that the Greeks did not have, nor does the word appear in the Greek New Testament. Augustine's use of the word

> *cor*, heart, equates it with *intima mea*, inward dwelling...the anima or soul....
>
> Heart is essentially *my* heart....the deepest place...in which my truth resides.[186]

Both Lou and Rilke take this "heart of Augustine" as their own spiritual point of departure. The Augustinian concept of the human person, qua feeling subject and author of inner life, figures as the indispensable—and distinctly psychological—ground of their various projects of cultural self and soul-definition. Lou's psychological aesthetics, as described in her "Basic Forms of Art," is avowedly confessional in character (is the artist capable of expressing "the secret mysteries in the soul"). The sense of uniquely personal inwardness cultured in and through—not the metaphysical or theological intellect or moral will—but the feeling soul, similarly founds her psychology of religion (Hillman's sentence "Heart is essentially *my* heart" recalls Lou's own quotation of the notion that the most religious of words is not "God," but "*my* God"). Throughout his poetic career, Rilke made a modern version of the inward, feeling-centered "heart of Augustine" so much his own as to virtually take out a new patent on it. It comes as no surprise, then, that *The Book of Hours*—the first book the poet consistently recognized as his own—clearly reinscribes "the heart of Augustine" and its unequivocal privileging of the faculty of feeling.

This privilege emerges in the very first poem in the *Book of Monastic Life*. After the poem's initiating image ("The hour bows down and touches me") and the soul's (passive) reception of a spiritual impulse, the phrase "I feel: I can" foregrounds *feeling* as the very first act of the "I": it is the immediate effect of inspiration and, coincidently, the enabling prerequisite of imaginative will. All subsequent create activity—central, as we have seen, to the self's own definition—flows from it. Several later poems explicitly reaffirm feeling as the privileged mode of relation to the godhead and the psychological faculty enabling authentic imagination. Here is the beginning of the eighteenth poem:

> Why are my hands fooling once more with brushes?
> When I *paint* you, God, nothing happens.
>
> I *feel* you. At my senses' horizon
> you begin to appear, hesitantly,
> like scattered islands.[187]

...and here the end of the thirty-ninth:

What mystery breaks over me now?
In its shadow I come into life.
For the first time I am alone with you—

you, my power to feel.[188]

Nor was Augustine a stranger to Rilke; the poet did, in fact, read "the holy Augustine"[189] repeatedly throughout his life. Yet despite the degree of kinship, the common ground between Rilke and Augustine is less solid than may at first appear. *In fact, the heart of Rilke's poetic sense of soul ultimately differs radically from Augustine's—the notion of soul which, rightfully or not, has widely come to be understood as "Christian."* Indeed, Rilke's sense of soul and the religion peculiar to it comes into its own by virtue of a decisive *break* with the orthodox Christian tradition founded upon Augustinian doctrine.

Rilke, as we have seen, aggressively inaugurated his independence from mainstream Christian norms in his *Visions of Christ*. It is a sign of his relative spiritual and artistic maturity that *The Book of Hours* offers a more constructively creative vision—and less purely deconstructive critique—of Christianity, and indeed rather readily absorbs elements of Christian iconography into its individual style. Even so, we must probe still more deeply into the bases of Augustine's (Christian) sense of self or soul, for Rilke's own more poetic religion emerges clearly only against the backdrop of the world view he transfigures. We can begin where we left off, with Hillman.

Augustine attracts Hillman's attention, after all, not because Hillman himself wishes to champion the feeling heart, but, on the contrary, because Hillman sees Augustine as the origin of a model of *overly* personal subjectivity that—even while it grounds and continues to dominate much modern psychology—finally proves anathema to archetypal psychology and the soul it serves. It is so because the feeling heart, as the center of personal subjectivity, can function in a manner inimical to the faculty that (more essentially than mere "feeling") counts as the defining act of the archetypally psychological soul—namely, imagination:

> And this heart of subjective feeling...holds imagination in its captivity. We judge our images in terms of their feelings....To test something in the heart has come to mean what we feel about it, and to weigh the heart refers no longer to the gravity and substance of its images, but mainly to our personal motivations and reactions that can be discovered in confessional introspection.[190]

If it is difficult to follow Hillman on this point it is not because his explanation is obscure but because the dynamic he describes still holds so much of our psychology in thrall. Even in the artistic sphere—by rights the stronghold of imagination—confessional writing that sometimes depends overmuch upon purely personal, autobiographical factors remains in vogue. Hillman's analysis, however, discloses that such modern phenomena derive from an ancient model that—in accord, once more, with Tarnas's discussion—*links the human with the divine subject.* When the reign of personal feeling draws religion and the name of God into its sphere of influence, we find ourselves in Augustine's realm of *feeling* become *faith*:

> Now we see what happens to the imagination in a heart of personal feeling. By personalizing the heart and locating there the word of God, the imagination is driven into exile. Its place is usurped by dogma, by images already revealed....When imagination is driven out, there remains only subjectivity—the heart of Augustine.[191]

This passage, quite accessible on one level, nonetheless invites question and amplification. How precisely does Augustine's overly personal heart of feeling exile imagination? What does it really mean to claim that the imagination's centrality is "usurped by dogma, by images already revealed"? What is the foundation of the omnivorous subjectivity Hillman describes? Inquiry into these vital issues requires looking more closely into the generic form of Augustine's most famous and influential work.

In his analysis, Hillman argues that the pervasive and domineering subjectivity associated with Augustine's "feeling heart" finds, not only its typical expression, but its essential authorization in a specific literary mode: namely, that of *confession.* Insofar as confession aims to reveal the inner truth of its author's subjectivity, it requires an unrelenting focus upon the self, and so, grammatically speaking, "a rhetoric of the ego, the first person singular." Hillman cites Augustine's own definition of the generic aim of his classic work: "Accept the books of my

Confessions. . . . There see me . . . there believe, not others about me, but myself; there mark me, and see what I was in myself. . . . "[192] The generic form of Augustine's *Confessions* thus encodes subjective veracity as the norm of literary truth and value. The problem with such a norm, as Hillman indicates, is that personal truth need not coincide with imaginative value, and matters of purely biographical concern can often effectively displace more purely imaginative matters as the center of interest.

Hillman undoubtedly has a point; even so, he somewhat overstates his case. Just as feeling and imagination can stir together, autobiographical interest and subjective veracity *need* not necessarily detract from imaginative value. Many excellent memoirs attest to this fact, not to mention classic works such as Wordsworth's *Prelude*. While it may indeed be the case that—theoretically regarded—the moment of interest in the image per se and the moment of interest in the person are mutually exclusive, practically speaking they often intertwine and may as well prod as undercut each other. In *The Prelude*, for instance, because the personal narrative itself focuses upon the development of imagination (the poem was originally subtitled "Growth of a Poet's Mind"), autobiographical and poetic interest tend to support rather than supplant each other.

It is not, therefore, the first-person form of address alone that, in Augustine, issues in a mode of subjective, personal consciousness inimical to imagination, but the *essential definition of self or soul* written into his peculiar style of confession—the soul-character established by the author's voice, the story he tells, and the metaphysical presuppositions that underlie both. For the Augustinian self—like any other—assumes definite form only in a determined relationship to how that self experiences and interprets its world and, too, what may lie hidden within or beyond that world—its God. In short, understanding Augustinian subjectivity, and "the feeling heart" at its center, necessitates some conception of the Augustinian world view, including the ideas of the meaning and purpose of human life prescribed by that world view.

All of this is transparently transcribed in the form and thematic content of Augustine's *Confessions*. Let us, once again, begin at the beginning, for—as in the case of Rilke's *The Book of Hours*—we can learn a great deal from Augustine's opening lines:

> *Can any praise be worthy of the Lord's majesty? How magnificent his strength! How inscrutable his wisdom!* Man is one of your creatures, Lord, and his instinct is to praise you. He bears about

> him the mark of death, the sign of his own sin, to remind him that you *thwart the proud*. But still, since he is a part of your creation, he wishes to praise you. The thought of you stirs him so deeply that he cannot be content unless he praises you, because you made us for yourself and our hearts find no peace until they rest in you.[193]

In most every way—voice, form, content—Augustine's first lines present a graphic contrast with Rilke's. Augustine, true to the style of one who puts such stock in scripture (words *already* writ and spoken) does not begin with his own inspiration, but quotes a psalm. Augustine's traditional text, moreover, puts God the Almighty first. The opening hails God as *the (sovereign) Lord*, perfect in majesty and strength, a theme sounded *ad infinitum* throughout the text, as in these lines, a few pages later: "What, then, is the God I worship? He can be none but the Lord God himself.... you, my God, are supreme, utmost in goodness, mightiest and all-powerful, most merciful and most just."[194]

As we have seen, the first poem of Rilke's *Book of Hours* does not mention God by name but centers rather upon the (human) self and its creative power. In Augustine, however, creativity is, essentially and irrevocably, one more aspect of God's sovereign majesty. Man may exercise an inferior degree of creativity when he acts "as a human craftsman, making one thing out of something else as his mind directs," but such activity is of a wholly different order and kind from the original, archetypal, divine instance, the *creatio ex nihilo* by means of which God produced the universe:

> You created heaven and earth but you did not make them of your own substance. If you had done so, they would have been equal to your only-begotten Son, and therefore to yourself, and justice could in no way admit that what was not of your substance should be equal to you. But besides yourself, O God, who are Trinity in Unity, Unity in Trinity, there was nothing from which you could make heaven and earth. Therefore you must have created them from nothing.... You were, and besides you nothing was. From nothing, then, you created heaven and earth.[195]

The doctrine of *creatio ex nihilo*, as Augustine expounds it here, posits an unbridgeable metaphysical gulf between God and the creation. The created world, though brought forth by God, is not of God's own substance. Although the creation manifests the work of God, and so may, in its order and beauty, refer us to him, God himself does not indwell his Creation. Made, not of God or divine substance, but out of nothing, the intrinsic value of the created world must then (in comparison, at least, with the worth of God himself) be counted as very slight, indeed, be next to nothing. Speaking of earth and the heavens, Augustine writes:

> It was you, then, O Lord, who made them, you who are beautiful, for they too are beautiful; you who are good, for they too are good.... But they are not beautiful and good as you are beautiful and good, nor do they have their being as you, their Creator, have your being. In comparison with you they have neither beauty nor goodness nor being at all.[196]

Returning, then, to the paragraph that opens the *Confessions*, we should not be surprised that Augustine's first paragraph—indeed the whole first four-paragraph section—makes no reference whatsoever to any thing of this world aside from man himself. Augustine—again in marked contrast to Rilke, and in line with Tarnas's discussion—does not initially concern himself with the creation at all, but exclusively with man's relationship to God, exemplified, naturally, in his own person. We have indicated something of Augustine's concept of God's essential nature above; what then, of the human being's?

Again, the contrast with Rilke proves stark. We meet Rilke's monk in his capacity as an inspired creator capable—in a manner akin to that of God—of shaping the world. Augustine, on the other hand, introduces us to man as an effect, not a cause, of creation: a "creature" made by the sovereign God ("Man is one of your creatures, Lord"). He is, admittedly, a special creature (though Augustine does not explicitly state this here, he does so elsewhere), one made "in the image of God," but such privilege does not belie (in fact is the precondition of) the human creature's defining feature. Having diverged from that image, he is a *fallen* creature, essentially or originally marked by *sin* ("He bears about him the mark of death, the sign of his own sin").

These then, are the basic metaphysical terms underlying Augustine's work: an omnipotent, transcendent creator **God**, an almighty being utterly beyond the sphere of change who stands as the origin and end of all conceivable value; a **created world** not made of divine substance and so, metaphysically and valuatively, nothing in and of itself; **man**, a creature made in the image of God, but originally marked by sin. The religious aim and character of man follows logically from these terms: the plot of Augustinian Christianity as unfolded in his *Confessions* cannot be anything other than the moral story of (a) sinful soul's search for salvific reunion with God by way of the expiation and renunciation of his transgressive nature. The last lines of Augustine's initial section articulate his book's aim:

> I shall look for you, Lord, by praying to you and as I pray I shall believe in you, because we have had preachers to tell us about you. It is my faith that calls to you, Lord, the faith which you gave me and made to live in me through the merits of your Son, who became man, and through the ministry of your preacher.[197]

In passing, let us note that we shall soon see the operative terms of Augustine's quest—*belief, faith, and the authority of tradition*—emerge as the flip side of his very "personal" approach to God.

Having sketched—albeit briefly—the foundations of Augustine's world-view, we are better prepared to understand more fully the underlying constitution and religious compass of his "feeling heart," and why and how the intellectual and moral gist of his faith—indeed his very definition of (the Christian) soul—intrinsically suppresses imagination. As we have repeatedly stressed, imagination and soul (as we have developed the archetypal ideas of these terms) are essentially medial in nature, unfolding in a dynamic creative movement that transects the spiritual and the sensible universes. Augustinian theology, however, gives rise to ontological and cosmological premises fundamentally inimical to the imagination, and inimical, too, to the archetypally psychological understanding of soul indissolubly linked to its creative function.

The doctrine of *creatio ex nihilo* produces an unstable dualistic world-view prone to collapse into a valuative monism. There is God (spirit, or divine substance) on the one hand, and, on the other, that which is not (of the essence of God): the formless matter which, in the riddling notion that plagues the whole theory, is really nothing at all, and yet out of which, nonetheless, the entire universe is made. Consequently, (the image of) things themselves do *not* possess an intrinsically meaningful relation to the godhead; there is no *real* symbolic correspondence between Creator and Creation, the sensible form of things in the world and the divine archetype. Rather, the very space of that relation—the intermediate sphere of images subsisting between the worlds of spirit and sense—is not recognized as authentically existent. Correlatively, the act of imagination (the symbolic movement between spirit and matter, visible and invisible things) identified with this realm can not be accorded any real noetic or religious value and can in no wise be construed as positively or genuinely *creative*, for it does not comport with the archetypal idea of *creatio ex nihilo* that is the sole prerogative of God. Instead, phenomena evidently allied to the imagination—myth and dream, for instance—are typically construed as "imaginary" in the sense of fundamentally unreal.

The same theological and cosmological presuppositions produce a "Christian" sense of soul that puts an inherently anti-imaginative morality at the very heart of the human being. When the beginning and end of things as well as the ultimate locus of all meaning and value are exclusively identified with an immutable, transcendental source, the nature of soul—insofar as it is understood as distinct or different from that source—*can only be construed negatively, as a fall away from God.* Undue intercourse with the created world—*itself irrevocably foreign to the divine*—inevitably entails sin. The religious life of the soul unfolds primarily as an *aversion*, or turning away from the world, back toward God, divine substance or source.

We must emphasize that this aversive movement cannot be imaginative, because imagination depends upon and recreates the symbolic *connection* of spirit and matter and is essentially a two-way motion between. The *moral aversion* in question here, on the other hand, confirms the *lack* of any real connection between spirit and matter. Whereas Imagination unfolds as a functional and substantial bridge between spirit and matter, moral aversion shoots the ontological and valuative gap, taking a leap of faith in order to land, ideally, once and for all, in the lap of God.

Christian morality, as explicated here, thus depends upon a degraded notion of soul that is—not only intrinsically unimaginative—but intrinsically anti-imaginative. Hillman contends that such a notion of soul is antithetical to the archetypal idea of soul itself, and so is one with the suppression of soul inscribed in our cultural history: "Ever since Tertullian declared that the soul (anima) is naturally Christian, there has been a latent Christianity, an antisoul spirituality, in our Western soul."[198] We are now in a position to comprehend why Hillman—for whom imagination counts as the heart of soul—construes Christianity as "antisoul." The Christian *theology* of an omnipotent, transcendent godhead—closely linked, as it is, with a dualistic *cosmology*—authorizes a personal *psychology* that invests faith in moral feelings, reasons, and church doctrines that need not and indeed *cannot* be imaginatively substantiated.

The seed and fruit of all of this is clearly legible in Augustine's *Confessions*, which unfolds in the form of a stream of subjective consciousness that absorbs all reality into its own self-centered narrative, undermining the autonomy of the imagination in the process. Nowhere do we find—as we do most everywhere in Rilke—images of things presented as symbolic significances in and of themselves; maintaining, that is, some degree of semantic independence from the author's *already formed* moral opinions. Augustine does relate the signal events of his life and, in so doing, recites all manner of objective detail (the theft of pears as a youth, the death of a treasured friend); yet, when those matters are not left as mere data points, the author inevitably interprets their significance in predictable moral terms strictly in keeping with doctrinal belief. The ultimate meaning of things themselves is never seriously in doubt and cannot rise to the pregnant ambiguity proper to symbolic value.[199] The images of the story tend to flatten into the allegorical instances of the Hand of God in all playing multiple variations on the single ubiquitous lesson of moral aversion: "If the things of the world delight you, praise God for them but turn your love away from them and give it to their Maker, so that in the things that please you you may not displease him."[200] And so the narrative drives forward under firm control of the authorial consciousness, inexorably directed toward the decisive moment, the true beginning and end of the story: the moment of Augustine's conversion.

In his *Confessions*, Augustine tells the story of how—due to pride, ambition, lust, and ignorance—he rejected the teachings of the church despite the fervent prayers of his devoutly Christian mother. In time, however, he grew both intellectually and emotionally more inclined towards those teachings, especially under the influence of the wise bishop, Ambrose. Despite a growing inner desire to join the church, his pride and sinful attachment (most particularly, his disinclination to chastity) blocked his way, resulting in a growing agony of guilt and uncertainty. In the climactic scene, Augustine has recently learned of the conversion of another respected man, and feels immense pressure to follow suit, but cannot. Racked with doubt and disgust at his own prevarication, he weeps, and suddenly—as in an audible vision—hears a child's voice saying, "Tolle, lege"—"Pick up and read." He hastens to find his copy of Paul's Epistles, and, opening it at random, reads the lines:

> Not in revelling and drunkenness, not in lust and wantonness, not in quarrels and rivalries. Rather arm yourselves with the Lord Jesus Christ; spend no more thought on nature and nature's appetites.[201]

Struck by the uncanny manner in which the words speak to the core of his own spiritual struggle, Augustine's *feeling heart* is illumined ("it was as though the light of confidence flooded into my heart and all the darkness of doubt was dispelled") and the conversion towards which the whole book tends accomplished in a moment of inner conviction.

The text of Augustine's conversion contains, in distilled form, the spiritual gist of his *Confessions* and the religion unfolded in it. We should note first that *Augustine's own imaginative inspiration—the child's voice—does not itself produce his conversion, but rather directs him to a scriptural authority.* The climax of the conversion experience issues forth, not in any poetically original conception or utterance, but in a moment of biblical *citation*. Furthermore, the lines from Paul that finally catalyze his conversion—and give voice to its chief spiritual content—articulate with great concision the fundamental tenets of "the Christian soul" as we have elucidated it here: *renunciation of sin* ("Not in..., not in..., not in...") coupled with *belief in doctrine* ("Rather arm yourself with the Lord Jesus Christ"), and finally, the coda that reiterates that this faith depends upon *a moral aversion to the world*—not only, indeed, to "nature's appetites," but to "nature" herself.

At the very center, then, of Augustine's conversion, is his acceptance of church dogma—specifically, as such pertains to the import of the salvific figure "the Lord Jesus Christ." This, we should be clear, is not an imaginative act; on the contrary, the very nature of dogma is that its acceptance requires surrender of individual initiative. Augustine's narrative does not show him finally converting to the Christian faith because he has an original creative imagination of Christ or the essence of his teachings; rather, his newfound *belief* turns upon his acceptance of *traditional notions and images of Christ as savior framed and authorized by others.* He may, in his inmost personal soul, *feel* the power of Christian faith as his heart is "flooded" with "the light of confidence"; he may, too, will it to be true for him, but he does not fundamentally reconceive or *re-imagine* it. Hillman again: "Now we see what happens to the imagination in a heart of personal feeling. By personalizing the heart and locating there the word of God, the imagination is driven into exile. Its place is usurped by dogma, by *images already revealed*" (italics mine). The synergy of personal feeling, moral duty, and dogmatic faith at the core of Augustine's conversion, and indeed the "Christian" sense of soul it typifies, cuts imagination out of the heart, and the heart out of imagination.[202]

RILKE THE ICON PAINTER

Controversy revolving around the role of imagination in spiritual life riddles the history of religion, especially monotheism. From the Mosaic commandment against graven imagery to the Muslim ban on representational art and the multiple iconoclastic controversies that vex the history of the church, strict regulation of the kinds and forms of spiritual imagination deemed acceptable figure centrally in the canon of Jewish, Christian, and Muslim identity. To a significant degree, indeed, monotheism constitutes and authorizes itself by way of such regulation, whether it be in the form of explicit taboos or—still more importantly—inherited norms of spiritual value that exert unconscious control over the collective psyche.

As James Hillman so forcefully contends, the fate of the image converges with the fate of the soul itself. Having looked more deeply into the indissoluble bond between the archetypal idea of soul and the creative imagination, we are now in a better position to understand how the doctrine promulgated at the Council of Nicaea in 787 prepared the ground for that exile of soul formalized roughly a hundred years later in Constantinople, heart of the Byzantine empire. In response to one of the recurrent controversies revolving around the worship of icons, the Council at Nicaea legislated the kind of images admissible to the church. Hillman comments:

> Now, at Nicaea a subtle and devastating differentiation was made. Neither the imagists nor the iconoclasts got their way entirely. A distinction was drawn between the *adoration* of images and the free formulation of them, on the one hand, and the *veneration* of images and the authorized control over them on the other.... At Nicaea a distinction was made between the image as such, its power, its full divine or archetypal reality, and what the image represents, points to, means. Thus images became allegories.
>
> When images become allegories the iconoclasts have won. The image itself has become subtly depotentiated. Yes, images are allowed, but only if they are officially approved images illustrative of theological doctrine.... Yes, the image is allowed, but only to be

venerated for what it represents, the abstract ideas, configurations, transcendences behind the image. Images became ways of perceiving doctrine.... representation, no longer presentations, no longer presences of the divine power.

The year 787 marks another victory in our tradition of spirit over soul.[203]

Not only are the general issues raised here central to *The Book of Hours*—the book is driven, more than anything else, by the desire to establish an imaginative relationship with God—but the related cultural history proves concretely relevant as well. Rilke steeps his poems in the religious atmosphere of Russian iconography and icon-painting, a milieu that bears the very persona through which Rilke's poetic voice finds the power and inspiration to speak. This tradition, in turn, is firmly rooted in Byzantine forms of religion and art. Rilke's own engagement with the debates revolving around the norms of icon-painting in his Russian context thus figure as another chapter of the controversy confronted in Nicaea; the rules of icon-painting he wrestled with are distant offspring of the doctrines promulgated in 787. Where, then, does Rilke stand; how are we to construe his understanding of the nature and significance of that archetypally religious image, the icon?

As we have seen, Rilke does exhibit deep respect for certain conservative positions associated with icon-painting. Coincidently, the practice of the veneration of icons, including the custom of parading particularly renowned icons through the streets, remained very much part of the texture of religious life in Rilke's Russia. Rilke himself witnessed such a spectacle in Moscow and "saw the beggars and their prayers to the Iberian Madonna, who all create their God with the same kneeling strength, over and over again, presenting him with their sorrow and their joy.... "[204] As the tone of this and many other passages from letters, poems, and stories indicate, Rilke profoundly respected the sacred character of traditional icons and was not averse to performing the traditional gestures of ritual devotion himself. In July of 1899, after visiting the Znamenskaya chapel in Moscow, Rilke wrote: "I will bow down before the Znamenskaya icon, I will bow three times and in the orthodox manner."[205]

At the same time, Rilke does exhibit certain iconoclastic tendencies. The sixth poem vehemently rejects the iconic conventions evidently endorsed in the fourth, implying that these ultimately generate "a wall" of religiously ineffectual images that set up a barricade around God and prevent the soul from realizing his near presence. In later passages, the monk apparently repudiates the notion that any image of God might—as Hillman would have it—fully embody divine presence. "There is no image I could invent / that your presence would not eclipse."[206]

It is no simple matter to reconcile Rilke's apparent indictment of traditional religious imagery with his obvious reverence for, and personal participation in, the numinous power of traditional iconography. The key to doing so may lie in looking more deeply into Rilke's understanding of the archetypal essence of the icon. Insofar as that essence reveals itself to be, in some wise, inherently paradoxical, the issue perhaps lends itself best to poetical resolution.

Not long before writing *The Book of Monastic Life*, Rilke wrote an important poem based on the Znamenskaya icon—one spoken, like *The Book of Hours* itself, in the persona of an icon painter. In this poem—a clear precursor to the poetics of *The Book of Monastic Life*—the artist prepares to paint an image of Mary in the signature Znamenskaya pose, her hands at her side, lifting in the gesture of prayer, a (smaller) image of the Christ encircled in the region of her heart. "Die Znamenskaja" begins:

> As though I were leading a blond child
> I want to trace a golden line
> about your face—a face like folding doors
> behind which a hundred lamps hang lit.

Rilke immediately transforms the act of tracing the literal contours of the face into poetic metaphor. As Brodsky[207] remarks, the image of the folding doors alludes to the "Royal Doors" which lead through the huge screen of the iconostasis to the hidden altar behind (an opening absent from the image in "We may not paint you") and so figure the act of painting itself as a kind of portal or gate to a holy place.

As the poem unfolds, the poet-painter continues to turn the outlining of the icon into an ongoing symbolic process:

> And then we wander around your raiment
> trembling, as we follow its folds
> and the hands that you still hold
> up at your sides like things;
> and the way around you grows long.

Virgin Orant, The Great Panagia of Yaroslavl

Brodsky: "The act of painting thus becomes an act of worship and a pilgrimage."

> Paint you small as we may
> inside the dark icon,
> when we plead: come, dwell here—
> the brush goes on endlessly
> and the path around your crown
> already moves it to despair.
>
> Do not believe I want to bound you
> with this weak and timid spur;
> your radiant grace spills
> over every contour.
> Do not believe I want to hem you
> at your blue mantle's rim;
> your gentle wonder wanders
> well beyond this one home.

Finally, the artist acknowledges that Mary can hardly be confined in the icon itself:

> You are spread far out
> over everything. You hold all room.
> And every morning the red sun
> slips out of your dark womb.

Still, in the crowning metaphor, the painter nonetheless expresses the belief that, although she is great, the Virgin may also become small, and likens the relation between the icon and Mary to that between the foliage of a tree and a dove that may alight in it:

> But—o forgive us—we believe
> you can be small like the doves,
> white and soft and tame like them.
> And then you come somehow
> into the images as into leaves
> and we find you therein—
> find you as if asleep
> and we kneel (may you correct us)
> and kiss you on the chin.[208]

Implicitly, the figure of the dove harboring in the leaves echoes the image-content of the icon itself: its depiction of God qua Christ harboring in Mary's heart, spirit nesting in the embodying soul.

What does the poem tell us about Rilke's understanding of the nature of the archetypal icon? As Freedman says, "The icon exists not by itself, only by the act of producing it."[209] And that act, clearly, is one of ongoing imaginative transformation. The icon thus figures as a *holding frame for imagination itself* in its sacred function—the endlessly unfolding creative relation to the divine which strives to see spirit in matter like a white dove in green leaves. The icon functions as a catalyst and symbol of religious imagination, by which phrase I mean to imply the inherently religious character of imagination itself. For Rilke the icon-painter, it is a reverent and inspired imagination that *produces* true religiosity, rather than—as the Nicaean Council would have it—religious truth known in some otherwise controlling and delimiting its spiritual purview.

That act of imagination, moreover, does not belong to the original icon-painter alone. Indeed, the true art of the icon inheres—not in delivering ready-made packages of divine presence for the viewer's passive consumption—but in eliciting the viewer's own spiritual activity, his or her imaginative re-creation of the icon and its meaning. In his essay "Russian Art," Rilke maintains that the icon fulfills

> what in the highest sense remains valid for every work of art, insofar as it concerns the one who feels and experiences it truly: that it is really only a potential, a provision of a space wherein the viewer must recreate what the artist originally created—a possibility that fulfills itself in the frames of these paintings by virtue of the religious feeling of those who pray before them. The people gaze countless Madonnas into the hollow icon, and their creative yearning constantly enlivens the empty ovals with mild countenances.[210]

When, at the close of the first poem of the *Book of the Monastic Life*, the monk declares that his iconic art may set loose or free the souls of its viewer, Rilke may have had just this sort of imaginative activity in mind.

In his essay "Rilke and the Art of Icon Painting," August Stahl elaborates the just-cited quotation from "Russian Art," interpreting its wider significance for the Rilkean opus as a whole:

> The concept that the icon does not delimit religious feeling, but—insofar as it points towards the absence of what is signified in the

> picture—lends it space or room, that the icon itself is thus empty or hollow, allows it to become one of the most significant symbol-bearers and symbol-producers in Rilke's poetry.[211]

After mentioning kindred image-concepts in Rilke's later work (the "empty mold" cited in a letter discussing *Malte*, the "open arms" that recur several times in his poetry, the "hollow forms" of the relief in the *Elegies*), Stahl continues:

> All these images have in common that they become symbols for what is missing or lost, for distance and absence and, at the same time, the longing of human being for all of this—the missing, the lost, the distant, the absent. The icon thus becomes the exemplary form for the representation of what is absent [*présence absente*] and the supplying of space for the human being's creative yearning.[212]

In accord with this understanding, Rilke's own position cannot exactly be equated with Hillman's. For Rilke, the iconic image does not—at this juncture anyway—immediately embody divine presence. Nor, however, does it figure as a mere allegory of some transcendent or doctrinal verity. Instead, the experience of the iconic image becomes an enactment of the soul's yearning for the divine and its aspiration to draw images of spirit into its heart. That is as much as to say *the icon functions as a symbol and bearer of—not only religious imagination—but soul itself.* It is naturally no accident that icons so frequently contain an image of Mary—herself a figure of the pure or virgin soul. The Znamenskaya, in particular, displays the yearning soul in its capacity to bear (images of) spirit or God within the secret, dark-encircled recess of the heart. As such, it may be considered revelatory of the intrinsic nature of the icon itself—as (so to speak) an iconic icon.

Stahl acutely recognizes that the iconic character underlying Rilke's art may be understood as a response to the spiritual predicament of his time:

> The traditional conflict concerning the possibility and impossibility, the permissibility or impermissibility of representation—that which we call the iconoclastic controversy and owe to the art of the icon—all of this becomes fruitful in Rilke's interpretation, an interpretation that seeks to overcome the turn of the century's far-reaching spiritual discomfort by pointing to the creative power of human beings.[213]

...a creative power nonetheless regulated (as it is not in Nietzsche) by the canons of humility and self-restraint inscribed in iconic traditions. The art of the icon consequently may be understood to both depend upon and elicit the combination of creative self-assertion and humility Lou Andreas-Salomé posits as the very essence of "the religious affect."

The accent on imaginative activity implicit in Rilke's iconic poetics implies that drawing soul back into the heart of religion—the historic stronghold of spirit—may require a change of heart: a conversion of religion into something other than a feeling faith ultimately subservient to established dogma. In his *Thought of the Heart*, Hillman aims not merely to critique Augustine, but to elaborate a more imaginative view of the heart based upon the work of the Islamic scholar Henry Corbin and *his* work on the twelfth-century Sufi mystic Ibn Arabi.

> Corbin...states quite clearly that the heart's characteristic action is not feeling, but sight. Love is of the spirit, quickening the soul to its images in the heart. The heart is not so much the place of personal feeling as it is the place of true imagining.... One turns to the heart because here is where the essences of reality are presented by the imaginal to the imagination. The passionate spirit of *himma* that moves through the heart is not the *passio* of personal confessional life.[214]

The center of Rilke's spiritual life may well be construed as the kind of imagining heart Hillman and Corbin evoke here. An organ of feeling, it is at the same time the vessel of the soul's imagination, its ability to image or see things—including God, even if only darkly, as through iconic glass. It is this capacity, this visionary heart of imagination that Rilke affirms in the last lines—indeed, the last word—of his fourth prayer/poem, which brings the *heart* and *sight* together in its concluding figure: "Denn dich verhüllen unsre frommen Hände / so oft dich unsere *Herzen* offen *sehen.*" ("For our pious hands hide you / as often as our open hearts see you.") It is not enough to feel faith in God. Rilke's monk desires greater intimacy: longs to see him, if not face to face, at least in the mirror of his own poetic soul.

We may say, then, that the act of imagination—as symbolized by the freely conceived and recreated icon—figures the heart of Rilke's *fin-de-siècle* religion and the core of his poetic soul. Moreover, just as the character of the Augustinian self determines the literary form and content of his *Confessions*, so is *The Book of Hours* cast in the mold of Rilke's essentially imaginal self. That Rilke does not speak *The Book of Hours* in his own voice, but employs instead the poetic persona of the monk, makes no small difference. Even if we were to presume that the monk's feelings and experience generally reflect Rilke's own, the use of this persona nonetheless inserts a crucial, ineluctable distance between the truth of our historical author's "real" personal self ("there mark me, and see what I was in myself," wrote Augustine) and the aesthetic sphere which his poem—and his monk—inhabits. While we may, if we choose, read "Rilke" into the *Book of Hours*, the generic conventions of the literary form do *not* require us to validate the truth of the poem by reference to the truth of its historical author's personality. On the contrary, we are invited to enter a specifically aesthetic sphere—one that may (in Lou and Rilke's aesthetic theory) be rooted in and emerge from the the author's personal psychology, but, at the same time, attains a critical degree of independence from it. We are invited, that is, into the transpersonal poetic sphere of images themselves, the imaginal realm that counts as the proper domain of both art and archetypal (not merely personal) psychology. Hillman again:

> One has recourse to the heart—not because it is where the truth of feelings reside or where one feels one's personal soul. No. One turns to the heart because here is where the essences of reality are presented by the imaginal to the imagination.[215]

Of course, Rilke's *Book of Hours* cannot be considered particularly exceptional in this respect. Any literary work that employs a persona achieves a like effect, setting off the realm of the imagination from that of historical and autobiographical truth. Rilke, however, did not choose just any persona, but a monk whose very identity is bound to the sphere of the image: one whose calling it is to make images that help forge a relation to God—holy images, icons.

The monk's imaginative character, moreover, inevitably infuses the form and texture of the book of his life. Though the *Book of Monastic Life* may be regarded as deeply "confessional," its generic grammar, logic, and rhetoric contrast dramatically with that of Augustine's *Confessions*. We have here no true story, no plot which—driving towards its inevitable religious conclusion—makes of every thing an epiphenomenal sign of the author's own moral development; no religious subject who, in his unrelenting zeal to work God's Elysian field, ploughs every image symbol under. Instead, we have a poetic self who constantly turns himself into other things—falcons, storms, songs, trees, ships, sandals (the list goes on and on), and turns God into those things, too, for the world of created things (earthly life) is not a matter of aversion for the monk, but the place of his rendezvous with God. Rather than telling a story of religious conversion which entails a withdrawal from the world, Rilke's monk spills his soul and pours forth symbolic images aplenty, his (im)personal confession one with the cornucopia of creation.

Indeed, just this is perhaps Rilke's most radical transfiguration of the traditional iconography of religion, one frankly announced in his book's very first poem. As we have seen, Rilke revered the religion of the Russian icon, and it was in part his connection with this spiritual landscape that enabled him to access the religious resources in his own soul. Yet the terms of his native poetic religion, the province of his spiritual imagination, could not stop at the boundaries of traditional religious subjects—Madonnas, saints, scenes from the life of Christ—for to do so leaves (in accord with Augustinian aversion) Creation itself out of the picture, stifling the imagination and denying the world soul. "No thing is too small," declares Rilke's monk, "for me to love / and paint great on a background of gold"—no thing unworthy, that is, of being seen as the leaf that bears the dove—as a holy image, or icon.

In his essay, Stahl makes special mention of the Greek name for the Znamenskaya Madonna—*Platytera. Platys* means great or wide in the sense of all-encompassing. Stahl comments:

> The Znamenskaja as Platytera remains for Rilke a sensible thought-model for religious questions. Just as the Madonna Platytera transcends all and so cannot be fully grasped in any particular thing and yet for just this reason remains present in all things, so can it become a symbol for the divine that is missing in all things and yet toward which—precisely because of this lack—all things nonetheless point.[216]

In thus grafting together the iconic traditions of religious orthodoxy with an all-embracing spirit of poetic imagination, Rilke, in his redaction of modernity, redirects the huge flow of spiritual energy channeled through monotheistic belief *toward*—as well as away from—the world. *The Book of Hours* draws upon the Russian religious sensibilities in order to restore a sense of soul to the manifest universe. In so doing, it reimbues the creation with a sacral significance and, in turn, revivifies the spirit of religion by nourishing it with the infinitely rich symbolic resources of the sensible world.

In this transaction, the greatest benefactor of all may well be the human soul itself, whose sacred mission it becomes to act as the central term of exchange between God and the creation. Rather than the originally sinful soul's religious life revolving around renunciation of its immoral ways, Rilke sees the fulfilling of its imaginatively creative function as both native to the soul and the heartbeat of its new religious life.

Just as he refuses to allow "images already revealed" to occlude his vision of God, Rilke's monk does not believe that the words of others can voice his own "original relation to the universe," or to God:

> I believe in all that has never yet been spoken.
> I wish to free my most religious feeling.
> What no one dared to wish for
> may for once come naturally to me....
>
> May what I do flow from me like a river,
> no forcing and no holding back,
> the way it is with children.
>
> Then in these swelling and ebbing currents,
> these deepening tides moving out, returning,
> I will confess you, I will announce you
> as no one before has.[217]

The last line identifies the motif of the Annunciation—already inscribed in "The hour bows down"—with the act of Confession, understood not as moral expiation (the cleansing of a soiled soul) but as speech that flows spontaneously from the soul's pure source. In one of his last great works, Rilke would give that unsullied spring a divine, mythic name: Orpheus. Meanwhile, here, in a poem toward the end of *The Book of Monastic Life,* which virtually identifies Rilke's God with the dark ground of the Russian soil/soul, the monk clearly enough identifies his spiritual mission to be the bardic one of poetic enunciation:

I was there with the first mythmakers and monks
who made up your stories, traced your runes.

But now I see you:
winds, woods, water,
roaring at the rim of Christendom—
you land,
to be left in darkness.

I want to utter you. I want to portray you
not with lapis or gold, but with colors made of apple bark.

There is no image I could invent
that your presence would not eclipse.

I want, then, simply
to say the name of things.[218]

Adumbrating more famous pronouncements in Rilke's *Elegies*, the monk gives voice to the soul of his book: the transfiguration of the spirit indwelling traditional (Russian) religious iconography into a more modern and inclusive idiom of poetic speech, one that plainly, and religiously, rechristens the creative imagination and ensouls the world. The spiritual harvest seeded in *The Book of Hours* would see Rilke through the rest of his life, even in those many dark hours when—estranged from love, or poor, or sick, or . . . just being himself—his modern self would face the true enormity of what it means to be alone.

Chapter 5

NOTHING BUT PRAYER

Toward the end of his section called "The Heart of Augustine," Hillman—addressing the narcissistic tendencies inherent in modern psychology—throws the godfather of its feeling heart a spiritual sop:

> In the practice of religion, confession is immediately followed by prayer.... confession corrects personal experience, but does not remove us from it. Augustine recognized that confession becomes mere autobiography unless it is as well a devotion to the divine in the heart.[219]

Rilke shares this insight with Augustine, and its truth inspires and shapes his *Book of Hours*. The character of the persona Rilke assumes as well as the style of the poems he utters reflects the uniquely privileged role played by prayer in religious consciousness.

Rilke, we may recall, originally called the volume simply *Prayers*. The dialogic tenor of the book first registers formally in "We may not paint you." This poem contains the first of many conversations with God, whom the monk addresses (significantly enough) in the familiar form of *du*. Just as Hillman sees confessionalism's first-person "rhetoric of the ego" as tending to restrict imagination, he sees the dialogic form of prayer as conducive to its dynamic activity:

> As Coleridge insisted, the intensity of Western subjectivism requires a personal divinity to whom we address our hearts. We are saved by these divinities, psychologically, for we are saved from the personalism of feeling by bringing those feelings to persons who are not we, who are beyond our notion of experience. We talk to them, they to us, and this "dialogical situation" (CI:

247) which constitutes prayer (in distinction to worship, idolatry, ecstasy) as a psychological act is, in Corbin's words (CI: 248), "the supreme act of the Creative Imagination."[220]

Note: Corbin's words[221]—not Augustine's. If Rilke and Augustine share the dialogic impulse of prayer, the common ground largely ends there. As we have seen, Augustine's psychology—even while carving a novel niche for the human person's feeling heart—does *not* see imagination as that heart's defining activity. Nor does Augustinian cosmology, in its strict dualism, invite recognition of imagination's native realm. Nor, finally, does Augustinian theology with its omnipotent God (who, in the beginning, creates everything out of nothing) leave much space for understanding human creativity as a quintessentially religious enterprise. Within such mutually interdependent psychological, cosmological, and theological frames of reference, it is in fact not easy to comprehend prayer as an expression of creative imagination. The intense difficulty of doing so finds poignant expression in the lives of Christian poets such as Samuel Taylor Coleridge and Gerard Manley Hopkins. These writers often experienced the demands of their poetic and religious commitments as mutually contradictory, and the friction thereby generated proved the source of immense and sometimes debilitating inner tension.

Rilke, however, presents a different story. Rilke had long been transforming his religious heritage into commitments that accommodated the imperative of his poetic vocation, a world-view that put the soul and its creative imagination at the very center of his spiritual as well as intellectual life. We have, in our discussion of Rilke as icon-painter, elaborated the *essentially religious character of the imagination*; conversely, and complementarily, we will contend that *The Book of Hours* makes a de facto case for the *essentially imaginative and creative function of prayer.* In the process of doing so, moreover, Rilke inevitably undermines some of the pillars of a more traditional faith. Here, as elsewhere, the poet's project of religious renovation is fundamentally aided and abetted—if not engineered—by Lou.

First and foremost, Lou's psychology of religion—arising out of the critical spirit of the middle and late nineteenth century—explodes the traditional image of the Almighty God. Lou's anthropologically inspired notion that, in the beginning, man created God (rather than vice versa) annihilates the metaphysical premises of God's absolute sovereignty. Lou realized that this perspective confronts the soul that would devote itself to God with a trying paradox, one that can readily appear to undercut the archetypal foundation of religion itself. Even so, in the difficult consistency that marks her thought, Lou regards internal resolutions of that paradox—hinged upon the logic of the back-effect—as the gist of true religiosity, the kind of advanced spiritual development achieved, most signally, by Jesus:

> In a word: here, for the first time, the contradiction inherent to the soul is resolved—the contradiction inherent in the picture of the human being kneeling before a man-made God, his own creation. The soul can only overcome this contradiction, which necessarily sticks deep in the heart of all religion, in moments of immeasurable, unconditional devotion and enthusiasm vis-à-vis God.[222]

In chapter 3, we sought to indicate something of the dialectical logic of the back-effect which Lou claims can, in time, produce such devotion. For our present purposes, it is most important to note that Lou does *not* see the divine fall from power as the putative end of God's reign in the heart, but rather as its beginning. Psychologically speaking, that is, surrendering the notion of God's unconditioned supremacy—the image of God as absolute power—figures as the accompaniment (if not the prerequisite) for an authentically spiritual relation to the godhead, one unaffected by those subtle—or not so subtle—forms of utilitarianism that originally color the archetypal act of devotion: prayer.

Speaking, still, of Jesus, Lou writes:

> Originally, it was—bluntly spoken—need that taught the human being how to pray: moved him, begging for help, to turn towards the Gods as the most powerful possible means of assistance. Here, however [in the contrary case of Jesus], "the one who is needed" is God himself, and this need becomes part of the devotee's innermost being; all else, on the other hand—the whole of life, becomes a means of fulfilling this high purpose.[223]

In other words, God is not to be revered for any power that might aid man practically, socially, or in any other less than purely spiritual wise, but for his very being—a being *not* necessarily understood as characterized by omnipotence. In another important passage from this same essay "Jesus the Jew" (Lou's favorite, and the one that initiated her relationship with Rilke), Lou clarifies her sense that attribution of unlimited power to God tends to come at the cost of the possibility of feeling close to God and consequently jeopardizes the intimacy conducive to love:

> The New brought into being by the great founders of religion is really never a new creation of divinities, but far more a new disposition of the heart towards them.... A new teaching incarnates itself every time in a single God-filled human being who unveils and reveals the God more clearly than before.... for him... all the disguises and dividing walls which have been built up around the God fall away, because the worshipping people did not love, but only needed God; and *with every accretion of power granted out of the unconscious grounds of their mere need, their souls grew still more distant from Him.* The great religious characters are therefore first necessary again to bring the God who has become powerful but not lovable once more near the world he rules. In the deep intimacy of the religious relationship realized by such personalities, and the inward feeling of unity that enables it, the pinnacle of religion once more comes naïvely and splendidly to light.[224]

We have seen again and again how much Rilke learned from Lou. Like Lou, Rilke—rather than throwing God out with the scientifically scented bathwater—seized the opportunity presented by the *Gotterdämmerung* of the late nineteenth century to re-create God in his own, less imposing image and, coincidently, draw nearer to him. A famous poem in his *Book of Monastic Life*—picking up on motifs introduced in "We may not paint you"—resonantly echoes Lou's line of thought:

> You, neighbor God, when sometimes I wake you
> with loud knocks in the night,
> it is because I seldom
> hear you breathe,
> and know:
> you
> are alone
> in the room.
>
> And when you need something, there is no one
> to put the drink into your hand:
> I am always listening.
> Send a little sign.
> I am very near.

Only a thin wall stands—
by chance—

between us; any moment, a cry
from your mouth or
from mine—
and it will fall
without a sound.

It is built of your images...[225]

Rilke's poem reverses the traditional order of reliance: God, like a child in his room, depends upon the will and the love of the human being to bring him the water of life. Rilke writes out of a keen awareness that the ongoing life of God, the spiritual efficacy of his image or God's reality in and for the soul, absolutely depends upon the rejuvenative force of the human imagination. The walls of conventional imagery that separate the soul from God not only cripple the soul, they parch God, threatening him with the kind of imaginative demise famously proclaimed by Nietzsche. God's disempowerment, however, does not negate his being or make it unworthy of love. On the contrary, the familiar vulnerability exposed when the wall of conventional images (the iconostasis once more?) falls draws the as yet unrevealed image of God into the heart. No longer the distant figure of God the Almighty, he is, in this moment, as familiar and close to us as the person next door: not so much *Lord* as *neighbor.*

A very traditional Christian notion, to be sure, in one aspect—and yet, in Rilke's formal application of it, not so.

The customary conception of prayer tends to construe this archetypally religious act as, most fundamentally, a form of petition. That characterization naturally derives from the assumption of God's omnipotence. Of course God can, if he so chooses, grant the supplicant's appeal—he has all the power in the world and more at his disposal. Relativizing God's power tends to undermines the petitionary basis of prayer and opens the door to an essentially different, more creative conception of its function. Lou's critique of a theology of sovereignty therefore indicates one direction we could follow as we search for premises that might ground an understanding of the creative function of prayer. As *The Book of Hours* displays dramatically, it is a direction Rilke himself followed.

Working, so to speak, from the other side of the equation, Lou's psychological aesthetics (intimately related to her psychology of religion) may also help frame an understanding of the essentially religious function of the creative imagination. The core of Lou's aesthetics, remember, inheres in her recognition of a dark, unconscious strata of the psyche that harbors, in a womb-like way, the seeds of thoughts and feeling the artist will ultimately bring to light and mature form in his art. Amalgamated with Rilke's notion of a dark God, this model can found an understanding of the creative act as revelation of the ground of the soul's own being and, simultaneously, the forging of dialogic contact with the hidden God.

The fifth poem (immediately preceding "You, Neighbor God") reads:

> I love the dark hours of my being.
> My mind deepens into them.
> There I can find, as in old letters,
> the days of my life, already lived,
> and held like a legend, and understood.
>
> Then the knowing comes: I can open
> to another life that's wide and timeless.
>
> So I am sometimes like a tree
> rustling over a gravesite
> and making real the dream
> of the one its living roots
> embrace:
>
> a dream once lost
> among sorrows and songs.[226]

In a sense, this poem (which may well be read as an autobiographical reflection of Rilke's relationship to his own "dreamcrowned" past) may be considered the most archetypally psychological poem in the whole book. It opens the monk's identity up to the *depths* of being that virtually define the soul, and to the meanings and reason (logos) inherent in its own nature. Hillman writes:

> Heraclitus (frg. 45) first brings together *psyche*, *logos*, and *bathun* ("depth"): "You could not find the ends of soul though you travelled every way, so deep is its logos." As Bruno Snell says, "In Heraclitus the image of depth is designed to throw light on the outstanding

> trait of the soul and its realm: that it has its own dimension, that it is not extended in space." Ever after Heraclitus depth became the direction, the quality, and dimension of the psyche.[227]

As Rilke's poem intimates, the depths of soul are not only outside of space, they are outside of time as well—even while figuring as the ground of temporal events. Those *unconscious* depths comprise the domain of the archetypal meanings (expressed, for instance, in "legends") that underlie and interpret the events of life. As we saw already in the third poem (likening God to an underground web of roots), those depths also harbor God. Indeed, a poem located roughly in the middle of the volume—employing a rather striking combination of Russian imagery with the technical language of psychology—explicitly identifies God with the unconscious:

> You are the murmurer asleep,
> sooty, on the tops of stoves.
> Knowledge exists only in time;
>
> you, though, are the dark Unconscious
> endlessness upon endlessness.[228]

Given such an imagination of God, the same creative act that dredges the poet's soul may readily double as a means of approaching and addressing the divine. The psychological ground of Rilke's spirituality thus helps empower his monk to move constantly and seamlessly between the mode of poetic confession and the hallowed—and hallowing—idiom of prayer.

Even in the face of all this good hermeneutical help, however, I am not sure that Lou's theories alone can serve, not only as a signpost, but as a complete map of the terrain we need to traverse in order adequately to construe the creative function of prayer. Precisely because Lou's spiritual thinking remains primarily a psychology of art and religion, and does not venture into a cosmological domain, we cannot really draw from it what may be, finally, a necessary metaphysical ingredient: namely, *an alternative idea of cosmogony itself.* So long as the traditional doctrine of *creatio ex nihilo* remains our archetypal image of creation (even if unconsciously so), it will, for reasons clarified in the last section, be difficult if not impossible to understand prayer as not only consonant with imagination but virtually identified with it, qualifying, indeed, as its "Supreme Act." How, then, to proceed? Perhaps we may take inspiration, not only from Hillman, but from the spiritual source he honors in *The Thought of the Heart*. If Augustine does not provide a framework within which we might comprehend prayer as creative imagination, evidently Corbin (and his source, Ibn Arabi) does. Let us, then, look and see if we cannot find Corbin picking up where Lou leaves off.

Before introducing Corbin's *Creative Imagination in the Sufism of Ibn Arabi* and endeavoring to read Rilke's *Book of Monastic Life* in the light of some of its most fundamental ideas, we should perhaps offer some justification for that interpretive move. Admittedly, we are hardly dealing here with a case of direct influence as is indubitably the case with Lou's ideas. I know of no evidence that, at this point in his life, Rilke had any special knowledge of Sufism. Nonetheless, grounds of justification are not hard to find.

First, we will soon discover that Lou's psychology of religion and Corbin's Sufism do share fundamental premises. Indeed, the affinity is so great that the latter could—theoretically, at least—be construed as a kind of cosmological extension of the former. This alone may serve as justification for exploring the shared spiritual territory. Moreover, so long as we are about the business of reading Rilke through the lens of Hillman's archetypal psychology, it can hardly be illegitimate to draw upon Corbin as well—a scholar whom Hillman cites (along with Jung) as one of the godfathers of archetypal psychology. Indeed, because we are interrogating a poet who transfigures, but does not reject, the monotheistic tradition, Corbin may prove an important link between the sources of Rilke's religious inspiration and the polytheistic premises that found Hillman's school of thought. Then, too, we might mention the evidence of Islamic influence in Rilke's later life and thought: for instance, the statement that "The 'angel' of the elegies has nothing to do with the angel of the Christian heaven (rather with the angel figures of Islam)."[229] We shall return to this remark at a later point. Its citation may stand as a signal that certain basic Sufi ideas—especially as these ideas contrast with Augustine's—may further our attempt to comprehend "those essential premises ... already given in *The Book of Hours*" which, by Rilke's own admission, ground the world-view implicitly inscribed in all his greatest work. For this, of course, is the last and primary justification—the necessary and sufficient condition—for reading Corbin: that his and

Ibn Arabi's compelling work on the creative imagination open doors to the heart of Rilke's poetic religion, enabling us better to understand the confluence of poetry and prayer.

Creation as Theophany

This much, at least, can be said with certainty: Corbin comprehends that the gist of the issue inheres in our archetypal idea of the nature of creativity and indeed creation itself:

> The terms "creative" and "creative activity" are part of our everyday language. But regardless of whether the purpose of this activity is a work of art or an institution, such objects, which are merely its expressions and symptoms, do not supply an answer to the question: What is the *meaning* of man's creative need? These objects themselves have their places in the outside world, but their genesis and meaning flow primarily from the inner world where they were conceived; it is this *world* alone, or rather the creation of this inner world, that can share in the dimension of man's creative activity and thus throw some light on the meaning of his creativity and on the creative organ that is the Imagination.[230]

Corbin sets out to elaborate the idea of creation at work in the Sufism of Ibn Arabi, taking the primordial divine act as his point of departure:

> To begin with: a Divine Being alone in His unconditioned essence, of which we know only one thing: precisely the sadness of the primordial solitude that makes Him yearn to be revealed in beings who manifest Him to Himself insofar as He manifests Himself to them. That is the Revelation we apprehend. We must meditate upon it in order to know *who* we are. The *leitmotiv* is not the bursting into being of an autarchic Omnipotence, but a fundamental sadness: "I was a hidden Treasure, I yearned to be known. That is why I produced creatures, in order to be known in them."[231]

From the first and in the beginning we remark these fundamental points, distinguishing the Sufi view from Augustine's:

1) "The true name of the Divinity, the name which expresses his hidden depths, is not the Infinite and All-Powerful of our rational

theodicies."[232] Corbin offers this remark after discussing the etymology of the name of God, *Al-lah*, which—according to his derivation—can be understood as a verbal noun denoting (a mode of being tending) "to desire, to sigh, to feel compassion." Thus, Ibn Arabi identifies God—not with omnipotence—but with the sadness of a primordial solitude, a sadness that generates an active yearning, "a movement of ardent desire." So arises the idea of a *pathetic* God endorsed by Corbin:

> In contrast to the deist God who had paled to an empty concept, or to the ethical God, guardian of the moral law, [Ibn Arabi] sets forth... the notion of a *pathetic God*, that is, a suffering and passionate God, a notion which has at all times been a dreaded stumbling block to the rational theology and philosophy of Christianity, Islam, and Judaism alike.[233]

2) The creation arises—not as something essentially extrinsic to (the substance of) God—but as an extension of the divine nature in its innate desire to know itself. God's primordial sadness expresses itself in a "divine Breath" (*tanaffus*) or "Sigh" of compassion that takes substantial form as the "Cloud" (*'amā*) which existentiates God's nature and supplies the ground of all creation. ("This Cloud, which the Divine Being exhaled... *receives* all forms and at the same time *gives* being their forms... through it is effected the differentiation within the primordial reality of... the divine Being as such."[234]) This contrasts most starkly with Augustinian cosmogony, and the ground of the difference becomes still clearer as Corbin elaborates more fully Ibn Arabi's idea of creation:

> Sadness is not the "privilege" of the creature; it is in the Creator Himself, it is indeed the motif which... makes the primordial Being a creative Being; it is the secret of His creativity. And His creation springs, not from nothingness, from something other than Himself, from a not-Him, but from His fundamental being, from the potencies and virtualities latent in His own unrevealed being. Accordingly, the word *tanaffus* also connotes "to shine," "to appear" after the manner of the dawn. The Creation is essentially the revelation of the Divine Being first to himself, a luminescence occurring within Him; it is a *theophany*. Here there is no notion of a *creatio ex nihilo* opening up a gulf which no rational thought will ever be able to bridge.[235]

Nor is Corbin less clear in naming the agent power of this theophanic creation:

> Thus Creation is Epiphany, that is, a passage from the state of occultation or potency to the luminous, manifest, revealed state; as such, it is an act of the divine, primordial Imagination.[236]

This marks another fundamental difference from the universe of the conventional "Christian soul." Imagination can no longer be regarded as extrinsic to the defining act of faith or belief, a degraded faculty that tends—like fantasy—to produce unreality. Rather, it qualifies as the original archetypal act of the divine, at once compassionate and creative.[237]

Imagination, however, cannot be so dignified without according it a place in the cosmic scheme of things; acknowledging an intermediate realm of being native to and reflective of its primordial creative act:

> For [the Sufis] the world is "objectively" and actually threefold: between the universe that can be apprehended by pure intellectual perception...and the universe perceptible to the senses, there is an intermediate world, the world of Idea-Images, of archetypal figures, of subtile substances, of "immaterial matter." This world is as real and objective, as consistent and subsistent as the intelligible and sensible worlds; it is an intermediate universe "where the spiritual takes body and the body becomes spiritual."... The organ of this universe is the active Imagination; it is the *place* of theophanic visions, the scene on which visionary events and symbolic histories *appear* in their true reality.[238]

Such a cosmology patently contradicts the dualism enforced by the edict of Constantinople. In making room for imagination, it invites the return of the soul to the world (or recognition that, in reality, it never left). It offers, as well, grounds for the precious hope that in seeking to reclaim the soul's own intermediate world, the spiritual pilgrim may simultaneously stage a close encounter with the divine and come to know God in and through the organ of his own imagination.

For Corbin makes clear, too, that the theophanic act of creation is in no wise the sole prerogative of God. Indeed, *the revelation it intends can only be fulfilled in and through beings who share God's ardent desire*: beings who yearn for knowledge of God and of themselves. Not only is primordial creation itself essentially continuous with God's compassionate will and substance, but the human being's own active imagination is so as well. God's own knowledge of himself and the ongoing act of creation (the two are one) are fulfilled only in and through the imaginative act of the human soul:

> To the initial act of the Creator imagining the world corresponds the creature imagining his world, imagining the worlds, his God, his symbols. Or rather, these are the phases, the recurrences of one and the same eternal process: Imagination effected in an Imagination, . . . an Imagination which is recurrent just as—and because—the Creation is recurrent. The same theophanic Imagination of the Creator who has revealed the worlds, renews the Creation from moment to moment in the human being whom He has revealed as His perfect image and who, in the mirror that this Image is, shows himself Him whose image he is.[239]

This interdependence of Creator and creature, of God and human being, figures as one of the great themes of Sufi gnosticism. It also comprises the very core of the spirituality infusing Rilke's *Book of Hours.* Rilke's own expression of the theme harks back to Lou; it is not difficult to grasp the kinship between this key Sufi tenet and the dialectical interaction of man and God that grounds Lou's psychology of religion. Correlatively, the Sufi articulation of what Lou calls "God-creation" builds upon a firm *cosmological* foundation and so proves less vulnerable to the charge of "psychologism" (the reduction of all reality to purely subjective phenomena) sometimes leveled at Lou's thought:

> The initial idea of Ibn Arabi's mystic theosophy . . . is that Creation is essentially a *theophany* (*tajallī*). As such, creation is an act of the divine imaginative power: this divine creative imagination is essentially a theophanic imagination. The Active Imagination in the gnostic is likewise a theophanic Imagination: the beings it "creates" subsist with an independent existence *sui generis* in the intermediate world which pertains to this mode of existence. The God whom it "creates," far from being an unreal product of our fantasy, is also a theophany, for man's Active Imagination is merely the organ of the absolute theophanic Imagination.[240]

The idea of creation as theophany—a showing forth, revelation, or appearance of God in and to the imaginative vision of the human being—functions as the founding inspiration of Rilke's *Book of Monastic Life* and pervades virtually the entire text. The motif implicitly informs the terms of the monk's first direct address of God and his first formal appellation: "du, Dämmernde, aus der der Morgen stieg" ("you, dawning one, out of whom the morning rose")...for dawn, as a process of revelation of what is already present, itself qualifies an archetypal image of theophany. In I, 18 ("Why am I fooling again with the brushes?"), the poet figures the monk's own nascent relation with God by way of a delicate poetic image of theophany: "At my senses' horizon / you appear hesitantly, like scattered islands." I, 45 ("You come and go") offers a fuller image of the theophanic idea of God as the luminosity of created forms shining forth in the (dark) vessel of the soul:

For all things
sing you: at times
we just hear them more clearly.

Often when I imagine you
your wholeness cascades into many shapes.
You run like a herd of luminous deer
and I am dark, I am forest.[241]

These are particular poetic occasions that in some way image theophany: the *appearing* of God in the creative imagination of the soul, divinity manifesting in the luminous dress of the forms of his own creation (dawn, islands, deer) reproduced in poetic speech. Yet no citation of specific instances can adequately convey how thoroughly the theophanic theme pervades and defines the poem. As we indicated in discussing Rilke as icon-painter, the spiritual mission informing *The Book of Monastic Life* coincides with the theophanic function of the monk's creative imagination. The monk does not wish to produce mere representations of God—paintings on a wall, images on a screen—but ("Imagination effected in an Imagination") wishes to marshal creative powers correspondent to those God himself exhibits in the monumental forms of nature and so effectively *reveal God by (re)producing the creation*:

I would have painted you: not on the wall
but in one broad sweep across heaven.
I'd have portrayed you brashly:

as mountain, as fire, as a wind
howling from the desert's vastness.[242]

The same theophanic impetus finds expression (albeit less dramatically) in the monk's vision of all creation seen in the form of a tree, which—in a manner once more commensurate with God's primordial act—blends compassion and imagination:

I find you there in all these things
I care for like a brother.
A seed, you nestle in the smallest of them,
and in the huge ones spread yourself hugely.

Such is the amazing play of the powers:
they give themselves so willingly;
swelling in the roots, thinning as the trunks rise,
and in the high leaves, resurrection.[243]

Initially, it may appear that the idea of the creation as a theophany belies or contradicts another chief motif of *The Book of Monastic Life*: namely, the darkness and hiddenness of God. Already in the third poem, the monk imagined God as the invisible root of things, concealed in inscrutable depths. Even so, "I find you there in all these things" locates God in *both* the invisible roots *and* the visible crown of creation. In fact, the hiddenness of God, the darkness that surrounds and figures as the background of any revelation, does not contravene the logic of theophany, but proves intrinsic to it and to the imagination that supplies its agent power. Dawn emerges only out of the dark shroud of night, and indeed, the primordial act of theophany manifests in the shape of a darkening *cloud* that simultaneously veils and reveals the light of divine presence.

Consonantly, Sufism, along with other gnostic schools, recognizes a paradoxical duality within divine nature itself which consists of a purely transcendent, unknowable aspect (*Theos agnostos*, the unknowable God) as well as its contradictory complement (the revealed God, *Deus revelatus*). This paradoxical nature characterizes too the very function of the Creative Imagination of which Corbin writes:

> When [the Creative Imagination] is true to the divine reality it reveals, it liberates, provided that we recognize the function with which Ibn Arabi endowed it and which it alone can perform; namely,

> the function of effecting a *coincidentia oppositorum* (*jamʿ bayna'l-naqīdayn*). This term is an allusion to the words of Abu Saʿid al-Kharraz, a celebrated Sufi master. "Whereby do you know God?" he was asked. And he replied: "By the fact that he is the *coincidentia oppositorum*." For the entire universe of worlds is at once He and not-He.... The God manifested in forms is at once Himself and other than Himself, for since He is manifested, He is the limited which has no limit, the visible which cannot be seen. This manifestation is neither perceptible nor verifiable by the sensory faculties; discursive reason rejects it. It is perceptible only by the Active Imagination.[244]

Rilke's God-image likewise embraces a paradoxical duality. Revealed again and again in all things, God is exhausted or present without reserve in none. This withholding of the *Theos agnostos* is the very condition of God's unity, and—in conjunction with the *Deus revelatus*—drives the monk's ceaseless incantation of symbols (*you gentlest law, you great homesickness, you forest, you song, you dark net*); the litany that both expresses the divine nature and falls perpetually short of doing so on account of that eternally indivisible and unknowable remainder. Indeed, Rilke, like Corbin, insists that the divine essence inheres in just this paradoxical character; maintains that God, the imageless source of all images, is indeed a *coincidentia oppositorum*:

> You are the deepest, who looms tallest
> the diver's and the tower's goal....
>
> You are the forest of paradox.[245]

This perspective proved no passing fancy for Rilke. A quarter of century later, he himself—by his own wish—was given back to the dark, sacred ground of things, buried under a stone that bore the inscription: "O rose, you pure contradiction / to be nobody's sleep / under so many lids." Evidently, the paradoxical vision Rilke first voiced so eloquently in *The Book of Monastic Life* was good for life—and beyond.

CREATIVE DEED

We may speak, and aptly so, of metaphysical ideas of theophany or *coincidentia oppositorum*. At the same time, we should exercise caution in so doing, for Rilke's monk does not begin with a fixed concept of God, nor does any such notion define the true end of his discourse. One cannot, in fact, place too much emphasis on any Rilkean *concept* of divinity, because doing so risks obscuring a still more essential dimension of his text: the dynamic imaginative process by which the monk unfolds his knowledge of God and of himself, effectively re-creating both in the ongoing course of his poetic deed.

That God can be truly known only in and through the *deed* of creation itself—an active doing incommensurate with mere assertion of faith or dogmatic belief—counts as one more of Rilke's principal poetic themes:

> Only in our doing can we grasp you.
> Only with our hands can we illumine you.
> The mind is but a visitor:
> It thinks us out of our world.[246]

St. Augustine, on the other hand, exhibits no such intellectual reservation. Reading the text of the *Confessions*, we are equipped from the outset with a host of concepts that define God's nature and serve to fix our idea of Him in our mind. ("What, then, is the God I worship? He can be none but the Lord God himself... supreme, utmost in goodness, mightiest and all-powerful, most merciful and most just."[247]) By contrast, in the initial poems of *The Book of Monastic Life*, Rilke's monk deliberately accents all he does *not* know. Each of the first three poems contains a phrase affirming one form or another form of non-knowledge: "I don't know whose"; "And I still don't know"; "More, I don't know." As these phrases indicate, the tone of self-assurance sounded in the very first poem—even while announcing a spiritual readiness and creative potential—by no means implies any sort of finished mastery. Most especially, the monk does not profess anything like a fully accomplished knowledge of God. Instead, the monk's very idea of God—no less than of himself—appears very much a work in progress and indeed one in its beginning stages. Instead of Augustinian certainty as to divine attributes, we are introduced to God by way of provisional images (a tower, the roots of a tree, the dawn) that function as the first strokes of a sketch likely never to be finished.

Nor is it only his idea of God that the monk presents in the form of a work in progress, but rather—in accord, once more, with Sufi doctrine—the very *being* of God himself. Several poems sound this theme. The fifteenth poem imagines God as a cathedral built up, block by block, by human hands:

Our hands shake as we try to construct you,
block on block.
But you, cathedral we dimly perceive—
who can bring you to completion?[248]

The lines clearly emphasize, too, the endlessness of the process, and though the monk does sometimes intimate (as in the closing lines of this poem) that the work may be rounded off, completed, the accent more frequently falls on the understanding that God cannot be construed as a fixed or immutable being but rather (like the soul itself) is ever *becoming*. The subsequent poem ends with the simple assertion—italicized for emphasis by Rilke himself—"Even when we do not will it / *God ripens*."

The monk's evocations of God inevitably follow the lines of certain metaphysical notions he has of the divine character, but those notions catalyze rather than strictly control or confine the imaginal process. For the monk, "God" is not primarily a concept that essentially pre-exists his prayers and pictures, but a living presence that—little by little, line by line, image by image—emerges in and through them. In this eminently poetic way, *The Book of Monastic Life* enacts the premise—at once theogonic and psychological—that founds it: namely, that God—insofar as he *can* be known by the human being—may be known, revealed, and indeed created in and through the human being's own Active Imagination and the dialogical intercourse it initiates. In this essentially theophanic impulse lies the seed of understanding *The Book of Monastic Life* as creative prayer, yet to comprehend the germinal force contained in that seed—to understand what drives the imaginative process—we must return, once more, to the seat of the soul: the power that resides in the heart.

Himma

No particular concept Rilke (or his monk) holds of God gives rise to *The Book of Hours*, nor does any particular image or set of images do so. Rather, the force of his desire—his *yearning* to enter into communion with the divine nature—engenders his poetic utterance. This irrepressible longing, this unquenchable thirst sounds through most every poem—and indeed most every line—of the book. When Augustine cites precedent for his mode of prayer, he emphasizes belief and positive knowledge ("As I pray I shall *believe* in you, because we have had preachers to *tell us about you*"); when Rilke's monk—rather uncharacteristically—likewise cites precedent, it is to highlight the heart of his religion, the force of the soul's longing: "Because once someone dared to want you / I know that we, too, may want you."[249]

This accent upon the soul's yearning does not in itself represent anything new for Rilke (we've already noted its signal importance in his earliest lyrics), but *The Book of Monastic Life* invests the theme with its own peculiarly religious inflection and urgency. Here, too, Rilke—even as he voices the imperatives of his own nature—takes a page from Lou's book. In the concluding paragraph of "Realism in Religion," she writes:

> Nothing is more amazing than the ease, even the pleasure, with which nearly every cultivated person of today is capable of swallowing down the vastest helping of doubts—so long as they're "modern" ones—without getting the slightest spiritual discomfort from it; they are like conjurers who swallow swords.... *May* it tear us to bits! If only we were less conjurers and more real people who feel in their innermost life what they think and do.[250]

The passage finds this echo in Rilke:

> So many are alive who don't seem to care.
> Casual, easy, they move in the world
> as though untouched.
>
> But you take pleasure in the faces
> of those who know they thirst.
> You cherish those
> who grip you for survival.
>
> You are not dead yet, it's not too late
> to open your depths....[251]

These passages reveal both Lou and Rilke (who explicitly references Nietzsche) writing out of a self-consciously historical sense of the plight of religion in the modern world and calling upon the soul's native religiosity to resurrect itself.

The soul's longing represents no barren desire, but rather constitutes the motive power driving its innate creativity. Naturally enough, the soul's longing flows from its spiritual center—the heart—and the Sufis call the force of desire as it projects forth from the heart *himma*:

> The power of the heart is what is specifically designated by the word *himma*...a word whose content is perhaps best suggested by the Greek word *enthymesis*, which signifies the act of meditating, conceiving, imagining, projecting, ardently desiring—in other words, having something present in the *thymos*, which is vital force, soul, heart, intention, thought, desire.[252]

It is this *himma*, this power born of the soul's desire, that can project the *thought of the heart* in the form of images that possess real (not merely subjective or purely psychological) being in the medial sphere of Idea-images. We can thus understand the heart, by virtue of this *himma*, to be the seat of the soul's central capability: its creative imagination. Hence Ibn Arabi calls gnostic knowledge of the workings of the Creative Imagination "the science of the Heart."

We naturally resist conceiving "science" in such a way. Wedded as we are (even if unconsciously so) to theological doctrines inimical to the imagination, it is difficult for us to comprehend how, precisely, "the figments of our imagination"—the mere projections of the heart's intentions—assume a real, substantial character, even if our experience constantly reveals to us this truth. Corbin therefore repeatedly emphasizes the theophanic character of—not only the primordial divine imagination—but the soul's own homologous act, which alone fulfills the original divine intention. Indeed, Corbin goes so far as to insist that even seemingly objective phenomena—the natural form, for instance, of a mountain or a flower—achieve fully actualized being only when (in accord with C. G. Jung's mythic conception of man as "the second creator of the world"[253]) they are recreated in the imaginative consciousness of the human being:

> Of course these forms (of flower and mountain) pre-exist, since nothing begins to be that was not before. But it is no less true that these forms were not created, in the sense of the word employed by Ibn Arabi, since they did not appear. And this precisely is the function of our *himma*, of our creativity, to make them appear, that is, to give them being. Here our creativity merges with the very core, the *heart*, of our being.[254]

It is not, moreover, only *our* own being or that of the world that *himma* opens for us. Insofar as "himma, creativity of the heart...is itself the Creator's theophanic imagination at work in the heart of the gnostic,"[255] *himma* is, too, the key to our intimate relation to God, the vital force underlying the soul's religious imagination.

In the last chapter, we spoke of icons as symbols of the human religious imagination. Given what we have said so far of *himma*, we should not be surprised to find Corbin exemplifying the workings of *himma* by reference to iconic art: "When in contemplating an image, an icon, others recognize and perceive as a divine image the vision beheld by the artist who created the image, it is because of the spiritual creativity, the *himma*, which the artist put into his work."[256] When Rilke, in writing "Znamenskaya," gives us a picture of the spiritual creativity involved in the painting of the icon, it is the workings of the icon painter's *himma* he so vividly images. And when the viewer of the icon (or reader of a poem-prayer) in turn activates her *himma* in order to recreate the work in her own imagination, she fulfills the act of spiritual liberation that Rilke's monk—at the end of his first poetic prayer—announces as the true goal of his artistic vocation.

The Sufi teaching associated with *himma*, the creative power of the heart, qualifies as a positive doctrine rather than one pessimistic or negative in tenor. The heart's desire to know God is not doomed to disappointment—the forms of its imagination of divine being are not considered irrevocably inadequate—because *the forms of the heart's longing for God flow from God's original desire to know himself in and through the beings he created.* That desire can be fulfilled because the creation—as an effusion of the divine being—intrinsically reflects that divine being; manifests as the mirror or shadow of God. "Everything we call other than God, everything we call the universe, is related to the Divine Being as the shadow (or his reflection in the mirror) to the person. The world is God's shadow."[257] And yet, even while the universe may be such a mirror, God cannot see himself in it *without* the mediation of the human being's creative imagination, which supplies the very organ of divine vision.

It is a Sufi proverb, and one Corbin repeatedly cites, that *the gnostic's heart is the eye of God* by which God reveals himself to himself. The universe may be an image of God, but that mirror-image is only activated—becoming both a process of divine reflection and human illumination—in and through human consciousness seated in the heart:

> It is said: "Neither my Heaven nor my Earth contains me, but the heart of my faithful believer contains me"...because the heart is a

> mirror in which the manifested "Form of God" is at each moment reflected on the scale of the microcosm.[258]

The force of desire, the *himma*, that issues forth in the monk's prayers manifests just this desire to reflect divine vision:

> I want always to mirror your whole immensity.
> I want never to be blind or too old
> to bear the heavy, lurching image of you.
>
> ...I would describe myself
> like a landscape I've studied
> at length, in detail;
> like a word I'm coming to understand;
> like a pitcher I pour from at mealtime;
> like my mother's face;
> like a ship that carried me
> when the waters raged.[259]

The monk's poetic logic reflects Corbin's Sufi statement. While the initial three lines here explicitly express the desire to mirror God, to contain God's image in himself, the concluding lines move—logically and rhetorically—to perform that function. The poem inserts the self, the "I," as a relay between God and the phenomenal world. In each of five concluding poetic figures, the monk imagines God relating to *him* in the same way *he* may relate to some concrete thing—God would see him the same way he looks at a landscape; God would strive to understand him just as he would a word. Moreover, the particular images he chooses are principally those of some sort of reflection and containment: a pitcher holds water as a ship does the human life of its passengers; and we would imagine the mutual love of mother and child to be reflected in the mother's face. Rilke's monk pictures himself as holding, in his gaze, the image of (the love of) God, not unlike the iconic Madonnas the poet so revered. And no wonder, for it is God himself who commands the monk to Write, to Paint, and to Go forth...

> And God said to me, Go forth:
>
> For I am king of time.
> But to you I am only the shadowy one
> who knows with you your loneliness
> and sees through your eyes.

He sees through my eyes
in all the ages.[260]

Truly grasping this essential gnostic insight—that God cannot know or see himself without the mirroring lens of the gnostic's heart—provides a framework within which we can comprehend Rilke's (or his monk's) repeated poetic insistence that God depends upon him as much as vice versa. Indeed, in the Sufi teaching, it is not only God's self-knowledge that depends upon the poet's or gnostic's creative imagination, but (as we've already noted) his very identity and *being*. Ibn Arabi's Sufism endorses the most radical form of interdependence of God, as Creator, and man, as creature: in the canons of Sufi sacred worship, the human vassal-vessel's creative imagination of God *is* the condition of his Lord's existence, *and* vice versa: "He is the vassal without whom his Lord would not be, but... he himself would be nothing without his Lord."[261]

The God spoken of here is not the *Theos agnostos*, that unknown and unknowable aspect of the godhead that remains above and beyond any and all acts of imagination. Indeed, Ibn Arabi specifically rejected the claims of those Sufis who professed knowledge of "The God who discloses Himself to Himself in His essence, in his own knowledge of His Names... isolated from any relation with their manifested existence."[262] Rather, the aspect of God at issue here is the one accessible to the soul, the form of the revealed God that can be known in and through the human heart. Sufis call the generalized version of the God disclosed in and through religious imagination the "God created in the faiths."

The "God created in the faiths" is not a purely psychological reality. Because the image the aspirant forms of God is, coincidently, "the form in which the Divine Being has chosen to disclose Himself to him," the reality of the "God created in the faiths" is anchored in the theophanic imagination of the Creator. Notice here, too, the plural form: Corbin's Sufi wisdom does not speak of the one God, or one true faith; quite the contrary. Respecting the *individual* character of the aspirant in whom any revelation of God is effected and the constitutive role of the individual in that revelation, Ibn Arabi's teaching inevitably recognizes a diversity of faiths:

> The theophany... takes the dimension of the receptacle that receives it.... That is why there are many different faiths. To each

> believer, the Divine Being is He who is disclosed to him in the form of his faith. If God manifests Himself in a different form, the believer rejects Him, and that is why the dogmatic faiths combat one another. "But when you meditate upon His words... *I am His foot on which he walks, his hand with which he feels, his tongue with which he speaks*... then you will say: the reality is the Creature-Creator, Creator in one dimension, creature in another, but the concrete totality is one."[263]

Rilke's monk expresses this syzygy in startlingly similar terms:

> What will you do, God, when I die?
>
> I am your pitcher (when I shatter?)
> I am your drink (when I go bitter?)
> I, your garment; I, your craft.
> Without me what reason have you?
>
> Without me what house
> where intimate words await you?
> I, velvet sandal that falls from your foot.
> I, cloak dropping from your shoulder.
>
> Your gaze, which I welcome now...
> will search for me hour after hour...
>
> What will you do, God? I am afraid.[264]

The relationship between the vassal and Lord, human being and God, creature and creator is thus very close, perhaps closer, even, than Rilke's monk imagines in his evocation of the neighbor God, for it is another Sufi saying that God's love is closer to man than his own jugular vein. Even so, to understand the essence of the imaginative relationship between the soul and God, it is not enough to speak in terms of near and far, of mirrors and shadows—poetic figures, that is, which reflect the structural relationship between the divine and human imagination. We must attend, as well, to the very act of speech that realizes that relationship, the word-deed that actuates the imaginative power of the heart, that sets it in motion; that archetypal expression of the human soul's desire for the divine—prayer.

Method of Creative Prayer

Corbin: "Thus we move toward our conclusion: Creative Imagination in the service of Creative Prayer, through *himma*, the concentration of all the powers of the heart."[265]

"Es gibt im Grunde nur Gebete"—"There is at root only prayer"—claims Rilke's monk, and the power of longing in his heart, his *himma*, overflows in line after line of passionate utterance—not pleading, not asking for the granting of some request—but expressing his soul's innermost core: his desire to know and see himself in God, and vice versa. "God is your mirror, that is, the mirror in which you contemplate your self, and you are his mirror," writes Corbin,[266] and the book of the monk's life unfolds as an "intimate dialogue" between the monk and his God, enacting that reciprocal envisioning, providing the discursive space and time within which it—and the theophany it effects—can manifest.

Corbin makes perfectly clear that Sufism does not conceive of prayer (as is so often the case in a more popular Christian context) as a form of petition. The ongoing, theophanic character of creation—and, most especially, the truth that the divine *and* the human imagination cooperate in it—naturally grounds an understanding of prayer's *creative* function:

> Prayer is not a request for something: it is the expression of a mode of being, a means of existing and of causing to exist, that is, a means of causing the God who reveals Himself to appear, of "seeing" Him, not to be sure in his essence, but in the form which precisely He reveals by revealing Himself by and to that form. This view of Prayer takes the ground from under the feet of those who, utterly ignorant of the nature of the theophanic Imagination as Creation, argue that a God who is the "creation" of our Imagination can only be "unreal" and that there can be no purpose in praying to such a God. For it is precisely because He is a creation of the imagination that we pray to him, and that He exists. Prayer is the highest form, the supreme act of the Creative Imagination.[267]

The monk's imaginative dialogue with God effects a gradual revelation of the divine nature; it is—as we have already witnessed—essentially *theophanic*. As such, it is, too, quintessentially *creative*. Rilke's monk hammers this point home in a poem that fuses motifs of creation as both *making* and *theophanic revelation:*

We are craftsmen: novice, apprentice, master,
and build you, you lofty center-nave.
And sometimes a serious stranger comes,
and, showing us a new grip,
ignites our work anew....

Then our many hammers sing
and—blow after blow—echo through the mountains.
Only at dusk do we let you go
when, finally, your shape begins to dawn.

God, you are great.[268]

Indeed, the entire *Book of Hours* supplies an exemplary instance of what Corbin, following Ibn Arabi, calls "Creative Prayer."

Not all prayer, however, qualifies as truly creative, and the Sufis have developed a certain protocol proper to its practice. What Corbin calls the "method of theophanic prayer" premises itself upon *dialogical* exchange that takes place in the space of an intimate conversation or "confidential psalm." This requires a sense of privacy; it is necessary to attain the seclusion and quietude that allows the orant and God to hear each other. Consequently,

> The Prayer recommended by Ibn Arabi...is not a public, collective Prayer, but a "divine service" practiced in private, a munājāt, an intimate dialogue...the condition of this personal divine service is precisely solitude.[269]

Had Rilke known of the Sufi method of prayer, he could hardly have followed its protocol more closely. *The Book of Monastic Life*—a kind of textbook example of creative prayer—qualifies too as what Corbin calls a "private liturgy." The monk himself constantly speaks of the difficulty of attaining the stillness and solitude requisite for entering creative communion with his God. I, 7 begins:

If only for once it were still.
If the *not quite right* and the *why this*
could be muted, and the neighbor's laughter,
and the static my senses make—
if all of it didn't keep me from coming awake—[270]

....and I, 13 (the same that ends with the figure of the self as landscape, word, etc.)—opens:

> I'm too alone in the world, yet not alone enough
> to make each hour holy.[271]

Here, and everywhere, the monk's prayer arises out of a fundamentally dialogical impulse. Even when his utterance may seem to verge toward the monological, the imagined recipient of his speech—the invisible other who is its origin and end—remains ever present at the very center of his heart's thought. In his mind, the true aspirant is the one who

> drives the loudmouths from the hall
> and clears it for a different celebration
>
> where the one guest is you.
> In the softness of evening
> it's you she receives.

In the space of solitude, the intimate conversation unfolds and—gradually—discloses the divine presence held in the expanding consciousness of the one who prays:

> You are the partner of her loneliness,
> the unspeaking center of her monologues.
> With each disclosure you encompass more
> and she stretches beyond what limits her,
> to hold you.[272]

Many of the monk's poems do not only exemplify a method of prayer, but themselves offer prayers about prayer, thematizing the conditions—both inward and outward—necessary for achieving effective (and that means *creative*) prayer. Poems about poetry and its writing are, of course, a familiar species and often the darling of literary critics, but the application of this kind of reflexity to the sphere of prayer—the genre of speech-act that virtually defines the essence of religion—less so. Not only does Rilke offer just this (justifying the title of the first book of his trilogy, for monastic life centers around the act of prayer), but he effectively does both at the same time, transfiguring the archetypal idea of prayer by way of its fusion with the act of poetry and vice versa. That fusion, and that revisioning, is made possible by discovering the common ground of both: the soul's creative imagination.

Yet let us return to Corbin, for he has more to say about Ibn Arabi's method of prayer that helps illuminate Rilke's own. Building upon the radical, existential interdependence of man and God, that method entails, not only dialogue, but a constructive "sharing of roles" in the course of prayer. Ibn Arabi writes: "If He has given us life and existence by His being, I also give Him life by knowing Him in my heart," and *both* moments (man's dependence on God, and vice versa) must be recognized, honored, and activated in the prayer. Ibn Arabi's method unfolds that mutual dependence in the form of an exchange of roles that develops in the course of three distinct and well-defined phases:

> As meditated by our shaikh... liturgical action breaks down into three phases; the first... is the action of the faithful toward or upon his Lord; the second... is a reciprocal action between the Lord and his faithful; the third... is an action of the Lord toward and upon the faithful.[273]

Here, too, Rilke follows suit. We have already remarked several poems in *The Book of Monastic Life* that emphasize the less orthodox order of dependence ("You, neighbor God"; "What will you do God, when I die"). Yet the monk's prayers consistently recognize his dependence upon God as well, though—precisely because it can more readily be taken for granted—this moment often registers more implicitly. It is also frequently braided with recognition of its enabling contrary and complement, and (still more notably) acknowledgment of the dialectic by which both man and God transform. While all these moments interweave throughout the monk's text, the general drift of his text does follow Ibn Arabi's progression of "liturgical phases."

As we have seen, the monk's creative agency strides out front and center at the beginning of the book, and "action of the faithful toward or upon his Lord" initially dominates his prayers—the monk must bring a childlike God a drink of water; he must rescue and feed God, pictured as a helpless fledgling fallen from the nest. Yet God, fed and strengthened by the monk's theophanic prayer, gains in strength and agency as the poem proceeds. I, 25 begins with an image of reciprocal action:

> I love you, gentlest of Ways
> who ripened us as we wrestled with you.[274]

This poem also explicitly recognizes that—as the Sufis say—*both* God and man are "First and Last" in the order of creation ("on the day you made us you created yourself") before (as befits the still relatively early placement of the poem) reasserting the privilege of human agency: ("Let your hand rest on the rim of heaven / And mutely bear the darkness we bring over you"). I, 45, though, ends with this more evenly balanced image of reciprocal action:

> You are a wheel at which I stand,
> whose dark spokes sometimes catch me up,
> revolve me nearer to the center.
> Then all the work I put my hand to
> widens from turn to turn.[275]

...while I, 51 ends with a statement that premises the being of both God and the individual upon an act of mutual understanding:

> I walk forever toward you
> with my whole being;
> For who am I and who are you
> if we do not understand each other?[276]

Over the course of the book, then—*in a dynamic that not only follows Sufi protocol, but also effectively manifests the working of Lou's "back-effect"*—God's "mute power" gradually increases, and indeed gathers impressive momentum in the last third or so of the book. The Old Testament God does put in an early appearance in I, 9, but that poem does not so much highlight God's power as evoke its fragmentation in the wake of Cain's fraternal murder. Yet this biblical God resurfaces toward the end of the book with much more of his original fearsome power intact. Coincidently, man becomes more subject to the action of the Lord toward or upon him:

> Your first word of all was *light*
> and time began. Then for long you were silent.
>
> Your second word was *man*, and fear began
> which grips us still.
>
> Are you about to speak again?
> I don't want your third word.[277]

I, 49 figures God as a powerful enemy "besieging" the city of the heart, one who "does not tire or diminish in size or strength," and will "overcome you /...working in silence." In I, 64, God's "mute power" issues forth from his hands to give law and order to the human mind, and images of God's force reaches a kind of transitory peak in the apocalyptic moment of I, 61:

> And those that labor—maybe you'll let their work
> grip them another five hours, or seven,
> before you become forest again, and water, and
> widening wilderness
> in that hour of inconceivable terror
> when you take back your name
> from all things.[278]

Rilke, though, had not traveled so far merely to fall back into the lap of biblical tradition. To be sure, Rilke's God-image grows out of biblical precedent; both the Old and New Testament (the latter inspiring several poems involving Mary and Christ) provide crucial precedent for Rilke's religious imagination. Yet even poems that acknowledge and herald, not God's weakness, but his power, do so in a highly unorthodox style that keeps the divine firmly within the circuit of the dialectical *exchange of roles* proper to theophanic method of prayer. In several of the cited poems, for instance, God's power premises itself upon his *silence*: the necessary condition of *the soul in prayer* becomes a principal feature of God himself, a veritable insignia of His way of working. Furthermore, even the culminating moments of "action of the Lord upon the faithful" are finally resumed into the cooperative, reciprocal relationship intrinsic to the theophanic vision. The apparently apocalyptic I, 61 ("Dear darkening ground") ends:

> Just give me a little more time!
> I want to love the things
> as no one has thought to love them,
> until they're real and ripe and worthy of you.
>
> I want only seven days, seven
> on which no one has ever written himself—
> seven pages of solitude.

There will be a book that includes these pages,
and she who takes it in her hands
will sit staring at it a long time,

until she feel that she is being held
and you are writing.[279]

The monk aspires to repeat (the seven days of) creation, and whoever reads the book that is the record of those days—and so herself repeats that creative act in her imagination—may feel the power of God working in and through her, revealing Himself in the process. This is pure theophany—"Imagination in Imagination"—caught here in the literary act.

For the monk's God does reveal himself in and through his creative prayer—not completely, and not in such a manner as renders him *wholly* visible, for the light in which he may be seen is always shrouded in darkness—but nonetheless, in such a way as to make his presence felt in all things. In the twilit atmosphere of a Russian cathedral, lighting votive candles, the monk sees God's "dark birthmark" in every icon, but still more powerfully in the figure of the elderly peasant farmer worshiping there:

I saw the farmer, old
and bearded like Joachim
...and felt you more tenderly than ever before
revealed without words
in everything and in him.[280]

"I was a hidden treasure, I yearned to be known. That is why I produced creatures, in order to be known in them." In the course of *The Book of Monastic Life*, God slowly but surely emerges as just such "a hidden treasure": what is most surely and powerfully known of him is his unassuageable longing to be known, the primordial yearning *manifested and reflected* in the monk's ceaseless desire to seek and find him. And find him he does, not only in the church, of course, but in all people and things:

The poets have scattered you...

I wander in your winds
and bring back everything I find.

The blind man needed you as a cup.
The servant concealed you.

The homeless one held you out as I passed.

You see, I am a seeker....

One that dreams of making you whole
and: of making himself whole in turn.[281]

This poem proffers an image of the soul of the poet as a kind of new Isis, wandering the earth in search of the scattered pieces of her beloved Lord. Seeking him, our pilgrim poet is also—by way of the logic of reciprocal action that remains the heart of his theophanic prayer—seeking himself.

We should emphasize again that the creative imagination itself qualifies as the primary agent of the "sharing of roles" essential to "the method of prayer." In an important passage, Corbin clarifies its twofold, medial function. Speaking yet again of the reliance of Creator upon creature *and* vice versa, Corbin writes:

> This sharing...results from...a twofold movement of descent and ascent: *descent*, which is Epiphany, the primordial existentiating Imagination; *ascent* or return, which is the vision dispensed...to the capacity of the receptacle....And it is this sharing...which is the work of theophanic prayer, itself "creative" in the same way as the theophanic Imagination....For one and the same agent underlies the secret of Prayer and the secret of the Imagination.[282]

Thus, the mutual desire (Corbin also calls this "transitive passion") flowing *between* Creator and creature, God and man, manifests itself in and through creative imagination as it eternally transmutes spirit into the form of sensible image, and, reciprocally, returns the image-form of all things to its spiritual source. This twofold dynamic remains central to *The Book of Monastic Life* to the very end, though—as the apocalyptic aspect of I, 61 indicates—the second moment, the ascent or return, emerges more prominently towards the end.

In the penultimate poem of *The Book of Monastic Life*, the soul calls God into the home of its longing, endless as the broad dark Russian plains:

An hour at the end of day
and the landscape lies prepared.
What you long for, my soul, now say it:

Be heather, and heath, spread far....

Be moor, be heath, be plain
so the Ancient One may come
whom I can barely distinguish from Night,
bringing his huge blindness
into my listening house. [283]

Once God enters into the home of soul, it is discovered that God remembers everything *except* the songs of the world:

I see him sit and ponder
but never beyond my reach;
for him, all is within,
heaven and heath and house.
Only the songs are lost to him,
which he no longer tries to recite;
for from the ears of thousands of gates,
Time and the Wind drank them up.[284]

Yet God cannot know himself without these songs, for it is these prayers, these soulful figures of the human creative imagination, that finally reveal God to himself by reflecting him in the mirror of the soul. The book ends with a short final poem that images the completing of the theophanic circuit, the flowing of poetic knowledge and inspiration back into the divine source from which it arose:

And still: it seems to me
as if I had saved each song
deep inside me.

While he is quiet, beard aquiver,
bent to win back himself
from his lost melodies—
then I come up to his knees:

and his songs flow rushing back
into him.[285]

This is, to be sure, a moment of religious communion, but of a rather unique kind. God's own divine substance is returned to him, but only after it has been consecrated by human memory and imagination. The soul of the world, remembered in the monk's songs, is given back to God—but only after God himself has—by virtue of the twofold imaginative act of the monk's creative prayers—been given back to the re-enchanted world.

THE DIALECTIC OF LOVE

> The experience of mystic love.... implies creative Imagination.... it effects a twofold movement; on the one hand it causes invisible spiritual realities to descend to the reality of the Image... on the other hand... the Imagination transmutes the sensible world by raising it up to its own subtile and incorruptible modality. This twofold movement... [is] at the same time a descent of the divine and an assumption of the sensible.[286]

We may now finally speak the word that underlies and sanctions the continual exchange between Creator and creature, the spirit-force that drives their mutual desire, the fire in the divine compassion, and the burning that kindles the heart's *himma*, inspiring creative imagination. Theophanic vision, and the intimate conversation between Creator and creature that unfolds it, is (as Corbin says) a "dialectic of love":

> Thus love exists eternally as an exchange, a permutation between God and creature: ardent Desire, compassionate nostalgia, and encounter exist eternally, and delimit the area of being.[287]

Because love is at the heart of Ibn Arabi's creative imagination, Corbin identifies him as one of the *fedele d'amore*—those "faithful in love" who, like Dante in his worship of Beatrice, practice a chivalric, mystic love. Rilke himself had always tended to blend erotic and religious love and, as his life unfolded, would ally himself more and more closely with the chivalric/mystic ethos of the *fedele d'amore*. Nor is the specifically erotic note absent from *The Book of Monastic Life*. Several poems involve the emerging sexuality of one of our monk's younger brothers—poems that delicately aim to foster the *purity of soul* that defines true chastity without (contra Augustine) condemning sexual desire as inherently sinful.

In the majority of the monk's prayers, however, the love theme remains implicit, intrinsic as it is to the dynamic of mutual longing, knowledge, and revelation at the heart of the relationship between the monk and his God. Corbin asks the pointed question: "How is it possible to love God?" and supplies this answer from Ibn Arabi:

> We can typify Him and take Him as an object of our contemplation, not only in our innermost hearts but also before our eyes and in our imagination, as though we saw Him, or better still, *so that* we really see Him.... It is He who in every beloved being is manifested to the gaze of each lover... and none other than He is adored, for it is impossible to adore a being without conceiving the Godhead in that being.... So it is with love: a being does not truly love anyone other than his Creator.[288]

This says a great deal about the spirit that inspires Rilke's *Book of Monastic Life*. It also speaks to Rilke's love for Lou, without whose human love Rilke's love of God could not have found its form.

We have, however, neglected one more crucial formal articulation of the intimacy subsisting between Rilke's monk and his God, one that may lead us toward the archetypal psychological ground of the monk's long love song and the soul-development it figures in Rilke himself. The third and last moment of "the method of theophanic prayer"—"action of the Lord toward or upon the faithful"—includes a rhetorical aspect we have not yet discussed; namely, what Ibn Arabi calls "the divine response." This term refers to those moments when the intensity of the prayer's dialogical impetus finally issues in God himself answering the orant, effectively speaking in his own voice ("The Divine Presence, to which the faithful makes himself present, and which he makes present to himself, is attested by a divine response"[289]). *The Book of Monastic Life* includes at least two instances of this: I, 53 ("And God said to me, Write"), and, still more exemplary perhaps, I, 59:

> God speaks to each of us as he makes us,
> then walks with us silently out of the night.
>
> These are the words we dimly hear:
>
> You, sent out beyond your recall,
> go to the limits of your longing.
> Embody me....
>
> Let everything happen to you: beauty and terror.
> Just keep going. No feeling is final.
>
> Don't let yourself lose me.

Nearby is the country they call life.
You will know it by its seriousness.

Give me your hand.[290]

If one listens with a psychobiographical ear, this may well be an especially moving poem: we can hear Rilke urging himself on toward the still largely nascent odyssey of his own life. Approaching his twenty-fifth birthday, the young poet had already accomplished much, but—psychologically, literarily, spiritually—much more lay ahead. One can hear the divine voice preparing Rilke for the trials and triumphs of his own future, foreshadowing, for instance, the experiences that find expression in his great Elegies: "For Beauty is nothing but the beginning of Terror."

While no longer immature, *The Book of Monastic Life* remains a preeminently youthful text; indeed, it is archetypally so. Its intensely idealistic spirituality and continual intimacy with eternal concerns; its uninhibited self-confidence and the element of pure spontaneity technically and thematically so important to it; its expansive motion and abiding sense of unlimited possibility; the annunciation of new beginnings, belief "in all that is as yet unspoken" and sense of futurity that pervades the work—all this speaks clearly of the book's chief archetypal sponsor: the puer aeternus, the archetype of eternal youth.

In light of the profound spiritual affinity subsisting between *The Book of Monastic Life* and Ibn Arabi's Sufism, it should then come as no surprise that Ibn Arabi's entire spiritual teaching issues forth under the guidance of the puer aeternus figure. This archetypal aegis is borne out in two distinct and equally fundamental cornerstones of Ibn Arabi's personal spiritual life. First of all, Ibn Arabi was known as "the disciple of Khidr," a mythical spiritual master who (like Orpheus) may or may not have also been a historical person and who (as Corbin writes) "is described as he who has attained the source of life, has drunk of the water of immortality, and consequently knows neither old age nor death. He is the 'Eternal Youth.'"[291] Secondly, the Lord that revealed himself to Ibn Arabi in his own personal mystic vision appeared to him in the likeness of the figure famously described by the Prophet in the Koran: "I have seen my Lord in a form of the greatest beauty, as a youth with abundant hair, seated on the Throne of grace; he was clad in a green robe; on his hair a golden mitre; on his feet golden sandals."[292] Corbin comments:

> The Image recurring both in the...prophetic vision and in the personal experience of Ibn Arabi is an image of the puer aeternus....well known to psychologists as a symbol of the same *coincidentia oppositorum.*[293]

While—given the image under discussion here—Corbin's invocation of the puer aeternus needs no explanation, his equation of the same with the *coincidentia oppositorum* requires some elaboration. As a contrast with the famous vision of the face of God in the Koran, Corbin had just invoked God's reply to Moses as it is recorded, as well, in the Koran ("Thou shalt not see me") and remarked: "Refusal of vision and attestation of vision: the two motifs together form a *coincidentia oppositorum.*" He understands the puer, likewise, as an archetypal figure of the paradoxical concatenation of the infinite in finite form; the entrance of eternality into the sphere of time—logically enough, for the very idea of "eternal youth" proves inherently paradoxical. In this wise, too, we can understand how the archetypal force of the puer that ignites and flows through Rilke's *Book of Monastic Life* at some level supports and coincides with the image of God as the "forest of contradiction" that emerges in it. Coincidently, the monk's puer power complements the more traditional image of God that appears more visibly in the text: God as senex, the old man with the beard.

Yet, once again, we must be careful not to reduce an archetypal image to a definition or static concept. What is most important about the numinous puer figures—be it Khidr or the vision of "my Lord" as a beautiful youth—is that *the spirit manifested in them drives the soul-development enacted in and through the method of creative prayer.* One of the chief elements thereof is spiritual freedom, most specifically, from religious orthodoxy. As we saw in chapter 1, Hillman himself identifies this liberating function as one of the gifts of the puer. Speaking on this theme, Corbin contrasts Moses, the senex-inspired author of religious law, with the religious impulse offered by Khidr, claiming, "The spirituality inaugurated by Khidr is free from the servitude of literal religion."[294] Exploring just what it means to be "a disciple of Khidr," Corbin writes:

> Khidr's "guidance" does not consist in leading all his disciples uniformly to the same goal, to one theophany identical for all, in the manner of a theologican propagating dogma. He leads each

> disciple to his own theophany, the theophany of which he personally is the witness, because that theophany corresponds to his "inner heaven," to the form of his own being.[295]

It follows logically that the method of prayer evolved by the disciple of Khidr, Ibn Arabi, eschews collective norms. ("Here," writes Corbin, "we have indicated the meaning of 'Creative Prayer' practiced as personal 'divine service.' If it is a 'plea,' it is such as an aspiration to a new creation" [296]). As Corbin remarks, "the internalization and individualization of liturgy go hand in hand."[297] The dynamic interchange enacted in the course of creative prayer not only effects theophany ("The gnostic does not receive a ready-made image of his Lord, but understands Him in the light of the Image which in the course of his intimate dialogue appears in the mirror of his heart" [298]); it is also, manifestly, a method of realizing the Self:

> Thus the "life of prayer" practiced in the spirit and according to the indications of Ibn Arabi represents the authentic form of a "process of individuation" releasing the spiritual person from collective norms and ready-made evidences and enabling him to live as a unique individual for and with his Unique God. It signifies the effective realization of the "science of the heart."[299]

In *The Book of Monastic Life*, Rilke goes far toward "releasing his spiritual person from collective norms." Articulating a spirituality which—unlike the traditional Christian faith he inherited—featured the creative imagination at its heart, Rilke effectively fuses the poetic and religious imperatives of his nature, transfiguring both in the process. In the very act of composing *The Book of Monastic Life*—painting its iconic images, writing its poems, speaking its prayers—Rilke coincidently revealed his own unique God, and wrote another, crucial chapter in the book of his own soul-making. Recalling the close relationship between the puer and Eros, the god of love, we can take one measure of his psychological and poetic progress by referring, once more, to the myth of Psyche and Eros.

If it is true, as we proposed, that this story supplies an archetypal foundation for the opus of Rilke's soul, it should be possible to identify distinct phases of Rilke's literary and psychospiritual career with distinct phases of the myth. Thinking in a speculative, symbolic spirit and exercising caution not to interpret these imaginal matters literally, we might propose that Rilke's early dream lyrics (especially *Dreamcrowned* and *Advent* and, to a lesser extent, *In My Honor*) date from the mythic phase *before* Eros and Psyche's initial meeting—a time when Psyche's beauty was *too* virginal (when she was admired, but inapproachable, as yet untouched by Love) and Eros himself unbound to relationship, the inspiration he provided erratic and facile. Most of the poems from this period possess a quality of a surface beauty, an aestheticism as yet undeepened by any fatal engagement with love. Negative puer qualities that typically predate any real psychic involvement—narcissism and a sensualism linked with emotional detachment—likewise manifest themselves in both Rilke's literature and life.

All this changed with remarkable rapidity once Rilke met Lou. Their encounter, felt by both as a numinous force of destiny, played out on all levels—physical and emotional, intellectual and spiritual. Mythically speaking, it corresponds to the coming of Eros and the period of his (and Psyche's) initial rapture—an extended rendezvous brought about as a direct consequence of *Psyche's sacrificial crucifixion. That* episode I would, in the same playful spirit, associate with Rilke's general surrender of his virginal spirit, but perhaps still more with the real spiritual crisis, the inner crucifixion worked through in his *Visions of Christ*. Imagine, for instance, the shift of consciousness experienced by the narrator of "The Fair" when he steps from the busy public life of the fair into the waxworks tent, and—in a kind of a trance that transports him into a purely psychic reality—relives the crucifixion. Does this not bear some analogy to Psyche's circumstance when, wrenched out of the public stream of life, she is arrayed in funereal garb and abandoned on the mountain crag?[300] And Rilke's *Visions of Christ* did, after all, serve as the vehicle of Lou and Rilke's fateful meeting.

The relationship with Lou brought the full archetypal power of Eros into Rilke's psychic life, and, too, brought real psychic involvement to his still puerile idealizations of love and life. The whole *Book of Hours*, but especially its first part, figures as the poetic fruit of that initial union. Still energized by the archetypal energy of the puer aeternus, the work—immeasurably enriched by the soul-full experiences of Lou, of Italy, of Russia—doubtlessly achieves the "increased interiority" Hillman designates as psyche's contribution to the puer impulse: the "intimate dialogue" of the monk's prayers creates a depth of inner soul-space undreamed of in Rilke's earlier lyrics. At the same time, the sense of direction and spiritual destiny afforded by eros is everywhere evident, driving the writing, the painting, the praying on toward the hidden yet everywhere manifest God, the new revelation. Hillman also calls the interiority effected by the psyche-eros union "a bridal chamber," a motif echoed by the Annunciation imagery in the very first poem of *The Book of Monastic Life*. Likewise, in the myth, Psyche, living in Eros' house, soon finds herself pregnant with his divine child: a new spiritual birth is in the offing.

Even so, mythically speaking, this is only the initial phase of the union of Love and Soul; still a preliminary, ideal phase of their relationship. It is one still premised upon Psyche's ignorance of the full reality of love; for all her rapture, she remains in the dark as to the real identity of her lover, and their idyll is only sustained by keeping all sorts of jealous realities (Psyche's sisters) at bay. That cannot go on indefinitely, and soon Psyche, having inevitably transgressed the impossible laws of an ideal love, tries, in vain, to grasp the revealed god in a consciousness as yet uninitiated in the trials she must sustain to truly hold him. Eros, burned, flies away, leaving Psyche desolate. Ahead of her lie all the seemingly impossible labors she must perform—archetypal encounters with toil, suffering, and death—before her sacred marriage with Eros may ultimately be consecrated by the gods.

Likewise for Rilke. A pure spiritual effusion, *The Book of Monastic Life* remains a youthful text, a song of innocence seasoned with experience rather than an aged blend. We are offered here only hints of the deep sorrows and profound fears that mark Rilke's later works; his own archetypal confrontation with the travails of sickness, poverty, suffering—and, above all, death—still lie in the future:

> I cannot believe that little death
> whom we busily ignore
> should still trouble us so.
>
> I cannot believe he is that powerful.[301]

writes Rilke's monk, but soon, as author of *The Book of Poverty and Death*, he will confront that power; and another, future persona—Malte Laurids Brigge—will plumb his own fear of it to the depths. A breathtaking accomplishment, *The Book of Monastic Life* is hardly Rilke's last word on things. Great poetic labor and many more chapters of soul-making lay ahead.

Inevitably, life itself moved matters along. Unhappy psychological and social inequalities fraying their love, Rilke and Lou grew apart; the end of their romantic relationship was already on the horizon. They would separate, provisionally, after the second Russian trip; not very long after that, a decisive break would come, precipitated by the poet's novel relationships with two intriguing young women.

But that is another chapter in the story. I wish to end this one with a final testimony to the love that inspired *The Book of Monastic Life*—and, simultaneously, to the profound kinship subsisting between Rilke's vision and the poetic genius of Sufi wisdom. First, Rilke's well-known poem to Lou, which found its way into the second part of *The Book of Hours*:

> Extinguish my eyes, I'll go on seeing you.
> Seal my ears, I'll go on hearing you.
> And without feet I can make my way to you,
> without a mouth I can swear your name.
>
> Break off my arms, I'll take hold of you
> with my heart as with a hand.
> Stop my heart, and my brain will start to beat.
> And if you consume my brain with fire,
> I'll feel you burn in every drop of my blood.[302]

...and, last, this poem by Sadi, which—cited at the very end of *Creative Imagination in the Sufism of Ibn Arabi*—Henry Corbin offers as his final word on the subject:

> If the sword of your anger puts me to death,
> My soul will find comfort in it.
> If you impose the cup of poison upon me,
> My spirit will drink the cup.
> When on the day of Resurrection
> I rise from the dust of my tomb,
> The perfume of your love
> Will still impregnate the garment of my soul.
> For even though you refused me your love,
> You have given me a vision of *You*
> Which has been the confidant of my hidden secrets.

"Singing Women (Summer Evening)"
Heinrich Vogeler, c. 1900

PART II

DEATH AND THE MAIDEN

"Death and Age," Heinrich Vogeler, 1896

CHAPTER 6

WHAT BRIDGES LEAD TO IMAGES

In the spring of 1900—roughly half a year after finishing The Book of Monastic Life*—Rilke and Lou returned to Russia. In some ways, this second and longer trip proved more satisfying than the first. Visits to Moscow and Tolstoy were complemented by a 2,500-mile journey through the Russian heartland that included steamer trips down the Volga and Dnieper rivers as well as significant stays in small Russian peasant villages. Even so, tensions between the two travelers mounted as the epic voyage wore on. Indeed, by the time it ended, Lou had become thoroughly exhausted by the emotionally demanding relationship with Rilke. Convinced that Rainer, no less than she herself, required "freedom and distance," she encouraged Rilke to accept a pending invitation to visit his friend Heinrich Vogeler at Worpswede, in part to oversee Vogeler's illustrations for the forthcoming edition of Rilke's prose book* Geschichten der Lieben Gott (Tales of God)*. Upon their return to Germany, Lou resumed her life in Berlin while Rilke immediately departed for the small artist colony set amongst the North German moors, arriving there on August 27.*

Rilke had always been enthralled by anima. Typical anima figures (maidens, mostly) overpopulate his early poetry, most intensively in his sequence *Girls' Songs* from *In My Honor*. Even so, Rilke's six-week stay in Worpswede in the fall of 1900 triggered a crucial deepening of his involvement with the anima archetype, one that marked a new phase of the poet's evolution. The novel developments associated with his sojourn were kindled by the poet's intimate connections with two women artists: Paula Becker, a painter, and Clara Westoff, the young sculptor who would, in time, become his wife.

Paula and Clara undoubtedly offered a welcome emotional sea-change from Rilke's increasingly vexed relationship with the older and more powerful Lou. Anima, according to Jung, can be associated with a whole host of feminine figures—maidens, sisters, lovers, nymphs, nixies—but not, generally speaking, with the mother. Lou—fourteen years Rilke's senior—had always been in part a maternal figure for Rilke, and his persistent emotional dependence upon her ultimately spelled the end of their romantic relationship. Paula (Rilke's age) and Clara (three years younger than he) presented an altogether different picture. In their lissome white or spring green dresses and their willing and sensitively appreciative receptivity, they were fresh and virginal enough to qualify as *Mädchen* (girls) in Rilke's poetic imagination. No sooner had he met them than Rilke began celebrating these maidens in prose (his ongoing diary) and verse. Instead of searching for the source of all mystery in the images of religious icons, Rilke began seeking for the springs of wonder—and, too, his own identity—in the reflective mirror of the girls' deeply gazing eyes:

The reddest roses never looked so red
as on that evening wrapped in rain.
Your soft hair was on my mind again...
The reddest roses never looked so red.

The bushes never darkened quite so green
as on that evening in its raininess.
I thought long upon your silken dress...
The bushes never darkened quite so green.

The trunks of birches never stood so white
as on that evening, rain everywhere,
when I saw your two hands—slender, fair...
The trunks of birches never stood so white.

The water mirrored there a land of black
on that evening I found rain-filled skies;
so did I find myself in your eyes...
The water mirrored there a land of black.[303]

While Rilke devoted a good deal of his attention to Paula and Clara, the poet's relationship to these young women can hardly be separated from all of these young artists' involvement with their natural surroundings.

The variegated elemental beauty of the Worpswede area and the relative simplicity of the human life so closely integrated with it had been the chief reason painters such as Fritz Mackensen and Otto Modersohn had chosen to settle there some ten years earlier. In the spacious colorful fields and woods and the impressively stark moorland that stretched to an almost infinite distance all around, Rilke himself—still internally preoccupied with Russia—found a landscape strangely kin to the vastness of that land and yet one possessed, too, of a unique order of intimacy.

On the last day of July, on the Volga River in Russia, Rilke had written:

> A broad stream, high woods along the one shore, along the other a deep moorland.... One discovers: land is huge, water is something huge, and above all, the sky is huge. What I have seen until now was no more than an image of land and river and world. Here, however, everything is itself. I feel as if I had been witness to the creation.[304]

Worpswede—itself a land of water and huge sky—provided a kind of inner continuity with the stream of Rilke's Russian meditations, often absorbing into itself the interest of the artists traversing it:

> We walked through the heath together, in the evening wind...for a while two ramble on together, deep in conversations that the wind quickly destroys—then one of them comes to a halt and after a few moments the other.... Beneath the vast skies the darkening colorful fields lie flat—wide hilly waves of rustling heather, bordering them stubble-fields and new mown buckwheat, which with its stalk-red and the yellow of its leaves is like richest silk.... Every moment something is held up into the vivifying air, a tree, a house, a slowly turning mill...or a hard-edged, jagged goat that walks into the sky. There are no conversations in which the landscape doesn't take part, from all sides and with a hundred voices.[305]

Wind appears repeatedly in Rilke's descriptive evocations of Worpswede. Carl Jung:

> The Latin words *animus*, "spirit," and *anima*, "soul," are the same as the Greek *anemos*, "wind." In Arabic, "wind" is *ruh*, and *ruh* is "soul, spirit." The Greek word *psyche* has similar connections; it is related to *psychein*, "to breathe".... These connections show

> clearly how in Latin, Greek, and Arabic the names given to the soul are related to the notion of moving air.[306]

Wind thus qualifies as one element of the Worpswede landscape associated with soul, though—as Jung indicates—it is a soul-spiritual element rather than one identified with the soul as distinguishable from spirit. This latter type characteristically involves some aspect of the reflective element lent by *water.* With respect to air, soul associates more closely with *atmospheric effect* rather than the pure activity of wind. Hillman writes: "Anima consciousness is mood-determined, a notion that has been represented in mythological phenomenology by images of natural atmosphere (clouds, waves, still waters)."[307] Whereas Eros and spirit are phenomenologically related to the element of fire ("fiery, phallic, spirited, directed, sporadic, unattached"), Hillman identifies anima with that which is "moist, vegetative, receptive, indirect, ambiguous; its consciousness is reflective and in flux."[308] The Worpswede moorland is risen from an ancient sea that still inundates it in time of flood and remains ever present in the dark waters underlying the moorland, water that—rising in vaporous dew and falling in frequent rain—continually saturates everything so that (as Rilke himself noticed) even wood and stone are continually vegetating and thus changing in color and form. Worpswede is a decidedly soulful environment—anything but the dry desert Bamford[309] identifies as the natural home of pure spirit. Even a casual perusal of the canvases of Worpswede's landscape artists reveals endless cloudscapes as well as waterways mirroring the land around: work that is nothing if not *atmospheric.*

Before we lose ourselves in the details of Worpswede's peculiar nature, though, we need to stress the paramount importance, for Rilke, of the Worpswede artists' overriding interest in nature per se. Worpswede after all, was primarily—though not exclusively—a colony of landscape painters, and the inspiration informing the work of an artist such as Otto Modersohn differs dramatically from—and is even directly opposed to—the founding norms of the tradition of icon painting so important to Rilke's *Book of Hours.* Icon painting focuses upon ideal or religious content represented by stylized saints, Madonnas, or other religious figures—spiritual matter not really conceivable in natural form. Consequently, many icons do entirely without natural landscape. When landscape features are included, they are highly stylized and of marginal interest. How radically different the practice of an Otto Modersohn, who not only worked directly from nature but—as Rilke discovered to his astonished delight—filled his studio with natural history cabinets so as to enable a continual close study of natural form and color.

The Worpswede artists were profoundly and passionately invested in the project of truly *seeing* nature—seeing things as they actually were in themselves, presented to the awakened senses in full imaginative reality. In this respect especially, Rilke took them as his teachers. His diary pages are filled with references to the art of seeing nature and the superiority of the Worpswede artists on this score. More, such seeing becomes in Rilke's mind, not merely a training of visual perspective, but a way of being so that the one who sees nature intensely enough becomes *like* nature:

> I am gradually beginning to comprehend this life that passes through large eyes into eternally waiting souls.... In how poor a sense do we actually *see* compared with these people! How richly these people must travel! And when once they truly arrive at themselves after this blissful apprenticeship-time, what a wonderful language they must possess, what images for everything experienced! Then they must confide themselves the way landscapes do, as with clouds, winds, things going down...[310]

Those "large eyes" are, presumably, Paula's. Consequently, as this passage (and countless others, in prose and verse) indicate, Rilke's interest in nature cannot well be sundered from his preoccupation with anima—a preoccupation outwardly figured by his attention to "the girls," and inwardly by his efforts to comprehend, assimilate, and express their mode of being and consciousness. Theoretically as well as practically, in fact, involvement with nature and anima are indissolubly linked—at least, when one is speaking of the German Romantic anima shared by both Rilke and the psychologist (Jung) who first formulated the formal concept. A "deep feeling for nature" figures as the *first* of the traits Ellenberger[311] identifies as characteristic of German Romanticism, one that shaped C. G. Jung's original notion of anima itself.

It is not only nature qua observable natural phenomena, but nature as the *state of being or consciousness* typified by natural phenomena that is relevant here. Hillman describes this as follows:

> The consciousness of this archetypal structure (anima) is never far from unconsciousness. Its primary attachment is to the state of nature, to all things that simply are—life, fate, death—and which can only be reflected but never separated from their

> impenetrable opacity. Anima stays close to this field of the natural unconscious mind.[312]

Rilke's literary evocations of his Worpswede experience reflect the various aspects of this characterization again and again. For instance, the poet begins both his "Worpswede Diary" and the small collection of poems he put together for his friend and host (*In and After Worpswede. Verses for my dear Heinrich Vogeler*[313]) with lines blending the motifs of fate and natural (un)consciousness:

> Destinies are (every day, this feeling grows)
> much *more* than accident, a little less than fate.
> Are—air, felt by a wingbeat,
> Evenings in the consciousness of a rose.[314]

In and after Worpswede stands as the only poem collection consistently representative of Rilke's Worpswede experience, and the whole of it may be read as a meditation on the interrelated aspects of anima. Following "Destines are" (an untitled piece), Rilke offers seven pieces centering on feminine characters, most all of them transparently anima figures. The first, "The Bride," celebrates Martha Schroeder, Vogeler's betrothed:

The Bride

> I have felt her presence in this house
> the blond bride, who suffered long, alone.
> All hours sing with her soft voice,
> and all sounds follow her step's tone.
>
> The objects which had to serve me every day
> were disappointed whenever I drew near
> and yearned for someone far more natural
> with whom their simplicity could be shared.
>
> Nothing in the house betrayed her loudly,
> yet all said "not you" as if in sign
> and when at dusk I walked the hallways, mirrors
> asked for her image instead of mine.[315]

Apart from a brief poetic jibe at Carl Hauptmann (a competitor for the girls' attention), this poem stands as the first lyric penned in that portion of Rilke's diary recording his days in Worpswede (the diary pages formally called the Worpswede diary begin shortly thereafter, with "Destinies are"). The poem flows from the circumstance of Rilke's residence in Vogeler's house, the marvelous white Barkenhoff that would soon be the bride's own. Its sense of containment and interiority and its portrayal of a consciousness indissociable from the simple presence of things themselves contrast rather sharply with the spiritual gesture of the initial two poems of *The Book of Monastic Life*. There, the hours "bow down" and touch the monk in his cloister, inspiring him with active creative power; here, the hours are already fully incorporated in (the voice of) the bride; there, the monk's creative consciousness soars clear out of the cloister of his material shell to trace ever expanding circles; here, the bride's consciousness remains entirely attached to and inseparable from the immanent domain and interior content of the house itself.

Designating the bride's mode of consciousness, Rilke calls her *eine Unbewußte*—translated here as "one far more natural." While this accurately denotes one level of relevant meaning, it hardly conveys the whole force of the German term, which means, literally, "an unconscious one"—the root term being the same as that employed by Freud. It is a term that recurs numerous times—always favorably inflected—in Rilke's writing at the time (a few days later, lamenting the losses typically implicated in growing up, the poet writes: "What has drawn him on / in darkness / all that is unconscious / must cease to be"[316]) and reflects his intimate involvement with "the natural unconscious mind" that Hillman—and Jung—associate with anima. Jung, in fact, once defined anima as "a personification of the unconscious,"[317] a definition that could readily be seen as one apt characterization of Rilke's "bride."

Rilke's residence in Heinrich Vogeler's house nourished the poet's anima fantasies in many ways, the psychic presence of Vogeler's betrothed being just one relatively minor instance. Vogeler himself, after all, qualified as a true devotee, and had long shown himself to be, if anything, still more anima-enthralled than Rilke. An inveterate lover and creator of anima figures, Vogeler drew, painted, and etched innumerable beautiful young maidens with long hair, gazing eyes, and flowing gowns, set amidst lush landscapes. He also depicted any number of still more gorgeously archetypal fairies and water nymphs—his triptych of the water nymph

Worpswede Landscape (top); The Barkenhoff

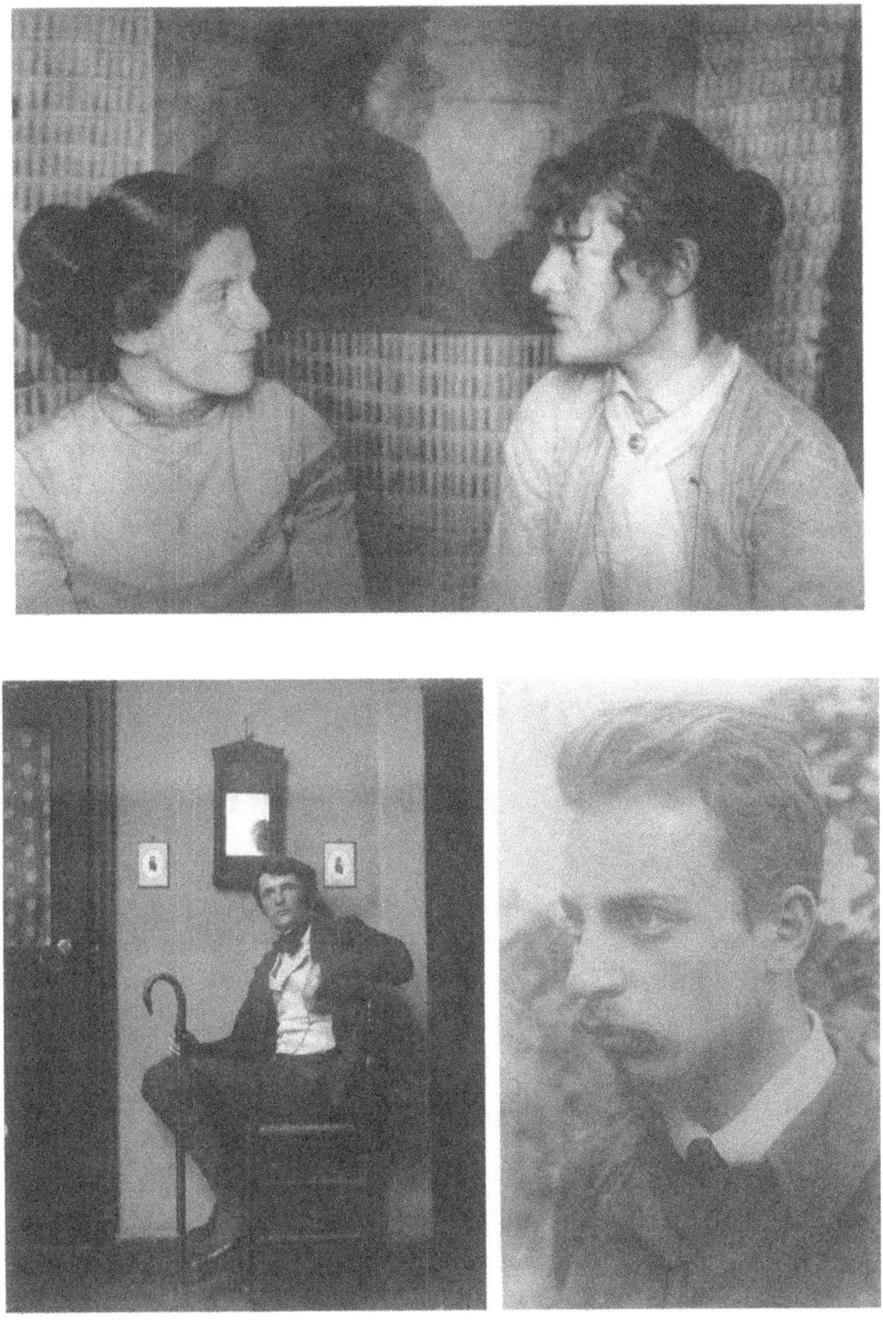

Paula Becker and Clara Westhoff (top);
Heinrich Vogeler, 1898 (bottom left); Rilke, 1900

Rilke in Westerwede, 1901

Melusine, for instance, whom Jung himself singled out as a particularly typical anima figure:

> Melusina comes into the same category as the nymphs and sirens who dwell in the "Nymphidida," the watery realm.... The birthplace of Melusina is the womb of the mysteries, obviously what we today would call the unconscious.... Melusina is clearly an anima figure.[318]

While this Jung passage—consistent with all that has been said above—associates anima with the unconscious, it would nonetheless be a mistake simply to *identify* anima with the unconscious—to do so, indeed, would be a fateful mistake like to the unwanted incursion into her realm that brings such misfortune upon the legendary Melusina's husband-lovers. Close to nature (in most portrayals, including Vogeler's, Melusina is mermaid-like, with a fishtail for feet) anima nonetheless adds a *reflective* moment foreign to nature herself. Hillman:

> Anima-consciousness favors a protective mimicry, an attachment to something or someone else to which it is echo. Here we see the wood nymphs that belong to trees, the souls which hover over waters, speak from dells and caves.... That we conceive anima in tandems is already given by her phenomenology....
>
> In these pairs... anima is the reflective partner, she it is who provides the moment of reflection in the midst of what is naturally given. *She is the psychic factor in nature.*[319]

Or, as Hillman states later, "Anima is nature now conscious of itself through reflection."[320]

A number of consequences follow from this critical elaboration. Anima—rather than being simply identified with the unconscious—becomes instead a function *bridging* the conscious and unconscious, a portal to the unknown:

> Anima as relationship means that configuration which mediates between personal and collective, between actualities and beyond, between the individual conscious horizon and the primordial realm of the imaginal, its images, ideas, figures, and emotions. Here anima functions as mediatrix... *as a bridge to everything unknown.*[321]

Rilke own experience of "the two girls" follows this script closely:

> How much I learn in watching these two girls, especially the blond painter, who has such brown observant eyes! How much closer now I feel again to everything wondrous and intuitive, as in those days of my "Girls' Songs." How much mysteriousness invests these slender figures when they stand before the evening or when, leaning back in velvet chairs, they listen with all their aspects. Since they are the most receptive, I can be the most giving. My whole life is full of the images with which I can talk to them; *everything that I've experienced becomes an expression for what lies deep behind experience.*[322]

Or, to put the matter more poetically, as Rilke does in his poem "Girls II":

> Girls, poets are those who learn from you
> to *say* that which you, alone, *are*...[323]

Still another principal aspect of anima registers in several of the passages cited above. Given her role as a bridge to the unconscious, the mode of language or expression associated with her cannot be discursive or theoretical language that bespeaks full intellectual consciousness. Rather, hers is a language that reflects her mysterious psychological source; a language of images. In "Girls I," Rilke deftly joins the idea of the anima as bridge to the unknown with her association with images:

> Only girls do not ask
> what bridges lead to images....
>
> From their lives every door opens
> onto a poet
> and onto the world.[324]

Indeed, Rilke at Worpswede was so attuned to the soul dynamics of the archetype that—in delineating anima and its connection with the unconscious and its expression in imagery—Hillman almost sounds as if he is quoting Rilke's last-cited diary entry:

> To consider anima as *the life behind consciousness from which consciousness arises* deepens our understanding of her strange expressions in images, emotions, symptoms. She projects herself into consciousness through expression; expression is her art....Anima here is not projection but is the projector.[325]

Despite the congruity between Rilke's and Hillman's writings, this last Hillman citation might be used to question one of the premises implicit in Rilke's "Girls" poems. Do the girls—anima figures—indeed require a poet to express what they, in themselves, are; or—as Hillman suggests—is a moment of imaginative expression inherent within the anima archetype itself? The question has, if you will, feminist implications hardly irrelevant to the dynamics of Rilke's actual relationship to Paula and Clara. Torgersen remarks how Rilke made a consistent practice of recording (in his diary and written missives) stories Paula or Clara had told him and subsequently re-presenting them, in literary form, as gifts to the girls.[326] Paula and Clara graciously received these gifts as such. Even so, the peculiar dynamic hints at the supposition that the girls' own initial expression was somehow inadequate; that, in the last analysis, it was theirs, not to give, but to receive.

As Hillman indicates, the reflective character of anima consciousness does not mean that it is *purely* passive. Anima's inherent receptivity reflexively empowers her—more or less spontaneously—to express herself, to project imagery. To be sure, a certain tension in this interplay of receptivity and activity inheres within the anima archetype itself. In Rilke's poem "The Bride," the mirrors ask for her (rather than him) because it is she who in her own mirror-like nature reflects *them* as much as vice versa: she it is who "provides the moment of reflection in the midst of what is naturally given" and so figures as the soul of the house. There is, after all, activity in the very act of reflection: a mirror gives back, produces and projects an image—albeit purely spontaneously.

The moments of passive reception and active projection are not always so perfectly coincident as in the simple mirror-image. Less simple forms of mimesis figure essentially in most forms of art, and most certainly in landscape painting and painted or sculpted portraiture. Rilke—not always merely overweening in his relationship to Paula and Clara—spins out the dynamic of this tension in one of his first detailed description of them, one that leaves room to recognize these anima figures as artists in their own right:

> [*After a Sunday evening gathering at the Barkenhoff that was ending with*...] jokes, clowning, sickening end of German conviviality. But the ending was beautiful in spite of all, and it was the girls in white who redeemed it. I opened the door to my room, which was growing cool and dark blue like a grotto. I pushed open my window, and then they came to join the miracle and leaned out brightly into the moonlit night, which enveloped their laughter-hot cheeks in cold. And suddenly they all became so poignant in their gazing. Half fully aware, i.e. as painters, half intuitively, i.e. as girls. Initially the mood seized them, the single note of this misty night with its almost full moon over the three poplar trees, this mood of faintly tarnished silver robs them of their defenses and forces them into the dark, yearning-filled life of girls.... Then the artist in them gains control and gazes and gazes, and when the artist has become deep enough in this gazing, they are once more at the threshold of their own being and miracle and glide gently back into their life as girls. That's why they always gaze so long into the landscape.[327]

Eleven days later, Rilke composed a poetic transcription of this perspective, one that still more clearly articulates the duality of unconscious and consciousness, receptivity and activity inherent in anima:

> To live half-unconscious, and half in haste
> to set down what one saw—how, and where;
> to act with purpose, and then once more to wander
> in the unknown, alone, and free of care—:
> *here these lovely girls fit this mold:*
> *half held in thrall, yet already seizing hold...*[328]

Having identified the duality, it should be emphasized that—both in Rilke's prose and in his poem—the unconscious, receptive moment comes first. The art of the anima and the creative consciousness associated with it premises itself upon a prior element of unconsciousness and pure receptivity and grows out of that—indeed, unfolds as a continual reflection upon and expression of that element. This continually transforming dynamic of consciousness of natural unconsciousness, this deepening development of the dark unknown, lies at the heart of anima and leads to one of Hillman's crowning definitions:

> Anima here is not projection but is the projector. And our consciousness is the result of her prior psychic life. Anima thus becomes the primordial carrier of psyche, or the archetype of psyche itself.[329]

Anima thus qualifies as the archetype of psychic consciousness, of psyche becoming (conscious of) herself—even as this process continually and interminably depends upon the ineluctable mystery of her prior unconsciousness ("the unknown"). Or, in still another formulation, anima is the archetype of soul coming into its own by way of creative imagination, the archetype of soul-making itself, seen through psyche's own deeply gazing eyes.

Psyche, however, cannot go it alone. In the myth that underlies our reading of Rilke's life, it is Psyche's relationship to Eros that drives her development; the soul-making at the heart of the anima archetype cannot dispense with its relation to Love. Nor did the god of love fail to visit the colorful fields and art studios of Worpswede, and the tale of Rilke's anima involvement there doubles as a love story. Rilke often played the part of Eros to Paula or Clara's Psyche. The colony's resident troubadour, he shared his lyric eloquence in mellifluous community readings, in privately shared prose and verse, in intimate conversation in the Barkenhoff's enchanted rooms, in walks along long winding footpaths, and sometimes—in yet more transparent shades of eros—in late visits to Paula or Clara in their studios under the cover of a moonlit night.

Rilke and the two girls, though, were not the only characters caught up in this stage of the Eros-Psyche myth, this chapter of the tale wherein Psyche (as yet the unmarried bride of Eros) resides in a magic, jewel-studded palace set apart from the "real" world—the luxuriously appointed house wherein she is ministered to by invisible attendants and receives visits from the unknown lover who comes to her at night, his identity concealed in the cloak of darkness. Heinrich Vogeler, too, had been living this myth, and indeed more literally so than Rilke. He had seen and immediately fallen in love with the innocent Martha Schroeder, a fourteen-year-old farm girl, and soon whisked her away from unsympathetic surroundings to raise her for his own. Miraculously, he seems to have succeeded; at the time of Rilke's visit, the couple had just been engaged. Vogeler, in fact, told Rilke of the betrothal a few days after his arrival. The engagement was not yet public, and since Martha and he could not yet live openly with each other at Vogeler's Barkenhoff, Vogeler was often away with her for days—and nights—at a time at Martha's brother's still more secluded place in Adiek, several hours from Worpswede. Even so, as Rilke well knew, the Barkenhoff—Vogeler's own elaborately crafted Jugendstil castle—was waiting for her. Rilke's imagination of her there as "The Bride," mistress soul of the place whom all visible and invisible things in the house yearn to serve, evokes Psyche in the myth no less than all the (at least partially undercover) comings and goings of Love.

And then there were Modersohn and Paula. Otto Modersohn's ailing wife had recently died, and he and Paula had already formed a close, albeit very private attachment. Even as Rilke was, in his own gallant way, paying court to Paula, Modersohn was pressing his more earnest suit. He did so, however, with great secrecy on account of the social impropriety of wooing Paula so soon after his wife's death. Otto and Paula communicated, in part, by leaving letters for each other hidden under a rock. It is also highly likely that he came quite frequently to her studio very late—after midnight—for intimate (though it seems clear from Paula's writings, not yet sexual) conversation. Shades of Eros and Psyche yet again: Love was in the air, but so far more felt than seen; declared only secretly, if at all.

Inevitably, though, another, less savory element of the myth also put in its appearance at Worpswede, though not very intrusively, at least at first. In Apuleius' tale, Psyche, beginning to tire of her lonely luxury, finally convinces Eros to allow her to receive visits from her sisters. These fine specimens aptly display many of the soul's less endearing sides. "Hatred, spite, suspicion, jealousy, rejection, enmity, deception, betrayal, cruelty... play their part in anima experiences" writes Hillman,[330] and Psyche's sisters import these traits into the psychological texture of the myth. Scheming enviously, desiring love for themselves, they ultimately persuade Psyche to imagine her unknown husband as a monster whom she—if she wishes to save both herself and her child (for she is pregnant)—must mercilessly kill.

Given the intricacy and emotional significance of all the interlocking relationships at Worpswede, the soul's vices seemed remarkably muted there during the period of Rilke's stay, though they would, in time, flare and tear "The Family" (for so the select group of artists—including Rilke—began calling themselves) apart. Clara and Paula, after all, were best friends; from the first, Rilke (interestingly enough) referred to them as "sisters." Despite Paula's secret attachment to Modersohn, some degree of jealousy undoubtedly percolated beneath the tranquil surface of the trio's (or the quartet's) mutual admiration. In this connection, one need only call to mind the famous scene of Rilke riding to Hamburg in a coach, gazing admiringly into Paula's receptive eyes with Modersohn sitting beside him, while Clara—physically the most robust of all—breathlessly overtook the coach on her bicycle and thrust a wreath of flowers into Rilke's hands so that he (as he blithely recorded in his diary) finished the ride feeling the strength of the sculptress's hands in his even while continuing to enjoy amorous eye contact with Paula. One can imagine Modersohn did not enjoy the ride half so much as he.

Faced with all these crisscrossing lines of character, it would be misguided to attempt to make archetypal psychological sense of it all by inflexibly "assigning parts" in the mythic play, as if one historical personage always played only one role. Far more sensible and meaningful is the general archetypal truth that the jealousy, envy, deception, and betrayal that counter Psyche's idealized—and still largely unconscious—relation to Eros were self-evidently on the scene. If (as is true, too, in the myth), they were waiting in the wings during the first phase of Psyche's erotic rapture, they would all too soon burst onto center stage and, tragically, take over the action. In all likelihood, it was Rilke's discovery of Paula's secret engagement that precipitated his drastically sudden departure from Worpswede and, ultimately, his marriage to Clara. In time, that marriage would sorely estrange Paula from both Clara (a loss she felt keenly) and Rilke. At a certain juncture, in fact, Paula would come to see Rilke (as per the myth) in the guise of the love-monster dominating and even devouring both Clara and her child. Reciprocally, Rilke would see Otto Modersohn very much in the same light—perhaps with still more justification, for Modersohn was certainly the more possessive of the two. One might imagine that this trait played a role in Paula's tragically premature death in the aftermath of the birth of her and Otto's child.

Nor should we neglect entirely mention of Lou, who, from her distant post in Berlin, nonetheless continued to play an important part in the drama. Despite her express desire to promote his (and her) freedom and initially encouraging Rilke to visit Worpswede, Lou quickly grew critical of Rilke's intimacy with Clara and Paula, feeling it was leading him astray. Though it is not the only way one can interpret Lou in this context, it would not be implausible to see her in the role of Aphrodite, Eros' mother, infuriated at the cheek of her son's sudden abandonment (never mind, as a fellow goddess reminded her, that it was she herself who had sharpened his love weapons) and jealously riled by his insufferable infatuation with a mere girl who, though pretty, was simple and innocent and—most impossible of all—mortal. When Rilke actually married Clara later, Lou's disapproval took dramatic form and turned into outright rejection.

Suffice it to say, then, that the negative elements attached to anima were hardly absent from the Worpswede scene. The darker side of the Psyche-Eros myth, the undertone of tragic potential written into its subscript, pervaded Worpswede along with its lighter registers.

Unavoidably so, perhaps, for the spiritual action does not go forward without the bitter alchemical addition of those elements. After all, it is Psyche's reprehensible sisters (and all the ugly forms of unconsciousness they bring into the picture) that compel Psyche to light the lamp of consciousness, to strive to see and to know her husband (Love) and, so, herself, while it is the imperiously jealous Aphrodite who ultimately sets her the tasks that define the heart of her soul-making quest. A few years down the road, Rilke himself would soon come to speak eloquently of how love without difficulty could hardly be understood as love at all.

We are in danger, though, of getting ahead of ourselves, for we have still more work to do to achieve a fuller understanding of Rilke's own experience of the "Worpswede phase" of the myth: that enchanted period associated with Psyche's initial (unmarried) brideship and Eros' secret comings and goings; that phase when the sisters—even after visiting Psyche, and beginning to scheme—had not yet thoroughly (albeit temporarily) poisoned Psyche's imagination. For while we have provisionally rehearsed Rilke himself in the role of Eros, that can by no means serve as a fixed or final cast. Eros and Psyche interact as archetypes *within* the soul-consciousness of individuals, not only in projected forms in connection with others. Coincidently, it is clear that the main action of the Worpswede scene for Rilke was—not only play-acting love—but (simultaneously and even more vitally) *becoming ever more intimate with Psyche*, probing and even penetrating her virginal being, and—in moments of deepest communion—becoming one with her, making her his own, and vice versa. To phrase the matter more analytically, Rilke's concentrated attempt to comprehend and assimilate the mysterious (un)consciousness of the lovely girl-artists; his relentlessly sensitive effort to come to see the world through their eyes, to know his own maiden being... this, to put it technically, was Rilke's concerted attempt to "integrate the anima."

Despite the human complications attendant upon the process, Rilke made crucial progress in this direction. What the poet learned in and after Worpswede—from Paula, from Clara, from the whole crew of artists and (for a time) fellow travelers—may well be almost comparable in importance to what he learned from Lou, though it was (and this is integral to the point) of a fundamentally different, less intellectual and spiritual nature. We can continue studying Rilke's anima lessons by drawing a contrast between the terms of Rilke's inheritance from Lou, and the nascent promise of Worpswede which—building upon and transforming the former—proved an indispensable point d'appui for all the still young poet's future evolutions.

In the last chapter, I proposed that, mythologically speaking, Rilke's love affair with Lou figured the advent of Eros in his psychic life. In this relationship with a woman of extraordinary spiritual and intellectual power—a woman with a masculine name—Rilke tended to be more on the receiving than the giving end of things, to play Psyche to Lou's Eros as much as—or more than—vice versa. Even so, if we focus upon Rilke's most significant early poetic achievement, the puer-inspired *Book of Monastic Life*, the chief archetypal energy integrated via Rilke's poetic work in this phase proved to be—not the more receptive type he acted in life—but the more active spiritual energy born by the other (Lou). This oppositional principal holds true for the Worpswede chapter of Rilke's life as well. Even as he took the more active, typically masculine role in relationship to Paula and Clara (ably playing Eros to the girls' Psyches), it was the girls' archetypal anima energy that his soul was inwardly—and transformatively—most deeply involved with, and most intent upon assimilating via the creative vehicle of his literary art.

The switch from Lou to Paula/Clara thus figures more—much more—than a change in the shifting winds of personal relationship. The archetypal psychological transformation it signifies correlates with other, more manifest differences. Lou—in addition to being partially a maternal figure for Rilke—was herself a writer and professional intellectual, and one profoundly invested in overtly religious concerns. As we have seen, her intellectual and literary projects—especially her inquiry into the psychology of religion—shaped Rilke's own kindred endeavors in the years of their greatest intimacy. In marked contrast to Lou, neither the sculptress Clara nor the painter Paula was particularly interested in religion per se. Coincidently, in striking contrast to the preoccupation with God evident in Rilke's "Russian" phase, Rilke's Worpswede writing largely neglects patently religious topoi. Very few poems in or immediately after Worpswede possess obvious religious content, and Rilke mentions God only three or four times in the almost one hundred pages of prose in his diary devoted to his Worpswede stay. The only really significant mention occurs in the last entry penned in Worpswede (the last, that is, which is not torn out), dated October 4, two days before Rilke's precipitous departure. It records a discussion with Paula about religion, and begins by transcribing Paula's revealing views on the subject: views Rilke listened to so carefully that he ventures to render them in Paula's own voice:

> "When you were first here I so often marveled that you [Rilke] used the name God... and that you were able to use it so beautifully. I myself was totally without that word. It's true I never felt any great need for it either. There were times, earlier, when I believed: he is in the wind, but for the most part I didn't experience him as a

> unified personality at all...I knew only aspects of God. And many of those aspects were horrifying....All the same it would be comforting to believe in a personality around whom all circles close, a mountain of power before whom all people and all countries of all people lie open...." And later on: "No, it would all be foreign doctrine, for me God will always be 'she,' Nature."

Rilke did not necessarily agree, and answered her in terms familiar from *The Book of Hours.*

> But I argued on his behalf. That his shortcomings, his injustice, and the deficiencies of his power were all matters of his development. That he is not finished yet. When was there time for him to become? Man needed him so urgently that he experienced and envisioned him from the very beginning as being. Man needed him complete and said: God is. Now he must get back to his becoming. And it falls to us to help him do so.[331]

Despite Rilke's counterargument, the weight of his literary work during his Worpswede days reflected the gist of Paula's view as much as his own and makes it clear that the immediate locus of the sacred had shifted somewhat for Rilke away from the name and spirit of God toward the soul of nature experienced in and through the eyes of two enchanting maiden-artists—or, at least, that the latter mediated relation to the former more and more. As the focus of his human universe shifted from Lou to Paula and Clara, the methods and metaphors of visual art correlatively replaced those of religion as the center of Rilke's spiritual attention, becoming the new *sister domain* modeling for him the heart of the poetic life. Nor was this destined to be a temporary alteration, but figured a growing trend that peaked only later (with Rilke's relation to Rodin) and indeed proved a lasting legacy, molding Rilke's poetry for the rest of his life.

I do not mean to imply, however, that the religious impulse that had always been a driving force in Rilke's life was summarily surrendered or discarded. Rather, in the sphere of his Worpswede influences, Rilke's intellectual and spiritual energies became progressively absorbed into and transformed by less patently religious forms of imaginative enterprise. Paula and Clara—as intellectually questioning as they were in their own rights—were primarily visual artists, dedicated to translating spiritual life into visual form (and vice versa). The powerful stream of their creative energy did not tend to flow from personal inner experience toward ideational and essayistic verbal forms—as it did for Lou—but rather from close observation and inward reverie towards the realized visual image. One of Rilke's poetic portraits of Paula and Clara tellingly transforms their very being as well as their capacity for speech wholly into visual contour, a trope reflective of the shift of emphasis occurring in the crucible of his own art:

> A girl... pale... just before the evening hour...
> and ever and again I experience the power
> of discovery. Not only girls themselves enchant me so,
> but the gentle lines of neck and and hair,
> standing out against the darkness there...
>
> For a long while, they live only in contour.
> And the words they share in the evening, too—
> with the meadow flowers or a child they knew—
> are all outline; simple, pure...[332]

Image, of course, had always been indispensable to Rilke; the deep fascination with icon painting that inspired *The Book of Monastic Life* figures one particularly potent case in point. Nonetheless, Rilke's Worpswede periods represents a significant turn in his sense of the character, autonomy, and value of the image, one most obviously signaled in the title of the major poetic work, *Der Buch der Bilder*, associated in part with Rilke's Worpswede sojourn.

I initially give the name of this work in German, because no single English translation quite captures the double meaning implicit in its key German word, *Bilder*. Snow aptly elaborates the word's significance:

> The word can designate a picture, a portrait, or any other form of pictorial representation (sculptural, architectural), and thus suggests a strong "belonging" to the visual world. But it can also designate an image that works as a metaphor—a figurative entity pointing to realities beyond or behind it. *Bilder* in this sense can populate the visual realm with traces, invisible connections, imaginings, remembrances, intimations of things lost or unrealized, waiting to be recalled or brought (back) to life.[333]

As Snow recognizes, the linked meanings of the term figure crucially in many of the poems in *The Book of Images (or Pictures)*—and no less so in verses in Rilke's diary and *In and After Worpswede*. All these writings contain poems directly involving literal sculptures, pictures, and portraits. *In and After Worpswede* includes, for instance, a series of poems directly based on Vogeler's pictures as well as a meditation on the nature of a portrait ("Bildnis") spoken by the figure in the portrait and beginning: "I am a picture/portrait/image [*Bild*] / Do not demand that I speak."[334] Most interesting (and manifestly at work in "Bildnis") is not merely Rilke's involvement with pictures per se, but the constant and intricate interplay between the more literal meanings of *Bild* in his work and the subtler, more figurative senses of the term that qualify it to be the privileged medium and element of, not only visual art, but exploration of (Rilke's) psyche's inner realms. As Rilke's diary indicates, this was a quite conscious preoccupation:

27 September

All feeling, in form and deed,
grows infinitely large and light.
I'll not rest until I win one fight:
to find images for my transformations.
The spontaneous song no longer is enough.
Now, for once, my words must strain
to make *outwardly visible*—perfectly plain—
all that barely flickers through the dreaming brain.[335]

This intimate involvement with the (in)visible image as, simultaneously, a vehicle of poetic expression and self-transformation proved key to the novel developments precipitated by Rilke's stay at Worpswede. It is also manifestly under the auspices of the anima archetype, for (as indicated in this chapter's first section) the language of image is preeminently the province of anima. Jung: "the feminine mind is pictorial [*bildlich*] and symbolic."[336] Or, in Rilke's own more poetic parlance: "Only girls do not ask / What bridges lead to images."

Artistically speaking, Rilke's new initiative translates into a concerted effort to render ever more graphically and concretely—in ever more fully realized images—the poet's inner states as well as objective phenomena. That *The Book of Images* represents a significant advance in this direction becomes clear when compared, for instance, with *In My Honor*, Rilke's prior collection of lyric poems. Speaking of *The Book of Images*, Heerikhuizen writes:

> In these poems has been achieved something that was not yet possible in the period of *Early Poems* [a later edition of *In My Honor*]. Each of these poems stands alone; each has a title and deals with one subject in contrast to the poems in *Early Poems* which... float one after another like colourful bubbles on the wind of desire.... In the latter, the subtle play of sounds and associations was wholly aimed at suggesting a fluid unity of all things; now one object at a time is evoked with words that draw an intellectually sharper picture and yet are so full of emotional value that access to intuitive spaciousness remains unhindered.[337]

In a late diary entry from Worpswede, Rilke himself registered his poetic and psychological "progress" in a poem that ultimately appears in *The Book of Images* under just that name:

Progress

And again my deep life rushes louder
as if there were broader banks it now flowed between.
To me things become more intimately related
and all images more completely seen.
Kin to what's nameless and without wishes,
with my thought—as with birds—I reach
from the oak into the windy heavens,
and in the pond's broken-off day
my feeling sinks, as if it stood on fishes.[338]

This remarkable piece details many of the key terms of Rilke's project of poetic and self-transformation even while itself providing a revealing instance of that progress. The poem rehearses salient elements of Rilke's evolving soul-concern: the ever deepening flow of soul life itself; the increased intimacy with things realized in and reflected by more fully realized image-vision; a thought-life that reaches into the realm of spiritual inspiration even while remaining rooted in the earth; and a feeling life acquainted with, and at least partially supported by, the watery element of the unconscious. While the poem may be less accomplished than kindred later productions (a poem such as "Evening," for instance, conveys more universal significance with less self-consciousness and more unified image-content), it clearly points in the direction of many of the best poems in *The Book of Images* and beyond to Rilke's great breakthrough in the art of the image, his *New Poems*.

Interestingly, in its original context in Rilke's diary, "Progess" does not bear the title later awarded to it ("Fortschritt"), but is named simply "Prayer" ("Gebet"). The original name, though, seems somewhat anomalous. In its rather muted, self-reflective tone and solid, self-contained image-form, the poem seems quite distant from the passionate *Gebete* ("prayers") comprising *The Book of Monastic Life*. The archetypal shift differentiating the two may be indicated by comparing the third and fourth lines of this poem with the imagery in the second half of "The hour bows down." In *The Book of Monastic Life*, the speaker's glance plays an active, self-willed masculine role vis-à-vis "the things" that come to it like brides. In "Progress" (or "Prayer"), on the other hand, it is more inner kinship with things than commanding creativity that is claimed. Nor, in the later poem, does the speaker profess to bring things into being by crafting and displaying his images of them. Instead, he merely affirms and appreciates his growing capacity to see more deeply and inwardly into things that exist without his intercession. These subtle yet weighty shifts bespeak the increasing influence of the feminine side of the syzygy in Rilke's creative mind, the new leading role awarded to the anima archetype.

Of course, one cannot rest a comparison of *The Book of Monastic Life* and *The Book of Images* on a brief passage or two. Still, painting with a broader brush confirms the archetypal shift we've begun to trace. The two books, in fact, are widely divergent—both stylistically and thematically—in ways consistent with their distinct titles, and the relevant contrasts reveal much about the significant psychopoetic shifts transpiring in the transition from Russia to Worpswede and beyond. Before sketching further terms of comparison, however, a caveat is necessary, for, in certain respects, at least, these two works are of quite different orders of creation.

The Book of Monastic Life, like most of Rilke's major poetic works (including the two other sections of *The Book of Hours*, *New Poems*, the *Elegies* and the *Sonnets*), originated in a burst of creative inspiration that provided the finished text with an indisputable underlying unity. *The Book of Images*, however, boasts no such inspired origin and, correlatively, exhibits far more heterogeneity than Rilke's other major works. The book was composed over the course of many years. The first edition includes work spanning the years 1898 to 1901, while the second and final edition—dramatically different from the first—includes work dated as late as 1906. The second edition, especially—the one by far more commonly known—is so varied both formally and thematically that it hardly qualifies as a unified work at all but, as Edward Snow states, presents itself more as a kind of "catchall," a barely coherent collection of pieces spanning "the great transitions in Rilke's early life": Lou and Russia, Worpswede, and—later—marriage and Westerwede, Paris and Rodin. Because multiple phases of poetic developments are inscribed in its irregular text, it is impossible to read it in quite the same way one can read far more unified work (such as *The Book of Monastic Life*) composed in the course of a few weeks. Indeed, since only four of the book's sixty-five or so poems (including "Girls" and "Progress") date from Rilke's time at the art colony, one might well question whether *The Book of Images* can rightly be significantly associated with Worpswede at all.

To be sure, any interpretation of Rilke's Worpswede period should draw heavily upon contemporaneous works (such as the poet's diaries and *In and After Worpswede*) and not depend overmuch on *The Book of Images*. Still, I would argue that the collection, while varied, is no mere miscellany, and that the post-Worpswede work in *The Book of Images* (which makes up the largest and most interesting part of the text) follows and builds upon the artistic and psychological developments set in motion in Worpswede, remaining texturally consistent with those developments. Consequently, I would argue that—despite the book's heterogeneity and apparently tangential association with Worpswede—it is possible to identify leading formal and thematic characteristics which earn *The Book of Images* its name, and to draw sharp contrasts between the dominant features of this book and those inscribed in the first part of Rilke's *Book of Hours*. In so doing, we will be hot on the trail of the anima developments at the heart of Rilke's pivotal Worpswede experience.

As we have seen, *The Book of Monastic Life* takes shape as a collection of poem-prayers uttered by a single persona (an icon-painting monk) involved in intimate conversation with God. The monk's "I" and its opposite—God, the divine "Thou"—accordingly figure as the dual foci of the text, formally and thematically. While individual images naturally provide the poetic substance of the work, the religious and formal apparatus tends to subordinate any particular image and poem to the spiritual impetus forming and driving the whole. As in the case of *In My Honor*, the poems are untitled and stand on their own as discrete works of art only imperfectly—just as any one of the series of images composing an iconostasis cannot really be comprehended outside its place in the whole.

In all these crucial respects, Rilke's *Book of Images* presents an altogether different picture. This assortment of diverse, individually titled poems—all of which do stand as self-contained pieces—is not unified by any consistent point of view or poetic persona. Rather, the heterogeneous collection offers a multiplicity of voices and perspective—a tendency that becomes explicit in one of the late, post-Worpswede sequences ("The Voices: Nine Leaves with a Title Leaf"[339]), which presents "songs" ascribed to a variety of figures ("The Song of the Beggar," "The Song of the Blind Man," of the Drunkard, Suicide, Widow, etc.). Just as there is no consistent "I" anchoring point of view, no dominant "Thou" emerges, either. While the collection does include poems of manifestly religious content, these pre- or postdate Rilke's Worpswede stay; moreover, even those poems that do treat of angels, saints, or religious rituals ("The Confirmed" or "The Last Supper") do not prominently feature the figure of "God." What does emerge, though, is—as the book's title promises—a host of images: images generally more concretely realized than had been the case in Rilke's earlier work.

In his diary, Rilke himself reflected upon the difference between the form of consciousness he bore with him upon the Russian journey(s) and the nascent, more consistently creative consciousness he was seeking to develop in Worpswede. An entry shortly after his arrival in Worpswede famously declares that "everything that has truly been seen *must* become a poem,"[340] and laments how little he actually saw—and so made—of Russia. On September 21, immediately after the verse "To live half-unconscious, half in haste / to set down what one saw—how, and where," Rilke wrote:

> I place great trust in this landscape, and will gladly accept from it path and possibilities for many days. Here I can once again simply go along, become, be someone who changes. On the grand tour it

> was a great burden to have to be someone who is firm, someone who stands, someone who remains immovable in the face of the profusely fleeting, the always unexpected....[341]

The "grand tour," of course, refers to the Russia journey—presumably the second, more extensive voyage from which Rilke had returned one month before. In this passage, Rilke indicates a psychological move commensurate with the shift inscribed in his poetic texts. Rilke's description of his frame of mind on the grand tour evokes ego consciousness (the self-consistent "I") in its traditional connection with the hero archetype.[342] He contrasts this with a more receptive, labile, mutable consciousness that can well be linked with anima consciousness—which, as Hillman reminds us, reveals itself as far more changeable, characteristically "reflective and in flux." What registers here—in both Rilke's self-reflective prose and the style and themes of his poetry—is a subtle yet profound move away from a sense of poetic self centered in the quasi-heroic ego (which entertains a complex kinship with the similarly masculine puer archetype) to one guided ever more deeply by a soul or anima-consciousness that does not so much serve or take direction from the ego as much as vice versa. Consequently, Rilke's Worpswede experience represents a watershed on the poet's path toward what Carl Jung called *esse in anima*, that state of being-in-soul Jung recognized as the telos of psychological life and the end of individuation.

It may seem strange to ground the idea of self-realization upon an archetype other than that of the ego, which naturally stands for the "I" in the popular and grammatical imagination. Correlatively, it may appear paradoxical to identify consciousness itself, not with the ego, but with anima insofar as the latter (as we have seen) remains so closely tied to the primordial *unconsciousness* underlying the mystery of human being. Nonetheless, in his book *Anima*, Hillman does precisely that. First, Hillman quotes Jung on reflection:

> "Reflection is a spiritual act that runs counter to the natural process; an act whereby we stop, call something to mind, form a picture, and take up a relation to and come to terms with what we have seen. It should, therefore, be understood as an act of becoming conscious."

...and then continues:

> Far-reaching consequences emerge from these passages. They indicate nothing less than an altogether other vision for the archetypal base of consciousness. If "becoming conscious" has its roots in reflection and if this instinct refers to the anima archetype, then consciousness itself may more appropriately be conceived as based upon anima than upon ego.[343]

In tune with this perspective, one of Rilke's diary passages provides an account of how Paula and Clara's way of being in nature (one Rilke was anxious to emulate) actively turns consciousness *away* from the ego or personal center towards less self-conscious participation in all that is forever happening in its natural surround:

> There is something like selflessness in this way of taking part in nature. I am gradually beginning to comprehend this life that passes through large eyes into eternally waiting souls. This daily attentiveness, alertness, and eagerness of the senses turned outward, this thousandfold seeing and seeing always away from oneself, this not-accompanying-oneself in the changing landscape with one's looks, this being only eye, without having to justify over whom.—This purity of life, this always being joyful because something always is happening, not that it has any bearing on one's own personality, but simply that there is motion and change.[344]

The notions Rilke expresses here are no passing fancies, as soon forgotten as recorded; on the contrary, the drift of these reflections—the idea that nature contemplation leads one away from the center of human personality—becomes a leading motif in the formal theoretical writings that grew directly out of Rilke's Worpswede experience: his 1902 essay "Concerning Landscape" and his monograph *Worpswede*, published in the same year. These later texts emphasize a perspective barely hinted at in Rilke's earlier diary entries: namely, the notion of nature as something essentially, radically foreign to the human being.

> But whoever was to write the history of landscape would find himself immediately, without aids, at the mercy of what was alien, unrelated, incomprehensible to him. We are accustomed to deal with forms, and landscape has no form, we are accustomed to deduce acts of volition from movements, and landscape, when it has movement, does not will. The waters flow, and in them the

> images of things fluctuate and tremble.... let it be confessed: landscape is foreign to us, and we are fearfully alone amongst trees which blossom and by streams which flow.[345]

The tone here, significantly darker than the tone of his diaries, doubtlessly reflects the difficult turns of events that mark the roughly two years intervening between these writings—events we will soon address. Nonetheless, for our present purposes, what is crucial is that, as the monograph develops, it is precisely nature's radical alterity, its *distance* (one of Rilke's favorite concepts) from our familiar human reality that ultimately qualifies it (or the language it supplies) to serve as the fit representative of the artist's deepest secrets, the medium in and through which the truest mysteries of the individual may be confessed. In the kind of paradox (indeed, enantiodromia) that we repeatedly encounter in this discourse on soul, nature—as that which is furthest from our usual human consciousness—turns out to be closest to the artist's heart. In the Modersohn chapter in *Worpswede*, Rilke, after a long passage on aesthetic theory that manifestly harks back to ideas inherited from Lou, writes:

> The artist is always he who wishes to say, who must say something most deeply his own, something solitary, something he shares with no one, and who always tries to express that with the most strange and distant things he can still oversee.... The object meeting this criterion changes from period to period, approaching every more closely actual Nature until, in our day, it coincides with her.[346]

In these reflections upon the complex and paradox-ridden relationship between nature and human personality, the "I" and the "not I," we verge once more upon a theme deeply congruent with the inner working of anima. In his book *Anima*, Hillman describes a psychological factor called the "personal coefficient," the loss of which leads to the clinically recognized phenomenon of "depersonalization"—a psychic state wherein all reality is experienced as fundamentally alien to the self and so void of intrinsic meaning. Classical theory understood the resultant disorientation as a loss of ego. Hillman, however, makes a convincing argument that it is not ego but anima that lends the events of life an inwardly felt, personal significance and so qualifies as the "personal coefficient" in the psychological equation. At the same time, Hillman refuses to identify anima with the sphere of purely personal meaning and human relationship, aggressively promoting anima as a bridge between human life and archetypal realities that transcend the realm of human feeling and personality. In one passage, Hillman rejects the idea that anima is most fundamentally a function serving human relationship:

> It seems odd that anima could ever have been considered as a help in human relationship. In each of her classical shapes she is a non-human or half-human creature, and her effects lead us away from the individually human situation. She makes moods, distortions, illusions, which serve human relatedness only where the persons concerned share the same mood or fantasy.[347]

In another, he aims to divorce anima from the realm of purely personal feeling:

> The feeling that is developed through soul-making is perhaps more impersonal, a detailed sensitivity to the specific worth of psychic contents and attitudes, than it is personal. This development does not proceed from the impersonal to the personal, related, and human. Rather the movement goes from the narrower embrace of my empirical human world and its personal concerns toward archetypal events that put my empirical, personal world in a more significant frame. This frame is given, not by feeling or relatedness, but by the anima whose mythologizing fantasy and reflective function remind of life, fate, death. She does not lead into human feeling, but out of it. As the function that relates conscious and unconscious, she occludes conscious feeling, making it unconscious and making the human, inhuman. She puts other things in mind than the human world.[348]

Rilke's life and art continually embody the difficult interplay of personal and impersonal factors intrinsic to anima. Rilke himself would come to speak of this tension in terms of "life" vs. "art," though in Worpswede he had not yet come to the point of starkly opposing these terms. In light of all we have seen so far, of course, it would be folly to deny the importance of the personal factor; the poetic and spiritual itinerary we are tracing could not conceivably have unfolded as it did in the absence of Rilke's human relationships to Lou, Paula and Clara, and others. At the same time, the dynamic Hillman articulates in the last cited passage also registers clearly in Rilke's poetic biography. Rilke's most intimate relationships did not begin or end solely in the personal sphere but catalyzed (and were catalyzed by) his connection with archetypal, impersonal factors, spiritual and imaginal realities that underlie and overlay the human realm, exceeding the bounds of ego consciousness. In *The Book of Monastic Life*, Rilke tended to sum these forces under the name of (the one) God, a spiritual entity closely linked to the one Self that half-creates it. In Rilke's anima-driven Worpswede phase, the poet's intensified focus on image translates into a heightened interest in forms and genres keyed less to the I-Thou consciousness constitutive of prayer than to more objective presentations of archetypal figures and imaginal soul realities. Insofar as interest in myth and folk tale qualifies as another German Romantic trait constitutive of anima for both Jung and Rilke,[349] Rilke's ongoing engagement with these genres of imagination at Worpswede figure as another manifestation of anima's increasing sway, and—correlatively—what Hillman calls "relativization of the ego," the loosening of the personal self's hold on the reins of consciousness.

Fairy tale—pure dream stuff run through the mill of art—is (like myth) a genre of pure imagination, subsisting with little mixture of historical reality. Heinrich Vogeler and Otto Modersohn's long and productive engagement with fairy tale impressed Rilke deeply, and the poet's essays on these artists pay repeated tribute to the imaginal fabric of the genre that so superbly links the world of the child and the mature artist. (Rilke's essay on Modersohn ends: "He is a quiet, deep man, who possesses his own fairy tales, his own German, northern world."[350]) Rilke's diary discloses that the poet experienced Worpswede itself—especially the world of the Barkenhoff—as wrapped in the magic aura of fairy. "This really is a fairy tale. I sit in a pure white house of gables that is overgrown everywhere with gardens..."[351]; and—just before inscribing his poem "Girls"—

> The round forecourt with the small urns was steeped in white... the silvery world stood, untouched by us, under cool skies, peopled by other beings, and we were not real as long as this lunar fairy tale, with its firmament of stars and forms, endured.[352]

Rilke's newly inspired interest in fairy tale entered his poetic work as well, though in hybrid rather than pure form. Several poems in *In and After Worpswede* draw upon the worlds of myth and fairy tale, offering clearly etched images of patently archetypal figures. In all of these poems, the hand of the anima, "whose mythologizing fantasy and reflective function remind of life, fate, and death" makes itself clearly evident. Take, for instance, the following lyric based upon a Vogeler picture titled "Death and Age." In its evocation of Death, the poem reveals Rilke's growing capacity to shape a poem around a single central, graphically realized image:

From a Worpswede Cycle: Of Death

...He goes before me. I can see him always
yet still fear overtaking him someday.
Bridge boards bend beneath his heavy steps
and his shoulders close the boulevard of trees.

He knows the way, as if the land were his
and the crossroad-arrow-hands—long, dark, slim—
seem to turn away from all the proper places
and secretly—from behind—point to *him.*[353]

While this poem retains the lyric "I," the more balladic "Knight, World, and Moor" (based on Vogeler's picture *On the Edge of the Moor*) dispenses with the first person altogether in its archetypal imaginations of the Knight, Life, and Death. Indeed, insofar as the knight may be taken as representative of the heroic masculine ego, the poem (and the painting) symbolizes the manner in which this ego is confronted with new realities that—in their breadth and variety—exceed the boundaries of the heroic ego's traditional province of control:

Knight, World, and Moor

As if born by dark voices, the moorland
rises up before the weary knight.
And he halts, and hears his heart beat,
beat on the doors of new days
he can barely comprehend.

"On the Edge of the Moor," Heinrich Vogeler, 1900

Of days so wide, one cannot ride around them,
and goals one aims for only in dreams,—
all at once, a thousand hands play the world for him
upon a thousand strings.
There are two things only: Life and Nonbeing,
but how much these mean is clear!
Life is: being the face of blind things
now transfigured; now, stained with tears.

Dying means: riding on the black earth,
on a heavy horse, bearing weapons
that, resting, shine—and making a heavy gesture
under the dark iron... [354]

Another poem pasted into the manuscript of *In and After Worpswede* was actually written before Worpswede—in July of 1899, after Rilke's first Russian journey—and as such presents a revealing formal and thematic contrast with "Knight, World, and Moor."

PRAYER TO SAINT GEORGE'S MIGHT AND NAME

Be greeted, Saint George; your dragon's wounds
gape—like a chasm or darkening maw.
St. George, who led a maiden dressed in silk
out of the Dragon's hold
into the roaring land...
St. George, into whose crown
courage climbs, like liquid sap
taut in the oak trunk in spring.
St. George, without peer:
May you give
your prophetic power to us
and your deep silver knighthood
come over all of us.
Live in us. Live.
Amen.[355]

Not only is the poem-prayer manifestly more religious than "Knight, World, and Moor," it offers a far more traditional picture of the saintly knight whose patently heroic deed remains the center of spiritual attention. True, in Rilke's version, he rescues the gentle maiden (a.k.a. anima), but the action and acclaim are all his, and she is a mere cipher.

That, however, is not the ultimate end of the tale of Rilke's dragon slayer, for Rilke revisits the topos in a tale he wrote in nearby Westerwede (where he was living with his wife Clara) a year after his seminal sojourn in Worpswede. "The Dragon-Slayer"—the closest Rilke ever came to pure fairy tale—bears witness to Rilke's novel interest in the genre in and after Worpswede. The tale begins with these prefatory lines:

> This story begins like a fairy tale, but leads deep into the midst of that which really is. And this it has in common with all authentic fairy tales, from which it diverges in many other respects.[356]

While the meaning of Rilke's opening salvo is clear enough, his introduction's last clause is less so. Perhaps it refers to the fact that, in his atypical tale, the knight—while he does slay a dragon—does not subsequently come to claim the appointed prize (the king's beautiful daughter) because something in the exhausting conquest itself—something the knight learned—prevents him from fulfilling the typical plot. Or perhaps it refers to the unusual point of view from which the tale is told: a kind of inward perspective that sees and experiences matters from within the psyche of the girl, the maiden who—unlike her father—knows the knight to whom she belongs (both by public decree and the private decree of her heart) will not come. And perhaps these differences in plot and in point of view are ultimately the *same* difference, because it is precisely in the space opened by them that the possibility of the maiden's own inner freedom—her discovery of her own, independent destiny—lies. "The Dragon-Slayer" thus unfolds as a story symbolizing the changing relationship between the heroic ego and the soul; a tale of the linked transformation of both under the aegis of the autonomy of the anima and her new historical horizons. It is also a story of impossible love, one Rilke would tell many times in many guises in the course of his life.

This issue of personal autonomy and individual destiny—especially that of a young woman—figures at the center of another poem that appears in both *In and After Worpswede* and *The Book of Images*, "The Singer Sings Before a Child of Princes."

In *The Book of Images*, "The Singer Sings" is grouped with a host of other poems that—while widely diverse—all share a close relation to another genre important to Rilke: legend. Indeed, while fairy tale lent its magic hue to Rilke's life and work at Worpswede, he inclined more naturally toward the genre that more evenly blends purely mythic and historical elements. Insofar as Ellenberger cites "a new feeling for history," as yet another aspect of the German Romantic anima—one related to but distinct from interest in myth and folktale—the encounter with the past inherent to the legend qualifies, once more, as a province within the domain of anima. This province (like all the others) is, too, a bridge fraught with tension.

Hillman, drawing upon Jung, speaks of anima as a culturally determined and determining factor that immerses us in the feeling of a peculiar history; speaks of anima, that is, as a "conservative ancestress who roots our human feeling in her historical soil." At the same time, he recognizes "another impersonal factor in anima which is individual, endogenous, and independent of the racial unconscious....(bringing) an individual fate and...style of feeling." This concatenation of historical influence and individual destiny figures as still another of the paradoxical conjunctions intrinsic to the anima archetype, determining "anima as an ancestrally ethnic dominant on the one hand, and, on the other, as an individually fateful constellation."[357] It is precisely this internal contradiction that Rilke elaborates in "The Singer Sings Before the Child of Princes," which gathers and rehearses many of the anima motifs we have been discussing.

The poem's opening echoes and combines motifs sounded in "Girls I" and "Girls II" while inflecting them with the historical tenor of legendary song:

> You pale child, every evening the singer
> shall stand in the shadows among your things.
> Over the bridge of his voice and the strings
> of the harp filled with his hands, he
> shall bring you legends that ring in the blood.

The next stanza gives a succinct account of the singer's strange relation to temporal reality, registering his claim that the fine cloth woven by the imagination *is* reality:

> Not out of time comes what he tells you,
> it's as if lifted out of tapestries;
> there never were such forms of love or strife
> and what never existed, he calls Life.

The poem then proceeds to perform a long and complex riff on the multiple valences of (the word) "image" (*Bild*). The poet imagines this "royal" child of princes so deeply and unconsciously steeped in her ancestry that the figures staring at her from portraits (*Bildern*) in the great hallway preempt every feeling gesture of her own soul. After inventorying all the child has inherited from her forebears:

> You have pearls from them, and you have turquoise
> from these women, who stand in their portraits
> as if lingering in a meadow at evening...
>
> You wear the jewels from their waistbands...
> and your small books are bound in the silk
> of soft bridal gowns...

...the singer laments:

> It's as if everything already happened.
> They have put their lips to the goblets
> as if you would never touch them with your own;
> stirred their passions to sample every joy
> and left not one grief , one sorrow, unnamed
> so that you now stand here
> and feel ashamed.

Even so, the singer comes to affirm the child's unique identity in the literal and figural face of all this rich yet oppressive past, declaring, in fact, that her true individuality rests upon this same layered ground:

> You, pale child, yours too is a life,
> the singer comes to tell you that you are...
> Your life is so ineffably your own
> because it is burdened with so many.

The poem's celebratory closing cinches the dialectal resolution of the tension of past and present, reaffirming the child's unique destiny as a kind of sublimation of the past. It does so, moreover, in terms that mirror the reflective consciousness instinct in anima:

> Past upon past is planted within you
> in order to arise from you, like a garden.
>
> You pale child, you make the singer rich
> with your destiny, which calls forth praise:
> so does a great garden party with many lights
> mirror itself in the astonished lake.
> In the dark poet, every thing
> is repeated: star, forest, house, gate.
> And your stirring form is quietly surrounded
> by the many things he'll celebrate.[358]

Weighty and somewhat overwrought, "The Singer Sings Before a Child of Princes" is not Rilke's most accomplished Worpswede poem. It is of special interest, though, not only because of its transparent mirroring of diverse anima themes but also because it is one of the very last poems Rilke wrote at Worpswede (he inscribed it in his diary on October

3) and because it reveals much about his relationship to Paula, to whom he dedicated the poem when it appeared in *The Book of Images*. When Rilke precipitously and unexpectedly left Worpswede a mere two days later, it was one of the poems included in a notebook he left—in lieu of a personal farewell—behind for her, one of the two "sisters in white" whose anima-nature made so indelible an impression upon the poet's own continually evolving psyche.

CHAPTER 7

BLACK GLINT

Evidence indicates that Rilke did not so much leave Worpswede as flee it. His departure was unanticipated, sudden, and secretive. The poet, after all, had recently decided to stay in Worpswede. His long September 27 journal entry includes an account of "The Family's" collective trip to Hamburg and concludes, "We arrived back in Worpswede by mail coach. Beautiful, still, starry night, festive and so apt for a homecoming. It was at that moment that I decided to stay in Worpswede."[359] Shortly thereafter, Rilke rented a house in which to spend the winter. Yet just a few days later—early on the morning of October 5—he left by mail coach for Berlin without bidding farewell to anyone. When Paula and Clara arose that morning, Worpswede's poet-in-residence was gone. Gone too—sooner or later—were two pages of his journal which Rilke evidently ripped out, destroying the only record that might have unambiguously revealed the true cause of his precipitous departure.

Rilke did, in short order, provide reasons to Paula, Clara, and the others by post. He cited the outward necessity of looking after the exhibition of Russian art he was midwifing (unsuccessfully so, as it turned out) and (in another letter) the more inward necessity of returning focus to Russian things and the lifestyle he had known before Worpswede. Such justifications were probably not entirely fabulated, but do little to explain Rilke's violent haste or the missing journal pages. More plausible, on the face of it, is Petzet's suggestion[360] that Rilke had somehow learned of Paula's secret engagement to Modersohn and that this most unwelcome revelation drove him, posthaste, from the haven that had just begun to feel like home.

While we shall never be certain of the cause of Rilke's departure, we do have definite poetic evidence of the deep psychological shift that marked its wake. Following the torn-out pages in his journal, we find the final two stanzas of a poem evidently written in Berlin between October 5 and the next dated entry on October 21. We know the whole of it because it later appeared, in its entirety, in *The Book of Images*:

Solemn Hour

Whoever weeps now anywhere in the world,
    weeps without reason in the world,
    weeps for me.

Whoever laughs now anywhere in the night,
    laughs without reason in the night,
    laughs at me.

Whoever walks now anywhere in the world,
    walks without reason in the world
    walks toward me.

Whoever dies now anywhere in the world,
    dies without reason in the world,
    looks at me.[361]

The tenor of keen despair sounded here diverges dramatically from the largely affirmative, reverential, and celebratory tone of the poems (e.g., "Progress" or "A Singer Sings") Rilke had been writing shortly before in Worpswede. To be sure, the poet's lyre had long known strains of darkness, but this poem, with its consistent reiteration of the phrase *ohne Grund* ("without cause or reason"), strikes a distinct note, conveying the sense of someone who has just had the spiritual wind knocked out of him, someone whose life has suddenly lost vital meaning and purpose, someone who has suffered—and is suffering through—psychological death. Another, less self-centered poem from the same journal entry imagines a woodscape pervaded by a like feeling of the utter senselessness born of death and decay, effectively shaping a world made wholly of that soul mood. "Apprehension" ("Bangnis") offers a good example of Rilke's poetic progress, his ability to lend feeling imaginatively palpable form:

Apprehension

In the withered wood there is a birdcall
that seems senseless in this withered wood.
And yet the rounded birdcall rests
in this interval that shaped it,
wide as a sky upon the withered wood.
Everything makes room inside the cry.
The whole land seems to lie soundlessly within it,
the strong wind appears to nestle inside,
and the moment, which still wants to go on,
is pale and silent, as if it knew things
which, for anyone, must mean death
risen out of it.[362]

Rilke liked to employ the image of a wood or forest as a representation of the region of the soul itself, the topos of the psyche. In the famous first *Sonnet to Orpheus*, the wood/world is *klar/aufgelöst*—language which denotes clarity and imaginative transparency. Here, however, this poem's obsessively repeated phrase—*welken Walde*—denotes a *faded* or *withered* wood, and conveys a psychic state of loss or degeneration, a movement *away* from vivid life. As in "Solemn Hour," the key (albeit behind-the-scenes) character puts in appearance only at the end: the world of this wood, the moment of this poem, is haunted by a premonition of death. It is death's invisible specter, uncannily heard in the cry of the bird, which engenders the undercurrent of angst that saturates and names the poem.

In early November, Rilke attended a performance of Maeterlinck's play *The Death of Tintagiles*. Immediately thereafter, Rilke wrote in his journal,

> From dreams we have learned that feelings are large and spacious. Often under the shelter of sleep actions take place that according to the rule of nature would have to rest in separate regions of feeling, and which in reality could only be played out in successive, shifting scenes. But in a dream everything takes place on *one* stage, *one* feeling stretches out far as a sky and remains arched over all events.[363]

Whatever merit the passage may have as dramatic criticism, Rilke had already put these ideas into practice in his lyric work; the title "Apprehension" clearly names the "one feeling" that "stretches out far as the sky and remains arched over all events."

A well-known lyric ("Klage") recorded on October 21 opens on the same chord:

LAMENT

O how everything is far away
and long gone by.
I believe the star
from which I receive light
has been dead for thousands of years.
In the boat which just
slipped by, I think I heard
something frightful being spoken.

...though the poem does take a more positive turn towards the end:

I would like to pray.
And surely one of all those stars
must still exist.
I think I might know
which one alone
endured—
which one stands like a white city in the sky
at the end of its road of light.[364]

A ray of hope shines through; still, how far Rilke has come from the eternally youthful vision of *The Book of Monastic Life*! There, the whole world was of the future, an open and unlimited promise of creative capability: here, the celestial glint of heaven is a thing of the past, and the hand of death rests upon the stars themselves. There, poetic consciousness likened itself to the eternal "silence of the stars" enfolding "the city of time"; here, fallen away from the infinite canopy of the all, the most it can dream of is to look from afar upon a single, distant glimmer of hope. There, the self was one with the world and all was made of prayer; here, the lonely, isolate poetic voice can only weakly intone a timid desire to pray.

Let us return, for a moment, to Maeterlinck's drama and Rilke's commentary upon it, for this will further help identify that "one feeling" that came, more and more, to characterize Rilke's soul mood in Berlin. In accord with his own anima-driven artistic praxis, Rilke applauded *The Death of Tintagiles* on account of the revolutionary manner in which it achieved "the displacement of the center of gravity from the external plot as such to the region of the soul." Rilke's articulation of the psychological ground of dramatic art is significant, but so too is his repeated reference to the *particular* feeling that played the leading role in the Maeterlinck's play:

> Maeterlinck's drama, with all its events and circumstances, with its tenderness and longing and infinitely fragile happiness, has been shaped inside one feeling, inside this great gray fear that manifests itself as the eternal vis-à-vis all events, that is already in existence when the curtain rises and that doesn't cease with the desperate curse of Ygraine.[365]

As "Solemn Hour," "Apprehension" and, to some extent, "Lament" indicate, Rilke is here painting a picture, not only of Maeterlinck's world, but of his own. That "gray fear"—sometimes great and terrible, sometimes small and niggling, and not seldom turning from one to the other with frightening alacrity—was fast becoming the dominant feature of his psychic state after his abrupt removal from Worpswede.

Nor, in light of the biographical facts, is it too difficult to see why. Whatever romantic hopes he had pinned on Paula were more or less shattered—if not by private, then soon by public discovery, for (at Modersohn's vexed insistence) she herself let Rilke know where things stood in mid-November. Meanwhile, although Rilke was trying to reestablish himself in Berlin, matters there too were tending towards unhappy endings. He had resumed some of his accustomed routines with Lou (walks, talks, social events, shared meals at the Andreas household), but the downward spiral of their emotional relationship continued, so much so that at one point Lou wrote: "Oh, if Rainer would just go away, *go away completely*! I'd be capable of a brutal act."[366] For all that, Lou remained a crucial liaison to all the "Russian things" still so important to Rilke. The fraying of their relationship accordingly endangered his Russian connections, psychologically and materially—all the more so since the threads of his own pet Russian projects (the staging of an art exhibit, translating Benois) were fast unraveling and coming to nought. Rilke's life, at this point, lacked a professional center. While his commitment to his art remained unquestioned, viable means of earning income appeared few, and dwindling.

That state of affairs undoubtedly contributed to the heart of the matter: the emotional limbo in which Rilke lived in the four or five months after his departure from Worpswede. For although Rilke had physically left the colony, he remained intimately involved—through correspondence, visits, and imaginative writing—with the Worpswede artists, especially Paula and Clara. Knowledge of Paula's engagement by no means immediately terminated their relationship, though—naturally enough—Rilke's correspondence reveals some diminution in the intensity of his communication with Paula and increasing investment in the relationship with Clara, who made no secret of her interest in the poet. Rilke lived torn between worlds, psychically and physically: between Berlin and Worpswede; between Lou and Paula and Clara; between past and future. The emotional crosscurrents were strong and racking, and it is hardly surprising that a young man (he was, after all, only in his mid twenties) of Rilke's melancholic temper found his life invaded by "great gray fear." On December 13, Rilke gave this tellingly grim account of himself:

> It is an infinite humiliation to enroll here the names of the last several days; but for just that reason I shall do so and do so briefly.
>
> If every death (like every life) has been allotted a certain portion of time, then days like the last ones will have to be counted up and deducted from its sum. For they are days spent beneath the earth, days in dampness and decay.... Such stretches of hopelessness, such gaspings of the soul. And should they once *not* come to an end, not cast away, not suddenly become untrue: if one had to name all this "I," this unspeakably disconnected, helplessly isolated consciousness that, cut off from the voices of silence, falls into itself as into an empty well, as into the depths of a pool that contains stagnant water and animals gestating in muck. What is one then.... it is so frighteningly easy to die in this state. It is dying itself.[367]

Rilke's personal state, however, was not simply that ("personal states" never are), but was rooted in the archetypal psychological development named, variously, the *nigredo*, the *mortificatio*, or—most simply and powerfully—"Death." In the sequence of developmental stages Jung traces in *The Psychology of Transference*—a book based upon a series of illustrations contained in a medieval alchemical text—the sixth stage, "Death," follows upon one called "The Conjunction." The relevant chapter begins:

> King and queen are dead and have melted into a single being with two heads. The feast of life is followed by the funereal threnody. Just as Gabricus dies after becoming united with his sister, and the son-lover always comes to an early end after consummating the *hieros gamos* with the mother-goddess... so after the *coniunctio oppositorum*, deathlike stillness reigns. When the opposites unite, all energy ceases: there is no more flow. The waterfall has plunged to its full depth in that torrent of nuptial joy and longing; now only a stagnant pool remains, without wave or current.[368]

This order of affairs resonates with Rilke's case. For while Rilke's slough of despond followed most immediately upon his Worpswede sojourn, the six weeks there—despite their deep significance—stand in the shadow of the watershed years with Lou. We have already spoken of the relevance of the incest analogy in connection with Rilke and Lou's love and borne witness to the "torrent of nuptial joy and longing" that transformed Rilke's life and art, including the manner in which the God of *The Book of Monastic Life* can be construed as, precisely, a conjunction of opposites, or *coincidentia oppositorum*. From one perspective, the intimacy with "the girls" or "sisters in white" at Worpswede could be seen as a last ripple of that great wave, the *imagination* of incestuous union consummated not as son-lover (as was, in part, the case with Lou) but as brother-lover. In both (overlapping) events, in the aftermath of initially intense and intimate intercourse, a cessation—violently abrupt as well as long and drawn out—ensued, a loss of love energy experienced as nothing less than the loss of life itself—Death.

It is striking that Jung and Rilke employ the identical metaphor to image this state of affairs: the living water of the soul becomes *a stagnant pool*. Jung further amplifies the condition: "The situation... is a kind of Ash Wednesday... a dark abyss yawns. Death means the total extinction of consciousness and the complete stagnation of psychic life."[369] Rilke's journal continues in a similar vein:

> It is dying itself. The growing indifferent and the balancing with the weight of one's own inertia an opposite pan full of doubts and

> putrescences. What good are the efforts one makes ever more sluggishly, ever more wearily, ever more laboriously.... One's will is there... but it is like a piece of conduit that has hit rock. One tries: uprisings, ascents, one wants to get moving, one stands for a while, and it all comes to this: one lies down, lies down...[370]

The pool, moreover, is not merely stagnant: it is (as Rilke's own wording indicates) *putrid*. The alchemical *mortificatio* is always simultaneously a *putrefactio*. Jung: "The picture represents the putrefactio, the corruption, the decay of a once living creature."[371] Jung continues to elaborate this idea—including its putative moral dimension—in a manner that explains the association of this stage with the alchemical *nigredo*, or *blackening* of the work:

> One cannot rid oneself of the impression that the death is a sort of tacit punishment for the sin of incest, for "the wages of sin is death." That would explain the soul's "great distress" and also the blackness mentioned in the variant of the picture. ("Here is Sol turned black.") This blackness is the *immunditia* (uncleanliness)...
>
> The *coniunctio* was incestuous and therefore sinful, leaving pollution behind it. The *nigredo* always appears in conjunction with *tenebrositas*, the darkness of the tomb and of Hades.[372]

Rilke, still from December 13:

> One becomes ever so humble, humble to the point of baseness. Humble like a dog with a guilty conscience. Flat, without feeling and filled only with fear, fear of everything that does and does not happen, of what exists and of any change in what one can scarcely bear.... Deluge and sin's malediction. And this again and again...[373]

The evidence seems clear: Rilke, after Worpswede, entered a distinct phase of soul life, the deep psychic travail characteristic of the *nigredo*. Though it was neither the first nor the last time he would experience and exhibit the classic symptoms of the syndrome, the period following Rilke's removal from Worpswede does mark a crucial dark dawn, one that ushers in the pitched and prolonged confrontation with fear, suffering, and (above all) death that lies at the threshold of both his psychological and poetic maturity. The seeds of Rilke's future literary career—from the finishing of *The Book of Hours* all the way through the *Elegies* and *Sonnets to Orpheus*—were planted at this time, sown in the soil of the emotional and spiritual challenges embedded in it. Moreover—as a direct effect of the train of inner and outer events set in motion by his departure from Worpswede—the outlines of Rilke's personal and professional life finally took lasting form.

It was in the months and years immediately following his departure from Worpswede that the lines of Rilke's poetic destiny began to emerge most clearly, a development that depended—like a photographic negative—on a dark background. The theory of the *nigredo* is unequivocal on this point: Death's black coat does have a silver lining.

Many alchemical texts testify to the indispensable value of the *mortificatio* or *nigredo.*

> *Mortificatio* is the most negative operation in alchemy. It has to do with darkness, defeat, torture, mutilation, death, and rotting. However, these dark images often lead over to highly positive ones—growth, resurrection, rebirth—but the hallmark of *mortificatio* is the color black.[374]

The Golden Treatise of Hermes gives the same thought more poetic—and more powerful— expression:

> O happy gate of blackness, cries the sage, which art the passage to this so glorious change. Study, therefore, whosoever appliest thyself to this Art, only to know this secret, for to know this is to know all, but to be ignorant of this is to be ignorant of all. For putrefaction precedes the generation of every new form into existence.[375]

This passage provides apt indication of the immense importance attached to the *nigredo* in the alchemical opus. Most often conceived as the beginning of the real work, it is the prerequisite of the process of alchemical transformation—which process Jung, of course, employed as a model of soul development or individuation. Only two other processes (each likewise identified by color) are as basic to the language of alchemy: the *albedo*, or whitening, and the *rubedo*, or reddening. Even so, the *nigredo*, typically regarded as the first, initiating step (followed by the purifying *albedo* and, finally, the fullness of life characterized by the climactic *rubedo*) retains the priority due its inaugural position. It is a privilege that Rilke, poet of the soul, intuitively recognized.

While Rilke may not have been consciously conversant with the language of alchemy, the poetry of his post-Worpswede phase nonetheless mirrors the archetypal dynamics encoded in alchemy's color theory. After Rilke wrote the long desperate journal entry on December 13 (it ends: "This had to be written as a sign for myself. God help me"), he recorded another, separate entry under the same date, a poem titled (in yet another permutation!) "Prayer," which begins:

> Night, silent night, into which are woven
> purely white things, red, brightly dappled things,
> scattered colors, which are lifted
> into one darkness, one silence,—bring me too
> into relation to that rich variety
> you persuade to become part of you.[376]

It is striking that Rilke, in his effort to come to terms with his excruciating despair, makes recourse to color imagery. It is still more so that he unerringly singles out the alchemical primaries: black (represented by the all-important "night" and "darkness"), white, and red—in that order—as he seeks imaginative means to signal to himself the possibility of his soul's revivification. This (separately dated December 13) entry consists entirely of this poem followed by a single closing sentence, one that glimpses light at the end of the dark tunnel: "After many incredibly heavy and vague days, today I experienced an hour of sunshine in the woods."

This poem, however, was by no means the first in this interim time to feature elements consistent with alchemical color theory, and certainly not the first to figure the singularly charged matter of the *nigredo*. This passage from the *Rosarium Philosophorum* (Jung's chosen alchemical text) reflects, once more, on "Prayer":

> O blessed Nature, blessed are thy works, for that thou makest the imperfect to be perfect through the true putrefaction, which is dark and black. Afterwards thou makest new and multitudinous things to grow, causing with thy verdure the many colours to appear.[377]

Jung writes:

> The appearance of the colours in the alchemical vessel...denotes the spring, the renewal of life—*post tenebras lux*. The text [the *Rosarium*] continues: "This blackness is called earth." The Mercurius in whom the sun drowns is an earth spirit.[378]

This further connection of blackness with earth illumines a poem already cited in the last chapter—"Knight, World, and Moor," recorded in Rilke's journal on October 28. The poem concludes:

> Dying means: riding on the black earth,
> bearing weapons, that, resting, shine,
> on a heavy horse, to make a heavy gesture
> under the dark iron....
>
> With this gesture to wake one's Mother
> and bury oneself in warm arms—
> (among the roots is just room enough)
> and—to raise a tree from one's heart,
> a red,
> rustling tree:
> such is Death.[379]

Rilke's writing not only makes explicit the natural connection of *death* with *black earth*, it also (though admittedly passing over the intermediate *albedo*) images the rebirth of life that may emerge from death's dark soil. The climactic *rubedo* that crowns the alchemical opus reappears here in the form of a red tree of life rising out of the buried (and presumably decayed) heart, from which blood-center the tree borrows the *rubedo*'s signature color.

In speaking of the transformative potential latent in the *nigredo*, we should not, however, pass too lightly beyond the heavy, dark, physical and psychical corruption that characterizes the substance of the *nigredo* itself. The psychic episode shears all means of spiritual flight from the soul, and—as imaged in a poem Rilke inscribed into his diary on November 7 (roughly a month after his departure from Worpswede, and a month before the dire December entry to which it is kin)—sends it plunging down and into the jealously insensate earth:

Fragments from Lost Days

> ...Like birds that get used to walking
> and become heavier and heavier, as if in free fall:
> the earth sucks out of their long claws
> the brave memory of all
> the great things that happen up high,
> and turns them almost into leaves that hold
> close to the ground,—
> like plants which,
> loath to grow upward, pull back toward the soil,
> sink lightly and softly and wetly
> into black clods and sicken there lifelessly,—

After this opening, the poem proceeds—in a somewhat loosely formed stream-of-consciousness style that bespeaks its psychic intensity—to chant an almost two-page-long litany of images of decay, affliction, and dismemberment: mad children; a face in a coffin; desiccated house-plants; brothels; hospitals; torn and withered garden huts that can no longer house secret lovers; drunkards; curses; buried corpses and dead flowers. All this (as the poetic voice tells us toward the end) figures the speaker's own existence, tortured as it is by some strange spiritual voodoo:

> And many a day's hours were like that.
> As if someone stitched my likeness somewhere
> so as to slowly torment it with needles.

Rilke's distress, however—even at its most intense—did not translate into utter hopelessness. Indeed, one sometimes has the sense of the poet giving full play to his darkest imagination in order to induce the transformation that (alchemically speaking) depends upon distillation of the psyche's black substance. Here, too, the silver lining shows through at the close:

> I felt each sharp prick of his malice,
> and it was: as if a rain fell on me
> in which all things change.[380]

Another Rilke poem ("Der Kahn" or "The Skiff") from the series based on Vogeler's pictures offers a version of the *nigredo* theme in connection with religious life. The poem evokes a figure who, if he is not

Death himself, is intimately connected with him, and who ministers to infants, the sick, the old, and the lost in strange (yet strangely effective) ways. This figure's treatment of the spiritually dispossessed is particularly potent:

> ...and on the wall
> he hangs those who have lost God
> like limp clothes soaked
> with black water out of stagnant ponds.

The image—fusing the signature *nigredo* motifs of blackness and stagnant water—may imply that only by being fully steeped in the element of death may spiritual life, perhaps, be resuscitated, a reading confirmed by the poem's conclusion:

> He who stands as the one most strange to Life
> is like the towers above a city
> watching all that shimmers, falls, and fades
> and around whom the evening wind circles as if in thirst,
> for in his hands he holds those bells
> that summon all to prayer.[381]

This poem lifts the *nigredo* theme out of the psychodrama of one individual's "lost days" into a wider, more collective context. Interpreting a passage from an alchemical text, Edinger writes: "This way of putting it implies that what is undergoing *mortificatio* and rejuvenation is nothing less than the collective God-image."[382] The same might be said of Rilke's "The Skiff."

Still, the crisis, and Rilke's response to it, remained deeply rooted in individual relationships. It is therefore fitting that Rilke's most extended and elevated treatment of the *nigredo* theme at this time unfolded in the form of a poem dedicated to Clara—a poem, in fact, drawn directly from an episode in Clara's own life, and spoken in her voice. "Requiem"—ultimately placed as the penultimate piece in *The Book of Images*—prefigures and prepares Rilke's later, far more famous and accomplished "Requiem for a Friend" to and for Paula. Indeed, in a strange twist of fate, the poem was composed on the date (November 20) Paula herself would die seven years later. The two requiems represent crucial incursions into the elegiac mode that would later issue in Rilke's famous masterpiece, the *Duino Elegies.*

"Requiem" revolves around a childhood friend of Clara's (whom Rilke did not know) who had just died at a young age. Clara's letter relating this circumstance and her personal response to it afforded Rilke the opportunity to confront the phenomenon of death at a safe remove from his own dark frame of mind. "Requiem" consequently has a markedly different tone and tenor than the poems issuing more directly from Rilke's own despair. The donning of a persona and the elegiac idiom both contribute to a poetic consciousness that seeks to *see through* the fact of death to its deeper archetypal character and spiritual meaning. Indeed, the intensely speculative form of imagination practiced in the poem qualifies as a distinct mode of soul-making, one which we will examine in depth in later chapters devoted to the *Duino Elegies*.

Rilke's more philosophical handling of the matter of death does not, however, mean that his "Requiem"—or the journal material which immediately preceded and prepared the writing of the poem—relies any less forcefully upon *nigredo* imagery. The relevant journal prose opens as follows:

> Clara writes today about a black wreath, and what she recounts is again a work of art. The way she speaks of this heavy black wreath that she took down unsuspectingly from the gable of her house and brought in out of the gray November air and that then became so monstrously earnest in her room, a thing unto itself, suddenly one thing more, and a thing that seems to grow constantly heavier, drinking up as it were all the grief in the air of the room and in the early twilight. And all this shall lie then in the thin wooden coffin of the poor girl who died in the South, in the hands of the sun. The black wreath may cause the coffin to cave in, and then its long tendrils will creep up along the white shroud and grow into the folded hands...and grow into the heart that, full of congealed blood, has also become black.[383]

The entire poem revolves around the figure of the black wreath. Not only is the blackening of the powerful life force represented by the ivy itself a most evocative *nigredo* symbol, its juxtaposition with the fact of young Gretel's death "in the hands of the sun" evokes perhaps the most classic alchemical image of the *nigredo*: the black sun, or *sol niger*. It is interesting to note, moreover, that the black wreath itself is a patently psychological phenomenon; viewed by the light of day, the ivy wreath (not itself dead) would appear, not black, but green. It is the darkness of Clara's room in the evening—a darkness symbolically identified with loss and grief—that lends the wreath its unnatural but powerfully evocative color. The poem begins:

> For an hour now, earth is more
> by one thing. More by a wreath.
> A while ago, it was light leaves. . . . I turned it:
> and now this ivy is strangely heavy
> and full of darkness, as if it had drunk
> future nights out of my things.
> Now I almost dread the coming night
> alone with this wreath I made,
> not suspecting that something enters existence
> when the tendrils twist around the hoop;
> and deeply needing to understand just this:
> *that something can be no more.*

From the outset, the poem strikes a metaphysical note. It queries the mystery of being and its negation, juxtaposing the *addition* of something to earthly existence with the *subtraction* of something else, and so poses the question of what it means *to be* and *not to be*. The whole poem seeks to solve the difficult spiritual arithmetic introduced here: to figure the relationship of (or *difference between*) life and death. Later, the poetic voice expresses confidence that the earth itself holds the answer to this problem of the relative weights of these two existential primaries. In a phrase italicized for emphasis, Clara assures the dead Gretel: "The earth is full of balance. Your earth." But how to formulate the equation figuring this sum? As the ending of one of his most famous *Sonnets to Orpheus* testifies,[384] it is a problem that occupies Rilke for the rest of his life and—as "Requiem" reveals—counts as a question of *destiny.*

The poem continues:

> Gretel, from the beginning of all things,
> it was destined that you would die so early,
> die still fair.
> Long before you were sent into life.

As Torgersen notes, the poem provides an early instance of Rilke's notion—drawn from Jacobson—of the *individual death* that figures the *authentic end of life*, the vessel of inner meaning or hidden destiny towards which true life tends.[385] The idea emerges as a central one for Rilke: we will encounter it at the end of this section on *Death and the Maiden* as a central leitmotif of Rilke's *Book of Poverty and Death*, and later on in *Malte*, before it gets woven into the very texture of the *Elegies* and *Sonnets*. In this poem, though, Rilke elaborates the idea by making audacious use of another tragic personal circumstance. Rilke conceives of the prior death of Gretel's two older siblings (a brother and sister) as a predestined tutelage and preparation for Gretel's own; imagines that these siblings passed on before her in order to show her how to die.

> Your brother and sister were invented
> only in order that you might become accustomed to it....
>
> For your death, these lives arose;
> hands, that bound flowers into bouquets,
> eyes, that perceived the redness of roses,
> and the might of human beings
> were made and destroyed
> and twice death was *prepared* and *performed*
> before it stepped from the dark theatre
> and directed itself towards you.

The phrase "prepared and performed" awkwardly translates a single, and singularly potent, German word, *gedichtet*, italicized in Rilke's original. The term means to compose poetically—or, in another, more literal definition, to *thicken*. Rilke's wording therefore implies that Gretel's siblings died in order to thicken the plot of her passage, to lend spiritual substance to the process of her dying. The alchemical resonance of Rilke's diction merits special note, for in alchemy the success of the *opus* depends upon the delicate and difficult process of distilling the black substance, capturing from the complex ferment the residual gist of the *nigredo*. Similarly, in the heated crucible of his poetry, Rilke—via Gretel and Clara—is slowly working towards the essence of death.

We have already indicated just how important the *nigredo* is in alchemy; psychologically, too, death is intrinsically *of the essence*. In his early, pathbreaking *Suicide and the Soul*, Hillman writes:

> Working at the death problem is both a dying from the world with its illusory sustaining hope that there is no death, not really, and a dying into life, as a fresh and vital concern with essentials. *Because living and dying in this sense imply each other, any act which holds off death prevents life.* "How" to die means nothing less than "how" to live.[386]

It is, indeed, no accident that Hillman inaugurates the entire project of his soul-centered psychology under the auspices of death and the question it puts to life. In so doing, Hillman makes clear the crucial difference—one we have implied yet not stated—between *physical death* and *death as a psychological reality*. To be sure, psychological reflections of death may ultimately derive from actual mortality, but the former nonetheless represent a distinct and independent order of reality. Hillman: "Death and existence may exclude each other in rational philosophy, but they are not psychological contraries. Death can be experienced as a state of being, an existential condition..." and, relatedly, "The fear of dying concerns the experience of death, which is separable from physical death and not dependent upon it."[387]

In *Suicide and the Soul*, Hillman argues that it is precisely in and through imaginations of death—be it in suicidal fantasy or (as in the case of Rilke's "Requiem") other means of forging direct connection with the other side—that soul reality distinguishes itself most sharply from mere corporeal existence:

> *Suicide fantasies provide freedom from the actual and usual view of things, enabling one to meet the realities of the soul.* These realities appear as images and voices, as well as impulses, with which one can communicate. But for these conversations with death one must take the realm of the soul—with its night spirits, its uncanny emotions and shapeless voices, where life is disembodied and highly autonomous, as reality.[388]

Rilke's "Requiem"—one of his first prolonged meditations on death—unfolds as just such a night-life conversation, mediated by vaguely eerie images and half-heard voices. In it, the dead Gretel represents and personifies death's perspective, but it is Clara's imagined voice we hear bridging the worlds of the living and the dead, querying the soul of her friend about the very heart of the death experience and arriving at knowledge through the momentum of her own questioning:

Was it frightening when it came near, beloved playmate?
Was it your enemy?
Did you weep upon its heart...?
...How did it look?
You must know...
It was for this you traveled home.

You know
how the almond trees bloom
and that lakes are blue.
Many things that exist only in the feelings
of a woman in the throes of first love,—
you know.

The lines attribute insight into essence—*the intimately entwined essences of death and of life*—to Clara, here Rilke's poetic persona. In so doing, they directly adumbrate not only the major theme of the *Duino Elegies* but particular passages of that work as well. In another section of "Requiem," Rilke moves from Gretel's initial experience of death (the *mortificatio*) to its lingering effects. In a strangely improbable train of thought, Rilke imagines "the black weight" of the ivy breaking through and into the coffin; winding around—and even into—Gretel's body:

But you are no longer closed.
You are stretched out and relaxed.
The doors of your body are left ajar,
and the moist ivy enters in....

like rows
of nuns
who guide themselves
along a black rope....
Through the empty halls
of your blood they press on toward your heart...
wandering, as if in prayer
into your heart, which, completely soundless,
and dark, stands open to all.

This passage displays the language of "Requiem" prefiguring, not only the *Elegies*, but other major Rilke works as well. The religiously sanitized version of the *putrefactio* Rilke offers here is bracketed by imagery of death's openness, revealing Gretel as a direct precursor of the Eurydice figure that appears first in Rilke's *New Poems* and later (inspired, once again, by the death of a young girl) in the *Sonnets*. Clearly, in "Requiem," Rilke is tilling fertile soil.

As befits "Requiem's" fateful occasion, we have been focusing intently upon images of death and its aftermath. In so doing, however, we should not lose sight of the intimate connection between death and the misery and melancholia that function as its psychological corollaries. Another Hillman passage helps clarify the intellectual segue between Rilke's own despair and the kind of redemptive imaginative colloquy enacted in "Requiem":

> Melancholy, that black affliction in which so many suicides occur, shows the pull of gravity downward into the dark, cold bones of reality. Depression narrows and concentrates upon essences, and suicide is the final denial of existence for the sake of essence.[389]

By citing Hillman's *Suicide and the Soul*, I do not mean to imply that Rilke himself was suicidal at this time. Even so, Hillman does make the powerful point that suicide represents a psychological choice—the only one—"which asks directly for the death experience,"[390] and shades of the theme did flicker suggestively around the fringes of Rilke's consciousness at this juncture. In early November, he wrote Paula that, though he had long since abandoned the custom of spending All Souls' Day at the graves of strangers or relatives, this year he had traveled to Wannsee to visit the grave of Heinrich Kleist (giving, in the letter, a brief and oblique account of Kleist's suicide).[391] The last, lengthy entries in Rilke's youthful diaries focus on Gerhardt Hauptmann's play *Michael Kramer*, a drama that centers upon a father's reaction to the death of his son—presumably by suicide. When Lou finally did break with Rilke in February, she assured him that he could, if it proved necessary, contact her in his darkest hour... and we learn from later correspondence that Pineles—the psychologist to whom she had spoken extensively about Rilke—had warned her about what he perceived as serious suicidal tendencies inherent in Rilke's character.

Clara's friend Gretel, to be sure, did not take her own life. At the same time, Rilke does patently portray her dying as, at the deepest soul strata, a matter of choice:

Life is only a part... of what?
Life is only a tone... in what?
Life has sense only when bound with many
circles of space, each larger
than the last—

Life is only the dream of a dream,
but wakefulness is elsewhere.
So you let it go.

Gretel, in Rilke's imagination, inclines towards death because it *completes* life, providing the mysterious key to the deeper, fuller reality without which Life—like the cry of the bird in "Apprehension"—must ultimately resonate with emptiness. In his analysis of Maeterlinck's play, Rilke had identified "great gray fear" as the one feeling that sets the stage for all others. He *also* declared that this fear—associated, as in "Apprehension," with death—"manifests itself as the eternal vis-à-vis all events." The realm of soul-essence ruled by death naturally partakes of a timeless quality so that to titer life with death is to transcend physical mortality, to touch eternity. "Requiem" is a poem wholly given over to just this gesture, the shamanic power of which finds embodiment in the figure of the black wreath and its portentous making.

The black wreath joins life and death by virtue of the simple fact that ivy—a remarkably fast-growing and tenacious plant symbolic of the irrepressible force of life—has been cut from the nourishing vine. In this particular case, moreover, it dramatically displays the sure mark of death in the mourning color lent it by the night. The *form* of the wreath contributes to the poet's symbolic treatment of the theme as well. Rilke, alias Clara, begins and ends the poem by remarking upon the *turning* action that shapes the wreath. The poem's third lines states: "Earlier it was light leaves... I turned it"; while the whole long poem concludes:

What have I accomplished today?
...I gathered ivy at evening and turned
and bent the vines together, until they took the desired form.
It still glints with a black radiance.
And my power
circles in the wreath.[392]

Fashioning a wreath requires, first, cutting a living continuum into discrete pieces, finite lines each with definite ends; then, bending and braiding those strands into the one seamless whole of a circle, a form that possesses neither beginning nor end. Wreath-making thus turns natural life into an artistic form which—twining life and death together—figures eternality, binding mortality to the timeless realm of soul or spirit beyond.

In "Requiem," Rilke offers an updated version of the creative power he wishes, as poet, to claim, a new image of the deep mission of art itself. We've marked, and remarked, the "widening circles" traced by the aspiring soul of his Russian monk who confidently presumes his plastic, shaping force to be the source of all future becoming. "Requiem" too shapes itself in a set of circles: one at the beginning and one at the end (naturally, the poem itself shapes a circle of thought) and, too, the figure of widening gyres (those "many circles / each larger than the last") in the middle. There is, however, a world of difference between the spirit of a falcon's flight and the power bound in a small black wreath woven by a grieving girlfriend. The former may soar over all things, but the latter has been potentized by a vortex of darkness. "Requiem" may be marred by many poetic awkwardnesses, but, as we've seen, it also foreshadows much of Rilke's greatest work. By way of Rilke's experience of the *nigredo*—the poet's encounters with the psychic space of death and its legion of foot soldiers (fear, despair, and grief, to name a few)—the plot of Rilke's art was clearly thickening; beginning to glint black.

Before, however, turning back to Rilke's life—most particularly, his life to come with Clara—we may round off this discussion of the *nigredo* by finishing Rilke's Worpswede diary, the last of the three (Florence, Schmargendorf, Worpswede) composing Rilke's almost three-year-long diary venture. The poet's final two journal entries record yet another dramatic encounter with death.

> *On the evening of 19 December 1900*
>
> Today was the dress rehearsal of Gerhardt Hauptmann's *Michael Kramer.* I sat with Lou all alone in the dark auditorium of the German Theater and waited. Churned up, furrowed open in my inmost being, I was like a plowed field, and when the great gesture of the sower extended out over me, I felt a sharp pang as the single seed dropped onto my bared heart. It was a day of conception.[393]

Near the beginning of this chapter, we excerpted Jung's comment on the picture of Death from the *Rosarium Philosophorum*, but stopped short of his mention of a fundamental fact: "the picture is also entitled 'Conceptio' ...an indication that this death is an interim stage to be followed by a new life."[394] Rilke clearly experienced his witnessing of Hauptmann's drama in just this manner—"a day of conception"—but to understand the *confluence* of new life and death enacted in it we need know something of the play itself.

Michael Kramer is a rather elderly artist, accomplished if not exceptional, but a revered teacher and an essentially noble human being. Kramer fathers a son who grows up disfigured by a hunchback, and, despite his parents' great love, the boy's physical distortion ends up seriously afflicting his psyche as well. He turns into a problem child, then into a brilliant but desperately dissolute young man, who near the opening of the play dies a shameful death, most probably by suicide. His grief-ravaged father, who had always cherished great hopes for his child, takes the corpse to his studio, and, slowly, laboriously, sets to work molding his death mask. In the process, Kramer witnesses—and participates in—death at work as it rips away the masks the son wore in life and reveals the hidden unsullied life of his child. In Rilke's words:

> And Michael Kramer realizes that he wasn't wrong: it *was* there, it *is* there. He wasn't carrying an empty ark into the temple back then when he presented his newborn to eternity. He was holding infinite treasures aloft in his trembling arms, and Life didn't touch them, never unlocked the chest.... But Death, like someone rich and powerful who knows the location of all gold, of all that is deepest and most hidden, has opened everything.[395]

Michael Kramer finds and gives shape to all of this in his hands. The death mask slowly turns into his masterpiece, redeeming the father and—in his eyes—the son.

Rilke regarded Hauptmann's play in an exalted light, declaring, in his journal, "I know of no experience in the theater that I could set beside it." Freedman remarks that Rilke and Lou "endlessly discussed Michael Kramer as though it were the century's masterpiece."[396] A year and a half after the play's premiere Rilke would dedicate the first edition of *The Book of Images* "to Gerhardt Hauptmann, in thanks for *Michael Kramer.*" Rilke's enormous regard for the work, however, finds faint echo in literary history. It is likely, in fact, that the play proved so compelling to Rilke not so much on account of its objective artistic merit—considerable though that may be—but because of the magnetic force of its central metaphor. The making of the death mask—no less than the fashioning of Clara's black wreath—offers a highly evocative symbol of death's transformative power, an archetypal image of the redemptive potential latent in the *nigredo.*

The gist of the matter here is contained, precisely, *in the head.* Edinger relates the intriguing etymology that associates the *nigredo* with head symbolism:

> A common term for the *nigredo* is *"corvus,"* crow or raven, perhaps because it is black and a carrion eater.... Related to *"corvus"* is the term *"caput corvi,"* head of the raven...[which is] synonymous with *"caput mortuum,"* dead head. It is not immediately evident why the *nigredo* should be associated with head symbolism. One reason seems to be the connection between the term "head" and top or beginning. Blackness was considered to be the starting point of the work.[397]

The importance of the head, however, does not consist solely in the priority of its position. In fact, its unique value tends to manifest most clearly in the somewhat macabre contexts in which the head, so to speak, *stands by itself.* Edinger states: "Decapitation or separation of the head from the body also belongs to the mortificatio." On the one hand, this process figures a distillation of understanding. Jung declares that "Beheading is significant symbolically as the separation of the 'understanding' from the great 'suffering and grief' which nature inflicts on the soul." Yet even this does not exhaust the independent significance of the head, for the head can also be seen as a metonymy of the whole man, the seed of human completion. Edinger: "From another standpoint, beheading extracts the rotundum, the round complete man, from the empirical man. The head or skull becomes the round vessel of transformation."[398]

As these citations indicate, the most common instance of relevant head symbolism may be found in instances of decapitations; the head of John the Baptist serves as one classic example. Yet a death mask, too, displays a head separated from the body, and—insofar as it is, like a wreath, manifestly a work of art—perhaps figures yet more powerfully the symbolic resonances articulated above. Certainly, Michael Kramer, in shaping the mask, distills knowledge from great suffering and grief, and—in Rilke's mind, at least—the head of his son becomes precisely "the round vessel of transformation" that enables, finally, redemptive release of the soul of his being. The poet's concluding comments on the play mark the transition from the sixth picture in the *Rosarium Philosophorum* sequence—the "Death" that is simultaneously "Conception"—to the seventh, "The Ascent of the Soul":

> From all the features of his dead countenance there now emerges, unafraid, his soul. And his father recognizes it: it is what he lifted high up back then with his trembling arms, without seeing it, believing—but now he sees it.... And that it *exists*, that is Michael Kramer's epiphany. He lives through a death, the loss of his only son, and the death is not that, not the loss: it is something that clarifies him, that makes the old man farseeing and full of wisdom and serene, a larger-than-life grief that changes all the measures and makes him incapable of ever again experiencing anything petty, insignificant, or fortuitous after something so triumphant, so immense. Whoever understands and honors Death correctly, grants Life greatness.[399]

Thus ends Rilke's Worpswede Diary. Thus begins the task that will occupy him for the rest of his life, for translating the (in)sight of the head into the thought of the heart necessitates a long, fraught, laborious journey. As Michael Kramer knows, Death's wisdom is not cheaply sold.

Chapter 8

THE LAST HOUSE

Clara and Rilke in Westerwede

The dynamics of the *nigredo* are hardly alien to anima and indeed typically transpire under her auspices:

> The encounter with *anima* and *animus* means conflict and brings us up against the hard dilemma in which nature herself has placed us. Whichever course one takes, nature will be mortified and must suffer, even to the death; for the merely natural man must die in part during his own lifetime.[400]

As Jung indicates, the encounter with the contrasexual other often catalyzes a train of events entailing sorrow, loss, and even psychological death—but anima is far more than a mere trigger in this regard. In fact, the whole psychological death experience remains *internal* to the anima archetype, comprising a crucial component of its defining phenomenology. Hillman:

> Anima is inward (hence "closed" and called "virginal" in religious and poetic metaphors of the soul)....To this interiority belongs a movement of deepening downward....which in the phenomenology of Kore-Persephone connects her with the realm of the underworld. She carries our death; our death is lodged in the soul.[401]

Rilke had always been closely attuned to the intimate relation subsisting between death and the maiden, and his anima-saturated Worpswede days saw him intensively involved on this score. In late September, he wrote a prose fragment imagining a young man covering his dead beloved's eyes with cold, heavy roses, and later—astonished—carrying away the two large, warm blooms that had drunk the precious exhalation of her dying beauty.[402] His November "Requiem" for Clara mines the theme and prepares the poet's later, highly accomplished treatment of the Kore-Persephone figures Alcestis and Eurydice in the *New Poems* and *Sonnets to Orpheus*.

So Rilke did come, in time, to master the poetics of this archetypal constellation. Even so, after his precipitous departure from Worpswede the poet found himself grappling on a very personal level with the "hard dilemmas" engendered by his own anima involvements. When first Paula, and then Clara, came to Berlin shortly after the turn of the year, the emotional tension born of his conflicting relationships with both women and with Lou intensified to an almost unbearable degree. Rilke could not resist the urge to resolve the situation one way or another—though, given the choice Paula had already made, and the way matters were going with Lou, his options at this point were more diminished than he might have wished.

Paula did not want to come to Berlin. Her mother, finally informed of her engagement, insisted that the young painter attend an extended cooking course in preparation for her married life. Paula arrived on January 13, and—freed, perhaps, from the burden of guilt on account of her official status as Modersohn's betrothed—immediately resumed intimate conversation with Rilke. The magnetism between the two had not dissipated. The morning after her first visit to his rooms in Schmargendorf, Rilke (as we know from a letter he immediately posted to Paula) refused to touch or move anything to preserve the aura of her presence.

Meanwhile, around the corner, Lou was seething. Frustrated to the point of hostility with Rilke's dark glooming (on January 5, she wrote: "I was mean to Rainer too, but that never bothers me"[403]), she still lobbied fiercely against his attachments to Paula and Clara. That task gained urgency when Clara arrived for a visit with her friends at the end of January. Rilke's "dark sister" naturally called on him—first in Paula's company, and later alone. The three friends went so far as to extend poetically scripted invitations to Otto, Vogeler, and Martha Schroeder to come to Berlin to celebrate Paula's February 8 birthday. Though the plan did not materialize (Vogeler was too busy with his own wedding preparations), the gesture had been made and "The Family," to some small degree, emotionally reconstituted. Lou's admonitions notwithstanding, the magic of Worpswede was reasserting itself. When Clara visited Rilke in his rooms on February 11, the two became lovers. A few days later, the young couple were engaged.

Despite the obvious emotional setup, it was, by all accounts, an unexpected turn of events—one that surprised even Clara herself. (The young bride-to-be told her mother that, shortly before, "she could have sworn it was only a friendship.") Nor did Paula, Clara's closest confidante, see the union coming. At first, taken aback and even saddened by the news (she perhaps rightly guessed that it would compromise her relationships with both her dear friends), Paula soon graciously accepted it. Lou, on the other hand, reacted in a dramatically different fashion.

Rilke visited her at her house on February 15. Lou, who was to leave the next day for Vienna, was appalled when he told her the momentous news, and strenuously tried to dissuade Rilke from taking what she saw as a serious misstep. Her efforts, however, were to no avail, and in an emotionally fraught exchange the erstwhile friends and lovers more or less took leave of each other. Unable to say the words out loud, Lou scribbled on a milk carton: "If some time, much later, you are in a very bad state of mind, our home will be open to you at your direst hour."[404] The next day, Rilke, in what could be read as a symbolic response, vacated his rooms in Schmargendorf, and moved into the hotel Clara had just left to go to her parents in Bremen. Evidently, Clara herself had doubts about the whole enterprise, but sent her final emphatic "Yes" from Hamburg, en route to Bremen. Though the outcome could well be construed as more of a dénouement than a proper climax, Rilke's emotional crisis had—for the time being anyway—been resolved.

Even so, when Lou sent him a letter from Vienna ten days later—a "Last Appeal" that articulated her fears for his emotional well-being and stipulated that—in the best interest of both of them—all contact between them must cease, Rilke was devastated. On February 27, the day after he received the letter, he wrote:

> I stand in the darkness as though blinded
> because my gaze no longer reaches you.
> To me, the day's mad turmoil is
> a curtain behind which you stand.
> I stare at it, and wonder if it will rise,
> that curtain behind which my life lives,
> my life's substance, my life's bidding—
> and yet: my death—[405]

Despite his forthcoming marriage, Rilke's *nigredo* was hardly a thing of the past.

The road to marriage proved a rough one for Rilke. Not long after the announcement of the engagement, Rainer contracted scarlet fever and had to be nursed by Clara's mother in the family home in Bremen. His illness delayed the wedding, which even so was held at the Westhoff house instead of the nearby church on account of the groom's condition. Further postponement, though, was out of the question. For one thing, by the time of the April 28 wedding, Clara was already close to two months pregnant. After the ceremony, the newlyweds escaped the Westhoff household to spend most of May taking a cure at the White Stag sanatorium near Dresden—a rather poor substitute for a properly romantic honeymoon.

Despite these difficulties, the Rilkes began their life together with optimism and determination. They were to live in a cottage in Westerwede, near Worpswede—an old ivy-covered building Clara had known since childhood. The cottage, though small, was secluded (not to say isolated) and seemed to suit at least Rainer's hermetic taste. In a letter, Rilke described the house and the life he hoped to live there:

> A house like this in the middle of the moor, without neighbors (except for a few unknown farmsteads) lying on no street and discovered by no one, is a good refuge, a place into which one can blend with a kind of inconspicuous mimicry, and designed, both forwards and backwards, in future and in memory, for a life full of peace and equilibrium.[406]

The cottage, though, required significant work. The versatile Vogeler helped plan the renovation and designed much of the new furniture Rilke, especially, desired in order to make the home their own. Work on that domestic front occupied much of the summer, a season that passed, it seemed, harmoniously enough. For one thing, Rilke appeared to show Clara due attention, even seeking to make arrangements to have her portrait painted "in her first bloom of beauty, before the second beauty of motherhood." The poet of *The Book of Images*—interested, as always, in lineage—wished to have a picture of his wife "so that the children and descendents may have an inheritance, and unmistakable evidence of that beauty and goodness."[407] The theme of inheritance was soon to assume poetic as well as biographical significance for Rilke.

Fall had often been a productive time of year for Rilke, and in Westerwede the creative energy of the season's storms combined with the poet's relative seclusion to inspire a major work: the second part of *The Book of Hours*, titled *The Book of Pilgrimage*. The thirty-four poems composing this work—though reflecting in part the poet's outward circumstances—certainly do not mirror the tranquil serenity evoked in Rilke's letter. Instead, *The Book of Pilgrimage* reveals the inner turmoil brewing below the peaceful surface of Rilke's life: the transformative alchemy of the *nigredo* continuing to cook in the crucible of the small, sequestered cottage that the poet strove—in vain—to make his home.

The writing of *The Book of Pilgrimage* (and, a year and a half later, *The Book of Poverty and Death*) bears witness to the constant depth of Rilke's religious instinct as well as the lasting influence of the Russian experience upon his poetic life. The linked sequence of thirty-four poems—composed between September 18 and 25, 1901—miraculously picks up the stream of inspiration that produced *The Book of Monastic Life* exactly two years earlier. Exhibiting fundamental continuities in form, voice, and theme, the two works (as well as the third to come) are clearly of a piece. Even so, the events of the intervening years could not help but make their mark, and telling rifts and differences distinguish the two books. Near the beginning of *The Book of Pilgrimage*, the poetic voice declares:

> I am still the same one who knelt before you
> in monk's robes...
> You filled him as he called you into being.[408]

But the poet protests too much, for the poems he utters furnish hard evidence to the contrary. Written in the midst of a period of dramatic outer as well as inner change, *The Book of Pilgrimage* reveals new dimensions of Rilke's ongoing soul transformation, psychological developments broadly associated with a *nigredo* phase that—despite the temporarily settled circumstances of Rilke's life—had by no means spent its force.

The book's first words transport us to a different scene:

> You are not surprised at the force of the storm—
> you have seen it growing.
> The trees flee. Their flight
> sets the boulevards streaming. And you know:
> he whom they flee is the one
> you move toward. All your senses
> sing him, as you stand at the window.

We have here no monk in a cloister, but the poet looking out of the window of his Westerwede cottage at an autumn storm. Only later does Rilke seek to reestablish his Russian persona, though the characterization remains weak and inconsistent. In *The Book of Monastic Life*, on the other hand, the poetic voice fuses seamlessly with its chosen persona from the start, establishing an identity centered in the creative will of the artist-monk who feels himself empowered to seize hold of and reshape all things. The poetic situation here, though, contrasts sharply with that one, signaling just how much Rilke's spiritual landscape had changed, notwithstanding any outward similarities between the northern moorland and the Russian plains.

In *The Book of Pilgrimage*, agent power is borne, first of all, by the figure of the storm. Frequent and violent on the open moors, storms appear repeatedly in Rilke's Worps/Westerwede-influenced poetry, most notably perhaps in the sequence "From a Stormy Night, Eight Leaves with a Title Leaf," written the prior November. Significantly, storm-power—while potentially indirectly creative—does not act *constructively* but typically wreaks destruction, which nonetheless may augur transformation. That *The Book of Pilgrimage* commences with a storm conveys much about the energy of the entire volume; Rilke's new creation seethes with the restless force of high winds.

Just as significantly, the opening poem immediately identifies the power of the storm, not with the poetic speaker himself, but rather with (the as yet unnamed) God. The gesture proves profoundly characteristic of the book as a whole. In dramatic contrast to *The Book of Monastic Life*, we find in its pages no confident affirmation of the self's creative autonomy and prowess, no daring assertion of God's radical dependence upon the self. On the contrary, the poetic persona consistently looks to God to restore a unity and presence it has lost. In this first poem, for instance, the poet views the storm from a distance, and, in the recurrent motif that lends the poem its title, expresses his desire to *move toward* the force he recognizes as somehow redemptive—a force, however, external to him, one he himself does not possess or control. The artist-monk stood as the creative center of all becoming; but here the poet initially assumes a position on the periphery of the destructive-creative vortex, witnessing transfiguration through a pane of glass.

The speaker's distance from the source manifests too, in the self-reflexive form of address that opens the poem. The peculiar self-address both eschews the authority of the first person and, coincidently, denies the Other (God) any immediate vis-à-vis by pre-occupying its usual place—the place of the "You." The rhetorical form—one that does not appear in *The Book of Monastic Life*—tends to close the poetic consciousness in on itself, separating it off from the phenomenal force of Nature and of God (here relegated to the third person). The poem's second stanza registers that estrangement as it is inscribed in the landscape itself:

> The weeks stood still in summer.
> The trees' blood rose. Now you feel
> it wants to sink back
> into the source of everything. You thought
> you could trust that power
> when you plucked the fruit;

now it becomes a riddle again,
and you again a stranger.

The poetic subject's self-consciousness and the existential isolation attendant upon it sound a peculiarly modern chord. The momentum of the poem seeks to confront and counteract the creeping sense of alienation, but the subtle *Entfremdungseffekt* nonetheless remains the ineradicable origin of *The Book of Pilgrimage*—one does not typically embark upon a religious journey if spiritually at home in one's own house. Moreover, the estrangement from God and from nature inevitably affects the relationship to others. The pilgrim's quest—even if commenced in the company of others—is one that must, finally, be taken alone:

Summer was like your house: you knew
where each thing stood.
Now you must go out into your heart
as onto a vast plain. Now
the immense loneliness begins.

The last sentence of this passage is full of portent for our poet. Against the background of Rilke's outer circumstances—his recent, seemingly solid commitment to his wife and their shared home—it strikes an especially somber, not to say troubling note. The mood evoked is, nonetheless, one well attuned to the season, for fall is the season of dying, the incipient loss of life and meaning characteristic of the *nigredo*:

The days go numb, the wind
sucks the world from your senses like withered leaves.

The poem—looking to God to fill the void, and to supply the active, creative agency unavailable to the poet—does manage an upbeat ending:

Through the empty branches the sky remains....
Be modest now, like a thing
ripened until it is real,
so that he who began it all
can feel you when he reaches for you.[409]

But such quiet acquiescence reassures only temporarily, for something more than modest passivity awaits he who moves toward the storm of transformation.

The second poem loses little in time in tearing the mask of calm self-possession off the poetic self.

> I am praying again, Awesome One.
>
> You hear me again, as words
> from the depths of me
> rush toward you in the wind.
>
> I've been scattered in pieces,
> torn by conflict,
> mocked by laughter,
> washed down in drink.
>
> In alleyways I sweep myself up
> out of garbage and broken glass.
> With my half-mouth I stammer you,
> who are eternal in your symmetry.
> I lift to you my half-hands
> in wordless beseeching, that I may find again
> the eyes with which I once beheld you.

Nothing like this appears in *The Book of Monastic Life*. These lines confess a wrenching loss of the connection with God, and, coordinately, a shattering of the unity and integrity of the poetic self. The poem continues to offer a string of grim self-metaphors calling up fear and loathing, annihilation and putrefaction:

> I was a house gutted by fire....
>
> I was a city by the sea
> besieged by pestilence
> which, like a corpse, hung heavy
> on the children's hands.
>
> I was a stranger to myself....

True, these lines are rendered in the past tense, and, as the poem continues, the persona claims to have salvaged some sense of integrity from its own wreckage. Even in so doing, however, he turns to God to resupply the wholeness he can no longer claim as his own:

It's here in all the pieces of my shame
that now I find myself again.
I yearn to belong to something, to be contained
in an all-embracing mind that sees me
as a single thing.
I yearn to be held
in the great hands of your heart—
o let them take me now.
Into them I place these fragments, my life,
and you, God—spend them however you want.[410]

The whole passage presents a rather striking inversion of motif of one of the late poems from *The Book of Monastic Life*:

The poets have scattered you.
A storm ripped through their stammering
I want to gather you up again
in a vessel that makes you glad.[411]

Here it is the poet who is to gather the scattered remnants of God instead of—as in *The Book of Pilgrimage*—vice versa.

The third *Pilgrimage* poem carries on in a similar vein.

Are you, then, the All? and I the separated one
who tumbles and rages?
Am I not the whole? Am I not all things
when I weep, and you, the single one, who hears it?

The self, however, is not only fractured; it is also orphaned, exiled, and—in yet another devastating rewriting of *The Book of Monastic Life*—not so much *cloistered* as *imprisoned*:

...I am the one who's been asking you—
it hurts to ask—Who are you?
I am orphaned
each time the sun goes down.
I can feel cast out from everything....
and all things stand like cloisters
in which I am imprisoned.

As if all this were not enough, the poem continues to develop an elaborate metaphor likening the experience of those who have lost God to that of insomniacs who suffer the horror of endlessly dark and hopeless nights:

> They see not the faintest glimmer of morning
> and listen in vain for the cock's crow.
> The night is a huge house
> where doors torn open by wounded hands
> lead into endless corridors, and there's no way out.
>
> God, every night is like that.[412]

Meaninglessness and disconnection, sickness and affliction, hopelessness and endless blackness: the telltale signs of the *nigredo* are hard to miss. Despite his marriage to Clara, despite the evidently pleasant homemaking, deep down, Rilke was still in the midst of it, suffering dark changes. Yet the process, while painful, did not cease to prepare vital self-transformation.

Because linked imaginations of God and Self are front and center in *The Book of Hours*, its second volume displays certain crucial *nigredo*-related motifs more clearly and dramatically than Rilke's earlier post-Worpswede lyrics. First and foremost among these may be the shattering of egoity implicit in the process, a traumatic dismantling which—as Jung explains—nonetheless prepares the poetic self to encompass the novel experiences triggered by anima and the unconscious (collective as well as personal) to which it is conjoined:

> With the integration of projections...the personality becomes so vastly enlarged that the normal ego-personality is almost extinguished....Positive inflation comes very near to a more or less conscious megalomania; negative inflation is felt as an annihilation of the ego. The two conditions may alternate. At all events the integration of contents that were always unconscious and projected involves a serious lesion of the ego. Alchemy expresses this through the symbols of death, mutilation, or poisoning, or through the curious idea of dropsy...[The king] suffers from a surfeit of the unconscious and becomes dissociated—"*ut mihi*

> *videtur omnia membra mea ab invicem dividuntur*" (so that all my limbs seem divided one from another).[413]

Insofar as imagery of death, dismemberment, pestilential poisoning and the like perforates the opening of *The Book of Pilgrimage*, the alchemical symbolism remains highly apropos. Nor will the figure of the king appear wholly irrelevant to Rilke's opus when we recall that *The Book of Hours* grew out of early work—for instance, the "King's Song" that opens *Dreamcrowned*—that explicitly identified the poetic self with kingship.

The death of the old king and the birth of a new one figures as one of the classic emblems of the regenerative forces implicit in the *nigredo* and its aftermath. For instance, in *Splendor Solis*, another alchemical text illustrated by a series of symbolic pictures, the seventh image, "The Drowning King," is followed by "The Ethiopian," a plate depicting a naked black man emerging from a river of mud to receive a red cloak (symbolic of the *rubedo*) from a pale queen.[414] Still, the king hardly qualifies as the only symbol relevant in this regard. Edinger:

> King, sun, and lion refer to the ruling principle of the conscious ego and to the power instinct. At a certain point these must be mortified in order for a new center to emerge. As Jung says, "Egocentricity is a necessary attribute of consciousness and is also its specific sin." On the archetypal level the *mortificatio* of the king or the sun will refer to the death and transformation of a collective dominant or ruling principle.[415]

In *The Book of Hours*, the ruling principle that must be overthrown to make way for a new order is imaged—not by king, sun, or lion—but by another traditional figure of sovereignty: the *father*. Rilke's version of the theme, moreover, proves especially provocative on account of the way in which he plays self- and God-image off one another. Seeking his own vocabulary of transformation, Rilke permutes these in a thoroughly heretical manner, one incomprehensible in terms of traditional faith yet nonetheless logical within the highly unorthodox psychology of religion—borrowed from Lou—that grounds Rilke's spiritual imagination.

In the fourth poem, Rilke himself (or his poetic persona) takes over the paternal identity that traditionally belongs to God in order to recast God in a new, more vital character as *his* son.

Unending one, you've shown yourself to me.

I love you as I would a son
who long since went from me,
because his fate called him
to a high place
where he could see out
over all things.

I have stayed home like an old man
who no longer understands his son
and knows little of the new things
that concern him now...

I am the father; but the son is more.
He is all the father was, and what the father was not
grows great in him. He is the future....[416]

The sense of promise and futurity persists as the predominant archetypal energy throughout *The Book of Hours*, but here, in its second part, the puer's radiance has been dimmed—indeed, almost extinguished—and rekindling it requires a kind of ritual sacrifice. In order to recuperate divine creative energy, Rilke must kill off the old king, the old father figure *to whom he nonetheless relates himself.* Barrows and Macy state, "The patriarchal God is rejected now with a vehemence that never occurs in *The Book of Monastic Life*."[417] At the same time, it is the old ego consciousness (first and foremost, his own) surreptitiously ruled by that God-image that Rilke so aggressively repudiates.

The fifth poem begins the hatchet job:

Does anyone love a father? Doesn't one turn away
as you turned from me, your face hardened,
wanting to escape these empty, helpless hands?

Isn't the father always that which was...

And while in his time he may have been a hero,
he is a leaf that, when we grow, falls away.[418]

The sixth finishes it off with a vengeance:

> His caring is a nightmare to us,
> and his voice a stone....
>
> Only when we notice that he is dying
> do we know he lived.

All this makes way for a final reaffirmation of God's new identity:

> That is a Father to us. And I—
> I should call you Father?
> That would open a gulf between us.
> You are my son.[419]

Naturally, Rilke's attempt to revivify a dead God-image dovetails with his effort to resurrect himself, to fashion a poetic self that could imaginatively live through death and incorporate the knowledge gained thereby into the fiber of the soul. This is more than the monk could do, for that persona predated Rilke's *nigredo*. The poetic self who declaimed, "I cannot believe that little death / should still trouble us so" could not truly fathom death's power.

Despite Rilke's radical heterodoxy, the Christian overtones of his new God-image—which naturally becomes his new ideal self-image as well—are unmistakable. Yet, while the particular archetypes involved are central to the canon of Christian belief, the archetypal wisdom embedded in the Christ/Son figure cannot be carelessly translated into orthodox religious terms. In the case of one such as Rilke, to do so would be—as Jung and his school recognized—to abrogate its validity entirely. Edinger:

> Mortification leads us directly into the imagery of Christ's Passion....However, the alchemical attitude to the Christ-image and the attitude of religious faith are very different. Jung: "...he recognizes in the transformation in which he himself is involved a similarity to the passion....it is not an 'imitation of Christ' but its exact opposite: an assimilation of the Christ image to his own self, which is 'the true man.'"[420]

And it is Jung who—in language aptly referencing *esoteric* Christian traditions—gives a précis of the archetypal dynamics we have been tracing in Rilke's text.

> The alchemists assert that death is...the conception of the *filius philosophorum*...the Gnostic Christ....This "son" is the new man, the product of the union of king and queen—though he is not born of the queen, but queen and king are themselves transformed into the new birth.
>
> Translated into the language of psychology, the mythologem runs as follows: the union of the conscious mind or ego-personality with the unconscious personified as anima produces a new personality compounded of both....Not that the new personality is a third thing midway between conscious and unconscious, it is both together. Since it transcends consciousness it can no longer be called "ego" but must be given the name of "self."[421]

I would modify Jung's language on one point here. Since it is precisely the "ego-personality" that suffers death, it cannot be this same ego-consciousness that weds anima. As per the Psyche-Eros mythologem, it is (in Rilke's case at least) the puer spirit, the transcendent fount of the "I" which figures as the true partner in the *hieros gamos* that births the "self" as "son"—the new God-image.

The process Jung describes does not unfold overnight, but is the work of a lifetime. In the case of our poet, that "self" ultimately came to bear an intimate relation to the mythic figure of Orpheus celebrated in the sonnet sequence that crowns Rilke's opus. While that poetic climax was still some twenty years in the future, the dynamic underlying its essential conception and gestation took form in the phase of Rilke's career we are interrogating now, a phase that hinges upon his term in Westerwede and its poetic fruit, the central volume of his *Book of Hours*.

The Book of Pilgrimage explicitly reconceives the divine as the "son," but where, one may well ask, does anima—that vital link to the unconscious—register in Rilke's text? While her presence may be discerned in subtle ways in what we've read already, one could reasonably expect more evident signs of her continued sway—for instance, the kind of erotic interchange we have seen to be so conspicuous a feature of Rilke's own anima encounters.

Rilke's text does not disappoint us on this score. Barrows and Macy, in their translation, move straight from the sixth to the ninth poem—one that continues to unfold Rilke's understanding of God as (his) son—in order "not to interrupt the sequence which seems all of a piece." It may seem so, but why then did Rilke himself "interrupt" it? The answer has something to do with anima, and the erotic interest she bears in her train.

It is true that the seventh poem in Rilke's sequence represents a unique exception to the poetic rule of his *Book of Hours*: it is the only poem in the entire work that dates not from Berlin, Westerwede, or Viareggio, but from another time and place altogether. In this position, Rilke inserts the love poem originally written to Lou not long after their first acquaintance in 1897, the poem beginning "Extinguish my eyes..." cited at the conclusion of the fifth chapter of this book. Why this anomalous insertion? To be sure, Rilke may have wished to preserve this poetic memento of the relationship with Lou (evidently one of Lou's own favorites) but such a motive does not alone explain the deeper logic of its specific placement.

In II, 5, the poetic self declares to God: "I want to love you." The whole project of *The Book of Hours*, including the rejuvenation of the God-image especially central to *The Book of Pilgrimage*, depends upon the "dialectic of love" discussed in the fifth chapter of this book. That dialectic, in turn, requires that the relation between the poetic persona and God be maintained as one between lover and beloved. Rilke's figuration of that same relationship as an essentially antagonistic (or at least uncomprehending) relation between father and son threatens this form; the momentum of the poem drives the son not toward, but away from his parent. In order to help recuperate that endangered love, and reclaim the relationship as one of intimacy rather than distance, Rilke interjects a poetic moment born of genuine youthful passion, transferring his burning love for Lou to a more universally respected beloved: God. It is Rilke's means of terminating (himself as) the father, and dramatically transforming the relationship of self and God around which the whole book revolves.

The love poem to God qua Lou sets the scene for another poem of kindred tenor which—drawing upon the potent force of biblical story—accomplishes that transfiguration with remarkable imaginative efficiency. The eighth poem of *The Book of Pilgrimage* reads:

> And my soul is a woman before you.
> And is like the cord of Naomi, is like Ruth.
> She goes by day about the sheaves of gleanings
> like a maid who performs deep service.

But by night she goes to the river
and bathes, and dresses well
and comes to you when all is quiet about you
and comes and lies down at your feet.

And when you question her at midnight, she says
in deep simplicity, I am Ruth, the maid.
Spread your wings over your maid.
You are the heir...

And my soul then sleeps until day
by your feet, warmed by your blood.
And is a woman before you. And is like Ruth.[422]

This key poem, openly declaring the poet's continued identification with the anima archetype in its first line and last lines, effectively reestablishes the erotic ground of the relationship between the poet and God. The biblical story of Ruth places a love scene (reminiscent, to some degree, of pivotal episodes in the Psyche-Eros myth) at the center of that relationship, and so too, at the center of the psychodynamics driving the poet's soul-making, the development of what Jung calls "the self."

The poem is full of portent. The story it reflects captures, on many levels, the thrust of the entire *Book of Pilgrimage*. It symbolizes the rejuvenation of an aging father (Boaz/God) via intercourse with an anima figure fresh from a bath in the waters of the unconscious—an anima figure, moreover, who is at the same time a wanderer who exiles herself from her homeland, a stranger in a strange land who finds God, not in her own house, but in foreign realms. The story possessed deep personal resonance for Rilke, for it evokes themes central to his own life, particularly in connection with his relation to Russia. When his own daughter was born several months after the writing of *The Book of Pilgrimage*, Rainer and Clara named her simply (in Rilke's words) "Ruth, without the addition of any other name."[423]

The theme of exilic wandering maintains an intrinsic connection to the *nigredo*, for death frequently looses us from our moorings. In Ruth's story, it is the death of her husband and brother-in-law that triggers her journey with Naomi. Edinger, though, remarks a more subtle alchemical connection. Traditionally, the process of putrefaction or blackening was said to last forty days; correspondingly, the biblical tradition consistently associates the same number with sojourns in the wilderness: the Israelite exodus from Egypt lasted forty years; Elijah's fast in the wilderness—like Jesus' temptation in the desert—lasted forty days. *The time of the* putrefactio *and the time of wandering in a wilderness of unknowing are one and the same.*

Let us return, though, to the place of the Ruth poem in Rilke's *Book of Pilgrimage.*

In addition to all symbolic and personal resonances just mentioned, the Ruth story proves a crucial intellectual pivot in the unfolding sequence of poems, engendering the idea of God as not only son but *heir.* The subsequent brief poem reads, in its entirety, as follows:

> You are the heir.
> Sons are the heirs because
> fathers will die.
> Sons, however, rise and grow.
> You are the heir.[424]

While it is natural to conceive of a son as an heir, the character of the inheritance here—*what* is being inherited, and from *whom*—cannot be comprehended unless this poem is read against the background of the previous one. It is the Ruth poem that debuts the line *Du bist der Erbe* ("You are the heir") which then recurs verbatim at the beginning of II, 9. In the Ruth poem's biblical backstory, however, these words refer, not to any son, but to Boaz, who as next of kin inherits Ruth as his wife. The inheritance is passed down, not from a father, but from a dead kinsman, and *what* is inherited is the woman, Ruth, the familiar stranger who comes to him under the cloak of darkness and sleeps at his feet—anima, and the love she brings. It is this that rejuvenates the elderly father figure, recasting him as husband and beloved, one who eventually engenders a son who carries the God-line forward. The father himself, qua old king, has little to offer except his death.

The tenth poem of *The Book of Pilgrimage* effectively culminates the whole sequence that opens the book. In it, Rilke capitalizes on the way the idea of an *heir* blends past and future. Preserving *what has come before* in the person of the one who moves toward *what is to come,* Rilke's God emerges as the promise of a future that will incorporate into itself all the riches of human experience. The poem attempts a more or less comprehensive inventory of poetic wealth, beginning with the beauty of each of nature's four seasons:

> And you inherit the green
> of vanished gardens
> and the motionless blue of fallen skies,
> dew of a thousand dawns, countless summers
> the suns sang, and springtimes to break your heart
> like a young woman's letters.
>
> You inherit the autumns, folded like festive clothing
> in the memories of poets, and all the winters,
> like abandoned fields, bequeath you their quietness.

...then proceeding to cultural history:

> You inherit Venice, Kazan, and Rome;
>
> Florence will be yours, and Pisa's cathedral,
> Moscow with bells like memories,
> and the Troiska convent...

...personal history in the form of the experience of lovers:

> And lovers also gather your inheritance.
> They are the poets of one brief hour...
>
> Awakening desire, they make a place
> where pain can enter...
> They bring suffering along with their laughter
> and longings that had slept and now awaken
> to weep in a stranger's arms.

...an experience that, naturally, culminates in death:

> They let the riddles pile up and then they die
> the way animals die, without making sense of it.
> But maybe in those who come after,
> their green life will ripen;
> it's then that you will inherit the love
> to which they gave themselves so blindly, as in a sleep.[425]

What is most crucial here is the manner in which Rilke is developing his God-image so that it encompasses the full range of human experience in its beauty—but, too, in its ineluctable transience, intrinsically marked by loss. Rilke's own emotional tribulation was maturing his tragic sense, effecting a wounding of the puer impulse that would like to refuse, forever more, to come down to earth, to acknowledge the mortality of time and the reality of suffering.

If, as Hillman[426] indicates, the negative senex is virtually identical with the negative puer (Augustine's God as sovereign and rigidly immutable father coincident with the incorrigible youth eternally above it all), then the death of the old king is likewise the death—or at least near-fatal wounding—of the puer and his native impulse to parade as that which can never be: *an immortal ego*. The *nigredo* catalyzed by the encounter with anima therefore promotes the cause of Psyche and Eros' eventual marriage by insisting upon *the difference between* the mortal and immortal self, humanity and divinity, time and eternity—in the interest, eventually, of bringing these more consciously and harmoniously together. In the initial, uninitiated state of affairs these opposites are often unconsciously joined in the *massa confusa* of young love. It is up to the crash-and-burn dynamic of the *nigredo* to destroy the illusion of seamless identity and so open a space of more conscious translation, the task of transformation that is the soul of art. It is, finally, this insight that figures as the heart of "And you inherit the green." The poem's underlying theme is the harmonizing of the temporal and the eternal, human endeavor and divine being, under the auspices of art:

> And painters paint their pictures only
> that the world, so transient as you made it,
> can be given back to you,
> in a form that endures:
> all becomes eternal.

The poem, of course, richly prefigures the *Elegies*—more consistently and closely even than Rilke's earlier "Requiem." Yet "And you inherit the green" and the *Elegies*, for all their thematic similarity, occupy different positions in the larger trajectory of Rilke's opus of soul-making. *The Book of Pilgrimage* remains attached to the youthfully elevated point d'appui of *The Book of Hours* even as it represents a dramatic turn in the *downward* spiral of Rilke's poetic and psychological life, a descent that eventually lands him ill and destitute in his version of the inferno (Paris). The *Elegies*, on the other hand, mark an advanced stage in Rilke's effort to redeem a human world long fallen away from divine presence.

To put the same matter in a different way, in *The Book of Pilgrimage*, Rilke, despite his recent trials, still retains the power rapidly to recoup the puer energy that provides a more or less immediate link with God or spirit. In *The Book of Monastic Life*, the divine and the human are intimate neighbors—lover and beloved—who cohabit the soul together. By the time of the *Elegies*, the divine has assumed the aspect of a terrible—and terribly distant—beauty whose approach (even while ardently desired) threatens the self with annihilation. *The Book of Pilgrimage* figures an in-between station: the immediate presence of a divine wholeness has—as the initial poems reveal—been lost, but not irrevocably so. The memory of the Russian mecca remains fresh, the promised land not yet so very far away.

The Russian vignettes in the volume—one poem that commemorates the long river trip on the Volga, another recalling the visit to the underground cloisters in Kiev—prove this. The latter carries forward Rilke's exploration of death—his concerted attempt to reconcile the fact of mortality with the truth of spirit—by exposing a false solution to the problem: the mummification of life figured by the underground monastic order may rob death of its sting, but steals too its salvific transformative power, its capacity to release a soul from the body and return it to spirit. The Volga poem, on the other hand, qualifies as one of the central ones imaging the underlying—and inherently paradoxical—idea of *pilgrimage*: that only the one who hears God calling from distant reaches and sets forth to seek him may find him close at hand, because God is (in) the spirit of the seeking, the wandering journey itself:

> To him you are new and near and kind
> and marvelous like a journey
> he makes in a quiet ship
> down a great river.[427]

Later in the sequence, this rather leisurely voyaging turns into the urgent seeking characteristic of pilgrimage:

> There will be no rest in the houses:
>   the stir
> of departure—

> ....So many are drawn now to move toward you,
> the roads are never empty.
> ....I have seen them moving like a tide.[428]

The very idea of pilgrimage derives its impetus from the restless puer, who—wounded or unwounded—provides the archetypal energy for the soul's quest:

> The puer aspect of meaning is in the *search*...the quest, or questioning, seeking, adventuring, which grips the ego from behind and compels it forward. All things are uncertain, provisional, subject to question, thereby opening the way and leading the soul towards further questing.[429]

In an essay titled "*Pothos*: The Nostalgia of the Puer Eternus," Hillman amplifies this perspective. Defining his subject, Hillman emphasizes that *pothos*—like the puer himself—may well be construed as a manifestation of Eros:

> The Greek word for this specific erotic feeling of nostalgic desire was *pothos*. Plato defines it in the Cratylus as a yearning for a distant object. Its associations in the Classical corpus are with longings for that which cannot be obtained.[430]

Hillman elaborates, too, how the phenomenon of inveterate wandering that so often embodies *pothos* associates with the restless puer spirit:

> For our purposes here, the puer eternus is that structure of consciousness and pattern of behaviour that (a) refuses and struggles with the senex—time, work, order, limits, learning, history, continuity, survival and endurance—and that (b) is driven by a phallicism to inquire, quest, travel, chase, search, to transgress all limits. It is a restless spirit that has no "home" on earth, is always coming from somewhere or going to somewhere in transition. Its eros is driven by longing.[431]

...longing, unhappily, not readily satisfied by present realities. Indeed, Hillman's points may well be considered unfortunately relevant to Rilke's domestic situation: the familial responsibilities he did not after all really wish to shoulder; his insatiable spiritual yearning.

In Rilke's text, the Volga poem is followed by two more crucial evocations of the idea of pilgrimage, and the more intimate imagery of these poems hits still closer to home. The poems transparently manifest the *pothos* so powerfully at work in Rilke's psyche while reflecting all too poignantly upon Rilke's own living situation: the radical schism between his professed desire to make his and Clara's house a spiritual home—a place of refuge that would, in its stability, provide free rein for the flights of his creative imagination—and the restless urge to be more truly alone, living the life of a perpetual pilgrim ever moving on.

The nineteenth poem effectively conveys the radical—and radically unsettling—force of pilgrimage:

> Sometimes a man rises from the supper table
> and goes outside. And he keeps on going
> because somewhere to the east there's a church.
> His children bless his name as if he were dead.
>
> Another man stays at home until he dies,
> stays with plates and glasses.
> So it is his children who go out
> into the world, seeking the church that he forgot.[432]

This poem images spiritual and domestic life as irrevocably at odds with one another and can be read as an ill omen delivered by the earnest householder and expectant father to himself. Yet the prior poem, positioned between this one and the Volga, more specifically evokes the actual character of the Rilke's own Westerwede house and provides, perhaps, still more telling commentary on the pathos—and *pothos*—inherent in his soul's situation:

> In this village the last house stands
> as lonely as if it were the last house in the world.
>
> The road, which the tiny village cannot stop,
> goes slowly onward into the night.
>
> The little village is only a transition
> between two vast reaches, full of foreboding,
> a crossing by way of houses instead of a bridge.

And those who leave the village wander long,
and many die, perhaps, on the way.[433]

Thus—unfortunately—Westerwede. For the home that was, in Rilke's imagination, built to last, did not, and all the high hopes originally attached to it—the locus of his married life with Clara—crumbled in a strikingly short period of time. To be sure, there was, by all accounts, a brief period of relative domestic bliss after Ruth's birth on December 12 (an interlude Rilke cherished the rest of his life), but disaster followed soon thereafter. The first serious blow was struck by family. Not unreasonably, the relatives who had been administering Rilke's deceased Uncle Jaroslav's estate decided that the monthly allowance set aside for Rilke—originally intended to fund his education—was no longer serving its stipulated function, and cut it off. This deprived Rilke of an important source of financial support and triggered a frenzied search for some means of maintaining the household. Despite a flurry of letters and appeals, Rilke had little luck in landing employment he regarded as viable. Though he was awarded a commission to write a monograph on the Worpswede artists, this success proved a signal exception, and his efforts to find a dependable position as an editor or art critic came to nought. Nor would Rilke even begin to consider (as his father urged) a bank post, or any day job that compromised his autonomy as a creative artist. All too soon, the financial pressure broke Rilke's rather fragile commitment to house and home.

Emotionally ill-equipped for marriage and still less so for the responsibilities of paternity, the sensitive poet soon chafed under the burdens of family life.[434] Many critics speculate that Rilke was not, after all, averse to finding a way out of a situation he had created—albeit with all good intentions—much too hastily. Already by April the decision had been more or less made: the household would be dissolved, and Rilke himself would move to Paris. Ruth, eventually, would find her way to her maternal grandparents. And Clara? Rilke half-hoped she, too, would come to Paris. In time, she did, and the two would maintain an active connection for years. Nor were they (in part on account of legal obstacles) ever divorced. Even so, their marriage was over almost before it had begun. They did not share a room in Paris, and Rilke soon grew reluctant to acknowledge his married state to those unaware of it. Not surprisingly, Lou was right after all, though—for better or for worse—she was not around to say "I told you so."

So, in the geography of Rilke's life, Westerwede (and perhaps even Worpswede as well) proved uncannily like the little village of the poem. No true destination in itself, it was but a crossing, a way station, a point of transition between two vast worlds: Russia and Paris (which Rilke once called "anti-Russia"); the land of God and the infernal City; (spiritual self-)possession and dispossession; the *The Book of... Life*, and *The Book of... Death*; a way station, too, between the two great teachers in Rilke's life: Lou Andreas-Salomé and Auguste Rodin.

And yet, as *The Book of Pilgrimage* shows, Rilke did make something of this world—which, while in-between, was in no wise listless like the state so named in the despairing journal entry of the December before Ruth's birth. In and through the failed experiment of marriage and householding, Rilke was learning (as his pilgrimage poems teach) that to be alone on the way somewhere was indeed *his* way, and that the long road ahead was for him both destiny and destination. He was learning, too, to go ever more deeply into the bridal chamber of the soul that is, likewise, always in between: in between time and eternity, the human and the divine, heaven and earth, past and future. Even in the midst of *falling away* from the youthful grace that could—like a falcon, a storm, or a god—soar confidently over and above the world in ever-widening circles, he was falling into a deeper, darker, more inward and fuller knowledge of self and world.

When Psyche, clinging to the wounded and fleeing Eros, falls to earth, she does not immediately lose sight of him; nor, in the long run, does she lose him forever. The provisional separation serves eventual re-union, the marriage which could not truly be consummated while she was living in dark passive unconsciousness and he had not yet suffered the wound through which—as Hillman writes of the puer—"these energies of eternity can flow." Both the fall to earth—preparatory to Psyche's long labors—and Eros' wound are traumatic yet necessary developments of the story. We will spend the second part of this book immersed in analysis of the former; let us here look, for a moment, at the significance of the latter within the context of archetypal dynamics already highlighted in this chapter.

King, Lion, Sun, Father—these are all are masculine energies, and all bear relation, as well, to ego-consciousness and the Hero. Rilke himself associates father and hero at the end of the fifth poem of *The Book of Pilgrimage*. The same poem that exclaims, "Does anyone love a father?" concludes: "And while in his time he may have been a hero / he is a leaf that, when we grow, falls away." But puer—the founding archetype of *The Book of Hours*—counts here, too, as a carrier of masculine spirit, of affirmation of the "I," one that bears the cross of its own peculiar relation to the heroic ego. The fracturing of egoity inscribed in the opening of *The Book of Pilgrimage* and indelibly woven into the texture of the whole finds symbolic expression in *nigredo* motifs we've discussed: the death and even dismemberment of the old king, or father, or hero. Yet puer cannot quite be placed in the same league in this regard, for the puer, by virtue of his indissoluble bond with eternity, cannot be killed in the same way. He can, on the other hand, like Eros, be wounded, and it may be that the *nigredo* experience has a role to play in distinguishing puer and hero so that the former, almost (but not quite) mortally wounded, may be loosed from the egotism that precludes Psyche's continued development and the spirit's ultimate union with anima. Hillman:

> Our hermeneutic scrutiny... will have to go where puer consciousness is embodied in heroic configurations. We can't keep them apart until we have discerned the necessity of the spirit's entrapment in the wounds of heroism. Hopefully, we may recover mythical images that lose the hero but save the wound.[435]

To lose the hero is to see him die, or at least mortally suffer, which may effectively free the puer from heroic entrapment, albeit in wounded form. So, in Rilke's *Book of Pilgrimage*, the puer spirit that inspires the entire *Book of Hours* survives Rilke's *nigredo*, though—to *some* degree—the heroism implicit in his poetic persona is burned off, and the "I" opened to suffering, more liable to near divinity through sorrow than creative strength. "Am I not all things, when I weep, and you the single one, who hears it?" writes Rilke. The spirit's wounds prepare it, ultimately, to enter more fully into soul: encourage the bleeding of eternity into time, heaven's condescension to come down to earth in the figure of the son.

So Rilke's book, as it moves past its pilgrim-center, contains poems adumbrating the future sacred marriage of eros and psyche even as it enters the long in-between phase of separation. II, 22 begins with typical puer images of future dawning:

> You are the future,
> the red sky before sunrise
> over the fields of time.

Yet even as it extends the litany of dawn...

> You are the cock's crow when night is done,
> you are the dew and the bells of matins,

...it segues almost seamlessly into anima imagery: characterizations reminiscent of Ruth and her story:

> maiden, stranger, mother, death.

...and, offers, in its last stanza, lines that couple a classically Rilkean characterization of anima *and* puer illimitability:

> You are the deep innerness of all things,
> the last word that can never be spoken.[436]

The final poem of the book—striking a note at once more personal and cosmological—relates spirit and soul by way of an archetypal image of puer wounding. In it, the speaker offers the bloodying experience of his earthbound travail up toward the sky: a heaven which, remade in his own image, is itself shattered—and yet, in that very dispersion, all the more available to enter with fecund power into the erstwhile barren earth:

> In deep nights I dig for you like treasure.
> For all I have seen
> that clutters the surface of my world
> is poor and paltry substitute
> for the beauty of you
> that has not happened yet.
>
> My hands are bloody from digging.
> I lift them, hold them open in the wind,
> so they can branch like a tree.
> Reaching, these hands would pull you out of the sky

> as if you had shattered there,
> dashed yourself to pieces in some wild impatience.
>
> What is this I feel falling now,
> falling on this parched earth,
> softly,
> like a spring rain?[437]

In an essay in *Puer Papers*, Hillman details the phenomenology of distinct puer wounds, including both *maimed hands* and *bleeding*. Interestingly, Hillman identifies *the gesture of gesture* itself with the former:

> One meaning that speaks particularly through the wounded hand has to do with gestures... for puer consciousness... life is a gesture of the spirit; life as *mudra*, a significant gesture.
>
> Damage to the hand discloses the fate of one who is purely and only puer: life as broken gesture, unachieved, a fragment that points beyond itself. At the same time, this damage offers the very possibility for moving from this fate into a human world where handicaps give soul.[438]

Rilke's closing poem, in the spirit of the puer, makes a gesture. The lifting of the poet's bloodied hands certifies his puer pedigree; at the same time, it signifies the opening of the spirit toward the soul by way of its wounding by the hardscrabble earth. That opening is, too, a *bleeding*, a spilling of vital, life-giving energy that—like the spirit-stuff spilled from the cross—"releases and reveals essence," rejuvenating the world. Hillman:

> The vitality of the puer spreads and stains like the red tincture of the alchemist's *lapis*. His bleeding is a *multiplicatio*, the infectious giving out of essence for the sake of transforming the world around.[439]

In his own epistolary discussion of his *Duino Elegies*, Rilke spoke famously of the task of transformation, and the final image of *The Book of Pilgrimage* adumbrates the end of the *Elegies* which likewise tells of "spring rain falling on the dark earth." It is often said that Rilke spent ten years in quest of that masterwork, from its formal inception in 1912 to its completion in 1922. The truth, however, is that the way was much longer than that—twice as long at least. Already in 1901, in Westerwede—even as his happiness was falling—our poet's pilgrimage was well under way.

CHAPTER 9

STRANGE VIOLIN

Rilke, 1902

Rilke could boast of at least one good reason for his move to Paris in August 1902. He had been commissioned to write a book about the man who would, in time, become his master: Auguste Rodin. After completion of his Worpswede monograph in May, Richard Muther had helped Rilke secure this new, more promising assignment. The monograph, and still more the association with Rodin, proved a turning point in Rilke's life. We shall deal with Rodin and all that emerged from Rilke's new discipleship in subsequent chapters. Here, however, we will focus on the concluding phase of the prior passage of the still young poet's life.

Despite the salutary, even healing power of the intense involvement with Rodin, Rilke's soul life did not turn on a dime, nor did dark dislocation cease to work within him. His circumstances, after all, were hardly enviable. Rilke was poor, as yet relatively little-known, and—for the time being—problematically separated from his wife and child. After his arrival in Paris, moreover, the poet found himself adrift in a strange and even terrifying environment. Although initially pleased with his humble quarters at 11 Rue Toullier, Rilke soon felt overwhelmed by the alien force of the city, which, unlike St. Petersburg, seemed to him to revel in its own inhuman scale. All was a rush of seemingly aimless activity, and, most disturbingly, exuded an air of sickness, affliction, and death. Huge hospitals, replete with insidiously suggestive little side doors, appeared everywhere: "I see now why they figure so often in Verlaine, Baudelaire, and Mallarmé.... You suddenly feel that in this vast city there are armies of the sick, hosts of the dying, whole populations of the dead." "Paris is hard," he wrote Vogeler in September. "A galley! I can't tell you how I loathe it"; and to Arthur Holitscher, a few weeks later, "Can you feel, that Paris is infinitely alien and hostile to me?"[440]

No wonder, then, that the poetry Rilke penned in the first half-year in Paris focuses ever more acutely upon archetypal motifs associated with the latter phase of his *nigredo*: a sense of the world as fallen or falling; estrangement; loneliness; chronic exilic homelessness; death. Indeed, it is in this Parisian period that Rilke's life and work crystallize around these themes, which remain permanent nuclear elements of his mature identity and poetic vision.

Rilke arrived in Paris on August 28, 1902. In September, precisely one year after writing *The Book of Pilgrimage*, Rilke wrote several autumn poems that reflected his still darker Parisian state of mind. The first of these, written on September 11, imaginatively links fall and intense *aloneness* in a context at once cosmological, psychological, and physical. The poet envisions the heavens themselves touched by the autumnal process of death and decay, and the falling of leaves augurs the whole earth's fall out of the cosmic fold into lonely isolation:

AUTUMN

The leaves are falling, falling as from far away,
as if distant gardens withered in the skies;
they fall with gestures saying "No."

And in the nights the heavy earth falls
from a multitude of stars into aloneness.

Indeed, the motion of falling appears latent in everything, and so defines the very heart of earthly existence:

> We are all falling. This hand is falling.
> And look at the others: it's inside them all.

...though the fall is not, finally, endless:

> And yet there's one who with infinite
> tenderness holds this falling in his hands.[441]

The poem's ending echoes the salvific impulse inscribed in *The Book of Pilgrimage*. It does so, however, in muted tones that, as Rilke's time in Paris wears on, will grow ever fainter in the face of the city's harsh realities.

"Autumn Day," composed ten days later, is one of Rilke's most famous poems. It, too, cushions fall's difficult message. Even so, the poem's last stanza remains subtly unforgiving:

> Whoever has no house, will never build one now.
> Whoever is alone now will long remain so,
> will stay awake, read books, write long letters
> and wander restless back and forth
> along the tree-lined streets, as the leaves drift down.[442]

Read against the background of Rilke's life, the poem takes on a poignant personal resonance. Rilke in fact no longer had a house, only a rented flat; he was indeed alone in Paris, while Clara was attending to the unhappy task of packing up what had been their abode; and yes, he would long remain alone, constantly given to restless wandering. Rilke had once imaginatively bound his future to the solid foundation of a family home. Here, quietly, implicitly, his poetic persona allies itself with dead leaves drifting aimlessly in city streets. The contrast could hardly be more dramatic.

As a matter of fact, as Rilke wrote "Autumn Day" he was in the midst of delicate discussions with Clara as to where she would live when she arrived, the next month, in Paris. Though the Rilkes had dissolved their household, the status of their relationship remained quite ambiguous. While still bearing both affection and regard for his wife and genuinely valuing her companionship, Rilke did not really wish to live a married life. Clara, on the other hand, still harbored hopes of a more firm and intimate attachment. Rilke's disinclination toward the same finds almost hostile expression in another poem written the same day as "Autumn Day":

Solitude

Solitude is like a rain.
Toward evening it rises from the sea;
from plains that are distant and remote
it migrates to the sky, where it always is.
And only then it falls from the sky on the city.

It rains down in the in-between hours,
when toward dawn all the streets turn around again,
and when those bodies that found nothing
leave each other sad and disappointed;
and when those people who detest each other
have to sleep together in one bed:

then solitude runs with the rivers...[443]

With respect to the Clara question, a provisional compromise was reached more or less at the last moment. When she finally arrived, they maintained separate quarters but lived under one roof, sharing the same address. It was to be last time the pair would do so. As "Solitude" reveals, Rilke, alone in an alien city, was refining his imagination of solitude as the natural element of the psyche.

Another famous poem from this period conveys Rilke's sense of living on the existential edge:

The Neighbor

Do you follow me, strange violin?
In how many cities have you run
after me, your lonely night speaking to mine?
Do hundreds play you? Does only one?

In all the big cities, are there men
and women who, without you,
would have already flung themselves in the rivers?
And why do *I* meet you, again, and again?

Why am I always the neighbor of those
who anxiously force you to sing

> and to say: life is heavier
> than the weight of all things.[444]

Here one can cut the melancholia with a knife. Seamlessly fusing themes of loneliness, restless wandering, heaviness, and estrangement from the current of life, the poem evokes the image of one who—no matter how far he travels—cannot escape the violin's haunting melody and is at home nowhere but in the sphere of its difficult truth. In *The Book of Monastic Life*, the neighbor—the one inevitably near at hand—was God himself, a pervasive sense of the marvelous presence of the divine. In "The Neighbor," it is a singer whose song is almost unbearably grave, yet whose fearful confession makes existence tolerable for those who, in the absence of that bittersweet expression, might throw themselves off the bridge of life altogether. The poem sounds a vaguely Orphic theme, figuring music as the ineluctable intermediary between life and death, but does so in an intensely melancholic key. The *pothos* of the eternal pilgrim reappears, but transmuted; attuned not to stirring hope, but to death-rich resignation.[445]

Two other poems from the same time and place echo the by now increasingly familiar theme of the one who, paradoxically, finds himself profoundly estranged from the life that surrounds him, reconciled only to what is distant and far off. The opening of "The Solitary" recalls the central pilgrim poems of *The Book of Pilgrimage*; nor is it any accident that the root word *fremd*—the first word of "The Neighbor"—appears once more in this poem's first line:

> Like one who's voyaged over strange seas,
> so am I among those forever at home;
> the full days stand mutely around their tables,
> but distant reaches draw me, full of dream.[446]

"The Ashanti," on the other hand, offers a kind of revealing negative of "The Solitary." The title refers to Africans from recently vanquished tribes who were (believe it or not) put on display in Paris's Jardin d'Acclimatation. Rilke, rather than abhorring the simple fact of their captivity, reviles their servile accommodation to those who gape at them, comparing them unfavorably with animals that "subside into themselves / indifferent to the new adventure / and alone with their untouchable blood."[447] For all its incredible insensitivity, the poem does image soul force utterly and irrevocably foreign to the reality in which it is—literally—caged. Imprisonment, after all, figures as the flip side of pilgrimage. The first—and perhaps most famous—of Rilke's *New Poems*, "The Panther," is right around the corner.

A last poem from this period, "Pont du Carrousel," features another figure set off against his surroundings, this time, however, in a positive sense:

Pont du Carrousel

The blind man standing on the bridge,
gray like a boundary stone of nameless kingdoms,
he is perhaps that one unchanging thing
around which the far-off stellar hours revolve,
the silent midpoint of the constellations.
For everything around him strays and struts and runs.

He is the immovable upright one
set down in many tangled paths;
the dark entrance to the underworld
among a surface-dwelling race.[448]

Precisely because he is, by virtue of his malady, cut off from the meaningless activity swirling around him, the blind man—still as a piece of sculpture—serves as a portal to other realms, a point of intersection between the visible and invisible worlds, motion and rest. In so doing, he becomes a kind of signpost for Rilke himself; for the poet's early Paris lyrics, while giving voice to his profound alienation and evolving identity as a wandering solitary, nonetheless generally maintain a safe aesthetic distance from the grotesque physical and psychical affliction so prevalent in his environment. Not so the epistolary prose he was already writing. In the near future, the poet would walk his readers through that "dark entrance" and, in both poetry and literary fiction, more freely image the hells he himself was experiencing—and, too, the destiny discovered in the realms of poverty and death.

Work on the Rodin book shone as a bright light in an otherwise dark existence. When Rilke finished it in mid-December, he fell into illness and depression. Though a significant accomplishment, the book brought little financial return. Rainer and Clara—their own relationship ongoingly ambiguous—continued to live on the edge of poverty in a city both of them reviled. Rilke's inner anxiety found symptomatic expression in his body and he was racked by recurrent attacks of influenza that left him physically and psychologically debilitated. When Paula came to visit in February, hoping, perhaps, to rekindle the vivacity of her prior friendship with Clara and Rainer, she was bitterly disappointed to find them mired in dull despondency. In a letter to Otto, she reported that the Rilkes "trumpet gloom, and now they have two instruments to do it on." Even their work—pursued with a willful dedication—seemed to bring them little joy.

Paula left Paris on March 18. Two days later, Rilke did likewise. Some time earlier, he had conceived the idea of getting away, of traveling to a warmer, more congenial place that might restore his spirit and body. It was a sure sign of his general distress that—pleading ill health—he needed to appeal to his father to help finance the trip. On March 20, Rilke boarded an overcrowded train for Italy, alone.

After a tiring journey through mountain tunnels, Rilke eventually found his way to Viareggio—a place he had visited some five years before—and soon began to enjoy the healing effects of the warmth of the sun, sea, and sand. On April 13, inspiration returned, and, in the course of a single week, Rilke composed the thirty-four poems comprising the third and last section of his *Book of Hours*, *The Book of Poverty and Death*.

Though Rilke composed this book under the southern sun, Paris figures as its principal locus and the horrors of urban experience supply its thematic background. Neither Russia nor the northern moorland is explicitly pictured in its pages, though the legacy of those vast spaces lives on in the text, serving as an antidote to the strangulating effect of city life. The first poem draws upon the imagery of the mountain tunnels through which Rilke traveled on his train trip south:

> Perhaps, I am pushing through heavy mountains
> in hard veins, like ore, alone;
> and am down so deep, I see no end
> and nothing far: everything grows near
> and all that nearness turns to stone.
>
> I know so little of pain, *how* or *why*—
> so this huge darkness makes me small;

> but if it's you, strike hard, smash through
> so your hand's whole weight breaks over me,
> and over you, the fullness of my cry.[449]

Once again, the initial situation of the poetic persona has altered dramatically, and in a manner that speaks volumes about the condition of the poet's own soul. The Russian monk, though presumably enclosed in a cell of stone, was not the least bit constrained by that circumstance. Filled with the breath of spirit, the monk's soul liberates itself from the bonds of matter and, by virtue of indwelling creative power, quickly rises above the physical confines of things. The pilgrim of Book Two—though distanced from the divine source of being—nonetheless retains full freedom of motion and assumes the identity of one *traveling toward* his spiritual goal. In *The Book of Poverty and Death*, however, the poetic self finds itself, not only imprisoned, but thoroughly immobilized, encased in stone. The monk's creative agency knew no bounds as he fashioned the icons of his art to emancipate the souls of others ("I hold it high, and know not whose / soul it will break from the mold"); the pilgrim retained the potent power of spiritual decision; but in this poem the self's active power is reduced to the issuing of an SOS, an anguished cry of pain. In the book of the "neighbor God," a sense of God's almost physical proximity symbolized intimacy with the divine; in *The Book of Pilgrimage*, God's presence was felt in the vast distances that offered themselves, like incense, to the wanderer. Here, however, all distance has disappeared—all space swallowed into a single sensation of a nearness that is not God, but dense matter that must be broken through in order to reestablish any connection whatsoever. No longer a religious artist or traveler, the poetic persona is initially not a person at all, but—in a rich figure of near soullessness—an *inanimate* vein of ore.

The book's second poem defines, still more closely, the outward and inward condition of the self's awful constriction. After reiterating the essential circumstance:

> You, mountain, here since mountains began...
> ...Your hardness encloses me everywhere.

...the poem suddenly translates its physical metaphor into the correspondent psychological state, one readily recognized from the early days of Rilke's *nigredo*...

Or is it fear
I am caught in?

...and then, without missing a beat, provides that psychological condition a geographical locus:

The tightening fear
of the swollen cities
in which I suffocate?

...You force me, Lord, into an alien hour.[450]

...*einer fremden Stunde*: the poem ends with the juxtaposition of two key words. For if this is *The Book of Hours*, its final volume begins in a time and place strange to its founding inspiration, an "hour" almost inconceivably removed from those "Russian hours" that originally gave the work its title. Consequent imagery reveals that time in these "swollen cities" is not, as it was imagined to be in Russia, filled with the sense of an eternal, and eternally creative, presence, but (in the kind of inversion typical of the *nigredo*) rushed, hollow, and—for all its frenetic human activity—void of real life.

The fourth poem opens:

Lord, the great cities are lost and rotting.
Their time is running out.
The people there live harsh and heavy,
crowded together in dark basement rooms.

Beyond them waits and breathes your earth,
but where they are it cannot reach them.[451]

Again and again, the poetic voice laments the inauthenticity endemic to big-city life, construing such cities as places corrosive to the soul, all but impermeable to the breath of God. III, 13 condemns this general treason in no uncertain terms:

The big cities are not true; they betray
the day, the night, animals and children.
They lie with silence, they lie with noise
and with all that lets itself be used.

None of the vast events that move around you
happens there. In city streets and alleys

your great winds falter and churn,
and in frenzied traffic grow confused.[452]

The anima figures so vital in the prior book are present here as well, but often in degraded forms signifying betrayal of the soul's spiritual substance. As Freedman aptly details, much of the imagery that registers the inversion (or perversion) of spiritual fullness revolves around sexuality and procreation, often provocatively linking conception and death. III, 4, for instance, concludes:

The young girls have only strangers to parade before,
and no one sees them truly;
so, chilled,
they close.

And in back rooms they live out the nagging years
of disappointed motherhood. Their dying is long
and hard to finish: hard to surrender
what you never received.

Their exit has no grace or mystery.
It's a little death, hanging dry and measly
like fruit inside them that never ripened.[453]

The eighth poem includes a more violent rendition of a related motif:

Are we only the sex
and womb of women who yield too much?
We have been whoring with eternity
and in labor we only give birth
by miscarriage to our own death;
a dead, crippled, miserable embryo.[454]

It may seem strange that Rilke consistently and directly links conception (or here, misconception) and birth with death, yet, as we've already elucidated, these opposites are intimately joined in the transformative logic of the *nigredo*; recall, for instance, that the sixth picture in the *Rosarium Philosophorum* was titled both "Death" and "Conception." The crucial idea of *death as integral to the spiritual conception of the self* thus finally arrives at the station of titular announcement in the last book of *The Book of Hours*, though much of the poetry sings the theme in a negative key, elaborating the ungodly way in which big city life deprives its denizens of authentic death and so authentic life.

The fifth poem images the rough treatment the city metes out to sensitive human natures:

> There, people live pale as white blossoms
> and die wondering at life's too great weight.
>
> ...They go about, degraded by their labor,
> serving senseless things without conviction.
>
> Given over to a hundred torments,
> assaulted by every hour's cruel stroke,
> they circle the hospitals, alone,
> anxiously awaiting admittance.

...and closes with repetition of the keynote theme:

> And Death is there. Not the one whose mystery
> greeted them, gently, in childhood...
> but one that hangs in them green and without sweetness,
> like a fruit that never ripens.[455]

The sixth poem, though—one of the crucial nodes of the whole volume—offers a positive formulation of the main theme:

> God, give us each our own death,
> the dying that proceeds
> from each of our lives:
>
> the way we loved,
> the meanings we made,
> our need.[456]

...while the seventh returns to the vital fruit metaphor to amplify it:

> For we are only the rind and the leaf.
>
> The great death, that each of us carries inside,
> is the fruit.
>
> Everything enfolds it.[457]

It is this "great death" that lends life direction and indwelling destiny. Valve of the soul, it is the synapse of matter (or body) and spirit, the visible and the invisible worlds, time and eternity:

> For its sake all that has been truly seen endures
> as something eternal, even while long gone...

...the shaping, even, of the receptacle of "the thought of the heart":

> Into it enters all heart-warmth and the mind's
> white heat...[458]

Rilke initially borrowed the notion of the *individual death* as sign and seal of the individual life—a soul life that fulfills its unique spiritual destiny—from Jacobsen. In *The Book of Poverty and Death* and the closely related *Notebooks of Malte Laurids Brigge* (which deals likewise with Parisian themes), Rilke not only made the idea his own but incorporated it as one of those essential postulates which ultimately anchor his whole world-view. Even as Rilke the man was suffering, the poet was about the business of distilling death's precious black gist from the dross of mortifying experience. For a relation to death is a crucial element of what makes soul *soul*, a chief catalyst of all its imaginative conversions.

Of course, neither Rilke nor Jacobsen invented the fundamental idea of death as the overseer of the spiritual life. Long ago, in the *Phaedo*, Plato declared that "true philosophers make dying their profession,"[459] styling the perspective on life lent by death the veritable insignia of authentic philosophy. In a modern context, Hillman inaugurated his psychology of soul-making with a book dedicated to a similar proposition, though one that includes Rilke's more explicit emphasis on the individual. In *Suicide and the Soul*, Hillman singles out "the importance of death for individuality," asserting, "the death experience is needed to separate from the collective flow of life and discover individuality."[460] *The Book of Poverty and Death*—for all the despair and killing spiritual violence imaged in it—figures as a literary precipitate of Rilke's own prolonged death experience and so a key moment in the saga of his soul, the development of his unique individuality. Even as the early interregnum in Paris marks a low point in Rilke's life, this very nadir—in accordance with the logic of the *nigredo*—figures as a kind of transformative point of departure, providing seed-stuff out which the rest of his life and art will grow.

The progress of the book itself records the crucial turn. Initially figuring itself as, effectively, a *prisoner* of the spiritual violence inflicted upon the soul by the city, the poetic self effectively recovers its power in the role of herald of *den Tod-Gebärer*, the one who gives birth to true death and so, paradoxically, confers new, true life upon humanity. "I wish to praise him," writes the poet, "as horns go before troops, so I will go and sound."[461] It is in this role that the poetic persona seeks, at one and the same time, to recollect itself and reestablish its relation to God, *the divine power invested here, finally, in the transformative power of death.* Declaring that he now speaks with two voices (one that "prepares all that comes from afar"—the force that breaks through his cocoon of fear—and another that hallows the loneliness of that poetic mission), the poet prays:

> May both voices accompany me,
> when I am scattered again in city and fear.
>
> They will serve me in the fury of our time
> and help me make a place for you
>
> wherever you need to be.[462]

In a certain sense, this brings the inspiration of *The Book of Hours* full circle. For in the first of the three books, the Russian monk's seemingly endless spiritual confidence does confront a strict limit. Death, and the fear it breeds, remains essentially beyond his purview—and beyond, too, the province of his God; indeed, the unwanted incursion of death's unknown force threatens to sunder the all-important unity subsisting between the monk and his God. For the most part, the monk suppresses this fear, only occasionally allowing it to break through: "What will you do, God, When I die? . . . I am afraid."

The next two books of the triptych, however, move to include elements that remain largely unconscious in *The Book of Monastic Life* within the realm of the soul's poetic making and breaking. The fracturing (or wounding) of egoity and the coincident distance placed between Self and God in *The Book of Pilgrimage* begins this process by creating a space wherein God can signify forces initially foreign to the self and its egoic consciousness, thus establishing the possibility of developing a *relationship* to those forces—a relationship in turn facilitated (as in the Ruth poem) by the anima function that provides the link with the divine and the unconscious mysteries it signifies. In *The Book of Poverty and Death*, as a consequence of Rilke's ongoing *nigredo*, his poetic soul-making aims to extract the spiritual substance of (the initially alien power of) death from the hard heart of the constriction and fear it breeds, and to realize the transformative—indeed, divinely rejuvenative—force it bears. Soul and God thus rendezvous behind what had been, so to speak, "enemy lines," claiming territory whose neglect would render the soul spiritually insecure and, ultimately, barren.

What then of poverty, the other titular theme of the text? A similar soul logic is at work here. Both poverty and death signify negation or absence—some form of nullity severing the soul's attachment to matter, and so ultimately clarifying its spiritual connection. In his *Mysterium Coniunctionis*,[463] Jung understands the alchemical career of the soul to include three decisive moments involving body, soul, and spirit. In the first, the soul unites with the spirit; in the second, the product of that union separates from the body; in the third and final phase, soul and spirit are reunited with the purified body. The second phase—the sheering away from body—is typically identified with death, but poverty figures as death's close cousin in this regard, for it too symbolizes a cleaving of the soul from materialist concern, a detachment from things or (more essentially perhaps) any *perspective* on things tainted by hollow worldliness.

And so we have *The Book of Poverty <u>and</u> Death*. The same poetry that aims to reconcile the soul's spiritual life with death—unfolding the vision of God as the *coincidentum oppositorum*—endeavors to identify real self-possession with a species of dispossession; inner wealth with what appears as outward want; true value with what, in the eyes of the world, may well appear worthless refuse, all that is *cast out*:

> You are the poor one, you the destitute.
> You the stone that has no resting place.
> You are the diseased one
> whom we fear to touch....
>
> Like flowering along the tracks, shuddering
> as the train roars by, and like the hand
> that covers our face when we cry—that poor.
>
> Yours is the suffering of birds on freezing nights,
> of dogs who go hungry for days.
> Yours the long sad waiting of animals
> who are locked up and forgotten.

You are the beggar who averts his face,
the homeless person who has given up asking;
you howl in the storm.[464]

This valuing of what's left out is yet another dynamic intrinsic to the *nigredo*. Edinger: "The dead, worthless residue is the stuff of the nigredo phase.... The worthless becomes the most precious, and the last becomes first." We certainly recognize this logic in Rilke who, speaking of the poor, writes:

They will live on....
no longer the pawns of time....
Theirs shall be the harvest; for them the fruits.[465]

Yet the concluding sentences of the Edinger passage are perhaps still more revealing of the inner impetus of Rilke's writing: "And the last become first. This is a lesson we each must learn again and again. It is the psyche that we find in the worthless, despised place."[466] That psyche, qua anima, names the inner space of soul, the inestimable worth of which may one day shine forth from those who realize its true virtue, or, as Rilke says in the most famous, single-line poem of the volume:

For poverty is a great radiance from within...[467]

From the black glint of Clara's wreath to the inner light of those who live in dire outward poverty, Rilke continued to plumb the alchemical agency of the *nigredo*: search for the sunrise hidden in the dark night of the soul.

In the last chapter we spoke of the wounding of the puer, and in so doing initiated the task of reimagining the post-Worpswede phase of Rilke's life in light of the Psyche-Eros myth. Yet the related incident in the myth—the wounding of Eros—represents only one of a whole series of events that collectively comprise the relevant chapter of the Psyche-Eros story. It is time to review both this chapter of the myth and its relevance to Rilke's soul history more fully. In so doing, we will naturally find our attention focused upon the character who proves the real moving force in this central passage: namely, Psyche herself.

Psyche inaugurates the relevant action by virtue of the quasi-heroic deed around which the entire mythic plot pivots. Acting upon the advice of her sinister sisters, she takes an unsheathed blade and a lamp in hand and—violating Eros' repeated injunction—illuminates the darkness shrouding her sleeping lover. Psyche expects to find the vile monster whom she has determined to slay, but discovers instead the divinely gorgeous god. Overwhelmed, Psyche at first seeks to "hide the blade in her own heart," but her knife refuses to commit such an awful and senseless deed. Finding herself curious about Eros' own magic weaponry, the still half-stunned Psyche then accidentally pricks herself on his arrows, falling desperately in love with him. As Psyche throws herself upon the sleeping god, the lamp sputters, searing Eros, who—burned in more ways than one—flees in wounded anger.

How may all of this relate to Rilke? As always, it cannot be a matter of a literal translation of the myth, but rather a highlighting of corresponding archetypal motifs against the background of the poet's life and work. No single event can readily be identified with the act of discovery that breaks the spell of darkness and initiates, not only this chapter of the mythic story, but Psyche's defining quest. At the same time, resonant parallels are not too difficult to find.

We spoke earlier of the code of secret love and concealed identity that pervaded the atmosphere at Worpswede. Paula's covert engagement to Otto; Vogeler's still half-hidden bond with Martha; Rilke's own ambiguous affection for Paula and/or Clara—all these relationships were premised upon the unmarried, virginal aspects of the "girls" —their status, that is, as "maidens" rather than women initiated into the rites of selfhood. In "Girls II," Rilke had written:

> None may ever give herself to a poet
> even if his eyes longed for women;
> for he can only think of you as girls:
> the feeling in your slender wrists
> would break beneath brocade.[468]

But the fall of 1900 through spring of 1901 was a time of just such breakage: a period that saw the breach of love's secret code, the lifting of the protective cloak of darkness, the "outing" of maidens and their lovers. When he learned of Paula's engagement, Rilke fled. Not so long after, though, he threw himself into Clara's arms (and/or vice versa), and the feeling in her (never really very slender) wrists was, like that in Paula's, soon symbolically "broken." Though the marriages of Paula and

Otto, Rainer and Clara, and Heinrich and Martha transpired against the background of dramatically varied personal circumstances, all were, in one way or another, courageous commitments to move toward a new, more fully realized relationship to love: attempts to seize the day, to take hold of the divine beast—if not by the horns, then by his feathered wings—and bring what had been shrouded to light. In Rilke's case, too, there was the added element of the standing up to Lou. In mythic terms, this must count in part as a decisive confrontation with the (step-)mother. The cord of the past had to be cut: for all its ambiguous, even tragic aftermath, Rilke's marriage did help initiate him into his own, self-chosen, individual destiny. For better or for worse, he would never look at love in quite the same way again.

It is, though, crucial to recognize that the principal consequence of Psyche's initiatory act is *not* union, but quite the opposite, *separation*, and the loss of love. Burned by the oil that lights the lamp of consciousness—wounded by Psyche's betrayal—Eros flies off. Psyche clings to his thigh, but soon falls to earth. Eros, like a great bird of prey, castigates her from the treetops before disappearing altogether, leaving Psyche absolutely devastated. And who would not be? The spirit of Love—dearer, far dearer to the soul than life itself—is fled and gone.

No wonder Psyche—after venting her despair in tormented lamentation—seeks solace in death, and throws herself off a bluff into the river. The river god preserves her life, but the only thing that really saves the soul is the god Pan's wise advice to seek solace from Love himself—the hope, that is, that she may live to see Love again. Accordingly, Psyche begins *wandering*: half deliberately (she is, after all, both seeking Eros and seeking refuge from Aphrodite's wrath) and half-aimlessly—she has no idea, really, where to find love or refuge, suspecting the bitter truth that neither can be found any place on earth. Happening upon a neglected temple of Ceres, Psyche tends to the shrine and appeals for sanctuary to the goddess herself, but is repulsed—and the like happens in a temple of Hera. The soul, estranged from human life yet cast off by the gods, can find no spiritual asylum, and has no recourse but to turn herself in to Aphrodite's cruel handmaids: Habit, Trouble, and Sorrow.

The episode of the myth triggered by Psyche's act thus encompasses a host of interwoven motifs: loss and separation, falling away from heaven to earth; devastating (even suicidal) despair and (psychological) death; lamentation, loneliness, and longing; homelessness, limbo, exile, pilgrim quest, and errant wandering. Nor is it difficult to relate this nexus of motifs to Rilke: the last three chapters of this book reveal the texture of Rilke's life and work after Worpswede to be woven of the dark, complex fabric of just these psychic matters. The initiatory separations—Rilke's flight from (Paula at) Worpswede, Lou's flight from Rainer and vice versa, Rilke's flight from wife Clara and child at Westerwede—are readily evident, and these critical schisms, these crises in life and love, bring the rest in train: all those psychic consequences Rilke voiced intricately in poetry and prose, from self-flagellating expressions of listless despair in Berlin to evocations of the landscape of godlessness in Paris. "No new life can arise, say the alchemists, without the death of the old." Taking its cue from the darkening of soul life that follows upon the spirit—Love's—departure, Rilke's writing during this critical, transformative period could be said to represent a small but vital corpus of the literature of the *nigredo*.

In his interpretation of the Psyche-Eros story, Erich Neumann divides the myth into five parts: the introduction, the marriage of death, the act, the four tasks, the happy end. While Neumann's discussion of the archetypal significance of the second of these—the marriage of death—is provocative, his identification of that theme with a single early episode of the story—the ritual "sacrifice" of Psyche that precedes her transportation to the house of Eros—seems overly simplistic. Surely, Psyche's later descent into the underworld should be considered a moment of that marriage. Psychologically speaking, moreover, another passage of the myth must also enter into the picture, for *the real centerpiece of Psyche's linked relations to both heaven (via Eros) and Hades is the psychological death she suffers after her own deed of discovery and the consequent departure of the wounded Eros.*

Neumann himself aptly highlights the enormous importance of this *nigredo*-related theme: the *coincidence* of Psyche's devastating loss of (and separation from) Eros and her initiation into a new order of consciousness:

> The knowing Psyche, who sees Eros in the full light and has broken the taboo of his invisibility, is no longer naïve and infantile in her attitude toward the masculine; she is no longer merely captivating and captivated, but is so completely changed in her new womanhood that she loses and indeed must lose her lover. In this love situation of womanhood growing conscious through encounter, knowledge and suffering and sacrifice are identical.[469]

It is, after all, the suffering consequent upon her loss of Eros that ultimately initiates Psyche's true, self-conscious quest and pursuit of individual destiny, and so marks the *in-* and *con-ception* of her independent spiritual career. To put the matter in terms consonant with those of the last book of *The Book of Hours*, it is only when Psyche finds herself utterly estranged from this world, with nothing left to lose and (psychically speaking) pregnant with death, that the next phase of the myth (and of Psyche's imaginative development) may unfold.

Soul, then, emerges as the active agent of the death experience that catalyzes its own future transformation, preparing the ultimate knowledge of death (figured by Psyche's successful journey into and out of the underworld) that in turn finally enables a reunion with Love. In between Psyche's initiatory *nigredo* and her climactic reunion with Eros lies what—from a soul-making perspective—may well be considered the heart of the myth: the enormous work of Psyche's labors. A reading of the four major works that constitute the core of Rilke's mature oeuvre (*New Poems*, *The Notebooks of Malte Laurids Brigge*, *Duino Elegies*, and *Sonnets to Orpheus*)—*a poetic sequence that effectively enacts the completion of each of those daunting tasks in turn*—comprises the content of Book Two of our critical opus. To conclude Book One, though, I wish briefly to discuss Rilke's own imaginative encapsulation of the first "half" of his soul-history, his own quasi-mythic rendition of the train of archetypal events—hinged around an encounter with death—that bring Psyche to the threshold of her destiny.

We have already touched upon the text of *The Dragon Slayer*, the fairy tale Rilke composed in Westerwede one week before he wrote *The Book of Pilgrimage* in the fall of 1901. The titular subject of the story represents a classic *nigredo* theme. Edinger elucidates the motif in the following terms:

> The blackness, when it is not the original condition, is brought about by the slaying of something. Most commonly it is the dragon that is to be killed. The dragon is "a personification of the instinctual psyche" and is one of the synonyms for the *prima materia*. This image links the alchemical opus with the myth of the hero who slays the dragon. Just as the hero rescues the captive maiden from the dragon, so the alchemist redeems the *anima mundi* from

> her imprisonment in matter by *mortificatio* of the *prima materia*. Or, as Jung, puts it, "the slaying of the dragon is the *mortificatio* of the first, dangerous, poisonous stage of the anima...freed from her imprisonment in the *prima materia*."[470]

First of all, this explication may help explain a moment of the Psyche-Eros story we have not yet noted. When Psyche, following Pan's advice, begins her wandering search for Eros, her steps are not so errant as they might first appear. In short order, she finds herself at the cities of each of her sisters, and—employing the cunning newly learned from them—sends them off to fall to their deaths from the cliff above Eros' palace in their own vain search for Love. The sisters may well be regarded as personifications of the instinctual psyche, "the first, dangerous, poisonous stage of anima." Psyche's own (quasi-heroic) slaying of them and all they represent (jealousy, betrayal, lust, the desire for power, greed, and the like) figures as a consistent ingredient of the painful but purificatory *nigredo*.

In *The Dragon Slayer*'s somewhat more classic plot, however, the slaying of the dragon who terrorizes the realm is left to youthful male heroes from foreign lands. The one who succeeds is to win the kingdom's princess as bride. Rilke's description of the princess confirms that (as is invariably the case in fairy tales) she may be identified with Psyche/Soul: "And this King's only child was a maiden of great youthfulness, yearning, and beauty." As noted in chapter 5, however, Rilke's tale—despite its thoroughly traditionally setup—contains novel twists profoundly revealing of the poet's own imaginal insight into the mythic chapter we are concluding here.

The interest of the tale revolves around Rilke's handling of the interrelated themes of soul, death, love, and distance. The first notable incident involves a young adventurer who, though mortally wounded by the dragon, manages to crawl away from the forest battleground. Found the next day, he is taken into a small, secluded house on the edge of a wood quite some distance from the royal castle. The Princess hears of this hero, who suffers greatly from burning wounds, and feels inexorably drawn to him. She wishes to go to him but cannot bring herself to do so. Instead she sends, by way of an old servant, costly linens, salves, and healing wine. After three days, and three journeys, the old servant returns with the precious salve. The youth has died.

This news, however, affects the princess still more deeply. Now, despite the protestations of the aghast old servant, who does his best to dissuade her, she insists upon visiting the dead one. She makes the journey under the cover of night in the company of the old man. Arriving at the dimly lit house, they find the dead hero laid out upon a large table, covered in a crude cloth. The old servant seeks to hide the awful sight of the corpse from the princess, but she brushes by him and goes to the makeshift bier

> strong and not amazed, as if the form and countenance of death held nothing unexpected for her. She leaned like an angel over him, closed his eyes, and touched the strange, cold mouth with the endless sweetness of her first kiss. Then her knees buckled and she lay and pressed her face in her ice-cold hands and prayed...and wept. When she rose again, she hardly knew where she was and stood alone, breathless with fear.[471]

This scene figures a kind of initiation. By virtue of this encounter—centered upon the symbolic first kiss—the maiden soul achieves an intimate, even carnal knowledge of death. When she finally leaves the hut to journey homeward (alone, for the old servant has fallen asleep and she cannot bear to wake him, so much does his slumbering figure resemble death) her consciousness has been profoundly transformed:

> The young princess had never been so alone. It seemed to her as if everything somehow stayed behind her, for nowhere did she see a house, and the barking of dogs she heard from time to time was already far away....When she thought back, she didn't recognize the past anymore, and there was no future. So she was driven forward like a lightweight leaf, set loose from life.[472]

The imagery of the passage foreshadows the "last house" poem in *The Book of Pilgrimage*; its last line adumbrates the close of Rilke's famous "Autumn Day," composed in Paris almost exactly one year later.

The Princess's long evening, however, is far from over. Walking on, alone, she suddenly sees a rider coming toward her, and instinctively hides herself in the dark, moist roadside shrubbery.

> So he rode past. The girl looked after him a long time. All at once, she knew: he had slain the dragon. And instantly the knowledge

> came over her like a great wave of calm. She was no longer a lost thing in this night, she belonged to this trembling hero who rode into the morning, and he, whom she as yet did not know, would search for her tomorrow.[473]

Tomorrow, indeed, the Princess wakes to great rejoicing. The people are celebrating; bells ring in their towers. All seems to call upon the hero, but he has not yet shown himself. In the midst of the joyful noise, the Princess realizes: he never will.

> The one, however, who was really his own, knew that he would not come. She tried to imagine him enveloped in the loud gratitude of the crowd, and could not. She saw him ride alone into the morning. She saw him ride and herself remain behind. But the one who remained behind was not the same one she had been. She had grown. She reflected upon the dead one she had kissed and on the living one who was lost to her, and, for the first time, her thoughts touched Life.[474]

Thus does Rilke's tale figure (knowledge of) death as integral to the conception of life—of life, *and of love*. For the nuanced telling of his tale recalls the plotting of the Psyche-Eros myth: the moment the Princess sees and falls in love with the unknown hero—first the dead, and then the living one—is the *same* moment she loses him, perhaps forever. Yet because the Princess has knowledge of death and disorientation already behind—or *in*—her when she loses the victorious dragon slayer, she can move rather quickly toward the soul's true goal: the internalization of (the image of) love, *inner* marriage with Eros. Neumann articulates this same idea:

> With Psyche's love that bursts forth when she "sees Eros," there comes into being within her an Eros who is no longer identical with the sleeping Eros outside her. *This inner Eros that is the image of her love is in truth a higher and invisible form of the Eros who lies sleeping before her.*[475]

While this theme remains largely implicit in the original version of *The Dragon-Slayer*—the one we have been quoting here—the *revised* version Rilke produced a few months later includes lines that read like a poetic translation of Neumann's critical commentary:

> And the Princess, who heard the noise of jubilation, suddenly knew that he would not come. She tried to imagine him enveloped in the loud gratitude of the masses, but could not. Almost fearfully she sought to hold the image of the solitary hero, the trembling one, as she had seen him. As if it were important for her life not to forget that. And with that her mood became so festive that, although she knew he would not come, she did not interrupt the chamber maids who adorned her.[476]

And so the soul, equipped with this *inner* image of love (gifted, in part, by death) prepares for its sacred union.

Rilke, after the faltering of his marriage with Clara, never repeated the experiment of marriage. Indeed, in the ensuing years, he appeared to play the flightier part of Eros again and again: falling in love with one beautiful, sensitive woman after another (Mimi Romanelli, Lou Albert-Lasard, Magda von Hattingberg, Baladine Klossowska, to name just a few of the most notable), but resisting emotional claims and fleeing when his partners, refusing mere subservience, pressed too close. Thus arises the Don Juanism implicit in Rilke's continued identification with the puer archetype.

Even so, one cannot oversimplify Rilke's story. Leaving aside, as we must, the diverse details of his various love relationships, we may revert yet again to a dynamic cited several times before. While naturally favoring the masculine role of Eros in life, Rilke's more feminine side—his anima—weaves ever more powerfully through the current of his work. Rilke explicitly and repeatedly identified with the archetype of "the woman in love," and it would be possible to claim that—after the energy that inspired *The Book of Hours* finally spent itself—the itinerary of Rilke's work, and the perspective from which he wrote, was given, primarily, by anima. This would correspond, once more, with the plot of our guiding myth, for the next phase of the myth centers squarely upon the soul.

As Psyche commences her labors, Eros (his wings clipped, himself a convalescent prisoner of his mother's wrath) is largely out of the picture and remains so until the labors, and the story itself, are almost complete. Even so, to be sure, Eros is everywhere present, inspiring and guiding Psyche—but, as Neumann implies, he is so as *inner* image lodged in Psyche's heart. Neumann, commenting once again upon the consequences of Psyche's initiatory act of discovery, declares:

> *Psyche emerges from the darkness and enters upon her destiny as a woman in love*...for she is Psyche, that is, her essence is psychic, an existence in paradisaical darkness cannot satisfy her. It is not until Psyche experiences Eros as more than the darkly ensnaring one, not until she sees him...that she really encounters him. And in this very moment of loss and alienation, she loves and consciously recognizes Eros.[477]

So, too, the Princess of Rilke's *Dragon Slayer*, equipped with the inner image of her impossible love at the story's end. So too, indeed, Rilke himself, ready—after kissing death, and losing (married) life—to embark upon the laborious poetic quest that would produce the *New Poems*, *Malte*, the *Elegies*, and the *Sonnets*; the itinerary of his soul's making bringing him ever closer to consummating the inner marriage of psyche and eros, the soul and love, Eurydice and (the image of) Orpheus.

The world would first need to alter
in the evening wind
before I could find my way to your kisses
that are like riding a river's tresses
and a day mirrored in a pond.

The path was long, and sharp the turn
that fixed its course,
and deep the song:
so our steps can meet
a great circle-dance must first come round—
one you begin, one I
complete.

RILKE
Alongside the Pictures

Opposite: "Kissing Pair," Ludwig von Hofmann

BOOK II

LOVE'S LABORS

Paris to Muzot

"The Prodigal Son," Auguste Rodin, c. 1884

PART III

BY BEAUTY AND BY FEAR

Chapter 10

STONE IN YOU AND STAR

Evening

The evening slowly changes the garments
held for it by a row of ancient trees;
you watch, and the realms divide from you,
one traveling heavenward, one that falls;

and leave you, at home in neither one,
not quite so dark as the silent houses,
and not so surely vowing the eternal
as that which becomes star each night and rises—

and leave you (inexpressibly to unravel)
your life, fearful and immense and ripening,
so that it—now bounded, now reaching infinitely far—
becomes alternately stone in you and star.[478]

Composed somewhere between 1902 and 1906 (probably in 1904, in Sweden), "Evening" dates from the time just before the writing of most of Rilke's *Neue Gedichte* (*New Poems*) and images the poet's own sense of his psychic situation at that critical juncture. No longer confidently installed in the limitless heaven of youthful aspiration, Rilke had become all too familiar with an earthly world fallen—or falling—away from eternal concern, yet steadfastly refused to surrender his native idealism altogether. Stone and star symbolize the opposite poles of universal being: distant, unbounded, eternally ethereal *spirit* on the one hand, and dense, delimiting, concretizing *matter* on the other. In "Evening," Rilke profiles himself as identified with neither one nor the other, but suffering the dynamically riven center in between. The poet thus positions himself as one who, exploring the human condition, continues to *be* and *make soul*. During Rilke's early Paris years—years which enfold significant stays in Italy, Scandinavia, and Germany—that ongoing odyssey features, as one central chapter, realizing the meeting of extremes: discovering, under the tutelage of the sculptor Rodin, the deep affinities linking stone and star.

Rilke did, in all likelihood, pen at least one "new poem" well before "Evening." Written in 1903 (or perhaps, near the end of 1902) in Paris, "The Panther" heralds the new poetic style which finds prolific issue in nearly two hundred poems—the vast majority written between the winter of 1905 and summer of 1908—comprising the two volumes of Rilke's *New Poems*: *New Poems* (1907), and *New Poems: The Other Part* (1908). Interestingly enough, the very first "new poem" Rilke wrote may well be the most famous.

THE PANTHER

IN THE JARDIN DES PLANTES, PARIS

The passing of the bars fatigues his gaze
so much, that it can hold no more.
To him, it is as if each bar were a maze
that led to another, and another barred door.

The quiet pacing of strong and supple limbs
that turn around the very smallest sphere
is like a dance of power around the rims
of circles, that hold a great will numb in there.

Only seldom does the pupil's curtain slide
soundlessly up—. Then an image enters,
ripples through the tensely stilled stride
and ceases where the rhythm centers.[479]

Even a cursory comparison of this poem with "Evening"—which appears in the second, enlarged edition of *The Book of Images* published in 1906—reveals the most salient elements of the style that distinguish Rilke's *New Poems*. While "Evening" does take an objective image as a point of departure, the poem progresses, not by adding objective detail, but by subjectively centered elaborations initiated by the interpolation "you watch." By contrast, "The Panther" begins and ends with accumulating layers of evidently objective description, a sticking with the image of "the thing itself" that earned such poems the new generic name of *Dinggedichte* (literally, "thing-poems"). Correlatively, no readily identifiable poetic self or lyric ego—generally signaled by an "I" or (as in "Evening") a self-referential "you"—makes any obvious entrance, or speaks to us from center stage. Rather, the poetic consciousness appears purely observant and detached, supplying (or so it seems) nothing more than the poetic record of what simply *is*.

The objectivity sought by the poem inheres and incarnates too in the poem's own linguistic medium. As Robert Hass[480] notes, before *New Poems*, the form of Rilke's poetic thought generally conformed to the pattern of the poetic line. This end-stopping (evident, as well, in "Evening") tends to lend an ideal quality to poetic voice and object. "The Panther," however, inaugurates a practice of strong enjambment which intensifies considerably in the course of Rilke's development of his new style. That syntactic enjambment, coordinated with a concentration and accumulation of concrete imagistic detail, lends the poem a peculiarly material quality foregrounding its own status as a made thing, a thought-object sculpted out of language.

On the face of it, it might seem unlikely that a sculptor could act as master to a poet. Nonetheless, Rilke did indeed assimilate fundamental elements of Rodin's monumental art into work with his own far more subtle medium and thereby accomplish the poetic breakthrough memorialized in his *New Poems*. He did not, however, achieve that remarkable translation overnight. The process took years to mature and to bear its ripest fruit. Meanwhile, as we have seen, Rilke's initial years in Paris were anything but easy, and "The Panther"—even while auguring a new phase in Rilke's poetical career—can be read to signify much about the psychic pressure Rilke continued to suffer there.

The poem—like "The Ashanti" and, too, the first in *The Book of Poverty and Death*—takes mental and physical confinement as its subject. Indeed, the progressive restriction evident in the trajectory of *The Book of Hours*—from the expansive motion of falcon or storm, to the witnessing of a storm from behind the windows of a house, to being immured in stone—is echoed and intensified in the progressive contraction traced in the concentric movement of "The Panther." The first stanza evokes the wall of bars which cuts the panther off from (perception of) the world;

the second conjures the "very smallest" circle of the panther's ceaseless pacing, figure of his pent will; and the third, the virtual center of eye and heart, wherein the world, in all conceivable extent, vanishes altogether. Many commentators, including Hass, have remarked how terrifying the poem is: the panther's physical and psychic isolation is such that it experiences a total eclipse of objective reality, an obliteration that inevitably threatens to extinguish, in turn, any sane subjectivity. Will numbed, perception rendered inoperative, the panther circles in what could well be a kind of incipient madness, and it is understandable why the stricken patient in the film *Awakenings*,[481] fighting mental and physical paralysis, might identify with Rilke's awful creation.

In the years intervening between Rilke's arrival in Paris in August 1902 and the completion and publication of the *New Poems* in 1908, many signal developments—aside from the central relation to Rodin and the poetry engendered by it—aided Rilke's quest to break through the dark bars that sometimes surrounded him. In June of 1903 (shortly after completion of *The Book of Poverty and Death*), Rilke, in significant psychic distress, reached out to Lou, and the reestablishment of their relationship—first in correspondence, and two years later in person—undoubtedly helped him forward. Relations with Clara—and, indeed, too, with Paula—proved (from Rilke's standpoint) more mixed blessings, but nonetheless continued to figure importantly in his life. In the fall of 1903, Rilke traveled with Clara to Italy, and it was during their extended stay in Rome that he made a material start with both *New Poems* and *Malte*.

As it turned out, the Italian trip proved the first in a series of sojourns and temporary residences in Italy, Scandinavia, and Germany that kept Rilke away from Paris for two whole years. After Rome, Rilke's long journey to Sweden and Denmark (facilitated by the educationalist Ellen Key) enriched the imaginative resources upon which Rilke might draw in working on *Malte* and opened new doors of friendship. Yet Rilke's relations with Lou, Clara, Paula, and even Scandinavia predated his arrival in Paris; not so the association with Countess Luise von Schwerin, struck up at the White Stag in Dresden where both the Rilkes (financed by new Scandinavian friends) and the Countess were taking a cure in early 1905. Countess Schwerin invited Rilke to her castle—Friedelhausen in Hesse—thus inaugurating the liaison with rich and titled nobility that was to prove hugely important in Rilke's life and work. Rilke did visit Friedelhausen in the summer of 1905, though only after two other important sojourns: his reunion with Lou in her new house in Göttingen, and several weeks of study in Berlin with the classicist Georg Simmel, which fortified and deepened the poet's relation to classical mythology. Then, too, these years saw the publication of his *Book of Hours* in 1905—an enterprise that established Rilke's lifelong connection with Insel Verlag—as well as the publication (in 1906) of new editions of *The Book of Images* and *The Lay of the Love and Death of Cornet Christof Rilke*: developments of great significance for Rilke spiritually, socially, and materially.

All the above-mentioned matters contributed to Rilke's inner and outer maturation, and diffused, deflected, or redirected the force of the *nigredo* that had literally laid him low in Paris. Even so, none of them (with the exception of his work on *Malte*, which we will engage in subsequent chapters) proved as essential to the poet's progress as his relation to Rodin and the work it bred.

The writing of most of the *New Poems* followed upon the *second* of Rilke's several periods of close collaboration with Rodin. In the fall of 1905—immediately after his trip to Friedelhausen—Rilke returned to Paris, and soon commenced an eight-month stint as Rodin's private secretary. During that time, Rilke—when not on tour lecturing on Rodin—resided as Rodin's guest at Meudon, literally living with the master's sculptures and (at least initially) conversing with him almost constantly. Thus stimulated, Rilke began writing many "new poems" at Meudon, and his artistic output only increased after a breach with Rodin terminated their formal arrangement in May of 1906. Once more ensconced in his own Parisian quarters on Rue Cassette, "new poems" flooded from Rilke's pen in the summer of 1906, and did so again in the spring and summer of the two subsequent years. Imaginative evidence thus suggests that Rilke took the next major step in his soul's journey in and through the gestation and creation of his *New Poems*, work which represented not only a poetic breakthrough, but a psychological one as well.

The *New Poems* were, indeed, new for Rilke; at the same time, the body of work evinces profound continuities with all that had gone before. Sometimes viewed as Rilke's dramatic entrance into the modern era, his *New Poems* nonetheless do not enact any decisive break with his earlier inward development. On the contrary, they represent a concerted carrying forward of the spiritual and poetic evolution we have traced from the *Visions of Christ* to *The Book of Images* and *The Book of Poverty and*

Death: Rilke's transformation of his native religious tradition into an essentially poetic spirituality centered upon the soul—qua anima—and its formative relationship to love and death.

The signs of this continuity are perhaps most clearly inscribed in the groups of poems that begin and end the first volume of *New Poems*. Edward Snow remarks that both volumes "are intricately composed books of poetry, and even the most famous poems...take on a very different feel when read in context."[482] Consequently, in reading *New Poems* (we will concentrate almost exclusively upon the initial volume), we may do well to pay some heed to the order and arrangement of the poems—a task which Rilke himself took very seriously. Let us begin, as usual, at the beginning.

EARLY APOLLO

As sometimes between still leafless branches
a morning looks through that is already
glorious with spring: so nothing in his head
could prevent the radiance of all poems

from striking us with almost fatal force;
for there's as yet no shadow in his gaze,
his temples are still too cool for laurel
and only later will the rose garden rise,

tall-stemmed, out of his eyebrows
from which petals—one by one—are loosed
to fall...

"Early Apollo" opens the *New Poems* by sounding one of Rilke's chief themes: the origin of song, and the divine impulse underlying all art. By way of its densely metaphoric exploration of that subject, the poem posits too the formative relationship between poetry and sculpture that inaugurated the author's new project. Rilke erects the figure of Apollo—Orpheus' father—at the portal of his verse, invoking the divine solar power that, if unshadowed, can strike with almost fatal effect. Viewed from one angle, the poem recalls the very first poem in *The Book of Hours*, which likewise invokes the virtually unlimited creative force of a masculine gaze, albeit one seemingly devoid of the destructive element latent in Apollo's. Even in "Early Apollo," though, the terrible clarity of the God's visage finally softens as the poem's close turns attention from the cold fire in his eye to the smile that begins to warm:

> ...upon the quivering of the mouth
>
> that's now still quiet; never used and gleaming
> and only with its smile something drinking
> as if his song were being infused in him.[483]

The concluding lines suggest that the God—rather than already containing all poetic power in himself—may in fact be imbibing the substance of song from another source. The closing gesture does not quite succeed in taking Apollo down from his imposing pedestal, but certainly does move him toward the human pole of things, turning the stone face of the divine into one that may receive as well as give, *and opening it to reanimation.* Whereas the poem's opening leads us to believe we could almost be slain by the divine force coursing through the poems we are about to read, its ending repositions Apollo as one who may be listening *with* us, drinking in lyric strains that could bring him and his ancient art back to real imaginal life.

From a certain perspective, "Early Apollo" could be seen to stand alone at the threshold of Rilke's gallery of "new poems"; from another, one could well look at it paired with the second poem, "Girl's Lament," in a manner roughly analogous to the Orpheus-Eurydice duo that opens Rilke's famous later sonnet sequence. For if Apollo stands as the figurehead of a divinely creative masculine spirit, the subsequent poem immediately holds up the feminine, human, emotionally labile and vulnerable side of soul, a complementarity that sets up an attractive magnetism. Of course, Apollo and the girl are not, like Orpheus and Eurydice, lovers. Even so, while it may not be exactly Apollo himself the young girl yearns for, it is—as the close of the poem clearly reveals—desire for connection with a divine masculine spirit which stirs her:

> Suddenly I'm as if cast out,
> and into something vast and ill-fitting
> this solitude transforms,
> when, standing on my breasts' hills,
> my feeling screams for wings
> or for an end.[484]

As we have seen, it is precisely Psyche who—before her fateful meeting with Eros, as well as after his wounded flight—is "cast out" and alone, and whose feeling heart yearns for her winged Love or, in lieu of that, the death she repeatedly seeks, after as well as before the commencement of her labors. "Girl's Lament" thus inscribes a kind of poetic frieze of a central moment in the Psyche and Eros story into the sculptural opening of Rilke's *New Poems*.

Nor is this by any means an isolated or accidental incident. In fact, "Girl's Lament" strikes an erotic tone that rings resonantly through—at the least—the next seven poems, all unabashed love poems expressive, most especially, of feminine desire. Shadowing "Early Apollo's" sunlit gaze, this sizable group effectively headlines the whole volume, which thus unfolds under the banner of another of Rilke's master themes: the soul's relationship to Love.

As announced in its title, the third piece ("Love Song") effectively fuses the themes of the volume's first two poems, figuring the love that binds beings together as an instrument of song and (as is implicit in the speech-act of the poem) vice versa. Evoking the deep attraction of one human soul for another, the poem nonetheless tacitly recognizes the *archetypal* and *cosmological* backdrop of love's deep music in the very design of the poem's central conceit:

> Yet whatever touches *you* and *me*
> blends us together the way a bow's stroke
> draws *one* voice from two strings.
> Across what instrument are we stretched taut?
> And what player holds us in his hand?
> O sweet song.[485]

Here, "you and me"—the human lovers—are indeed material to the song, but hardly the whole story. In and of themselves, they are neither the divine musician nor the form of the instrument upon which he plays. The subsequent poem, "Eranna to Sappho," harps on a similar theme, evoking (as so many of these poems do) the strange—and strangely removed or *distant*—spiritual space the soul enters upon being touched by divine eros: "Your music / launched me far. I don't know where I am." Its conclusion, moreover, makes dramatically explicit the mythological dimension of any love scene:

My sisters think of me and weave,
and the house is full of trusted footsteps.
I alone am distant and given over,
and I tremble like a plea;
for the lovely goddess burns in the middle
of her myths and lives my life.[486]

Who is this "lovely goddess"—Venus, or perhaps Psyche herself, hearing "trusted footsteps" in Eros' palace? In any event, the lines once more clearly evoke Rilke's own abiding sense of the mythic, archetypal ground of the love poems that open his volume.

That Rilke would choose to place a group of love poems at the outset of his *New Poems* makes perfect sense, because it is precisely one of the boons of love to "make all things new," to foment revolution in the inner precincts of the soul and turn the world upside down, or inside out. Rilke's eighth poem, "Sacrifice," says as much, even as it dedicates the life of the soul to the *spirit* of love symbolized (as in "Evening") by the stars:

How my body blooms from every vein
more fragrantly, since I first knew you...

Look: I feel how I'm moving away,
how I'm shedding my old life, leaf by leaf.
Only your smile stands like pure stars
over you and, soon now, over me.[487]

Is it possible to identify a biographical source for these love poems? Not really. Composed between 1905 and summer of 1907, they were written during a period of time when Clara, Lou, and Paula were all part of Rilke's life, but not in a sexual or tangibly erotic wise; nor had any other significant romantic relationship yet blossomed. Nonetheless, "Love Song" is a far cry from the almost bitter "Solitude," its harmonious musical instrument a redemptive transfiguration of the neighbor's strange violin. The poems thus reveal Rilke's ongoing—and somehow refreshed—interior involvement with the myth of love, which he would engage, in life as well as art, more or less continually for the rest of his years. Rilke met Mimi Romanelli, the first of many flames to come, in the fall of 1907, not long after the last of these love poems were written.

In the deliberate arrangement of *New Poems*, the love poems blend into a group that revisit another of the watershed themes in Rilke's lifework: the complex and often vexed relationship to Judeo-Christian tradition so dramatically featured in his early *Visions of Christ*. The handful of poems here reveal yet again Rilke's keen sense of the need to rejuvenate religion and the impossibility of resting content with inherited images of God and spiritual sovereignty. The first, "Abishag," features an aging king who—while physically dependent upon a beautiful young maiden for the warmth of life—remains impotent, incapable of inspiring and sharing love. Linking the erotic and the biblical sets of poems, it suggests the decrepitude and insufficiency of the old patriarchal religious authority and its ultimate dependence upon a historically subordinated feminine soul-element.

"Joshua's Council" carries a kindred thrust. The poem is notable for its reminiscence of Joshua's willed domination of God ("they thought back to how high-handedly / he shouted to the sun in Gideon: stand: / And God went off, cowering like a serf"), but still more for his portentous disappearance at its close. The departure of the old patriarch (the only one who still lives in confidence of his God) again evokes—and with still more incisive rhetorical force—the end of an old religious order:

> But they saw him, as if silent for years,
> ascending to his mountain stronghold;
> and then no more. It was the last time.[488]

The next poem, "The Departure of the Prodigal Son," revisits and entirely revalues this theme of *departure*. In traditional tellings of the tale, the moral of the story revolves not so much upon the son's departure as upon his *return* and the unexpected welcome he receives at the hands of an evidently loving and forgiving father. As its title advertises, Rilke's version focuses exclusively on the occasion of the son's *leaving*. Indeed, not only does the body of Rilke's poem omit any reference to the son's return, it makes no allusion—explicit *or* implicit—to any father or God. Wholly internalizing the biblical topos, Rilke translates it into *an entirely psychological language and scene devoid of any apparent religious markers*. One could, perhaps even imagine this radical excision as a literary historical enactment of the son's departure. In any event, in Rilke's poem, it is the *going away* itself—not any putative return—that promises (perhaps!) the spiritual revivification which (as in "Sacrifice") figures as the overall aim of the *New Poems*.

Departure of the Prodigal Son

Now to go away from everything
tangled, that is ours, and yet—not so—
that, like water in an ancient spring,
mirrors us, trembling, and disturbs the picture-show;
from all of this—that would continually cling
to us, as if thorned—to part; and leave;
and this and that,
which we no longer perceive
(so familiar is it, so commonplace)
witness suddenly; gently, and with grace
as if from the beginning, and close-up;
and see the impersonal face
of suffering hid in the too-full cup
of childhood, spilt out across the land—:
and then, to go, still, hand from hand
as if tearing flesh from off the bone
and to go: where? Into the unknown,
far along a warm, unfamiliar strand
that behind each act like a windblown
backdrop remains indifferent: sea, or sand;
and to go: why? Out of instinct, out of urge,
out of impatience; dark expectation's surge,
out of the inability to understand:

To take all of this on and—in vain,
perhaps—let go of what's been learned, to die
alone, knowing nothing of the reason why—

is this the way to make life new again?[489]

If, for a moment, a reader might imagine that the Rilkean *vita nuova* could conceivably be achieved via conversion from an Old to a New Testament perspective, the next poem immediately disabuses her of that notion. Providing what is probably the *New Poems*' most dramatic and direct link to Rilke's own literary and spiritual past, "The Olive Garden" counts as a reprise of themes sounded in Rilke's third Vision of Christ, "The Jewish Cemetery." The former poem is assuredly far more violent in its disaffection; nonetheless, this "new" poem offers a devastating picture of religious disillusionment aimed at the heart and soul of Christianity. By force of disbelief, the poem converts a sacred landscape (Gethsemane, or the olive garden) into a thoroughly disenchanted, spiritually barren one, and its final lines issue a biting indictment of the ingrained tendency of traditional worship to promote no real imagination of God, but loss of self as soul and, withal, true parentage. All told, it offers an incisive reminder of the point d'appui of Rilke's own spiritual journey.

THE OLIVE GARDEN

He went up under the grey leaves
the leaves—all grey—covering the olive-lands
and laid his heavy dust-covered brow
deep in his hot dust-covered hands.
After everything, this. And this was the end.
Now I must go, even while growing blind—
and why is it your Will that I must say
you are, when I myself no longer find

you. I no longer find you—no, not in me—
not in others; not in this stone.
I find you no longer. I am alone.

I am alone with all human pain
which—through you—I sought to lighten,
you who are not. O unspeakable shame!

Later—they said—an angel came.

Why an angel? Ah, what came was night
which leafed indifferently through the trees
as the disciples stirred in their dreams.
Why an angel? Ah, what came was night.

The night that came was no uncommon one—
hundreds such go dully by.
Dogs sleep in them, and stones lie—
Ah, a sorrowful one, ah, any one
that waits until morning, not knowing why.

For angels do not come to such pleaders;
nights don't grow around them, like large rooms—
those who lose themselves are lost by all—
cut off from their fathers by a wall
and shut out of their mothers' wombs.[490]

The last of this set of biblical poems, "Pietà," may also be understood to reflect upon an earlier Christ Vision, insofar as it revisits—albeit in a quite different key—the problematic of Christian (a)sexuality. Portraying Magdalene holding the dead Jesus, bitterly lamenting the erotic union that was not—and now, never will be—consummated, Rilke's version of the famed tableau focuses upon the soul (Magdalene) in its primary relations to love and death. A compelling and provocative work that has proved a model for others, Rilke's "Pietà" may be interpreted in a variety of ways.

The poem (like "The Olive Garden") can be read as a repudiation of central Christian norms, though (like "Abishag") doing so in a manner recursively related to the first major group of "new poems": Magdalene's speech may be heard as a general complaint lamenting the absence (or at least suppression) of a truly feminine-erotic element in the *dominant* ethos of Christian love. Her passion may appear selfishly jealous:

But look, your hands are torn—:
Dearest, not from me, not from my biting.
Your heart stands open and anyone may enter:
it should have been a way in kept for me.

...but nonetheless accurately reflects a constitutive difference between two distinct varieties of love: *eros* and *agape*. While the latter, by definition, applies to humanity (or indeed all being) at large, eros, in its true relation to soul (a *psychological* relation that goes beyond general instinctual desire), remains inherently individual and individuating. As Rilke's moving "Pietà" intuitively suggests, a soul-making spirituality—one premised upon the transformative interaction of psyche and eros—cannot dispense with its patron love-God in the name of any more "universal" truth, especially one whose figurehead does not (unlike, for instance, Orpheus) manifestly require feminine consort.

The conventional Christian image of divinity—centered on Jesus Christ and his privileged relation to deity—remains bedeviled by lack of gender parity, not only its worship of a univocal Father God, but in the spiritual son's corresponding lack of an alchemical sister-soul. In

Christian iconography, the principal feminine other is, of course, Mary, but—by archetypal definition—a mother figure cannot finally double as the mystic *soror* or feminine consort needed to fill out a balanced picture of the whole of love and clearly image it as process of dynamic, dialogical transformation. Inevitably, the void attracts attention, and both popular and esoteric culture repeatedly inclines toward filling the missing anima position with the most likely candidate: Magdalene. Whatever the objective merit of Dan Brown's *Da Vinci Code*,[491] the author of "Pietà" would probably not have been the least bit surprised at the cultural phenomenon it represents, symptomatic as it is of one of our culture's most deeply seated psychospiritual needs. For Rilke's "Pietà" presents a picture of spirit—and spirituality—that has declined to enter into a relationship with soul on erotic terms; has refused it most intimate, individualizing intercourse. The concluding lines of Rilke's poem suggest that, in the last analysis, neither Magdalene nor Jesus, neither the human soul nor orthodox Christian spirituality, can survive that forfeiture intact.

> Now you are tired, and your weary lips
> have no desire for my aching mouth—
> O Jesus, Jesus, when was our hour?
> How strangely both of us are perishing.[492]

The place of the "Pietà" in *New Poems*—in combination with the thrust of the biblical and love poems that immediately precede it—encourages the foregoing reading, but Rilke's dramatic tableau can be seen differently as well. In general, after all—and in Rilke in particular—eros cannot be simply identified with sexuality so that denial of one necessarily translates into denial of both. On the contrary, for Rilke, denial or cessation of physical love often figures as a chief means of the soul's concentrated interiorization of eros. In this perspective, his Magdalene could be seen as an adumbration of Rilke's later idolization of women lovers (such as Gaspara Stampa or Marianna Alcoforado) whose love proved great precisely because it remained unrequited (or, in Hillman's terms, "impossible"). The soul, denied an exterior love-object, bears the mission of love forward in itself, in interior marriage (the model, of course, for nuns who style themselves as "brides of Christ").

It is, however, not only a figure of love Magdalene holds in her hands, but one of death as well. Rilke's poetic sculpture can therefore also be viewed as an image of the soul, qua anima, beginning to bear the relation to death which—as we saw in the last section of this book—along with love, initiates the soul's own spiritual awakening. While Rilke (after "Early Apollo") begins *New Poems* with a set of love poems, he ends it with a comparably impressive set focusing squarely upon the soul's relation to death and spiritual rebirth.

The continuity of the thematic concerns binding the *New Poems* to the archetypal world of "Death and the Maiden" emerges in graphic relief in the three narrative poems Rilke composed in Rome in 1904—"Tombs of the Hetaerae," "Orpheus. Eurydice. Hermes," and "Birth of Venus." Interestingly enough, though these are the first "new poems" Rilke wrote after "The Panther" and the only other ones that predate Rilke's later stay at Meudon, they are grouped with one of later vintage ("Alcestis") towards the very *end* of *New Poems*, a placement indicative of their weight and import for the volume as a whole. The poems pick up where the *nigredo*-infested *Book of Poverty and Death* left off: reimagining the soul's relation to death and (re)birth. In all of these works, Rilke consistently represents the soul by way of archetypal anima figures, but whereas *The Book of Poverty and Death* offers images of women whose relation to death and sex has been prostituted, and who are consequently incapable of true life-giving, these poems—following along the path cleared in poems like "Requiem"—offer the opposite: images of feminine figures truly embracing (or being embraced by) death's eternal kingdom, and reconnecting soul and spirit.

"Tombs of the Hetaerae" ends with a figure of such reconnection. Imagining the hetaerae as "river beds" filled with clear water, the poem ends with (once more) a *starry* world of spirit opening up above the calmly reflective element of the soul:

> They filled with smooth clear water
> across the whole expanse of their wide course
> ...while on high
> the starry nights of a sweet country
> blossomed into heavens that closed nowhere.[493]

"Orpheus. Eurydice. Hermes" takes as its point of departure the famous marble relief (a Roman copy of the 420 BCE Greek original) Rilke had viewed in the Louvre. The poet's Eurydice figure embodies still more powerfully the means by which the soul's exclusive relation to death impregnates it with the seed of its own spirit, engendering a species

Orpheus. Eurydice. Hermes

of interiority and self-containment virtually definitive (as we will discuss later in this chapter) of real being:

> She was in herself, like a woman near birth,
> and thought not of the man, who walked ahead,
> and not of the path, which ascended into life.
> She was in herself. And her having died
> filled her like abundance.
>
> Like a fruit ripe with sweetness and night
> she was filled with her great death,
> which was so new that she understood nothing.
>
> She was in a new virginity
> and untouchable.[494]

The imagery of ripe fruit (a favorite motif of Rilke's, borrowed, perhaps, from Paula's still-lifes) contrasts dramatically with the "little death, hanging dry and measly / like a fruit inside them that never ripened" of *The Book of Poverty and Death.*

Before Rilke, retellings of this myth tended to center upon Orpheus, treating Eurydice largely as a ghostly foil. Rilke's focus on Eurydice's inner experience—and indeed his imaging of her consciousness as by far the more compelling and spiritually relevant—represents an almost revolutionary gesture dramatically confirming the central place of soul in his work. In fact, the poem verifies the lead role played by (the feminine) psyche at this stage of his psychological development—and, indeed, during the whole latter half of his creative career—a prominence correspondent to Psyche's lead role in that portion of the myth revolving around her quest for (lost) love and the performance of her labors. "Orpheus. Eurydice. Hermes" adumbrates Rilke's consummating work, *Sonnets to Orpheus*; and when he returns to the myth almost twenty years later, Orpheus can function as the poet's God *only* because he is indissociably conjoined with Eurydice and has thoroughly absorbed into his being all that Eurydice, in this early poem, is just beginning to be and understand. "Be forever dead in Eurydice"—the meaning of this key phrase in the famous thirteenth sonnet (Part II) clearly flows directly from the form of consciousness Rilke explores in this crucial early "new poem."

In a manner consonant with this general theme, we may observe that the series of three poems beginning with "Tombs of the Hetaerae" reveal the soul qua anima *bearing* the relation with death in place of male figures unable or unwilling to do so. A determinate sequence prevails. In the first, "Tombs of the Hetaerae," the said role is not consciously assumed; indeed, as the title indicates, most of the poem focuses upon the tombs of the hetaerae and deals only indirectly with the soul and spirit of the women themselves. "Orpheus. Eurydice. Hermes" portrays Eurydice as just becoming conscious of the profundity of her connection to the realm of death—a connection so deep as to leave her indifferent to any life that would leave it behind. In "Alcestis" (the last of the three in placement and time of composition), the bride—dying in place of her husband, Admetus—takes the relation to death upon herself as a matter of conscious and deliberate choice. Speaking to the messenger God—Hermes—who has come to take Admetus' soul to the realm of shades, she declares:

No one can stand in for him. Take me.
I *am* a stand-in. No one's life is over
the way mine is. What remains to me
of all I was here? I'm *already* dying.
Didn't she tell you, when she charged you,
that the bed that waits inside there
belongs to the underworld?[495]

Questions revolving around the nature of death and its integral relation to soul, spirit, love, and sex are crucial to Rilke's vision. We will revisit them (and two of these poems) in another context in the next chapter—and again in the course of reading *Malte*, the *Elegies*, and the *Sonnets*—for Rilke's ever deepening contemplation of death remains the heartbeat of his evolving spiritual career, the pulse of his poetry. For now, we may say that, in the *New Poems*, Rilke's anima moves towards an ever more positive construction of death's transformative potential, and, too, toward more concrete poetic realizations of its imaginal character.

In "Death Experienced," an important poem placed near the center of the book, Rilke figures life as a stage filled with superficial action, a charade in which the figure of Death—duly costumed and disguised—participates. When Death's departure from the stage of illusion allows a glimpse of its truth, reality breaks through:

But when you [Death] went, a streak of reality
broke in upon the stage through that fissure
where you'd left: green of real green,
real sunshine, real forest.[496]

As an agent of initiatory transformation, the experience of death guides the soul towards the inner renaissance that defines the telos of Rilke's *New Poems*, that "making life new again" subtly symbolized—in the famous poem immediately following "Death Experienced"—by the suddenly revivifying color of fading blue hydrangeas. The writer of the *New Poems* may still be suffering the *nigredo*, but the poems reveal him already turning his experience of death's darkness into more brilliantly living color.

Accordingly, after "Tombs of the Hetaerae," "Orpheus. Eurydice. Hermes" and "Alcestis"—three poems centering upon death—Rilke, in the collection's penultimate piece, offers a poem of (re)birth. In "Birth of Venus" the poet paints the emergence of the Goddess of love and of beauty with such exquisite detail that we witness her born on the page. The poem inevitably recalls Botticelli's iconic masterpiece; indeed, Rilke's Venus incarnates the very idea of renaissance. Nature itself comes back to life under the influence of her archetypally feminine energies:

> Behind her,
> as she strode swiftly on across the young sands,
> all morning long the flowers and the grasses
> sprang up, warm, confused,
> as from embracing.

Even so—as the poem continues to its conclusion—a dead dolphin, coughed up by the sea, signals the ineluctable connection of beauty, birth and death:

> But at noon, in the heaviest hour,
> the sea rose up once more and threw
> a dolphin on that selfsame spot.
> Dead, red, and open.[497]

We will discuss the very last poem of the book, "The Bowl of Roses," in the next chapter. For now, suffice it to say that this poem picks up on and utterly transforms the image of openness that closes "The Birth of Venus." The roses (though neither corporeal women nor Goddesses) are manifestly feminine in nature, so that it is fair to declare that—just as the book virtually opens with poems expressive of the (feminine) soul's desire for love—it ends with peculiarly feminine consummations. Anima energy thus envelopes and authorizes Rilke's *New Poems*, which—like Rilke's roses—unfurl as so many figures of soul.

Still, to understand the nature and kind of consummation the book ultimately reaches—and to comprehend the main body of the text—we will have to look more closely at what we have, so far, left out. That includes the (largely) excluded middle, important poems that help shape the "torso" of the text; and—still more crucially—issues that cannot be approached by way of chiefly thematic analysis. Both matters will be taken up in subsequent sections of this chapter. Here, let us close this preliminary exploration with brief indications on both scores.

As far as the body of the text is concerned, in between the beginning and ending groups of poems mentioned so far, other more or less tightly knit groups (medieval, animal, human types, historical, portraits, things, places) work intricate, interweaving variations on Rilke's leading themes.

After "Pietà,""Song of the Women to the Poet," closely echoing Rilke's earlier "Girls II," links the soul qua anima and the archetypal poet; the next poem ("The Poet's Death") interrogates that poet's own relation to death. Then, in the impressive "Buddha," the motif of *distance* already introduced in the love poems assumes a still more powerful spiritual valence as Rilke recurs, once more, to the symbol of the star:

> As if he listened. Stillness: something distant...
> we check ourselves and cease to hear it.
> And he is star....

...and, too—at the poem's close—to the castaway state of the soul experiencing the inaccessibility of spirit:

> For what tears us roughly to his feet
> has circled in him for a million years.
> He, who forgets what we experience
> and who experiences what casts us out.[498]

While it is impossible to trace all the thematic lines of force written into the *New Poems*' intricate designs, what has already been said may suffice to reveal the many strong threads that bind the *New Poems* to Rilke's prior soul work even while providing some sense of the volume's novel force and twist. Let us close this preliminary review of some of the *New Poems*' principal themes by returning to the one early biblical poem we did not mention.

Like the first and immediately prior Old Testament poem, "Abishag," "David Sings Before Saul" features an aging sovereign who leans upon a youthful figure—David, the young psalmist or poet-singer. The poem accordingly registers Rilke's continued allegiance to the rejuvenative force of the puer impulse; yet, unlike "Abishag," "David Sings Before Saul" ends on a conciliatory note, seeking a balance and fusion of youth and age, puer and senex, that might achieve the kind of spiritual illumination figured—yet again—by the star. David speaks these closing words:

> Can you feel, now, how we reconfigure?
> King, King, heaviness becomes spirit.
> If only we hold on to one another,
> you to youth, King, I to age,
> we are almost like a star that circles.[499]

Rilke's imagination of David and Saul in this poem resonates with overtones of his own relation to the much older Rodin. And what exactly did Rilke take from the old master? We made some small start on this subject in our analysis of "The Panther," but the primarily thematic inquest we've pursued in this section—while confirming the coherence of Rilke's ouevre and, especially the continued relevance of the Psyche-Eros mythos—nonetheless cannot in and of itself achieve this chapter's chief aim: laying bare what it is, exactly, that makes *New Poems* new, catapulting Rilke into a *new* phase of the Psyche-Eros story. Rilke's own Rodin book eloquently articulates why this is so:

> It is possible, if one so desires, to explain and illuminate most of Rodin's works by associating ideas with them...With Rodin subject matter is never attached to a work of art like an animal to a tree....
>
> [But] when the first inspiration comes from the subject matter, when the impulse to create is given by a classic legend, part of a poem, a scene from history or some actual person, such material is transformed more and more...into something concrete and anonymous: translated into the language of the hands, the demands which then arise all have a new meaning, which depends solely on the conditions of plastic realization.[500]

Or, to put the matter more succinctly:

> His art was not based upon any great idea, but upon the conscientious realization of something small, upon something capable of achievement, upon a matter of technique.[501]

Pursuing Rilke's own lead, let us continue by focusing yet more closely upon the specific gravity of Auguste Rodin's influence upon the still young poet-singer's life and work, for only so are we likely to approach the heart and soul of his *New Poems*.

"*Il faut travailler, rien que travailler*"—"one must work, nothing but work"—this was the old master's credo, embodied in a life of ceaseless labor, day in and day out, shaping the unyielding element of stone. The young poet, weary of a creative life dependent upon fickle inspiration, aspired to follow the master's model and enthusiastically adopted Rodin's

Rodin with sculpture of Victor Hugo, ca. 1900 (top);
Rilke and Clara in Friedelhausen, 1906

Rilke in 1906 (top) and at the Hotel Biron in 1908

Rilke in the Hotel Biron, 1908

motto as his own. Shortly after his arrival in Paris, Rilke—despairing of adequate expression in French conversation—confessed his conversion in a letter to the sculptor:

> It was not only to do a study that I came to be with you,—it was to ask you: how must one live? And you replied: by working. And I well understand. I feel that to work is to live without dying. I am full of gratitude and joy. For since my earliest youth I have wanted nothing but that. And I have tried it. But my work...has become...a festival connected with rare inspirations; and there were weeks when I did nothing but wait with infinite sadness for the creative hour. It was a life full of abysses. I anxiously avoided every artificial means of evoking the inspirations....but I didn't have the courage to bring back the distant inspiration by working. Now I know that it is the only way of keeping them.—And it is the great rebirth of my life and of my hope that you have given me.[502]

In the aftermath of his failed experiment at householding, this missive signaled Rilke's single-minded devotion to the work of the artist and a new *niveau* of interest in the conscious crafting of his poetic art.

Unfortunately, the far more immaterial substance of the poet's art offered less concrete resistance, less solid ground, than the sculptor's, and it was vain to imagine that Rilke could work with the same almost superhuman constancy as Rodin. Nonetheless, the still suffering poet did what he could, deliberately drawing up lists of things to write about and—"on assignment" from Rodin as once, in Italy, from Lou—visiting Paris's botanical gardens and following strict instructions to observe everything as closely as possible. Inevitably, though, the poet's attempt to renovate his work habits ran up against his own still formidable psychic walls. While "The Panther" stands out as an early victory, the endeavor initially met with only partial success. Nonetheless, as Rilke's letter implies, the example of Rodin's prodigious—and prodigiously creative—labor represented more, far more, than a purely *practical* model for the poet, and his voluntary apprenticeship to this new master effectively signified a dramatically new phase of Rilke's poetic psychology, one that culminated in the concentrated and prolonged poetic effort that finally produced—as its first rich harvest—the *New Poems*.

Before parsing the concrete features of Rodin's art (and they are quintessentially relevant to Rilke's poetic progress), we must first duly acknowledge the signal importance of this more general fact: for Rilke, the great sculptor of *The Gates of Hell* was himself a portal, initiating the poet into a novel maturity defined by *a new concept of* and *practical commitment to* his soul's poetic mission.[503] Modeling a vision of the making of things as a concerted, almost endless work of love, Rodin effectively ushered Rilke into the next chapter of his own soul-history. Still racked by the handmaids Trouble and Sorrow, the young writer's poetic psyche—finally facing the Goddess's dread music—commenced its daunting, yet thoroughly transformative, labors.

When Psyche, despairing of finding Eros on her own (and despairing, too, of finding refuge from the angry Goddess's wrath) puts herself into Venus' vengeful hands, she initiates a novel and crucial phase of her mythic story. No longer wandering quite so errantly—momentarily worshipping at this, then that God's ancient, neglected altar—Psyche does not (as she half-expected) find herself immediately condemned to death. Instead—in a motif familiar from numerous fairy tales, those eminently imitable bibles of the psyche—she is set a series of tasks necessary for the fulfillment of her distant goal. To be sure, these tasks are all seemingly impossible; to be sure, she cannot accomplish them without almost supernatural aid. Even so, the agents that assist Psyche—even while working under the higher auspices of love—are elements of her own undiscovered capacities, and the preeminent fact remains: in this phase of the myth, the soul is deliberately *set to work*. The psychology proper to this phase of the myth can thus be conceived as *a psychology of labor*, the more so, of course, because Psyche is pregnant all the while. Cognizant of Eros' omnipresence in the background, we could also construe this penultimate stage of Psyche's career as her labor(s) of love. Given that the true end of the work is not only reunion with Eros, but, coincidently, the remaking and rebirth of self, the labor(s) of love Psyche performs may well be considered the marrow of the whole project of soul-making.

Psyche does not, however, set out, full of determination, immediately after Eros' departure. Devastated by his abandonment of her, she attempts to kill herself. Though it is the kindly river spirit who saves her body, it is another God who, at this pivotal moment, rescues her soul:

> The kindly stream...caught her in his current and laid her unhurt upon a bank deep in flowering herbage. It chanced that at that moment, Pan, the god of the countryside, sat on the river's brow

> with Echo, the mountain goddess, in his arms, teaching her to make melodious answer to sounds of every kind... The goat-footed god called Psyche to him...[504]

Pan proceeds to assuage Psyche's suicidal grief *by wisely counseling her to seek out Eros*, sagely sending her on her way in quest of love.

In his commentary on the myth, Neumann makes clear Pan's pivotal importance:

> Let us not forget who it is that Psyche first meets after Eros has forsaken her and after the river has frustrated her attempt at suicide... *it is (Pan) who gives Psyche the lesson with which she goes on living, and which profoundly influences the whole ensuing action*... Pan is the god of natural existence, taught by "long old age and ripe experience"... Psyche's true mentor. His figure remains entirely in the background, and yet this "old sage" determines Psyche's development."[505]

"It is the great rebirth of life and hope you have given me," wrote the young poet to the old sculptor. Clearly, if we are to seek Rodin's archetypal likeness in the texture of our myth, it is to the great God Pan we must look: Pan, whose name means "all," bearer of instinctual wisdom and the primal energy indwelling the whole panoply of natural forms; Pan, the sweet player of pipes amorously teaching the nymph Echo "to make melodious answer to sounds of every kind"; Pan, the old sage whose wise advice first rescues Psyche from self-destruction and whose agents (ants, reeds, eagles) possess the innate knowledge of things necessary for the successful accomplishments of her tasks.

If Pan can effectively mentor Psyche on account of his "long old age and ripe experience," Rodin likewise functioned as a positive senex figure for Rilke, acting as an "old sage" who helped balance the puerile elements of Rilke's personality. In this respect, too, he counts as a pivotal, threshold figure, mediating between Rilke's "eternal youth" and the arduous labors of love that inaugurate the poet's maturity.

Age alone, however, hardly defines Pan's—or Rodin's—purview. Above all else, Pan stands as the preeminent God of Nature, the archetypal embodiment of all Nature represents—including endless creativity. In this respect, too, Rilke's own description of the master sculptor makes amply clear the archetypal connection linking Pan and Rodin. If Pan's very name signifies the plethora of forms characteristic of his domain,

Rilke marvels repeatedly at the incomparable abundance issuing from Rodin's superhuman generativity. Correspondingly, in his monograph, Rilke speaks of "that deep agreement with Nature, which is characteristic of Rodin" and—after quoting Rodenbach's description of him as an "elemental force"—elaborates the analogy:

> And indeed, there is in Rodin a deep patience which makes him almost anonymous, a quiet, wise forbearance, something of the great patience and kindness of Nature herself, who, beginning with some negligible quantity, traverses silently and seriously the long pathway to abundance.[506]

True, the picture Rilke draws here—while consonant with the particularly gentle, sage and bucolic Pan imaged by Apuleius—hardly tallies with the God's often more rambunctious and even disorderly energies. Even so, the goat-footed God's ubiquitous sexuality—which styles him as an earthly cousin of Eros—itself finds ample expression in the sculptor's work, and it may well be supposed that Rodin's supremely steadfast will and consummate control proved the necessary counterweight to the virtual pandemonium perpetually surfacing in the body of his work. Rilke again:

> [Sculpture] surely possessed the power to bring help to an age tormented by conflicts which lay, almost without exception, in the realm of the invisible. The language of this art was the body. And when had this body last been seen? Layer upon layer of clothing had been laid upon it like constantly renewed varnish, but beneath these protecting incrustations the living soul, breathlessly at work upon the human face, had transformed the body too. It had become a different body. If it were now uncovered, it would probably reveal a thousand forms of expression for all that was new and nameless in its development, and for all those ancient secrets which, emerging from the Unconscious, like strange river gods, lift their dripping heads from out the wild current of the blood.[507]

Here, though, we are already verging upon discussion of the peculiarity of Rodin's art, parsing the specific psychology of the sculptural technique that enabled Rilke—who assimilated it into his own idiom—to accomplish his own conflicted soul's first great task.

The peculiar appeal Rodin's medium held for Rilke derived, in part, from the poet's own intensely contracted state, the soul-implosion triggered by the *nigredo* he continued to suffer. Rilke began his *Book of Poverty and Death* by imaging himself immured in stone; the art of the sculptor who works to *liberate forms of life* from the dense resistance of matter thus answered to the poet's deepest psychic need. Though no immediate panacea (*The Book of Poverty and Death*, after all, postdates Rilke's initial engagement with Rodin), the model of Rodin's artistic praxis could offer an interior avenue of escape from the psychic cul-de-sac Rilke had run into—or, more precisely, help him find a way through that dark tunnel to the light that shone at its end.

Rilke on Rodin:

> Ultimately, it was this surface [of the body] which became the subject of his study. It consisted of innumerable effects of light falling upon the object, and it appeared that each of these effects was different and each remarkable. At one place the light seemed to be absorbed, at another to give a lingering greeting, at a third to pass coldly by.[508]

In his monograph, Rilke emphasizes again and again that Rodin's is an art of *living surfaces*. Still (as the "strange river god" passage cited previously discloses) that should not for a moment disguise the psychic depths plumbed and lifted to expression in the gestures that animate the sculptor's forms. "Human life, its blood and heartbeat, its weeping and speaking, is confronted with and folded into bodily form . . . these moments are fashioned into plastic shapes that contain them."—so Ralph Freedman glosses Rilke's own careful reading of Rodin.[509] Under Rodin's tutelage, Rilke studied—with unprecedented intensity and focus—the technical craft of making visible the indwelling soul of things, the mysterious translation between spirit and form that lies at the heart of art.

It was crucial that the end result amount to something more than work expressing mere feelings. Rilke, by his own admission, had had more than enough of that and craved, not to leave feelings behind, but to realize their mode of objective existence; to make, as the poet said, "things out of feelings," to lend ever more *concrete* existence to the soul's innate longings. Consequently, Rilke's turn to sculpture represented yet another remarkable step in the trajectory of his own relation to the poetic image, one following directly upon the line of advance that leads from the iconic imagination informing his *Book of Hours* to the more purely painterly sensibility trained at Worpswede. A passage from Rilke's Rodin book indicates the poet's own sense of the religious underpinnings of these transformations:

> Necessity had created [the strange sculpture of the medieval cathedrals]. Fearful of the invisible tribunals of an oppressive faith, men had sought refuge in these visible forms, had escaped from the unknown to this concrete embodiment. Still seeking reality in God, men showed their piety, not any longer by inventing images for Him and seeking to picture the All-too-distant one, but by bringing into His house, laying in His hand and on His heart all the fear and poverty, all the timidity and the gestures of the humble. This was a better way than by painting, for painting was also an illusion... they desired something more real, something simple...
>
> And looking from the plastic art of the Middle Ages back to the antique, and again beyond the antique to the beginning of eras whose age cannot be reckoned, did it not seem that at every hopeful or disquieting turning-point of history the human soul had ever and again demanded this art which gives more than word and picture, more than similitude and appearance, this simple becoming-concrete of its longings or its apprehensions?[510]

The passage lays bare Rilke's own conception of the psycho-spiritual ground of art.

Rodin's own more modern art figures a further development of the sculptural impulse:

> Whilst at work upon the Brussels Exchange, Rodin must have felt that buildings no longer attracted sculpture to them, as did the old cathedrals... The piece of sculpture was a thing standing apart... something which could exist for its own sake alone, and it was well to give it absolutely the character of an object round which one could pass and which could be observed from all sides. And yet, it must in some way be distinguished from other things... made, by some means, untouchable, sacrosanct,

> separated from the influence of accident or time . . . part of the calm permanence of space and its great laws. It must be fitted into the surrounding air as into a niche and thus be given a security, a stability, a sublimity due to its simple existence and not to its significance.[511]

Thus did Rodin's sculpture stand in the gallery or Meudon and so too does Rilke's "Early Apollo" seem to stand, regally independent, in poetic space. It is of course no accident that the first of Rilke's new poems is literally a piece of sculpture, but all his *Dinggedichte*—indeed, to a significant degree, most all of his *New Poems*—exhibit a similar free-standing quality.[512]

In the case of Rodin, Rilke perceived that the secret of achieving this effect lay in the master's ability to shape matter so as to endow *every least part* with vitality so that the whole form radiated with the vibrancy of some thing that *is*, possessing not merely representational form but real being. The technical means of accomplishing this—the art of *modèle*, or modeling planes of space to creative activity at the surface—became, as Rilke wrote, "the fundamental element of his art . . . the cell of his world."[513] Translating the lesson into his own medium, Rilke fashioned poetic objects out of "an endless variety of living surfaces," catching soul-life in its innumerable "moments of transition" and, by organizing and balancing these in the delicate motions of syntax, revealing the spirit of the thing itself.

"Roman Fountains" offers a consummate instance. Composed of deftly modeled strokes of sound and meaning that constantly shift and play off each other in the sinuous syntax of the *single* sentence that symbolizes its overall unity, the poem takes transition as its culminating theme as well as its principle of form:

Roman Fountain

Borghese

Two basins, one rising above the other
out of an old, round, marble rim
and from the one above, water bending softly
down to water standing in wait below the brim

receiving that gentle speech in silence
and secretly, as in a hollowed hand,
showing it sky behind green and darkness
like some unfamiliar object, and

itself spreading gently—circle after circle—
without homesickness in the lovely shell;
only sometimes dreamily, drop by drop,

letting itself down the moss hanging low
into the last mirror that makes its well
smile softly with transitions from below.[514]

To read this poem is to walk around a piece of poetic sculpture. One follows the gradual, careful construction of the object—registering first one facet or gesture, then another, and constantly adjusting the mind's eye to the continually transforming relationships, filling out the imagination of the thing as the whole shape fills out in space. Rilke's words refuse to stay flat on the page but immediately insist on an almost palpable three-dimensionality so that one could say—if the analogy were not too trivial—that the *New Poems* acts almost like a pop-up book. In structure and motion, the poem mimes or performs its object: the sonnet's stanzas act like basins which conduct consciousness—like water—down from one to the other, reflecting even as it moves and falling, finally, into the last vessel, the last word, that somehow completes the thing and contains it all.

Rilke's poetic procedure here bears *some* resemblance to that exhibited in the poetic painting "Die Znamenskaya"; however, the imagination producing the earlier piece self-consciously composes with line or contour rather than shape, and the iconic object never fills out in the same way. In part, it does not do so because the center of attention never rests exclusively on the thing itself: from the first, it advertises its dependence upon the hand producing it, and much of the evolving interest of the poem inheres in the dialogue that develops between the poetic persona (the icon-painter) and spiritual subject *represented* by the object—namely, Mary. Not so in "Roman Fountain," in which, characteristically, the authorial consciousness remains anonymously unobtrusive, effectively out of the picture altogether, so that (as Rilke's "cathedral quotation" stipulates) the religious value of the thing itself inheres in the sheer reality of its simple presence.

Rilke himself, of course, had anticipated just such a development in his *Book of Hours*. Even while inspired by orthodox art, his icon-painting monk had professed the wish to worship his God in a manner not mediated by any representational form, let alone typical religious imagery. "There is no image I could invent / that your presence would not eclipse. / I want, then, simply to say the names of things."[515] In the *New Poems*, Rilke is doing just that—though of course, it is anything but a simple matter. His Roman Fountain's own "simple presence" emerges as the dynamic resolution of numerous delicately balanced planes of poetic force evoked by a concatenation of deft poetic gestures.

Rilke explicitly recognized too that it is just such balancing of internal motion that reconciles change and life in time with the permanence of space and so contributes to the sense of self-contained presence investing the art object:

> Movement was not contrary to the spirit of sculpture; only such movement as is incomplete, as is not balanced by other movement, such movement passes beyond the object itself... However great the movement in a piece of sculpture, whether it comes from infinite distances or from the depths of the heavens, it must return to the marble, the vast circle must be closed.... This distinguishing characteristic of things, complete self-absorption, was what gave plastic art its calm.[516]

Not only so, but the sense that movement in the art object *does* indeed come "from infinite distances or from the depths of heavens" contributes integrally to its evocative power, creating it as a veritable incarnation of eternal measure and lending it extension into spiritual space. Discussing the "monumental principle" of Rodin's sculpture, Rilke writes that the master

> was able to create things which were visible afar off, things surrounded not merely by the immediate atmosphere but by heaven itself. With one living surface he could catch and reflect the distances as with a mirror and could form a gesture which appeared immense, forcing space to participate with it.[517]

"Roman Fountain," too, does this, both formally and thematically ("and secretly, as in a hollowed hand / showing it sky behind green and darkness"), as does "Early Apollo" in the very first lines of the *New Poems*:

As sometimes between still leafless branches
a morning looks through that is already
glorious with Spring: so nothing in his head
could prevent the radiance of all poems

from striking us with almost fatal force;
for there's as yet no shadow in his gaze...

and—more succinctly, in "Buddha":

As if he listened. Stillness: something distant...
We check ourselves and cease to hear it.
And he is star.

Each of these instances (and myriad more could be cited) reveals Rilke's mastery of the art of gesture, modeling the surface of his language into metaphoric expressions that give us insight into various aspects of the (poetic) thing itself, lending it both *cosmic dimension* and *concrete reality*. In his *New Poems*, we find Rilke working toward material reality that—rather than falling away from spiritual essence—incorporates it into the body of poetic substance. Indeed, we can by now begin to catch a glimpse of how Rilke's Rodin-inspired art responded to the falling of earth away from heaven, the dividing of carnate and eternal concern integral to the *nigredo*. Rilke's artistic attempt to incorporate heavenly space into the smallest facets and features of poetic body can be seen as a step toward closing that gap, bridging the space *between stone and star* which, in reality, is no void, but the place of human life, the soul-life that fills and spills out of the sculpted volume of Rodin's sculptures and Rilke's *New Poems*. One of Rilke's own favorite symbols of that soul is *the smile* which brings the speaking mouth to gestural expression: the smile that warms the distant God Apollo's lips and flashes from the faces of adolescent girls going round on a carousel like a promise of an indescribably distant, yet ever present love. The smile animates the human world with the joy of inner (re)union, countering and complementing the tears of sorrow that fall, eternally, from the flight of love away from the world.

That space between earth and heaven, mortal flesh and immortal spirit is, too, *the distance opened between Eros and Psyche consequent upon the former's wounded flight*. As Psyche begins her labors, the convalescent Eros is nearby, and yet—because Venus has taken pains to confine him to her house—remote and inaccessible. In concrete terms, then, Rilke's Rodinesque art, his animate blending of the worlds of stone and star, figures a stride forward on Psyche's long path toward her close yet distant divine love.

It is naturally no accident that Rodin's work—hardly less than Rilke's own—revolves around the relation of the soul to love: only so could the sculptor have become the poet's model and master. Numerous sculptures indicate this truth—his iconic "The Kiss," "Magdalene and the Christ" (a source for Rilke's own "Pietà"), "Fugit Amor," "The Eternal Spring." The prevalence of erotic energy and manifest anima figures ("Psyche and Spring," "The Eternal Idol," "The Interior Voice") is such that Rilke himself could see a dynamic kin to that unfolded in Eros and Psyche as the thematic and spiritual center of Rodin's art, the master gesture inscribed in the body of the sculptor's prodigious work:

> Running parallel with the whole history of the human race, there was this other history, innocent of covering, of convention, of rank and class—which knew only conflict. It, too, had had its historical development. From being a mere instinct, it had become a longing, from being an appetite between man and woman, it had become a desire of one human being for another. And as such it appears in Rodin's work. It is still the eternal conflict of the sexes, but woman is no longer the forced or willing animal. Like man, she is awake and filled with longing, it is as though the two made common cause to find their souls.[518]

Soul-searching and soul-making: in Rodin and Rilke, the two are one. It is time to turn to more explicitly to the relation between Rilke's newly learned sculptural art and the larger trajectory of his poetic soul, to interrogate the place of his *New Poems* in the plot of Psyche's spiritual career.

Chapter 11

ENCHANTED ONE

First, let us rehearse Psyche's initial task, assigned by the furious Venus:

> Taking corn and barley and millet and poppy seed and chick peas and lentils and beans, all jumbled and confused in one heap, she said to her: "I cannot conceive that any serving-wench as hideous as yourself could find means to attract lovers save by making herself their drudge; wherefore now I myself will make trial of your worth. Sort that disordered heap of seeds, place each kind of grain apart in its own place, and see that you show me the work completed before the evening."[519]

Psyche is overwhelmed. After Venus' departure, she sits "in silent stupefaction" in front of "that disordered and inextricable mass." Fortunately, though, the ants, those "nimble nurslings of the earth," pity the poor, lovely girl whom they know to be Love's own spouse, and take action:

> Wave upon wave, the six-footed hosts, one by one, with the utmost zeal, separated the whole heap, grain by grain. And after they had parted and distributed the several grains, each after their kind, they vanished swiftly from sight.[520]

So Psyche—or that part of the soul represented by the ants—completes the task. How does the symbolism inherent in it illuminate the poetic work Rilke accomplishes in his *New Poems*?

Much depends upon one's understanding of the seeds. In his reading of the myth, Neumann initially construes the heap of seeds as an undifferentiated mass of seminal—and so anonymously *masculine*—power. In this connection, he alludes to Bachofen's notion of "hetaerism," a cultural and psychological stage characterized by instinctual and indiscriminate sexuality driven, primarily, by masculine appetite. As Neumann indicates, the phase of Psyche's sexual service to the unknown Eros—a phase wherein he is both the God of love *and* a phallic serpent-monster—bears some relation to this hetaerism. Psyche's initial task involves a *sorting* of that indiscriminate generative force, or "putting order into masculine promiscuity."[521]

Tellingly, two of the three "new poems" Rilke wrote in Rome in the beginning of 1904—the first "new poems" after "The Panther"—reflect this theme. As we've seen, one even takes hetaerism—or rather its *end*—as its subject. In Rilke's "Tombs of the Hetaerae," death terminates lives defined by the instinctual hurl of the bodies of young men and the equally indiscriminate rushing of "grown men's torrents," releasing every *thing* associated with the hetaerae into an imaginative afterlife of its own. Toward its close, the poet remembers the hetaerae themselves as river beds into whom boys and men heedlessly poured their fluid desire; the poem's finish, however, imagines a transformation. Rather than the headlong flow of waterfalls cascading from the slopes above, the masculine water—once encountering the variegated floor of the river bed—takes on definition and even reflective clarity:

> And sometimes boys broke out of the mountains
> of childhood, came down in timid falls
> and played with the things on the bottom...
>
> Then they filled with smooth clear water
> across the whole expanse of their wide course
> and began eddying in their deep places;
> and for the first time mirrored the shore
> and distant birdcalls—[522]

An elaborate metaphor, to be sure, but one that nonetheless aptly illustrates the theme of unrestrained male libido differentiated and transformed upon reception by a psychic vessel.

In "Orpheus. Eurydice. Hermes"—the other most relevant 1904 poem—the archetypal poet himself may not be quite so indiscriminate in his desire. Even so, his possessiveness establishes an erotic dominance that Eurydice must escape in order to come into her own:

She was no longer the blond wife
who echoed often in the poet's songs,
no longer the wide bed's scent and island,
and that man's property no longer.[523]

Even Rilke's "Spanish Dancer" (a poem of later vintage) can be seen as provoking the all-consuming fire of masculine desire in order, at last, to reveal her control over and disdain of it as she "stamps it out with little furious feet."

Yet it is not finally denial of undifferentiated seminal energy that characterizes Psyche's first task, but, as Neumann stresses, an *ordering* of the creative potential inherent in it: "Psyche possesses within her an unconscious principle which enables her to select, sift, correlate, and evaluate, and so find her way amid the confusion of the masculine."[524] In this connection, we would do well to recall the prominence—perhaps even archetypal dominance—of masculine puer-energy in the early phase of Rilke's career, most notably in *The Book of Hours*. That book begins with a nod to pure inspiration ("The hour bows down and touches me") and a gesture asserting the grand sweep of peculiarly masculine potency ("Nothing was completed, until I beheld it / all becoming stood still. / My glances are ripe, and like a bride / to each comes the thing that it wills.") It virtually ends with a paean to St. Francis which concludes:

And when he died, as carelessly as if he had no name
then he was dispersed: his semen ran
in streams, and his semen sang in the trees
and looked at him quietly from the face of flowers.
(It) rested and sang. And when the sisters came,
they wept over the man so dear to them.[525]

This climax celebrates a kind of anonymous and indiscriminate seminal power which—while not wholly identical to the less spiritualized force Neumann alludes to—can well be considered kin to it. Moreover, the closing characterization of the feminine element and its relation to that seminal force confirms that we are here definitely *not* yet entered into the sphere of Psyche's psychology of labor.

The sisters' gesture of passive weeping, while not incommensurate with Psyche's general state of mind, does not comport with the *action* that distinguishes her tasks. It is a far cry from the ants' industrious sorting, an ordering that is, as well, *a distinguishing of essence.* Though it is obviated when heaped in "an inextricable mass," seeds do possess an ideational as well as energic character: they represent the archetypal ideas of things, the formative force that impels the growth of organic matter and shapes it into distinct kinds. To sort seeds is to know the germinal form of a host of things: to tell what is what, to identify, and so effectively *name* them. As the botanical example of Linnaeus demonstrates, classification and taxonomy go hand in hand.

The Book of Hours does herald the *naming of things* as Rilke's chosen spiritual project. It does not, however, concentrate on actually performing that task. Preoccupied as he is with the all-important dialogue between the creative Self and God, Rilke's iconic monk cannot lend much attention to the concrete details of the manifest universe, even though that universe—theoretically, at least—serves as the crucial point of rendezvous. To be sure, trees, rivers, mountains, and forests repeatedly appear in *The Book of Hours*, but do so as generically conceived *topoi* rather than specifically or concretely realized things. No *Dinggedichte*—or any poems remotely resembling them—appear in *The Book of Hours*; indeed, the energy of the volume is so caught up in the singularly grand sweep of inspiration that produced it, that *no titles* (*names* of poems) distinguish its individual parts, which—unlike Rilke's *New Poems*—are not made to stand on their own.

The loose, seamless, almost liturgical flow of *The Book of Hours* could hardly be more antithetical to the poetic ideology informing "New Criticism," which conceives the ideal poem as an immaculate, freestanding object. The *Dinggedichte* of Rilke's *New Poems*, on the other hand, presage its central tenets. Though concentrated and prolonged bursts of creative energy produced most of the *New Poems*, the self's own inspiration no longer functions as a major theme: indeed, as we've noted, the poetic self tends to disappear into the particular matters at hand. To be sure, neither Rodin's art nor Rilke's *New Poems* lack scope or sweep, but—as Rilke's theory insists—the method of this art incorporates heavenly space into the body of specifically realized objects, and Rilke's poems—as indicated by the simple *labeling* characteristic of most of the titles—*name things themselves.* As a consequence, the style, form and feel of the book as a whole differs drastically from that of *The Book of Hours.* The latter is an extended prayer, a long incantation; the *New Poems*—like some natural history cabinet—is truly a *collection.*

In fact, the gestalt of the two books diverges so much, it is almost as if the *New Poems* were authored by an entirely different principle or person—and, indeed, it is so. In lieu of the grand gesture of puer inspiration, the close work required to identify the essence of each kind of thing—the hand- and footwork necessary to discern the seed-form of things themselves—bears the stamp of a feminine principle of order, the sorting action of Psyche's first labor. The ant, not the falcon, is in creative control.

Particular *New Poems* thematize, more or less explicitly, the spiritual and poetical transformations implicit in these differences. Performing one of his astonishingly imaginative riffs upon a portal or gate and the figures carved into it, Rilke articulates two critical and closely linked motifs: on the one hand, the *decentralization and dispersion of divine energy*, and on the other, its *concrete embodiment*. The second part of "The Portal" includes these telling lines:

So the darkness of this doorway strides acting
onto the tragic theatre of its depths,
as boundless and seething as God the Father
and just as He transforming wondrously

into a Son, who is distributed here
among many small, almost unspeaking roles....[526]

These revealing lines—in addition to making the above-mentioned points—remind us too that the aesthetic premises underlying Rilke's *Dinggedichte* apply, not only to the paradigmatic instance of poems about tangible objects, but to a wide variety of poetic subjects, including poems evoking the essential nature of particular human roles or types. One of these in particular graphically reveals the marked distance between the poetic ground of Rilke's *Book of Hours* and his *New Poems*, and, too, the place of *The Book of Images* in between:

The Poet

You're withdrawing from me, hour.
The beating of your wings leaves me bruised.
Alone: what shall I do with my mouth?
my night? my day?

I have no loved one, no house,
no place to lead a life.
All the things to which I give myself
grow rich and spend me.[527]

The opening line evokes the *withdrawal* of the source of inspiration invoked at the outset of the *Book of Hours*; the second line conjures images of its putative persona: winged Eros. The middle four lines distill tonalities sounded in *The Book of Pilgrimage* as well as *The Book of Images* (e.g., "Autumn Day"). The last two lines figure, as well, an inversion of generative relation between the *poetic self* and the *things* with which it is concerned. In the earlier work, the former is the sole possessor of agent force, and performs all getting and spending, but—emblematically—here, in Rilke's *New Poems*, poetic *subject* and *object* have virtually changed places in this regard.

Correlatively, the next poem in the volume ("The Lace") makes clear we are not speaking, really, of a loss of spiritual presence as much as its transfer—via intervention of the feminine persona—to the object(s) of devoted attention. Rilke's lacemaker sacrifices her capacity for vision in the course of accomplishing her fine and detailed handwork. Even so, that deed invests the thing she has crafted—small though it may be—with the spiritual grace or blessedness (*Seligkeit*) we might normally reserve for the human subject.

You long departed and finally blind,
does your blessedness live on within this thing,
into which, as between bark and core,
your huge feeling flowed, as if made small?

While the *vision* of the lacemaker, as the price of the work, may go lost, her *soul* does not. On the contrary, her unreserved giving of herself to her task vanquishes the usual tyranny of time and utility and enables her soul to live indefinitely on in the (material) thing itself:

Through a tear in fate, a tiny gap,
you drew your soul out of your stretch of time;
and it inheres so in this delicate work,
that the thought of usefulness makes me smile.[528]

Following immediately after "The Poet," "The Lace" extends and elaborates the logic of that poem, and in so doing supplies a virtual *ars poetica* of Rilke's new style of poetic work, especially its most human, least distant pole. (The poem begins: "Humanness: name for wavering possession...") The poem allegorizes Rilke's own surrender of the vision that, rising in expanding circles, could take in everything in the broad sweep of a single, commanding glance. At the same time, it banks upon fulfilling that vision by descending towards—and actually entering into—the body of the All, imaginatively discriminating the essence of each and every object. The author of the *New Poems* stitches his soul into the material fabric of his work, wholly investing it in the texture of each thing-poem and, indeed, lending it his eyes as well. Does not "The Panther" or "The Roman Fountain" enable its sensitive reader—looking through Rilke's poetic lenses—to see the thing itself? That means the *soul* of the thing—and, reflected in it, the poet's own, eluding the ravages of time through the intricate lacework of his poetic lines.

We began this section by referencing Neumann's interpretation of the confused seeds as indiscriminate seminal—and so masculine—force. Yet Neumann himself adds a second, "more universal" interpretation of the labor, one that regards the seeds as potencies inherent in the feminine nature—and so the soul—itself.

> The confused heap of seeds, fruits, and grains also represents the disordered welter of fruitful predispositions and potentialities...present in the feminine nature...Psyche's act brings order into them and so for the first time enables them to develop. An unconscious spiritual principle is already at work within Psyche. It works for her and by putting order into matter makes it serviceable to her.[529]

The reading we have pursued has already moved on to this other level of interpretation. The lacemaker who works "putting order into matter" is not necessarily handling confused masculine energies, but cultivating creative potential intrinsic in the soul and its own making. To probe still more deeply into the connection between Rilke's *New Poems* and the archetypal character of Psyche's first labor, we now turn to another source, a book dedicated to sorting the seed-ideas guiding Psyche's self-development, a psychological text devoted to classing and naming the art of soul-making's chief poetic methods.

Hillman's *Revisioning Psychology* may well count as archetypal psychology's most foundational text. Prefaced by an introduction that begins "This book is about soul-making," its four main chapters discuss topics central to that endeavor. Hillman himself suggests a curricular categorization of his chapters, identifying each with a traditional department of knowledge (mythology, psychiatry, philosophy, and the humanities) even while warning that this somewhat artificial division should not be taken too seriously. In the speculative spirit that marks Hillman's own enterprise, I wish to propose a different, complementary means of conceiving the structure of the book. Each chapter may be understood to correspond, not only to a principal means of soul-making, but, coincidently, to one of Psyche's four labors. This rereading requires no reshuffling of pages. Hillman's four chapters are—so far as Psyche's labors are concerned—in perfect order. Let us begin reading Hillman's book, looking—initially—at the theoretical perspectives offered in his first section as windows into the world of Rilke's *New Poems*. Later, toward the end of this chapter, we will—by way of that prior analysis—return to the pregnant yet cryptic symbolism of Psyche's first labor.

Hillman's first chapter ("Personifying or Imagining Things") unfolds a passionate critique of the monotheistic premises of our dominant spiritual culture and the disenchantment of the universe that follows in its wake. Hillman's sketch of the nature and genesis of "our modern world view" tallies closely with Tarnas's:

> This view confines the idea of subjectivity to human persons. Only they are permitted to be subjects, to be agents and doers, to have consciousness and soul. The Christian idea of person as the true focus of the divine and the only carrier of soul is basic to this world view. The Christian concentrated focus upon actual living persons has also come to mean that the psyche is too narrowly identified with the ego personality. Also basic to this modern view of persons is the psychology of Descartes; it imagines a universe divided into living subjects and dead objects. There is no space for anything intermediate, ambiguous, and metaphorical.[530]

Hillman's archetypal psychology articulates an alternative world view founded—not upon the one God and his psychological representative, the ego—but upon a "polytheistic psychology" revolving around the soul qua anima and the multiplicity inherent in its nature and relations. Hillman's erudite chapter delves into the involved historical backgrounds of both world views: on the one hand, the exfoliation of monotheism in Mersenne and Descartes, the philosophy of nominalism, and the rationalism of modern science as well as modern ego-psychology; on the other hand, the fount of soul-vision in Greek mythology and later movements it helped spawn—Renaissance classicism and Neoplatonism, Romantic poetry, and, too, modern psychopathology. For Hillman, the crux of the difference between these traditions is clear: the former suppresses soul and the principal activity defining its life—creative imagination:

> The modern vision of ourselves and the world has stultified our imaginations. It has fixed our view of personality (psychology), of insanity (psychopathology), of matter and objects (science), of the cosmos (metaphysics), and of the nature of the divine (theology). Moreover, it has fixed the methods in all these fields so that they present a unified front against soul.... What is needed is a revisioning, a fundamental shift of perspective out of that soulless predicament we call modern consciousness.[531]

While the manifestations of an alternative soul-centered tradition are multiple, for Hillman, at least, Greek mythology remains its wellspring and chief source of continuing inspiration. This privilege derives from both its temporal priority and the incomparable wealth of imaginative resource that allows it to reflect the native complexity and plurality of soul. "Greece," writes Hillman "provides a polycentric pattern of the most richly elaborated polytheism of all cultures.... This fantastic variety offers the psyche manifold fantasies for reflecting its many possibilities."[532]

Hillman makes clear that his psychology's "return to Greece" should not be taken literally, but emerges as a response to a cultural crisis—the inability of monocentric consciousness to negotiate the spiritual breakdown consequent upon the repressions inherent in it, to negotiate the multiple and fragmented psychic reality that constitutes the lived reality of the modern soul. Hillman:

> *Polytheistic psychology refers to the inherent dissociability of the psyche and the location of consciousness in multiple figures and centers.* A psychological polytheism provides archetypal

> containers for differentiating our fragmentation and, what is of utmost significance, offers another perspective to pathology....
>
> When the monotheism of consciousness is no longer able to deny the existence of fragmentary autonomous systems and no longer able to deal with our actual psychic state, then there arises the fantasy of returning to Greek polytheism. For the "return to Greece" offers a way of coping when our centers cannot hold and things fall apart.[533]

Hillman's last line alludes, of course, to a cultural moment imagined by Yeats, but it could as well have referred to Rilke confronting the fragmenting of consciousness triggered by his *nigredo*, the falling apart of self and world characteristic of his Parisian nadir. Nor must one attribute any foreign polytheology to Rilke in order to acknowledge that his Paris poetry reflects the premises of Hillman's "polytheistic psychology" and its critical distance from monocentric forms of thought—a distance which steadily increases as we progress from Russia to Worpswede to Paris.

We have recorded Rilke's repudiation of dominant Judeo-Christian tenets up to and including the composition of his *New Poems*; the varied means by which the soul of his poetry counters a too narrow identification of psyche "with the ego personality" and, correlatively, the deadening division of subject and object. We have repeatedly remarked the erasure of the "I" in the *New Poems*, which practice coincides with a dispersion of consciousness among "multiple figures and centers"—all the subject-objects of the *New Poems*, of course, but as well, the nine persona poems ("The Song of the Beggar," "The Song of the Blind Man," etc.) that comprise the best part of the last section of *The Book of Images*. Given this fundamental confluence between Hillman's and Rilke's initiatives, it should perhaps come as small surprise that Rilke's most advanced work along these lines to date—the *New Poems*—should openly exhibit a major debt to Greece and the classical tradition that founds archetypal psychology. Rilke's studies in Berlin with the esteemed classicist Georg Simmel in 1905 undoubtedly acted as an important stimulus for some of the poet's ancient myth-influenced work. At the same time, Rilke's own miniature "return to Greece" unfolds energies *internal* to the evolving opus of his poetical soul.

It is not a question here of a preponderance of poems on classical subjects, but a matter of the relative prominence, importance, and stylistic treatment of those subjects throughout the corpus of the *New Poems*. The defining terms of Rilke's interpretation of Rodin's art—the emphasis on the balancing of internal motion and unity of form—reveal the strongly classical dimension inherent to his new aesthetic, a predilection borne out by the significant number of sonnets in the collection. Moreover, while it is true that poems on biblical themes far outnumber Rilke's classical subjects—especially in the second volume—many of these cut against the grain of monotheistic religious tradition rather than endorsing it. On the other hand, a pivotal work such as "Orpheus. Eurydice. Hermes" introduces Greek mythological personae who positively fuel Rilke's imaginative development and who reappear many years later as the leading figures of his culminating masterpiece. Finally, Rilke deliberately erects a poetic statue of—not Moses, or Christ, or David—but the God Apollo at the portal of his verse. He does so not once, but twice—in both volumes of his *New Poems*—and if the preeminent influence of sculpture on the *New Poems* makes a classical figure a more natural choice for this position, this fact too bears just witness to the underlying affinity with pagan antiquity. It is, after all, towards Greece, not Jerusalem or Nazareth, that we naturally look to see divinity sculpted in stone, imaged in the face and form of the living body. If the art of Rilke's *New Poems* is unthinkable without Rodin, the master sculptor's own art would be simply inconceivable divorced from its classical origins.

All of this harks back to the heart of this religious—or mythological—matter: the regard—or lack thereof—for the manifold nature of soul inscribed in these different spiritual traditions and the relationship to image or imagination implicit therein. In an earlier chapter, we commented upon the Judaic prohibition against graven images, Islam's ban on representational art, and the iconoclastic currents that continually roil Christian baptismal waters. Greece and pagan Rome present a different case altogether. Commenting upon the classical predilection for crafting personified images, not only of Gods, but of archetypal presences such as Fame, Hope, and Night, Hillman contends, "The personifying of the ancient Greeks and Romans provided altars for configurations of the soul" and quotes Plotinus ("the greatest of all Platonist philosophers") on the need to provide "containers" for the multiple features of the soul of the All:

> I think, therefore, that those ancient sages, who sought to secure the presence of divine beings by the erection of shrines and statues, showed insight into the nature of the All; they perceived that, though this soul is everywhere tractable, its presence will

> be secured all the more readily when an appropriate receptacle is elaborated, a place especially capable of receiving some portion or phase of it, something reproducing it, or representing it and serving like a mirror to catch an image of it.[534]

This ancient impulse to provide receptacles for soul, to supply "a place especially capable of receiving some portion or phase of it," and to do so repeatedly in order to mirror soul's myriad nature, animates Rilke's *New Poems*. The chief *method* of so doing—at once a psychological way of being and seeing *and* a poetical technique—Hillman calls *personifying*, and this primary mode of soul-making saturates Rilke's *New Poems*.

Hillman deliberately distinguishes his central concept from the more familiar "personification" and its key conceptual correlatives—anthropomorphism and animism. These latter notions all imagine human thought projecting soul-life from within itself onto exterior forms which, in themselves, are presumed soulless. As such, they stem directly from the disenchanted view of the cosmos which cannot imagine soul in the world any other way. Personifying, however, arises out of different premises. Hillman:

> Where these three terms (personification, anthropomorphism, animism) assume thought makes soul, personifying recognizes soul as existent prior to reflection. Personifying is a way of being in the world and experiencing the world as a psychological field where persons are given with events, so that events are experiences that touch us, move us, appeal to us.[535]

Elsewhere, Hillman defines personifying still more succinctly as "the spontaneous experiencing, envisioning and speaking of the configurations of existence as psychic presences."[536]

Hillman's sentence captures the essence of the world of the *New Poems*. The way of being in the world that Hillman names "personifying" virtually defines Rilke's *vita nuova*, his new way of life. Everywhere, Rilke's poetic method reveals psychic presence in things. From Apollo's first radiant but almost lethal glance to the last roses in the bowl that arrest us with ineffable beauty and modesty...

> Look at that white one, blissfully opened
> and standing there amid its spread of petals
> like a Venus balanced on her shell;

> and the blushing one, which as if flustered
> turns across to one that is cool...[537]

...we are perpetually seized by the soul of the world as it speaks through the face of things, or silently addresses us through the infinitely expressive gestures of its living body. To be sure, the spectacular self-assurance of a Spanish dancer or the subtle yet infinitely meaningful motions of a blind woman rising from her tea may be more or less readily recognized as animated by a living soul, but Rilke, as we've seen, extends the same understanding to everything—every object as well as every subject—because this Cartesian distinction dissolves in the perpetually personifying art of these poems. Even "inanimate" things are viewed as filled with expressive life—the water in a Roman fountain does not simply ripple gently out from the center of its basin but "smiles gently with transitions"; the shadow of a mere portal enters into religious drama ("so the darkness of this doorway strides acting / onto the tragic theater of its depths"), and the stairs of the Orangery ascend

> Like kings who in the end still stride
> almost without purpose...
>
> just so, alone between the balustrades,
> which have bowed thus since the beginning,
> the stairs climb...[538]

These of course are just isolated instances: not only could equally convincing ones be found in almost all the *New Poems*, most every one—like "The Roman Fountain"—is actually *made* of multiple instances of such animating gestures which, in connection with one another, confer a palpable sense of psychic presence upon the poetic object. The poems, as well as the things they name, are (revealed as) ensouled. Rilke's *New Poems* may have been his most "modern" work to date, but the living marrow of his work bespeaks the classical origin of its spiritual designs.

Hillman emphasizes that the soul-consciousness enacted by means of personifying is simultaneously a *mythological* consciousness. The very act of personifying arises within, and gives rise to, a world of living myth: "To enter myth we must personify; to personify carries us into myth."[539] Likewise, a mythological consciousness informs Rilke's *New*

Poems from the start: the moment one enters the book, one encounters the God Apollo's brilliantly cold gaze, and we've already elucidated the subtler inscriptions of Psyche and of Eros in the love poems that follow. Nor do the mythic strains fade. On the contrary, towards the book's climactic end, those strains crescendo in a sequence of major poems on classical themes: "Orpheus. Eurydice. Hermes," "Alcestis," "The Birth of Venus."

That much said, the mythic dimension of the *New Poems* does not depend on manifestly mythological topoi. The personifying activity animates everything so that myth functions primarily—not as subject matter which, in unappreciative hands, can be as soul-dead as anything else—but as a style of consciousness that revivifies the world. In mythic consciousness, writes Cassirer: "There is nowhere an 'it' as a dead object, a mere thing." Hillman adds, "Subject and object, man and Gods...are not apart and isolated, each with a different sort of being, one living or real, the other dead or imaginary."[540] The universal coin of all these transformations—the soul *element* and *act* that enlivens all, and supplies the life of myth—contributes that second key concept in Hillman's title: *imagination*. "Mythic consciousness is a mode of being in the world that brings with it imaginal persons. They are given with the imagination and are its data. Where imagination reigns, personifying happens."[541] Personifying, mythological consciousness, imagining things—these are *rhetorical, topological, and facultative or psychological* ways of naming the creative deed of the soul (re)vivifying subject and object, self and world through the primordial act of imagination.

For all his theoretical acumen, however, Hillman cannot *show* us exactly how it is done as concretely and immediately as can our poet. "Imagining Things"—the phrase makes up the second part of Hillman's title, and his own analysis places an unmistakable accent on "imagining." In the midst of our reading of Rilke, though, we may well be encouraged to hear that title in a different, more provocative way. If we stress—or at give at least equal weight to—the *second* word of the clause, we might endow Hillman's relatively innocuous clause with a whole new meaning: "imagining *things*." On the face of it, what phrase could more aptly caption the task Rilke fulfills in his *New Poems*, the volume that pioneered the genre of *Dinggedichte*? Conversely, what work can better or more concretely illustrate Hillman's meaning than these poems which—with unparalleled intensity and precision—bring his revisioning of psychology to bear on the atomic unit of the world, the very nature of "the thing" itself? Let's return once more to Rilke's poetry, and look yet again at exactly how this personifying, this "imagining things" is actually, poetically done.

If the reader were to review the above-cited instances of Rilke's personifying—or, still better, the *New Poems* as a whole—she might well remark that the author's poetic method depends enormously upon metaphor and simile. In his Rodin book, Rilke lays great weight upon his subject's discovery of "the fundamental element of his art, as it were, the cell of his world."[542] In the case of the sculptor, this is "the exactly defined plane, of varying size and emphasis, from which all else must be made." In the poet's case, it is the countless tropes of likeness that shape the landscape of his work. Similes and metaphors of varying length and complexity—some that snap into place in a word, others (as at the end of "Tombs of the Hetaerae") extending over multiple lines and even stanzas—create Rilke's poetic volume. It is no accident that the first word of the first poem is *Wie* ("As if"), introducing a complex trope comparing Apollo's gaze to the sun shining through leafless branches in spring and, too, to the radiant force of the whole collection of poems the reader has just begun—*as if* the effect of opening the volume of *New Poe.ms* were like that of walking into a gallery of sculpture, where, in that initial instant, the power of all the figures assails you at once.

The prevalence of metaphor in Rilke's *New Poems* should come as no surprise, especially given the classical premises of Rilke's aesthetic. Did not Aristotle, after all, declare it the soul of poetry? Metaphor defies literalism, the notion that the matter in question is what it is, and nothing more. (So is it that some modern poetry, estranged from the world of spirit, tends to eschew excessive figuration. So is it, too, that in the fundamentalist account of creation, the seven days are the seven days, and nothing more.) By revealing that one thing can be seen as something else, metaphor releases things from the fixity of static definition and releases them into *the fluid transitional domain between phenomenon and idea, matter, and spirit that is, in fact, the sphere of the soul itself and its defining act of creative imagination.* As an act, literally, of translation ("metaphor" means "carrying over"), the metaphoric imagination belongs to this medial soul-sphere the *exclusion* of which—as Hillman himself states from the outset—defines the modern world: "This modern view...imagines a universe divided into living subjects and dead objects. There is not space for anything intermediate, ambiguous, and metaphorical."[543] But just this is the space created and inhabited by Rilke's *New Poems*.

It is easy to see Rilke's metaphors effectively "making soul": the magic happens, again and again, right in front of your eyes. Often, inanimate matter—like a flight of stairs—acquires psychic and spiritual lift by virtue of the symbolic imagination: the whole poem "The Stairs of the Orangery" extends the initial simile likening the flight of stairs to the stride of a certain kind of king. Conversely, of course, a complex psycho-spiritual state is accorded material weight and imaginative visibility. "The Swan" provides another instance in which Rilke begins with invisible soul-spiritual matters and moves from there to metaphoric embodiment:

> This toil and struggle—passing on, heavy
> and as if bound, through things still undone,
> is like the makeshift walking of the swan.
>
> And dying—this no longer grasping
> of that ground, on which we daily stand,
> like his nervous settling himself—:
> into the water, that receives him gently...[544]

Such lines display the heart of Rilke's poetic genius. Imaginatively speaking, these metaphors are a real stretch—who would think of likening the labor of life to the gait of a swan, or (still more startling) the experience of death with the insecurity of the swan's existence on land and (finally) the ease with which it glides upon the water? Yet, upon reading Rilke's lines, we intuitively grasp the sense of his metaphors and their imaginative truth grips us. This process of translation between spirit and matter is not merely an aesthetic exercise, but carries epistemological weight. This poetic imagination comprises the soul's own method of understanding, its way of *knowing* self and world in the space of their relation.

The world of the *New Poems*, then, is not the world of things themselves insofar as they may be seen simply as objects. In his introduction to his translation of *New Poems*, Edward Snow writes: " 'As if's' proliferate through the poetry, keeping the reader's attention fixed not so much on the object world as on the zone where it and the imagination interact."[545] Rilke's is a world of soul that lives in the imaginative transformation that moves upon the face of the world, playing upon the facets of things as upon the instruments of vision. Rilke's incessant similes serve, not only as a symptom, but as an artistic tool of that vision, the "technical" means by which he molds imaginative form out of the linguistic confluence of inner and outer reality.

Likeness in difference constitutes the essence of metaphor, and one of Rilke's most exquisite new poems, "The Gazelle," imaginatively (metaphorically!) explores this theme in relation to the nature of poetry itself. Rilke artfully evokes the way in which the distinct parts of the gazelle's body move together in balanced, rhythmic beauty; so much so that the animal's very form and motion manifest the essence of concord (*Einklang*—literally, one sound) or rhyme.

> Enchanted one: how shall the concord
> of two chosen words attain that rhyme
> which ripples through you like a spell?

Thus poetry—and indeed, the "love songs" at its lyric center—merely echoes what lives in the animal:

> From your forehead rises laurel leaf and lyre
>
> and all you are already moves in simile
> through songs of love...[546]

The gazelle, a living likeness of the *unifying motion* inherent in the imaginative *act* of metaphor, figures the heart and soul of poetry itself.

The poem, however, does not end there; more transformations follow. In the psychological quality of its rapt, tense attention, the gazelle is likened to both a loaded gun ready to fire and a maiden bathing in the forest who, startled by a sound, turns in fear and (perhaps) erotic expectation. Where beauty reigns, dangerous love is present, too. Everything in Rilke's quintessentially poetic world is charged—if not with the grandeur of God—with the shimmering, quicksilver life of soul and its endless, and endlessly breathtaking, transfigurations. Like the open roses

> ...that shed everything.
> And *what* they shed: how it can be
> at once light and heavy, a cloak, a burden,
> a wing and a mask—it all depends—
> and *how* they shed it: as before the loved one.[547]

In Rilke's poetry, only the blink of an eye intervenes between the revelation of naked truth and the putting on of yet another metaphoric veil.

In his mythopoetic world—a world in which gazelles wear crowns of laurel—imaginative disclosure and disguise virtually coincide.

In light of all we have just discussed, we perhaps had better revisit our commonsense notion of that last word of Hillman's chapter title, "things." To do so, moreover, would only be following in Rilke's own tracks. When, in 1905, Rilke revisits the subject of Rodin and prepares a lecture which ultimately appears as "the second part" of his Rodin book (published as such in the second edition of the monograph in 1907), he begins—with great rhetorical flourish—by deferring mention of Rodin's name in favor of a long discourse about "things." Taking the instance of a childhood plaything as paradigm of a real "thing," Rilke unfolds its essence as follows:

> In the legends of saints, you found a holy joyfulness, a blessed humility, a readiness to be all things, qualities which were already familiar to you because some small piece of wood had once shown you them all, assuming and illustrating them for you. That small, forgotten object, willing as it was to represent any and every thing, made you familiar with thousands of things by filling a thousand roles, by being animal and tree, and king and child; and when it ceased to play its part, all these things were there.[548]

For Rilke in his *New Poems*, the objectivity of "things" does challenge the poetic self to pass beyond the precincts of its mere feelings, to extend its reach to touch what appears outside its own egotistical border. At the same time, in the act of so doing, that self comes to realize that "things" are not mere objects, but (no less than God) are essentially and inalienably both *products* and *vessels* of imagination. In other words, things are—literally—metaphors. This does not make the real, sensible world over into something "imaginary." It does redefine its essence to be (made) of the substance of imagination—i.e., imaginal.

In his first chapter, Hillman repeatedly emphasizes the reality of the imagination, for the soul's world *is* the world of image—not image as reproduction of some prior more substantial or authentic being, but as the archetypal essence of the "thing itself." Establishing the reality of the imaginal figures as one of the lynchpins of archetypal psychology:

> Since we can know only fantasy-images directly and immediately, and from these images create our worlds and call them realities, we live in a world that is neither "inner" nor "outer." Rather the psychic world is an imaginal world, just as image is psyche.[549]

The theme of the ultimate *reality* of the imagination—and so, too, its preeminent spiritual and religious *value*—finds inscription as well in Rilke's *New Poems*, and perhaps nowhere more powerfully than in the poem directly following "Gazelle."

It is once more, an animal *Dinggedicht*, but here that animal is, by definition, imaginal:

THE UNICORN

> The saint looked up, and the prayer
> fell back like a helmet from his head
> for soundlessly the never-believed-in neared...

Yet again, a simile at the beginning, one that introduces a scene which can be read as a kind of allegory of Rilke's own line of spiritual development from *The Book of Hours* to *The New Poems*. The saint's prayer may be understood to stand for a traditionally religious relation to the divine, an address to a God in whom the saint "believes." Yet it falls back "like a helmet from his head" (a most provocative simile) when "the never-believed in" nears. The unicorn approaches as a figure of purely imaginal reality, an image of image and imagination—the soul-stratum of being that, as Hillman tirelessly argues, has no honored place in orthodox Christian doctrine. Here, however, the imaginal creature confronts the saint as an arrestingly present, substantial reality that can in no wise be denied. The center of the poem describes, in vivid and affecting color, this living thing as it presents itself to the senses (its "thin leg's ivory undercarriage," the "moonlit" horn, "the muzzle with its rose-gray down") before finally turning at its close to the all-important (and, in Rilke, recurrent) feature—the look or gaze:

> But its gaze, which no thing impeded,
> cast images into space
> and closed out a blue legend-cycle.[550]

The unicorn's "gaze" recalls not only early Apollo's, but as well that of a different saintly figure (or is it the same one?)—Rilke's Russian monk. Indeed, still more so, for the same *plural* German word (*Blicke*) occurs both in "The Unicorn" and in the first poem of *The Book of Hours*. It implies multiple and discrete "looks," whereas the term Rilke employs in "Early Apollo"—*Schauen*—can be more accurately understood as a constant cast of vision or "gaze." In any event, in "The Unicorn," as in *The Book of Monastic Life*, the relevant "looks" manifest creative power. Here, however, Rilke figures that power as still more *explicitly, purely, and concretely imaginative*: the unicorn "casts images into space"—very much like the poet-sculptor of the *New Poems*.

In "The Unicorn," the monk's world of creative prayer has not exactly been left behind, but its style and substance has been transformed *almost* beyond recognition. Instead of the poetic prayer unfolding as a dialogue between the poetic self ("I") and a God whose simple being would eclipse any image he could create, Rilke's poetry reveals the shudder of divinity to be embodied in *the anonymous soul-inspired imagination of the thing itself*, and the undeniable force of its present reality. This particular thing—the unicorn—figures *the act of the imagination, the imaginal core of (the very idea of) "the thing itself,"* and, simultaneously, *its inherent luminosity, its numinous thrust.*

Rilke's closing allusion to "a blue legend cycle" reinforces, on a general level, the poem's affirmation of imaginative, mythic reality, but traditional symbolism can help us begin to provide a more specific interpretation of his cryptic utterance. Alchemy construes the unicorn as a symbol of (masculine) spirit and conceives an integral synthesis or fusion of the trinity of body, soul, and spirit as the aim of its transformative work. According to myth, moreover, the unicorn, when pursued by hunters, seeks and finds refuge with the virgin Mary—the pure soul—and indeed is only capable of being "caught"—or reflected—in her mirror. Such a motif recalls the first part of our discussion of Psyche's first labor (the winnowing of primitive masculine force) and images the spiritual scenario underlying the *New Poems* as a whole (and prefigured in the Plotinus passage quoted earlier): momentary capture or embodiment of the elusive magic of spirit in and through the pure (virgin) anima-element of soul.

Featuring prominently in both *Malte* and *Sonnets to Orpheus*, the unicorn remains a figure of great symbolic relevance for Rilke, and we will have ample excuse to return to this mythic motif again. For now, however, let us merely note that the sequence of three consecutive animal poems—"The Panther," "The Gazelle," and "The Unicorn"—can be read as a kind of triptych. "The Panther" paints a picture of the soul's great will trapped in a perceptual cage, denied all real connection to the world, incapable of sustaining imagination—a figure, perhaps, of the spiritual state of the modern human subject. The gazelle's (in a sense, equally self-contained) motion embodies not frustration, but incarnate beauty, the unity of soul and form; and its nervousness reflects a tense, virginal, open attentiveness to whatever may break into the magic circle of its forested seclusion. The unicorn, lastly, manifests the startling entrance into soul-consciousness of the numinous presence of the (imaginal) thing itself, a moment of authentic spiritual experience, an epiphany. The soul *imprisoned in* and (at the same time) paradoxically *cut off from* the body of the world; the soul gracefully united with that body in a poetry of living motion; the body and soul filled with spirit in a moment of epiphanic vision: this triptych reveals the art of the *New Poems* to be—not only poetic sculpture—but a cabinet of icons of soul-nature, and so religious painting of a high order.

This almost impermissibly allegorical reading of these animal poems may help highlight a point I hope is evident enough: namely, despite the spiritual and poetic distance separating these works, *New Poems*—in strict accord with the profound unity underlying Rilke's entire oeuvre—may well be read as a logical development of the spiritual premises that ground Rilke's *Book of Hours* and, subsequently, the transitional *Book of Images*. In his novel collection of *Dinggedichte*, Rilke levies his considerable poetic force against a modern worldview that, believing in an essentially transcendent deity, or no divinity at all, denies the soul to the world and sets the human subject off against a world of inanimate object-things. In Rilke's poetic universe, though all things may not be so quintessentially gorgeous as the gazelle, all could well be addressed with the single world that begins his animal triptych's central love song: "Verzauberte..."—"Enchanted one..."

Yet what of Rilke's own psychological circumstance, and, too, the imagery of Psyche's labor? Can Hillman's thoughts on "Personifying or Imagining Things" help further interpret the cryptic symbolism of the myth and assist in framing a therapeutic understanding of the relevant stage of Rilke's soul-history?

If we look once more at the place Rilke landed in Paris (not literally, but psychologically speaking) as indicated by his own literary figures—a self fractured and dispersed among the effluvia of the world, fallen into isolation and imprisoned in the unyielding element of its own fears—we can perhaps glimpse how the gesture of personifying may respond to—and even flow from—that divided state. Hillman argues that personifying bears a special and unique relation to *psychopathology*, which generally manifests in connection with a *disassociation* or *fragmentation* of consciousness. Personifying—precisely because of the polytheistic element of multiplicity inherent in it—can both derive from internal fragmentation and effectively "treat" it by turning the profile of malady into a source of healing creative expression. It does so in part by establishing multiple points of contact between the (pluralized) subject and the manifold objects that can reflect those (most likely confused or undifferentiated) soul states. Personifying, writes Hillman, can provide a new-old way

> a) of revivifying our relations with the world around us, b) of meeting our individual fragmentation, our many rooms and many voices, and c) of furthering the imagination to show all its bright forms.[551]

He details the operative mechanism as follows:

> By actively imaging the psyche into multiple persons, we prevent the ego from identifying with each and every figure... each and every impulse and voice.... Therapy works through the paradox of admitting that all figures and feelings of the psyche are wholly "mine" while at the same time recognizing that these figures and feelings are free of my control and identity, not "mine" at all.[552]

Once more, one must think of all Rilke's persona poems from *The Book of Images*, all written in the voice of figures (the beggar, blind man, and widow; the suicide, orphan, and leper) who are both manifestly Rilke's own, children of his soul, and yet not really "him" or "his" at all ("What, then, was mine: mine, my own?" laments the riven widow). And the personae of his *New Poems*—Eranna and Sappho; Jesus in the olive garden; the lacemaker, or blind woman—all Rilke, and at the same time... not. Moreover, because personifying tends to dissolve the distance between subjects and objects, seeing one as the other, its psychological initiative cannot be limited to the former category, but extends to relations with all the things of the world. In this rich plurality of relation, and the imaginative *discrimination* required to make it count, we find, at last, the key trace of Psyche's labor:

> Personifying helps place subjective experiences "out there"; thereby we can devise protections against them and relations with them. Through multiplicity we become internally more separated; we become aware of distinct parts. Even should unity of personality be an aim, "only separated things can unite" as we learn from the old alchemical psychologists. Separation comes first. It is a way of gaining distance. This *separatio* offers internal detachment, as if there were now more interior space for movement and for placing events, where before there was a conglomerate adhesion of parts or a monolithic identification with each and all, a sense of being stuck in one's problem.[553]

"Then, taking corn and barley and millet and poppy seed and chick peas and lentils and beans, all jumbled and confused in one heap, she said to her.... Sort that disordered heap of seeds, place each kind of grain apart...." That "disordered and inextricable mass" of seeds symbolizes Psyche herself, her internal state; and her first labor entails its progressive differentiation. Psyche's first animal helpers, the ants, admirably perform the work: "The six-footed hosts rushed to the rescue, and...*separated* the whole heap, grain by grain. And after they had parted and distributed the several grains, each after their kind, they vanished...." Psyche's initial task, then, consists of precisely the alchemical *separatio* Hillman describes, the act of distinguishing and ordering the seed-ideas that comprise the contents of (un)consciousness, the spiritual stuff of the soul.

And Rilke? "A conglomerate adhesion of parts or a monolithic identification with each and all" may be a most unflattering description of the soul-form of Rilke's *Book of Hours*, but nonetheless contains a grain or two of truth. Certainly, by the time Rilke begins its last book, when his erstwhile monk finds himself encased in a stone composed of the marrow of his own fear, it might be fair to speak of psychic immobility, or "being stuck in one's problem." But Hillman's continuation clarifies just how Rilke's *New Poems* help remedy the situation: "Essential to this internal separation is naming the personalities, as if only by naming the animals in Eden could Adam become who he was..."[554] and as if Rilke could only become who *he* was, or could be, by *naming* the animals in Paris: not only the panther, but the gazelle, the swan, even the unicorn; and not only the animals, but the plants (the blue hydrangea, and the roses in the bowl); and not only animals and plants, but places (the square in Furnes, Bruges' quay) and persons (the prisoner, the courtesan, the convalescent, the grownup), Gods (Apollo, Venus, and Hermes), and prophets (Jesus, Buddha); passages (death, illness, birth) and indeed, all things (the Roman fountain, the tower, the rose window, the cathedral, the carousel). Who, after all, had declared the great God Pan's decease?

This naming, this interior separation and ordering, certainly does supply "internal detachment." Edward Snow notes the "icons of indifference that figure so prominently in the *New Poems*," adding that they "live in the imagination whose desire for relation they refuse."[555] ("Even if we threw ourselves down before him / he'd remain deep and idle like a beast"—Rilke's "Buddha") Yet one could also speak of the relation they cannot refuse as it has already conceived them—even while the degree of detachment they figure does help create "more interior space for movement and for placing events": the event of death, or love, or the fading of blue flowers; imprisonment, spiritual estrangement, or the summer rain. Indeed, this *expansion of inner soul space*—to the degree, indeed, that it contains the All—counts as the grand concluding theme of the *New Poems*. The last poem—"The Bowl of Roses"—finishes with this description of the open roses:

> And aren't all that way, simply self-containing,
> if self-containing means: to transform the world outside
> and the wind and rain and patience of Spring
> and guilt and restlessness and muffled fate
> and the darkness of the evening earth
> out to the roaming and flying and fleeing of the clouds
> and the vague influence of distant stars
> into a handful of inwardness.
>
> Now it lies carefree in these opened roses.[556]

The *New Poems* thus climaxes in a gorgeous moment of what Edward Snow calls "ontological redefinition"—a revisioning of the nature or essential being of things themselves. Insofar, moreover, as the roses—no less than the hetaerae, Eurydice, Alcestis, or Venus—exhibit a tangibly feminine nature, this redefinition proceeds under the aegis of anima, entails the revelation of a world *in* and *of* soul. All that might appear outside of soul—physical matters of the earth, as well as the spirit-realm of distant stars—has been imaginatively converted into the coin of soul-consciousness, that "handful" of inner knowing and being that constitutes the distillate of the soul's poetic alchemy, its process of self-making.

Even so: why does the inner opening accomplished via Psyche's *separatio*, her internal process of discrimination, qualify as her initial labor? Because, of course, it brings Psyche one significant step closer to Love. Hillman:

> Personifying not only aids discrimination, it also offers another avenue of loving, of imaging things in a personal form so that we can find access to them with our hearts...The image of the heart—"l'immagine del cuor"—was an important idea in the work of Michelangelo...and refers to a mode of perception that penetrates through names and physical appearances to a personified interior image, from the heart to the heart.[557]

It is not only the love poems at the beginning of the *New Poems* that bring it under the aegis of love, but the way of imagining or seeing things that informs the whole. Rilke's poems embody, in vivid "objective" image, the "thought of the heart" that is no longer merely (Augustinian) feeling, but—manifestly—a creative and imaginative expression of the soul of the world.

"The Panther" figures a particularly interesting instance in this regard, because it represents almost a photographic negative of Michelangelo's *l'immagine del cuor.* The poem's concluding lines reveal the heart as the ultimate center of perception, though in this sad and terrible instance, the moment the image would finally register there, it disappears. The panther's isolation is not merely sensory: the negation of imaginal reality the animal experiences amounts, as well, to something like a total loss of (the possibility of) love. Yet for Rilke to picture this so livingly, to personify it in an image that, at one and the same time, appears eminently objective *and* subjective or interior, discloses a mode of understanding or knowing that, springing forth from the heart, itself surely counts as a labor of love, especially when—as in the volume of Rilke's *New Poems*—it is repeated again, and again, and again. *Rien que travailler.*

The *New Poems* represent a breakthrough in Rilke's art and life—not the first, or the last, but a pivotal watershed at the virtual heart of his poetical and spiritual career. Interestingly enough, it was during the gestation and composition of these generally selfless poems that, psychologically speaking, Rilke's own identity achieved more definite, mature, and lasting form. As detailed at the outset of this chapter, many developments contributed to Rilke's ability ultimately to turn the lead of his *nigredo* into gold, but none (with the exception of the writing of *Malte*) went to the heart of the soul-matter as did the work involved in the creation of the *New Poems*. If we were to liken Rilke's life-work to the building of a cathedral, all that had gone before could be compared to the design of the building as well as the digging and laying of its foundation. Rilke's *New Poems*, though, could represent the first real masonry—the quarrying, cutting, and putting in place of the first stones.

So let us close, then, with one more stone, one poem (the first) from the "Other Part" of Rilke's *New Poems*. It is another, and still more famous, Apollo, and a poem that can stand for the style of Rilke's vital soul-transformation, his successful joining of the worlds of stone and star:

Archaic Torso of Apollo

We never knew his unheard-of head
wherein the eye-apples ripened. Still
his torso glows like a streetlamp, fed
by the gaze that (but turned in) will

always hold its fire. Else the surge
of the breast couldn't blind you, or the gentle twist
of the loins reveal the invisible urge
to smile that shudders through Creation's midst.

Else this stone would stand deformed and knif-
ed off at the shoulder's steep rock-face
and not ripple like a panther's fluid pelt

and not burst through form's constricting belt
like a shining star: for there is no place
that does not see you. You must change your life.[558]

The figure—another statue—is not only (once more) stone, but is fractured, broken—nominally, at least. But here the loss of the head translates into a concentration of creative energy all through the body: the force of conception, no longer limited to the head/ego, finds distribution all through the being. This does not, however, dilute creative agency, but rather seems to intensify it, to excite a shudder in the loins.

The poem, indeed, symbolizes *breakthrough*—a breaking through of the kind of psychic constriction figured in the first poem of the *Book of Poverty and Death*, or imprisoning the panther. As figured in "Evening," stone and star represent the extremes of spirit and matter, contraction and expansion, divinely immeasurable expanse, and concrete, earthly, finite form. Yet the poet's Greek God bends these poles together, and makes of them one unified soul-filled thing. Far from being trapped or confined in and by the stone, Apollo's power is concentrated in it, only to burst out again like a star of limitless force and luminosity.

In accord, finally, with the poetics of personifying allied with Psyche's first labor of love, the poem lends the statue a life and power of vision which subsequently redounds upon the human subject or viewer—which may be Rilke, but is also, patently, us. Rilke's poem *is* the statue, and in reading and seeing it, we encounter the soul force embodied in the beautiful thing. Are we living with this degree of intensity, embodying soul as fully, as powerfully, as it is? If not, why not? Reading Rilke can be a risky proposition: if you do so deeply, honestly, and courageously, you may have to change your life.

Chapter 12

DÖDEN . . . DÖDEN

Twin births of the poet's fateful move to Paris in August 1902, Rilke's New Poems *and his novel* The Notebooks of Malte Laurids Brigge *consumed most of the poet's creative energy for the better part of the twentieth century's first decade. Rilke finished the second and final volume of his* New Poems *in 1908 and—after agonizing delay at the close—finally concluded work on* Malte *in January of 1910. Both works were published in the year of their completion.*

"So, then people do come here in order to live; I would sooner have thought one died here." The opening of Rilke's novel unforgettably captures the psychological milieu of Malte's Paris—an atmosphere of decrepitude and dismay that was, too, the poet's own. Rilke first formally conceived the project of his novel while ensconced in the Villa Strohl-Fern in Rome in January 1904, but the poet's early, most difficult days in Paris clearly supply the book's imaginative point of departure, and key passages in it are drawn from letters dating from that period. At that time, Rilke—we may once again recall—had entered a late and peculiarly intense phase of his life-defying *nigredo*. Having fled wife, child, and house in Westerwede, the poet found himself alone in an alien city, overwhelmed by what he experienced as an utterly hostile environment. Gloom-driven and recurrently ill, the impoverished refugee confronted the wrenching end of his not so eternal youth, and—Rodin's inspirational example notwithstanding—sometimes seemed on the verge of losing his bearings.

To some degree, Rilke's psychic situation at this critical juncture resembles the formative crisis in the life of his contemporary Carl Jung. In the aftermath of his decisive break with Freud in 1907, Jung suffered a putative breakdown which—despite the drastic disorientation involved—ultimately figured as a crucial watershed in the great psychologist's life and work. In his book *Healing Fiction*, Hillman notes the event of Jung's crisis and—still more crucially—the fundamental terms of the psychologist's response:

> At this moment in his life, Jung was spiritually alone. But in isolation he turned neither to a new group, nor to organized religion, nor to refuge in psychosis, nor to security in conventional activities, work, or family: he turned to images. When there was nothing else to hold to, Jung turned to the personified images of interior vision. He entered into an interior drama, took himself into an imaginative fiction and then, perhaps, began his healing—even if it has been called his breakdown.[559]

Rilke seek refuge in a group? The monkish heretic return to a religion he had so deliberately left behind? To the family he'd just abandoned, or to journey-work he scorned? Rilke, like Jung, could find no conventional refuge for his spiritual distress. Like the great psychologist, Rilke found a creative means of addressing his psychic circumstances: with perhaps a still more practiced hand, the poet too "turned to his images."

Rilke did so in a twofold guise. In the *New Poems*, he sought relief from his psychic constriction by way of a decided turn toward the objective world, seeking in the poetic essence of things themselves mirrors that might reflectively differentiate various facets of his own psyche and forge connections with the world-soul. In *Malte*, on the other hand, Rilke essayed an intensely *subjective* approach to the same internal situation, artistically exploring—not so much *things* in what initially appears as outer *space*—as the imaginative face of human *time*. Here, it not so much the *lyric idea of the object* that provides Rilke his point of departure, but instead the web of inner and outer events comprising a *personal history*—albeit one that need not, in any literal sense, be "true." While *New Poems* and *Malte* both traffic in "personified images of interior vision," it is in the quasi-narrative form of his extraordinary novel that Rilke most obviously "took himself into an imaginative fiction" and—revising the story of his life—"began his healing."

On paper, however, that "healing" distinctly resembles a breakdown. Reflecting Rilke's own depressed condition, Malte's notebooks hardly offer any pleasant *Bildungsroman* or gentle remembrance of things past. Plunging into the heart of darkness, Rilke—via his literary persona—delves into the subliminal roots of the psyche's worst fears, confronting head on the specters of madness and death that terrify the self with images of its own extinction. Yet it is precisely the extremity of Malte's state—and Rilke's unsparing portrayal of the sometimes gory details of his psychic distress—that generate the book's radical transformative power. Hillman:

> The true revolution begins in the individual who can be true to his or her depression. Neither jerking oneself out of it, caught in cycles of hope and despair, nor suffering it through till it turns, nor theologizing it—but discovering the consciousness and depths it wants. So begins the revolution in behalf of soul.[560]

So, too, does Rilke begin his *Malte*, the significance of which reaches beyond the bounds of his personal biography, comprising another crucial evolution of the soul-based spirituality—the "revolution in behalf of soul"—at the heart of his poetic opus.

In the previous chapter, we quoted this pointed Hillmanian criticism of modernity's prevailing worldview:

> The modern vision of ourselves and the world has stultified our imaginations. It has fixed our view of personality (psychology), of insanity (psychopathology), of matter and objects (science), of the cosmos (metaphysics), and the nature of the divine (theology). Moreover it has fixed the methods in all these fields so that they present a unified front against soul. What is needed is a revisioning, a fundamental shift of perspective out of that soulless predicament we call modern consciousness.[561]

The *New Poems* undertake just such a revisioning, focusing most centrally (though not exclusively) upon "matter and objects." In *Malte*, on the other hand, Rilke's (re)visionary quill takes dead aim at "our view of personality (psychology)" and its intimate correlative—psychopathology. Confronting age-old spiritual and social norms as well as the founding tenets of the emergent field of psychology itself, Rilke's *Malte* reclaims the subject of sickness, the *pathos* of the psyche, for the soul itself.

On the face of it, *The Notebooks of Malte Laurids Brigge* tells—in the voice of Malte himself—the "story" of a young Dane living in Paris. As its title indicates, the book does not unfold in the form of a continuous narrative, but is comprised of an episodic collage of entries in Malte's notebook. The very first of these—the only one to bear a date and place—advertises the manifest connection between the lives of the novel's author and its protagonist. Rilke (or Malte) heads the entry "September 11, Rue Toullier." The date corresponds to the period of Rilke's initial months in Paris, during which time the poet himself resided at (where else?) Number 11, Rue Toullier.

The book begins:

> So, then, people do come here in order to live; I would sooner have thought one died here. I have been out. I saw: hospitals. I saw a man who swayed and sank to the ground. People gathered round him, so I was spared the rest....
>
> And what else? A child in a standing baby carriage. It was fat, greenish, and had a distinct eruption on its forehead....The child slept, its mouth was open, breathing idioform, pommes frites and fear. It was simply like that. The main thing was, being alive. That was the main thing.[562]

In an earlier section of this book, we spoke at length about the images of death, putrefaction, illness, and fear that saturated Rilke's psychology in the dark period of his *nigredo*. Malte's condition—inward as well as outward—mirrors the same, and his morbid fears quickly assume frightening depth and scope. Rilke's novel thus takes the soul's illness as its point of departure. In conformity with the historical origins of the field of psychology itself, *psychopathology* figures as *Malte's* main gateway into the sphere of soul.

In *Revisioning Psychology*, Hillman eloquently and passionately articulates the foundational role played by psychopathology in the life of the soul.

> A psychological book or a psychological system that does not fully validate psychopathology, or lays it to one side as a separate field called "abnormal psychology," is insufficient—even dangerous. It divides in theory what is not divided in actuality. To treat

> pathologizing as secondary and extraneous rather than as primary and inherent, neglects the reality that pathologizing is not a field but a fundament, a strand in all our being, woven into every complex. It is a belonging of each thought and feeling, and a face of each person of the psyche...Erikson's statement that "pathography remains the traditional source of psychoanalytic insight" and Freud's that the "starting point" is the symptom are not merely methodological, i.e. about the soul's analysis. These are ontological statements, statements about the soul's very being, a source of whose native insight is its native pathology.[563]

Or, to state the gist of the matter most succinctly, "The psyche does not exist without pathologizing."[564]

The term "pathologizing" is Hillman's own. In *Revisioning Psychology*, he defines it thus:

> I am introducing the term pathologizing to mean the psyche's autonomous ability to create illness, morbidity, disorder, abnormality, and suffering in any aspect of its behavior and to experience and imagine life through this deformed and afflicted perspective.[565]

The idea of pathologizing clearly figures as one of the cornerstones of Hillman's psychology, and indeed represents the *second* primary mode of soul-making elaborated in *Revisioning Psychology*. If critical power offers any measure, Rilke's poetic opus effectively corroborates its fundamental importance. For if the first chapter of *Revisioning Psychology*—"Personifying or Imagining Things"—zooms unfailingly in upon the poetic center of Rilke's *New Poems*, Hillman's second chapter—"Pathologizing or Falling Apart"—does the same for the *The Notebooks of Malte Laurids Brigge*, defining *the* psychodynamic force driving the writing of Rilke's extraordinary novel.

For Malte certainly does pathologize. His notebooks teem with images of death, illness, decay, deformity, degradation, and suffering. All—whether directly attached to Malte's own person or not—mirror the morbid, even deranged side of his own psyche. The images are disturbing, frightening, sometimes even downright horrific. What end, one may well ask, do such images serve; what role can such ugly stuff play in Rilke's "healing fiction"?

At this juncture, we need to clarify a key point. Despite the patent affinity between Malte's psychology and Rilke's own, the autobiographical resonances of Rilke's text should not mislead us into any careless conflation of our historical author and the protagonist of his novel. Rilke himself complained of readers who uncritically identified him with Malte, ignoring that—however much "Rilke" we may find in it—*The Notebooks of Malte Laurids Brigge* represents a deliberately styled piece of *fiction*. Malte is, not Rilke himself, but his imaginative creation or fantasy.

This distinction is especially critical when it comes to construing the psychological—even, if you will, *therapeutic*—value of pathologizing. True enough, the difference cannot always be readily maintained. In the case of creative artists and thinkers, in particular, the line between "fantasy" and "reality" may sometimes blur, entailing confusion that can lead to real madness (cf. Hölderlin, Nietzsche, and countless others). In Rilke's case, however, the line seems more or less firmly drawn in black ink, certified by the consistent conscious artistry marking Rilke's poetic prose. If nothing else, history vindicates the truth that *imagining* the possibility of Malte losing his mind did not result in Rilke losing his, or compromise the poetic identity vital to his soul—on the contrary.

The chief value of pathologizing, in fact, inheres in the manner in which it stimulates imagination, distorting and even destroying rigidified literal realities that pose as the whole truth of the matter—whatever matter is at hand—and so opening a door into the invisible precincts of the soul. Hillman:

> The soul sees by means of affliction.... The crazy artist, daft poet, and mad professor... are metaphors for the intimate relation between pathologizing and imagination. Pathologizing processes are a source of imaginative work, and the work provides a container for the pathological process.[566]

For Rilke, *The Notebooks of Malte Laurids Brigge* served as just such a container. Another Hillman passage invites a still more precise formulation of exactly how:

> As there are archetypal fantasies of health and growth, of being saved and of coming home, so there are similar imaginal motifs of falling ill, being wounded, *going mad. Although falling sick may belong to medicine, the fantasy of it belongs to the soul.*[567]

With this understanding as a backdrop, let us then turn back to the novel's text and analyze more closely how Rilke's pathologized fantasy of illness and madness—Malte Laurids Brigge—proves a means of psyche finding and making soul.

In accord with Rilke's prior spiritual development, *The Notebooks of Malte Laurids Brigge* represents a genre of (healing) fiction uniquely attuned to dictates of the soul qua anima. A medley of poetic evocations of the beauty and horror of Malte's Paris environs, recollections of his Danish childhood, essayistic reflections on various and sundry topics, and (in part II) retellings of French and Russian history, *Malte* does *not* offer a plot hinged upon its hero's outward deeds. The principal "action" of the book—if it can be termed as such—unfolds in the form of Malte's imaginative musing. Malte—himself a poet—does record definite events, past and present (a grandfather's death, the onset of illness, scenes on the street) but it is not so much the events themselves, nor their (decidedly loose) temporal sequencing, that supplies the book's substance but the ongoing process of reflection they engender, a stream of consciousness in and through which Malte seeks to mirror and so comprehend his own soul-reality. In a very real sense, it is just this *imaginative creation of soul history*—Malte's own—that qualifies as the chief subject and "action" of the book. Just as there are poems about the making of poetry, Rilke's *Malte* represents a healing fiction that takes the writing of healing fiction—in the form of notebooks comprising a very personal history—as its overarching theme.

Malte's own soul-making goes hand in hand with a process of pathologizing that at one and the same time enables and fatally endangers his poetic imagination. Even while providing raw material for his life and work, Malte's Parisian environs threaten his psyche with imaginative extinction, even incipient madness. "'Soul' refers to that . . . which makes meaning possible. . . . the deepening of events into experiences,"[568] writes Hilllman, but such alchemy requires time and patience, ingredients in short supply in Malte's frenetic urban milieu. Not unrelatedly, Malte remains constantly ghosted by the specters of death that—it seems to him—haunt its too busy streets.

After living in Paris for a month, Rilke himself wrote to Clara:

> The many hospitals that are all about here frighten me. . . . One suddenly feels that in this wide city there are legions of sick, armies of dying, populations of dead. I have never felt that in any city

> and it is strange that I feel it just in Paris, where...the drive to live is stronger than elsewhere. Is this drive to live—life? No,—life is something quiet, broad, simple. The drive to live is hurry and pursuit. Drive to have life, at once, whole, in an hour. Of that Paris is so full and therefore so near to death. It is an alien, alien city.[569]

Those hospitals and that death-drive reappear in Rilke's novel, stimulating the constant sense of dread that permeates Malte's psyche. Near the beginning of the book, Malte expresses his own fear of ending up in the huge hospital known as the "Hôtel-Dieu," remarking—with morbid irony—the awful sense of hurry its presence generates:

> I am afraid. One has to take some action against fear, once one has it. It would be very nasty to fall ill here, and if it occurred to anyone to get me into the Hôtel-Dieu I should certainly die there.
>
> This hotel is a pleasant hotel, enormously frequented. One can scarcely examine the facade of the Cathedral of Paris without danger of being run over by one of the many vehicles that must cross the open space as quickly as possible to get in yonder.[570]

If Malte finds the pace of life in Paris positively antithetical to the digestive process that turns "events" into "experiences," neither does he find that he himself has managed the transformation well in his own past life and work. Malte, the writer, possesses an acute sense of how difficult it may actually be to accomplish this seemingly simple alchemical act and, correlatively, laments how little real poetry he himself has so far achieved. Once again, we hear Rilke himself in and through the voice of his main character:

> Ah! but verses amount to so little when one writes them young....For verses are not, as people imagine, simply feelings (those one has early enough), they are experiences. For the sake of a single verse, one must see many cities, men, and things, one must know the animals, one must feel how the birds fly and know the gesture with which the little flowers open in the morning...[571]

...and much, much more as well. While the whole litany of mnemonic requisites is too long to cite here, Malte's crucial closing comment upon it cannot be passed over:

> And still it is not yet enough to have memories. One must be able to forget them when they are many and one must have the great patience to wait until they come again. For it is not yet the memories themselves. Not till they have turned to blood within us, to glance, and gesture, nameless and no longer to be distinguished from ourselves—not till then can it happen that in a most rare hour the first word of a verse arises in their midst and goes forth from them.
>
> But all my verses had a different origin; so they are not verses.[572]

Malte the poet, then, struggles against lifestyles too impatient to allow a true deepening of life and thought, but that is not all. He wrestles with a whole panoply of inner and outer circumstances that block, belittle, or belie the reality of the soul: superficial materialisms blind to the underlying, invisible truth of things; religious habits that preach conformities lethal to the soul as well as norms of learning that reason it out of existence; the stifling conventions of a social life that suppress all traces of real individuality. Soon, we shall interrogate these forms of soul-suppression in Malte's own Danish past, but for the character in his Parisian present, some appear at large as the face of the world. Immediately after the passage pertaining to the making of verses, Malte lashes out at a modern existence largely devoid of psychological imagination and indeed a whole soul-dead history of being. In his positively apocalyptic (and puer-infused!) gesture, Malte takes upon himself the burden of finding a new beginning, a new point of departure for creative work that might make life count once more:

> It is ridiculous. Here I sit in my little room, I, Brigge, who have grown to be twenty-eight years old and of whom no one knows. I sit here and am nothing. And nevertheless this nothing begins to think and thinks, five flights up, on a grey Parisian afternoon, these thoughts:
>
> Is it possible, it thinks, that one has not yet seen, known and said anything real or important? Is it possible that one has had millennia of time to observe, reflect and note down, and that one has let those millennia slip away like a recess interval at school in which one eats one's sandwich and an apple?
>
> Yes, it is possible.

> Is it possible that despite discoveries and progress, despite culture, religion, and world-wisdom, one has remained on the surface of life? Is it possible that one has even covered this surface, which might still have been something, with an incredibly uninteresting stuff which makes it look like the drawing-room furniture during summer holidays?
>
> Yes, it is possible.
>
> Is it possible that the whole history of the world has been misunderstood? Is it possible that the past is false, because one has always spoken of its masses just as though one were telling of a coming together of many human beings, instead of speaking of the individual around whom they stood because he was a stranger and was dying?
>
> Yes, it is possible....
>
> Is it possible that there are people who say "God" and mean that this is something they have in common?—Just take a couple of schoolboys: one buys a pocket knife and his companion buys another exactly like it on the same day. And after a week they compare knives and it turns out that there is now only a very distant resemblance between the two—so differently have they developed in different hands. ("Well", says the mother of one, "if you always must wear everything out immediately—") Ah, so: Is it possible to believe one could have a God without using him?
>
> Yes, it is possible.
>
> But if all this is possible—has even no more than a semblance of possibility—then surely, for all the world's sake, something must happen. The first comer, he who has had this disturbing thought, must begin to do some of the things that have been neglected; even if he is just anybody, by no means the most suitable person: there is no one else at hand. This young, insignificant foreigner, Brigge, will have to sit down in his room five flights up and write, day and night: yes, he will have to write; that is how it will end.[573]

So does Rilke's fearful, ailing Malte —a most unlikely (anti-)hero—throw down the gauntlet and declare his own "revolution in behalf of soul."

Very well, but where, exactly, is Malte to begin? Right where he is, inwardly as well as outwardly: with a description of the *symptoms*, physical and psychical, of his fearfully distressed condition, for these are "the *via regia* into soul."[574] Malte enters the world of soul through the door of his fears, the gate of the afflictions that define, in no small measure, the contours of his personal history.

Hillman:

> Now we come to a fundamental in the relation between soul and history. An event becomes an experience, moves from outer to inner, is made into soul, when it goes through a psychological process, when it is worked upon by the soul in any of several ways. Plato gave us main ones: dialectic, certain kinds of mania including love and ritual, and poetry, *to which we can add sickness or pathologizing as the thanatological activity of the psyche. We can take in the world by putting it through sickness, by symptom-making we can turn an event into an experience.*[575]

This passage helps construe the "revolutionary logic" implicit in Malte's pathologizing. If the social and historical norm reflects an essentially soulless state of being, a return to soul requires recourse to distinctly abnormal attitudes and behaviors; if the conventional state of well-being hides spiritual sickness, one may have to fall ill to revivify spiritual life. Pathologizing cuts a path into the depths of the soul, the unconscious drives, impulses, affects, and images that lie below or behind that "drawing room" surface of things, the ordinary events of the day world and the conventional rationales that organize it without necessarily supplying meaning. Underneath or inside what physically speaking is merely the form of matter, and socially speaking is a matter of form, pathology circumvents and derails the mechanical business of life, disrupts the order of the day. Through the symptomizing activity of the soul, it manifests—sometimes physically, always psychically—what commonly remains unmanifest, locked in the dark, stirring movement in the soul. Moreover, as the rational ego normally rules day consciousness, pathology naturally operates by subverting its autonomy and control: fearful and ailing, we are no longer up and running, but laid low, and made subject to another, hidden order of experience.

After the first notebook entry's famous evocation—or invocation—of death and fear, Malte's second entry offers a picture of himself suffering insomnia in his room:

> To think that I cannot give up sleeping with the window open. Electric street-cars rage ringing through my room. Automobiles run their way over me. A door slams. Somewhere a window-pane falls clattering; I hear its big splinters laugh, its little ones snicker.[576]

"These"—as Malte writes in the following (third) entry—"are the noises. But there is something here that is more terrible: the stillness." Malte continues to liken silence in Paris to the tense moment of awful expectation just before the collapse of a burning building:

> The firemen no longer climb their ladders, no one stirs. Noiselessly a black cornice thrusts itself forward overhead, and a high wall, behind which the fire shoots up, leans forward, noiselessly. All stand and wait...for the terrific crash. The stillness here is like that.[577]

In accord with the metaphoric and dreamlike logic of Malte's art, these scenes supply precise and compelling images of the character's mental state. Unable to wall out external noise or frenzy, Malte finds his own consciousness constantly flattened, overrun; subject to the fury of some consuming fire, he may even be on the verge of collapse.

Viewed from a pathologizing perspective, however, even such an evidently disastrous state of affairs may not be without redeeming features. One more Hillmanian definition of soul:

> It is as if consciousness rests upon a self-sustaining and imaging substrate—an inner place or deeper person or ongoing presence—that is simply there even when all our subjectivity, ego, and consciousness go into eclipse.[578]

Reading between the lines, we might suppose that this "imaging substrate" registers its presence and asserts its relative autonomy *only* when the ego goes "into eclipse," *or at least surrenders its usual quotient of control.* It is consequently logical—even if not particularly rational—that it is precisely in his afflicted and indeed precarious psychological condition that Malte discovers the capacity of imaginative vision proper to that inner, deeper self—his soul.[579]

Malte's next (fourth) entry clearly evokes that "inner place or deeper person" described by Hillman as an analogue of the soul:

> I am learning to see. I don't know why it is, but everything penetrates more deeply into me and does not stop at the place where

> until now it always used to finish. I have an inner self of which I was ignorant. Everything goes thither now. What happens there I do not know.[580]

The chord sounded in this crucial passage figures as a kind of bass line for the whole novel. *The Notebooks of Malte Laurids Brigge* in fact represents—to approximate the phrase Rilke originally employed as a title for his *Malte*—the journal of that other, inner self. "The soul" writes Hillman, "sees by means of affliction."

Of course, the realities Malte perceives from his new, pathologized perspective are not exactly comforting. He sees, for instance (in the fifth entry) how much people's faces resemble masks, observing that some people "wear the same face for years; naturally it wears out, it gets dirty, it splits at the folds," while other people "put their faces on, one after the other, with uncanny rapidity, and wear them out." The entry closes with Malte's deeply disturbing encounter with a poor woman on the corner of the rue Notre-Dame-des-Champs. The woman had "completely collapsed into herself, forward into her hands." Disturbed by the echoing noise of Malte's approach along the empty street, she

> startled and pulled away too quickly out of herself, too violently, so that her face remained in her two hands. I could see it lying in them, its hollow form. . . . I shuddered to see a face from the inside, but still I was much more afraid of the naked flayed head without a face.[581]

We'll return to this image again later: for now it is enough to note just how terrifying it really is.

Despite the nightmarish reel of his mind, Malte's pathologized vision *does* perceive psychic realities indicated, but not revealed, by physical appearances, and it is precisely the fearful aspect of those invisible truths that may open access to still deeper levels of soul-understanding. "Since pathologizing is frightening, we are obliged to follow fear, not with courage, but as a path that leads deeper into awe for what is at work in the depths of the soul,"[582] writes Hillman. At sufficient depth, in fact, we may perhaps come to touch upon the *individuality* characteristic of soul's essential nature, that uniqueness of (human) being Malte so misses in life and the impersonal history he has studied.

Hillman again:

> Perhaps our psychopathology has an intimate connection with our individuality, so that our fear of being what we really are is partly because we fear the psychopathological aspect of individuality.[583]

Malte's own peculiarly morbid obsessions, moreover, possess a special privilege in this critical regard:

> Pathologizing is present most profoundly in the individual's sense of death, which he carries wherever he goes. It is also present in each person's inward feeling of his peculiar "differentness," which includes, and may even be based upon, his sense of individual "craziness." For we each have a private fantasy of mental illness.[584]

In going by way of imagination deeper into his own fears—especially his fear of death—and in spinning out potent fantasies of his own mental illness, Malte plumbs the roots of his individuality. If he—like Jung—can come through the dark night with faculties intact, perhaps he may emerge as one of those most "singular" persons, that strange individual around whom the historic crowd gathers and stands. And—if not Malte—then perhaps the individual whose "private fantasy of mental illness" he represents—Rilke.

Rilke and Hillman both recognize pathologizing as a path into soul. Both recognize, as well, that society continually finds means of barring that path, of blocking or diverting the psyche that would move down and in that frightening fashion. One such bar Hillman discusses involves professional psychopathology's attempt to colonize and contain the soul's pathologizing by way of scientistic nominalism. Instead of focusing upon how particular symptoms emerge out of the concrete soul history of an individual patients, psychology—especially eighteenth- and nineteenth-century psychology—displayed a rabid penchant for *classifying* diseases and, consequently, treating individuals as a mere instance of some generally and abstractly defined term. Hillman observes that most of the terms comprising the now familiar vocabulary of psychopathology—*alcoholism, autism, catatonia, claustrophobia, masochism, schizophrenia*—were coined in those prior centuries. Rilke, emerging out of that same nineteenth-century milieu, makes precisely the same point, albeit more poetically, weaving his critical perception of this tendency into Malte's unique symptomatology.

After the encounter with the faceless woman at the corner of Rue Notre-Dame-des-Champs, Malte, in the next entry, openly confesses the fear that underlies his life. "I am afraid...if it occurred to anyone to get me into the Hôtel-Dieu I should certainly die there." Yet it is not only a fear of death in general that grips Malte, but dread of the kind of institutionalized death that—instead of confirming the individuality of his life—would deny and destroy all trace of it. After writing about the omnibuses rushing to get into the Hôtel Dieu, Malte remarks upon the extraordinary size and impersonality of the hospital:

> They are dying there in 559 beds. Factory-like, of course. Where production is so enormous an individual death is not so nicely carried out; but then that doesn't matter.... One dies just as it comes; one dies the death that belongs to the disease one has (for since one has come to know all diseases, one knows too, that the different lethal terminations belong to the diseases and not to the people; and the sick person has so to speak nothing to do).[585]

Malte could have taken such words right out of Hillman's mouth. Or vice versa.

The Hôtel Dieu passage reveals that although Malte finds premonitions of death everywhere on hand in Paris, the streets of that city do not reveal to him the deeper meaning of death—what it means to and for the soul—and it is just this disconnection that constitutes the peculiar dread of the place. To find images that reflect the reality of death more deeply, images which—neither sanitized nor homogenized—reflect both death's enormity and its vital connection with the soul's individuality, Malte must think back to his Danish childhood. For in that childhood lie both the source of Malte's overriding fear of death and, as well, imaginal perspectives that may help address it.

After the Hôtel Dieu passages, Malte continues:

> When I think back to my home, where there is nobody left now, I imagine that formerly this must have been otherwise. Formerly one knew (or perhaps one guessed it) that one had one's death within one, as a fruit its kernel...

and proceeds to illustrate his point with a story:

> My grandfather, old Chamberlain Brigge, still looked as if he carried a death within him. And what a death it was: two months long and so loud that it could be heard as far off as the manor farm.[586]

In Malte's telling, the dying man's body seems to grow in size; it fits in no room, on no bed, and the ailing patriarch constantly shouts demands at everybody in the house. His voice seems to grow louder with the passage of time; it roars out of the manor, and—haunting pregnant women, frightening calving cows into stillbirth, and rivaling the church bells—drowns out all other life in the village until half-mad townspeople fantasize about killing the chamberlain to silence the unbearable voice of his death.

His grandfather's death proves terrifically traumatizing, and Malte's account renders the full—and fully pathologized—force of it. Yet what matters most to Malte is—not the particular character of that death (though this is significant)—but that it indubitably qualified as Chamberlain Brigge's own, unfolded an unmistakable expression of his unique individuality. Malte's account closes:

> That was not the death of just any dropsical person; it was the wicked, princely death which the chamberlain had carried within him and nourished on himself his whole life long. All excess of pride, will and lordly vigor that he himself had not been able to consume in his quiet days, had passed into his death, that death which now sat, dissipating, at Ulsgaard.
>
> How the chamberlain would have looked at anyone who asked of him that he should die any other death than this. He was dying his own hard death.[587]

Hillman: "One has one's death, each his own, alone, singular, toward which the soul leads each piece of life by pathologizing. Symptoms are death's solemn ambassadors...and life mirrored in its symptoms sees there its death and remembers soul."[588]

To be sure, the episode of Chamberlain Brigge's death reveals not so much Malte's character as his grandfather's. Yet, another story—one told later in the novel—culminates in something akin to the birth of Malte's sense of his own irreducibly unique selfhood. Significantly, the incident once again revolves around weirdly pathologized imagery.

In his notebooks, Malte relates how, when he still a quite young child, he happened to be drawing at a table when his most treasured crayon (the red one) rolled off and fell to the rug beneath his chair. Malte clambered down and—unable to see well in the semi-darkness under the table—awkwardly groped for the crayon. Suddenly, Malte saw *another* hand not his own emerge from behind the adjoining wall and grope feelingly toward his. At first hypnotized and then horrified by the apparition, Malte just managed to pull his own hand away, and rose—white as a sheet—out from under the table.

Seeing his fright, Mademoiselle (Malte's caretaker) rushed to him. The boy wanted to tell her what he had seen, but could not, and the whole occult experience remains Malte's own treasured secret. On rare occasions, he considers telling the secret to a person who matters greatly to him—his beloved Mama, or his cousin, Erik, whose friendship he craves—but the story remains untold until he records it in his notebooks, where (as Malte himself acknowledges) he relates it "after all only for myself." After telling the story itself, Malte continues with this crucial passage:

> It is of course imagination on my part to declare now that I already felt that something had entered into my life, directly into mine, with which I alone should have to go about, always and always. I see myself lying in my little crib and not sleeping and somehow vaguely foreseeing that life would be like this: full of many special things that are meant for *one* person alone and that cannot be told.[589]

Malte's account of the individuating force of the secret recalls a kindred episode in Jung's *Memories, Dreams, Reflections.* In that soul history, Jung recalls how as a young boy he hid a fetish in the rafters of the attic and, subsequently, how a comforting sense of his own specialness constellated around the nucleus of that personal secret.[590] In Jung's case, the secret itself does not involve dramatic pathologizing; nor, of course, does pathologizing represent the *sole* means of access to the depths of personality. It does, however, figure as a basic, even indispensable one. Sooner or later, after all, even the most physically and psychologically robust individuals avail themselves of the body's own way of pathologizing, and get sick.

Malte follows his telling of the crayon episode with recollections of a crucial *class* of experience vital to his individual development: "those illnesses that set themselves to prove to me that this was not my first private experience." Malte's description of one prolonged fever makes clear the psychological force of his recurrent episodes of childhood sickness: "The fever rummaged in me and brought up from way down adventures, pictures, facts of which I had been ignorant... I lay there overloaded with myself." The same fever, in fact, gives rise to a scene distinctly reminiscent of Chamberlain Brigge's death: "Then rage seized me.... And then I yelled, half-open as I was, I yelled and yelled...."[591] The soul of the growing child, no less than the dying grandfather, evidently had need to resort to extreme measures to break through to expression.

That extremity does, of course, raise a crucial question. While his childhood in Denmark roots Malte's own individuality, the cited episodes—by no means happy ones—hardly imply that the Danish environment proved naturally hospitable to the child's soul life, or, in general, positively fostered individual expression—on the contrary. Why did Chamberlain Brigge yell so terribly? Why was Malte so often ill? In discussing the psychological crisis in Carl Jung's life, Hillman emphasizes that the images conjured by that crisis stemmed from a particular cultural milieu ("Hellenistic with gnostic coloring"), and that the historical specificity of those images figured importantly in Jung's healing. Why (aside from his personal acquaintance with the place and his reverence for Jacobsen) did Rilke choose a Danish character for his novel; psychologically speaking, what comprises the specific character of the Danish environment that bore his Malte? Looking more deeply into this matter will shed light not only on Malte's Danish past but, reflectively, upon his Parisian present as well. Most important of all, it will help construe root causes of the uniquely pathologized style basic to Malte's highly individual character, the destiny particular to his afflicted soul.

Malte grew up in Ulsgaard, the very house in which his grandfather Chamberlain Brigge so dramatically died. In fact, Malte, his father and mother, and his paternal grandparents shared the manor as long as the old chamberlain and his wife were still alive. Though impressive in death, Malte's grandfather by no means figured as the totemic head of the household. That title clearly belonged to his most formidable spouse, Countess Margarete Brigge, "the real mistress of Ulsgaard," and a glimpse of her character can go some ways toward acquainting us with the psychological climate prevailing in young Malte's Danish environs—at least at Ulsgaard.

That climate was frigid. The damning adjective can be applied without reservation to Mrs. Margarete Brigge herself, whom Malte introduces in these coolly devastating terms:

> Mrs. Margarete Brigge had always been, as far as my recollection of her goes, a tall unapproachable old lady. I cannot picture her except as much older than the chamberlain. She lived her life in our midst without consideration for anyone. She was dependent upon none of us; she had always about her a sort of lady companion, the ageing Countess Oxe, whom by some benefaction she had put under a boundless obligation. This must have been the single exception in her life, for she was not given to good deeds. She did not like children, and animals were not allowed to come near her.
>
> I do not know whether there was anything else she did like.[592]

The Countess's personal foibles naturally accord with this picture of near perfect coldness and imperious self-control. The Countess was possessed of a phobic hatred of wine stains on the white tablecloth, bitterly upbraiding all who offended on that score. Nor could she tolerate the least sign of sickness or injury. When a cook cut herself and appeared with a bandaged hand, the Countess complained that the whole house smelled of iodoform and wished to dismiss the unfortunate servant—permanently—at once. Similarly, Malte reports that when his mother fell fatally ill, Countess Brigge sequestered herself in her own part of the house and severed all relations with the rest of her family, her own son (Malte's father) included. Roughly a year later, the Countess herself passed away, the style of her death perfectly mirroring her life and offering the starkest possible contrast with her husband's, which, as Malte tells us, followed soon after:

> She died on the approach of spring, in the city, one night. Sophie Oxe, whose door stood open, had heard nothing. When they found Margarete Brigge in the morning she was as cold as glass.
>
> Immediately after that the chamberlain's great and terrible sickness set in. It was as if he had awaited her end, that he might die as inconsiderately as he had to.[593]

So much for Countess Brigge's cold silence, and the opposite it finally provokes in her husband: the bellowing rage spilling forth from him at death. So much, as well, for the generous size of Malte's immediate family. This journal entry—appearing shortly before the end of the first part of the book—makes clear the slightly staggering truth that Malte lost his beloved mother and both his paternal grandparents within the course of a single year—reason enough for a long-standing fear of death. Malte's remaining parent, moreover, could do little to inhibit the invisible growth of that fear because—outward appearance to the contrary—it was in good measure his own.

Malte's notebooks show his father—the Countess Margarete Brigge's son—to be far more correct and courteous than his mother, but only marginally less cold. The general tenor of the relation between father and son emerges clearly in Malte's account of still another of his fevers, this one contracted while his his mother and father are away at a great ball. The domestics cannot quiet the wildly crying boy and, as a last resort, send for his parents. Malte quickly calms down in his mother's arms, but his father does not respond sympathetically:

> "He has high fever," I heard Maman say timidly, and my father took my hand and counted my pulse. He wore the uniform of the Master-of-the-Hunt with its lovely, broad, watered blue ribbon of the Order of the Elephant. "What nonsense to send for us," he said, speaking into the room without looking at me.[594]

In Malte's notebooks, that uniform—notable in its perfect formality and ceremonial badge of mastery or control—comes to stand as a symbol of the man himself.

When Malte's mother is dying, Dr. Jespersen, the local priest, visits the household. Malte's words recounting the visit reveal much about the character of religion in his environment as well as his father's consistently decorous relation to God himself, one epitomized by reference to that indispensable uniform:

> In our house Dr. Jespersen had to content himself with being a sort of private person; but that was exactly what he had never been. As far back as he could think, his profession had been the soul. For him the soul was a public institution which he represented, and he saw to it that he was never off duty, not even in his relations with

> his wife, "his modest, faithful Rebecca, being sanctified by the bearing of children," as Lavater expressed it in another case.
>
> As for my father, his attitutude to God was perfectly correct and of a faultless courtesy. At church it sometimes seemed to me as though he were positively Master-of-the-Hunt to God himself.[595]

Such descriptions provide a fair sense of Malte's father; yet it is, once again, the circumstance of death itself that proves most revealing. By the time of his father's passing, Malte himself has grown and gone abroad and—arriving too late at the deathbed—can pay respects only to the corpse laid out on a bier in his father's flat. The corpse is garbed—naturally—in the uniform of Master-of-the-Hunt, and indeed everything about it likewise redressed according to the dictates of due decorum. Malte writes:

> They had hurriedly told me that he had suffered a great deal: nothing of this was to be seen. His features were set in order like the furniture in a guestroom which some visitor has left. I had the feeling that I had already seen him dead several times: I knew it all so well.[596]

Once more, we discover all signs of suffering—all that might disturb the appearance of order and control—mercilessly hidden or covered over. In his usual wry yet subtly hard-hitting manner, Malte lets us know that as far as he is concerned, his father—for whom life had been so much a matter of proprietary form—had passed his days in a world that resembled a state of living death.

As Malte continues to sit by the corpse, something remarkable transpires—something that reveals yet another dimension of—not only Malte's father's character—but the entire lineage he represents. Two doctors arrive and look nervously at Malte (he was supposed to have left for breakfast) before one curtly explains, "The Master-of-the-Hunt had one more wish." Malte continues:

> It was strange that the Master-of-the-Hunt still had wishes.
>
> Involuntarily I looked again at the fine, regular countenance. And I knew then that he wanted certainty. Fundamentally he had always desired certainty. Now he was about to have it.
>
> "You are here for the perforation of the heart: if you please."[597]

And so, with Malte looking on, the doctor proceeds to pierce his father's breast and heart with a short, sharp instrument—to make sure, absolutely, scientifically sure, that he was dead. Evidently, the Master-of-the-Hunt's desire for control was such that he could not leave death itself in death's own hands.

Correlatively, Malte's father was hardly a poetic character. On the contrary, here was a man who fantasized that the thrust of a scientific instrument could stand in for contemplation of the true mystery of death. Medical perforation of the heart—central organ, as we've seen, of the soul itself—symbolizes mechanical murder of the life of creative imagination.

The Master-of-the-Hunt's inordinate desire for outward command, however, hides a flip side: a state of inner helplessness and uncontrollable dread. Malte himself finally realizes this in the wake of something that happens shortly after his father's death. Going through his father's things, Malte finds a small folded piece of paper in his wallet. He soon realizes that the writing upon it (his father's own) consists of an account—not *composed* by but *carefully copied over* by his father—of the death of Christian the Fourth. According to this account, three hours before his death, the king—exerting enormous effort—sat up in bed and strove to say something to the attending doctor. For some time his words remained unintelligible, but finally his speech became distinct:

> The king, as soon as he heard that they understood him, opened wide his right eye, the one that remained to him, and expressed with his whole face the single word his tongue had been forming for hours, the sole word that still existed. "Döden," he said, "Döden." ["Death... Death."]

Malte has just mentioned that his father had maintained both a peerless and fearless exterior. Yet below that impressive mask, he, no less than the dying king, had been consumed with an almost unspeakable fear of death, a dread he carried, like some form of personal ID, in his wallet. Rather than the outward glory of the family line, that fear, that dread, represents the true legacy the Master-of-the-Hunt bequeaths his sensitive, undecorated son, who (as Malte himself realizes) always compared unfavorably with his father in the eyes of others.

These brief portraits form a picture of the kind of mind-set that dominated Malte's psychological environment—at least at Ulsgaard. His grandmother and father are cold personalities obsessively attached to the formally established order of things, rigidly intolerant of anything that threatens to breach that decorous facade or endanger conscious control over it—animals, children, wobbly wine glasses, weakness, injury, illness, death. One can well imagine that the environment ruled by such a mentality would be extremely repressive—denying, confining, concealing, or destroying any spontaneous unconscious impulse or independent sign of soul. Malte's father "always desired certainty," and "suffered no comparisons"—but Malte, like the soul itself,

> is the "patient" part of us . . . is vulnerable and suffers . . . is passive and remembers. [Soul] is water to the spirit's fire, like a mermaid who beckons the heroic spirit into the depths of passions to extinguish its certainty. Soul is imagination.[598]

. . . and, like the sickness that stimulates it, is not welcome in his father's house. Although suffering somewhat different circumstances, one of Malte's distinguished literary predecessors and countrymen nonetheless conveyed the heart of the matter succinctly: "Denmark," Hamlet declared, is "a prison."

Malte's discovery of the paper in his father's wallet makes quite clear what could anyway have been readily surmised: a deeply concealed fear underlies his consciousness, shaping it in the form of a defense against all those unseen forces—captained by Death, the ultimate unknown—it can neither comprehend nor control. Why, though, may this kind of (after all not unfamiliar) mind-set figure as specifically Danish in texture and form? Not, certainly, on account of any lack of darker, less visible realities congenital to Danish nature. In fact, Malte's father's mentality most likely arises in part as a defense against darker realities that press all too closely and persistently against the walls of consciousness in his native land.

Denmark lies far north of the equator. Every year its people face the long winter season when darkness encroaches upon and threatens to overwhelm the reign of light. As a consequence, the Danish experience long hours of twilight—that liminal state belonging neither to day nor to night, neither to life nor to death, but conducive to passage between those worlds; a twilight hospitable to the presence of those spirits traditionally at home in liminal soul-realms. The most widely recognized form of these are the kind that open Shakespeare's famous play and haunt its tormented hero: ghosts.

Rilke himself—no stranger to occult concerns—was keenly aware of these matters. In response to a critical questionnaire, the poet cited Denmark's familiarity with ghosts as one reason for choosing this place as the imaginative backdrop for his novel. Nor are ghosts left out of the novel itself. Malte's second recollection from childhood—preceded only by his account of his grandfather's death—takes place at Urnekloster, his *maternal* grandfather's house, some years after Chamberlain Brigge's death. Urnekloster, as Malte describes it, represents a world fantastically different from Countess Margarete Brigge's Ulsgaard, the flip side, as it were, of the Danish coin. It is only natural that the lengthy episode set there culminates in eerie events fully worthy of the prolonged Danish dusk.

Certainly, the people gathered around the table for dinner in the great hall at Urnekloster are of an entirely different cast than the Countess or her son. Though Count Brahe—Malte's other grandfather—calls them "the family," Malte writes that "although these four persons were distantly related to one another, they in no way belonged together."[599] Yet, in their own peculiar fashion, the members of this motley crew do cohere, for they are all eccentrics with at least one foot firmly planted in (or, as the case may be, one eye fixed upon) another world—not, by any means, the conventional Christian heaven—but a twilit realm of purely psychic and indeed occult realities.

It is indeed a strange lot. One old uncle is a kind of alchemist who receives corpses from prison "which he cut up and prepared in some mysterious fashion so that they withstood putrefaction." Malte knows relatively little about his aunt Mathilde Brahe, except that she is in constant correspondence with an Austrian spiritualist, Baron Nolde, and "would not undertake the slightest thing without first soliciting his consent, or rather, benefaction." A little boy roughly Malte's own age, a distant cousin named Erik, possesses only one movable eye, and is the only one on intimate terms with Count Brahe. The old Count himself proves a remarkable character who blithely maintains ongoing connection with individuals who happen to be long deceased. "Chronological sequence," writes Malte,

> played no role whatever for him, death was a trifling incident which he utterly ignored, persons whom he had once received into

> his memory continued to exist, and their dying off could not alter that in the least.[600]

The whole ensemble of characters represents a spirit entirely antithetical to the order of rational consciousness and formally established convention definitive of Malte's father's world. No wonder Malte's father has never previously visited Urnekloster. No wonder, either, that after what happens there, neither he nor Malte will ever see the house again.

The central incident occurs during dinner in the great hall:

> We had just reached dessert when my eye was caught and carried along by a movement going on, in the half-darkness, at the back of the room. . . . as I looked on with a feeling entirely new to me of curiosity and consternation, there stepped into the darkness of the doorway a slender lady in a light-colored dress, who came slowly toward us . . . I caught sight of my father, who had jumped up and now, his face pale as death, his hands clenched by his sides, was going toward the lady . . .

Count Brahe restrains Malte's father. After the ghost disappears, the old Count exchanges these words with his horrified and angry son-in-law:

> "You are violent, chamberlain, and uncivil. Why don't you let people go about their business?"
>
> "Who is that?" broke in my father with a cry.
>
> "Someone who has every right to be here. No stranger. Christine Brahe."
>
> And again there was that same curiously attenuated silence. . . . But then my father broke away with a gesture and rushed from the hall.[601]

What does the appearance of a ghost signal? While seeming to bridge the world of the living and the dead, the visible and invisible worlds, the presence of ghosts by no means indicates a peaceful connection between the two—on the contrary. When Hamlet's dead father appears, he does not do so because all is well but to let it be known that there is something rotten in the state of Denmark; to make his son aware of an unpaid debt owed to the world of the dead. When in 1908, Rilke—still more or less in the middle of writing *Malte*—writes his requiem to Paula Becker, her ghostly appearance likewise bodes ill, leading Rilke to wonder if there is anything he can do to help put her soul at peace.

We know what is amiss in Hamlet's Denmark, but what about Malte's? Given all we've so far discussed, we may well suppose that the question extends beyond the bounds of the unfortunate cause of Christine Brahe's death, embracing, more generally, the *disharmony or disjunction between the world of the dead and the world of the living* that her apparition implies. Malte's Denmark suffers some vital disruption of the natural connection between these—and related—realms; conscious and unconscious, visible and invisible, spiritual and material realities repel and polarize. Figuratively speaking, it is almost as if the long Danish twilight—rather than happily *bridging* the realms of day and night, light and darkness, life and death—had forced them unusually far apart, creating a fateful schism; as if the middle passage were not the domain of the living soul moving creatively back and forth between in—let us say, ritual mourning, or elegiac verse—but were a no man's land of tortured souls.

To be sure, the reality of purely psychic phenomena (ghosts, visions of entities no longer physically present, and the like) figures as an important and recurrent theme in Malte's Danish reminiscences. Yet the literal reality of such phenomena accedes to importance only in an environment deficient in the "natural" activity proper to the intermediate soul realm. That in-between world, after all, is the realm of pure image (image, that is, without corporeal body necessarily attached), and it is the human activity native to its domain—*creative imagination*—that Malte—consciously or not—misses in his Danish homes.

For if, in certain respects, Ulsgaard and Urnekloster remain polar opposites, the chief residents of both evince a similar lack of imagination and a marked tendency to take things—whether physical or psychical in nature—*literally*. Malte's father tries to impose his literal interpretation upon death itself, yet the alchemical uncle—working madly to achieve preservation of bodily remains—seems to have an equally materialistic notion of immortality. Nor is Mathilde Brahe's slavish obedience to Baron Nolde's occultism any less unimaginative than the most sterile rationalism.

Malte himself indicates the endemic lack in several passages. Toward the beginning of the first long Urnekloster passage, Malte describes the dining hall as a place inherently inimical to image: "With its darkening height, with its never quite clarified corners, it sucked all images out of one without giving one any definite substitute for them. . . . One was like a vacant spot."[602] Far more decisive, however, is a later recollection that records a like void in Malte's upbringing. Malte confesses, "The telling of stories, the real telling, must have been before my time. I never heard anyone tell stories."[603] Hillman details just how pyschologically significant that void may be:

> I have found that the person with a sense of story built in from childhood is in better shape than one who has not had stories, who has not heard them. . . . One knows what stories can do, how they can make up worlds and transpose existence into these worlds. One maintains a sense of the imaginal world, its convincing real existence, that it is peopled, that it can be entered and left.[604]

One would not—we may imagine—even need a tortured spirit, a ghost, to prove it. Malte, in recollecting his childhood and (re)telling the story of his life, is endeavoring to redress an old wrong, and to realize that (in Hillman's words) "imagination is a place where one can be." For insofar as "soul is imagination," in the absence of such a place, the soul—ghost-like—can be nowhere at home.

The character of Malte's Danish past supplies the crucial backdrop for the psychological condition in which we find him in Paris. The soullessness in his past encrusts his present. A legacy of frigidity, literal-mindedness, and fear bars the door to the imaginative life of his soul, access to which figures as matter of life and death for Malte as poet and man. No wonder Malte's psyche is desperately driven to employ whatever means may be necessary to open that door even though the prospect of doing so fills him with a literally maddening terror; no wonder his psyche requires extreme—indeed psychopathological—measures to break down, out, and through. Hillman:

> For the soul to be struck to its imaginal depths so that it can gain some intelligence of itself, or, as we would say more dryly today, "become conscious of the unconscious"—pathologizing fantasies are required. A bloodied or obscene image in a dream, a hypochondriacal fantasy, a psychosomatic symptom is a statement in imaginal language that the psyche is being profoundly stirred, and these pathologized fantasies are precisely the focal point of action and movement in the soul.[605]

In dire need of such intelligence and such action—the pathos of soul so denied in Denmark—Malte (like Rilke) moves to a dramatically different place, a locale in some wise so foreign to his experience that he would sooner die than live there.

Yet live there he does, and Malte's Paris represents a place still more radically antithetical to the Ulsgaard of Countess Margarete and The Master-of-the-Hunt than eccentric Urnekloster. If Ulsgaard's reigning dignitaries *repress* any sign of death, illness, or decay, in Malte's Paris such signs are *all over* everything, defining the physical surface of the city itself. If Ulsgaard's ruling spirits enforce a rigid division between acceptable exteriors and inadmissible insides—if its ruling mentality represses the dark interior of (un)consciousness, the world that underlies its formal facades—in Paris that other reality erupts and, defying all containment, all boundary, spills out onto the streets, so that little if any difference exists between the world above and the world below, what's "inside" and what's "out"—as if Paris were a person whose face-mask had been torn off.

Even in Urnekloster, where underworld realities are recognized, they are confined to accepted boundaries and assimilated to the conventions of that peculiar house. Counte Brahe remains on "civil" terms with the ghost of Christine Brahe; the alchemical uncle confines himself to his room when experimenting on his corpses; Mathilde Brahe's spiritualism has its appointed place and does not in the least disturb the order of the day. In Urnekloster, the eerieness connected with death and decay has been largely domesticated. In Paris, however—in Malte's mind at least—it breaks out all over.

Here, Malte's everyday reality continually dissolves into a kind of spectral waking dream or nightmare. People dressed in hospital gowns float by in the window like ghosts; men and women faint in the streets or die before your very eyes at the next table in the café. Epileptics dance on bridges while blind men shout in the boulevards; grotesquely bandaged inhuman forms sit next to you in the public clinic; and everywhere, and nowhere, are the poor and homeless, the outcast class who, with strange, incomprehensible signs, beckon Malte, claiming him as one of their own. Paris, for Malte, resembles Dante's inferno, the dolorous city of death, the underworld itself.

In his book *Dreams and the Underworld*, Hillman allies the underworld with dream. Construing the underworld as a realm of invisible image foreign to the corporeality of day consciousness and the willful machinations of the ego that operate on and in it, Hillman privileges this realm as the native domain of the psyche. He describes one primary means of access to this realm in the following terms:

> The transition from the material to the psychical perspective often presents dream imagery of sickening and dying. The hospital and doctor's office are not only dream places of getting better. They are places where the collapse of the corporeal is given refuge. The rotting and blackening processes of alchemy, dreadful wounds and suppurating sores...and other such shocking imagery point to where something material is losing substance and thrust, where a physical impulse or animal drive is descending toward the underworld.[606]

Hillman's words brings tangibly and forcibly to mind innumerable passages from *Malte*: the first entry, with its hospitals and image of human collapse; Malte's miserable, terrifying experience in the waiting room of a public clinic; his excruciatingly precise description of the putrefying remains of the wall of a half-demolished house; the "purulent sore" on the breast of King Charles VI (complete with the precious iron amulet embedded in the "pearly border of pus" and the worms emerging upon its removal); and many more. All these images, of course, represent signal instances of *pathologizing*, which process is thus revealed as the *via regia* to the altered perspective of the underworld.

Another passage from *Dreams and the Underworld* forms another vital link with Malte the poet:

> Underworld images are nonetheless visible, but only to what is invisible in us...psyche. Psychic images are not necessarily pictures and may not be like sense images at all. Rather they are images as metaphors. An image in poetry.[607]

This reminds us of Malte's own peculiarly poetic way of seeing—one focused, we may recall, through the lens of his affliction. Whether the matter at hand is a distraught woman with her face in her hands or an epileptic painfully crossing a bridge, Malte's mode of perception consistently departs from the merely physical facts, moving—albeit almost insensibly so—into a realm of purely psychical or imaginal/metaphorical reality. On some level, we do actually see the woman's flayed face, but the image remains a purely imaginal—not natural or physical—reality. Moreover, insofar as that which defines physiognomic *outside*—the face—suddenly reveals an utterly incomprehensible *inside* while that which is normally *inside* (what's behind the face/mask) suddenly presents an unthinkable *outside*, the image has enormous—and enormously terrifying—symbolic force, capturing in a moment the gist of Malte's Paris and the horror it holds. Malte's pathologizing thus triggers his psychological as well as poetic imagination, and—opening the gates to the underworld—offers access to a whole realm of soul truths previously banished or barred from his well-ordered Danish consciousness.

Even so, these are (to borrow an image from one of Rilke's masters) the Gates of Hell. Reading Hillman, it sometimes seems too easy to forget what *Malte* reminds us of most forcibly: the nightmarish terror often accompanying descent to the underworld; the loss of conscious control, and the overriding fear that one may entirely lose oneself there, and never come back.

At this point, we must refer once more to that crucial, difficult, and ambiguous difference which a careless reading of Hillman can all too readily gloss over: namely, that between a fantasy of underworld experience, on the one hand, and a full-blown psychosis on the other. In extreme forms of psychosis, unconscious imagery from the depths of the soul rises up and totally overwhelms the ego so that the difference between hallucinatory imagery and ordinary reality entirely disappears. Admittedly, the line between poetry and lunacy, creative imagination and wholesale madness cannot always be clearly or surely drawn. Jung's putative "breakdown" serves as one case in point, and history hardly lacks instances of genuine madness overtaking the most brilliant artists and thinkers. In connection with *Malte*, however, it appears as though Rilke composed his "healing fiction" in part to draw just that line in the sand. One may well imagine that Rilke created *Malte* so that he himself might explore the underworld realm vital to his soul without literally going mad himself.

Malte himself does fear madness. That fear more or less coincides with the dread of death that haunts Malte's Parisian existence, for both madness and death entail irrevocable loss of one's own conscious sense of self or definite identity. Malte's perspective on things counts as slightly deranged from the outset, and—as the novel progresses—he does seem in palpable danger of going under and losing his sanity altogether. Malte, after all, does have a real problem, one that continually vexes and endangers his Parisian existence. Try as he may (and he does try), Malte *cannot contain himself*; cannot, that is, secure a place from which his own consciousness may maintain a creative connection with the spectral underworld without becoming wholly absorbed by it.

Such containment implies an ability to create an interior space that remains (relatively) distinct from all incursions from the outside. Toward the beginning of the book, Malte does claim to be newly conscious of "an inner self." Even so, the crush of his fraught existence continually threatens Malte's sense of identity, and the urgent necessity to *contain and so define* himself generates a host of compensatory fantasies. Malte dreams of keeping a small shop in Paris, divided from all that is going on outside by a protective sheet of glass; he fantasizes about a cozy, secluded ancestral home in the mountains surrounded only by a few old and treasured things. Malte does in fact enjoy the refuge of a special reading room in Paris—an especially valued retreat precisely because one needs an identity card to enter so that the poor and homeless that haunt him are excluded. Even here, however, Malte harbors a deep anxiety that, as he becomes outwardly and inwardly ever more like those outcasts, he will no longer have access to such safe havens—places (like the reading room where he sits reading poetry—another treasured mark of difference and distinction) which confirm for him who he is by excluding who and what he is not.

The poor and homeless both terrify and attract Malte because (in his mind at least) they abide beyond the pale. Living wholly beyond the bounds of conventional consensus reality, these outcasts figure as denizens and ciphers of that other underworld Malte dreads and—at the same time—finds himself irrevocably and fatefully drawn toward. Indeed, as the "action" of the novel proceeds, that underworld more and more threatens to swallow Malte whole. Even his childhood recollections—his imaginative attempt to go behind the frigid form of consciousness he has in some wise inherited, and confront the debilitating fear of death it concealed—even this threatens merely to fuel the underworld fires that seem on the verge of consuming him. For as Malte probes ever deeper into the sources of his own unconscious, repressed childhood fears—sources of angst he had thought he had forgotten or left behind—reemerge in a tangle of insane and incoherent memories. At one desperate point, Malte confesses: "I have asked for my childhood, and it has come back, and I feel it is just as difficult as it was before, and that it has been useless to grow older."[608]

Concomitantly, in Paris, Malte finds himself literally driven away from all physical and psychological refuge, hounded out of every locale that might offer some place he could call (even provisionally) his own, any retreat set apart from the underworld reality of the Parisian streets. His chronically smoking stove drives him out of his own shabby room; nor can he find rest in the Louvre on account of the guards and the homeless drifters that somehow find their way in. Out on the streets once again, Malte finds himself, unwittingly, in the midst of a carnival. His description of that experience superbly displays how thoroughly the underworld logic of dream pervades Malte's Paris:

> For it was a carnival and evening, and the people all had time and roved about, rubbing against each other. And their faces were full of the light that came from the show-booths, and laughter bubbled from their mouths like matter from open sores. The more impatiently I tried to force my way forward, the more they laughed and the more closely they crowded together. Somehow a woman's shawl hooked itself to me; I dragged her after me, and people stopped me and laughed.... Someone threw a handful of confetti into my eyes, and it burned like a whip. At the crossings people were wedged fast, shoved one into the other, and there was no forward movement in them, only a quiet, gentle swaying back and forth, as if they copulated standing. But although they stood, and I ran like a madman along the edge of the pavement where there were gaps in the crown, yet in truth it was they who moved while I never stirred. For nothing changed.[609]

Such a passage brings forcibly to mind Freud's interpretation of "the psychological underworld," which he allies with the id. Hillman cites Freud's definitions—which both complement and compete with his own—in his *Dream and the Underworld*. Freud calls the id "a chaos, a cauldron of seething excitement" that "cannot say what it wants." Likening that incapacity to the inability of the dead in the mythological underworld to speak in anything but a whisper, Hillman notes Freud's claim that "it would be possible to picture the id.... under the domination of the mute but powerful death instincts." In the id, just as in Rilke's waking dream, "there is no recognition of the passage of time," and

> the denizens of the underworld are, in Freud's language, "instinctual cathexes seeking discharges...'" And finally, this id, like the Homeric underworld, is completely cut off from the external world, dealing with it only "through the medium of the ego."[610]

If that ego goes into total eclipse, all connection with "the external world" does as well—precisely the condition of madness and of death that Malte so obsessively contemplates and fears.

It goes without saying that—in and of itself—such a world of death does not serve the soul's individuation but obliterates it, even as Malte's distinct consciousness goes lost in the undifferentiated sea of swaying bodies. We arrive, then, at the shores of paradox. For earlier, we supposed that the ego must to some significant degree surrender its control of consciousness in order for the soul to enter the underworld of imagination and have its poetic say. If, however, that loss of control approaches total eclipse, self and soul may all too easily flow down the dark river Styx into the oblivion of real madness or literal death.

Malte shows himself to be all too aware of this second outcome: for him it is no mere theoretical possibility, but a clear and increasingly present danger. Finally managing to escape the carnival, Malte seeks shelter in his favorite café. Yet there—even there—he is pitilessly denied refuge or safe haven. Almost immediately upon sitting down, Malte perceives—not so much physically as psychically—that, at the adjacent table (the one he himself usually occupies) sits a man who is dying.

> The connection between us was established, and I knew that he was stiff with terror. I knew that terror had paralyzed him, terror at something that was happening inside him. Perhaps one of his blood-vessels had burst.

Malte forces himself to look directly at the man, because he "still hoped it was all imagination."

But his vision of the man with the "grey strained face," distended nostrils, and "wasted temples out of which everything had been taken" confirmed his worst fear:

> Yes, he knew that he was now withdrawing from everything: not merely from human beings. A moment more and everything will have lost its meaning, and that table and the cup, and the chair to which he clings, all the near and the commonplace, will have become unintelligible, strange and heavy.[611]

Malte cannot take it. He springs up and rushes out. Vainly perhaps, because wherever he goes in Paris, the specter of death pursues him.

Naturally, we cannot know if the man in the café was indeed dying, or whether Malte's perceptions amounted to pure projection of his own inner paranoia. Malte's inner, psychical state decisively colors and shapes the world around him, which consequently threatens to lose its objective character altogether. Malte's Paris increasingly comes to represent the *reverse* psychic situation from that prevailing in his native Denmark, at least in its dominant, Ulsgaard variety. If his father's rational consciousness denied—and so split itself off from—all unconscious unknowns; if outer form appeared radically disconnected from interior truth; if his father and grandmother held sickness taboo, and refused death a part in life, Paris fatefully turns Malte's (un)conscious tables as the historically repressed underworld roars up and subsumes his conscious life. No longer forcibly cleft in two and held apart by his father's or grandmother's iron will, unconscious and conscious, night and day, inside and out, death and life, meet and merge in one undifferentiated dreamlike continuum auguring, it seems, naught but the chaos of madness.

Malte's pathologizing appears to have brought him to a fatal pass, yet his hope does not wholly die. Despite the gravity of his affliction, Malte retains a glimpse of light at the end of his dark tunnel, a crack in the roof of the underworld which, if he—like a bee—could pass through, might allow him to achieve a transformed, redeemed vision of things. Immediately after his encounter with the man in the café, Malte writes:

> If my fear were not so great, I should console myself with the fact that it is not impossible to see everything differently and yet to live... Despite my fear I am yet like one standing before something great... Only a step, and my deep misery would be beatitude. But I cannot take that step, I have fallen and cannot pick myself up again, because I am broken.[612]

Malte continues to provide the biblical topos that offers a different perspective on his miserable state, puts his sickness and his suffering in a rather different light:

> By the great force of my disease is my garment changed: it
> bindeth me about as the collar of my coat....

> My bowels boiled and rested not: the days of affliction prevented me....
> My harp also is turned to mourning, and my organ into the voice of them that weep.

Job, it may be argued, was righteous; Malte simply sick, gripped by fear, half-mad, his fantasies of beatitude and identification with Job naught but psychic inflations compensating for his crippling sense of personal insufficiency. Undoubtedly, such a verdict could hardly be judged "wrong," and yet, at the same time, Malte—plunged deep into the heart of our human fear of the unknown—may nonetheless bear profound archetypal truth in his character. His travail, and the psychological cross he carries, are not his alone.[613]

In any event, despite Malte's despair, despite his inability to take the step that might transform his agony into ecstatic vision, he does see the possibility of doing so. Correlatively, he begins to contemplate images of figures who, in some manner, have achieved that step and point the way toward a more integrated consciousness that would hold life and death together as part of a more comprehensive order and would regard misery and affliction, not with distancing scorn, but with a love that embraces the whole. In an entry that appears not long after the escapade in the café, Malte sees a statue of "the saint in the Pantheon, the solitary, saintly woman" and weeps at the image of this roof-top presence who "watches over the sleeping city,"[614] holding all of it in her compassionate gaze. Later in the same entry, he mentions "Baudelaire's incredible poem, 'Une Charogne'"—in which the poet finds an almost transcendent beauty investing the repulsive physical reality of a dead and worm-eaten dog.

Malte, however, knows he is no saint, nor is it clear that he as yet can even lay claim to the title of poet. While the saint and master poet may serve him as distant ideals, in order to move toward a more integral vision of love and more inclusive beauty, Malte requires images closer to home, figures from his own past who may reveal to him that not only fear, but love too has a place in his own personal history. In addition to cold-as-glass grandmothers, stiff fathers and bonafide eccentrics, they too play a role in his past. Not surprisingly, most all are feminine—and on his *mother's* side of the family.

As his Maman related, her sister Ingeborg possessed a joyful spirit: "She made us all happy.... your father, too, Malte, literally happy." Full of light herself, Ingeborg apparently had no need to shrink from darker truths. Although she died at a young age, she—in marked contrast to Malte's father—did not allow the specter of death to overwhelm or subdue her. Malte's Maman again:

> When we were told she was going to die, though she seemed to be ailing only a little, and we all went about hiding the truth, she sat up in bed one day and said, as if to herself, like a person who wants to hear how something sounds: "You mustn't put such a strain on yourselves; we all know it, and I can set your minds at rest; it will be all right just as it comes; I don't want any more."[615]

Ingeborg's sitting up in bed recalls the similar gesture (as recorded in the account Malte's father carried in his wallet) on the part of Christian IV, but the affect and content of the subsequent words could hardly be more different. Malte's mother, in fact, charges her son to understand Ingeborg's remarkable equanimity in the face of death, for "it would be good if there were someone who understood such things."[616]

Rilke's Maman herself clearly plays a key role in his soul history. In general, she emanates a loving warmth that contrasts starkly with her husband's coldness, and one cannot help but feel that her own death and even gradual derangement (as her illness progressed, she would not eat anything that was not run through a fine sieve on account of all the small needles she imagined were lying about all over) must have evolved as a reaction to her husband's faultlessly correct yet soulless sovereignty. To a significant degree, the healing force of Malte's reminiscence revolves around remembrance of her image; in her best moments, his Maman shows herself capable of—not only deep affection—but an intuitive (albeit unorthodox) religious soul-intelligence. The following passage, centering around Malte and his mother's rolling out of exquisite and treasured pieces of lace, reveals an intimate connection with the "new poem" on the same topic:

> "They surely got to heaven, whoever made this," I said admiringly. I remember it occurred to me that for a long time I had not asked about heaven. Maman drew a long breath, the laces were assembled again.
>
> After a while, when I had already forgotten about it, she said quite slowly: "To heaven? I believe they are completely in all this. If one sees it so, that may well be an eternal beatitude. One does know so little about it."[617]

At some deeply unconscious level, Malte's Maman provides an image of a universe alternative to the one signified by his father or grandmother—a soul-filled cosmos that does not see heaven elsewhere, away from this earth. She even provides an imaginal prefiguration of the type of the saintly woman watching over the sleeping city. Yet as fundamental as her role in Malte's personal history remains, another related figure proves no less—and indeed perhaps still more—crucial. If Maman supplies Malte with a subliminal connection to the archetype of the divine mother, it is her youngest sister, Abelone, with whom Malte first falls in love and so will—in time—permit us to pick up the thread of our guiding myth once more.

Chapter 13

TAPESTRIES, ABELONE...

The Lady and the Unicorn

The Notebooks of Malte Laurids Brigge could well be considered the most patently psychological of all Rilke's major works. Replete with detailed descriptions of the symptoms of his own mental condition as well as seminal memories of early childhood, Malte's imagination often assumes an almost psychoanalytic character. Only so could we, in the foregoing chapter, pretend to carry Malte's own "self-analysis" a step further, tracing the origin of his illness back to the peculiar nature of his early family life—including Malte's parental *imagos*, the formative relation between his cold and controlling father and his less rational but more beloved *maman*.

In point of biographical fact, the psychoanalytic movement—burgeoning even while Rilke was hard at work on *Malte*—did not fail to touch Rilke himself. His closest confidante, Lou, was swept up by it, and in 1912, just before the inception of his *Duino Elegies*, Rilke himself seriously considered entering into a course of analysis. Explaining his decision not to do so to Lou (whose counsel seconded his own decision), Rilke wrote:

> You know perhaps, dear Lou, that since sometime early in the year Gebsattel has had my wife under treatment,—with her it is a different matter, her work has never helped her, while mine, in a certain sense, was from the beginning a kind of self-treatment.[618]

Though Rilke's comment by no means applies exclusively to *Malte*, it is in his highly personal novel that Rilke's method of "self-treatment" most closely approximates professional psychology's most classical form of the same.

Indeed, Rilke's literary response to his formative psychological crisis could well be seen as revealing greatest generic affinity with the norms, not of Jungian, but of Freudian analysis. Freud, after all, discovered the nascent shape of his praxis in good measure in and through the process of writing a book. Freud wrote his *Dora: An Analysis of a Case of Hysteria* in 1901 and published it in 1905,[619] a time period more or less contemporaneous with *Malte*'s inception. In its rigorous diagnosis of symptom and typical regression to childhood scenes, Rilke's *Malte* mimics the genre of case history pioneered in Freud's seminal text, the literary form of which decisively shaped what soon became the classic method of (psycho)analysis.

Yet if the similarities between Rilke's *Malte* and Freud's *Dora* are notable and significant, the generic distinctions between the two works are still more so. Indeed, once the "family resemblance" between Freud's case history and Rilke's novel has been duly noted, elaborating the dramatic differences between them can serve to set in clear relief the unique—and deeply radical—psychological initiative embodied in Rilke's highly original text.

First and foremost, Rilke's *Malte* does not present itself as the record of a scientific analysis but, unreservedly, as a literary fiction. This clearly identifies *Malte* as a work of imagination that does not pretend to empirical truth. As Hillman points out in his book *Healing Fiction*, the claim to objective veracity implicit in the genre of the case history itself must always remains suspect, premised as it is upon an inherently and intensely subjective process of recollection. Hillman, indeed, goes so far as to insist that the purely imaginative dimension always comprises the heart and soul of any truly psychological process of remembering so that analysis itself always unfolds, not empirical truths, but "healing fiction":

> Freud's crucial discovery that the stories he was being told were psychological happenings dressed as history and experienced as remembered events was the first recognition in modern psychology of psychic reality independent of other realities. It was, further, *a recognition of the independence of memory from history and history from memory.* There is history that is not remembered—forgetting, distortion, denial, repressing; there is also memory that is not historical.[620]

Much of *Malte* patently falls in this latter category. Indeed, the *whole* of the book does so—if more ambiguously so—for even when *Malte*'s author narrates incidents based on Rilke's actual life or objective historical events, he manifestly reinvents everything in the writing. "To be correct," writes Hillman,

> this remembering-what-never-happened must rightly be called imagining, and this sort of memory is imagination. *Memoria* was the old term for both.[621]

Rilke's *Malte*—eliding the difference between recollection and invention *and redressing (personal) history as fiction*—carries Freud's "crucial discovery" to its logical psychological conclusion, unequivocally privileging imagination as the authentically therapeutic agent in his "self-treatment."

As Hillman indicates, imagination or *memoria* may form the hidden core of Freud's *Dora* no less than Rilke's *Malte*. Even so, the veneer of scientific objectivity characteristic of the former makes an enormous difference, giving rise to basic generic distinctions that carry inestimable psychological force. The crucial category of authorial point of view represents one critical instance. *Dora* provides an account of Sigmund Freud's analysis of a young woman. It is thus the good doctor himself who—building upon what Dora offered in conversation—recounts relevant details of Dora's life and, too, interprets their significance. In Malte's case, by contrast, the one telling the story (or writing the notebooks) doubles as the main character; author and subject of the personal or "case history"—"analyst" and "analysand"—are one and the same.

Generically speaking, Rilke's *Malte*—first person through and through—represents a form of self-analysis.

Of course, it may be argued that Malte remains Rilke's invention and cannot be spoken of as the "true" author of his notebooks; that the distance between Freud and Dora finds some parallel in that between Rilke and his literary persona. Perhaps, but these are very different, indeed quite incommensurate distances. The line between Freud and Dora, two distinct historical persons—doctor and patient—remains preeminently clear; that between "Rilke" and his imaginative creation (Malte) inevitably tends to blur. Most importantly, interrogations of the difference between Rilke and Malte—as relevant as they may be to psychobiography—*remain outside the purview of the work of poetic art itself and the psychology inscribed in its literary form.* Not so for Freud's *Dora*, the voice, form, and style of which depend utterly upon the manifest difference between (on the one hand) the professional persona of its author/narrator and (on the other) his subject—or object—of study (Dora).

A host of critical correlates flow from this difference. First, insofar as the putative author of the *Notebooks*—Malte—doubles as its subject, the authorial persona can no longer readily occupy a post outside the origin of the tale he tells or naturally pose as a detached, quasi-omniscient narrator. It is just this position that Freud assumes in *Dora*, and, too, just this position that founds and authorizes the classic method of psychoanalyis. Analysts who take the utmost care to maintain a pose of entirely impersonal objectivity (keeping, for instance, the slightest trace of their own personal history out of the charmed analytic circle) aspire to the authorial position claimed and staked out in Freud's *Dora*.

The norm of the more or less omniscient narrator—the one who can know what is really going on precisely because of his outside perspective—triggers vital generic spin-offs.

Perhaps the most primary of these involves the very extra-literary conception of psychology itself. Insofar as the detached objectivity—even anonymity—that characterizes the omniscient narrator mirrors the typical stance of the neutral investigator, it is, in good measure, precisely the assumption of this position that empowers psychoanalysis to *conceive of itself as science* in the first place, and to *compose* itself accordingly. Scientific language—for example, the diagnostic classification and naming of mental disease—flows naturally from the position of detached knowing, and the dependence upon abstract terminology figures as one of the earmarks of scientific writing. Freud's very title provides a signature case in point. While its main title might lead us to believe that the book is really about Dora, Freud is no Flaubert, and his volume no *Madame Bovary.* In fact, Freud's subtitle subtly undercuts the apparent importance accorded to Dora as an individual person and reveals the book's real investment, which lies, not in delineation of living character, but in descriptive investigation of a certain *class* of mental illness: *Dora: An Analysis of a Case of Hysteria.*

The position of relative omniscience presumed by Freud in *Dora* helps enable another, equally determining element of style: namely, the importance accorded to the *plotting* of the story. As a general critical term, plot (or "emplotment," as Northrop Frye calls it) prescribes not merely the bare sequence of events that constitutes "story," but *why* events unfold as they do, the causal logic—rooted in character and intention—that organizes and impels the action. In *Healing Fiction*, Hillman explains the relevance of the idea of plot to psychological praxis:

> In our kind of fictions the plots are our theories. They are the ways in which we put the intentions of human nature together so that we can understand the *why* between the sequence of events in a story.
>
> Telling us why is Freud's main aim with his case histories. All his narrative skills are assembled only for the sake of plot. Freud devised a plot that fits all his stories.[622]

Hillman is referring here, of course, to the Oedipal myth that grounds Freud's theory. We will have more to say about the connection between plot and myth in general—and Freud's Oedipus in particular—shortly. For now, we need note only the main point: the defining role played by plot in the genre of case history, its dominant function as a means of organizing story so that the ordering of events conforms to and reveals the master teller's underlying knowledge of the whole.

With respect to both the generic factors just discussed (language and plot) Rilke's *Malte*—and the form of self-analysis it represents—diverges sharply from the model presented in Freud's *Dora.* Given Malte's mental state, it would certainly be possible for the author of his story to venture into the terrain of scientific diagnosis, to avail himself of technical terminology in his attempt to grasp the nature of his malaise. Yet Malte's position as both author *and* subject of his story problematizes the strict subject/object division inherent in such naming; nor is Malte as a character (or Rilke as a writer) inclined in that direction. Instead,

Malte presents his own personal history from the inside out, sharing his episodic stream of consciousness without label or professional classification. His language, poetic from beginning to end, remains in the realm of image, evocation, innuendo. Malte, after all, is himself a poet whose writing *is* his life, and (for Rilke, too) is far more a genuine *character* than "a case."

Nor, by any means, does *Malte*'s fragmented, episodic style readily lend itself to the driving force and explanatory power of strong plotting. Indeed, the manifest infirmity of that element of Rilke's fiction is so great as to threaten its very coherence. The book, like Malte himself, seems ever on the verge of falling apart, and it stretches the limits of that genre to call Rilke's book "a novel" at all. Narrative threads, of course, weave throughout the book, but one cannot claim that these threads are patterned "for the sake of plot," or that the causal narrative logic organizes and drives the writing. In fact, Malte's plot does such a poor job of this that, when it came to finishing his "novel," Rilke had great difficulty in settling upon a satisfying conclusion, and only decided upon one of two entirely different scenarios at the last moment. Still, some critics—Rilke's best biographer included—feel he may not have made the best choice.

Let us return, however, to Oedipus, for the generic distinctions we are drawing ultimately derive from this mythic source—the innumerable ways, both overt and covert, that the Oedipus myth molds the poetics of (psycho)analysis.

It is not difficult to see how the Oedipus myth establishes the defining *subject* and *goal* of analysis. "The basic content of the conflicted soul lies in childhood and its passions in regard to parents. Self-knowledge consists in uncovering this truth."[623] Yet the myth does more than determine the ostensible content of analysis: it decisively shapes the generic form which contains, reflects, and reciprocally engenders its defining *method*. Hillman:

> It is not, however, the contents of the myth that keep analysis Freudian. It is the method. Analysis is Oedipal in *method*: inquiry as interrogation, consciousness as seeing, dialogue to find out, self-discovery by recall of early life, oracular reading of dreams. The methods of an analysis are the *methods* of this myth.[624]

Let us briefly examine how the mold of that method inheres in the poetics of *Oedipus Rex*, focusing, once again, upon the formative—and interrelated—elements of plot and perspective.

Sophocles' tragedy unfolds Oedipus' story with astonishing economy and power. Incident follows incident in quick, predetermined causal order. Plot is not only "strong," but all-powerful, for it unfailingly unfolds fate, and fate—seemingly inescapable—dominates the play, dictating its action every step of the way and culminating in Oedipus' tragic—and blinding—insight into his own identity. The telos of conscious (self-)knowledge and the revelatory process of plot remain inextricably linked.

What, exactly, drives the action of the play so forcefully forward? Oedipus himself, of course, and his proudly unrelenting desire to solve the problem presented to him: the reason for his city's sore distress. Initially, Oedipus believes himself to be entirely uninvolved in that problem—no part of its *cause*—even while resolutely, heroically, dedicated to its solution. He assumes, that is, the stance of one capable of objective investigation, presuming his own self to comprise no part of the object of study. Oedipus' method, accordingly, begins on a rational, quasi-scientific basis, and his intellect—the tool of mind by which he famously solved the enigma of the Sphinx—figures as his principal means of approach. "The dominant characteristic of this blind man Oedipus lies in how his mind works, his superior *heuriskein*: discovering, finding, or figuring out."[625] No less a riddlemaster than Dr. Freud, the king who would find a cure for the ills of the city does not avail himself of anything resembling "the thought of the heart," but consistently confronts the problem—all his problems—*head-on*.

Having said so much, we may perceive how the poetics of Freud's *Dora* (and, implicitly, those of the analytic method in general) ultimately flow from the profession's Sophoclean source. The generic form featuring an impersonal and detached author/interrogator; conceptual language serving the problem-solving intellect; strong emplotment irrevocably linking present symptoms to experiences of early childhood (in accordance with the causal logic of fate)—all may be construed as legacies of the myth Freud chose as the ground of analysis.

One could hardly contend that Rilke's *Malte* altogether excludes Oedipal elements; quite the contrary. Malte's repeated recollections of childhood and conscious insistence that this childhood supplies his spiritual foundation; his evident distance from his father and enormous affection for his mother; the keen analytic eye Malte casts upon his inner and outer world and his perpetual dissection of reality—all these qualify as Oedipal elements in Malte's text, engendering its underlying affinity with psychoanalysis. Yet, as the significant generic differences we have so far identified indicate, Rilke's *Malte* does not tangle with Oedipus in order to submit to this tragic hero's myth. Rather, Malte's very affinity with psychoanalysis may be read as means of gaining leverage in order to wrest psychology all the more strongly away from its Oedipal ground. Having closed with Oedipus, Rilke's *Malte* executes a wrestler's twist, throwing the classic tragic hero to the mat. Before psychoanalysis had even fully established itself, Rilke had pulled its founding myth out from under its club-feet.

Despite the discontinuous character of Malte's writings, his book by no means lacks significant structure. For one thing, his *Notebooks* divide into two almost exactly equal parts. Thematically as well as formally, the book hinges upon the figures placed at its center, for it is here that Malte first invites us to view the intricately woven lines of the non- (or even anti-) Oedipal *myth of love* that underlies *The Notebooks of Malte Laurids Brigge.*

Sophocles' *Oedipus*, after all, is not much concerned with love. Oedipus' incestuous relationship with Jocasta does figure as a crucial element of the plot, a necessary link in the iron chain of the tragic hero's fate, but hardly qualifies as the chief focus of the play. *Oepidus Rex* is all about Oedipus: his proud mind and blinding (un)consciousness, his fateful search for what turns out to be *self*-knowledge.

The most crucial points of difference between Rilke's *Malte* and *Oedipus* do, however, emerge against similar backgrounds, for *Malte* and *Oedipus* share more than a focus on family. Sickness, a pathologized state of being that demands attention—even a cure—furnishes the point of departure for both texts. Both protagonists, too, initiate a kind of investigation, and pursue a more or less prolonged inquiry into the character and cause of a pervasive affliction. From the first, however, they differ dramatically in their *attitude towards illness, their relation to pathology.*

Like Malte, Oedipus does acknowledge his affliction from the outset, responding to the citizens' plea for help with this telling preamble:

I pity you, children. You have come full of longing,
but I have known the story before you told it
only too well. I know you are all sick,
yet there is not one of you, sick though you are,
that is as sick as I myself.
...My spirit groans
for city and myself and you at once.[626]

Unlike Malte, however, Oedipus imagines the *origin* of the illness to lie entirely outside himself. He has no notion that he himself may be its source, and that it is the sickness, the pathology of his own soul that qualifies as the root cause of the affliction he laments. His pride and intelligence cast a long dark shadow over his past and future life, but a shadow that he—a worshipper of the sun-God, Pheobus Apollo—cannot, in his solar splendor, see. The action of the play, however, inexorably drives him on toward self-discovery, constraining him, at last, to turn and face the terrible illuminative force of his mind. Blindness defines Oedipus' character, at the beginning as well as the end of the play—in ignorance as well as knowledge—and the climactic moment when he literally tears out his eyes fulfills his awful fate.

Malte, too, embarks on a kind of vision quest, but departs from a quite different platform. Malte (as he himself confesses) "is learning to see," but his is a darker line of sight, already attuned to the in- and underside of things, the sources of sickness in himself as well as the world. Perhaps because Malte is, from the first, keenly aware of his own illness and vulnerability, all too conscious of the specters and shades that darken his mind, his "play"—even if it be read as tragedy—does not drive blindly toward a sudden tragic reversal of fortune, the moment of fateful self-revelation. In fact, at the crossroads posted midway through the book of his life, Malte takes a decisive turn toward a different, less *self-centered* end, beginning his exploration of—not the myth of the classic tragic hero—but the myth of love.

Confronting Oedipus' legacy, Hillman poses some crucial questions:

> Because we proceed like Oedipus, we think like Oedipus, and we find what he found...Were we to imagine therapy differently—say, as a work in love with the mythologem of Eros and Psyche

> paramount...therapy's methods would display an altogether different nature. Would we still be assessing a human soul in terms of its origins, and would origins be equivalent to parents and childhood? Would we still be trying to "find ourselves," our true story, our identity? Would we still be solving riddles?[627]

If we were to look to Rilke in answering these questions, the response would be: *Yes...and no.* Rilke's *Malte* metamorphoses Oedipal method, effecting a vital generic transformation born of the intervention of another myth, the myth introduced in the figure of Abelone and Malte's memories of falling in love.

To be sure, Malte's initial attraction to Abelone could well be perceived as strengthening, rather than challenging, the Oedipal undertones of Malte's psychology. Abelone is, after all, his mother's younger sister, and Malte only really becomes aware of her after his mother's death. (Malte introduces her with the words "It was in the year after Maman's death that I first noticed Abelone."[628]) In the first phase of their relationship, moreover, Abelone serves primarily as a vehicle through which Malte's mother may be better remembered. ("At first our relationship consisted in her telling me of the days of Maman's girlhood. She set great store by convincing me how valiant and young Maman had been.") All of this could well suggest that Abelone indeed represents a stand-in for Malte's *maman*, and so identify Malte's love for her as thoroughly consistent with Oedipal themes.

Initially, perhaps. Even so, the more crucial point is that Abelone, and Malte's memory of his youthful love for her, fundamentally transfigures his book, dramatically refocusing its attention. Illness, fear, death, family, the city, poverty, beauty, religion—before the Abelone entry, Malte's notebooks engage all these topics, but *not* erotic love, which earns naught but the most passing mention in most of the first half of the text. After Abelone's entrance, however, Malte's text becomes another story altogether.

Whether or not Malte's initial love for Abelone represents displaced love for his mother ultimately matters very little, because—regardless of her relationship to Malte's *maman*—she immediately becomes a bridge for Malte to other images, images of soul, of anima, images of women—the soul—in love, *even love itself.* Indeed, even before Malte tells us that Abelone reminded him of his mother, sharing memories of her girlhood with him, he tells us that "Abelone had one good point: she sang"—and tells us, too, that there was divinity—masculine divinity—in her voice: "There was a strong unswerving music in her. If it is true that angels are masculine, then one may well say there was something masculine in her voice: a radiant, celestial masculinity." This, after all, was Malte-Psyche's introduction to erotic love:

> I endured this music, on which one could ascend upright, higher and higher, until one imagined that for a while this must just about have been heaven. I did not suspect that Abelone was to open yet other heavens for me.[629]

If Eros enters with Abelone, he can do so because she herself also represents anima, the feminine (side of) Psyche that evokes, receives, and partners love's inaugural address. The feminine element had by no means been entirely absent from the text of Malte's psyche prior to Abelone's appearance. The scene—famously drawn from Rilke's own biography—of little Malte pretending (with his mother's glad collusion) to be a little girl manifests it. Even so, after Abelone's appearance, the anima elements in Malte's psyche take on a less aberrant, more developed form and assume a whole new level of prominence in the text.

If Abelone herself provides a *personal-historical* point of reference for Malte's anima development, the scene evoked in the passage subsequent to her introduction—the final one of the first part, half of its central hinge—supplies a potent *archetypally artistic* image of the same. Naturally enough, Abelone's personal presence, the guidance and guardianship of her soul, mediates Malte's evocation of the scene:

> There are tapestries, Abelone, wall tapestries. I am imagining that you are here; there are six tapestries: come, let us pass slowly before them.... a lady, in various costumes, but always the same.... On the left a lion, and, on the right, so clear, the unicorn.[630]

While interpretations of the famous *Lady and the Unicorn* tapestries vary greatly, its central character remains clear: the tapestries represent diverse aspects of the feminine soul, various faces or gestures of the soul qua anima. In Rilke's reading, at least one of the tapestries—the one he places fourth—makes explicit reference to the soul's nascent relation to love: Malte makes special reference to the motto inscribed on the lady's tent, *A mon seul desir. All* the tapestries, however—while by no means offering images pertaining exclusively or primarily to romantic love per se—involve the soul's relation to (masculine) spirit as such is symbolized by the lion and, most importantly, the unicorn. The whole series thus remains suffused with an erotic—or, more precisely, *psycherotic*—aura. At the end of the first half of his notebooks and, too, the beginning of the second, Malte reframes his writing, placing it under the aegis of the soul qua anima and eros, Psyche and (her) Love.

Malte's memory of Abelone, in fact, acts as a psychic door, opening up imaginative memory (*memoria*) of a whole host of figures of girls and women in (or regrettably not in) love—from young single girls living alone in the city to the whole radiant pantheon of famous women lovers and authors (Bettina von Arnim, Gaspara Stampa, Christine de Pisan, Sappho) who populate the second part of the text. Of Bettina von Arnim, for instance, Malte writes, "Abelone...was like a preparation for her and has now become merged for me in Bettina, as if in her own unconscious being." He remembers Bettina and her love in the following terms:

> Just now, Bettina, you still were; I understand you. Is not the earth still warm with you, and do not the birds still leave room for your voice?...Or is not the whole world of your making? For how often you have set it afire with your love.[631]

James Hillman formally proposed the Psyche-Eros myth as archetypal psychology's own in a long essay entitled "On Psychological Creativity"—the first of three long essays comprising his book *The Myth of Analysis*. Malte's text does not only inscribe archetypal elements of the myth into its literary texture, but, too—as the above passage reveals—foregrounds its quintessentially *creative* function, so foundational for psychology. Yet Rilke, as we have seen, had been weaving together psychology, art, love, and creativity ever since Florence. As indispensable as love's cosmically creative function may be, we will need to look elsewhere to identify Malte's *novel* contribution to Rilke's poetic and psychological development; to construe the original moment of his spiritual career the book represents.

The first Abelone passage in the *Notebooks* evokes Eros's arrival, but Malte's attention by no means remains focused upon that initial moment. As the text progresses, Malte consistently focuses upon dynamics inherent in the latter half of the myth itself, the phase commencing after Eros' departure. The very first entry of the book's second part—deliberately spinning off *The Lady and the Unicorn* tapestries—sounds the pathbreaking themes:

> For centuries now, they [women] have performed the whole of love; they have always played the full dialogue, both parts. For the man has only imitated them, and badly. And has made their learning difficult with his inattentiveness, with his negligence, with his jealousy, which was also a sort of negligence. And they have nevertheless persevered day and night, and increased in love and misery. And from among them, under the stress of endless needs, have gone forth those powerful lovers, who, while they called him, surpassed their man; who grew beyond him when he did not return, like Gaspara Stampa or like the Portuguese nun, who never desisted until their torture turned into a bitter, icy splendor.[632]

In chapter 11, we discussed Rilke's assimilation of Rodin's concept of Art as Work, a Task requiring ceaseless labor. In *Malte*, Rilke not only applies a similar understanding to the intimately related work of Love, but inflects that understanding in a quite distinctive manner. The historical privilege accorded to *woman's* part in the work of love; the (distinctly feminine) virtue of *patience* exhibited in it; the suffering—indeed torture—inherent in love's labor, especially in the context of that most challenging, *unrequited* kind of love—Malte repeatedly elaborates these interrelated motifs in the latter half of the book. For instance, he pictures Charles XI, King of France...

> turning the pages of the little book by Christine de Pisan which is called "The Way of Long Learning." ... The book always opened for him at the simplest passages: where it spoke of the heart which for thirteen long years, like a retort over the fire of suffering, had only served to distill the water of bitterness for the eyes.[633]

Like themes figure prominently in Hillman's discussion of *The Myth of Analysis*. In a section of the aforementioned essay titled "The Suffering of Impossible Love," Hillman writes:

> We can recognize another consequent of a psyche without eros from felt experience. We suffer. This torment of the soul in its relationship to eros is a major theme in the tale of Eros and Psyche.... the psyche is tortured by love.[634]

Suffering implies affliction or illness, a sickness of body or soul; *torture* indicates an almost pathological intensification of the same. In broaching the topic of the suffering of (impossible) love, we begin to tie together two of Malte's—and Hillman's—chief themes, connecting the psyche's *pathologizing* with its innate, intense, irreducible desire for erotic union.

Hillman elaborates the subject further:

> For our psyche to unite legitimately with the creative and bring to sanctified birth what carries it, we evidently need to realize both our loss of primordial love through betrayal and separation and also our wrong relation to eros—the enthrallment, servility, pain, sadness, longing: all aspects of erotic *mania*. As Jung says, "for always the ardour of love transmutes fear and compulsion into a higher free type of feeling."[635]

Again and again, our poet sings of just these manifestations of erotic mania in his great woman lovers, and, too, the transmutation effected in and through their lovesickness. That transmutation takes both a physical and mythical form in the person of Byblis, whose legendary love for Caunus drove her to pursue him until "she reappeared beyond her death as a spring, hurrying on."[636] Malte imagines all his great women lovers as undergoing like transfiguration. ("What else happened to the Portuguese nun, save that inwardly she became a spring? Or to you, Heloise? To you all, lovers, whose laments have come down to us. . . . ") Striving to comprehend the spiritual careers of his great woman-lovers, he introduces a critical distinction:

> Fate loves to invent patterns and designs. Its difficulty lies in complexity. But life is difficult because of its simplicity. . . . the woman who loves always transcends the man she loves, because life is greater than fate.[637]

Malte reiterates this theme several times in his text, most often in connection with a celebration of Sappho and the deep and enduring import of her (distinctly poetic) life of love. We have seen, however, how *fate* rules the *life* of another ancient figure, and, in fact, arrive here at a juncture crucial to our ongoing exploration of competing myths of analysis. For the psychopathological phenomena of *fear* and *compulsion* noted by Jung play central roles in Oedipus' tragedy as well as Malte's notebook, but—as Hillman's continuation of the above-cited passage duly notes—act very differently in the two texts.

> "The ardour of love transmutes fear and compulsion into a higher free type of feeling." Seen against the Oedipal background, these torments cannot redeem, since in that myth compulsion overcomes love; in our tale, despite the same phenomena of torment, love—because it finds soul—overcomes compulsion.[638]

"Love—because it finds soul—overcomes compulsion"—in this phrase lies something of the deepest meaning of Malte's Notebooks, *a distinct lesson of love unaddressed by Psyche's first labor.* We touch here upon something crucial to—not only the psychology inscribed in *The Notebooks of Malte Laurids Brigge*—but an understanding of the significance of that book within the larger context of its author's psycho-spiritual career, something germane to the archetypal significance of Psyche's *second* labor of love. In delving into the riddling symbolism of that task, we will, moreover, find ourselves compelled to continue addressing Oedipus—if only, at the last, to leave him more definitively behind.

Venus was not the least bit pleased by Psyche's successful completion of her first charge and promptly set her another—apparently no less impossible—task:

> Do you see that grove that fringes the long banks of the gliding stream, whose deep eddies come rushing down from yonder mountain? There wander sheep whose fleeces shine with hue of gold, and no man guards them as they graze. I bid you take a wisp from the wool of their precious fleece as best you may and bring it to me with speed.[639]

The golden rams being fearsome beasts, Psyche hears Venus' words as a sentence of doom. She proceeds to the spot—not, initially, to try her luck with the rams, but to end her sorrows by casting herself off a cliff. However, just as the ants came to Psyche's rescue before, another agent of Pan—a green reed—intervenes on her behalf this time, and reveals to her how she may successfully complete the dread mission:

> "Psyche, racked though thou art by so many a woe, pollute not my sacred waters by slaying thyself thus miserably, nor at this hour approach those terrible sheep. For they borrow fierce heat from the blazing sun and wild frenzy maddens them, so that with sharp horns

> and foreheads hard as stone, and sometimes even with venomous bites, they vent their fury in the destruction of men. But till the heat of the noonday sun has assuaged its burning, and the beasts are lulled to sleep by the soft river breeze, thou canst hide thee beneath yonder lofty plane tree, which drinks of the river water even as I. And when once the sheep have abated their madness and allayed their anger, go shake the leaves of yonder grove, and thou shalt find the golden wool clinging here and there to crooked twigs."[640]

Psyche follows the reed's sage advice and—collecting strands of radiant stuff—accomplishes her second labor, returning to Venus with a quantity of golden wool.

In his commentary on the myth, Neumann understands this labor (like the first) as presenting an essentially erotic problem. The solar rams represent the masculine principle at the height of its unqualified power and yet, at the same time, incapable of entering into any constructive relationship to the feminine. On the contrary, if confronted at the zenith of its blazing force, the masculine can only burn up and destroy the feminine. Neumann, indeed, identifies the rams not with the life-giving power of the sun, but with its opposite: "The rams of the sun, symbols of the destructive power of the masculine, correspond to the negative masculine death principle. . . ."[641] At the high noon of that heated force, the cosmos reveals itself as drastically polarized—the extremes of light and darkness, fire and water, masculinity and femininity, death and soul life, appear irreconcilably divided.

Not surprisingly, Psyche's new helper contributes vital medial elements to this schizoid world-picture. While not necessarily an anima-figure per se, the reed nonetheless does possess anima-like attributes: not outwardly powerful, but supple and resilient; yielding readily to the wind, but firmly rooted in the moist element typically associated with "natural unconsciousness." Most crucially, though—and most closely linked with anima intelligence—the counsel the reed offers Psyche reconnects the realms of water and heavenly fire, passivity and activity, night and day, effectively bridging the worlds of soul and spirit. Following the reed's advice, Psyche—resting until *dusk* under the shade of the plane tree whose roots drink from the waters of the unconscious even while its "lofty" crown touches the sky—moves into a liminal position kin to the place (likewise, beneath a tree) Rilke's Orpheus occupies at the opening of his *Sonnets*.

Before, however, receiving the reed's aid, Psyche—inhabiting a hopelessly polarized cosmos—imagines herself condemned to a head-on confrontation with the raging rams, fated to surrender her life to the "the negative masculine death principle." *The initial frame of Psyche's second labor thus offers a potent image of Malte's soul-situation in Paris at the outset of his Notebooks.* Heir of a hopelessly divided consciousness—legacy of his Danish past—Malte is terrified by the specter of death, and the image of the irresistible violence it inflicts upon human consciousness repeatedly paralyzes him with fear. Nor does he, intially, know any way out of his psychic dilemma. He *must* face the source of his fear—what else, after all, is he doing in Paris?—but in the absence of any effective strategy for doing so, the prospect overwhelms him. Nowhere amid the city's teeming streets can he seem to escape, deflect, or counter the awful force of death's violent sway. Like Psyche, who, when informed of her second task, initially sought to throw herself off a cliff into the river, Malte seems fated to fail in his appointed mission, and go under.

Yet he does not—at least not right away. His frame of mind, in fact, alters dramatically in the course of his notebooks, *a change that pivots around the tapestry of anima-influence embroidering the novel's central hinge.* Just as the reed's wisdom transmutes an impossible task into a manageable labor, Abelone's—or rather anima's—decisive intervention, while not altogether banishing Malte's fear, does, ultimately, fundamentally transform it. This transfiguration forms the thematic gist of of whatever *plot* underlies Malte's loosely structured story.

It is, for instance, in the *latter* half of the text that Malte records his recollection of the events following upon his father's death, including his discovery of the slip of paper recording Christian IV's fateful last words—"Döden . . . Döden." This telling entry is immediately followed by another pivotal one that begins: "Since then I have reflected a good deal on the fear of death, not without taking into consideration certain personal experiences of my own." Rehearsing those experiences does make Malte's primordial terror of death rise, once more, to the conscious surface of his psyche. Even so, he has—by virtue of the imaginative work already done, the anima-enabled *memoria* recorded in his notebooks—gained *reflective distance* that prevents him from being entirely overwhelmed by fear. Meditating upon the fear of death—"fear that increases only when the force that engenders it increases"—the passage ends:

> We have no idea of his force, except in our fear. For it is so utterly inconceivable, so totally opposed to us, that our brain disintegrates at the point where we strain ourselves to think it. And yet, for some time now I have believed that it is *our own* force, all our own force that is still too great for us. It is true we do not know it; but is it not just that which is most our own of which we know the least? Sometimes I reflect on how heaven came to be and death: through our having distanced what is most precious to us, because there was still so much else to do beforehand and because it was not secure with us busy people. Now times have elapsed over this, and we have become accustomed to lesser things. We no longer recognize that which is our own and are terrified by its extreme greatness. May that not be?[642]

The reference to "us busy people" recalls Malte's early evocations of his Parisian existence and the pervasive and deep-seated fear underlying it; but here, in this later portion of the book, Malte moves toward a deeper, more constructive relation to death. As we will see later, death—rather than a wholly incomprehensible killing force—becomes a true mystery for Malte, a problematic but potent source of self-revelation that plays a central role in the still greater, more all-encompassing mystery of love.

Even while highlighting how anima figures catalyze Malte's imaginative progress, we should not forget the related part played by pathologizing in Malte's soul-drama. That part, too, finds apt and revealing inscription in the imagery of Psyche's second labor. The sun-crazed rams can readily be seen to figure a pathologized force, but the mythic picture must be grasped more comprehensively—*in fact, the entire scene of Psyche's second labor may be seen to present a psychic or imaginal picture of what (physically speaking) we call a fever,* like to those so frequent—and formative—in Malte's youth. An intemperate heat burns (kindled, perhaps, by the fire of love?). If well advised, the soul takes refuge in cooler elements, seeking the healing rest that will allow it, eventually, to rise refreshed, having (ideally) incorporated into itself the psychosomatic changes wrought by the fever. The ailing psyche convalescing under the plane tree gains reflective time and space that enables soul to enter into more constructive communion with the spirit's fire. This psyche may (like the kindred long-suffering patient we find so variously pictured in Malte) therefore be accorded her place in our mythological picture of the pathologized and pathologizing imagination. The soul finds refuge in the kind of protected place Oedipus the King disdained, and avails itself of the sort of private time he would *not* take. And therein lies his tragedy, and—perhaps, by way of dramatic contrast—the secret of the *exiled* Oedipus' (and Malte's?) ultimate redemption.

While apt, Neumann's interpretation of the force figured by the golden rams ("the negative masculine death principle") remains partial and somewhat abstract. How, psychologically speaking, might we imagine that fierce solar strength manifesting in human life? How come to a more concrete characterization of the nature and effects of that kind of *compelling* masculine power? To be sure, Malte's text provides a wide variety of related imagery; the chamberlain's intemperate, infernal death howl provides one signal instance. Still, to gain a clearer, more comprehensive picture of the archetypal force in question, we can do no better than to revisit Sophocles' *Oedipus Rex*.

Oedipus, after all, is a solar hero, and an intimate connection binds Oedipus, his pathology, and the (blinding) power of the sun. The tragedy unfolds under the aegis of Oedipus' chief divinity, the sun-God Phoebus Apollo. It is Apollo's frightful oracle (predicting the killing of a father by his son) that sets the fateful trap which springs shut in the course of the play; it is Apollo to whom Oedipus appeals in his search for a cure to the city's ills; it is Apollo whom Oedipus finally blames as the deity responsible for his demise. The Chorus inquires: "O doer of dread deeds.... What daimon drove you on?" Oedipus answers: "Apollo it was, Apollo, friends, / Who brought these ills."[643]

The God Apollo, however, does not act only at a distance: Apollo is Oedipus' tutelary spirit because Oedipus' psychology is purely Apollonic. Oedipus' penchant for clarity, consciousness and the light of reason, moreover, hides a dark shadow: *blind, ruinous anger.* Confronted with the seer Teiresias' "obstinate" refusal to divulge all he sees, Oedipus, in fact, behaves very much like a sun-crazed ram. The scene reveals the proudly "rational" hero as a real hothead, one whose vaunted rational faculties are quickly consumed by a tempestuous rage that drives him—looking neither left nor right—to most rash conclusions:

Teiresias
You blame my temper but you do not see
your own that lives within you...
Oedipus
Who would not feel his temper rise
at words like these...
Teiresias
I will say nothing further.
Against this answer let your temper rage
as wildly as you will.
Oedipus
Indeed I am
so angry I shall not hold back a jot
of what I think. For I would have you know
I think you were complotter of the deed
and doer of the deed save in so far
as for the actual killing.[644]

This outburst finally leads Teiresias to declare Oedipus himself to be the criminal responsible for the blight of the city. Once he finally understands the accusation, Oedipus grows still more furiously irrational, accusing in turn his trusted brother-in-law and adviser Creon of raising this plot against him. All Creon's reasoned denials fall on deaf ears. Oedipus, in fact, tells Creon he intends to kill him on the spot. "I do not think you have your wits about you." answers Creon. That fit response avails nothing, however, and only the intervention of Jocasta and the Chorus prevents the atrocious deed.

Creon's murder, though, would not have been the first committed by the intemperate solar hero. Oedipus, of course, long ago did kill his father, Laius (as well as several of his servants). Meeting at a crossroads, neither would so much as move aside, and, in this early case of senseless "road rage," fatal violence erupted. In his reading of the play, Hillman notes that the locale where father and son met (near Mt. Cithaeron) was the legendary home of certain nymphs that, if they seized upon an unfortunate traveler, would drive him mad. Noting, too, that such nymphs were most dangerous at noon—especially summer noon—Hillman connects Oedipus' blind fury to the heat of the sun:

> The entire drama is under the blaze of noon... Were they both, father and son, susceptible to nympholepsy, to noon's shadow, that high solar madness called *superbia*, a soullessness or absence of anima, psychologically inept?[645]

Superbia, the Latin word for pride, is considered "the original and most serious of the seven deadly sins, and ultimately responsible for all the others."[646] *Oedipus Rex* certainly bears out such an assessment, even as it reveals the death and destruction wrought by masculine energy run mad, meting out, not love, but death to the feminine, to mother and to wife.

In the imagery of the golden sheep, the Psyche-Eros story thus incorporates an Oedipal moment into the train of its symbolism. Indeed, *the lesson of the second labor may consequently be understood as an aversion to and avoidance of (Oedipus') Apollonic psychology, or, alternatively, a fundamental transfiguration of it.* The learning of the whole lesson hinges, ultimately, upon anima and the feminine virtue of patience: the ability of the psyche to wait out the high noon of aggression and approach the masculine at a more propitious moment, a time when love—instead of death—may follow upon the meeting of contrary principles. Neumann:

> The reed whispers to her [Psyche] with his Pan-like vegetative wisdom... wait, be patient. Things change. Time brings counsel. It is not always high noon... Evening comes, and night, when the sun returns home, when the masculine principle approaches the feminine and Helios "journeys to the depths of the sacred dark night, to the mother and to his wife and many children."
>
> Then, as the sun is setting, there arises the love situation in which it is natural and safe to take the golden hair of the sun rams.[647]

Sophocles' tragedy offers no redemption for its shattered hero—a man driven by the fire of spirit, but whose clear eye was not moistened by the waters of soul. Blind Oedipus, though, does live on into another play, and in *Oedipus at Colonus* we see Oedipus' two daughters—Antigone and Ismene—leading the blind old man into a new land. Here, the feminine takes the lead, symbolically as well as literally, and—twenty years later—Oedipus himself has learned something of Psyche's second lesson. In his very first speech of the play, Oedipus declares:

> Suffering and time,
> Vast time, have been instructors in contentment...[648]

and, towards the close of his life, the aged father bears witness to the bond of love shared with his daughters, which breathes as the redeemed life of his text:

> Children, this day your father is gone from you.
> Everything about him dies; this rigorous attention
> to his needs may now be dropped. I know
> how hard it was. yet it was made lighter by one
> word—love [*philein*].[649]

The two Oepidus plays reflect, to a significant degree, two archetypal energies featured in Psyche's second labor: the golden rams thrashing madly about at high noon, and Psyche waiting patiently under a tree by the water until dusk when she may safely venture forth to gather the strands of wool. If, however, it took Oedipus twenty years and an unending toll of destruction to learn the lesson of Psyche's second labor, an aversion to Oedipus the King's Apollonic brand of spiritual heroism informs the method of Malte's *Notebooks* from the beginning.

The descent of the sun from its zenith at noon is also the sunset of the heroic ego, the *Untergang* (going under) into the dark, the liminal realm of shade and shadow, repository of images of fear, illness, and love. Malte's *nigredo*, his psychopathological falling apart, entails, too, a falling away from the world of Oedipus' fearless self, the *superbia*, or pride, of the heroic ego that cannot wait to see the truth in the single-mindedly naïve conviction that it will make him (as well as his city) free. Malte's is another way, another longer path, one of deliberate delay and travail, indulgence in chastening fears and suicidal uncertainties, a plumbing of the underworld depths of fear and the fear of death that amounts, too, to the sufferings of what often appears an impossible—and yet for all that still shining—love.

The soul-wisdom that does not grasp—like Psyche with her knife and lamp—impatiently at spirit, knowingly avoiding its killing force; the daimonic restraint that—suffering the slow alchemy of impossible love—concentrates and cultures love within: in our prior mention of Rilke's great woman lovers, we have, in fact, already touched upon some of the main lines of Psyche's second labor in Malte's text. Here are others:

> And still it is not yet enough to have memories. One must....have the great patience to wait until they come again.
>
> For centuries now, they have performed the whole of love....And they have nevertheless persevered day and night....
>
> I see his life, which at that time began its long love to God, that silent, aimless labor...He had found the philosopher's stone, and now he was being forced ceaselessly to transmute the swiftly made gold of his happiness into the lumpy lead of patience. [650]

These three passages from the beginning, middle, and end of *Malte* display the book's consistent dedication to the underlying theme of Psyche's second labor. Reflecting (respectively) upon poetry, love, and religion, they indicate the intrinsic unity of those primary concerns. Poetry infuses the text, formally and thematically, from start to finish; woman love-poets *whose legendary patience and self-surrender draw the sun of love into their own hearts* emerge, half-way through, not only as erotic heroines, but as religious mystics for whom the paths to love and God are one.

The confluence of art, love, and religion recalls Rilke's Russian-influenced *Book of Hours*, but the bearer of the news has changed. The supremely self-confident, Romantic-medieval artist-monk has become the extraordinarily vulnerable, ill, and angst-ridden modern city-dweller whose difficult relation to a distant divine is mediated by a host of anima images (Abelone, Gaspara Stampa, Bettina, Sappho, etc.) who point to him "the way of long learning." That monk's iconic prayers have transmuted, too, into myriad longer lines that—despite often being darker and deeper—nonetheless remain tinged with gold. All Malte's poetic sentences weave his own intricate tapestry; his text is a braiding of innumerable shining strands of thought gathered at Malte's mental dusk, the twilight of his suffering heart. Malte's entire project, after all, is one of *recollection*: that *imaginative retrieval of soul history* we have previously recognized as a form of *memoria*.

In *Malte*, we do not—as in *Oedipus*—witness the protagonist's story unfolding, rapidly, in a persistent present tense, the high noon of dramatic action. In fact, we've already mentioned any number of ways in which the very *genre* of Rilke's writing, the method of his mind, effectively *enacts* the lesson of Psyche's labor, incorporating its meaning (including its aversion to Apollonic consciousness and solar heroism) into the literary form of his text. In addition to Rilke's disavowal of any plot that would tie his character up in a chain of fateful, causal logic, we've already mentioned his relative disinterest in literal truths of any sort (including the literal truths of his own childhood) as well as his avoidance of a too lucid conceptual language that would attempt to make matters reducible to the claims of pure reason.

From an archetypal psychological perspective, the relative weakness of Malte's plot may be a positive virtue, enabling forms of exploration and emphasis discouraged by those generic forms devoted to narrative rehearsal of the achievements of a heroic ego. Hillman, sampling alternative narrative styles, describes the *picaresque* novel in the following terms:

> Its central figure does not develop (or deteriorate), but goes through episodic, discontinuous movements. His narrative ends abruptly without achievement for there is no goal...There are tales within tales that do not further a plot, showing that psychic history goes on in many places at once.[651]

Rilke's *Malte*—though no classic picaresque—does share these important stylistic elements, and indeed (as the numerous vignettes from French and Russian history illustrate) accents discontinuity to a still more radical extreme. Yet more relevant to *Malte* is Hillman's reference to a generic style proceeding not from the archetypal perspective of heroic ego (as in heroic epic), or the senex perspective of scientific detective (as in Freud), but

> from the point of view of the anima which, as I see it, would stay with images and fantasies themselves, never translating them or organizing them into narrative through plot, but responding to them in a metaphorical style where consciousness is one of innuendo, reflection, echo, tone, and elusive movements.[652]

We find pages and pages of this[653] in *Malte*, who—as a scribbler in his private notebook—is under no external compulsion to tell a coherent story. Rather, the musing life of his text is often far more like that anima-consciousness figured in the famous *Lady and the Unicorn* tapestries:

> Young girls... find themselves before these tapestries and forget themselves a little. They have always felt that this existed, a subdued life like this, of leisurely gestures never quite explained.[654]

Likewise, Malte's dreambook is sequence of pictures, a tapestry of images no theory can ever wholly compass or explicate.

Traditional psychoanalysis, taking its cue from its founding myth, remains under the sway of another, more heroic Apollonic archetype. In his *New Poems*, Rilke had already engaged that legacy by placing Apollo at the threshold of both volumes—a complex gesture, because Rilke's Apollo is not Oedipus'. Already in "Early Apollo," Rilke evokes the killing power of the God's too clear gaze, and ends by diverting focus from the unforgiving eye to the mouth softened and made receptive by the fall of a figurative flower petal. Then, in "Archaic Torso of Apollo," Rilke gives us a fragmented God who has spectacularly lost his head and limbs, organs of cognition and action. His force remains, to be sure, but only in a radically transfigured shape.

Malte takes these transformations still further. In its profoundly poetic mosaic, we are—despite the surface resemblance to certain features of psychoanalysis—actually in a different archetypal landscape altogether, an entirely different geography opened by a different myth. Rilke himself employed the term "mosaic" in reference to Malte's composition, and the etymology of this word aptly evokes resonances with the lesson of Psyche's second labor: *mosaic* means, literally, "patient work worthy of the muses." The nine muses, of course, are feminine figures, and mother of them all is Mnemosyne.

The Notebooks of Malte Laurids Brigge represents a concentrated reclamation of *memoria* as primary faculty of the soul—more central than *rational understanding* or *will*, the other two terms of an Augustinian trinity. *Memoria*, moreover, represents the soul's principal means of engendering and exploring the *imaginal* reality that constitutes its true ontological ground. As Hillman discusses in the second chief essay in his *Myth of Analysis* ("On Psychological Language"), what we typically call "the unconscious" can perhaps be much better comprehended under the older, less scientific aegis of *memoria*.

> If we further pursue these ideas of *memoria*, we arrive at a remarkable parallel between the "inner world" we speak of in our psychology and the "fields and dens and caverns" of *memoria* described by Augustine, "innumerably full of innumerable kinds of things..." What we today call "the unconscious" and describe in spatial metaphors, though it is boundless and also timeless, which "contains" "contents"—images, personages, and affects, now called complexes—and which has a collective historical as well as ahistorical archetypal structure, at the unfound center of which, and around which, all else moves, the *imago Dei*: this unconscious appears hardly to differ from what was once called by Augustine *memoria*.[655]

One critical difference between *memoria* and the "the unconscious" inheres in the purely *negative* definition of the latter. "The unconscious" takes meaning only in dualistic opposition to what it supposedly is not—namely, conscious(ness). Not only does the whole rubric tend to deny "unconsciousness" positive agency, it implies a fundamentally dualistic psychology that elides or marginalizes the imaginal heart of the soul:

> Of all terms of analytical language...the unconscious is the first we should renounce....it makes sense only within a definition of consciousness that excludes the memorial imagination. It is useful only within a fantasy of opposites through which the psyche is divided against itself between head and body, ego and shadow, day side and night side.[656]

...and, we could add, life and death, the visible and invisible worlds, Denmark and Paris. In the last chapter, we saw how Malte's own psyche was "a house divided: on the one hand conscious, on the other, unconscious." Rilke, in his mosaic of Malte, provides a picture of a typically divided nineteenth-century consciousness, one that has lost the traditional deep sense of *memoria* as Platonic reminiscence, and forfeited recall of those substantial idea-images which inherently relate the human to the divine world. Hillman:

> During the nineteenth century in particular this faculty [of *memoria*] lost touch with ruling consciousness. We lost our imaginal ego, the ego which speaks for this aspect of the soul. Instead,

> we identified wholly with the rational, volitional ego. Memoria became unconscious. It became the Unconscious.[657]

Malte suffers the consciousness embodied (for instance) by his eminently rational father; suffers, intensely, the pathologies it breeds: above all, the crippling fear of the great Unknown (Death) which in turn blocks the soul's path to love and the spirit of God. Malte's childhood world—one where stories were no longer told—was one that had lost touch with the imaginal ground of the soul, its faculty of memory relegated to "the unconscious" Malte finally is forced to rediscover in his terrifying experiences of the Parisian underworld.

A traditional psychoanalytic remedy for Malte's "case" might involve recall of "unconscious" childhood material, an attempt to "bring to light" the character of Malte's relations to—most especially—his father and mother, to come to a more "enlightened" understanding of the sources of his deepest fears. Yet Malte's own notebook, his imaginative writing, preempts and displaces any purely analytic approach to his soul or—for that matter—to the poetic soul of his author. For it is *memoria* itself, the imaginative remembering of history, that may heal the rifts born of Malte's typically divided nineteenth-century consciousness, not so much by "making the unconscious conscious" as by housing the soul in the imaginal, that sphere and that creative agency which—essentially liminal, metaphorical—dissolves rigidly polarized structures of consciousness, letting the sun of love descend into the receptive twilight of Malte's Danish soul.

Malte's reminiscences, while they do embrace memories of his early family life, do not analyze those figures or see them, in and of themselves, as determinants of fate. Those figures and scenes lead not to theoretical explanation, but to other memories, and other less personal histories that perpetually broaden and deepen Malte's contemplation of the archetypal foundations of his being: Abelone leads to Bettina, Bettina to Sappho and beyond. The process of *memoria* loses its principally analytic dimension; responsive to alternative anima initiatives, Malte's process of reminiscence becomes more and more quintessentially historical, mythical, poetic. The subject ceases, in fact, to be Malte himself (the ego or "I"), becoming more the archetypal themes he—through the vehicle of the *imaginal ego* he represents—explores in ever-widening circles. Hillman:

> The imaginal ego is more discontinuous, now this and now that, guided as much by the synchronistic present as by the causal past, moving on a uroboric course, which is a circulation of the light and the darkness. It includes the downward turns, the depressions, recessions, and fallings-away from awareness. Psychopathology has its place; it is necessary. . . . The movement of the imaginal ego should be conceived less as a development than as a circular pattern.[658]

This "movement of the imaginal ego" finds apt illustration in the way Malte circles back to themes of love and death, illness and art, childhood and religion, poverty and beatitude, again and again—in personal history, in political history, in cultural history—weaving in ever richer hues the dream-tapestry of his mind, proffering, in all sorts of subtle tonal variations, not the "language of psychology" but the speech of the soul.

This perspective offers another means of understanding the significance of Malte's descent into the depths, his seemingly mad insistence that the light of reason, the driving force of the solar mind, be gathered, recollected, in the dream-shadows of what could—but should not—be called the "unconsciousness."

> Perhaps the phenomena of the so-called unconscious which do not fit into our definition of consciousness and therefore have become "pathological" and "un"-conscious are better conceived as twisted paths into *memoria*, as ways leading back into lost areas of the soul, its imagination, and its history. Freud showed that symptoms lead to discoveries and that psychopathology is a vehicle for entering the depths.[659]

So did Rilke, whose *Malte* perseveringly traveled those "twisted paths."

In view of our interpretation of Psyche's second labor, we should perhaps make special note that—even beyond Malte's personal preoccupation with death—"the destructive power of the masculine" is by no means altogether absent from the historical interest inscribed in his text. Ulsgaard, it is true, seems to burn under the star of a cold—not hot—anger, though its ruling spirits appear no less soulless for all that. Perhaps it is in part that very frigidity which inclines Malte's imagination to dwell upon historical times and places seething with murderous intent—as if the psyche might learn to counter masculine violence only when that deadly force (those sun-crazed rams) came out into the open. The historical scenes Malte narrates in the second half of the novel (sixteenth- and seventeenth-century Russian history, and thirteenth- and fourteenth-century French) revolve around a hub of deadly force, as if only against the backdrop of such intensity, such a surfeit of fear and of death, might the patient psyche find its way to the deeper mystery of love.

Evoking "that heavy, massive, desperate age.... in which the kiss of reconciliation between two men was only a signal for the murderers who were standing around,"[660] Malte places in its center Charles VI ("le Bien Aimé"), insane for most of his reign, yet nonetheless described by Malte as "this silent patient man, who was only there in order to let God... act over his head."[661] In Malte's imaginative remembering, Charles recalls his innocent witness of a scene of war-slaughter—"the triumph of death"—even while passing from that memory into a dawning experience of "the mystery of love."

> This they had impressed upon him as the beginning of his glory. And he had retained the memory of it. But if that had been the triumph of death, this, his standing here with his weak knees; upright in all these eyes: this was the mystery of love. He had seen by the others that that field of battle could be comprehended, immense though it was. But this which was happening now would not be.[662]

In Malte's text, the door to that mystery is opened, more often than not, by a kind of *stage-hand*; issues forth under the aegis of *drama*.

The third and final long essay composing Hillman's *Myth of Analysis*, "On Psychological Femininity," discusses the precept of feminine inferiority—beginning with Eve—underpinning the thought-structures upon which psychology traditionally rests. Transforming those structures involves, too, surrendering the Apollonic consciousness associated with them, and opening the psyche to another archetypal God who entertains much closer connections with women, and in fact embodies the essentially *bisexual* character of the psyche.

> Dionysus is mainly a god of women.... Though he is male, and phallic, there is no misogyny in this structure of consciousness because it is not divided from its own femininity.... Dionysius "in one of his appellations, is 'man and woman' in one person. Dionysus was bisexual in the first place.... " This figure and his spirit

> can inform consciousness so that it can at last move away from the line we have been following from Adam and Apollo . . .[663]

We've repeatedly noted the privileging of the feminine in Malte—Malte's own looking to the feminine side of his nature for a nourishing soul-consciousness. In the present context, Malte's embrace of his own difficult symptoms and his willing suffering of them emerges as an essentially Dionysian impulse:

> The symptom becomes a votive offering, a thing through which one pays one's debts to the bisexual dominant, the God of one's bisexuality. . . . Our afflictions and psychopathologies evoke the feminine side as carrier, sufferer, as nurse to that sufferer and to the child. . . . the Dionysian approach . . . would not separate the bisexuality in the symptom, not attempt to get consciousness out of the suffering, extract the active male light from the passive suffering.[664]

Yet Malte's pathological suffering does not figure as the only Dionysian element of his character.[665] Dionysius, after all, is also *the God of theater*, and theater and theatricality permeate Malte's text. The long story of Malte's childhood love of masks and costumes and the almost tragic denouement of that love; the evocation of Ibsen's art, and the famous actress Eleanora Duse's; visits to the ancient amphitheatre in Orange and repeated musings revolving around dramatic metaphors . . . despite the lyric and narrative character of Malte's notebooks, theater and performance are everywhere, and most of all in Malte's poetic method, his perpetual mimesis, or constant metaphorical enactment of scene after scene after scene recalled in imaginative memory. The logic of psyche and of dream, after all, is inherently Dionysian or dramatic: "The unconscious produces dramas, poetic fictions; it is theatre," writes Hillman, and "If the structure of Dionysian logic is drama, the particular embodiment of Dionysian logic is the actor. . . . "[666] Likewise, Malte, spinning and enacting poetic fictions in his diffused Dionysian universe, laments:

> Inside and before you, O my God. . . . are we not without action? We discover, indeed, that we do not know our part. . . . And thus we go about, a laughing stock, a mere half-thing, neither existing, nor actors.[667]

The Dionysian dimension of Malte's art represents yet another decisive distancing from the Apollonic consciousness characterizing analysis. "Dionysian consciousness understands the conflicts in our stories through dramatic tensions and not through conceptual opposites; we are composed of agonies not polarities..."[668] writes Hillman, but

> The analytic viewpoint tends toward divisions: conscious from unconscious, cure from neurosis, individuation from collectivity, even eros from psyche. The aim may be synthesis, but the means and method are division. Dionysian consciousness proceeds otherwise....The affliction would not be divided from its own potential of nursing, which is constellated by the suffering and the childishness. *The torn and rendered suffering, rather than cured by the medicine of Apollo, becomes an initiation into the cosmos of Dionysus.*[669]

That *dramatically* torn cosmos is Malte's. It is, moreover, one centered upon the act of *initiation*, an opening onto the mysteries of love and of death that lie at the heart of human being. No wonder, then, that—in Malte's inventive memory—King Charles VI looks to the medieval mystery plays for a glimpse of those deeper realities he, in his divine madness, so avidly seeks:

> No one knew to what temptation he yielded then, when he asked about the Mysteries and could hardly wait for them to begin. And once it came time, he lived more in rue Saint-Denis than in his Hôtel of Saint-Pol.[670]

As Hillman notes, this initiatory character is written into the very structure of the Psyche-Eros myth: the suffering in it, the imaged transformations, are elements of what is, essentially, a kind of mystery play:

> The myth of the [psyche-eros] process "arranges" suffering; yet this suffering is neither blind nor tragic, as with Oedipus....The suffering in our tale has something to do with initiation, with changing the structure of consciousness....This gives us a wholly different view....of the ground of neurosis in our time. Neurosis becomes initiation...and our developmental process in psyche and in eros, leading to their union, becomes the mystery.[671]

That mystery—so different from the Apollonic end of self-knowledge, revelation of the egotistical character of the heroic subject—figures as the ultimate subject of Malte's scene-paintings and dramatic enactments. Commenting on Psyche's second labor, Neumann writes: "these (golden) hair-rays are the fructifying powers of the masculine, and the feminine . . . is the great Weaver who plaits the threads of the sun seeds into the web of nature."[672] Malte—exhibiting the transfiguration of death that transpires in the course of the *Notebooks* even while foreshadowing the Eurydice of Rilke's later *Sonnets*—writes similarly of Bettina, who "spread out in everything as though she were after death. Everywhere she settled deep into existence, belonging to it, and whatever happened to her has eternally been in nature . . . "[673] and of Sappho, whose love transcended fate, and whose "heart became part of nature."[674]

In such poetic meditations, Rilke was clearly looking forward to another figure who fused the light of father Apollo with the darker, more dismembering vision of Dionysius. Yet before we come, eventually, to the figure of Orpheus—whose poetic consciousness cannot be separated from his Eurydice—Rilke had another giant step to take on his own "path of long learning," one that would entail still closer encounters with the dramatic mysteries of love as well as death. It should always be remembered, however, that the conception of *The Duino Elegies* takes place against the background of the tortured yet elegant soul tapestry that is Rilke's own "healing fiction," that intricate (t)issue of his imaginal ego, *The Notebooks of Malte Laurids Brigge.*

The last entry of the book—Rilke's rewriting of the parable of the prodigal son—sounds yet again the theme of (unanswered) love that dominates the book's latter half. Even here, though, one can hear an echo of Oedipus, or rather the desire to leave his archetypal world behind, that mythical world in which family is—literally—fate. Oedipus, after all, sought to escape his prophesied patricide by never going home. ("I will never come near my parents," vows Oedipus.[675]) Malte's prodigal son, however, does just that. That return—far from acknowledging the lasting power of the son's family upon him—does quite the opposite, annulling the hold upon him exerted, always, at a distance. Neutralizing that force by way of the prodigal's return represents a kind of fateful release, a way of cutting the son loose to worship his own God(s), providing him psychic time and space within which to live and write his own archetypally poetic myth of soul.

Many of Malte's privileged themes—love, poetry, theater, antiquity, memory, the restoration of cosmic unity—come together in the meditations of one of Malte's imagined figures, an older man who translates fragments of Sappho. His imagination fired by his love for one of the young women in his circle, the man—engaged in his work of translation—muses upon the ancient world:

> Never before has he been so certain of antiquity. He could almost smile at the generations that have mourned it as a lost play in which they would have liked to act. Now he instantaneously grasps the dynamic significance of that early world-unity, which was something like a new and simultaneous assumption of all human work. . . . There, it is true, the celestial half of life was really fitted against the half-round bowl of terrestrial existence, as two full hemispheres connect to form a perfect orb of gold.[676]

The unity proves, in the man's mind, to be transitory—and yet, even so, a window onto the infinite future glimpsed by Malte's own eternal yearning which (persisting shades of the puer) refuses the limitations of past accomplishments. The man places an apple on a plate. "How my life stands round about this fruit, he thinks. Around all that is finished that which has still to be done rises and takes increase." So Malte's "revolution on behalf of soul" goes never-endingly on.

"Orpheus," Cima da Conegliano

PART IV

BEING AND SONG

Chapter 14

THIS LANDSCAPE THAT PROPHESIES

In Apuleius' tale, Psyche is granted scant opportunity to enjoy the fruits of her initial labors. No sooner does she complete one seemingly impossible task than disdainful Venus sets her another, plunging the overawed and distraught heroine into despair once more. Just so Rilke, after finishing (finally) *The Notebooks of Malte Laurids Brigge*, hardly went tripping happily onward in his life of work. Relieved and gratified that the seemingly interminable toil on *Malte* was at last behind him, the poet nonetheless soon found himself in the midst of another prolonged personal crisis. Unable to produce much significant work for the better part of two years (the *Collected Works* include *no* poems completed in 1910 and only a handful written in 1911), Rilke found himself repeatedly racked by depression and self-doubt, and even half-seriously wondering if it would not be better if he were to give up writing altogether.

Malte, after all, had proved a travail on many levels, and the author continued to wrestle with the psychological legacy bequeathed him by his own fictional creation. In a hopeful moment soon after the book's completion, Rilke spoke of *Malte* as "something like a basis," telling his publisher, Kippenberg, that "Now everything can really begin. After (Malte) almost any songs are possible."[677] Yet as a barren reality set in, Malte's dark odyssey assumed a more problematic place in the poet's mind. After *Malte*, Rilke felt "like Raskolnikov after the deed,"[678] existentially uncertain of how to go on. In August of 1910, Rilke wrote to the Princess Marie von Thurn und Taxis-Hohenlohe: "I shudder a little when I think of all the violence I put through in *Malte Laurids*, how I landed with him back of everything in consistent despair...so that nothing more was possible, not even dying."[679] As late as December 28, 1911, he was writing Lou:

> You see, I am still in a hurry to get to myself; and there is a point of departure: Malte Laurids Brigge.... Can you understand that after this book I have been left behind just like a survivor, helpless in my inmost soul, no longer to be used? The nearer I came to the end of writing it, the more strongly did I feel that it would be an indescribable division, a high watershed, as I kept telling myself; but now it turns out that all the water has flowed off toward the old side and I am going down into an aridity that will not change.[680]

Even so, all this—Rilke's infertility, his ongoing internal dialogue with Malte and continual self-questioning—ultimately proved part of the agitated calm before a creative storm. In the two years following his completion of the *Notebooks*, Rilke—as he himself at some deep level knew—was preparing, both inwardly and outwardly, for the next giant step on his soul's path. Like Psyche before the dizzying peak rising above the waters of the Styx, like Moses before the God-shrouded mountain, the poet stood before what he himself would soon come to perceive as his greatest, life-defining task: the writing of the *Duino Elegies*. The opening of that famous poem—itself a cry of despair—thundered in Rilke's ear on the balcony of Duino Castle high above the Istrian Sea in January 1912:

> Who, if I cried out, would hear me among the angelic orders?

Developments crucial to the conception of the *Elegies* began unfolding even before *Malte*'s nominal ending. In December of 1909, Rilke met the Princess Marie von Thurn und Taxis-Hohenlohe, and the rapport quickly established between them turned into a lifelong friendship. Rilke's relation to the Princess cemented his identity as a kind of court poet, one uniquely privileged to travel and dwell among the aristocratic circles of the old nobility. While his connection with Kippenberg's Insel Verlag solidified the poet's professional and financial identity, the patronage of Princess Marie provided the impecunious and troubled peripatetic with a bastion of material, social, and spiritual support that proved essential to the progress of his career. *Malte*, the literary record of the near-destitute foreigner astray in the city, found its point d'appui in a poor Parisian apartment. The *Duino Elegies*, on the other hand, were destined to be conceived in the imposing castle bearing that name, and (in the words of

Rilke's own inscription) forever remain "the property of Princess Marie von Thurn und Taxis-Hohenlohe."

Not all Rilke's myriad relationships with women proved so mutually fulfilling as the one with Princess Marie. His problematic love life remained a principal source of creative unrest for the man who, at one and the same time, deeply craved intimate connection with a beloved feminine other and yet veered sharply away from any human commitment that might infringe upon his emotional freedom. His intermittent relationship with the Venetian Mimi Romanelli remained one of the most vexed in this regard. While Rilke possessed a talent for transforming actual or potential lovers into devoted friends, Mimi proved intransigent in this respect. When—after his first, rather unhappy stay at Duino—Rilke visited her in Venice in the spring of 1910, the resulting discontent issued in one of Rilke's patently paradoxical rejections:

> For the first time I think of you only in bitterness.... Never forget that solitude is my lot, that I must not have a need for anyone, that all my strength in fact comes from my detachment.... I *implore* those who love me to love my solitude.[681]

Mimi would be far from the last to suffer the double bind integral to Rilke's philosophy of impossible love. Other women still more important to the development of the *Elegies*—most signally, Magda von Hattingberg and (above all) Baladine Klossowska—would do likewise. As the relationship with Magda most clearly reveals,[682] it is almost as if one part of the poet's psyche remained fixated upon the phase of unconscious union Eros and Psyche enjoy *before* the lighting of her lamp—and so destined to replay, again and again, the consequent drama of Eros' wounded flight—in order that *another*, more anima-infused side of his soul might pick up the myth further on, and carry it still further forward. Rilke's relationship with Marthe Hennebert—the poor eighteen-year-old he found in the rain in a Parisian alley in June 1911 and took under his half-paternal wing—recalls his erstwhile friend Heinrich Vogeler's relation to a farm girl by the same name and fits into the above-mentioned mythic mold. So does Rilke's enthralled reading of Goethe's letters to Auguste von Stolberg (a young correspondent the aging poet assiduously avoided meeting in person) in August of the same year. All such matter fueled the poet's erotic imagination and kept the fire of love—so central to the *Elegies*—burning.

Another passing love interest incidentally paved the way to a different sort of development in Rilke's life. In Munich in September of 1910, Rilke met a wealthy young woman—Jenny Oltersdorf—who invited him to join her on a trip to North Africa. Rilke, already beset by depression and looking for a new window on the world, grasped at the opportunity despite misgivings about the erotic implications of the proposed journey. In writing to Kippenberg to request funds for the trip, he expressed the hope that the excursion into "the Orient" might prove as revelatory and vital to him as his earlier travels to Russia and help him turn the present uncreative corner of his life.

In the short run, certainly, those hopes were disappointed. The relationship with Jenny proved predictably problematic, and the roughly two-month journey ended ignominiously in illness in Alexandria. Nevertheless, the trip to Algiers, Tunis, and especially Egypt excited Rilke's interest in Islamic culture and (as we will shortly discuss further) awakened spiritual impulses that would, in conjunction with a later journey to another country with Islamic heritage, eventually bear abundant poetic fruit.

It was not, though, a new love, but rather an old one that Rilke turned to in the winter of 1911–12 in Duino, unable, as yet, to break the back of his depression. Beset by demons of poetic sterility, gloom, and self-recrimination, Rilke reached out to Lou and once more unburdened himself in long letters to her. Professionally speaking, this was a formative and stimulating time for Lou, who, in September of 1911, had attended the Third Psychoanalytic Congress in Weimar and solidified her relationship with Sigmund Freud. It was at this point, as well, that Rilke seriously considered entering into psychoanalysis with one of Lou's colleagues (and Clara's analyst), Dr. Emil Freiherr von Gebsattel. Accordingly, in the weeks immediately preceding the inception of the *Elegies*, psychology—in its professional guise as well as Rilke's own personal articulation of it—was much on the poet's mind.

Even so, it was neither the specters of psychoanalysis nor the vagaries of romantic love that inspired the work which—figuring as a kind of prelude or anteroom to the *Elegies*—finally broke the poet's extended dry spell and heralded what was to come. On January 15, in Duino, Rilke began writing a series of poems recording (as the sequence is titled) *The Life of Mary*. Though the work arose in part out of a (failed) desire to meet Vogeler's request to resuscitate the idea of producing a collaborative work on the subject, Rilke would never have composed his new *Marien-Leben* if the topic had not been, at the time, close to his heart. Rilke's

Life of Mary issued from a stream of meditation on specifically religious subject matter that Rilke (reviving, in some wise, his Russian period) pursued with some intensity and breadth in the post-*Malte* years that incubated the *Elegies*. The *Elegies* have often been treated to markedly philosophical interpretations, but—while Rilke did read the work of his friend Rudolf Kassner (to whom the Eighth Elegy is dedicated)—he did not read Kant or Hegel, but (in addition to Goethe, Hölderlin, and numerous other literary sources) the Bible, the Koran, St. Augustine, and (most immediate source of his *Marien-Leben* sequence) a German translation of Pedro de Ribadeaneira's *Flos Sanctorum* (*Lives of the Saints*). The historic force of the *Elegies* can be most truly heard against the sounding board of the traditions represented in these texts, for—though deep reflection infuses the cycle with true philosophical energy—the *voice* that resounds in these great poems is primarily that of a prophet, albeit one whose proclamation issues forth from the space of an almost deafening silence on the part of God and his divine emissaries.

The path of the religious hermit and the artist had been inextricably twined in Rilke's poetic imagination since his fateful early years with Lou and the voyages to Italy and Russia that engendered his *Book of Hours*. True, his preoccupation with patently religious subjects abated somewhat "in and after Worpswede" to make room for an equally intense focus upon the mysteries of visual art and, too (especially in *Malte*), his own brand of depth psychology, but these involvements never annulled Rilke's religious interests. Rather, the streams of religion, art, literature, and psychology ran ever more deeply together, forming a powerful confluence in the river of the poet's soul. *Malte* retains a deeply religious register, and the *New Poems*—for all the modernity of their thing-like form—hardly neglect religious topoi. Despite all its attendant difficulties, Rilke's journey to North Africa in 1910–11 refreshed and invigorated his religious imagination by inaugurating his first direct contact with a spiritual culture he had heretofore known only at a distance: Islam.

The subject of the Muslim religion was by no means entirely new to Rilke. The poet had spent significant time with Lou's husband, Friedrich Carl Andreas, a prominent scholar of Islamic culture, and Lou herself had devoted an essay to "The Problem of Islam." An important poem from the second volume of the *New Poems* displays not only Rilke's general interest in Islam, but his acquaintance with the Koranic verse that—rendering an account of the central event in the life of the prophet Mohammed—inspired Rilke's poetic version of the same.

MOHAMMED'S CALLING

Such majesty could not be mistaken.
Yet when the Angel stepped into his hideout—
erect, and pure and radiant as flame:
he put off all his old ambition and begged

to be allowed to remain what he was—a merchant
inwardly confused by his travels.
He had never read before—and now
such a word, too much even for a wise man.

But the Angel, commanding, pointed again
and again to what was written on his page,
and would not yield and once more beckoned: *read.*

Then he read: so deeply, the Angel bowed.
And he was already someone who *had* read
and—obeying—could and did fulfill the Word.[683]

"Mohammed's Calling" bears upon the future conception of the *Elegies*, not only because of the appearance of the angel in it (angels had appeared in every cycle of poems Rilke had written), but because of that superhuman messenger's main action: the issuing of an irresistible summons to a divine cause. Though the poem itself does not forge a link between the mission of religious prophecy and artistic calling, the equation inheres in the fact of Rilke's writing of it. Not long after Rilke's North African journey ignited his interest in Mohammed's spiritual legacy, the poet himself made that equation explicit in a letter to Marie von Thurn und Taxis-Hohenlohe. Speaking of his own sense of vocation, Rilke writes: "It must come upon the artist, at least as well as upon Mohammed...the task, which is always there and always exact and always demanding."[684] A little more than a half-year later, Rilke would hear the call that would define, with precision, the great "task" (*Aufgabe*) of his life, the prophetic mission that would preoccupy the poet for ten of the remaining fourteen years of his life.

When, three years after writing "Mohammed's Summoning," Rilke traveled to North Africa, his novel experience of the vital force of Islamic faith in North Africa helped provide a context of religious feeling that nurtured and deepened his own sense of spiritual mission. The poet's sense of the *immediate presence of divine power* in the Islamic world resounds in the very first letter Rilke wrote on the journey, posted from Algiers. Preferring the Turkish, Moorish, and Arabic portion of the city to the French, he ends his description of the locale that exhibited "an existence out of 1001 Nights" with the exclamation "Allah is great, and there is no power but his in the air."[685] A letter to Clara written a month later sounds a similar chord:

> I have come over for a day into the "holy city" of Kairuan, after Mecca the great pilgrim center of Islam.... One feels the simplicity and vitality of this religion in a wonderful way here, *the Prophet is like yesterday*, and the city is his like a kingdom.[686]

Two months later, at the very end of his voyage, Rilke offered this review of its rewards:

> In any event it is worthwhile to have felt God from Mohammed's side (this perhaps most usable God) and try one's own hand at one's own humanity next to these people in the mosques, in the bazaars and everywhere outside in the unobstructed world-space, or to put one's hand on the surface of the Earth somewhere, on the pure star Earth—: dear God, I suspect that I am taking a good deal with me, new arrangements, although practically the whole time I've been a confused man.[687]

Rilke was right: he did take away "new arrangements" (the German noun, significantly enough, is *Ordnungen*, the word that ends the first sentence of the *Elegies*) from his voyage. Yet even if we, for the moment, restrict our attention solely to the matter of the religious background of the *Elegies*, the work that immediately preceded the *Elegies* reveals that Rilke's North Africa experience alone did not provide sufficient impetus for the breakthrough that birthed that vision.

THE BIRTH OF MARY

O what must it have cost the angels
not suddenly to jubilate—as one cries out—
for they knew: in this night, the mother of the child,
the one soon to appear, would be born.[688]

Another angel, another prophetic moment—at least insofar as the "Birth of Mary" (the first poem in Rilke's thirteen-poem cycle *The Life of Mary*) portends all that is to follow, including the bearing of he who is himself the Word incarnate. Much later, Rilke wrote famously to his Polish translator that "the 'angel' of the Elegies has nothing to do with the angels of the Christian heaven (rather with the angel figures of Islam),"[689] but the poet's own protestation must be taken with a grain of salt. Even if we grant Rilke's justified claim that his elegy-angel does not possess distinctly Christian features and should not (as often happens in Christian iconography) be overly humanized, the angels in *The Life of Mary* (especially Gabriel) function as numinous ambassadors of the divine and so count as *one* foreshadowing of Rilke's angel. More importantly, it does not, in the last analysis, make good sense to insist upon *any* particular religious pedigree for Rilke's angel, because the poet's relation to religion—including Islam—did not hinge upon formal theology at all. Recognizing that Islam, for Rilke, was "no religious-social complex, but a ground-idea," Kuschel offers a version of that religion's appeal to Rilke's sensibility that resonates with the tenor of the poet's North African correspondence:

> Rilke's reception of religions (whether Judaism, Islam, or Buddhism) is highly selective, filtered through his own traumatic experience of Christianity and a very specific poetic-artistic disposition....In pre-Christian as well as post-Christian religions, he recognized an interpretation of God which directly confronted the human being with God's greatness, immensity, and incomprehensibility. In prophets like Jeremiah, Moses, or Mohammed, he recognized men who were "bound to face directly the full force of the enormity of the divine."[690]

Rilke's own relation to Christianity remained more ambivalent than this citation perhaps implies and cannot be excluded from the list of those religions which shaped—positively as well as negatively—the poet's own sense of divine presence. Even while Rilke—under the influence of his novel involvement with Islam—would soon confess himself to be professing "a rabid anti-Christianity,"[691] the poet's lifelong reservations about his childhood religion seldom prevented him from availing himself of Christian figures when these offered him means of translating his own religious feeling into telling imagery. Rilke accordingly continued to draw upon Christian texts as sources of inspiration in the years leading up to the *Elegies*. Not only had Ribadeneira's *Lives of the Saints* and Augustine's *Confessions* been treasured companions for years, but renewed reading of these works formed the immediate background of the poet's writing of *The Life of Mary* and so, too, of the *Elegies*.[692] Rilke, moreover, drew the Greek epigraph for *The Life of Mary* from yet another Christian source—an iconographic text titled *The Book of the Painter of the Mountain of Athos*—which directly recalls the Byzantine sources of *The Book of Hours*. The original Greek reads, "the storm is within," though Rilke himself most likely understood it in the mistranslated form in which it appears in the German version he himself read: "the space [*Raum*] is within." The epigraph reveals the profound ties linking *The Life of Mary* and the *Elegies*, for its potent words could as easily have been prefixed to the latter poem cycle as to the former.

The writing of *The Life of Mary* effectively jump started the *Duino Elegies*. Indeed, work on the two cycles overlapped. Rilke wrote *The Life of Mary* between January 15 and 22, 1912, and began the *Elegies* on January 21. The initial inspiration, however, by no means sufficed for realization of the elegy cycle as a whole. In early 1912, Rilke completed the first two Elegies, and composed fragments of four others, but the bulk of the work remained unaccomplished.

In fact, even the story of the *conception* of the *Elegies* cannot well be restricted to events preceding January 21, 1912. In order to round out that conception and fill out the seed-form that, a decade later, would finally issue forth in the completed cycle, Rilke himself required yet another source of religious inspiration, yet another journey to another place that would—more than Kairouan, and even more, perhaps, than Duino itself—embody the vision that ultimately found expression in the *Elegies*. As the poet himself testified, his journey to Spain proved one of the most meaningful of his life, one that would fulfill his hopes for a voyage the significance of which could compare with his spiritually pivotal voyage to mother Russia.

In November 1912, Rilke commenced a roughly four-month journey, spending the vast majority of his time in Toledo—the city of El Greco—and Ronda, a village in the country's southernmost region. In this land of richly mixed religious heritage, Rilke deepened his relation to Islamic culture and religious tradition. Never before had the poet's correspondence directly mentioned the poet reading the Koran, but a week or so after his arrival in Ronda on December ninth, Rilke wrote to Princess Marie: "I am reading the Koran, in certain places, it assumes a voice that, it seems to me, I am inside of, as it were, with all my strength, like the wind in an organ."[693] Two days later, he wrote to Lou: "Here I read the Koran, and marvel, marvel. . . . "[694] Still earlier, in Toledo, Rilke (always the religious eclectic) had steeped himself in *Old* Testament stories—the only reading, he felt, truly commensurate with the legendary, even biblical character of the landscape. Echoing and intensifying the religious feelings recorded on his North Africa journey, Rilke's Spanish correspondence repeatedly reveals him marveling at the divine presence seemingly incarnate in the surrounding landscape, the visionary force which the poet found almost overwhelming. His first letter after his first day in Toledo set the tone. It was, he wrote to the Princess, "a day out of Genesis":

> What it is like here, that, dear friend, I shall never be able to say (it would be the language of angels, their use of it among men) but *that* it is, that it *is*, you will just have to believe me. One can describe it to no one, it is full of law, yes I understand at this moment the legend that when on the fourth day of creation God took the sun and set it, he established it right over Toledo.[695]

Ten days later, he penned this passage to the Princess:

> This incomparable city is at pains to keep within its walls the arid, undiminished, unsubdued landscape, the mountain, the pure mountain, the mountain of vision,—monstrous the earth issues from it and directly before its gates becomes world, creation, mountain and ravine, Genesis. Again and again this region makes me think of a prophet, of one who rises from his meal, from hospitality, from being with others, and upon whom at once, on the very threshold of the house, prophesying comes, the immense seeing of ruthless visions.[696]

These words, even while recalling the nineteenth poem of *The Book of Pilgrimage* written twelve years earlier, transparently reflect Rilke's own struggle with the angelic power of his *Elegies*, the prophetic call that summoned him to his great, almost impossible task.

Prophetic voice was hardly anything new to Rilke. His Russia-inspired *Book of Hours* rings with prophetic tones; indeed, to some degree, the voice of the *Elegies* harks back to that of Rilke's icon-painting monk. Both poems place the issue of the speaker's individual relation to spiritual source front and center, and attention to that fundamental religious concern remains·intense and all-encompassing. Even so, the poetic voices in the two poems differ dramatically, inevitably reflecting the weighty force of all that had transpired in the intervening years—most signally, the extended *nigredo* that, like some black sun melting Icarian wings, had mercilessly cast the poetic puer down to earth.

Provocatively enough, the lead message of the *Elegies*—even as it flows from the texture of Rilke's religious experiences in North Africa—directly *contradicts* the ringingly affirmative spiritual declarations delivered in his letters from abroad. If the epistles from North Africa and Spain revel in Rilke's sense of immediate divine presence ("Allah is great, and there is no power... but his in the air"; "The Prophet is like yesterday"; "a day out of Genesis"), the great organ chords that open the *Elegies* resound in a clashingly contrary key. The *Elegies* commence, not with confident affirmations of inspiration and creative power, but with a cry of keen, almost hopeless despair. Remaining tuned, primarily, to the tone of *loss* intrinsic to their generic form, the opening lines make fairly clear what, exactly, the speaker so fervently mourns. If *The Book of Hours* begins with a moment of spiritual touch, an empowering contact between the supersensible and the human worlds, the *Elegies* open with a cry expressing *disconnection and estrangement from spiritual sources*, an expostulation recalling—not Michelangelo's Sistine moment of divine transmission—but the crucified Christ's wrenching expostulation: "My God, my God, why hast thou forsaken me?"

Yet it is not only (to borrow Charles Wright's[697] term) "the heavenly way" that seems to have been lost. Partly, perhaps, because Rilke (unlike Wright) never bought into Augustine's cosmological dualism, estrangement from the celestial sphere inevitably brings in its train a correspondent alienation from the earth and the whole sphere of quotidian relations as well:

> Alas, whom
> can we turn to? Not angels, not humans,
> and the clever animals already see
> how little at home we are
> in the interpreted world.[698]

For Rilke, the soul bereft of tangible spiritual converse cannot readily compensate with earthly joys—in part because that world, too, has forfeited its innocence. Its pristine nature has been covered over with imputed meanings lacking imaginative color and force. If, at the onset of Rilke's poem, we are not exactly in the domain of what T. S. Eliot famously called "the waste land," we are nonetheless—in Rilke's contemporary poem—certainly in the precincts of that same mythic topos.

The opening of the *Elegies* registers Rilke's spiritual predicament in the aftermath of his writing of *Malte*. Despite his enchantment with Islam, Rilke could not all of a sudden become a "believer" in this or any other faith. He could not, like Eliot, become a convert who reinvested his spiritual life in the dogmatic truths of an established religion. As Rilke himself repeatedly reaffirmed, the *Elegies* represented the logical next step in the line of spiritual and poetical development—the saga of soul-making—we have been tracing from his *Visions of Christ* and *The Book of Hours* through *Malte*. The centrality of the soul and its creative imagination; anima development leading toward inner vision of the (invisible) essence of things, a *non-dualistic* vision that sees heaven in earth; a penetration into the imaginal sphere that likewise reconciles the living and the dead—these are some of the essential elements of Rilke's evolving world-view, *the integral nexus of which he could not find articulated in traditional exoteric religious sources*. Rilke's religious reading offered spiritual and imaginative inspiration, but not, in fact, world views—*Weltanschauungen*—providing intellectual and cosmological frameworks for his evolving vision as medieval theology did for Dante. Rather, Rilke—acting in accord not with ideological program, but rather with inner necessity—sought to assimilate the spiritual force and value of religious tradition to his peculiarly modern—and peculiarly *psychological*—individual consciousness: to transmit a vision of human purpose and destiny as weighty as those delivered by the ancient prophets, and yet true to the historical horizon of his experience and the fundamentally altered relation to the spiritual world implicit in his twentieth-century soul.

Just so, the poet faced a potentially insurmountable obstacle in pursuing his vision. Having proceeded so far along the lines of the essentially Romantic project of internalizing the divine, Rilke could not revert to worship of some external transcendent deity. Yet, in a certain sense, he had, in *Malte*, come to the end of his most intensely subjective line of advance—an end that (as the earlier cited letters reveal) sometimes appeared to him as a *dead end*: a road, or pilgrim path, going nowhere. Even so, a later letter provides a more balanced perspective, giving voice to the positive vision that could, conceivably, arise out of the negative force of Malte's incessant pathologizing, his neurotic obsession with toil, suffering, and death:

> What is expressed in the suffering that is written into Malte Laurids Brigge... is really only this: how is it possible to live when after all the elements of this life are utterly incomprehensible to us? If we are continually inadequate in love, uncertain in decision and impotent in the face of death, how is it possible to exist?...I myself sometimes thought of [Malte] as a hollow form, a negative mold, all the grooves and indentations of which are agony, disconsolations and most painful insights, but the casting from which, were it possible to make one (as with a bronze the positive figure one would get out of it), would perhaps be happiness, assent,—most perfect bliss.[699]

The question then remained: how might Rilke make that cast, construe and accomplish the next step on his soul's path?

The whole cycle of *Elegies* itself constitutes the poet's final answer, but the poem's very conception takes place under the aegis of the spiritual character announced in its dramatic opening, that numinous ambassador of the divine who—even while distant and terrible—proved the indispensable condition of our poet-pilgrim's progress:

> Ah, even as we wait upon help from human beings, with a single step
> an angel climbs down to us
> over our prone heart.[700]

Rilke included these lines in a letter to Princess Marie written in December of 1912. Künkler comments upon them in light of Rilke's own reading of Malte:

> The underside of life, however, which the poet explored [in *Malte*]...led, after conclusion of the novel, to a crisis, a loss of balance which—as he came more and more to understand—could only be restored by the angel.... Only his help would render fulfillment of the task "to make life possible again" thinkable. In order to transform the negative into the positive, new gravitation points of hope, capacity, and knowledge were necessity. The angel of the first Elegies opened a new space and provided a new measure.[701]

How does the angel provide this new space and measure? Another, later passage from Rilke offers further perspective on that question. In mid-January, Rilke wrote: "I, who—through involvement with things—have so accustomed myself to what is here, I must certainly (and it is just this that makes these years so difficult for me) skip over humans and go directly to learning about angels."[702] Kuschel comments:

> Rilke no longer wished to be satisfied—as in the *New Poems*—with the observation and expression of the substantial quality of things that exists on this side. He wished to go beyond to lend expression to the invisible, the region which comprehends all that exists here. The first two Elegies had conjured this "invisible" reality as the space of the angel where life and death flow together as one. The human would thereby be, to some degree, leapt over.[703]

Kuschel draws most directly upon this passage from the First Elegy:

> But the living
> all make the same error: they distinguish too strongly.
> Angels (it's said) often don't know whether they are moving
> among the living or the dead. The eternal current
> whirls all ages with it through both realms forever,
> and their voices are drowned in its soundless roar.[704]

The angel offers the possibility of the transcendence of the putative contraries of life and death, visible and invisible worlds. If one were to consider the question of his necessity from the standpoint of Rilke's evolving oeuvre, one might also say that the angel answered the demand of finding a synthesis of the *objective* impetus that impelled Rilke's *New Poems* (with its focus upon things in themselves and their standing in cosmic space) and the intensely *subjective* exploration of ways of seeing and being—harrowed and shaped by illness and death—pursued in *Malte*. Rilke implies as much—and more—in this perhaps most famous explanation of his angel's raison d'être:

> External world and vision everywhere coincided as it were in the object; in each a whole inner world was displayed, as though an angel who embraces space were blind and gazing into himself. This world, seen no longer with the eyes of men, but in the angel, is perhaps my real task—*at least all my earlier experiments would come together in it.*[705]

However one inflects the formulation of the problem, the pressure of the polar opposites (life and death, subjective vision and objective appearance, inward and outward or heavenly and earthly realms) demands that its "solution" make reference to another plane, some tenor of transcendence. Thus the necessity of the organ of supersensible vision, the angel.

Even so, the angelic idea alone cannot lift the human being out of paradoxes that tear at the psyche. The "new measure" of hope, capability, and knowledge figured by it remains initially inaccessible to the human soul. The very spiritual power that offers indispensable help in solving the existential problem—the face of the divine that can ultimately supply a transcendental ground for the authenticity of human being—appears out of reach, the terrible beauty of its touch auguring near annihilation.

> Who, if I cried out, would hear me then
> among the angelic orders? And even if one
> suddenly took me to heart: I'd be consumed by the strength
> of his more powerful being. For beauty is nothing
> but the beginning of terror...[706]

The opening of the Second Elegy strikes a similar chord:

> Every angel is terrible. Even so, alas,
> I call upon you, almost deadly birds of the soul,
> knowing what you are. Where are the days of Tobias...

The poem continues to recall that ancient time when an archangel could—without undue disturbance—consort with men, before proceeding to lament the gulf that now cleaves the spiritual and human worlds:

> Were the archangel, that perilous one, now
> to emerge from behind the stars and take one step down towards us
> the pounding of our own heart would crush us. Who are you?[707]

How may the human soul come to bear the force of angelic power and (like Jacob) wrestle it to earth? How may psyche come to know—not only things in themselves, and not only the images constitutive of its own soul history—but something of the transcendent spiritual source of its own real being, the power uniting the realms of life and death, heaven and earth? In phrasing the matter thus, we approach once more the imaginal terrain of our guiding myth, and may look to it yet again for illumination of the nature of what is, after all, another station of the soul's archetypal cross: Psyche's third labor of love.

Psyche's third task appears still more impossible and life-threatening than her second. Declaring her wish to test whether Psyche possesses "a stout heart and prudence beyond the prudence of woman," Venus sets her a truly superhuman challenge:

> "Do you see the high mountain peak that crowns yonder lofty cliff, wherefrom the swarthy waves of a black stream flow down till, caught in the neighboring valley's walled abyss, they flood the Stygian swamps and feed the hoarse streams of Cocytus? Go, draw me icy water even from where on the high summit the fountain's farthest waves well forth, and bring it to me with all speed in this small urn." So saying, she gave her a small jar carved out of crystal, and threatened yet more cruel torments if she failed.[708]

Psyche wastes no time in climbing to the top of the mountain, "sure that there at least, if all else failed, she could put an end to her miserable existence." Arriving there, she

> perceived how vast and difficult was her task, and how fraught with death. For it was a rock of measureless height, rough, slippery, and inaccessible, and from jaws that gaped in its midst it vomited

> forth a hideous stream that...rushed secretly into the neighboring valley. To right and left from crannies in the crag there crept forth fierce dragons, with long craning necks and eyes sworn to unwinking wakefulness...And even the very waters had voices that forbade approach.

Psyche is completely overwhelmed by the awful prospect that confronts her. Understandably enough, she takes leave of her senses:

> Psyche felt herself turned to stone by the impossibility of her task. Though she was present in body, her senses had flown far away from her and, quite overwhelmed by such vast inevitable peril, she lacked even the last solace of tears.

All, however, is not lost. Once again, Psyche receives help from divine nature, though here her accomplished assistant is Jove's own minion rather than earthier Pan's:

> But the anguish of her innocent soul was not unmarked by the grave eyes of kindly Providence, for the royal bird of highest Jove suddenly spread both his pinions and came to her with timely aid.

Honoring "Love's godhead in the woes of his bride," the eagle departs "the shining paths of the high vault of heaven," and addresses Psyche thus:

> "Dost thou, simple-hearted and all unversed in such labors, hope to have power to steal or even touch so much as one drop of that most holy and also most cruel fountain? Thou hast surely heard tell...that even the gods and Jove himself dread yonder Stygian waters, and even as you mortals swear by the divinity of the gods, so the gods swear by the majesty of Styx. But come, give me that urn!" Straightway he seized it and caught it to his body...

Soaring on his great wings, the eagle—deftly avoiding the dragons and mollifying the voices of waters by telling them he is doing Venus' own bidding—attains his aim. "So he took of the water and Psyche received the full urn with joy and bore it back with all speed" to Venus.

Mission Impossible accomplished, once more.

The symbolism comprising this, Psyche's third labor, is rich and riveting. Neumann begins interpreting it as follows:

> This labor is a variant of the quest for the water of life, the precious substance hard to obtain.... The essential feature of this spring is that it unites the highest and lowest: it is a uroboric circular stream that feeds the depths of the underworld and rises up again to issue from the highest crag of the "huge mountain."[709]

These words highlight the relationship between defining elements of the scene and the contours of the spiritual challenge confronting Rilke as he endeavored to conceive his Elegies. The affinity flows from the image of the holy stream itself, the *endless current* pouring from its inaccessible and elevated origin down into the underworld, connecting *the sublime source of life* with the river of *death* below. Neumann continues:

> The problem is to capture in a vessel the water of this spring... Aphrodite regards the task as hopeless, because to her mind the stream of life defies capture, it is eternal movement, eternal change, generation, birth, and death. The essential quality of this stream is precisely that it cannot be contained. Psyche, then, as feminine vessel, is ordered to contain the stream, to give form and rest to what is formless and flowing; as vessel of individuation, as mandala-urn, she is ordered to mark off a configured unity from the flowing energy of life, to give form to life.[710]

This approaches the heart of the matter, for Rilke no less than Psyche. How may the individual soul not only view, but come to contain—incorporate in the vessel of its limited consciousness—the almost infinitely powerful spiritual sources of its own being; the sublime origin of its life, its death, and, too, the very possibility of love?

In viewing the stream from Aphrodite's (Venus') perspective, Neumann initially gives his interpretation of it a rather strongly biological inflection. Continuing his line of thought, he expands his understanding:

> [I]n addition to its general meaning as the uncontainable energy of the unconscious, the life stream possesses a specific symbolism in relation to Psyche. As what fills the mandala-urn this stream is male-generative, like the archetypally fecundating power of innumerable river gods all over the world. In relation to the feminine psyche it is the overwhelming male-numinous power of that which penetrates to fructify, that is, of the paternal uroboros.[711]

"Overwhelming male-numinous power": in the context of reading Rilke's *Elegies*, the phrase inevitably evokes the figure of Rilke's angel—at least if not too much stress is placed upon the "male" term. Even in that respect, however, the phrase is not off-target. Angels figure as representation of spirit and generally incline, in character and representation, more toward masculine than feminine qualities. Rilke's own angel, in fact, reveals features that answer—at least partially—to Neumann's description. After directly posing the question "Who *are* you?" in his Second Elegy, Rilke begins to sketch angelic nature in distinctly masculine contours:

> First successes, Creation's own darlings,
> mountain ranges, peaks reddening at the dawn
> of all beginning,—pollen of blossoming godhood,
> shafts of light...[712]

Rilke addresses "male-generative" energy still more directly in the Third Elegy, specifically invoking one of those "innumerable river gods" Neumann refers to:

> It's one thing to sing the beloved. Another, alas,
> that hidden, guilt-ridden river-god of the blood![713]

Rilke's angel and his river-god are, however, by no means one and same. In accord with the difficult dynamic of impossible love, Rilke (in the Third Elegy in particular, and the whole cycle in general) associates connection with spiritual source with movement *away* from a (Freudian) psychology dominated by natural libido. Unlike Neumann, Rilke does not generally identify "male-numinous power" with the unending fount of biological desire, but (while wrestling with the undeniable power of that natural force) reserves a more supernatural character for his numinous, angelic source.

If not entirely commensurate with Neumann's reading, Rilke's writing is, if anything, more in accord with the symbolism in the myth. The origin of the stream upon a high mountain-top ("a rock of measureless height") as well as the role played by the far-seeing denizen of the heights (the eagle) implies not a purely chthonic, but a sublimely transcendent spiritual source. The stream figures a power that may flow into and circulate through natural life—and death—but itself remains a holy, supernatural spring. With that caveat in mind, we can proceed to read the final sentence of Neumann's paragraph: "The insoluble problem which Aphrodite sets Psyche, and which Psyche solves, is to encompass this [overwhelming male-numinous] power without being shattered by it."[714]

This sentence resonates ringingly with Rilke's *Elegies*, and expresses the gist of the challenge Rilke confronted in conceiving and accomplishing his great poem cycle. The problem of capturing in an urn the mysterious "water of life" that flows from the awful fount is, too, the problem of facing the angel. How may (the vessel of the human) Psyche manage to contain something of the angel's numinous power without being destroyed by the terrible beauty of that transcendent source—the illimitable, invisible, divine force that spans the highest and lowest realms of being, connecting and uniting the peak experiences of Life and the river valley of Death?

As the myth implies, the challenge is almost superhuman. After a decade and a half of dedicated poetic labor and spiritual striving; after numerous journeys and immersion in religion and psychology, art, literature, and philosophy; after adventures and misadventures in life and in love; after real and imagined confrontations with illness, death, and the soul's dark night, Rilke—ensconced in the sublime landscape of Duino, the castle poised upon a cliff towering high above the Istrian sea—heard the voice of the angel, and made a beginning. "Who, if I cried out...."

The angel, however—while posited—reigns in absence. The angel of the first two Elegies remains unremittingly distant: angelic existence is conceived, and yet, at the same time, the task of drawing nearer and tapping that divine power is envisioned as virtually impossible.

It does not continue to be so—to the same degree—throughout the whole cycle of poems. The poetic voice comes to be on rather more familiar terms with the angel in the later Elegies. In the Fifth, for instance (the last to be composed), the poet twice directly addresses the no-longer-quite so-terribly distant angel ("Angel! O take it, pluck it, that small-petaled herb of healing," and, at the end of the poem, "Angel! Suppose there's a place we don't know of, and there..."[715]). In order, then, to progress—in order, in the long course of time, to accomplish the task embodied in his *Elegies*—the poet required some way of approaching that sublime source more closely; needed some means, imaginatively speaking, of bringing his prophetic vision of the angel down to earth in more palpable, comprehensible, even visible form. After the initial burst of inspiration that birthed the *Elegies* subsided, Rilke needed...Toledo.

"You have been entered there, Marina, on my internal map: somewhere between Moscow and Toledo I've made room for the influx of your ocean."[716] So Rilke wrote to the Russian poetess Marina Tsvetaeva in May 1926, roughly half a year before his death. The passage is only one among many that bear witness to the truth that, right up to the end of his life, Rilke regarded his experiences in Toledo as among the most significant of his existence, qualifying it as the only place he might mention in the same breath as Russia or Paris.

The question remains: Why so? Rilke's relation to Russia (inseparable from his relation to Lou) supplied him spiritual compass, and transmitted to him his founding myth of culture. Paris, city of Rodin and locus of Rilke's (and Malte's) *nigredo*, was his home for years and his place of perpetual return. Rilke's sojourn in Toledo, by contrast, lasted roughly a month (a short period, even though his three-month stay in Ronda may well be regarded as an imaginative extension) and—while it did pique his interest in Islam—did not stimulate immersion in the Spanish language or culture in general. What, then, accounts for Toledo's signal influence upon the poet's imagination?

Rilke's attraction to Toledo originated in a quite specific domain; inhered, almost exclusively, in *the imaginative geography of the locale*, the expressive *landscape* incarnated in the city and its immediate surround. Toledo, for Rilke, was not really a populated city or country at all, not so much a region or locus of culture as a single, extraordinarily rich symbolic *image*, a *topos* experienced less as a historical place than a visionary painting.

Rilke actually *saw* Toledo long before he arrived there, in physical fact, in November 1913. Five years previously, on October 16, 1908—having recently finished his *New Poems: The Other Part*, and still at work on *Malte*—Rilke visited the Salon d'Automne in Paris. Ignacio Zuloaga, a Spanish painter Rilke admired, directed Rilke there in order that he might view the work of one of Zuloaga's countrymen, little known at the time. It was there Rilke saw the city of his dreams in the color and form of El Greco's proto-expressionist landscape, *View of Toledo*.

The imaginative force of El Greco's visionary landscape—painted near the end of the artist's long life, and the only landscape of his on record—seized Rilke immediately. He wasted no time in communicating his impression of the work to Rodin:

"View of Toledo," El Greco, 1561

My dear Rodin:

I am returning from the Salon, where I spent an hour in front of El Greco's "Toledo." This landscape appears to me ever more astonishing. I must describe it to you, as I saw it. Here it is:

The thunderstorm has discharged its force and suddenly descends behind the town, which climbs steeply up the slope of a

> hill to its cathedral and still higher up to its quadratic and massive castle. A torn light ploughs the earth, moves it, raises it up and allows pale green meadows to stand out here and there behind the trees, like sleepless nights. A narrow river, motionless, leaves the massive hill and—terrifyingly—threatens the bushes' green flames with its black, nocturnal blue. The rising city, shocked, stretches upward with its last strength as if to push through the atmosphere of fear.
>
> One should have such dreams.[717]

Naumann gives an apt account of the painting's impact on the poet:

> Rilke never forgot this impression. Through El Greco's picture, the city of Toledo received a lasting and definite character in Rilke's mind, and became familiar to him. It became for him *the* chosen place which he—for inward reasons—required, so that on September 27, 1911 he could write to the Princess von Thurn und Taxis: "You know that I have a singular yearning: to travel to Toledo."[718]

That yearning was only intensified when, in Munich in December of 1911 (and so shortly before the onset of the Elegies), Rilke saw another impressive El Greco picture of Toledo—this time, the *Laocoön*. The only El Greco painting on a mythological theme, the work portrays the doomed Trojan seer and his sons struggling with serpents atop a mountain with the city of Toledo in the background. "And the Laocoön, the Laocoön: you can imagine what it was to me: I sat in front of it for hours, saw ever more clearly that... just this drama must play out in front of Toledo...."[719]

The two El Grecos exercised a decisive influence upon Rilke's imagination. In September of 1912, looking forward to his journey to Spain, Rilke wrote to Sidonie Nadherny: "Whenever I may think of looking [*Schauen*], I always inwardly believe Toledo to be necessary, Greco..."[720] By Rilke's own oft-repeated admission, it was, first and foremost, El Greco's paintings that excited a sense of keen anticipation (Rilke's own word was *Vorgefühl*) with respect to the Spanish city, and finally sent the poet—following an inner calling—to Toledo.

Naturally, Rilke harbored doubts as to whether his actual experience of Toledo would answer to his high expectations. Yet—as we saw from the correspondence cited earlier—the place lived up to his long-cherished image of it. If anything, Toledo's reality exceeded Rilke's dream of it.

Rilke's letters describing Toledo are full of superlatives; again and again, he characterizes its power as surpassing all limits, perpetually *going beyond*. Correlatively, the image of Toledo itself quickly became identified, internally, with Rilke's own conception of the next step on his soul's journey—a step so far beyond all that had gone before, it was nigh unthinkable, and yet, at the same time, a comprehensive summation. In December, from Ronda, he wrote to Lou Andreas-Salomé:

> The decision took shape to go on this journey through Spain, actually just for a stay in Toledo, and on arriving there, breathlessly exposed to the really infinitely anticipated which yet infinitely surpassed all anticipation,—I believe myself already almost torn out of my dullness and on the way to a broader participation in what validly exists,—there are no words with which I could tell you *how beyond everything* this city stood before me in the midst of its untamed landscape, through and through the next thing, that which a moment before would not yet have been bearable, at once chastening and consoling, like Moses when he came from the mountain with horns of light—, and yet again, little by little recalling everything in my life that was ever necessary, strong, pure, reliable.[721]

Earlier in this chapter, we spoke of the religious intensity—indeed, the prophetic power—Rilke saw incarnate in the landscape of Toledo, a theme sounded again in this passage and yet again when (in another letter to Lou) Rilke likens Mohammed to "a river through a primeval mountain breaking through to the one God."[722] In late November, still in Toledo itself, Rilke, in a letter to Elsa Bruckman, lends this theme classic formulation: Toledo, for him, was "a landscape that does not speak, but prophesies, and over which the spirit of its greatness comes, everywhere...."[723]

Toledo's magical appeal—its prophetic force—inhered in no single aspect of the landscape, but in the *dramatic whole* the image of the city and its surround presented to Rilke's physical and spiritual senses. The key elements of that whole archetypal scene find powerful expression in El Greco's paintings of Toledo—first and foremost, his *View of Toledo*. Look at the picture, its chief features faithfully registered in Rilke's letter to Rodin: a massive hill (in letters written after Rilke's arrival in Toledo, he consistently upgrades the hill to a hoary mountain) thrusting up into a storm-charged sky; a black river pouring with "terrifying" power down into the valleys of sleep far below; and the city in between, its cathedral and tower symbolizing the containing power of human consciousness, striving upward even while being caught in the sublime play of force connecting highest heaven and darkest earth.

We have encountered a very similar imaginative landscape before in the context of our reading of Apuleius' fable. Indeed, the flow of this entire chapter has been tending toward just this convergence of two apparently disparate symbolic representations, for *El Greco's* View of Toledo *doubles as a visual image of (the scene of) Psyche's third labor.*

In this, above all, lies Toledo's enormous, fateful significance for Rilke. Ever since he became fascinated by Byzantine icons; ever since Worpswede, Rodin, and Cezanne, visual art had played a decisive role in shaping Rilke's poetic imagination and (spiritually speaking) leading him onward. Long before he visited Toledo in the flesh (and before, too, the literary inception of his *Elegies*), El Greco's painting had announced an inner necessity by offering an archetypal image of the next enormous step on Rilke's soul path, a dreamlike condensation of the psycho-spiritual content defining his prophetic mission. Like the scene in Apuleius' tale, it offers a symbol of human consciousness face to face with the primordial sources of (its) being, implicitly confronting it with the task, not only of withstanding the tremendous forces unleashed in the expressionistic landscape, but of framing and containing the cosmic lines of force, effectively uniting "the highest and the lowest," above and below, and so capturing something of the holy mystery of the water of life.

And the *Laocoön?* This painting, too, is of a piece with these themes, though it places a marked accent upon the *tragic* potential inherent in the scene. Laocoön was the Trojan priest who foresaw the consequences of allowing the Trojan horse into the city and lobbied against that fateful act. In so doing, he angered Neptune, one of the Gods who destined the outcome of the war. Neptune consequently sent serpents to destroy Laocoön and his sons, a divine sign that sealed the city's doom. Rilke describes El Greco's painting in the following terms:

> Imagine a spacious picture, in the foreground, on top of a brown, stony region of the earth rashly and tragically darkened by the clouds, Laocoön, enveloped by the serpent which he attempts to fend off: one son already fallen; one on the left, standing,

> bent still tautly backward by the strong arc of the second serpent which is already reaching his heart; two sons on the right as yet uncomprehending (so suddenly did it all come and take the upper hand), and through all of that, through the standing and the falling and the resistance, through and through all the tense in-between spaces of this despair—Toledo is seen as if cognizant of this drama, thrust up on its unquiet hill, pale in the light of the sky falling down behind it—an incomparable, unforgettable picture.[724]

Why did this second image of Toledo so transfix Rilke's attention? It may be seen as a kind of complement of El Greco's *View of Toledo*, even a kind of holographic completion of the archetypal scene of Psyche's third labor. Laocoön was a *seer-soul* who sought—by force of higher consciousness—to alter destiny, and (in Neptune's view, anyway) wrest primordial power from the Gods. The scene of his death is set upon a high mountain above Toledo—once more a site comparable with the high crag in the scene of Psyche's labor. Though there is no rushing stream here, the serpents destroying Laocoön may well be likened to the dragons guarding the dread fount in Apuleius, the devouring force of the unconscious powers that threaten to destroy any mere mortal who seeks to draw from the well of divine power. In Rilke's view, the city of Toledo in the background witnesses the tragic scene, implicitly aware of the cosmic conflict it dramatizes, the real possibility of the demise of the seer who—without proper divine backing—oversteps his bounds. The painting (which Rilke contemplated deeply not once, but several times) most likely appeared to the poet as a kind of mirror of the very real dangers implicit in his own great task, the prophetic task which he—looking with the innermost eye of the soul—saw embodied in the imaginal landscape of Toledo.

In tenor and intensity, Rilke's experience of Toledo approached the mystical. Moved by the sense of sublimity Toledo inspired in him—its terrible beauty, transcending normal human measure—Rilke quickly came to associate Toledo with the being he identified as the guardian spirit of his prophetic mission: the angel. Virtually the first words flowing from Rilke's pen after his arrival in Toledo forge the connection: "*What* it is *like* here, that, dear friend, I shall never be able to say (it would be language of angels, their use of it among men), but *that* it is, that it *is*, you will just have to believe me."[725] Consistently, Rilke's famous evocation of the visionary character of his angel (already partially quoted earlier) takes Toledo and its landscape as likeness and point of departure:

> "Working after Nature" has in such a high degree made that which is into a task for me, that only very rarely now, as by mistake, does a thing speak to me, granting and giving without demanding that I reproduce it equivalently and significantly in myself. The Spanish landscape (the last I experienced to the utmost)—Toledo—drove this attitude of mine to its extreme: since there the external thing itself—tower, hill, bridge—already possessed the incredible, unsurpassable intensity of the inner equivalents through which one might have been able to represent it. *Appearance* and *vision* everywhere coincided as it were in the object, as though an angel who embraces space were blind and gazing into himself.[726]

The German word for "appearance" in this passage is *Erscheinung*, literally, "shining forth." Recalling the discussion in chapter 5 of this book, we may remark that Rilke's letter amounts to saying that Toledo appeared to him as a form of *theophany*—a shining forth of divine substance. The angel, coincidentally, qualifies as the agent or mediator of theophanic vision, repeated and concluded in the vassal/vessel of the poetic imagination. This insight could supply one means of making serious intellectual sense of Rilke's contention that *his* angel has nothing to do with Christianity, but rather with Islam.[727] Given Rilke's limited background, however, such an argument could not confidently proceed upon grounds of Rilke's conscious knowledge of such matters. Moreover, as we will soon see, there are persuasive grounds for believing that certain Christian images of angels influenced Rilke's own far more than the poet wished to acknowledge.

Evidence for the connection between Rilke's Spanish experience and the evolving image of his elegy-angel need not rest solely upon the content of his letters. During his stay in Ronda—a time that involved poetic reflection on his Toledo experience—Rilke composed a poem that clearly manifests relevant crosscurrents. "To the Angel" begins by contrasting angelic strength, constancy, and luminosity with human opacity and hesitation:

To the Angel

Calm, strong candelabra placed there
on the rim: above, night shows its face.
But we diffuse ourselves in unillumined
stuttering here, by your broad base.

The resonance with the *Elegies* sounds throughout, but most strongly in the last two stanzas of the poem:

Angel, do I cry, do I mourn?
Yet how then might the lament be mine?
Alas, I cry—pound with two wood hammers.
But am I heard? *Nein, nein, nein.*

My cry cannot reach your hearing if
you do not feel me, because I *am.*
Shine! Shine! Make me more visible
among the stars. For I vanish...among them.[728]

The vision of the angel in this poem—even while consistent with that inscribed in Rilke's first two Elegies—draws upon visible images unavailable to Rilke before his visit to Toledo. Rilke traveled to Toledo, after all, to see, not only the landscape of the city, but the El Greco paintings housed there. Angels frequent El Greco's canvases—for this premier painter of the Counter-Reformation, they are more common than trees—and El Greco's potent angelic images undoubtedly influenced Rilke's developing conception of the same. Naumann, for instance, suggests El Greco's painting *The Burial of the Count of Orgaz* (from the Santo Tomé in Toledo) as one possible visual source for Rilke's "To the Angel," describing this striking painting (one highly regarded by El Greco himself) as follows: "An angel carries the soul of the dead up to heaven and thereby stands 'on the border' between the earthly group of mourners and the divine realm."[729] Another Toledo "resident," *The Baptism of Jesus*, includes yet another instance of an angel on the border "connecting through gaze and gesture the earthly proceeding with the eternity of God the Father"[730] and likewise suggests itself as a possible precursor of Rilke's poem.

Yet the painting that most impressed Rilke during his stay in Toledo (one he visited repeatedly) inspired—not "To the Angel"—but another related Ronda poem which borrows the name and subject of the great

El Greco known, in Rilke's time, as *The Assumption of Mary*. Greco's elongate canvas, hung in the Church of San Vicente in Toledo, exhibits an extraordinary vertical motion spanning icons of heaven and of earth, as a powerful angel, his feet still touching earthly flowers, "arches his back as though to drive the Virgin up into the heavenly realm."[731] In a journal entry in Ronda, Rilke himself described the angel in the painting: "He [the angel] reaches sensibly into the supersensible, only his reach is unending...has its beginning and disappears in endlessness."[732] This visualization, so consonant with the transcendent character of Toledo itself (the city which, as Rilke put it, everywhere "reaches beyond itself"), indicates that—despite Rilke's own anti-Christian pronouncement—El Greco's angels did intersect Rilke's developing imagination of angelic being. Yet even in the context of this painting, Toledo itself plays an important part: like the Laocoön, El Greco's "Assumption" features Toledo as background and witness of its central event.

Rilke's own poetic "Assumption of Mary" focuses less upon the angel than upon Mary herself. The following lines, especially, evoke themes Rilke develops in the later Elegies:

> Ah, you draw yourself out of the chalices of flowers,
> out of the birds that describe the line of flight;
> out of the full and open being of children,
> out of the utter and the cud of the cow—;
> all things lose an element of mildness,
> only the heaven within grows greater now.[733]

Mary here represents the pure (virgin) soul's capacity to absorb angelic energy in the act of her own transcendence, and may thus serve as a figure mediating between the human psyche's imperfections and divine beatitude. Consequently, Mary (the subject, we should recall, of the poem sequence that helped catalyze the *Elegies*) prefigures the possibility of Psyche's own successful completion of her tasks, her own ultimate "assumption" and sacred union with divine Eros.

Rilke himself—while by no means ready for such divine consummations—evidently required such inspiring images to orient his vision and carry on. El Greco's images provided Rilke needed spiritual nourishment, and helped sustain his fraught and laborious visionary quest. Another important passage from one of Rilke's letters—drawing upon both Ribadeneira and, again, upon El Greco's *Assumption*—brings together the figure of Mary, angelogy, and the city of Toledo in a revealing concatenation of figures and influences:

> "A woman of Heaven and of Earth" said the Jesuit Ribadeneira... of the Virgin Mary; that could be applied to this city, "a city of Heaven and of the Earth," for it is really in both, it goes right through all existence. I tried recently to make this intelligible in one sentence to P. by saying that it is there in equal measure for the eyes of the dead, the living, and the angels,—yes, here is an object that might be accessible to all three of those so widely different visions; over it, one feels, they could come together and have one and the same impression.[734]

This single sentence offers an apt description of the high task Rilke set himself in the *Elegies*: the poet aimed to create an (art) object that synthesized and integrated the earthly time-space world of the (living) human soul with the divine spiritual world as well as the world of the dead. In accord with his image of Toledo qua the Virgin Mary, the poet aspired to a vision of being that bridged heaven and earth and all correlative contraries (invisible and visible, inward and outward, the temporal and eternal worlds); strove—*in the form of another sort of "unravished bride," "the mandala-urn" of soul consciousness embodied in the poem*—to *contain* the holy water of life that flows from sublime heights down into the dark river of death, circulating ceaselessly in between. The *Duino Elegies* were to be the crystal vessel in and through which Rilke might ultimately accomplish Psyche's third labor of love, and his *angels*—those "almost deadly birds of the soul"—were (his) psyche's *eagles*: agents of that higher, that divine vision without whom success could not be conceived.

In subsequent chapters, we will look more comprehensively at the shape, design, and poetic texture of Rilke's cycle of elegies, the art-work in and through which he strove to attain his singular object. Realizing the full scope of the vision prefigured in Toledo required almost a full decade. In Ronda, however, Rilke did achieve a poetic sketch of the locale that inspired and guided his quest: a poem expressive of his fierce desire to become one with the Spanish city and the vision it vouchsafed him.

Spanish Trilogy I

From this cloud—look! that so tempestuously
covers the star that just shone there—(and from me),
from the mountains yonder, where now the night's
high winds howl for a while—(and from me),
from this river in the valley's cleft, catching
glimmers of the torn light of the sky—(and from me);
from me, and from all of this to make
a single thing, Lord: from me and from the feeling
the cattle breathe in the pen at dusk, enduring
the huge, black, no-longer-being-there
of the world—from me and every gleam
of light in the many darkened houses, Lord:
to make one thing; from the strangers, for I know
no one, Lord, and from me and from me
to make *one* thing; from those who are sleeping,
the strange old men in the hospital who
cough so importantly in their beds, from
children drunk with sleep on the bosoms of strangers,
from many vaguenesses and always from me,
from nothing but me and all I don't know,
to make that thing, Lord Lord Lord, that thing
which, cosmic and earthly like a meteor
collects heaviness solely from the sum
of its flight, weighing nothing but arrival.[735]

The first poem of Rilke's triptych "The Spanish Trilogy" provides *one* summation of Rilke's visionary experience of Toledo. It serves as well as a testimony to El Greco's enduring hold upon the poet's perception of the place. Naumann points out that the poem's initial litany of images parallels rather closely Rilke's 1908 description of El Greco's *View of Toledo.* Storm-charged cloud, mountainous landscape, the river flowing into the valley: all reappear in the poem written five years later.

What stands out in the poem, though (and is *not* present in Rilke's much earlier epistolary description) is the poet's repeated inclusion of himself as an element—one among others—that must be integrated into a unified moment of vision objectively represented as a single "thing." The piece has resonances with both Rilke's prayerful *Book of Hours* and his *New Poems*. Indeed, it figures as a fusion of the styles characteristic of those volumes even while demarcating spiritual territory proper to the new scene of Rilke's work. In his letters, Rilke referred to Toledo as "star-ish" (*sternisch*) and the climax of this poem—based upon an actual experience in Toledo—offers an interesting variation on one of his leading *New Poem* themes.

Standing on the bridge arching over the River Tagus one evening, Rilke witnessed a meteor shoot through the sky. The visionary moment provided Rilke with a poetic opportunity to revisit the motif that famously concludes his "Archaic Torso of Apollo," revising it in accord with the spiritual logic proper to the new phase of his work.

> ...from nothing but me and all I don't know,
> to make that thing, Lord Lord Lord, that thing
> which, cosmic and earthly like a meteor
> collects heaviness solely from the sum
> of its flight, weighing nothing but arrival.

Instead of a stone sculpture "becoming alternately in you stone and star," a meteor—an actual cosmic body that is, at one and the *same* time, stone and star—plunges from heaven to earth, becoming, suddenly, neither—nothing but the force of its arrival. Rilke experienced the poetic moment as yet one more compelling image of his task: a shooting of the divide between heaven and earth, spirit and matter, eternity and time. To become one with the object that races from cosmic reaches of eternity to die into the earth's atmosphere—and yet, in that very act, to make a lasting impact, to transform into invisible influence; to make, and so become *one* with that thing (not only in a moment of objective perception, but in the very ground of his own human being), thus realizing the meteor's "cosmic-earthly" destiny in the fiber and fabric of his whole soul: such was Rilke's prophetic mission. Toledo provided him a shining glimpse of that mission, and "the thing" he made of it all (including himself) weighs no more than the path of a poem and the force of its invisible arrival—in us.

Chapter 15

WHO, IF I CRIED . . .

Rilke harbored a keen sense of the underlying unity of his oeuvre, and viewed the *Duino Elegies* as the culmination of his poetic work to date. Roughly a year before his death, Rilke wrote the Polish translator of his *Elegies*:

> I regard [the *Duino Elegies*] as a further elaboration of those essential premises that were already given in the *Book of Hours*, that in the two parts of the *New Poems* tentatively played with the image of the world and that then in the *Malte*, contracted in conflict, strike back into life and there almost lead to the proof that this life so suspended in the bottomless is impossible. In the *Elegies*, starting from the same postulates, life becomes possible again, indeed, it experiences here that ultimate affirmation to which young Malte, though on the difficult right path "des longues etudes," was as yet unable to conduct it.[736]

On a thematic level, certainly, it is easy to verify crucial elements of the continuity Rilke posits here. The *Elegies* transparently carry forward the meditation on the mysteries of death, (impossible) love, and poetic vocation so central to Rilke's previous work, especially *Malte.* As our ongoing engagement with the Psyche-Eros myth indicates, deeper continuities subsist as well. In the course of the next three chapters, we will detail how the *Elegies* unfold a further stage of the intimate yet deeply fraught intercourse between the *soul* and the transcendent *spirit of love* that underlies the whole of the poet's oeuvre.

Within the context of these deeper continuities, however, the *Elegies* do accomplish a dramatic leap. Reaching toward unprecedented heights and depths of thought and emotion, the poet of the *Elegies* attains to a whole new *niveau* of poetic consciousness. Accordingly, interpreting the *Elegies* is no mean task—indeed, represents a mission nearly as daunting as the poem's original transcription—for it requires construing that consciousness; entering into the form of spiritual vision that birthed a work that (even while often seeming to defy comprehension) exerts tremendous power. Recognizing, in advance, the challenges involved and the partiality of any potential success, we may nonetheless begin exploring the *Elegies* by querying the cycle's distinguishing characteristics, interrogating the terms and conditions that serve to set the *Elegies* apart from Rilke's prior work. In so doing, we will be attempting to delineate the signal features of an epochal poem, one that (like its contemporary *The Waste Land*) towers as one of the landmarks of modernity.

Let us begin with—not so much the *heights*—but rather the *depths* of consciousness plumbed in the *Duino Elegies.*

The very form of the poem—its elegiac mode—attests to the archetypal experience of devastating loss that underlies it. As its initiating cry ("Wer, wenn ich schriee...") announces, the *Elegies* issue forth from a state of profound despair, spiritual desolation, and incontrovertible isolation. On one level, of course, this is nothing new for Rilke. The poet had been diving in dark seas ever since his departure from Worpswede, and (as his letter implies) his *Malte* descends so deep into the elements of fear and doubt as to render questionable the very possibility of resurfacing. Even so, there are multiple degrees and kinds of *nigredo*, and the voice of the *Elegies* plunges still deeper and holds its breath yet longer—long enough, indeed, for consciousness to finally implode under pressure. In his *Malte*, Rilke dramatizes the possibility of consciousness falling apart; the *Elegies* speak, with unremitting intensity, from the standpoint of a consciousness effectively in the midst of a comprehensive existential shattering, or—proleptically—looking out from the far side of such experience. The curve of Rilke's career itself helps makes clear that the *Elegies* issue forth from the very nadir of the poet's (seemingly) unending *nigredo*; sound out of the deepest core of his soul's dark night.

In this respect, the *Elegies* manifest a development driven, primarily, by the inner logic of Rilke's own poetic destiny. Even so, certain "outward" circumstances fed into the soul's inner motions. While the events discussed below postdate the 1912 inception of the *Elegies* as well as the Spanish voyage the poet embarked upon later that same year, the experiences they represent nonetheless weave themselves into the texture of the whole, helping to dye its dark background.

The first relevant matter involves Rilke's persistently problematic love life. Despite (or because of) the failure of his marriage[737] as well as subsequent liaisons of varying duration and intensity, Rilke, in the post-Malte, prewar years, continued to cherish a thoroughly idealized image of "the unknown beloved," the feminine companion who would answer his soul's inveterate yearning *without* placing undue demands on his restless and resolutely independent spirit.[738] In the aftermath of his short-lived relationship with the actress Hedwig Bernhard in 1913, Rilke almost seemed to surrender the idea. In a poem from the winter of that year, "the future beloved" becomes

> You, beloved, lost in advance, you
> who never arrive . . .[739]

Not long after the penning of this poem, however, the "unknown beloved" miraculously *did* arrive in the only way truly open to her—not in person but by post.

In January of 1914, Rilke received a letter from a pianist—one Magda von Hattingberg—thanking him for the spiritual solace and artistic inspiration she found in his *Tales of God.* The simple yet intimate tone of the letter struck a deep chord with Rilke, and the poet answered it immediately. The ensuing correspondence quickly escalated in volume and intensity. In his third letter, Rilke wrote that he would like to "write you in one sitting all the possible letters that could be written in a year," and, in fact, in a series of "giant" letters, Rilke—surrendering all reserve—poured out his heart and soul to the woman he heralded as Benvenuta, "the welcome one." Magda, a capable artist in her own right, responded accordingly. In short order, the two became epistolary lovers. Rilke:

> We know we love each other as though from a pre-earthly time, from childhoods preceding all ages of existence; we love each other out of primordial being as the stars would love one another if they knew of their splendor. And I now know, too, that I want to stir no feelings toward you except those of the most unreflecting state of childhood so I may search there for the purest rays of my heart to take to you.[740]

Duino Castle

Magda von Hattingberg (top); Rilke, ca.1918

Yet the dénouement of the literary affair proved regrettably predictable. A little more than a month after the first fateful letter, Rilke and his Benvenuta met in Berlin. The lovers spent the better part of almost three months in each other's company: first in Berlin, then later in Munich, Innsbruck, Basel, Paris, and Duino. Despite quietly auspicious beginnings (including many hours passed with Rilke listening to Magda at the piano), the real-life relationship, inevitably falling short of impossible expectation, could not finally stand the test of human time. After a difficult fortnight at Duino in May (Princess Marie did not take to Magda) and a brief concluding interlude in Venice, Rainer and Magda parted. Rilke soon returned to Paris, alone once more.

The relationship with Magda deepened Rilke's relationship to music and the realm of nonverbal sound it opened. Even so, the breaking of beloved illusions it entailed proved, in its wise, shattering—the crushing of hopes that could no longer be nursed, even in dream.

In the aftermath of the Benvenuta affair, he wrote to Lou:

> So here I am, back again, after a long, broad, heavy time, a time in which once more a kind of future became past... What finally turned out so absolutely to my misery began with many, many letters, light beautiful letters that came rushing out of my heart: I can scarcely remember ever having written such letters before... If sometimes during these last few years I was able to plead my case by saying that certain attempts of mine to gain a more human and natural foothold in life had failed because the people concerned did not understand me... now after these months of suffering, I stand condemned in an altogether different sense: having to admit this time that no one *can* help me, no one.[741]

Rilke had long felt a cleavage between the ideal aims of his art and the exigencies of human life and love; the Benvenuta affair drove that sharp wedge home with splitting force. Nonetheless, a week after the above-mentioned letter to Lou, Rilke wrote an important poem confirming his sense that the way forward lay, not in abandoning the work of love, but, on the contrary, in withdrawing the centrifugal force of his outward projection of it, better *interiorizing* and so truly *realizing* it for the first time. Revolving around the contrast between the work of seeing (*Anschauen*) and more heartfelt labor, the poem concludes:

For see—looking erects a border.
And the world so intently looked upon
wants to flourish in love.

Work of the eyes is done,
now do heart-work
on all the images imprisoned inside you; for you
overpowered them: but even now, do not know them.
Learn, inner man, to look on your inner woman,
the one drawn out of
a thousand natures, this
first now attained but
never yet truly loved form.[742]

These lines offer Rilke's most explicit embrace of (not some particular anima figure but) the psychological idea of the anima archetype per se. Correlatively, its title—"Wendung," or "Turning Point"—foregrounds the truly pivotal importance of anima in the *Elegies* and indeed all Rilke's late work.

As valid and necessary as Rilke's inward "turning" might have been, it nonetheless took form as a kind of psychological salvage operation in the aftermath of the Benvenuta affair—one that could offer, at best, partial success. In fact, the further course of Rilke's life and work demonstrates that his love was not so rarefied as to render other human beings dispensable. In the end, Rilke would not find a way of completing his *Elegies* until inspired by another, somewhat more successful relationship with another woman artist—the passionate, intelligent, devoted painter he came to call Merline. That encounter, however, lay in the distant future, on the far side of a catastrophe of an entirely different order: one that—inwardly as well as outwardly—threatened total annihilation.

When was it (I often ask myself) that I had Johannes Kalckreuth show me your house—I still see its quiet street and how simply it showed its face out of the garden—when was it? A few days later fate broke out of the foggy world, this world-noise which overnight drowned out one's thinking back and on beyond which no one is yet able to think...Who might say what is really happening to us now...To me it is an unspeakable suffering and for weeks I

> have been understanding and envying those who died before it, that they have no longer to experience it from here; for somewhere in space there will surely be places from which this monstrosity still appears natural, as one of the rhythmic convulsions of the universe which is assured in its existence, even where we go under. And indeed we are going under, into the midst of it, into the most existent—here one must look upon the fullness of destruction ...[743]

Thus Rilke to his friend Helene von Nostitz on October 21, 1914—roughly a month and a half after the outbreak of World War I. The war shook the foundations of the world—most immediately, and most devastatingly, the European world. The cataclysmic destruction it entailed inevitably engulfed the poet born and bred upon the continent's newly bloodied soil.

If Rilke had long been accustomed to reflecting upon—and even dramatizing—suffering, if he had long made death a favorite subject of poetic investigation, the phenomenon of the war brought such hard matters home with unparalleled force and intensity. True, the poet did initially greet "the war god" with enthusiasm, even composing hymns in his honor at the outset of the conflict. Reality, however, quickly sank in.[744] Already in late August 1914, Rilke spoke of the war as that "monstrous generality."[745] In September, it was "the nameless human doom that is happening unceasingly day and night."[746]

In point of fact, the war quickly plunged Rilke into a state of prolonged spiritual as well as material dispossession. Traveling in Germany when the war broke out in the late summer of 1914, Rilke found himself suddenly cut off from all the belongings he had left in Paris—the only semblance of a normal home he might claim. For the next five years, Rilke, based mainly in Munich, found himself confined to what he came to call his "German prison," struggling—often in vain—to maintain a modicum of inner balance in the face of the incomprehensible violence set loose in the world.

Rilke lost friends, and the sons of friends, in the war. In time, he lost, too, the thread of his most cherished work. The poet particularly lamented how the war tended to annihilate, not only physical persons, but the very possibility of maintaining individual consciousness in the midst of collective violence. In July of 1915, Rilke wrote again to Helene von Nostitz:

> Writing now means somehow prevailing over oneself, for what to write when everything one touches is unspeakable, unrecognizable,

> when nothing belongs to one, no feeling, no hope; when an enormous provision, gotten I know not where, of suffering, despair, sacrifice and misery is used up in large amounts, as though everybody were somewhere in the whole mass, and the single person nowhere; nowhere any longer is the measure of the individual heart...the unit of the earth and the heavens and all expanses and abysses.[747]

In November of the same year, building upon momentum generated from some shorter poems, Rilke managed to draw upon his own inner memory of that measure sufficiently to compose the dark and difficult Fourth Elegy. His creative momentum, however, proved short-lived. In January 1916, at the age of forty, Rilke was conscripted into service in the Austrian army. Though friends soon succeeded in rescuing the physically delicate poet from "torture" in the barracks—securing an appointment in the War Archives instead—the traumatic experience destroyed whatever inner equilibrium Rilke had managed to maintain. A full year later, he wrote to Lou: "Rest and work are still nowhere to be found in me following the Vienna rupture."[748] In fact, after writing the Fourth Elegy in 1915, Rilke—despite unfailing intention—would not resume work on the cycle until well after the war was over. While the last phase of Rilke's stay in Munich witnessed him actively, if tentatively, engaged in pacifist politics (his apartment was searched twice), he did not succeed in picking up the thread of his magnum opus until February 1922—more than six long years after he had composed the Fourth Elegy during that bitter Munich fall.

When, however, Rilke did finally accomplish the *Elegies*, the end result bore the traces of the devastating force of the war experience. Indeed, in the midst of the war itself, Rilke—even while succumbing to the numbing effects of the conflict—inwardly sought to turn the impenetrable darkness to account. The continuation of the October 14 letter to Helene von Nostitz attests as much:

> And indeed we are going under, into the midst of it, into the most existent—here one must look upon the fullness of destruction and suddenly know something of death. Perhaps this is what is meant by the terrible war, perhaps this experiment is going on before some unsuspected observer...who is examining this like a hardest

> sort of stone, and confirming the existence of a further degree of hardness of life under this upboiling death.[749]

One might well nominate the poet of the *Elegies* for the role Rilke describes here. If the war experience did not alone precipitate the poet's dive "into the midst of it," the existential ground of being that—paradoxically—finds itself linked with "the fullness of destruction" and death, it nonetheless lent its fateful power to the plunge already underway.

Malte, too, moved in this direction, but with a difference. Rilke's prewar novel takes the acute neuroses of a fictional protagonist as its point of departure. That particular persona—even while lending character to Rilke's existential explorations—delimits somewhat its range of application. In the *Elegies*, on the other hand, the poet, speaking more nakedly in his own voice, takes undisguised aim at the universal lineaments of human being—or, at the least, at the very fundaments of modern consciousness. One can suppose *Malte* to be about pathology, or personal history, or any of a number of other interesting and compelling matters, but most every reader understands more or less immediately that the great subject of the *Elegies* is nothing less than the nature and destiny of humanity, the contours of modern consciousness per se as these appear silhouetted against the abyss; the existential core of human being that begins to reveal hidden features even as its accustomed faces are torn away in the apocalyptic storm of the soul's dark night.

A letter to Princess Marie von Thurn und Taxis in 1915 provides further hints about Rilke's innermost attitude during the war years, the perspective from which he might seek, ultimately, to come to terms with the devastation in and around him:

> Ah, Princess, a few years earlier and I might have been able to bring up in my heart, then not yet so downfallen, visions that would have withstood even such a time, a *Stundenbuch* [Book of Hours] state of mind that would have had the power to treat the simply incomprehensible like *that* which in its essence transcends all understanding; for what do I seek more than the one point, that of the Old Testament, at which the terrible coincides with the greatest, and to show it up now...For even though no one cares to admit it openly, consolations would be needed, the great inexhaustible consolations, the possibilities of which I have often

> felt at the bottom of my heart, almost frightened to be containing them, the boundless, in so limited a vessel.[750]

This passage contains a number of provocative indications. We address these, one by one.

Notable first of all is Rilke's religious point of reference, his invocation of biblical precedent as a backdrop for reframing and redressing present tribulation. In the last chapter, we emphasized the religious cast of mind that prepared the inception of the *Elegies*. Here, I would make the related case that the quasi-tragic poetics of the *Elegies* owes a considerable debt to the one religious figure that haunted Rilke his entire life: a figure, it is true, that most people (unlike Lou Andreas-Salomé) do not see as belonging to the Old Testament but who, in Rilke's mind, did not really belong to the New Testament either—namely, Jesus Christ.

We have already noted that Rilke, in the wake of his Toledo-inspired enthusiasm for Islam, professed a "rabid anti-Christianity." Yet it was never so much Christ himself as the conventions of the church that Rilke reviled without reservation. He did so—at least in part—because he felt those conventions betrayed the real substance of Christ's own spiritual legacy. As his early *Visions of Christ* showed, Rilke himself wrestled mightily with the spiritual inheritance symbolized by the "tiny gold cross" chosen for him as his very first gift. His early *Visions* reveal a profound identification with the sublime and tragic figure of the solitary Christ even as they aggressively repudiate many central features of Jesus' Christian profile—most centrally, his deification.

As far as the *Elegies* themselves are concerned, Rilke's interior revisioning of Christianity accompanied their writing, from start to finish. Rilke's *Life of Mary* jump-started the *Elegies*, and his "Young Workman's Letter"—composed in the same burst of inspiration that produced the late Elegies—reveals that questions pertaining to Christianity's spiritual legacy preoccupied the poet to the end. Correlatively, several biographical details indicate that his own fraught relation to the figure of Christ remained very much on Rilke's mind in those years just before and after the onset of the war that count as part of the seed-time of the cycle as a whole.

When, soon after the outbreak of the war, Rilke discovered that the belongings he had left behind in Paris were indeed lost to him, the poet—who perpetually practiced non-attachment—professed not to mind overmuch. He did, however, confess troubling sorrow at the loss of a very few dearly treasured items.

> Two or three things, it is true—the daguerrotype of my father, an old picture of Christ that I have had standing before me since boyhood, and certain letters and particular irreplaceable books among all my several hundred—still follow me from afar.[751]

If Rilke had no use for conventional Christianity, he nonetheless still cherished *the relation with the image of Christ* that—by his own admission—had traveled with him virtually his entire life.

A still earlier episode testifies to the inner connection binding Rilke's *Visions of Christ* and his *Elegies.* In July of 1913, Rilke visited Lou in Göttingen. The two old friends spend twelve deeply meaningful days together; as Freedman writes, "a new spirit revitalized an old communion."[752] The first two Elegies had already been in Lou's hands for some time; when he left Göttingen, however, the poet made the significant gesture of leaving behind for Lou his old *Visions of Christ*—the work that had forged their initial bond. Lou's response (it arrived by post a few days after Rilke's departure) speaks for itself:

> Yes, I did indeed read the Christ Visions (they must be the same ones I keep copies of in my safe-deposit box at the bank) and they have made me see for the first time quite wonderful connections. So difficult to describe in detail in a letter! They read far differently from your two recent poems, the present elegies—and yet everything you have created has advanced along the same steady course between these Christ visions in the past and the approaching Angel visions.[753]

If the *Elegies* strive to plumb the heart of the mystery of human being per se, Rilke's implicit engagement with the figure of the Christ contributes substantially to the poem's archetypal power. Carl Jung helps us understand why:

> Christ...is the still living myth of our culture...our culture hero, who, regardless of his historical existence, embodies the myth of the divine Primordial Man...the psychological position of the Christ symbol (is) quite clear. *Christ exemplifies the archetype of the self.*[754]

We cannot here plunge into any extended discussion of what Jung calls "the myth of our culture"; even so, we can go so far as to cite certain signal features of that myth which find transparent echo in Rilke's *Elegies.* The most relevant, and most central, derive from the events of the Passion itself. Does not the poet of the *Elegies,* like the archetypal figure of the Christ, take it upon himself to *carry the cross* of humanity, to bear the agonizing weight of—if not its moral sin—its persistently vexatious ignorance and agonizing imperfection? Torn apart by the opposites that rend—even while they constitute—the ground of his being, does not the poet suffer (no rack of wood and nails but) a veritable *crucifixion* of consciousness? Does he not—like Christ on Holy Saturday—descend into the underworld and aim to emancipate the souls of the dead? Does he not—after the travail of *death and entombment*—ultimately find himself—and through himself, his earthly world—*risen* once more into a new spiritual life, redeemed and redeeming in the invisible sphere of the Word, the *Weltinnenraum* (inner world-space) that may perhaps be compared to Christ's "kingdom . . . within"?[755]

To claim the relevance of these Christian motifs to the *Elegies* does not for a moment imply subordination of Rilke's poetic and psychological initiatives to Christian influence but rather vice versa. The *Elegies* no more subscribe to any doctrinal beliefs than do Rilke's earlier *Visions,* which—as we saw in chapter 2—work to deconstruct the founding tenets of the popular faith. As noted, Rilke particularly objected to the deification of Christ—whether declared by Jesus himself or his disciples. Already in 1893, in "Christ on the Cross," Rilke articulated his conviction that Jesus' human greatness was betrayed if not negated by that gesture:

> He would have stayed so godlike as a man;
> as god he seems so human now, so small![756]

A kindred opinion finds expression in our 1915 letter to the Princess. The same passage we are reading continues: "It is certain that the divinest consolation is contained in humanity itself—we would not be able to do much with the consolation of a god."

In accord with this sentiment, Rilke's *Duino Elegies* effectively *restyle* Christ's Passion as *a work of human soul-consciousness.* In reading the *Duino Elegies,* we experience the signal events of the Passion—the carrying of the cross, the crucifixion, entombment, and resurrection—as they are *reenacted in transfigured form* in the inner space of the speaker's decidedly *human* subjectivity—a self-consciousness archetypally *psychological* and *poetic* at one and the same time.

That Rilke's *Elegies* make no allusion whatsoever to the events of the Passion or any other Christian topoi does not abrogate the archetypal relevance of the above-mentioned motifs or invalidate the mythic significance their mention lends to the *Elegies*' image of Self. That lack of explicit allusion does, on the other hand, highlight the near-perfect degree to which Rilke *interiorizes* the reigning mythos of western culture, unfolding it entirely within the psychological milieu of his own unique—and quintessentially modern—individuality: the soul-history of his own poetic consciousness.

If Rilke had long lived his life with an image of Christ figuratively "standing before him," in his *Elegies* he finally does justice to that image—insofar as he, Rainer Maria Rilke, could do so within the limits of his nature and destiny—those individual limits that were, too, the source of the poet's strength. It is thus fitting that when—after dream-crushing romantic disillusionment and the shattering horror of the war; after all the interminable barrenness and destruction and waiting—Rilke finally finished the *Elegies*, his celebratory announcement employed religious metaphor. To Lou he wrote: "Think! I have been allowed to survive up to this. Through everything. Miracle. Grace."[757]

If Rilke professed little interest in "the consolations of a god," he did crave relationship with some species of transcending verity, did reach toward an enduring spiritual reality that subsists beyond the distressing evanescence of mortal existence. The letter to the Princess declares as much, affirming his desire to reconnect with "that which in its essence transcends all understanding." At the same time, Rilke's resolutely psychological attitude, his refusal to credit ideas not passed through the filter of his own soul-experience, rendered recourse to traditional theological notions problematic and the whole issue of his relationship to any transcendent sphere particularly fraught. Both Rilke's inveterate spiritual thirst and the challenge it portends find voice in his letter's express desire to rediscover "the great inexhaustible consolations, the possibilities of which I have often felt at the bottom of my heart, almost frightened to be containing them, the boundless, in so limited a vessel."

We are here, once more, in the domain of Psyche's third labor—confronting, again, the task of containing something of the illimitable spiritual source of life (and death) within the frangible vessel of the human soul. In the course of this chapter, we have so far sought to accent the abysmal *depths* of experience tapped in the *Elegies*. Now, it is time to reacknowledge the corresponding *heights* to which Rilke's poetry aspires, its phenomenal reach toward a visionary power and perspective that might comprehend not only one individual's soul-experience but the order of the entire universe, the reason inherent in the cosmos: the invisible yet meaningful relations subsisting between human beings and angels, birds, beasts, trees, man-made things, and the eternal realm of the stars. This metaphysical register qualifies as a further outstanding feature of the *Elegies*' archetypal appeal, that distinct species of *universality* that, so far as Rilke's oeuvre is concerned, helps put the *Duino Elegies* in a class by itself.

We quote yet again—but with a difference!—this critical passage from Hillman:

> The modern vision of ourselves and the world has stultified our imaginations. It has fixed our view of personality (psychology), of insanity (psychopathology), of matter and objects (science), of the cosmos (metaphysics), and the nature of the divine (theology). Moreover it has fixed the methods in all these fields so that they present a unified front against soul. What is needed is a revisioning, a fundamental shift of perspective out of that soulless predicament we call modern consciousness.[758]

We've shown how the *New Poems* and *Malte* bring a contrary soul-*full* perspective to our view of matter and objects, of personality and insanity. The *Elegies* (even while including elements of those prior initiatives) do likewise in connection with the grand subject of *the cosmos*, the generally intelligible order and meaning of the universe, including—most vitally—the defining place and purpose of human life in the context of the whole.

No less than the primal experience of loss, this recourse to metaphysical contemplation of cosmic order counts as a characteristic feature of the *Elegies*' generic mode. Keyed to an emotively charged confrontation with death, the classic elegy strives to redeem human loss by comprehending it as part of a greater spiritual whole. By virtue of the nature and magnitude of that task, the elegy often bears real philosophic weight, its tone of lament incorporating repeated reflective turns as the poetic mind endeavors to come to terms with the endemic suffering of the soul.

In the universe of Rilke's *Duino Elegies*, all this transpires under the auspices of the being that stands as representative and guarantor of that higher spiritual order: the angel. If the *Elegies* strive towards "that ultimate affirmation to which young Malte... was as yet unable to conduct [life]" it was (as we saw in the last chapter) Rilke's conception of the angel that opened the possibility of making that giant—and gigantically difficult—step. The angel does so in his capacity as emissary of divine being, sign and guardian of the invisible intelligibility of the cosmos. To be sure, at the outset of the poem, the poet laments his inability to realize any viable connection to that order; nonetheless, the angel—even "in absentia"—certifies its reality and the promise of meaning it bears. The poet's urgent need to reforge his broken bond with the invisible spiritual reality symbolized by the angel drives the energy of the whole elegy cycle; the existential drama of the poem revolves around the all-important—and initially open—question as to whether he (and, by implication, we ourselves) can succeed in that heroic attempt.

Rilke's angel, however, could not have come into his own in any old poetic form. The transparently metaphysical character of Rilke's chosen genre proves instrumental in containing—as in a crystal jar—the vision and voice the angelic presence (or absence!) inspired.

That voice, after all, differs markedly from Malte's. Compare, for instance, the respective openings of the two works: Malte's laconic "So, then, one does come here in order to live; I would have sooner thought one died here" and the *Elegies*' urgent "Who, if I cried out, would hear me among the angelic / orders?" On the one hand, we hear Malte's sardonic declaration, the statement that drolly shares his feeling opinion; and on the other, the *Elegies*' heartrending expostulation, the interrogative that throws opens the doors of the heart and—even as it streams out into the seeming void—puts the question of the self to the cosmos, and vice versa. The query, rhetorical as it may be, introduces a *speculative* note which—while by no means wholly foreign to *Malte*—remains more fundamentally and consistently characteristic of the *Elegies* as a whole, a metaphysical inflection naturally suited to the genre. We need not put too fine a point on what, on some level, is obvious: the *Elegies*, while prophetic in tenor, are deeply reflective philosophical poems, their imaginative fabric cut from a rich cloth of ideas.

The generic difference thus hinted at is no minor matter; on the contrary, it ultimately amounts to a distinct style of seeing and speaking, a whole new method of poetic soul-making. Something of the gist of the difference between Rilke's elegiac mode and the respective styles of his two prior major works (*New Poems* and *Malte*) emerges in this important passage from Hillman's *Revisioning Psychology*:

> In chapter 1, which was mainly a reflection from the imaginative psyche, the *phantasia* of the archetypes emerged. We saw there the many images of their persons, their appearances as mythical figures, as *daimones* and Gods. Chapter 2, mainly a reflection from the affective psyche, brought out the *pathos* of the archetypes. We saw there that Gods are in the styles of our suffering, in the *casus*, the way things fall, shaping our case history into their myths. Now this chapter, mainly a reflection from the intellectual psyche, presents the *logos* of the archetypes so that we may recognize the Gods and their myths in our ideas.[759]

"This chapter" refers, naturally, to chapter 3 of Hillman's book, "Psychologizing or Seeing Through." Just as the first two chapters of *Revisioning Psychology* elaborated psychological initiatives integral to the art of, respectively, Rilke's *New Poems* and *Malte*, this third mode of soul-making underlies the poetics of Rilke's *Duino Elegies*, shaping, from within, the cycle's inimitable idiom.

Hillman, for his part, unapologetically declares the preeminent importance of "psychologizing." His third chapter begins:

> The question before us in this chapter is even more essential to the psyche than those with which we have been engaged. Now we shall be asking not only what is psychology itself, that discipline named for the soul, but what is *psychologizing*—the soul's root and native activity. Our inquiry will now proceed by means of ideas rather than persons, although the archetypal connection between persons and ideas should emerge...
>
> By emphasizing ideation, we shall be assuming the passionate importance of psychological ideas. We shall be showing that the soul requires its own ideas, in fact, that soul-making takes place as much through ideation as in personal relationships or meditation.[760]

It will surprise no one if we declare the *Duino Elegies* a philosophical poem, one particularly concerned with the realm of ideas. Tremendous critical energy has been expended upon deciphering the intellectual riddles implicit in Rilke's dense text and its array of formidable concepts. Yet a real interpretive danger inheres in the work's intellectual appeal, for a critical approach that attacks Rilke's putative metaphysics head-on can too easily neglect the poem's all-important *psychological* point of departure, its origin in *soul-experience* manifested, first of all, in the expression of anguish that opens the poem.

The *Elegies*—in accord with the tenets of the genre—enact a work of mourning. The cycle begins by giving voice to the despair of a soul that has largely lost connection with the spiritual world. Suffused with suffering, the entire poem nonetheless vibrates with the energy of the soul's hope of achieving some kind of reunion or reconnection with its spiritual source by way of poetic reflection upon its own nature. One does not, however, *mourn* what one does not yearn for and in some way *love*. From the first, the *Elegies* unfold within the universe of the human psyche's fraught relation to the transcendent spirit that in one aspect may be named *Angel*, and in another, cosmogonic *Eros*, the spirit of love itself.

The train of reflection pursued in the *Elegies* thus begins and ends in the precincts of the soul, building ineluctably upon the whole course of Rilke's psychospiritual career to date—including his intense involvement with anima and the whole soul-stream of the Psyche-Eros mythologem. While the *Elegies* certainly do represent a dramatic new chapter in that ongoing soul history, to construe Rilke's "ideas" outside the context of its mythic unfoldment risks abstraction that violates the archetypal premises of Rilke's vision. For Rilke's ideas, "abstract" as they may sometimes seem, do remain consistently psychological in origin and character; are quintessentially *psychological ideas*.

Psychological ideas, in Hillman formulation, are "those that engender the soul's reflection upon its nature, structure, and purpose." Expanding upon their character and thematic reach, he construes them as fundamentally *archetypal* in character:

> Major psychological ideas echo the deepest questions of the soul, bringing it to reflect profoundly about its nature and destiny. These ideas can more readily be called archetypal because they perpetually recur with powerful fascination both in the history of psychology and in our individual psychological history.... Some of

> these archetypal ideas arise from the soul's relation with death, the world, and other souls; with its body, its gender and generation; with virtue and with sin, with love, beauty, and knowledge; with Gods, with sickness, with creation and destruction, with power, time, history and future; with family, ancestors, and the dead.[761]

It is easy to recognize the signature of many of these archetypal concerns in Rilke's *Elegies*; indeed, the sheer scope of the poem cycle's archetypal interest features as one aspect of its compelling power. Even so, it is not solely or even primarily thematic purview per se that defines an idea as archetypally psychological, but rather the form of spiritual activity associated with it, the *reflective* motion that is, simultaneously, *interiorizing*:

> True psychological ideas circulate within a psychic field, arising from the psyche and returning to it. They self-reflect. That is their internality and is what gives them their ability to interiorize events. An event that is psychologized is immediately internalized; it returns to the soul.[762]

In another articulation:

> Archetypal ideas are primarily speculative ideas, that is, they encourage speculation, a word which means mirroring, reflecting, visioning.[763]

This last passage in particular clues us in to the intrinsic affinity between the character of Rilke's angel and the dominant mode of soul-making pursued in his *Elegies*. As we saw in the last chapter, the language of vision proved vital to the *Elegies*' conception, and—in one important letter—Rilke clearly associated his own idea of the angel with a self-reflexive interiorization of vision ("object and appearance came everywhere together, *as if an angel were blind and looking into himself*"). Correlatively, perhaps Rilke's most explicit characterization of the angel in the *Elegies* themselves culminates in a figure that foregrounds the angel's specular and reflective character:

> . . . and then suddenly, singly,
> *mirrors*: scooping their outstreamed beauty
> back into their own faces.[764]

Hillman himself—as his chapter title advertises—consistently construes psychologizing in terms of metaphors of vision, interpreting its principal activity as a kind of *seeing through* things. Hillman's favorite metaphor for the act of "seeing through" matches the phenomenal figure which Rilke—as his italicization of "mirrors" implies—most strongly identifies with angelic being:

> Best of all is glass. Glass in dreams, as windows, panes, mirrors, presents the paradox of a solid transparency; its very purpose is to permit seeing through.... Only when the alchemist could put his soul substances in a glass vessel and keep them there did his psychologizing work effectively commence. Glass is the concrete image for seeing through.[765]

"Only when the alchemist could put his soul substances in a glass vessel"—the phrase recalls a familiar task. In accord with the argument underlying this book, *psychologizing or seeing through* does not only represent the mode of soul-making characteristic of Rilke's *Duino Elegies*, but represents too (as we shall discuss further below) archetypal psychology's amplification of Psyche's third labor of love.

The association suggested here between the act of *ideation* and *angelic being* need not rest solely on textual evidence drawn from Rilke and Hillman. That association is, in fact, eminently traditional. In Platonic teaching—the language of which provides our very word "idea"—ideas themselves are, like Rilke's angel, numinous beings belonging to the supersensible noetic realm. Indeed, by Platonic pedigree at least, ideas, like angels, belong less to the soul than to the spirit (qua *nous* or divine mind), though their divine essence permeates soul-life as the substance and ground of its being. The very idea of psychologizing thus signifies *an activity intent upon capturing ideational or spiritual essence—which, in some wise, transcends soul as its source—in the vessel of the psyche.*

Of course, it is not only the idea of "ideas" but the founding terms of "archetypal psychology" itself that hark back to Greek roots. Hillman himself notes how—in keeping with Platonic tradition—ideas may be seen as the very face of the divine so that commerce with them assumes a distinctly religious character:

> Should the Gods express themselves in the psyche through its ideas, then *our occupation with ideas is at least partly a religious occupation*, a means of addressing the ideational face of the Gods

> and redressing our mirroring of this face. . . . psychologizing ideas involves us with the divine.[766]

The principal religious sources for Rilke's inspiration were not Greek, but Hebraic, Christian, Islamic. Nonetheless, this unspoken classical undercurrent—one that forcefully reemerges in *Sonnets to Orpheus*—helps explain (if it needs explaining!) why the philosophic quality of Rilke's *Elegies* does not conflict with their profoundly religious, indeed prophetic tenor; on the contrary. In the *Elegies*, philosophy, religion, art, psychology, literature, and history are not distinct fields, but confluent currents in a single stream of poetic discourse.

Let us, however, return for a moment to the key phrase italicized above: *Psychologizing figures an activity intent upon capturing ideational or spiritual essence—which, in some wise, transcends soul as its source—in the vessel of the psyche.* This formulation qualifies as another, less metaphorical means of seeing how *psychologizing* itself functions as a translation—into the theoretical language of archetypal psychology—*of the mythic act of Psyche's third labor.* No wonder, then, that Hillman's own discourse on psychologizing ultimately converges, not only with the angelic theme of Rilke's *Elegies*, but with the lead role played by the mission or *task* of the *Duino Elegies* in the drama of Rilke's soul history:

> Since ideas present archetypal vision, I do not ever truly have ideas; they have, hold contain, govern me. *Our wrestling with ideas is a sacred struggle, as with an angel*; our attempts to formulate, a ritual activity to propitiate the angel. The emotions that ideas arouse are appropriate, and authentic, too, is our sense of being a victim of ideas, humiliated before their grand vision, our lifetime devotion to them, and the battles we must fight on their behalf.[767]

In the case of Rilke, we may see that devotion in the poet's decade-long struggle to complete his *Elegies*, an epic quest that endured, not only through personal travail, but through the searing tragedy of World War I.

The four-tiered structure of Hillman's *Revisioning Psychology*, no less than the fourfold character of Psyche's labors, itself represents one expression of an archetypal idea. Corresponding fourfold schemes manifest in myriad forms throughout intellectual history: Aristotle's four causes (*material*, *efficient*, *formal*, and *final*); Aquinas' *sensible*, *acquired*, *material*, and *agent* intellects; Jung's *sensation, feeling, thinking, and intuitive* functions; Rudolf Steiner's *physical*, *etheric*, *astral*, and *egoic* sheaths—to name only a few. Yet the most famous and intellectually influential of all such four-tiered structures may well be Plato's exegesis of the so-called "divided line," immediately preceding and preparing the parable of the cave in *The Republic*.

Socrates, Plato's persona, declares: "We predicate 'to be' of many beautiful things and many good things saying of them severally that they are, and so define them in our speech."[768] As this, the opening of his argument, declares, Plato openly premises his theory of knowledge upon ontological grounds, a theory of *being* which (as his argument reveals) itself rests upon the ultimate reality of divine *ideas*. Significantly enough, the close association between ideas and *vision* we remarked in both Rilke and Hillman finds its paradigmatic articulation in Plato's exegesis of the divided line, the whole of which depends upon the analogy between *seeing* and *knowing*. By virtue of its indissoluble relationship with the sun, one of the "divinities of heaven" and "author and cause" of the light by which we see, Plato opines that the creator has "lavished" by far the "greatest expenditure" upon the eye, "the most sun-like instruments of sense." The sun itself appears to Plato as a visible image of the highest good, "the idea of the good" itself, and this understanding in turn leads to a crucial enabling metaphor: "As the good is in the intelligible region to reason and the objects of reason, so is this [the sun] in the visible world to vision and the objects of vision."[769] This primordial division into the visible or sensible world, on the one hand, and the intelligible or supersensible spheres on the other (the former, illuminated by the sun, viewed as an image of the latter) figures as a kind of philosophical analogue of the biblical firmament dividing "the waters which were under the firmament from the waters above the firmament,"[770] and remains central to the cosmology and epistemology Plato develops in his divided line.

As Plato's argument unfolds further, each of these original two (the intelligible and sensible) spheres finds itself further divided in two, yielding four distinct grades of being or reality. The first—or rather last and lowest—grade consists of *images*—shadows, reflections in water, and the like; the second, the actual *sensible objects or things* themselves (plants, animals, man-made things) which figure as the origin of those images. These two together comprise the realm of the sensible or visible world, while the top two levels comprise the supersensible, invisible, or ideal world. The third (next to highest) level pertains to archetypal ideas that—while they may be visibly represented by forms such as a circle—are themselves essentially ideal and supersensible in character, while the highest level represents the pure essence of the ideas themselves as such transcend any form of sensible representation. The four "affections of the soul" refer, then, to the modes of knowing correspondent to each of these four grades of ontological reality: *intellection* or *intuition* (the highest grade), *reason*, *understanding* or *belief*, and *conjecture* or *picture-thinking.*[771]

To some degree, the intellectual ground plan of Hillman's *Re-visioning Psychology* and the order of Rilke's opus from the *New Poems* through the *Sonnets* reflect the archetypal structure of Plato's divided line, tracing theoretical and poetical paths through the whole span of soul-being. The consonance of *vision* and *knowledge* in all three authors provides a degree of common ground that manifests in certain telling correspondences. Why, for instance, did the *third* major work of Rilke's maturity—the *Elegies*—prove so demanding, requiring the intervention of a superhuman rank of spiritual being (the angel)? Was it not because the *Elegies* represent a step over that central threshold dividing the intelligible from the sensible realms? Rilke's angel was himself a numinous spiritual being, an invisible intelligence, whose function it was (as Rilke himself said) to enable "representation of the supersensible," extension of vision into the unseen realm of ideal or intellectual form:

> Where once a solid house stood,
> a thought-form presents itself athwart our vision, belonging
> wholly to the mind...[772]

Hillman, for his part, duly progresses in his third chapter to a topic "even more essential to the psyche than those with which we have been engaged....the passionate importance of psychological ideas." Indeed, it is inevitably in just this chapter that he unabashedly acknowledges the Platonic ancestry of archetypal psychology's own epistemological premises.

> The archetypal position...suggests nothing less than an archetypal *episteme*, an archetypal theory of knowing....this theory of knowledge would follow the implicit connection between *episteme* and *eidos* in Plato, that is, we would start off by looking at all

> knowledge as the expression of ideas that have psychic premises in the archetypes.[773]

To be sure, other levels of possible correspondences are more problematic. Take, for instance, the question of the nature and order of the two lowest levels of the divided line—the half representative of the visible or sensible world. Plato's *second* level of knowing involves knowledge of sensible *objects*; the first or lowest, knowledge of the reflected *images* of those objects. Focus upon sensible things themselves, however, would seem to correlate most closely with the objective *Dinggedichte* of Rilke's *New Poems* as well as Hillman's discussion of "Imagining Things" in his first chapter, while the exploration of the more subjectively inflected realm of psychopathology pursued in *Malte* as well as Hillman's second chapter corresponds more closely with the realm of shadows Plato relegates to the level of picture-thinking (*eikasia*) often associated not only with "opinion" but with what we might call fantasy and even illusion. In *Malte*, after all, right from the beginning, we are in the realm of images so strongly and patently colored by Malte's own individual state of mind that any notion of purely "objective reality" recedes from view. Accordingly, it would seem that—if we abide by the sequencing so far presented in *this* book—Rilke and Hillman *invert* the order of things comprising the bottom half of Plato's divided line.

This impression both should and should not be cause for critical concern. On the one hand, we should in no wise feel too strictly bound to sequence when it comes to the relevant Rilke and Hillman texts. Hillman lays little if any stress on the respective order of his first two chapters, the themes of which in any event intertwine. Meanwhile, Rilke's *New Poems* (both parts) and *Malte* were conceived and accomplished more or less concurrently, and so represent complementary initiatives simultaneously pursued rather than temporally distinct projects. The same could be claimed, in some wise, for the full cycle of *Elegies* and the *Sonnets*, insofar as both were completed in a single remarkable burst of inspiration.

Even so, the overall order of Rilke's texts should in no wise be considered arbitrary. The critical, original "dividing line" appears to be the one drawn through the middle of Rilke's mature work, the "watershed" distinguishing the *New Poems* and *Malte*, on the one hand, from the *Elegies* and the *Sonnets* on the other; works devoted primarily to the sensible and psychical worlds, and those more immediately associated with and inspired by more ideal orders of noetic vision. We have already spoken of the "supersensible" vision afforded by the angel, and the transcendental inflection of Orphic vision—dealt with in subsequent chapters—announces itself in the first line of the sonnets. "A tree rose up / O pure transcendence."

But let us return, for a moment, to the *New Poems* and *Malte*. If the "proper ordering" of these two Rilke works remains ambiguous, Plato's scheme admits no such uncertainty. The reality of sensible objects must precede—ontologically and valuatively—the reflected images or shadows of the same. We could, it is true, force our reading of Rilke to fit this schema: an argument could be made that the objective insight essayed in the *New Poems* could in some wise represent a "higher" order of knowledge than the shadowy specters of fear and misery triggered by Malte's tortured fantasies. Certainly, the *New Poems*' concern with the ideal form of objects as they may be artistically realized in (sculptural) relation to cosmic space seems close to and in some wise preparatory of the angelic perspective introduced in the *Elegies* no less than do Malte's explorations of affliction and death.

To think along such lines, however, seems misguided, and risks passing blithely over underlying differences that set the poet's informing world view dramatically apart from that of the philosopher. While it may be suggestive to invoke the metaphoric resonances evoked by reference to Plato's divided line and the graded soul-reality it images, it should likewise be observed that the character of poetic insight achieved in the *New Poems* has virtually nothing to do with Plato's notion of "belief," and that Plato's lowly estimation of "picture-thinking" does not *begin* to compass the nature and value of the soul work Rilke accomplished in *Malte*, his imaginative fiction. We verge here upon an immense rift dividing the distinctly *psychological* perspective informing Rilke and Hillman's vision, on the one hand, and Platonic idealism on the other, a decisive divide hinging upon the irreducible unit of psychological experience—the image.

Hillman, for his part, despite the Platonic pedigree of archetypal ideation, would undoubtedly look askance at any attempt to make his thought conform to a system of metaphysical hierarchy. More fundamentally, the founding premise of archetypal psychology—that all the soul's knowing begins and ends *in the image*—turns Plato's epistemology willy-nilly upside down. As the structure of *Revisioning Psychology* indicates, this inversion does not necessarily obliterate all ideas of distinct kinds, or even grades, of psychological insight. Nonetheless, even while championing the preeminent importance of ideas, Hillman redefines those founding archetypal ideas as intrinsically and inherently psychological in nature—and that means, ultimately, embedded in the realm of image and—coincidently—psychopathology. "Because ideas express our complexes and their archetypal cores, ideas always have a psychopathological aspect."[774]

For Hillman, the soul never entirely transcends the lowest level of Plato's schema, because that is where the soul qua psyche abides, and what it *is*; image remains psyche's ontological ground, and all is else is pure metaphysic. Because the realm of image remains foundational, *"higher" levels of knowledge may only be admitted insofar as they are enfolded and incorporated into the soul's bottom line, reappearing as aspects of the cardinal faculty of imagination.* The idea of reason, for instance, need not be wholly rejected, but it can no longer be "pure" or pristinely dialectical (proceeding in and through ideas alone), but is transfigured into thinking by way of *archetypally psychological* ideas: "psychologizing, or seeing through."

Much the same may be said for Rilke.[775] Even while the *Elegies* and *Sonnets* attain to degrees of intellectual and intuitive vision that set them apart from Rilke's earlier works, these poems do not leave the realm of image or the endemic suffering of soul behind—if anything, they penetrate more deeply into it. In a passage from his ninth *Sonnet to Orpheus*, Rilke directly (even if not deliberately) references the category of "images...in water" that Plato associates with the lowest level of his divided line, yet affirms that Orphic knowledge consists, in good measure, in true vision into this most difficult and ambiguous order of things:

> Even if the reflection in the pool
> often blurs before our eyes:
> Know the image.[776]

Plato's exegesis, on the other hand, knows little or nothing of the deep truth of image or the dignity (even divinity) of creative imagination. Whereas Ibn Arabi's Sufism posits a medial imaginal realm *between* the realm of idea and sense, the image has no *real* place in Plato's scheme; ranked *below* the physical object itself, "image" tends to imply "imaginary" in the sense of invented, deceptive, and ultimately unreal. Imagination per se (if we consider it addressed at all in Plato's dialogue) consequently finds itself relegated to the lowest level of knowledge, beneath the beliefs or understandings constituting conventional and utilitarian perception of objects. A Cezanne painting of a bowl of apples, fruit of years of patient contemplation, would—in a strict construction of Plato's scheme—possess less reality, less insight into the thing itself, than anybody's conventional knowledge of the apple as a source of nourishment. No wonder Plato, obedient to the strictures of his uncompromising "logocentric"[777] idealism, would ban the poet from the Republic altogether.

How then, construe the root of this radical cleavage? The differing opinion of image stems from divergent archetypal ideas: conflicting myths of the nature, origin, and destiny of the human soul.

Plato's philosophy conceives the soul to be a native, in truth, of the noetic sphere of being; imagines, correlatively, the soul's sojourn here on this earth as a forgetful fall from those higher heavenly reaches. Accordingly, realizing the soul's destiny requires, above all, return to its celestial home—an epistrophe that necessitates leaving this temporal realm behind and attaining to vision cleansed of the obscurities bred of earth's insubstantial shadows, the deceptive puppetry of life in the cave. The ethical philosopher may feel obligated to return from the higher reaches to help educate and enlighten others, but this only confirms that the earth—in its intransigent mutability, its nature as a stage of passing show—does not count as the soul's true home, and that authentic knowledge of itself must come, not from here, but elsewhere.

The tradition of depth psychology, on the other hand, possesses a conspicuously different vision of the nature of the soul qua psyche, one rooted in the very element of earth that Plato effectively disdains. True, depth psychology does not dissemble the dark unconsciousness inherent in psyche's natural state, or deny the confusion, suffering, and death inherent in earthly existence. Even so, Jung's chthonic vision regards the figurative cave—the space in or under the earth-world—as no loathsome cell of ignorance, but the womb of imaginal life, tomb of buried treasure, and psyche's rightful ancestral home. The soul as vessel of imagination, containing not merely celestial vision but infinite depths; the soul that achieves (not mere opinion but) real imaginative knowledge of the mutable, constantly transforming earthly world—embodied knowledge that is, too, *underworld* knowledge of the shadows born of the encounter with death—Plato does not credit such vision, occluded by the light. Nor could the divine philosopher ever worship the "dark God" like to a web of roots that Rilke—deeply psychological poet that he is—discovered in Russia, and never really left behind.

Apuleius, though, is another story. The ancient sage's remarkable tale likewise posits an earthly origin for the human soul named Psyche, albeit one that is, too, originally touched—and even engendered by—eternal love and beauty.

At the very beginning of his tale, Apuleius gives an account of Psyche's birth, recounts the popular legend inspired by her astonishing beauty: "It was certain they said, that heaven had rained fresh procreative dew, and earth, not sea, had brought forth as a flower a second Venus in all the glory of her maidenhood."[778] Because Psyche's beauty naturally indwells her mortal and her earthly origin—because her existence here is not essentially a fallen one but rather graced by a nigh divine beauty—Psyche contains within herself the seed of the transfigurative redemption of the mortal (temporal) sphere, a redemption that does not take the form of abandonment of the earth, but of its *transformation* (*Verwandlung*) and consequent realization of its connection with authentic being.[779] Psyche, of course, suffers the contradiction inherent in her nature: she represents the paradox of quasi-divine beauty residing in a mortal frame, and is crucified because of it. Yet that crucifixion is the necessary preliminary to the redemptive transfiguration which requires a relation to not only divine Reason (logos) but divine Love (eros) as well.

Let us put the gist of the matter in dramatic or narrative terms. Plato's divided line and parable of the cave tell a story of one chief character—the soul—ascending from darkness to light as it climbs the ladder of Reason—and perhaps, ultimately, descending once more to guide other benighted souls. Apuleius' tale, on the other hand, speaks of not one but two chief protagonists, Psyche and Eros, the Soul and the Spirit of Love. Given that one boasts heavenly pedigree while the other is born and bred on earth, the quest for spiritual consummation takes the form of a ***dual** motion of ascent and descent*; simultaneously an upward striving *and* a penetration down and in; and ultimately a sacred marriage (*hieros gamos*) of above and below that achieves both transcendence of *mere* mortality *and* a transformative immanence of spirit in the body of the world soul.

We are back, here, in the frame of Rilke's favorite El Grecos, back in the landscape of an ideal city (Toledo—Rilke's "Republic") kin to the figure of the Virgin Mary, "a woman of heaven and earth" connecting (along with her accompanying angel) the heights *and* the depths, the worlds of spiritual life and physical death, eternality and mortality, in one integral vision. We are back, too, in the terrain of Rilke's mature poetic opus (*New Poems, Malte, Elegies, Sonnets*), which reads as if the whole cosmic scale of being and knowing figured by the divided line were *interiorized within* the human psyche, *imploded* within the *creative imagination* of the soul, and as if the poet were scaling it—climbing ever high *and* lower, ever further up and ever further down and in.

We cannot, however, pretend to ascend too soon; cannot too summarily dismiss the desperate plight of the denizens of the cave by waving a magic, mythic wand over the terrible infelicities that plague earthly existence. Rilke does not. While his psyche, his archetypal human soul, may glimpse its destiny in the image of "a woman of heaven and earth," Rilke—despite his first two names—hardly claims, at the outset of the *Elegies*, the purity or wisdom embodied in the Life of Mary. Instead, as we have seen, his poem begins with bitter lament of the kind of sorrowful condition Plato portrays in his parable of the cave: evokes the human soul estranged from its spiritual source, a prisoner—in love as well as life—of mutable realms that render all bliss purely transient, and all knowledge deceptively uncertain.

The redemptive transfiguration of the human soul and of the earth qualifies as the great theme of the *Elegies*. Rilke's cycle works toward the idea of a distinctly human—and distinctly poetic—consciousness capable of reconnecting the dual realms of heaven and earth, spirit and matter, angelic being and earthly existence, eternity and time, life and death, invisible idea and manifest thing. That consciousness, however, does not appear fully achieved at the outset; the psychic vessel capable of receiving the water of life appears incompletely formed and is riven by the contradictions that comprise its being. The soul-making work of the *Elegies*, inscribed in the sequential form of the cycle, unfolds by means of *psychologizing or seeing through* the conditions that bind the soul to purely temporal existence, to a conflicted state of non-being, ultimately enabling, not abandonment of its earthly state, but its poetic *transformation*. Rilke may not be a Platonist, but the parable of the cave may be quite relevant to his initially uninitiate psyche after all, and the need for the *illumination* provided by ideas equally urgent *so long as those ideas—passed through the alembic of the thought of the heart—are* ***archetypally psychological*** *ideas* unfolding (rather than betraying) Rilke's linked imaginations of the earth, the angel, and their poetic intermediary—the soul of the human being.

Chapter 16

FULL SPHERE AND ORB OF BEING

We have sought to evoke both the depths and the heights inscribed in the imaginative geography of Rilke's *Duino Elegies*: the abyss of being that elicits the poet's cry of anguish as well as the steep reach of mind—inspired by the numinous angel—which he essays. The *Elegies* express both agony and ecstasy, and the cycle's existential drama enacts the turning of one into the other as the soul's mortal tribulation finally becomes the ground of its poetic celebration. This archetypal passage from darkness to light—this transformation of a self shrouded in ignorance into one in spiritual possession of itself—may well be understood as a path or process of *initiation*.

Rilke himself was familiar with the concept of initiation, especially in connection with those ancient mystery schools whose ritual practices typically revolved around some kind of (simulated) death experience. In a 1923 letter, Rilke alludes to initiation in a long passage that resonantly echoes his *Elegies*:

> I reproach all modern religions for having handed to their believers consolations and glossings over of death, instead of administering to them the means of reconciling themselves to it and coming to an understanding of it. With it, with its full unmasked cruelty; this cruelty is so tremendous that it is just with it that the circle closes: it leads right back again into the extreme of a mildness that is great, pure and perfectly clear.... But toward the experiencing of this most profound mildness which... could perhaps little by little penetrate and make *transparent* all the relations of life... mankind has never taken even the first steps,—unless in its oldest, most innocent times, whose secret has been all but lost to us. The content of

> "initiations" was, I am sure, nothing but the imparting of a "key" that permitted the reading of the word "death" without negation; like the moon, life surely has a side permanently turned away from us which is not its counterpart but its complement toward perfection, toward consummation, toward the really sound and full sphere and orb of being.[780]

This passage implies that the telos of Rilke's poetry includes—as one important aspect—some form of recovery or (better) contemporary rebirth of ancient mystery wisdom. In a 1913 essay that sets out to describe "the essence of a poet," Rilke declares "What else but *prehistory* [*Vorzeit*] breaks out in hearts assaulted by such forces?"[781] Consonantly, his *Duino Elegies*—even while cutting a distinctively early-twentieth-century figure—are infused with the aura of mystery shrouding those "oldest times," most especially toward the elegy cycle's end.

The last four *Duino Elegies* all make some mention of ancient culture. Egypt in particular emerges as a crucial point of reference as the poetic imagination spirals towards climax. In the pivotal Seventh Elegy, the poet draws upon Egyptian symbolism as he strives to articulate the goal of his poetic quest—a renewed vision of the archetypal nature of the human being. The relevant passage opens with lines rich in Hölderlinian overtones:

> Each dull turn of the world leaves such disinherited,
> to whom neither the past nor the coming life lends substance.
> For to humans even what comes next lies far away.

As the passage continues, Rilke evokes the destruction and disorientation bred of the war even as he bends historical time back on itself; imagines his own contemporary vision *reconnecting* with ancient forms of knowledge potently symbolized by that venerable icon of ancient Egypt, the Sphinx:

> This ought not baffle us but strengthen our defense
> of a still recognized form.—This once *stood* amidst men,
> stood amidst Fate, the destroyer, stood
> amidst Not-Knowing-Whither, as if it were alive there,
> and arched stars closer from safeguarded heavens.
> Angel, now *you* shall see it, too—*there!* In your gaze
> it stands secured at last, erect for eternity.

> Pillars, pylons, the Sphinx, the cathedral's
> gray upward striving from a vanishing or alien city.
> Miracles! O stand in wonder, Angel, for it was *us*...[782]

In the Tenth Elegy, too, the sphinx appears as a symbol of the true spiritual stature of humanity. In this elegy's allegorical landscape, the newly departed youth and his Lament-guide encounter

> ...the exalted Sphinx—: visage
> of the hidden chamber.
> And they marvel at that kingly head, which silently,
> for all time, has weighed the human face
> in the stars' balance.[783]

Why the prominence of the riddling figure of the Sphinx? A passage from Edouard Schuré's book *The Great Initiates* offers perspective on this question:

> A man's head emerges from a bull's body with lion's paws, and folds its eagle wings at its sides. It is...a portrayal of the living unity of nature's kingdoms....In this composite...are also contained the four animals of Ezekiel's vision, representing the four constituent elements of the microcosm and macrocosm: water, earth, air and fire, the foundations of esoteric science. This is why, in subsequent centuries when the initiates saw the sacred animal lying on the steps of the temples or in the recesses of crypts, they felt this mystery come to life within them...For before Oedipus, they knew that the answer to the riddle of the sphinx is Man, the microcosm, the divine agent who includes within himself all the elements and forces of nature.[784]

Schuré's entire book revolves around the theme of initiation. As the cited passage suggests, the human being himself stands as both *subject* and *object* of initiatic vision: he is the *subject* undergoing the travail of initiation, the ultimate *object* of which is not some excarnated state of bliss but authentic self-knowledge, revelation of the true scope and character of his own (human) being. In the logic of initiation, moreover—as Rilke's own letter implies—knowledge of death functions as the portal to any realization of the cosmological nature and purpose of humankind. It is only by transcending identification with purely temporal being (which does *not* mean permanent detachment from the sphere of earthly life) that the initiate comes into the larger self-consciousness reflective of—and integral to—the whole cosmic order.

Rudolf Steiner—a contemporary of Rilke's who explored the ancient mysteries far more deliberately than the poet—construes the process of initiation as fundamentally twofold in nature, consisting essentially of processes of *purification* or *catharsis* and *illumination*.[785] Both of these—and indeed their confluence—may readily be seen at work in Rilke's *Elegies*, reflecting the depths of soul and spiritual heights the poem explores. The poet's extended lament works to purge or cleanse dark soul-emotion, enabling, finally, spiritual illumination: a "seeing through" to the other side that (prospectively, at least) "makes *transparent* all the relations of life."[786]

The *Duino Elegies*, however, represent a quite unique instance of initiatory experience. Rooted in existential circumstance, recognizably human emotion, and intellectual reflection, the *Elegies* begin and end as a testament of soul-experience; remain profoundly *psychological* in character even as they reach toward the spiritual ground of human being. Coincidently, the soul-consciousness inscribed in the poem lives and breathes through the medium of language; is originally and intrinsically *poetic* in nature. This psychological and poetic texture is not in itself exceptional, *but it is so when (as in the* Elegies*) it simultaneously serves as vehicle and vessel of initiation*, for the degree and kind of *embodiment of consciousness* thus effected is by no means the norm when it comes to accounts of initiatic vision.

While some poets are mystics, most are not; nor are most mystics poets. In the *Elegies*, we do not merely possess record of a mystical rebirth of consciousness; *we have the form and substance of the initiatory experience itself* ***enacted*** *in and through language.* The *Elegies* do *not* recount spiritual experience which transpired some other time, some other place, some other way; biography and literary history bear witness to the truth that *the writing of the* Elegies *was—and is—the (initiatory) thing itself.* Like the lacemaker of his "new poem," Rilke gave not only his eyes but his soul to his work, and the genius of that soul continues to live transformed in the ongoing life of his poetic word, most palpably perhaps in the subsequent work it has inspired.[787] As Rilke himself recognized, the *Elegies* reach far beyond the limited consciousness we designate by his proper name; precisely because he so fully embodied his vision in language, it can belong as much to us—his readers—as to him.

That much said, we would do well to attend in detail to the salient specifics of Rilke's initiatory text, the archetypal *poetics of his Elegies*. We shall therefore interrogate more closely how Rilke's poetry—the sum of the speech acts inscribed in his language—works to purify and (ultimately) illuminate the soul-consciousness remaking itself in and through the writing of the poem. We begin by revisiting the topic of the *Duino Elegies*' generic form.

Already in the last chapter, we alluded to the touchstone of the elegy form—lamentation of loss leading to contemplation of some larger spiritual whole. Now we can enter into more detail on this score. Rilke's *Duino* cycle self-consciously participates in the rich tradition of the classical German elegy distinguished by the likes of Goethe, Schiller, Hölderlin, and others. In his definitive study of the form, Ziolkowski describes the essence of the sub-genre in the following terms:

> The classical German elegy would seem to be an extended poem in elegiac distichs, organized as a first-person framework embracing a central meditative core and moving from thematic tension toward resolution.... The characteristic elegiac tension... arises from a contrast within the meditative core between two ostensible opposites: the real and the ideal, present and past, freedom and necessity, society and nature, temporality and timelessness—in effect, any duality that obsesses the writer and his times.

Though Rilke's *Elegies*—like his *Sonnets to Orpheus*—permute the metric typical of the genre, the signal features of Ziolkowski's description (the first-person framework, the meditative core, the thematic tension) cast a fitting generic mold for Rilke's cycle. Ziolkowski elaborates further:

> The elegy is an extended poem because it does not merely state this opposition apodictically: it permits *the elegiac tension* to *emerge fully* through meditation. *The poetic persona* of the framework is introduced initially as still very much enmeshed in the tensions of the poem... But by the time the poetic persona reappears in the concluding part of the framework, it has been *elevated through meditation*, whose intensity produces a timeless state of entrancement, to *a higher level of consciousness at which a resolution is seen as possible.*[788]

All this fits Rilke's *Duino* cycle to a T. We may accordingly employ Ziolkowski's generic description as a template for investigating Rilke's initiatory poetics, examining—one by one—our author's distinctive styling of its defining elements: first, the *elegiac tension*; second, *the (first-person) poetic persona*; thirdly, the poetic means of *developing* the elegiac tension (allowing it "to emerge fully") and the commensurate means of its *elevation through meditation*; and, lastly, the character of that *"higher level of consciousness at which a resolution is seen as possible"* (in the vocabulary of initiation, the illumined state of being). These are complex, integrally interwoven matters; nonetheless, we shall do what we can to shed light on them. At many points, we will find apt cause to refer again to the mode of soul-making Hillman calls psychologizing, for initiation, too, involves "seeing through."

Rilke's *Elegies* revolve around not one single oppositional tension but a set of closely related contraries. Komar provides one terse formulation: "The tension for Rilke is generated between his desire to reach beyond the human to the transcendent realm of the angels and his intense appreciation of the physical world to which he is bound."[789] Building upon our discussion in the last chapter, we might similarly construe the key tension to be that subsisting between the two "halves" of Plato's dividing line—that primordial stroke through the heart of the universe that separates the intelligible from the sensible world, the more enduring invisible order of being from the visible, earthly realm subject to incessant change and mutation. To gain a still deeper and more comprehensive understanding of the whole gamut of metaphysical differences that underlie Rilke's *Elegies*, however, it may be enlightening to refer to yet another ancient text—one that covers much the same ground that Plato does but in its own distinctly illuminating wise; a text, moreover, steeped in the aura of ancient Egyptian lore so relevant to the mood of Rilke's late *Elegies*.

The collection of writings known as the *Corpus Hermeticum*—originally attributed to the quasi-mythical sage Hermes Trismegistus but actually composed in the second and third centuries near Alexandria—represents a compelling confluence of ancient Egyptian myth and mystery wisdom, Greek philosophy, and biblical culture. The eleventh text—*Mind to Hermes*—begins with the fabled Trismegistus requesting—and receiving—instruction in metaphysics and cosmology from the Divine Mind (Mind or *Nous*) itself:

> "Since people have said many contradictory things of all sorts about the universe and god, I have not learned the truth. Make the truth plain to me, master; it is you alone on whom I may depend to reveal it."
>
> "Mark my words, then, Hermes Trismegistus, and remember what I say. I will not hesitate to speak what occurs to me. Hear how it is with god and the universe, my child.
>
> "God, eternity, cosmos, time, becoming.
>
> "God makes eternity; eternity makes the cosmos; the cosmos makes time; time makes becoming. The essence (so to speak) of god is [the good, the beautiful, happiness,] wisdom; the essence of eternity is identity; of the cosmos, order; of time, change; of becoming, life and death. But the energy of god is mind and soul; the energy of eternity is permanence and immortality; of the cosmos, recurrence and counter-recurrence; of time, increase and decrease; of becoming, quality (and quantity). Eternity, therefore, is in god, the cosmos in eternity, time in the cosmos, and becoming in time."[790]

This passage offers much to think about to any mind that has not (as is unfortunately too often the postmodern prejudice) *a priori* decided that all metaphysic is mystifying nonsense. How does the teaching offered to Hermes compare to that propounded in Plato's divided line? The respective intellectual visions are quite complementary, though to coordinate them we must construe Hermes' (or Mind's) "god" as a transcendental source of the grades of Being and Knowing elaborated in the Divided Line rather than one of the levels of the Line itself. Thus we would have—corresponding to the four levels of Plato's line—the following Hermetic scheme:

	God	**(wisdom; mind and soul)**
1.	Eternity	(identity; permanence and immortality)
2.	Cosmos	(order; recurrence and counter-recurrence)
3.	Time	(change; increase and decrease)
4.	Becoming	(life and death; quality and quantity)

Because of its cosmological specificity, Hermes' teaching may permit us to understand the fundamental tension underlying the energy of Rilke's

Elegies more fully. The primary opposition remains the same, inhering in the critical difference between the enduring order of the cosmos—indeed eternity itself—wherein spiritual being (the angel, for instance) *is* what *is*, perpetually or everlastingly; and the "lower" earthly realms of Time and—especially—Becoming, the world of multiple distinct things and persons that live, change, and die.

That all too transient world of becoming is, of course, the earthly world in which we dwell—and the world the poet of the *Elegies* finds himself in at the outset of the poem, his psyche beset by existential despair on account of the awful cleft between himself and the higher spiritual state of being represented by the angel. Hermes' teaching—like Plato's parable of the cave—helps us interpret the deeper reason for that despair. Attributing *identity* (self-consistent being) to eternity implies, correlatively, that within the realm of becoming—*when that realm is isolated from the larger order within which it is embedded*—neither objects nor human subjects *are what they are in and of themselves*, but instead are riven by (internal) difference; afflicted by flux. Rilke laments states of impermanence, division, and inauthentic existence in myriad ways in the *Elegies*: he bewails the love that disappears even as it is tasted (Second Elegy); regrets the condition of nigh ineradicable division *within* the self as well as that between the self and its world seemingly characteristic of the human state ("That's what Fate means: being opposite, and nothing else, and always opposite"—Eighth Elegy); and excoriates the utter superficiality of life lived and experienced as if it were naught but a passing show, a banal soap opera of bourgeois boredom (Fourth Elegy) or a carnival of cheap thrills (Tenth Elegy).

Even so, Hermes' teaching (again, like Plato's) does not lead us to regard that alienated condition as an inescapable fate, for the difference between mortal and eternal life is by no means an incontrovertible one. Hermes (or rather "Mind") declares: **"Eternity, therefore, is in god, the cosmos in eternity, time in the cosmos, and becoming in time."** Ideally, a fundamental *continuity* subsists between all the levels of being, with each level *participating* in every other. Indeed, the source of spiritual desolation and despair—in Rilke no less than in Plato or Hermes—lies not in the order of the universe, but in the darkened vision of the soul trapped in what appears to it as a purely phenomenal reality devoid of deeper meaning; a *psyche* unable to relate its experience of the flux of thought, sensation, and emotion to those higher orders of consciousness (actually *internal* to its own being) attuned to the cosmic order; *human* *being* mired in sensational circumstance so that space, time, and causality—the categories of existence—seem to operate upon it from some source *external* to itself, while the soul itself—its very life—seems hopelessly cut off from any sense of intelligible meaning or purpose.

Hence the need for the literary trajectory traced in the *Elegies*. It is the function of Rilke's purificatory poetics to initiate the individual soul or psyche into the higher orders of consciousness implicit in its being—*not* so as to abandon and betray its earthly existence, but so as to *see through* the appearance of its *purely* transient nature, *reconnecting* both soul and world to that "really sound and full sphere and orb of being." Beholding things and events within the context of the cosmic soul-space *both concealed and revealed* by them, the poet's illumined vision—prospectively at least—transfigures both the self and the things of this world. The precondition and basis of that transformation, however, remains deeper insight into the "essence" of the realm of becoming itself; the intimate knowledge of things that can only be attained by way of a penetration into the integrally related quintessences of *life* and (most especially) *death*.

All of this is more easily said than done, of course, so we had better turn our attention directly to further salient specifics of Rilke's literary deed: the poetic means by which the *Elegies*—working constantly through the plastic element and force of the creative Word—strive to accomplish the great task of self- and world-transformation.

How may we characterize Rilke's poetic persona, the *subject* of initiation, the brand of consciousness that moves through and shapes the work as a whole? That persona finds expression in the form of voice that speaks the poem; in the stance the poetic consciousness takes toward its world and the themes it chooses to make its own; and in the cast of imaginative characters conjured in the course of its quest for self-understanding.

We remarked earlier that Rilke's *Elegies* appeared more or less contemporaneously with Eliot's *The Waste Land*, and—like that other modern classic—takes a sense of spiritual desolation as its point of departure. Despite that initial thematic resonance, the style of the two poems differs drastically. *The Waste Land* is most certainly not a classic German elegy, and Eliot's voice varies dramatically. After the poet's initial lyric statement ("April is the cruelest month, breeding / Lilacs out of the dead land"), a different voice speaking a different language soon chimes in (*"Bin gar keine Russin, stamm' aus Litauen, echt deutsch"*)—just the first of a whole medley of distinct voices that speak (in) the poem. ("Stetson! / You who were with me in the ships at Mylae!".... "My nerves are bad to-night. Yes, bad. Stay with me".... "O O O O that Shakespeherian Rag."[791]) *The Waste Land* is no solitary bard's song, but snatches of often seemingly unrelated voices sounding together in strange and haunting harmony.

The voice that speaks the *Elegies*, on the other hand, remains singularly consistent. The tone and gesture of that voice does range all over the rhetorical map—now bitterly lamenting, now coolly observing, now jubilating; even so, it remains unmistakably one and the same voice throughout, manifestly the lyric poet's own. This unity of voice helps shape the poem as *a vessel of constant reflection.* The steady stream of speech flowing from a single well of consciousness enables the specular ideation that supplies the Elegies' mental substance, casting the poem as the transparent mold of the poet's own *psychologizing*, his interior and interiorizing process of "seeing through."

> Seeing through does not depend on the field of psychology nor require the language of psychology...Essential to it are *qualities of reflection which are conscious, intentional, subjective, signifying, interior, deep.*[792]

It would be hard to find a string of adjectives that offers a better description of the character of Rilke's poetic voice—a voice thus preeminently suited to unfold what Ziolkowski terms the *meditative core* of the classic German elegy.

The formal difference between the poetic voice(s) speaking Eliot's *The Waste Land* and Rilke's *Elegies* translates into fundamental thematic differences as well—differences that reciprocally condition our sense of the character of the poetic self. In *The Waste Land*, the fracturing of the poet's voice helps transmit a pervasive sense of spiritual disorientation bred of cultural exhaustion.

> What are the roots that clutch, what branches grow
> Out of this stony rubbish? Son of man,
> You cannot say, or guess, for you know only
> A heap of broken images...[793]

Rilke's *Elegies*, too, let it be known that many traditional sources of spiritual value no longer supply the human being a sense of real integrity, either because, like the angel at the outset, they are inaccessible, or because, like temples or traditional objects of worship, they are thoroughly outworn. This truth, however—while a vital and vivid register of the poem—does not finally set its dominant tenor. Rather, Rilke's *Elegies* ultimately highlight *the rejuvenative potential inherent in the depths of the individual soul and its relation to the cosmos.* Manifestly informed by all sorts of tradition, Rilke's persisting puer spirit nonetheless ensures that his poem remains relatively less bound and tied to historical culture than *The Waste Land*. Perhaps still more importantly, the *Elegies*—unlike a classic existentialist/absurdist piece such as Beckett's *Waiting for Godot*—do *not* communicate the sense that the cosmos lacks spirit or meaning; that the self is alone in a universe bereft of life or intelligibility; that the underlying elegiac tension between time and eternity, human and angelic existence remains unbridgeable. Indeed—despite the tone of despair that opens the poem—the First Elegy quickly provides contrary evidence, evoking senses of spirit instinct in the world at large.

After lamenting estrangement from both the angelic sphere and "the interpreted world," and halfheartedly invoking the routines that give the human being some residual sense of belonging, the poet feelingly remembers another, more promising aspect of the cosmos:

> O and the night, the night, when the wind full of worldspace
> gnaws at our faces—, for whom *won't* the night be there,
> desired, gently disappointing, a hard rendezvous
> for each toiling heart?[794]

The night and (in many later passages) the stars it holds; the cosmic space borne upon the wind that harbors inscrutable purposes—these are features, not of a universe void of meaning, but of pregnant mystery. The poet's initial despair is thus quickly leavened by more than a hint of hope, a sense of pervading possibility that provides spiritual refuge. Indeed, the poetic self quickly identifies itself with the mission of hearing the spirit that speaks in and through things, interpreting that hermetic sense which contains, too, answer to the archetypally psychological question that drives the whole poem: namely, the question of the nature and destiny of the human soul.

Feeling the unfolding spring, gazing at a star, hearing a violin, the poet declares: "All that was mission." A later, related declaration of purpose picks up on the early image of (something like) the wind, a traditional symbol of the voice of spirit:

> Voices, voices. Listen, my heart, as before now
> only saints had listened, while that vast call
> raised them off the ground; yet they paid no heed
> and kept on kneeling, those impossible ones,
> listening wholly absorbed. Not that you could bear
> God's voice—by no means. But listen to the wind's breathing,
> that uninterrupted news that forms from the silence.[795]

The poet here affirms his identity as a kind of religious prophet even while transfiguring the terms definitive of traditional religious mission. Deprived of immediate access to the voice of God or his angelic messengers—the sort of divine proximity that defined prophecy for the likes of Moses and Mohammed—he nonetheless affirms the quiet yet constant spiritual channel that may (if he tunes in) flow in and through him, the oracle lodged—not at Delphi or Sinai—but in the heart of his own being and the speaking face of the world.

While Rilke's poetic self is not (à la Eliot) fractured, its constant vacillation between hope and despair is by no means uncomplicated; the consistency of voice that facilitates deep psychological reflection hardly mires Rilke's *Elegies* in any *simple* egocentricity. While beginning in the first person ("Wer, wenn ich schriee . . . "), the *Elegies* do not remain narrowly centered upon a single subject. "I" quickly metamorphoses into the collective "we" and subsequently, in the train of urgent existential questioning, to "you." Though this second person functions primarily as a form of reflexive self-address, it does—like the "we"—invite the reader into the speaker's inner dialogue, especially on account of its specifically familiar form (*du*). The shifting pronouns—persistent throughout the cycle—function as one means by which the poem seeks to reach beyond the potentially restrictive bounds of its first, personal subject. Yet the *interpersonal* interest fostered by the pronoun play is by no means the only or even principal method the poet employs to widen the orbit of his speech so as to engage not only matters of personal concern, but truths of the modern psyche per se.

If we listen closely to Hillman, the first *word* of Rilke's *Elegies* may be heard to indicate the more important means by which the poet expands the reach of his subject(ivity). Hillman writes:

> Dissolving *what* into *who*, we follow one of the main styles of the questioning used with the oracles at Delphi and Dodona: "To what god or hero must I pray or sacrifice to achieve such and such a purpose?" The questions of why things are as they are, how they came about, and how to settle them—even those of what is going on and what it means—find ultimate issue in revelation of the particular archetypal person at work in the events.[796]

Rilke, it is true, does not routinely refer his most pressing questions of fate or destiny to one or another Greek God—the Second Elegy, in fact, ends by declaring that "we" moderns can no longer image the drama of the human heart by way of such figures. Still, the poem's opening "who" does evoke the being of the angel—even if he initially cannot be directly *in*voked.

The last elegy likewise opens—and no less powerfully—with direct reference to the angelic sphere: "Someday, emerging at last from the dark and difficult vision / may I break into jubilant praise to assenting Angels!" The poet's initial expostulation of despair and his climactic (if prospective) affirmation bracket the *Elegies*, setting them in an angelic frame. From first to the last, that silently divine interlocutor's putative presence (or absence) provides the crucial archetypal backdrop to the play of consciousness staged in and through the *Elegies*. The angel stands for the reality of the spiritual world, and the poet—even while questioning his access to that reality—never seriously doubts its authentic existence in its own supernal domain.

While the angel remains the chief spiritual character addressed in the *Elegies*, he is by no stretch of the imagination the only archetypal figure addressed in it. The poetic self reflects upon itself by way of reference to a whole panoply of archetypal figures—figures that serve to differentiate what could otherwise be a monolithic subjectivity. The angel, the lover (especially the woman in love), the hero, the youthfully dead, the girl, the acrobat, the mother, the father, the bird, the beast, the Lament—all of these, and more, represent archetypal characters whose *interaction* unfolds much of the "action" of the poem, the metaphysical psychodrama it stages. Hillman:

> Their [the archetypes'] tales and their figures move through phases like dramas and interweave one with another, dissolve into one another.... Their process is in their complication and amplification, and each individual's psychic process involves attempting to follow, discriminate, and refine their complications. Here is an ongoing Protean movement...[797]

...and, too, an apt description of the dramatically fluid play of consciousness enacted in Rilke's *Elegies.*

The diversity and complexity of archetypal form does not disperse Rilke's poetic consciousness. Despite overlapping archetypal planes, the outline of the *Elegies*' chief subject—the poetic self—does not dissolve or fragment into unrecognizability; nor does it (like the polyphonic voice of Eliot's *The Waste Land*) edge toward incoherence. The voice of the *Elegies* laments disillusion born of inner conflict and infirmity, but *not* radical disassociation. The poem's constant psychologizing—carried by the consistently reflective and unified character of the poetic voice—ensures that *the play it stages remains palpably and coherently interior*; remains, that is, contained within the soul space of an essentially unified poetic self that qualifies as author and subject of the poem, prophetic bard and half-tragic hero.

At the same time, this poetic self cannot *begin* to see or explore itself except in terms of diverse and diversely interacting archetypal figures. On January 23, 1912, immediately after writing the First Elegy, Rilke confessed as much in a letter to Annette Kolb:

> And then: I have no window on human beings, definitely. They yield themselves to me only in so far as they are able to make themselves heard within myself, and during these last years, they have been communicating with me almost entirely through two figures, on which I base my conjectures about human beings in general. What speaks to me of humanity, immensely, with a calmness of authority that makes my hearing spacious, is the phenomenon of those who have died young, and, still, more unconditionally, purely, inexhaustibly: THE WOMAN WHO LOVES. In these two forms humanity gets mixed into my heart whether I will or no.[798]

No wonder then, that, in the first elegies, the poet repeatedly associates those intuitions of meaning that lend him a defining sense of mission with these two archetypes.

After his initial invocation of "the night full of world space," the poet immediately asks, "Is it easier for lovers?" Evoking the spring, the stars, and the sound of a violin, the poet subsequently declares:

> All that was mission.
> But were you up to it? Weren't you always
> distracted by expectation, as though each moment
> announced a beloved's coming? (But where would keep her,
> with all those huge strange thoughts in you
> going and coming and sometimes staying the night?)
> No, in longing's grip, sing women who *loved*...[799]

...and proceeds to elaborate upon the theme of impossible love exemplified in the figure of Gaspara Stampa, the first in a litany of woman lovers cited in the letter to Annette Kolb. The lengthy meditation upon love—its initiatory power, and the limiting compulsions it tends to impose—represents the first sounding of one of the *Elegies*' founding archetypal themes.

The poet's deliberation on love leads directly into the more formal declaration of mission cited earlier: "Voices, voices. Hear, O my heart, as only / saints have heard...." This passage, in turn, culminates by directly connecting that defining sense of mission with the *other* type of being named in Rilke's letter, the youthfully dead:

> But listen to the wind's breathing,
> that uninterrupted news that forms from silence.
> It's rustling towards you now from all the youthfully dead.
> When you entered a church in Rome or in Naples
> didn't their fate speak quietly to you?[800]

Just as the archetypal figure of the woman in love centers Rilke's initial exploration of the love theme, the advent of the figure of the youthfully dead enables his first probe of another of the poem's founding themes: death. In the following passage, the poet imagines how it might feel to see and experience things, so to speak, from the other side:

> ...Strange,
> to see all that was once so interconnected
> now floating in space. And death demands a labor,
> a tying up of loose ends, before one has
> that first inkling of eternity.[801]

This passage, in turn, leads—after an important reference to angels moving in realms of life and death—to a final, concluding stanza that reveals how the *interweaving* of archetypes grounds the poet's sense of self as soul in motion. After speculating that human beings need the informing spirits of the youthfully dead in order to realize, intellectually and practically, who "we" are ("could we be without them?"), the poet asks:

> Is it a tale told in vain, that myth of lament for Linos,
> in which music first pierced the shell of numbness:
> shocked Space, which an almost divine youth
> had suddenly left forever; then, in the void, vibrations—
> which in us now are rapture and solace and help.[802]

Spender and Leishman provide a most helpful note here. "Sometimes the origin of song and music in general was connected with his [Linos'] dirge, and it was said that those who had been benumbed with fear and horror at his death were reawakened to life by the song of Orpheus."[803] The legendary figures of Linos (himself related to Adonis) and Orpheus bring together themes of love, death, nature, spirit, and rebirth in connection with the archetypal theme of song, opening a mythic window on the all-important question of the nature and destiny of the human being. The Linus-Orpheus story or "saying" (*Sage*) indicates that *the horror of death and the transience it imparts to all things may, in some fashion, be redeemed by song: the striking of a soul chord that bridges the gulf separating spirit and mortal body, the Orphic lyre that—remembering love—draws new life out of the womb of death.* The rhetorical question that *concludes* the first elegy thus provides a kind of framing answer to the one that opens it: if no angel will hear the human being's cry of spiritual distress, *the lament itself*—the sorrowing music—may come to fill the void. The archetypal elegiac poet plays upon emptiness as upon an instrument, and draws succor from the sound and motion of his own voice, the poetic voice which—reaching beyond the human voices that drown us—remains consciously and melodiously haunted by imaginal spirits.

Responding to the rift that underlies its experience of loss and engenders its defining thematic tension, the elegiac voice naturally pours forth in *lamentation*. The poet's voice does not, however, merely reinscribe that fissuring difference; rather, *the sounding* of the pain and sorrow it causes sets in motion the act of redress. In his essay "Rilke und Hölderlin: Hermeneutik des Leids" (Hermeneutic of Pain), Manfred Koch articulates a peculiar ontology common to Rilke and Hölderlin; one we may well regard as intrinsic to the elegiac mode itself. Querying why—in the aftermath of disastrous wars—so many educated Germans turned for solace to the work of just these two poets, Koch writes:

> Nowhere else in the history of German literature does poetry—in the face of threatened or indeed already realized loss of religious certainty—claim to interpret the very ground of the human experience itself as do Rilke and Hölderlin. Nowhere else is the transcendental homelessness of the modern human being... so lyrically conjured in the hope that *just this articulation of the loss of sense and meaning will nonetheless simultaneously lend voice to what may heal and restore meaning to life.* Nowhere else is there offered a comparable ontology of pain and suffering, or—to put it another way—nowhere else do just those experiences that afflict and indeed almost destroy the human being emerge as the signature of humankind's unique place in the whole of being...
>
> The turn of thought that perhaps most closely ties Rilke to Hölderlin follows from the metaphysical distinction thus awarded to pain: the idea that the conscious heightening of tearing division may make underlying oneness that much more palpable; that extremes of opposition will first release the power to bind and unify.... In [Hölderlin's] *Hyperion*, the hero of the title expresses the certainty that "göttlich erst in tiefem Laid das Lebenslied der Welt uns tönt" ["the world's song of life first sounds its divine tone in deep sorrow"]. In the lyrical melody of this prose sentence—as the sound-echo indicates—sorrow or pain [*das Laid*, i.e., *Leid*] is the ground of song [*das Lied*]; the tones of lament are simultaneously also already the divine tones of an all-unifying life.[804]

Eloquently stated, but just how *does* the tone of lament help move consciousness towards a restorative unity and wholeness? The end of Rilke's First Elegy—resonantly echoing *Hyperion*—hints at an answer: Rilke's final sentence highlights how ritual lament *may lead us out of the precinct of personal suffering* into the company of the likes of Linos and Orpheus; *into, that is, the archetypal realm of myth.*

By its very nature, myth possesses the capacity to bridge the difference between an individual's particular experiences (including those of loss and pain) and the *types* of experience common to many and thus representative of a more general and unifying order of things. Even the most common understanding of myth gives us to understand that it does *not* belong primarily to the order of facts or manifest events—the domain of empirical life and death Hermes construes as the world of becoming. Even though mythic structures do constantly *pervade* most all aspects of our material culture, myth itself (like fantasy, fable, and fairy tale) originates elsewhere; is rooted in a more purely *imaginal* sphere. In essence, myth registers *archetypal* patterns of being as they unfold within that mysterious, anterior sphere Hermes identifies—not with events *in* time, but with Time itself. To elucidate this more clearly, we resort to a literary critical elaboration.

In its *most* basic sense, "myth" is not some specialized genre of literature, but rather an underlying form of temporal motion constitutive of literature itself. Frye:

> [M]yth to me means, first of all, *mythos*, plot, narrative, or in general the sequential ordering of words. As all verbal structures have some kind of sequence, even if, like telephone books, they are not read that way, all verbal structures are mythical in this primary sense.[805]

Frye admits that this most elementary equation of myth and literature borders on the tautological; nonetheless, it does set in relief how *the very act of **giving voice** to sorrow—and **inscribing** that mourning in the form of a continuous sequence of writing—moves the raw experience of pain into another sphere: the sphere of ritual, myth, and literature wherein significant forms of repetition may shape sequences of signs or gestures into meaningful patterns.*

Above and beyond its most basic meaning, *mythos* qua *plot* implies, not any random progression, but the ordering or unfolding of a sequence of events in (verbal) time in accord with some overarching reason or intentional logic. In the classical form of myth, that reason (which may at times appear anything but rational!) derives from the numinous, transcendental characters called Gods. The Gods, for their part, personify cosmic principles—Hermes' higher-order "patterns of recurrence"; reflect, that is, a level of *archetypal* intelligence that can lend individual experience a degree of intelligibility, a quotient of sense or meaning that flows from participation in that larger, more permanent order of things. By means of effectively translating between enduring principles embedded in the intelligible order of the cosmos and the ever-changing flux of material and historical affairs, myth—in its most positive construction—plays an indispensable role in the creation of meaning in human life. Joseph Campbell:

> It would not be too much to say that myth is the secret opening through which the inexhaustible energies of the cosmos pour into human cultural manifestation. Religions, philosophies, arts, the social forms of primitive and historic man, prime discoveries in science and technology, the very dreams that blister sleep, boil up from the basic magic ring of myth.[806]

We are moving here toward one means of construing how—in accord with framework provided by Hermes' cosmology—the poetics of the elegy *begin* to move the consciousness of the speaker (and his reader) out of its initial alienated state into one attuned to more inclusive orders of consciousness. That end may be furthered by empowering the soul to participate in—not *only* individual experience of the transient world of becoming, the realm of appearances and singular events that all too easily come and go without evident meaning or order ("Tomorrow, and tomorrow, and tomorrow / creeps in this petty pace from day to day," intones one early model of alienated ennui)—but in the anterior sphere of Time itself *that is, too, the sphere of myth and the archetypal intelligences* that underlie personal experience.

"Is it a tale told in vain," asks Rilke, "that myth of lament for Linos..." The poet's own novel repetition of that original, archaic act of mourning aims to supply a resounding "no" to this rhetorical question. Rilke's poetic voice—pouring forth in the time-honored form of lament—helps transport consciousness out of a purely individual and existential frame of reference into a mythic one that enables connections with more enduring orders of things. Yearning to sound "the divine tones of an all-unifying life," that voice strives to connect the writer's singular existence with *both* the poetic tradition that reaches back to the beginning of human time (*Vorzeit*) *and* the higher and deeper reasons for being latent in the cosmic spaces of the night and the perduring stars the poet so repeatedly invokes.

It is not only, however, the archetypal form of lament that gives rise to the mythic resonances of Rilke's poem. The cast of archetypal characters that preoccupies Rilke's poetic imagination also contributes immensely to the mythic quality and power of his voice. Crucially, that cast enhances Rilke's capacity to *develop* the thematic tension underlying the *Elegies*, thus allowing that tension "to emerge fully." Indeed, Rilke's whole *cycle* of elegies exceeds the typical standards of the genre in this regard. Komar aptly comments:

> In the *Elegies*, Rilke not only permits his thematic tension to emerge through meditation but also dramatizes that meditation to enact the development of a poetics he has subscribed to since his early works.[807]

In accord with this insight, we would do well to interrogate more closely the dramatic and mythic means by which Rilke elaborates the fraught relation between the human psyche and the transcendent sphere of spirit. That transcendent sphere, of course, finds its initial, most spectacular symbol in the angel, but—as we have glimpsed already—the angel does not remain the sole representative of the energies of spirit in the poem. Rilke's cast of types (including those two singled out in his letter to Annette Kolb) allows the poet *to explore movements of accommodation and reconnection between the embodied human psyche and transcendent registers of being*—and to do so within a sphere of poetic meditation that remains palpably interior to the soul itself. At the same time, this mythic unfolding involves a consistent counterpoint: namely, those constantly repeated instances of persistent *disconnection* and spiritual failure that reinscribe and (à la Koch) even intensify the division between human and angelic being at the core of the cycle's originating tension.

Let us continue, then, by looking more closely at the mythic emplotment of the *Elegies*. We begin by touching base—yet again—with the mythic stream that flows through not only the *Elegies* but the whole of Rilke's poetic opus.

The sequence of Psyche's labors plots a course of increasing danger; each succeeding task effectively ups the spiritual ante. In her first two labors, Psyche does not directly confront spiritual sources: the mass of seeds contain seminal power in a benign—though confused—form; nor (due to the sage advice of the reed), does Psyche come face to face with the solar rams, but instead rests in the shade by the river until she can gather the golden fleece, unhindered, at dusk. In her third labor, however, Psyche herself must climb the dizzying mount and look directly into the dread fount of her own being, the sacred stream that is the spring of both life and death. The perilous prospect of capturing and containing "the water of life," the illimitable potency of spirit, in her own poor human being initially petrifies her: "quite overwhelmed by such vast inevitable peril, she lacked even the last solace of tears."[808]

The condensation of the myth does not allow for detailed elaboration of how Psyche must *overcome* herself in order to avail herself of the visionary power instinct in the eagle; how her mortal vessel may be clarified and prepared to contain the substance of spirit; how she may find the wings to navigate around the mouths of dragons. In the myth, so to speak, it happens more or less all at once, but the moment of Psyche's success conceals endless spiritual and psychological struggles, innumerable doubts and defeats as the soul attempts to make itself equal to the task. We may also suppose that if at first Psyche is stupefied—not even able to weep in grief and despair at how impossible it all is—the unseen path of her travail would nonetheless entail opening the floodgates of the heart: that her way to the fount would be, too, a trail of tears.

So, too, with Rilke's *Elegies*. We may note here that at least one of the two central archetypes Rilke singles out in his letter to Annette Kolb directly reflects the mythic undercurrent that flows continuously through his oeuvre. *The woman in love—especially the one whose love (a la Gaspara Stampa) appears impossible—finds her archetypal original in our mythic Psyche*, type of the embodied human soul. Accordingly, the *Elegies* begin in the precincts of the soul still suffering a devastating separation from the source of its spiritual life and love; still straying, homeless, in a kind of no-man's-land where (s)he can find shelter in no temple, nor succor in any god; slave to trouble and sorrow and bereft—*almost*—of hope. Rilke, however, unlike Psyche, did *not* lack the solace of symbolic tears. Ritually mourning his outcast state, his soul, weighed down by travail, sought its long and difficult path towards the heights—and depths—of spiritual vision.

Because the metaphysical difference between divine Eros and mortal Psyche mirrors—albeit with certain significant distinctions—that between the angel and the human soul, Apuleius' tale may figure as a mythic prototype for construing the means by which Rilke develops the thematic tension at the core of his *Elegies*. The Psyche-Eros story as a whole, especially the sequence of Psyche's labors, dramatizes the quest to wed or fuse the polar yet complementary energies of the protagonists, to contain and indeed incorporate the *transcendent and illimitable spirit* of eternal love in the vessel of the *mortal psyche*, transforming both in the process. Psyche's third labor, in particular, represents a relatively advanced and particularly fraught phase of this whole alchemical process. Psyche, little concerned with duration of her own existence, *ascends* the hoary mount of spirit, and, aided by Jove's own eagle, ultimately does manage to *contain* the "water of life" in her clear vessel. As befits the work corresponding to this labor, the soul work of the *Elegies* consistently involves a like dual motion: a *transcending* of the partialities that may render the soul incapable of approaching and sustaining a relation to spirit, and a complementary yet apparently contradictory delimiting, a *containment within finite bounds* prescribed by the human soul's earthly existence. The synergistic effect of these motions—imaginally enacted via the play of a host of archetypal figures in a variety of settings—issues in the *psychologizing* that unfolds in and through the poem, for (as we have already discussed) psychologizing represents the soul's intellectual effort to assimilate the truths of spirit into the fabric of its being. In Ziolkowski's terms, psychologizing doubles as the mode of meditative movement by which the elegiac poet strives to resolve the tension that engenders the poem as a whole.

In *Revisioning Psychology*, Hillman describes psychologizing as a mode of soul-making involving four steps—*interiorizing*, *justifying*, *mythologizing, and ideation*. He sums the whole integrated process in a sentence: "We tell ourselves a justifying story as we penetrate inward by means of ideas."[809] This mantra helps construe how psychologizing works to wed spirit and soul, for it is spirit (in the form of love, or other divinity) that provides life's *justifications*, the ultimate ends mediated by *idea(l)s*, while soul provides the *inner* space within which it may *plot* and unfold its reason(s) for being.

If we reflect for a moment on Hillman's mantra, we will see how aptly it describes the heart of what is going on in Rilke's *Elegies*. On the face of it, all four aspects of psychologizing—*interiorizing*, *justifying*, *mythologizing*, and *ideation*—are transparently and powerfully at work in the poem. The only sticky point, perhaps, may involve the storytelling dimension, for the *Elegies* are not exactly narrative. Even so, the sequence of the whole does trace a sort of plot—one that continuously revolves around the interaction of the *transcending* and *delimiting* or *containing* gestures associated with Eros and Psyche and (in Rilke as well as Apuleius) a whole cast of related and supporting archetypal characters.

Each of the ten elegies remains internally complex, yet each one pivots around specific archetypal figures and themes. Concomitantly, often one of the two primary types of energy—transcending or delimiting—*predominates* in any given one, *even as these archetypal energies continually transform and evolve synergistically* as the whole sequence unfolds. The First Elegy, for instance—after indicating spiritual limits suffered by the modern human being in contrast to the sublime power of the angel—highlights motions of transcendence. The poem proffers multiple images of *release* from purely temporal constraints—forms of spiritual progress enabled by connection with the spirits of great (women) lovers and the youthfully dead. The succeeding Elegies, however, by no means harp constantly on that consoling string, and give still greater weight to the *limitations* that constrict the consciousness of the human being.

Both Komar and Boney[810] have offered outlines of the overarching plan or plot of the *Elegies*, the underlying patterns of development and repetition that structure the cycle as a whole. While their methods and results differ somewhat, both definitively recognize the Fifth Elegy as the central hinge of the cycle. My own vision of the larger plot of the *Elegies* likewise sees the Fifth as the pivotal nadir of the cycle's movement—a structural fulcrum that (after the general foundation laid down in the First) sums and accentuates human deficiencies rehearsed in the Second through Fourth even as it sets the stage for a generally more uplifting second half. The Sixth instigates a more positive, upward motion that soars to a high point in the Seventh; the Eighth (in accord with the cycle's version of negative dialectic) sounds more or less of a full-scale retreat which, nonetheless, the Ninth recoups in its definitive resolution of the cycle's thematic rifts. The Tenth diverges from the rest in mode; it does not function as part of the main line of the poet's rhetorical argument, but (as Boney suggests) offers a kind of summary of the entire cycle in mythological form.

This skeletal plotting, of course, amounts to little more than the crudest sort of outline—one offered for the purposes of general orientation but inevitably missing all those significant particulars that can only be engaged via close encounter with each of the elegies, reading them in detail one by one. Unfortunately, that sort of reading would require—at the least—a book unto itself, and cannot well be accomplished here. Nonetheless, to advance our comprehension of how the cycle of Elegies develops its originating tension, we can endeavor very roughly to sketch the contours of the archetypal drama that unfolds in each of the elegies in turn, reserving the lion's share of our interpretive energy for a close reading of one of them—the Seventh—that represents the high point and thematic crux of the whole.

We have already parsed both the despair and, still more materially, the signs of hope introduced in the First Elegy. The Second through Fifth Elegies—while certainly including positive developments—foreground limitations that threaten to render the human psyche incapable of realizing its destined end, inadequate to the task of holding, within itself, the undying substance of the spirit. The transience of even the most inspired kind of human feeling; the sometimes uncontrollable power of unconscious instinct; the internal divisions that cripple human will; the impermanence that seems to afflict the core of our very being—Rilke's poems give poignant—even agonized—voice to all these difficulties, and more.[811]

> Every angel is terrifying. And yet, alas,
> I sing to you, almost fatal birds of the soul...[812]

Rilke's Second Elegy reintroduces the angel, emphasizing once more the distance between angels and men and women, the chasm that has opened between the vacillating heart of the modern human being and the angel's constant numinous power. Carrying forward the meditation pursued in the First Elegy, the poet focuses once more on lovers, for it is love's inspiration above all that promises reconnection with the realms of eternity wherein angels abide.

> Lovers...I ask you about us. I know
> you touch so fervently because...
> your embraces almost promise you
> eternity.[813]

Yet the lovers addressed in this second elegy are not necessarily those (like Gaspara Stampa) whose long-suffering hearts have learned phenomenal endurance, but more ordinary human beings who cannot *hold* high notes, whose most elevated feelings quickly fall prey to the ravages of time:

> For our part, when we feel, we evaporate; ah, we breathe
> ourselves out and away; with each new heartfire
> we give off a fainter scent. True, someone may tell us:
> you're in my blood, this room, Spring itself
> is filled with you... To what end? He can't hold us...[814]

The evanescence afflicting the motions of the heart goes to the core of our very being:

> O smile, going where? O upturned look:
> new, warm, receding surge of the heart—alas,
> we *are* that surge.[815]

This Second Elegy, while recognizing the divine fire love sparks in the human heart, doubts whether the *vessel* of our heart(h)s can hold or nourish that divine flame; fears (if we may alter the element of the metaphor) that the spirit's holy water must incessantly evaporate like dew upon the face of human life.

Still, the whole weight of the elegy does not fall upon the theme of how unequal (our) Psyche may be to (divine) Love. A contrapuntal motif also makes itself heard in the poem, an acceptance of limit as the condition of our specifically human being as—true to the dialectical psychologizing of the *Elegies*—the Second Elegy counterpoints the images of spiritual ascent or release evoked in the first:

> If only we too could find some defined, narrow,
> purely human place, our own small strip of fertile soil
> between stream and stone! For even now our heart
> transcends us...[816]

Acknowledging that we human beings have become so estranged from the realm of the gods that the movements of our own hearts, in love, threaten to exceed our compass; confessing too that we can no longer even consort with the divine via mythic images of the Gods, the poet would nonetheless delimit a territory that may rightfully be claimed as our (human psyche's) own, a space of containment that may—in the last analysis—secure our place in the scheme of things.

The Third Elegy deepens and complicates the archetypal ground of love. This Elegy introduces the masculine type of the youthful lover (shades of the puer) and sets him in relation to—not only his feminine counterpart, the girl or maiden, but a whole host of unconscious forces that fill out his nature, lending it archetypal depth and drive. Evoking the unruly force of instinctual desire, the elegy thus shows eros at work in the element of psyche, revealing, too, *erotic power conditioned* by a whole complex of ancestral *psychic* forces—a theme that resonates with the mythic image of the *wounded* Eros confined in his great mother's house while Psyche labors on.

At the end of the poem's first stanza, the poet does posit a provisional linkage between desire and destiny:

> You stars,
> does not the lover's delight in his beloved's face
> come from you?[817]

At the same time, multiple ancestral energies complicate love's celestial directions. As the poem's penultimate stanza makes clear, love's seminal impulse seldom flies straight as an arrow, but may readily be diverted down all kinds of archetypal corridors:

> O girl,
> *this*: that we've loved, *within* us, not that one person yet to come,
> but all the weltering brood; not some single child,
> but the fathers who lie like mountain-ruins
> within us; and the dried-up riverbed
> of former mothers—; and the whole
> soundless landscape beneath our cloudy
> or cloudless fate: all *that*, O girl, claimed him first.[818]

This archetypal complexity does confuse the course of love. Even so, it does not necessarily dull its force, and the immense drive the youth bears within himself makes him a forerunner of the hero who appears in the Sixth Elegy.

The final stanza of this Third Elegy, though, returns to *the girl*, highlighting that it is the psyche qua anima that evokes the forces of the collective unconscious in the youth:

> And you yourself, unwittingly—: you have conjured
> primal times in your lover. What feelings
> writhed up out of beings long vanished!

At the same time, the poem's concluding lines emphasize how—in accord with the dialectic that informs the whole cycle—she is assigned the task of *constraining* the chaotic force of those ancestral spirits, of *balancing* wild ancestral desires with a more measured energy. It is remarkable how frequently one or another form of the German root *halten* (halt, hold, contain) appear in the *Elegies*. Correspondingly, this elegy—like the preceding one—ends with a plea for that psychic containment finally necessary for the forming and maintaining of the soul's spiritual interior.

> ...Oh gently, gently
> show him the love that adheres to a calm, everyday task,—lead
> him
> close to the garden, give him those nights
> that even out the scales....
> Temper him [*Verhalt ihn*]....[819]

If the Third Elegy elaborates the complex—and often conflicted—archetypal ground of erotic drive, the Fourth focuses more upon *present* forms of consciousness, and the inveterate confusions that so often obscure human vision and enervate human will. Migratory birds read sure signs of inner event from the face of nature, but we are somehow incapable of seeing past appearances, and so experience difficulty in plotting and sustaining any elevated course of action. Our timing flawed, we cannot hold ourselves up in air—the element of intelligible purpose—but fall out of connection with the cosmic course of things into a shallow, unreflective surface that passes for life. Even lovers, whose feeling would seem to give them wings, quickly come up against barriers raised by incessant internal conflict; even they, whose hearts would lift, cannot see the inner contours of their feelings, and find themselves beaten down by unseen obstructions in psychic space.

In this elegy, then, Eros' severe wound threatens to prove lethal. Love's kindling inspiration dies in diversion and delay as the arrow—rather than rising singingly toward its transcendent target—falls weakly away from the slack bowstring.

At the end of the Third Elegy, "the garden" functions as a place of earthly refuge, soothing in its mundane limit. In the Fourth, however, that *too* familiar place becomes part of the scenery of the habitually unexamined life's inauthentic show:

> Who hasn't sat anxiously before his heart's curtain?
> It rose: the scenery for *Parting.*
> Easy to understand. The familiar garden,
> swaying slightly: then—the dancer.
> Not *him!* Enough! However light his entrance
> he's in disguise and turns into a burgher
> who enters his kitchen to reach his living room.[820]

The poet disdains this poor spectacle, but refuses to abandon the theatre altogether. He insists upon remaining in the audience, even if he is all alone ("for there is always looking"); insists, indeed, upon *looking* so hard that the force of his gaze effectively transfigures people (or the memory of them) into figures of the imagination—puppets—whose movements visibly depend upon higher agencies—angels, even:

> ...what if I do choose
> to wait in front of the puppet stage—no,
> to stare with so much force that finally, to counteract
> my stare, an Angel will arrive...[821]

Hillman: "Seeing through, is a process of deliteralizing and a search for the imaginal in the heart of things by means of ideas."[822] The poet, of course, has been psychologizing from the outset, but here, in this elegy that focuses attention upon life's typical appearances, the *critical* force of the act of *seeing through* reveals itself with special clarity. In the Fifth and Tenth Elegies, too, the poet will conjure carnivalesque images revealing life's outward appearance as a poor show—poor, that is, *unless* consciousness penetrates, by means of ideas, down and into the ground of things, opening inner horizons of time and space that are not purely physical, or merely metaphysical, but psychological, of the nature of the soul itself.

"The physical," writes Hillman,

> which appears as well in the metaphysical, refers to a literalism, the fantasy of a real stuff, matter, or problem that *is* what it is and cannot be seen through. The enemy of *psyche* is physis, however it appears.[823]

Rilke:

Nothing
is what it is. O childhood hours,
when behind each shape there was more
than mere past, and before us—not the future.[824]

...when time, in other words, was subject not to flat chronology, the timeline of literal events, but to the fluid order of the imagination, the creative play (which Rilke had long associated with childhood) that reinvents the being of things.

This order of vision, at once critical and creative, may be attained only when the soul opens the hidden trap door of life.

But this: one's death,
the whole reach of death, even before one's life is under way,—
to hold it gently and not feel anger:
is indescribable.[825]

The Elegy glimpses a vision of life informed, in advance, by knowledge of death—the kind of vision (vouchsafed, too, by the youthful dead) that does *not* think or see in terms of the rigid contraries of life and death, above and below, spirit and matter. Transmuting the force of desire (Third Elegy) into the power of an unwavering gaze, the elegy enacts a ritual dance of *seeing through* the show of things, entering into the backstage of the soul where (in the spirit of revealing ideas) angels and puppets play.

This, however, is not the usual way of seeing or acting—even for those who are entertainers themselves. Though the Fifth Elegy was composed many years after the Fourth,[826] the two share kindred themes, imaging life—à la Plato—as something akin to a shadow puppet play, a show void of real spiritual substance. The Fifth's placement in the sequence makes sense, moreover, not merely on account of its connection to the Fourth Elegy but, too, because it serves as an effective center of the whole cycle, riveting our poetic attention upon yet another archetypal kind.

Rilke did not mention acrobats in the 1912 letter to Annette Kolb. The poet's intimate acquaintance with the Picasso painting that inspired the Fifth Elegy postdates that letter by several years. Still, his wandering acrobats—like the woman in love or the youthful dead—stand as typological representatives of the human condition, albeit in a more negative guise. While the lover and the youthfully dead represent sources of inspiration that can guide the poet *beyond* the normal limits of the psyche, Rilke's acrobats typify the human being constrained, against his or her will, by those limits. In the poet's imagination these performers cut a figure not far removed from that of those hapless human fowl who—at the opening of the Fourth Elegy—rise into the sky only to fall, miserably, back down again. The acrobats make a ritual act of repeating that almost pitiful motion, the heavy human being's painfully truncated mimicry of flight, a pretense of belonging in air. While capable now of executing her intent, the human actor has lost the purpose of her doing altogether; her mechanized will, in fact, is no longer her own:

> But tell me, who *are* they, these wanderers
> (more rootless even than we ourselves) seized early on
> and urgently wrung—for whose possible sake?—
> by some never satisfied will.[827]

"Ritual," writes Hillman,

> offers a primary mode of psychologizing, of deliteralizing events and seeing through them as we "perform" them. As we go into a ritual, the soul of our actions "comes out"; or to ritualize a literal action, we "put soul into it." Here not only can the priest and the alchemist point the way; so too can the actor, the entertainer, and the ball-player... *Ritual brings together action and idea into an enactment.*[828]

Hillman could well have included the poet in his list; for a faithful devotee of the art like Rilke, writing (whether it be poems or letters) certainly qualifies as a ritual act. Nor is it an accident that metaphors of performance—in the persons of puppets or acrobats—stand at the heart of the *Elegies*. By the same token, however, Hillman's words may help explain what, exactly, is so sad about Picasso's—and Rilke's—family of acrobats. As performers, they typify the kind of ritual action we expect to be filled with the style of soul; they are not so much "real people," or even concrete characters, as metaphors for the soul in motion, revealing the essence of the human being as artistic act. Consequently, when the heart goes out of the performance—when art is reduced to technical efficiency so that, no longer revealing inner striving, it becomes mere outward show—we feel ourselves most bitterly let down. Just there, where we most expect and look for a glimpse of soul to refresh our eyes and thrill our hearts, we find it lacking—and nothing conveys a greater sense of emptiness, or a more poignant sadness. It is all the more so, of course, when children—those archetypal bearers of the unbridled imaginative potential of soul—are involved. Then, the heartbreaking sense of the lostness of being foreshadows tragedy.

Still, bearing witness to this—seeing and feeling the archetypal suffering of the soul cut off (as from a mother) from all emanations of love, and bereft of spiritual purpose—the elegiac poet may catch a glimpse, too, of the young acrobat's smile, that inextinguishable promise of the soul's ultimate joy, psyche's future (re)union. *This exhibits once more the formal secrets of the elegy: how the soul-force engaged in* ***giving voice*** *to suffering may break through the numbness, reviving—in the sound-wave of its trembling vibration—the nascent sense of life and love's impossible possibilities.* This healing imagination of being, moreover, is vouched for by nothing less than death—or rather the spirits of the dead themselves—who know, already, the other side of life's delible coin. The end of the Fifth Elegy, sanctified—like the smile *sealed in the glass vase*—by the gaze of the angel, recalls the end of the Fourth, but expands the soul-space to include—not only the child and death, but angel, acrobat, and lover—in the magic circle of potential redemption. The concluding passage, beginning

Angel! Suppose there's a place...

ends the poem with that most common and most rare thing—a true smile, the Rilkean promise of whatever we may know of paradise.

Chapter 17

HAMMERS OF THE HEART

Beginning with the Sixth, the *Elegies* tend to take on an increasingly positive tone. While a keen sense of human limits persists—most painfully in the Eighth—the poet generally treats those very limits less as reasons for despair and more as the conditions for uniquely human accomplishment, *the opening and expansion of that soul-space that creates and preserves existential meaning.* Even so, the mortal psyche becomes a fit vessel only in its ever more intimate conjunction with some immortal source, a spirit that will not die—the kind of spirit psychologically embodied by the hero.

The Sixth Elegy opens with a symbol that counters the image of aborted flight that begins the Fourth. The fig tree does not waste energy in uncertainty or flowery show but successfully turns life's primordial drive (sap) into fruitful consummation. True, the poet once more laments the typical human being's habitual belatedness:

> ... But we, for our part, linger,
> ah, flowering flatters us; the belated inner place
> that is our culminating fruit we enter spent, betrayed.[829]

Here, though, we're immediately offered those energetic alternatives invoked in the First Elegy: we may draw inspiration from the youthfully dead (who, like the fig, do not flower, but proceed more directly toward life's consummation), and—strangely akin to that redeeming type—the self-transcending energy of the hero, whose very existence is uplift and ascent ("Sein Aufgang ist Dasein"—ascent is his existence). That spiritual drive—one that perpetually exceeds the limits of a too human love—embodies eros' uplift, and impels poetic consciousness ever onward beyond its prior bound. Indeed, the hero epitomizes the characteristic motion by means of which the poetic consciousness (to employ Ziolkowski's vocabulary) gains *elevation*. Before continuing our run through the sequence of elegies, we shall do well to inquire more deeply into the psychological and poetic ground of that all-important process—one central to the poetics of the classical German elegy, and spectacularly rendered in Rilke's towering example of the form.

While the imagery of Psyche's third labor and Hillman's notion of psychologizing help construe the mode of soul-making central to the spiritual path laid out in the *Elegies*, we can—and must—be still more specific on this score. It is possible to articulate more precisely and concretely the logic of soul-transformation most constantly at work in the poem; to elaborate the alchemical operation that enables the uninitiate psyche torn by the ravages of time and circumstances to become, by the cycle's end, the poetic initiate capable of sustaining a relation to both the enduring truths of the spirit (the ideal or noetic realm associated with the angel) and the abiding contingencies characteristic of earthly existence. Not surprisingly, the necessary operation qualifies as the one that, in its very nature, fuses the *idealizing* impetus underlying Platonic philosophy with the ineradicably *psychological* character and destiny of the human soul.

It is both correct and necessary to assert that the *Elegies* repeatedly involve dual motions of ascent and descent, transcendence and limitation. Even so, as Psyche's climb up the mountain crag (and the winged nature of her eagle-eyed helper) implies—it is the former that frames and sets the dominant tone of not only the crucial First Elegy but the entire cycle. Rilke's *Duino Elegies* embody a variety of psychological acts, but the alchemical process called *sublimatio* plays the leading role and proves especially instrumental to the all-important transformation of consciousness effected in and through the cycle of poems.

Edinger:

> Just as *calcinatio* pertains to fire, *solutio* to water, and *coagulatio* to earth, so *sublimatio* is the operation pertaining to air. It turns the material into air by volatizing and elevating it. The image derives from the chemical process of sublimation in which a solid, when heated, passes directly into a gaseous state and ascends to the top of the vessel.... All images that refer to upward

> movement—ladders, stairs, elevators, climbing, mountains, flying, and so forth—belong to *sublimatio* symbolism.[830]

Launched arrows, levitating saints, high mountain ridges, ladders, flights of stairs, pillars, towers, birds on the wing; the sublimity of angelic being; the hero whose very being consists of ascension ("Sein Aufgang ist Dasein"), and (perhaps most prevalently) the element of *air* itself and its intimate associates *wind* and (empty) *space*—the *Elegies* are replete with *sublimatio* imagery.[831] No wonder: if Psyche's third task involves *rising* to the task of containing spiritual substance in the vessel of soul consciousness, it only stands to reason that this would require—more quintessentially than anything else—a spiritualizing of the psychosomatic vessel; that purificatory or cathartic process Steiner identifies as one of the bases of initiation.

Quoting and commenting on a passage from Paracelsus, Edinger writes, "'In the process of sublimation . . . the spiritual is raised from the corporeal, subtilised, and the pure separated from the impure.' Here *sublimatio* is described as a purification." He offers this psychological elaboration of the relevant alchemy:

> When matter and spirit are intermixed in a state of unconscious contamination, they must be purified by separation. In this impure state, the spirit must first seek its own purity and will see all that pertains to flesh and matter—the concrete, the personal, the desire-laden—as the enemy to be overcome.[832]

This elucidates a dynamic readily evident in—and central to—the *Elegies*, and especially manifest in Rilke's treatment of love. In accord with his mythical premises, love provides the spirit and the energy for Rilke's visionary quest. Without it, (his) Psyche would not know where to begin. Yet Love, in the myth, is not merely human, but a divine force that drives Psyche forward on the path of self-transcendence, the path of becoming who she is—realizing her being—by way of the act of perpetually *going beyond herself*, repeatedly transcending her present state. And so Rilke sings not just ordinary human love, but impossible love on the model of Gaspara Stampa:

> Isn't it time . . . we tenderly loosed ourselves
> from the loved one, and, unsteadily, survived:
> the way the arrow, suddenly all vector, survives the string
> to be more than itself? For abiding is nowhere.[833]

Not only does this passage exhort us to achieve freedom from "the personal, the desire-laden," the specific symbol chosen to exemplify that dynamic offers a particularly pointed image of the *sublimatio*. *Arrows* belong to *Eros*—the shafts in Cupid's quiver. Like the birds that went before ("maybe that the birds / will feel the extended air in more intimate flight"), and will reappear, repeatedly, afterwards, arrows—long, slendered *feathered* shafts—are what they are ***in air***, lifting up and away from the solidity of earth. Fuel of the spirit's fire, element of wind and breath, air is also the medium of transmission between heaven and earth, water of the eagle wings that, "leaving...the shining paths of the high vault of heaven, swooped past Psyche's face," bringing her the gift of spirit vision.

Numerous other passages parsing the poet's thoughts on love also evoke the *sublimatio*. Even as the poem's author repeatedly laments the tendency for personal feeling to literally evaporate into thin air ("Like dew from the morning grass / that which is ours lifts away from us / like heat from a smoking plate"[834]) or dissolve into impersonal space ("I felt the space in your faces / even as I loved it, turn into world-space / where I no longer found you"[835]), the subtilizing process implicit in such experiences ultimately furthers the psyche's nascent relation to more timeless realms of thought and feeling.

As vital as it is, love is hardly the only force driving the process of purification at work in the poem. Given the transcendental inflection of ideation, it should come as no surprise that psychologizing itself bears an intrinsic relationship to the *sublimatio*. Edinger:

> The body is "made perfect" by spiritualizing it. Psychologically, this corresponds to a way of dealing with a concrete problem. One gets "above" it by seeing it objectively....Just to find suitable words or concepts for a psychic state may be sufficient for a person to get out of it enough to look down on it from above.[836]

Edinger himself continues to make the natural link between the *sublimatio* and Plato's metaphysical legacy:

> Heaven is the abode of the eternal Plátonic forms, the universals, the archetypal images. Hence, whenever a dream or life situation is interpeted from the archetypal standpoint, it is promoting *sublimatio*.[837]

Still more relevant to the psychologizing characteristic of Rilke's *Elegies* are both this follow-up passage:

> Plato's idealism, as well as all later idealistic systems, strive to present life in terms of eternal forms and universal ideas in order to overcome the galling human bondage to the contingencies of matter. Reason, which gives people a standpoint outside their personal likes and dislikes, becomes an indispensable agent of the *sublimatio* by teaching them how to be reflective spectators of themselves.[838]

...and this literary amplification, compliments of Schopenhauer:

> [It is] indeed wonderful to see, how man, beside his life in the concrete, always lives a second life in the abstract. In the former he is abandoned to all the storms of reality and to the influence of the present; he must struggle, suffer, and die like the animal. But...in the sphere of calm deliberation, what previously possessed him completely and moved him intensely appears to him cold, colorless, and, for the moment, foreign and strange; he is a mere spectator and observer. In respect of this withdrawal into reflection, he is like an actor who has played his part in one scene, and takes his place in the audience...[where] he quietly looks on at whatever may happen, even though it be the preparation for his own death.[839]

This latter passage readily calls to mind Rilke's Fourth Elegy, in which the poet deliberately takes a seat in the audience in order to watch the puppet-play of life, self-consciously persisting even if the colorless performance dissolves into no more than "greyish drafts of emptiness." The sense of "foreignness" articulated by Schopenhauer also evokes the cast of mind informing the penultimate section of the First Elegy, which section clearly expresses, too, the *relation to eternity* that underlies and drives the energy of the *sublimatio.*

> True, it is strange to dwell on earth no longer...
> Strange, not to go on wishing one's wishes. Strange,
> to see all that was once so interconnected
> now floating in space. And death demands a labor,
> a tying up of loose ends, before one has
> that first inkling of eternity.[840]

As both the content of this passage and subsequent lines imply, the perspective offered here is one identified with that other principal archetype cited in Rilke's letter to Annette Kolb—the youthfully dead. *Consequently, the two most fundamental (and integrally related) themes underlying the* Elegies—*Love and Death—as well as their principal archetypal representatives—the woman in love and those who died young—are deeply and intrinsically connected with the transcending force of the alchemical* sublimatio.

Despite the pertinence of the Edinger and Schopenhauer citations, however, the idea of *reason* they express by no means applies without reservation to Rilke's *Elegies*. Edinger speaks of "the galling human bondage to the contingencies of matter." While that phrase may be aptly applied to purer forms of Platonic idealism, Rilke's deeply psychological brand of "reverse Platonism"[841] can hardly be counted as such. One can indeed find good grounds to speak of "the galling human bondage to the contingencies of matter" in the *Elegies*; at the same time, it should be recognized that these are never *wholly* transcended in Rilke, and indeed (as we will soon discuss more fully) become the ground of his distinctly poetic vision of human being. Relatedly, while the *Elegies* do (à la Schopenhauer) include repeated critical moments of dispassion and detachment, the "deliberation" the poems carry out can hardly be deemed consistently "calm."

Even so, if we take into account still another facet or model of the *sublimatio*, we can grasp how life's troubling entanglements—as well as the passionately black moods of grief and despair they inspire—actually *fuel* that alchemical process. Edinger:

> One aspect of *sublimatio* overlaps with *separatio* symbolism—namely, its use as an extraction procedure. For instance, mercury can be extracted from certain compounds by heating.... This "expulsion of the quicksilver" is done by *sublimatio*, which releases the spirit hidden in matter.... The expulsion of the quicksilver can also be experienced... as the extraction of *meaning* from heavy moods, from concrete events, or from the factuality of nature.[842]

In connection with this extraction motif, Edinger mentions a young woman who dreamed she saw "a girl like the one in Munch's lithograph, 'The Cry.' Her mouth is a circular opening." In accord with the anguish depicted in the lithograph, the girl is "surrounded by more circles of black lines." Nonetheless, "Out of her mouth comes a horde of doves or white pigeons." Edinger comments:

> This dream informs the patient that the anxiety she is enduring is part of a larger transformation process, in which the ego is heated by horror in order to bring forth a new birth, the "sublimate," represented by the flock of doves. Dreams of birds generally refer to *sublimatio*, and bird phobias may indicate fear of a necessary *sublimatio*. They are also often connected with a fear of death, death being the ultimate *sublimatio* whereby the soul is separated from the body.[843]

"Wer, wenn ich schriee . . . " Rilke's *Duino Elegies* commence, too, with a *cry*, and if the poet's angst does not quite amount to horror,[844] his open mouth certainly expresses a kindred existential agony. Commensurately, the "transformation process" performed by the poem similarly issues in a kind of new birth; achieves a redemptive *conception* of human being empowered in large measure by "the ultimate *sublimatio*"—(knowledge of) death.

Naturally, those archetypal images of the flight of the soul—birds—abound in Rilke's *Elegies*. In the First Elegy, the very element of the *sublimatio* expands when a lover surrenders unduly personal forms of attachment; then "the birds / will sense the increase of air with more passionate flying."[845] The Second Elegy virtually begins with the poet calling the transcendent beings that inspire the poem—angels—"fast tödlich Vögel der Seele"—"nearly fatal birds of the soul." At the outset of the Fourth, migratory birds figure an unattainable singularity of lofty purpose, while the opening of the Seventh—highlighting transformation already achieved—makes the originating figure of poetic voice (the cry) over into the image of a bird in flight. The whole passage is pure *sublimatio*:

> No longer, voice. No longer let wooing send forth your cry:
> you're past that. Even though your cry would be clear as a bird's
> when first Spring bears him aloft, almost forgetting
> that he's a cautious creature and not an unsheathed heart
> being flung into brightness, into passionate skies.[846]

The last—Tenth—Elegy has its bird/call too, one that enigmatically "extends / into the distance the ancient glyph of its desolate cry,"[847] but I want to conclude this brief survey of *sublimatio* images by following up on the reference to the poet's two most central organs—the voice and the heart—inscribed in a passage from the Ninth Elegy.

In a dramatic moment towards the conclusion of the cycle—at the end of a stanza in the Ninth Elegy wherein the poet declares his mission—he proclaims:

> Between the hammers our heart
> lives on, as the tongue,
> even between the teeth, remains
> unceasing in praise.[848]

These lines, too, articulate a classic (though somewhat hidden) form of the *sublimatio*. Edinger:

> A text says, "If you do not make the bodies subtle, so that they may be impalpable to touch, you will not gain your end. If they have not been ground, repeat your operation, and see that they are ground and subtilized." Thus, *sublimatio* can mean "grinding" or "hammering" to bring about an attenuation of the material. Very fine powder approaches a gas in its consistency.[849]

The emotional climax of the whole cycle—the opening of the Tenth Elegy—reiterates the theme in very similar terms:

> Someday, at the end of the nightmare of knowing,
> may I emerge singing praise and jubilation to assenting angels.
> May I strike my heart's keys clearly, and may none fail
> because of slack, uncertain, or fraying strings.[850]

Many English translations obscure the language of the *sublimatio* here, but the relevant German phrase is "klar geschlagenen Hämmern des Herzen"—"clear-struck *hammers* of the heart." In an image that recalls the Orpheus-haunted closing of the First Elegy, the telltale hammer pulverizes or pounds the matter of the heart into waves of sound; the instrument of the *sublimatio* doubles as the agent—and action—of poetic vocation or praise.

Though Edinger never mentions the *Elegies* in his elucidation of the *sublimatio*, he does cite the second stanza of Rilke's twelfth Sonnet to Orpheus (Part II) as an archetypal instance of an impending *sublimatio*, one announced by the figure of a hammer about to strike.

Whatever's locked in stasis is already stiff and dry;
can it think itself safe in that innocuous grey?
Wait, from far off, something even harder warns the cold clay.
Woe—the absent hammer lifts high![851]

The poem—which would not have been possible without Rilke's prior work on the *Elegies*—naturally entertains a close connection with the related *Duino* passages we have just been reading. The sonnet, which begins "Wolle die Wandlung" ("Will (or want) metamorphosis"), closes with the suggestion that you "change yourself into wind." One would be hard put to conceive a simpler or clearer image of the *sublimatio* or the immense spiritual challenge its signature alchemy entails.

Crucially, the *sublimatio* process so essential to the *Elegies*' poetics manifests not only in *what* objects appear in the poem's images—ladders, birds, arrows, etc.—but, as well, in the treatment of those objects, the handling or styling of the imagery. In his *New Poems*, Rilke's *Dinggedichte*—as that very term connotes—*thickened* or *densified* the element of thought into concrete objects, a poetic process kin to the alchemical operation known as the *coagulatio*. The *sublimatio*, as we've illustrated, effects the opposite process: not a coagulating of thought into physical body or thing, but a subtilizing or aerating of thing into thought.

Not only do Rilke's *Elegies* include great swaths of language that unroll the poet's meditations without reference to *any* physical objects at all (the tree in line fourteen is the first truly tangible thing that appears in the poem), but the *Elegies* rapidly transform the objects that do appear into complex figures of thought. The physical nature of things (so carefully and slowly built up in many of the *New Poems*) does not hold the poet's interest. Instead, his poetic praxis precipitously sublimates objects into (often extended and multiple) metaphors that mirror some idea or train of reflection pertaining to the soul's own nature, destiny, and development. As the poet himself puts it: "Where once a solid house stood / a thought-form presents itself...."[852]

The arrow in the First Elegy provides one instance we've already discussed—an especially illuminating one, perhaps, because here it is readily evident that the "object" under discussion is not only the arrow, but the self or soul-consciousness it symbolizes. This, unsurprisingly, is not the exception but rather the rule in the poetics of the elegies. At every turn, the pervasive *sublimatio* transforms things, events—all sorts of matter—into objects of thought carried along in the self-reflexive meditative current constitutive of the self's own consciousness, and definitive of the inward soul-space opened in and through the poem.

Further examples abound. The fig tree in the Sixth Elegy—quickly likened to the tube of a fountain—symbolizes a desirable form of soul entelechy; the bird likened to the Etruscan soul in the Eighth figures consciousness peculiarly divided between spirit and body. Frequently, more or less concrete terms are immediately linked with highly abstract ones, a compounding (if not confounding) of spirit and matter that evokes a complex idea: e.g., the "trees of life" in the Second Elegy, the "rose of onlooking" and the "cheap winter hats of Fate" in the Fifth. The extended metaphors involving the last two provide excellent examples of how Rilke—like Paris's Madame Lamort—"winds and binds" labile material so that it finally volatilizes into elaborate forms of the soul's intellectual speculation.

The sublimating tendency we're sketching here not only manifests in the handling of particular images, but indeed defines the very texture and consistency of the whole poem. The metaphysical energy patent from the first in the language of Rilke's *Elegies* ("For Beauty is nothing / but the beginning of Terror") tends to lift everything up into the realm of thought, the sphere of self-reflective idea. As an incredible phrase such as "Never nowhere without no" indicates, the tendency toward abstraction occasionally reaches truly rarefied heights—evidence of the potent force of the alchemical *sublimatio* that powders the stuff of life into thought, elevating all things—most critically, the soul itself—through poetic meditation. The acme of that process—and the spiritual high point of the cycle—is reached in the Elegy that picks up the energy of the hero, and runs with it.

If the Fifth Elegy stands as both the center and nadir of the cycle, the Seventh represents a pivotal moment in the development of its informing vision, achieving a virtually decisive resolution of its generative thematic tension. In this Elegy, the combined action of love and death—working through the vessel of poetic voice—sublimates soul-consciousness so that it is capable of *comprehending* within itself the connection between the eternality of cosmic space and the actuality of earthly existence, the unity of being that bridges visible and invisible worlds.

In her analysis of the *Elegies*, Kathleen Komar sees the Seventh Elegy as a dramatic turning point in the poem, though in a somewhat different guise:

> In the Seventh Elegy, the speaker reverses the entire direction of his activity.... Rilke sees as futile what he took to be his task as the *Duino Elegies* began, i.e., the reaching of the transcendent realm.... The poet radically shifts his focus from the transcendent realm to the earthly realm... decisively changes his poetic aim from that of transcendence to that of transformation of and within the physical world.[853]

I cannot agree with this assessment. While the Seventh does mark a turn toward the earth as a field of activity, the poetic consciousness embraced in the late Elegies arises as a result of the alchemical changes wrought in and through the work of the earlier ones—most notably, the pervasive purificatory, transcendentally inflected *sublimatio*. More specifically, the relation to the earthly realm celebrated in the Seventh Elegy derives its value and authenticity from the connection with the (transcendent) realm of spirit forged—in good measure—through the *sublimatio*. The resolution of the underlying tension between the angelic and the human sphere, the transcendent and the immanent world, cannot, after all, take form as a repudiation of one pole in favor of the other, and the pivotal Seventh Elegy carries the vital work of reconnection forward in a series of almost dizzying poetic leaps.[854]

Incorporating the hero's ascendant power into its lead figure, the Seventh Elegy begins (as we've noted already) with a soaring *sublimatio*—the likening of *the poet's own voice* (and so his own persona) to the flight of a migratory bird lifting into "intimate heavens" ("die innige Himmel"). The initial lines[855] allude to the poet's "cry" ("Werbung nicht mehr, nicht Werbung, entwachsene Stimme, / sei deines, *Schreies* Natur; zwar *schrieest* du rein wie der Vogel"), and so recall the opening of the entire cycle ("Wer, wenn ich *schriee*... "). Here, though, the poet apparently disclaims the "wooing" of the transcendent audible in the First Elegy. This renunciatory gesture does not, however, signal a relinquishing of all transcendentally inflected aims; rather, the poetic voice professes to have "outgrown" wooing external sources of power because—by virtue of all that's gone before—it has incorporated tremendous spiritual strength into itself, attaining an exceptionally *elevated* form of consciousness.

From the heights of its "inner sky," the poet's voice naturally dips into the language of love: "Like him... you'd also woo—: invisibly, / so that some silent mate might learn of you..." The ecstatic force of love that bears up—and is borne upon—his song descends from those heights to embrace earthly creation: "O and Spring would understand—, annunciation / would echo everywhere." Here, and in the long passage that follows, the poet's love song moves between that "inner heaven" and the burgeoning world of the earth by way of poetic meditation upon *those archetypal patterns of time* called seasons. Once more (as in the Fourth Elegy[856]), Rilke draws upon the imagery of the seasons—those mythic molds of the cycle of the year—to bridge above and below, the invisible and visible worlds.

Nor are the seasons by any means the only archetypal ideas entering into the poet's recollections. The passage commencing:

> And on ahead, the Summer.
> Not only all of summer's dawns—, not only
> how they change into day and gleam with genesis.
> Not only the days, so tender around flowers...[857]

evokes a sense of primordial beginning; indeed, it echoes, in a more intimate key, the passage in the Second Elegy in which the angels—"Creation's darlings"—are likened to the "dawn-red ridges of all genesis." The echo—faint as it may be—exhibits the poetic voice absorbing and owning numinous power of the kind originally attributed to the Angel alone. The whole earthly creation, after all, echoes or mirrors the poet's expression of love ("da ist keine Stelle, / die nicht trüge den Ton Verkündigung"—there is no place / that would not echo/carry the tone's annunciation). The Elegy thus represents the energies of creation *participating* in the soul-space opened by poetic voice which therefore effectively *contains* them; Rilke's long, flowing lines conjure and so include (archetypal qualities of) spring and summer in their gorgeous texture. The passage, in fact, showcases the imaginative ground of the process by which Rilke interiorizes reality, absorbing "external" nature into the poetic soul-space he calls—in an earlier poem we'll soon discuss further—*Weltinnenraum*.

The poet's train of thought does not, however, confine itself to terrestrial and diurnal phenomena and the human experience associated with them. Those archetypal patterns of time—the seasons—open a window onto another, "higher level" of reality as well:

Not only all of summer's dawns...
Not only the days...
Not only the calm reverence in these outspread powers...
not only the paths...
not only, after late thunderstorms, the pulsing clarity,
not only the onset of sleep and, near dusk, a premonition...
But the nights! Those towering summer
nights! And the stars, the stars of the earth!
O to be dead and to know them endlessly,
all the stars: for how, how, how to forget them![858]

Already in the First Elegy, *night* (here, in accord with the ongoing *sublimatio*, described as "die hohen...Nächte"—"the towering nights") stood for a reality above and beyond the order of time, a cosmic *space* instinct with the breath of spirit. In the concluding lines of this passage, the long *sublimatio* inspired by the force of love climaxes by invoking the "ultimate *sublimatio*"—death—to empower imagination of *enduring* knowledge, knowledge keyed to the cosmic overtones underlying corporeal existence.

In Rilke's symbolic universe, the *angel*, *night*, and (those most traditional images of eternity) *the stars* that fill the night are all emblematic of the upper reaches of mind or soul: the upper half of the divided line Plato calls the intelligible realm and which Hermes (according to our system of correspondences) calls quite simply "eternity" and "the cosmos." As the unifying substratum of the whole cosmos and the illimitable container of the All, *space*, too, belongs to this realm. "The Angels are...the very embodiment of abstract space, completely realized being and, as such, an atemporal infinite," writes Weigand. She continues:

> For both [Rilke and Eliot] the most significant moments in life are those wherein life, temporal life, is suspended, and the human being apprehends eternity in his sensation of space...the "objective correlative" of mystic experience.[859]

Death naturally represents—symbolically as well as literally—*the suspension of temporal life*; as we've discussed before, it consequently serves as a portal between the mortal, mutable, physical realm and that of eternity. Correlatively, the kind of unending knowledge of the stars death proffers in this elegy certainly qualifies as one of Weigand's "most significant" mystic moments.

Even so, that moment does not represent a mode of transcendence of the type premised upon a simple abandonment of the "lower" plane of things, a rising above and leaving behind of earthly existence in the name of union with a purely incorporeal, spiritual reality. After all, Hermes teaches that death is—along with life—of the essence of the realm of becoming. Indeed, its nature as a portal reveals it as the invisible *link* between the realms of transience and eternity, the highest and lowest rungs of Hermes' cosmological ladder, and so "the key to initiation... the really sound and full sphere and orb of being."

It is of utmost significance that Rilke speaks first, not of any old stars, but of "die Sterne der Erde"—"the stars of the earth." The expression—recalling the theme we explored in connection with "Evening," "Archaic Torso of Apollo," and "The Spanish Trilogy"—represents yet another, higher octave of fusion of spiritual and material realities, a conjoining of heaven and earth, eternal being and the world of becoming. More specifically, Rilke's figure implies *an incorporation of the eternal order of the cosmos into earthly existence and a consequent illumination and sacralization of the concrete world.* While this mystical moment may not achieve a final resolution of the thematic tension underlying the *Elegies*, it certainly represents a preliminary visioning of the same.

Rilke's immanentist initiatives do (à la Komar) repudiate any notion of "transcendence" premised upon a *persistent* cosmological dualism. Even so, his poetic method reflects the alchemical truth that "only separated things can unite," and his (prospective) reunification of spiritual and corporeal substance derives its power and validity from the foregoing processes of sublimation, *the purifying of the psychic vessel or human soul-consciousness that functions as both place and agency of that reconnection.* Correlatively, if the unific character of space often offers itself as the ground (or "objective correlative") of mystic experience in Rilke, experience of space often depends upon, not an abandonment of time or (as often in Eliot) reducing temporal pattern to a form of stasis that mimics space, but an imaginative expansion of time. The poetic movement of the Seventh Elegy—moving through an evocation of the archetypal soul-experiences associated with spring and summer into the mystical space of night—illustrates Weigand's comment that "the space which Rilke opens to man is reached not by abandonment of the realm of time, but by infinite expansion of it."[860]

In the fourth stanza of the Seventh Elegy, the poet amplifies his immanentist vision. First, the poet's voice reaches yet further into the earth to include the dead in its all-encompassing embrace.

> And thus: I'd call my lover. But not only *she*
> would come... Other girls would come from crumbling graves
> and stand before me... For could I limit
> my call to just one? The interred seek
> the earth's surface forever.—[861]

The dead, here, are specifically dead *girls* because these represent the soul qua anima and its privileged relation to death.[862]

Shifting quickly, the poet's fluid, ever-mobile voice issues cryptic proclamations concerning childhood, the nature of destiny, and the consummate value of earthly existence:

> You children, one *present* thing
> truly grasped would count for so many!
> The whole of destiny crowds into childhood;
> how often you'd overtake your lover, panting,
> panting from the blissful chase, aimless, breaking into freedom.
> Life here is magic![863]

This last declaration—"Hiersein ist herrlich"—counts as one of the signature moments of the whole cycle. In stark contrast to the wrenching lament that initiates the *Elegies*, the poet here jubilates, proclaiming for all to hear the irreducible value of concrete existence, the almost illimitable worth of *being here*.

Realizing that value, however, depends upon the insights the poet offers in the immediately preceding lines. The condensed force of such paratactic, gnomic utterances dizzies the mind, but then again, *density* is an anagram for *destiny*. While Rilke does not supply the underlying logic that links his chief motifs here, our prior discussions provide the backdrop necessary for discerning those links. *Childhood* symbolizes *imaginative* consciousness not ruled by extrinsic convention or categories of perception; the concept of destiny as an unfolding of "das Dichte der Kindheit" accordingly implies a plotting of life responsive—not to externalized forms of time and causation—but to the inner imperatives of the soul. It is, naturally, that same imaginative capacity—one instinct in, not only childhood, but in anima as well—that can grasp the deeper meaning of things *here* ("ein hiesig...ergriffenes Ding"), which meaning depends upon their (symbolic) participation in an ensouled (and ensouling) reality. Correlatively, it is, finally, the soul qua anima (represented, consistently, by the figure of girls—*Mädchen*) that testifies to those epiphanic moments when authentic spiritual being—a reality that transcends the order of temporal succession—reveals itself in and through the human being's earthly existence. In accordance with logic of *The Book of Poverty and Death*, it does so even—or especially—when that existence may appear degraded, dispossessed, and devoid of outward worth:

> Even you knew it, you girls,
> who seemed deprived of it, who were trapped in the city's
> vilest streets, festering there, or cast aside
> for rubbish. For to each of you there was an hour, perhaps
> not even a full hour, but between two intervals
> a space not marked by the measures of time—
> when you had an *existence*. Everything.
> Veins filled with existence.[864]

It is anima (as we've iterated again and again) that lends soul a self-reflexive quality of *interiority*. Consequently, the ringing affirmation of *esse in anima* registered in the above lines naturally paves the way for the declaration that opens the next stanza:

> Nowhere, Love, will World exist but within. Our lives
> pass in transformation. And all the while the outside realm
> diminishes.[865]

These lines—another one of the *Elegies*' signature statements—display the interdependence of two crucial leitmotifs; reveal the all-important process of *Verwandlung* (*transformation*) as a concomitant of the transportation of things from an externalized visible order of space, time, and causation into an *interior, imaginal soul-space* opened in and through the act of psychologizing, the flow of poetic reflection, the creative activity of the word. Rilke's *Elegies* do validate and celebrate earthly existence, but only insofar as that existence is absorbed into the ongoing work of the poet's soul-making and consequently recreated in transfigured form.

Rilke, moreover, does not represents that work of interiorization and transformation as a purely individual subjective matter that leaves the historical world untouched. On the contrary, the Seventh Elegy understands that work to be of the essence of the historical moment, a defining feature of (the term, here, is Rilke's own) the zeitgeist, or spirit of the time. As such, his poetic initiative presumes to embrace not only quotidian things, but the whole flow of historical and material culture, including icons of past forms of religious worship—those objects representative of more traditional means of connecting human life with the divine, giving the sacred place on earth:

> The Zeitgeist is building vast reservoirs of power, formless
> as the thrusting energy it wrests from everything.
> It no longer recognizes temples... Where one of them still
>   survives,
> an object once prayed to, revered, knelt before—,
> it's already reaching, secretly, into the invisible world.
> Many no longer see it, yet without the gain
> of rebuilding it greater now, with pillars and statues, *within*! [866]

We arrive, now, at that passage already cited in the last chapter, that (new) section wherein the poet's meditation moves from *history* to *prehistory*, from evocations of the zeitgeist to imaginations of the transhistorical archetypal form of the human being.

> Each dull turn of the world leaves such disinherited,
> to whom neither the past nor the coming life lends substance.
> For to humans even what comes next lies far away.
> This ought not baffle us but strengthen our defense
> of a still recognized form.—This once *stood* amidst men
>   ...as if it were alive there,
> and arched stars closer from safeguarded heavens.[867]

Only now—after tracing the soul qua anima's association with eros (the love motif), nature and the world of creation, death, childhood, existentiality, interiority, history and prehistory; only now—after absorbing all these intrinsically related modes of being into its all-unifying life—does the poet's voice venture to offer its vision to the angel, dare to hold a type of itself up as a mirror to that divine reality. Before this moment, the poet's voice had—in this Elegy—restricted its list of rhetorical respondents to the human realm; addressed itself to children, girls, and the beloved—but not to the angel. Here, at last, he turns to that ever-present, silent interlocutor:

> Angel, now *you* shall see it, too—*there!* In your gaze
> it stands secured at last, erect for eternity.
> Pillars, pylons, the Sphinx, the cathedral's
> gray upward striving from a vanishing or alien city.[868]

We've already indicated something of the symbolic significance of the sphinx, that ancient emblem of the underlying unity of human consciousness and universal nature, microcosm and macrocosm. Now we may mention too that pillars and cathedral spires represent classical *sublimatio* images. Striving to picture the enduring type of human consciousness that reflects—and so in a sense incorporates into itself—a heavenly order of intelligence ("the established heavens"), the poet once more resorts to images associated with the *sublimatio*, that royal means of assimilating truths of the spirit into the substance of the soul.

The reconciliation between the angelic and human spheres thus achieved entails not (as Weigand said of Rilke's relation to time) an abandonment of the human psyche's native sphere of concern, but an *almost* illimitable expansion of it: the maturation of a type of consciousness that *comprehends within itself* the whole spectrum of being, *interiorizing* space, time, and the order of cause Rilke most often called Fate. The human being or soul does not cease to belong to the realm of earthly being, the existential sphere of visible life and death, but aims to realize the hermetic truth that *becoming is in time, time is in the cosmos, the cosmos in eternity, and eternity in god, or mind or soul.*

In a 1913 poem, Rilke first articulated the idea of *Weltinnenraum* (inner-world-space) so vital to the *Elegies*. The crucial passage echoes the opening of the Seventh Elegy:

> *One* space spreads through all creatures equally—
> inner-world-space. Birds quietly flying go
> flying through us. O, I that want to grow!
> the tree I look outside at's growing in me!
>
> I have a house within when I need care.
> I have a guard within when I need rest.
> The love that I have had!—Upon my breast
> the beauty of the world clings, to weep there.[869]

Rilke's philosophy, though, is not without precedent. Hermes teaches:

> Inwardly, a soul full of mind and god fills this universal body in which all bodies exist, but outwardly soul surrounds the universe and brings it to life. Outwardly, the universe is this great and perfect living thing, the cosmos; inwardly, it is all living things.[870]

Later in the discourse, Hermes offers what may almost be regarded as a précis of Rilke's poetic method:

> So you must think of god in this way, as having everything—the cosmos, the universe—like thoughts within himself. Thus unless you make yourself equal to god, you cannot understand god.... Go higher than every height and lower than every depth. Collect in yourself all the sensations of what has been made, of fire and water, dry and wet; be everywhere at once, on land, in the sea, in heaven; be not yet born, be in the womb, be young, old, dead, beyond death. And when you have understood all these at once—times, places, things, qualities, quantities—then you can understand god.[871]

...or, as Rilke might prefer to say, you might understand *yourself.* For his *Elegies*—transporting us in fact into a whole universe of elemental sensations, into the minds of fathers, mothers, and the womb itself; into the mind of the dead and the realm beyond death—follow a like procedure, with one crucial caveat.

Despite the immense expansion of consciousness enacted in the *Elegies*, Rilke resolutely resists any hint of self-deification. The modern poet remains keenly cognizant of the bounds of specifically human truth, the line that divides divine consciousness per se and the imperfect human being's peculiar mode of mirroring or reflecting eternal being within itself and in the forms of its own creative activity. Consequently, the penultimate section of the Elegy closes by acknowledging the difference in scale that sets divine consciousness off from human. At the same time, it affirms (in the last of its long train of metonymic moves) that art, culture, indeed the human psyche itself belongs to the same meaningful measure, reaching *up* (note the vocabulary of the *sublimatio* yet again!) to touch—at the least—the lower limits of divine being:

> But one tower was great, was it not? O, Angel, it was,—
> even next to you? Chartres was great—, and music
> rose still higher, soared beyond us. But even
> just one woman in love, alone, at night, at her window...
> didn't she reach your knee?[872]

The final section of the Seventh Elegy continues the poet's address to the angel and, in so doing, effectively brings this Elegy full circle. The poet begins by declaring he has outgrown the "wooing" of angelic presence that opened the First Elegy (recognizing, even then, that descent of that terrible beauty could destroy him); the Elegy's concluding lines accentuate that defensive gesture:

> Don't think I'm wooing!
> Angel, even if I were, you'd never come. For my call
> is always full of 'Away!" Against such a powerful
> current you cannot advance. Like an outstretched
> arm is my call. And its raised hand, tensed
> as for grasping, remains before you
> always, defense and warning.
> Ungraspable One—palm out, wide open.[873]

This closing gesture is a complex one, and, we may perhaps best approach its meaning by recalling like motifs inscribed in Rilke's earlier work.

In a series of angel poems in his *Frühe Gedichte* (Early Poems), Rilke depicted a maturing human consciousness taking over some of the spiritual functions provided by angelic guardians, thus freeing the latter for other forms of service. While the end of the Seventh Elegy is more aggressive in tone, it nonetheless reflects a kindred motif. In a rather more concrete allusion, the hand gesture that concludes the Seventh Elegy also echoes the penultimate image in the *Book of Pilgrimage*:

> My hands are bloody from digging.
> I lift them, hold them open in the wind,
> so they can branch like a tree.
>
> Reaching, these hands would pull you out of the sky
> as if you had shattered there...[874]

To be sure, significant differences mark the two passages. Here, at the end of the Seventh Elegy, the poet's hand is no longer bloodied or damaged; his exhaustive course of soul development has gone a long way toward integrating the transcendental energies of eros and the puer spirit into the fabric of his psyche. Even so, the way the hand—even as it warns away—remains *open* to the above—indeed, open for grasping—signifies an ongoing reception of spiritual substance. In turn, that receptivity will enable (as augured by the earlier poem) "the...giving out of essence for the sake of transforming the world around."[875] If Rilke makes a gesture of "warding off" the angel, it is not because he is surrendering interest in spiritual knowledge but because he is claiming his own, distinctly human version of the same as the signature of his true poetic estate—as always, Rilke's art dramatizes the act of the individual soul coming into its own. Moreover, though Rilke has discarded the traditional language of religion, the inspiration informing this and all the Elegies remains (as he himself insisted) continuous with that underlying *The Book of Hours* and—we might add—the commensurate Sufi understanding that ("Angel, I'll show it to you...there!") the heart of the gnostic is the mirror and eye of God.

If the Seventh Elegy dramatically expands human consciousness so that it virtually contains Creation within itself, the Eighth—in accord with the difficult dialectic of the whole—radically contracts that consciousness once again, casting the far-flung heart of the poet rather brutally back down to earth. The celebratory tone disappears, replaced once more by steady lamentation as the poet effectively surrenders the claim to inner vision. The archetypal agents enabling that vision—lovers, children, girls, the dead—while mentioned in the poem, remain patently extrinsic to the form of human consciousness in it; the poet essentially pulls the archetypal ground out from under the feet of his representative human being. The consciousness evoked in this Elegy—torn once more by opposites of inside/outside, subject/object, self/world, life/death—harks back to the states of mind depicted in the Fourth and Fifth Elegies and to the superficial existence bewailed in those prior poems:

> Always turned so fervently toward creation,
> we see only the reflection of the Open,
> which our own presence darkens....
> That's what destiny[876] is: being opposite,
> and nothing else but that and always opposite.[877]

Even the *interior soul space* within which the poetic voice might *lift* seems to have gone lost. The consonance of interior containment and upward flight belongs, in this elegy, *not* to the human being, but to those tiny creatures (e.g, the gnat) born from externally exposed seed, whose all-encompassing womb is nothing other than the air itself. Birds—hatched from eggs held in round nests perched high in trees—also fare rather better than we. Like the soul of a dead Etruscan—one part enclosed within a coffin, another belonging to the airy space outside—birds participate in both the *containing* world of earth and the *uplifting* sphere of air. As for human beings:

> And how confused is any womb-born creature
> that has to fly. As if frightened
> of its own self, it zigzags through the air
> like a crack through a teacup.[878]

The synergy of psyche and eros momentarily broken, we are once more estranged from earth as well as heaven, and, in that hapless homelessness, "live our lives, always taking leave."

While the Eighth Elegy can hardly be construed as anything other than negative in tenor,[879] the extreme divisiveness it registers does—in accord with the "hermeneutic of sorrow" Koch describes—prepare a further, more final stage of reconciliation. The poet, it is true, does not quite regain the elevation attained in the Seventh Elegy. Rebounding from the depressive letdown/reality check of the Eighth, the Ninth Elegy nonetheless does reaffirm and consolidate the vision achieved in the Seventh even as it etches the defining limits of human consciousness more sharply.

> ... why then
> *have* to be human—and, fleeing destiny,
> long for destiny?...
>
> ... because *life* here [*Hiersein*] compels us, and because everything here
> seems to need us, all this fleetingness
> that strangely entreats us. Us the *most* fleeting . . .[880]

The poetic voice in the Seventh Elegy—lifted by love—ranges freely through cosmic space and (pre)historical time, traversing "intimate heavens," blooming meadows, and vile city streets; revisiting childhood and the mind of the dead; imagining distant pasts and prospective futures. The Ninth contracts and concentrates that vision, reinforcing the difference between angelic and human consciousness:

> You can't impress [the Angel] with lofty emotions; in the cosmos
> that shapes his feelings, you're a mere novice.[881]

The Ninth accordingly concerns itself more intensively with the limits of the here and now; most especially, the impermanence characteristic of earthly existence, the quality of life amidst the world of becoming that—incessantly marked by death—is also the world of things that constantly come and go, perpetually pass away.

The *singularity* characteristic of our fleeting earthly existence nonetheless possesses its own valence of unique, incontrovertible value:

> Once for each thing, only once. Once and no more. And we, too,
> only once. Never again. But to have been
> once, even though only once:
> this having been *earthly* seems lasting, beyond repeal.[882]

Coincidently, the Ninth Elegy's focus on the here and now bears its own spiritual dividends: the earthly destiny of the human being emerges all the more definitively against the background of evanescence and—simultaneously—the kind of irrevocable, singular facticity that cannot but recall the mythic resonance of the event of the incarnation.

Still, while the poet clearly moves to reclaim human life's existential significance, vexatious uncertainties remain. As a consequence of the Eighth's reinstatement of the cycle's thematic tension, the Ninth Elegy finds the poet wrestling once more with an acute sense of a persistent gulf separating earthly existence and "that other relation"—life in the eternal spirit realm symbolized by the stars. At first, the poet hints that the soul's own signature experience—Psyche's hard labor—may itself bridge the difference between temporal and eternal spheres:

> Ah, but what can one carry across?...
> The pain, then. Above all, the hard labor of living,
> the long experience of love,—all the purely
> unsayable things.[883]

Yet the poet continues to question whether such "purely ineffable things" may indeed qualify as the soul's true dowry in its marriage to spirit. "But later, under the stars, what does it matter...." he exclaims—implying that such inarticulate soul-stuff may not be currency valuable enough to pay eternity's high toll, or suffice to bring the manifold perishable things of the earth themselves into some relation to spirit. To accomplish this indispensable end—*indispensable, because human being often seems the most perishable of all such things*—the soul must avail itself of one of its truest gifts: the poetic word:

> What if we're here just for saying: *house,*
> *bridge, fountain, gate, jug, fruit tree, window,—*
> at most: *column, tower?*... but for *saying*, understand,
> oh for such saying as the things themselves
> never hoped so intensely to be.[884]

On one level, this mission statement is far from new for Rilke. Already in the *The Book of Hours*, the poet announced, "I want, then, simply / to say the name of things," and the *New Poems* accomplished a later stage of that extended poetic experiment which—truth to be told—is anything *but* simple.

The *Elegies* imagine taking that experiment to a new level. True to form, they highlight the spiritual dimension of the mission of naming, stress poetic saying as the privileged means of realizing, not *identification* of human and angelic being, but the symbolic *connection* between them:

> Praise the world to the Angel...
> Tell him of *things*. He'll stand more amazed; as you stood
> beside the ropemaker in Rome or by the potter along the Nile.[885]

We will shortly revisit Rilke's vision of the nature of *things* in the work that he himself declared revealed the philosophy of the *Elegies* in poetic action: *Sonnets to Orpheus*. Here, though, we will simply propose that Rilke's poetic saying—in no wise a mere labeling—implies an unveiling and bestowal of being, a christening that confirms and completes creation by revealing the visible world as a form of *theophany*—the shining forth of a divine essence that may or may not be called "God."

An old Jewish legend may illuminate the relation between the angelic and human being implicit in the *Elegies*—especially the unique privilege accorded to the human being. The legend portrays hosts of angels responding to God's creation of the human being with utter bewilderment. Why, they wonder, did God create such an imperfect being when hosts of angels serve him in Heaven? In answer, God bends down to Earth and plucks a single red rose that had just begun to unfold. "Behold," God exclaims, "can any among you say what it is that I hold in my hand?" The legions of angels remain silent, for none can know or say. "I have made the human being," proclaims God, "so that there might be one being in the universe who can know and speak what it is I have created!"[886]

As in this legend, Rilke's archetypal human being fulfills her problematic destiny in the act of naming; finds her appointed place and function in a universe no longer evidently foreign to any spiritual order of intelligence but rather instinct with the breath of being, the creative life of the nourishing Word. For *here, now, in the Ninth Elegy, the poetic word—the saying of things—emerges as the chief vessel and vehicle of the great task of transformation outlined in the Seventh Elegy*—yet only now formally announced as our redemptive commission:

> And these things
> that keep alive on departure know that you praise them;
> transient,
> they look to us, the *most* transient, to be their rescue.
> They want us to change them completely, in our invisible hearts,
> into—O endlessly—us! Whoever, finally, we may be.[887]

Rilke's poetry aims to see through both human and non-human things—and, coincidently, *transform* them by the very act of translating their visible nature into the invisible interior of soul where they inevitably serve as symbolic figures and expressions of creative consciousness itself. That metamorphic act—reconnecting matter with spirit in and through the speech of the soul—enters all things into the stream of an "all-unifying life" (Koch) and so bears a positively *resurrective* force:

> Earth, isn't that what you want: to arise
> in us *invisibly*? Isn't it your dream
> to be invisible someday? Earth! Invisible!
>
> What, if not transformation, is your urgent charge?
> Earth, my darling, I will!

After once more invoking (as in the Seventh) spring, the archetypal time of rebirth, the poet's confession (or profession) of love flows on:

> Nameless now, I am betrothed to you forever.
> You've always been right, and your most sacred tenet
> is Death the intimate Friend.[888]

On one level, the connection between death and (the task of) transformation appears self-evident: new forms require the passing of the old. Nonetheless, a passage from an esotericist may help deepen our understanding of the mythic ground of that all-important connection:

> Before the Fall, death did not play the role of liberating consciousness, through the destruction of the forms which enclose it, that it has played since then. Instead of the destruction of forms, their continual *transformation* took place. This was enacted by the perpetual action of life effecting the metamorphosis of forms.... This perpetually liberating creative action of life was—and still is—the function of sacred magic.[889]

The first sentence here implies the role death has played *after* the Fall—one that Rilke well recognized as indispensable to creative activity as well as spiritual life. Moreover, Rilke had long conceived of death—comprehended in its underlying *unity* with life—as precisely that which enables "perpetually liberating creative action" "effecting the metamorphosis of forms."

The passage of our esoteric author continues to highlight the redemptive power of transformative activity even as it suggests its mythic source:

> And it is this transforming function, opposed to the destructive function of death, that Moses' Genesis designates by the symbol of the Tree of Life.... The Tree of Life is the source of the miracles of generation, transformation, rejuvenation, healing, and liberation. Conscious participation with it... is the great work of sacred magic.[890]

"A tree rose up.... " We are already looking forward here to that great companion work of the *Elegies*, *Sonnets to Orpheus*, for—as we will discuss in the next chapter—the tree in the poet's ear is no less mythically extraordinary than the archetypal poet-god himself. And if anyone doubts that Rilke himself regarded art as a form of sacred magic, this late poem—one deeply related to the *Elegies*—should put that doubt to rest:

Magic

Such creations arise out of indescribable transformations.
Feel! and believe!
We suffer it often—the flame turns to ash;
and yet, in Art, dust is turned once more to flame.

Here is magic. In the realm of enchantment
the common word is elevated
and is nonetheless real as the call of the dove
to its invisible companion.[891]

In the German, the last line reads, "der nach der unsichtbaren Taube ruft"—literally, "that calls up (or after) the invisible dove." Thus the dove's call—exactly like the poetic call sounded in the *Duino Elegies*—doubles as a love song, a wooing of an unknown beloved, *and* the calling up of its own essentially *invisible* prototype, emblem of the entire invisible world itself.

This conjunction of the power of love in the soul and the magic of the poetic word—so organic to the discourse of the *Elegies*—recalls us yet again to the myth of Eros and Psyche.

Insofar as Psyche is born of earth, it follows that her (our) destiny—the transfiguration resulting from her quest for and ultimate marriage to Love—could entail, as well, the transformation of the earth that bore her, and of all the things and creatures that accompanied her on her long and arduous path. This poetic end—the assumption of the earth into a type of invisibility that signifies its spiritual ground—entails imaginative action that realizes the undying connection between the things of this earth and the invisible ideas that form and, through the mediation of the imaginative life of the soul, constantly transform them. Having gained archetypal ground, Rilke's poetic psychologizing thus finally gives elegiac expression to the ultimate aim that first took definite form in Spain. Inspired but not dominated by angelic being, the *Elegies* enact a vision of *the Word*—the carrying force [*tragender Strom*] of poetic voice or speech—becoming a river of creative life that doubles as the *inner soul place and time* where the invisible and the visible worlds, spirit and matter, heaven and earth, eternity and evanescence, being and becoming, angels and human beings, rendezvous.

> Look, I am living. On what? Neither childhood nor future
> diminishes . . . . Supernumerary existence
> wells up in my heart.[892]

Participating in an order of Time defined (not by meaningless succession but) by unlimited imaginative possibility, the poet's soul—purified by the travail of sorrow and elevated by poetic meditation—is illumined by the eternal presence of hope. Hermes, we may recall, named *quantity* as one of the essential features of the world of becoming; "supernumerary" (*Überzähliges* means literally "beyond number") existence suggests a higher-order spiritual being pouring through the poet's consciousness even as he affirms his human existence in the world of the here and now. "Überzähliges Dasein / entspringt mir im Herzen": Here is the Thought of the Heart. Psyche's crystal jar filling... and spilling holy water.

In his discussion of the *sublimatio*, Edinger writes:

> Modern individuals have had entirely too much *sublimatio*.... They need descent and *coagulatio*. The relative freedom of the sublimated state is an important achievement in psychic development, but only a part. It can be disastrous to be stuck in the sky. Ascent and descent are both needed. As an alchemical dictum says, "Sublimate the body and coagulate the spirit."[893]

We have elaborated at length the importance of the *sublimatio* in Rilke's *Elegies*; however, the poems unfold a dialectic of transcending and containing motions, and the balancing *coagulatio* requires its due. "Upward movement eternalizes, downward movement personalizes," adds Edinger. A passage toward the end of the Second Elegy,

> If only we too could find some defined, narrow,
> purely human place, our own small strip of fertile soil
> between stream and stone. For even now our heart
> transcends us....[894]

registers one early instance of numerous moments—akin to the alchemical *coagulatio*—that *balance* the *sublimatio* so prevalent in the poem. Without such counterforce, the poet intent on liftoff could indeed become "stuck in the sky." As we have just seen, a kindred contraction or condensation of consciousness certainly is woven into the texture of the culminating Ninth Elegy, and it is finally (not one or the other but) the *combination* of these seemingly contradictory motions that most fully describes the inner alchemy of the *Elegies*. Not surprisingly, alchemy recognizes the integral amalgam of the ascending motion of the *sublimatio* and the descending, incarnating motion of the *coagulatio* with its own name:

> Upward movement eternalizes; downward movement personalizes. When these two movements are combined, we get another alchemical process, namely, *circulatio*.[895]

Circulatio imagery does indeed appear in the *Elegies*, and does so—logically enough—more in the later than the earlier ones. The "bent bough" of the fig tree hailed at the beginning of the Sixth "drives the sap downwards and up";[896] significantly enough, it is this balanced internal motion that allows the tree (unlike the less self-contained human being) to bear ripe fruit as the sap "leaps from its sleep, scarce waking, / into the joy of its sweetest achievement." Rilke likens the bough of the fig tree to "the pipe of a fountain," and the ecstatic opening of the Seventh Elegy contains its own fountain-form *circulatio*:

> ...then, the trill, the foreplay
> of the fountain whose strong upward jet is always already
> caught by falling...[897]

The very last image of the entire cycle also includes mention of *both* rising and falling, After invoking "the rain / that falls on the dark earth in the early Spring," the *Elegies* conclude:

> And we, who always think of happiness
> *rising*, would feel the emotion
> that almost baffles us
> when a happy thing *falls*.[898]

The poet's own accent on *rising* and *falling* signifies the importance of these paired, dual motions, though in this final instance he seems to oppose rather than integrate them into a true *circulatio*. If, however, Rilke's ending appears to give a kind of precedence to the coagulatory descent, it is by way—as Rilke himself implies—of compensation for a historic imbalance. One might also observe that the initiating image of falling rain—while stressing descent—includes a covert *circulatio*. One would be hard put to imagine a better image of the *circulatio* than the cosmic circulation of the life-giving element of water between heaven and earth which, in its turn, helps drive *the cycle of seasons*—yet another (temporal rather than spatial) *circulatio* motif woven into the fabric of the poem.

The relevance of the *circulatio*—like that of its associated alchemical processes—cannot be limited to a set of specific instantiating images. Rather, it functions as an underlying psychospiritual dynamic shaping the transformations of consciousness that comprise the heart and soul of the poem.[899] Even as we have set in relief the constant interplay of transcending and delimiting motions in the *Elegies*, Edinger construes the *circulatio* as "*sublimatio* and *coagulatio*...repeated alternately, again and again." He amplifies this idea:

> Psychologically, *circulatio* is the repeated circuit of all aspects of one's being, which gradually generates awareness of a transpersonal center uniting the conflicting factors. There is a transit through the opposites, which are experienced alternately again and again, leading finally to their reconciliation.[900]

...before offering this still more pregnant elaboration of the *circulatio* by Jung himself:

> Ascent and descent, above and below, up and down, represent an emotional realization of opposites, and this realization gradually leads, or should lead, to their equilibrium....This vacillating between the opposites and being tossed back and forth means being contained in the opposites. They become a vessel in which what was previously now one thing and now another floats vibrating, so that *the painful suspension between opposites gradually changes into the bilateral activity of the point in the centre*.[901]

All of this applies tellingly to Rilke's *Elegies*. What "floats vibrating" in the "vessel" of the psyche may well be identified with the "vibration" (*Schwingung*—literally, "swinging between") that "attracts and consoles and helps" at the end of the First Elegy, adumbrating the advent of Orpheus. "Bilateral activity of the point in the centre" may be an awfully unpoetic image for "the place where the lyre / lifted, resounding—; the unheard of center" spoken of in Rilke's penultimate Sonnet to Orpheus, but is nevertheless a deeply kindred conception.

Another passage that Edinger offers as descriptive of the *circulatio* supplies the *cosmological* perspective necessary to complement the *psychological* one described by Jung. *The Emerald Tablet of Hermes* declares: "It ascends from the earth to the heaven, and descends again to the earth, and receives the power of the above and below. Thus you will have the glory of the whole world."[902] We are here back, once more, in the visionary realm of Rilke's own "View of Toledo." His poetic re-imagination of the prophetic force and meaning of El Greco's symbolic landscape—the *Duino Elegies*—clearly strikes the hammers of the heart to sing, at last, "the glory of the whole world."

As highlighted in the last chapter, Rilke conceived of the task of his *Elegies* to be a spiritual responsibility of the highest order, a religious mission kin to that bestowed upon Mohammed when the angel summoned him to his prophetic calling. In completing his *Elegies* (and, coincidentally, his unanticipated *Sonnets*) Rilke fulfilled that high mission. To be sure, he did not singlehandedly found a new "religion"; nor could that ever have been his aim. Nonetheless, his ten commanding elegies do—in the difficult, almost runic language appropriate to what may well be understood as a truly esoteric text—transmit the fundamental premises of a *soul-centered Weltanschauung* profound enough to offer an alternative to the religious doctrine that still dominates western culture. To draw out the lines of that world view still more fully, it would undoubtedly be helpful to probe more deeply into other ancient and modern esoteric currents (hermeticism, gnosticism, Sufism,[903] alchemy, depth and archetypal psychology, anthroposophy) intrinsically related to Rilke's poetic vision.[904] In the spirit of that endeavor—and in the interest of displaying yet more clearly the difference between Rilke's vision and prevailing spiritual norms—I give in some length these thoughts from Jung via Edinger on the *Emerald Tablet:*

> The above passage from the *Emerald Tablet* gives a clear expression of the difference between the alchemical attitude and the Christian religious attitude. Jung... writes: "[In the *Emerald Tablet*] it is not a question of a one-way ascent to heaven, but, in contrast to the route followed by the Christian Redeemer, who comes from above to below and from there returns to the above, the *filius macrocosmi* starts from below, ascends on high, and, with the powers of

> the Above and Below united in himself, returns to earth again. He carries out the reverse movement and thereby manifests a nature contrary to that of Christ and the Gnostic Redeemers."
>
> The difference in the images corresponds to the difference betwen religious faith and psychological empiricism. In another place, Jung puts it this way: "(From the religious viewpoint)... man attributes to himself the need of redemption and leaves the work of redemption, the actual *athlon* or *opus*, to the autonomous divine figure... [From the alchemical viewpoint] man takes upon himself the duty of carrying out the redeeming opus, and attributes the state of suffering and consequent need of redemption to the *anima mundi* imprisoned in matter." And again "[The alchemist's] attention is not directed to his own salvation through God's grace, but to the liberation of God from the darkness of matter."
>
> The alchemical *filius philosophorum* begins and ends on earth...[905]

"Because"—as Rilke says—

> ...being here amounts to so much, because all
> this Here and Now, so fleeting, seems to require us and strangely
> concerns us. We, the most fleeting of all.[906]

The Edinger-Jung passage may serve, if nothing else, to help allay modern qualms (such as Komar's) about the role of transcendence in Rilke. For when the poet-initiate returns to earth to (in Komar's words) "sing the living, the physical and limited world," he must—if he is to fulfill his redemptive task—successfully contain in the vessel of his soul knowledge of above *and* below, the "glory of the whole world." The poet cannot show the angel a mere clod of earth—symbol of primary matter yet to be worked on—but "the word he has worked for, the yellow and blue / gentian"—flower of the liberated *anima mundi's* deep poetic wisdom.

> Through nine openings
> With a great rumble in the mountain wall
> It bursts from the ground there and floods the fields
> In a rushing sea.

These lines from Book I of Virgil's *Aeneid*[907] celebrate the remarkable river Timavo (or, in Latin, Timavus). After traveling twenty-three miles underground, the Timavo wells forth from nowhere in an astonishing flood. Is it mere accident that Rilke wrote not only the initial Elegies, but, as well, the opening of his Tenth at Duino Castle, which stands no more than a couple of miles from the Timavo's tremendous springs? Traveling long and far down the subterranean channels of the soul and finally issuing forth from "nine openings," the voice of the Tenth Elegy wells forth in a veritable poetic flood:

> Someday, emerging at last from this terrifying vision,
> may I burst into jubilant praise to assenting Angels!
> May not even one of the clear-struck keys of the heart
> fail to respond through alighting on slack or doubtful
> or rending strings! May a new-found splendor appear
> in my streaming face! May inconspicuous Weeping
> flower.[908]

The opening lines of this last Elegy contrast dramatically with those of the First. Bitter lament of the human soul's estrangement from spiritual realms has given way to ecstatic jubilation attended—prospectively, at least—by an angelic audience. The voice of the poet, the *stream of reflection* that bears not only his psyche's pathos—the enormous, purifying force of pain—but, too, its logos—the speculative insight welling forth from the spring of psychological ideas—pours forth in celebration. The poetic soul, it seems, has found its source, the holy stream that—like the Timavo, and the craggy fount in Psyche's third labor—runs both above and below, uniting the soul's spiritual life with death's unending realms.

The body of the Tenth Elegy (composed ten years later, in 1922) embarks upon a journey into the realm of death, taking the elegiac spirit of Lament as a guide to the other side. First, though (looking back to Fifth Elegy) Rilke treats us to some scenes of humankind's unreal city: burlesque images of life as a fair of senseless pleasure, entirely ignorant of all that lies behind its gaudy placards and facades—depths opened only by the door of death. After that, however, the poetic self—associated, once more, with one of Rilke's leading types, the spirit of the youthfully dead—journeys at the side of the Lament into the domain of shades.

We cannot linger at all the sights visited on this journey, most all of which reflect, in one way or another, idea-images already touched upon in this chapter: temples, birds, sphinx-like faces, starry destinies, images of rising and of falling (e)motion. We shall, however, revisit the last place to which the elder Lament brings the dead youth, for it is similar to one we have seen before:

> ...the elder Lament
> leads him in silence as far as the wide ravine,
> where they see shimmering in moonlight:
> the Font of Joy. She names it
> reverently, saying, "Among the living
> it becomes a powerful stream."
>
> They stand at the foot of the mountain.
> And she embraces him there, weeping.[909]

No dragons, or eagles, to be sure—but hasn't Rilke been addressing the psyche's fears and terrors, as well as its spiritual visions, all along? And has this not always been the *Duino Elegies*' elevated, indeed prophetic aim: to approach the font of the water of life, and contain it in the vessel of the poetic soul, the invisible inner space formed by the *Elegies* themselves? To *see* life *through* death's clear mirror, and, in the stream of song, to be—on both sides. Here. Now.

CODA

In his book *The Great Code: The Bible and Literature*, Northrop Frye speculates upon the degree of authority commanded by various artists:

> If we are listening to music on the level of say, Schumann or Tchaikovsky, we are listening to highly skillful craftsmanship by a distinguished and original composer. If then we listen to, say, the "Kyries" of the Bach B Minor Mass or the Mozart Requiem, a certain impersonal element enters. What we hear is still "subjective" in the sense that it is obviously Bach or Mozart, and could not possibly be anyone else. At the same time there is a sense of listening to the voice of music itself. This, we feel, is the kind of thing music is all about, the kind of thing it exists to say.... It is the voice of drama itself that we hear in Shakespeare or Sophocles.[910]

The Russian poetess Marina Tsvetaeva felt similarly about Rilke and lyric poetry. In the spring of 1926, Rilke—at the urging of Boris Pasternak—sent her copies of the *Duino Elegies* and *Sonnets to Orpheus*. Tsvetaeva soon responded: "Rainer Maria Rilke! May I call you that? You, Embodiment of Poetry, must know that your name is a poem itself."[911] As J. D. McClatchy's remarks in the introduction to this book indicate, Tsvetaeva has not been wholly alone in her estimation. Nor has any work been more central to Rilke's reputation than the *Duino Elegies*.

It is one thing to recognize artistic stature, another to account for it. In his own most illuminating attempt to render such account in connection with the unsurpassed authority of the Bible, Frye proposes that we

> turn again to the traditional but still neglected theory of "polysemous" meaning. One of the commonest experiences in reading is the sense of further discoveries to be made within the same structure of words. The feeling is approximately "there is more to be got out of this," or we may say, of something we particularly admire, that every time we read it we get something new out of it. This "something new" is not necessarily something we have overlooked before, but may come rather from a new context in our experience.[912]

All this may well apply to the *Elegies*. This reader, at least, finds its well of meaning bottomless, its suggestive potential nigh inexhaustible.

Frye has more to say about the substantive source of that superabundance of meaning:

> The implication is that when we start to read, some kind of dialectical process begins to unfold, so that any given understanding of what we read is one of a series of phases or stages of comprehension. In the Middle Ages these phases were classified in definite schemata, starting with the literal or immediate sense and going on to a series of further senses, usually three, that is, four including the literal.[913]

Frye continues to cite Dante's exposition of the time-honored scheme consisting of *literal*, *allegorical* or *mythical*, *moral*, and *anagogical* levels of interpretation. Analyzing the biblical verse "When Israel came out of Egypt, and the house of Jacob from a people of strange speech, Judaea became his sanctification, Israel his power," Dante writes:

> For if we inspect the letter alone the departure of the children of Israel from Egypt in the time of Moses is presented to us; if the allegory, our redemption wrought by Christ; if the moral sense, the conversion of the soul from the grief and misery of sin to the state of grace is presented to us; if the anagogical, the departure of the holy soul from the slavery of this corruption to the liberty of eternal glory is presented to us.[914]

By this time, four-tiered schemes should hardly be unfamiliar to the reader of this book. While I shall leave the enterprise of exploring correspondences between this medieval scheme and those already noted in this book (Plato's divided line, Hermes' cosmology, Hillman's four types of soul-making, for instance) to the reader's own imagination, it may be illuminating to venture an interpretation of Rilke's *Elegies* along these same medieval lines. We might, for instance, construe the *literal* level of the *Duino Elegies* as *the totality of its referential significations* (objective contents such as descriptions of acrobats, birds, and seasons as well as more subjective contents including evocations of states of despair and joy); the *mythic or allegorical* level as *the purifying of the vessel of the soul to receive the holy water of life*; the *moral* level as the urgent need to accomplish *the task of transformation*; and the *anagogical* level as the transition from a state of existential despair *to the illumined state of human being* when—in communion with angelic presence and indeed the whole orb of being—"supernumerary existence wells up" in the poet's heart and issues forth in his creative word.

Many texts, of course, could—with a greater or lesser degree of profit—be interpreted along the lines of such a scheme. Frye's argument, however, suggests that the extraordinary authority of the Bible rests in part upon the way it represents *each and every* level so richly and fully. I would propose that the same could be said of Rilke's *Duino Elegies* and, even more aptly, of the whole corpus of Rilke's mature work, an opus which itself organically assumes the shape of another four-tiered topography of soul.

Another discussion in Frye's book may offer yet another window on the stature and authority of Rilke's *Duino Elegies*. In his first chapter, Frye ventures an exposition—based upon Vico—of the chief modes of linguistic expression successively embodied in distinct phases of history. Vico identifies three such modes—the *poetic*, the *heroic* or *noble*, and the *vulgar*; Frye renames these the *hieroglyphic*, the *hieratic*, and the *demotic.* To provide a relatively concise synopsis of these stages—and so avail ourselves of a critical tool that can further our understanding of the special power and appeal exercised by Rilke's *Elegies*—we can do no better than to quote Frye's most salient passages on each in turn.

Of the first phase, Frye writes:

> I think we can see in most Greek literature before Plato, more especially in Homer, in the pre-Biblical cultures of the Near East, and in much of the Old Testament itself, a conception of language that is poetic and "hieroglyphic," not in the sense of sign-writing, but in the sense of using words as particular kinds of signs. In this period there is relatively little emphasis on a clear separation of subject and object: the emphasis falls rather on the feeling that subject and object are linked by a common power or energy.... The articulating of words may bring this common power into being.... A corollary of this principle is that there may be a potential magic in any use of words. Words in such a context are words of power or dynamic forces.[915]

In contrast to this initial phase, Frye characterizes a second one in the following terms:

> With Plato we enter a different phase of language, one that is "hieratic," partly in the sense of being produced by an intellectual elite.... In this second phase language is more individualized, and words become primarily the outward expression of inner thoughts or ideas. Subject and object are becoming more consistently separated, and "reflection," with its overtones of looking into a mirror, moves into the verbal foreground. The intellectual operations of the mind become distinguishable from the emotional operations; hence abstraction becomes possible, and the sense that there are valid and invalid ways of thinking, a sense which is to a degree independent of our feelings, develops into the conception of logic.... Thoughts indicate the existence of a transcendent order "above," which only thinking can communicate with and which only words can express....
>
> The first phase of language, being founded on metaphor, is inherently, as Vico says, "poetic"; the second phase, which is Plato's, retreats from the poetic into the dialectical, a world of thought

> separate from and in some respects superior to the physical world of nature.[916]

Frye notes, too, that—whereas the first phase naturally inclines toward forms of distinctly poetic speech, *continuous prose* emerges as the natural vehicle of the second, hieratic phase.

As for the third, demotic or descriptive phase—one that likewise depends primarily upon continuous prose—Frye writes:

> This third phase of language begins roughly in the sixteenth century, where it accompanies certain tendencies in the Renaissance and Reformation.... Here we start with a clear separation of subject and object, in which the subject exposes itself, in sense experience, to the impact of an objective world. The objective world is the order of nature; thinking or reflection follows the suggestions of sense experience, and words are the servomechanisms of reflection....
>
> Hence this approach treats language as primarily descriptive of an objective natural order.... The criterion of truth is related to the external source of the description rather than to the inner consistency of the argument.[917]

In addition to these primary modes, Frye proposes two more that represent more modern incarnations of the "hieroglyphic" and "hieratic" modes. "Poetic or literary writing" and "'existentialist writing" represent manifestations of (respectively) the first and second phases within the historical time frame dominated by the third.

Even in this most abbreviated form, Frye's discussion offers much food for thought. Within the context of our present interest, it naturally provokes the question: which mode—or modes—best characterize Rilke's *Duino Elegies*?

In *Transcending Angels*, Komar explicitly asks—and answers—this question. Drawing upon Frye in the conclusion to her book, Komar writes:

> As the *Elegies* open, a Platonic mode of thought has immobilized Rilke's creativity, and this paralysis generates his poetic crisis. He perceives a transcendent realm beyond his human world—beyond his comprehension, but, more specifically, beyond his language. Rilke knows that language has moved from what Frye describes

> as its first stage...to its second...in which thought and language become separate from both the natural world and the transcendent world. This dialectical separation creates Rilke's poetic crisis.[918]

Komar thus—with good reason—identifies the *Elegies* as basically *hieratic* in spirit. Though she does not explicitly discuss Frye's subsidiary modes, it is fair to presume she would agree that the *Elegies* qualify as a modern version of the same—what Frye calls existentialist writing. *At the same time*, Komar tacitly recognizes that the *Elegies* are manifestly poetic and literary writing, a text that embodies the ideals of a quintessentially lyric poet and so (despite its hieratic character) *aims* towards the restoration of an essentially poetic universe. Komar:

> Only in the poetic word can subject and object, consciousness and world be rejoined. As long as he is engaged in the intellectual investigation of this problem, Rilke must operate in the second, Socratically determined phase of language. To enact his solution, however, Rilke must recapture the first "poetic" phase or archaic mode of language.[919]

In Frye's mind, at least, Rilke would hardly be alone in such an attempt. He construes a like intent to be the chief aim of modern literature (especially modern poetry) in general:

> [I]t is the primary function of literature, more particularly of poetry, to keep re-creating the first or metaphorical phase of language during the domination of the later phases, to keep presenting it to us as a mode of language that we must never be allowed to underestimate, much less lose sight of.[920]

Komar herself, however, does not feel the *Elegies* succeed in that attempt. Putting great weight on the Tenth Elegy, she understands the cycle as a whole as registering "the impossibility of using language archaically in a Platonic intellectual world."[921]

Komar's interpretation of the *Elegies* as a kind of dialogue between hieratic and poetic modes is apt and insightful, but I disagree with her main conclusions in two major respects. First of all, I see *Sonnets to Orpheus*—not the Tenth Elegy—as chiefly representative of Rilke's endeavor to realize the poetic ideals finally affirmed in the *Elegies* and (as we shall explore in subsequent chapter) regard that attempt as largely successful. Secondly—and still more pressingly pertinent to our understanding of the *Elegies* themselves—while Rilke's mind-set does derive in part from hieratic/existentialist premises, his rhetorical style is not at all consistent with those, and indeed suggests that that this mode—even when strongly leavened with poetic elements—does *not* in fact stand as the *Elegies*' main literary historical point of departure.

The *Elegies*, after all, do not read in the least bit like a Platonic dialogue or (despite their intellectual probity) any form of continous philosophical argument. Indeed, another historic ingredient is at play here, one we—following Frye's own mode of exposition—have so far left unmentioned.

Frye wrote *The Great Code* in order to account for the literary character of the Bible. After rehearsing his version of Vico's three primary modes of linguistic expression, Frye turns his attention to the Bible itself. Finding that "the origins of the Bible are in the first metaphorical phase of language, but much of the Bible is contemporary with the second-phase separation of the dialectical from the poetic," Frye finally decides, "the Bible fits rather awkwardly into our cycle of three phases, and we need another conception or two to account for it." Following Frye, we shortly discover those new conceptions to be essentially *rhetorical* in kind.

Frye continues:

> One of the verbal genres that are prominent throughout the second phase of language is rhetoric in the sense of oratory. Oratorical rhetoric is "hieratic" in the sense that it tries to draw its audience together in a closer unity, but is "hieroglyphic" in that it makes extensive use of figuration and devices usually associated with verse, such as antithesis and alliteration. Thus oratorical rhetoric...as we have it in the history of literature, represents a kind of transitional stage of language between first-phase metaphor and second-phase argument....Hence oratory at its best is really a combination of metaphorical or poetic and "existential" idioms: it uses all the figures of speech, but within a context of concern and direct address that poetry as such does not employ.[922]

We touch here upon the rhetorical gist of Rilke's *Elegies*. That element of *moral concern* suffuses the entire cycle, simultaneously engendering and flowing from its preoccupation with the rightful destiny of the human being. At the same time, an element of direct address is native to the

Elegies' poetic idiom and is indeed inscribed in the very cry that opens the poem; if Rilke does not expect an angel to hear his cry, he does expect *us* to do so. As Robert Hass, in his discussion of the *Elegies*, writes:

> [Rilke's] poems have the feeling of being written from a great depth in himself. What makes them so seductive is that they also speak to the reader so intimately. They seem whispered or crooned into our inmost ear.[923]

Frye, though, has more to say about the *oratorical* character of the Bible:

> The essential idiom of the Bible is clearly oratorical.... Oratory on the highest level of oracle, exhortation, *kerygma*, or whatever the most appropriate term is, has to be seen from both of its two aspects—metaphor and concern....
>
> The linguistic idiom of the Bible does not really coincide with any of our three phases of language, important as those phases have been in the history of its influence. It is not metaphorical like poetry, though it is full of metaphor.... It does not use the transcendental language of abstraction and analogy, and its use of objective and descriptive language is incidental throughout. It is really a fourth form of expression, for which I adopt the now well-established term *kerygma*, proclamation.[924]

Rilke's *Elegies*, of course, is a work of literature—but is it merely that, or is it not "more" as well? Profoundly oratorical, steeped in the dual elements of metaphor and concern, do the *Elegies* not, like the Bible, issue forth in that "fourth form of expression.... *kerygma*, proclamation"? From the opening declamatory question:

> Who, if I cried, would hear me among the angelic
> orders?

to the signature affirmations of the Seventh Elegy:

> Life here's glorious! [*Hiersein ist herrlich!*]

> Nowhere, beloved, can world exist but within.
> Life passes in transformation.

and the Ninth:

> Just once,
> everything, only for once. Once and no more. And we, too,
> once. And never again...
>
> Are we, perhaps, here just for saying: House,
> Bridge, Fountain, Gate, Jug, Olive tree, Window,—
> possibly: Pillar, Tower . . . but for saying, remember,
> oh, for such saying as never the things themselves
> hoped so intensely to be.

the *Elegies* issue vatic pronouncements. Indeed, the above lines suggest a form of declamatory speech itself—proclamation, even—as the telos of the time; *proclaim, that is, the deed of proclamation, the mission of the Word, to be of the essence of the human commission and the heart of our moral concern:*

> *Here* is the time for the Tellable, *here* is its home.
> Speak and proclaim.

And if the prototypical scene of *kerygma*, proclamation, requires accompanying hosts of angels, the triumphal opening of the last Elegy adds that to Rilke's repertoire:

> Someday, emerging at last from this terrifying vision,
> may I burst into jubilant praise to assenting Angels![925]

Frye again:

> Kerygma is a mode of rhetoric... though of a special kind. It is, like all rhetoric, a mixture of the metaphorical and the "existential" or concerned but, unlike practically all other forms of rhetoric, it is not an argument disguised by figuration. It is the vehicle of what is traditionally called revelation.[926]

It can hardly be altogether incredible to construe the *Elegies* as an essentially prophetic text, a vessel of revelation. As detailed in chapter 14, such was Rilke's original aim—one he pursued, in part, by immersion in the Bible as well as the Koran. The question of whether or not Rilke's *Duino Elegies* represent a genuine revelation is naturally one every reader must answer for him- or herself. Nonetheless, with respect to rhetorical mode, the *Elegies* present themselves—above all—as just that, consistently exhibiting an oratorical style much closer to the Bible than to Plato or Kierkegaard or even Goethe. If that style is not wholly without substance, this may go some ways toward accounting for the tremendous authority and power of Rilke's great opus.

The mode Frye calls *kerygma* does not consist exclusively of those signature moments of direct proclamation. Instead, the accompanying requisites of that mode tend to mold the literary character of an entire text: its rhythm, its discursive strategies, its overall shape or gestalt. Though we cannot delve into a complex analysis of these features here—for that one should read Frye—we can provide some critical indications of special relevance to the *Elegies*.

Frye, for instance, writes:

> Continuous or descriptive prose has a democratic authority: it professes to be a delegate of experiment, evidence, or logic. More traditional kinds of authority are expressed in the discontinuous prose of aphorisms or oracles in which every sentence is surrounded by silence.[927]

In this connection Frye cites not only the Bible but the Yoga Sutras of Patanjali, wherein "every sentence is a gnarled, twisted, knotty aphorism demanding a long period of study, able to carry a whole commentary by itself." Something of the same quality attaches to Rilke's poetic periods. Take, for instance, this passage from the Fourth Elegy, characterized by consistent parataxis culminating in a kind of koan:

> Angel and Puppet: then, finally, the play begins.
> Then what we keep apart, simply by our
> presence here, conjoins. Then from the separate
> seasons of our life that one great wheel
> of transformation arises. Above us, beyond us,
> the angel plays. The dying—surely they
> must guess how full of pretext
> is all that we achieve here. Nothing
> is what it is.[928]

This whole episode unfolding as the poet "waits before the puppet stage"—like many more passages of similar design—recalls too Frye's discussion of one of the Gospels' chief discursive techniques—the pericope. Frye describes the pericope as short discontinuous units wherein

"Jesus appears in a certain context or situation that leads up to a crucial act...or to a crucial saying, such as a parable or moral pronouncement." He elaborates:

> The rhythm of the Bible expands from a series of "kernels"...In the wisdom literature this kernel is the proverb or aphorism; in the prophets it is the oracle...in the Torah it is the commandment; in the Gospels it is the pericope...
>
> The Gospels are...a sequence of discontinuous epiphanies. In the pericope one may distinguish the kernel, as we have called it, the miracle, the parable, or the aphorism, and a "husk," a setting in which it takes place.[929]

The *Elegies* likewise consist of relatively discontinous series of settings or situations (external or internal, or both) which function as the "husk" for some Rilkean kernel: that grain of aphoristic wisdom ("Destiny is nothing more than what's packed into Childhood"), oracular pronouncement ("Being Here is glorious!"), commandment ("Speak and proclaim") or even miracle: ("Pillars, pylons, the Sphinx...Wasn't all this a miracle?").

This discursive amalgam of spiritual essence and mundane container (or divine intelligence and human vessel, logos or eros and psyche) finds expression in other, related elements of biblical rhetoric, including voice and rhythm. Frye:

> Traditionally, the Bible speaks with the voice of God and through the voice of man. Its rhetoric is thus polarized between the oracular, the authoritative, and the repetitive on the one hand, and the more immediate and familiar on the other. The more poetic, repetitive, and metaphorical the texture, the more the sense of external authority surrounds it; the closer the texture comes to continuous prose, the greater the sense of the human and the familiar.[930]

Once more, this rings profoundly true of Rilke's *Elegies*, and yet does so—as, indeed, in all the above cases—with a difference.

We've illustrated the oracular aspect of the *Elegies*; the passage from the Seventh structured by that long string of eight "Not only" clauses provides one instance of the cooperation of repetition, metaphor, and oracular tone. Still, the sense of *the human and the familiar*—produced in part by the way the continuous current of poetic voice contains and counterpoints the text's semantic parataxis—remains equally strong in Rilke. Indeed, a good deal of the *Elegies*' uniquely appealing power consists in the way its language effects constant, invisible transitions between the humanly familiar and the most strange; the way the momentum of the poem constantly leads from the precincts of intimately personal thought and feeling to unbounded spaces of cosmic depth and dimension that authorize, finally, impersonal, oracular saying.

Taking a passage in the Seventh Elegy as his point of departure, Robert Hass eloquently evokes this movement:

> Look at how he bores into us. That caressing voice seems to be speaking to the solitary walker in each of us who is moved by springtimes, stars, oceans, the sound of music. And then he reminds us that those things touch off in us a deeper longing. First, there is the surprising statement that the world is a mission, and the more surprising question about our fitness for it. Then, with another question, he brings us to his intimacy with our deeper hunger. And then he goes below that, to the still more solitary self with its huge strange thoughts. It is as if he were peeling off layers of the apparent richness of the self, arguing us back to the poverty of a great, raw, objectless longing.[931]

All this speaks to a companionable but critical difference between the voice of the *Elegies* and that of its biblical prototype. "Traditionally, the Bible speaks with the voice of God and through the voice of man," states Frye, but—while this may not be so far from the truth of Rilke's *Elegies* and their inspiring angel—the idiom, the styling of the relevant voices and their relationship, remains radically distinct. Though God does speak in Rilke's earlier *Book of Hours*, the angel of his *Elegies*—rhetorically speaking—remains silent, nor could one truly imagine the phrase "Thus saith the Lord"—employed by Biblical prophets—popping up in the *Elegies.*

Why not?

Rilke's principal *subject* and *organ of speech* is not the same as the Bible's. It is neither Israel in its relation to Jehovah, nor the Son of God who is One with Father and through whose Grace we may be also. Instead, it is the poet himself, *the individual human soul in its relation to the world of spirit.* Correspondingly, Rilke's voice is not so much "the voice of man" channeling "the voice of God," but (as Hass so well evokes) *the voice of Psyche, the human soul in its archetypal longing for union with the Spirit of Love and the fulfillment of Being that union confers.* Marina Tsvetaeva—even as she heard Rilke's as the voice of poetry itself—instinctly recognized this correlative truth. "You," she wrote to Rilke, "are a topography of soul."[932]

This most fundamental difference between Biblical and Rilkean idiom effects innumerable others in form and rhetorical style. Many of these flow from the truth that—whereas God is indubitably one with the fullness of Being and Truth, and the Christ of the Gospels, the Word incarnate, just as indubitably in full possession of it—the human soul, like Psyche on her quest, is not. In and of herself, she is intrinsically lacking, even empty—which need not be a negative designation, for nothing (including the universe) can be filled if there is no receiving void. Accordingly, we most frequently encounter Psyche on one or another phase of her long and arduous journey in search of the Spirit of Love, one or another stage of the travail she endures as she strives for union with that numinous source of being.

So it is that Rilke's utterance assumes the elegiac form of lament, for that quintessential expression of loss and longing doubles as the archetypal voice of the soul. So it is too that most of his oracular pronouncements have a significant element of uncertainty and openness and indeed—rhetorically speaking—often pose themselves as questions rather than wholly positive answers. ("What if we're here just for saying...?") Not only does the cycle's first, most famous proclamation ("Who, if I cried...?") frame itself as question; *all* of the Elegies in the cycle's first half (One through Five) feature questions at either the beginning or end of their first stanzas, and the question form remains ubiquitous throughout the poem. The triumphal declaration that opens the very last Elegy ("Someday, emerging at last from this terrifying vision, / may I burst into jubilant praise to assenting Angels!") phrases itself in terms of a subjunctive futurity characteristic—not of accomplished conclusions—but of the soul's prospective hopes and dreams.

That note of futurity brings us back to the issue of the shape of literary and historical time implicit in Vico and Frye. Frye diagrams his revision of Vico as follows:

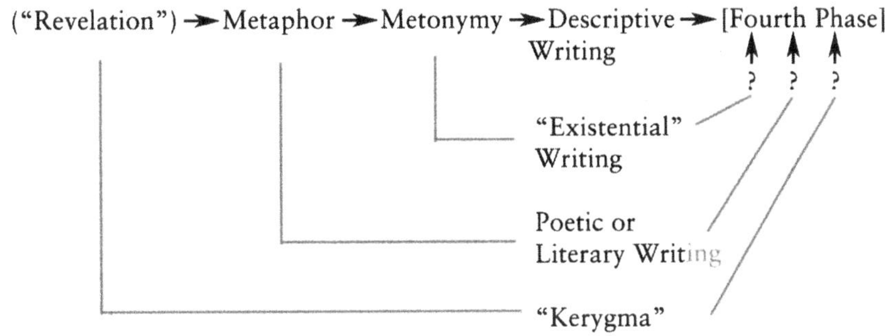

Rather drolly, Frye notes:

> In my diagram [the Bible] appears chronologically prior to metaphorical language: it is not, and it is partly my own lack of ingenuity in such matters that so represents it. But it has been traditionally believed to come from a time out of time, so the arrangement is not too misleading from that point of view.[933]

So much for the placement of "the first term" in Frye's scheme; but what of that enigmatic last term?

According to Vico, after the sequence of ages (in Vico, the mythopoetic, heroic, and demotic), there is a *ricorso*, or return, at which point the whole historical process begins again. Frye's enigmatic "Fourth Phase"—which he himself does not explicitly discuss—represents his own cipher of Vico's *ricorso*. Frye, of course, complicates matters somewhat: his diagram indicates no simple recursion (which would after all be inconceivable) but intimates a new age or stage which—even as it returns to archaic beginnings (Rilke's *Vorzeit*) and, too, that suprahistorical biblical "time out of time"—sums the influence of all subsequent developments in the horizon of its new future.

As we've seen in the course of our discussion, Rilke's *Duino Elegies*—even while going back before the beginning of time—contains strong currents of all the modes in the texture of its integral revelation. Perhaps those rather runic question marks and arrows in Frye's scheme may thus be envisioned as pointing towards Rilke's own miraculous text even as Rilke—and his *Duino Elegies*—direct us towards our future. As the poet well knew: "Denn auch das Nächste ist weit für die Menschen." For even what's next is far for humankind.

Chapter 18

PURE TRANSCENDENCE

"Petrarch," Florentine School

Amidst the political turmoil broiling in postwar Germany, Rilke departed for a lecture tour through Switzerland in June 1919. At the time, he had no definite intention of taking up permanent residence in the region. Still, despite initial resistance to the postcard-perfect scenery, Rilke soon responded to the beauty and relative serenity of this country that had largely escaped the ravages of war. After much peregrination, he decided to settle in Switzerland and, by virtue of the legal and financial aid provided by a host of new friends and admirers, finally achieved that aim. So it was that Switzerland became the poet's chief abode for the last five years of his life as well as the place wherein—after unending frustration—he would finally fulfill his poetic mission, the completion of the *Duino Elegies*.

The great event, however, required still more time and trouble. Nor did Rilke manage it without the help of new love. Shortly after his arrival in Switzerland, he revived a long-dormant acquaintance with an artist then living in Geneva, Baladine Klossowska. In the summer of 1920, their rekindled friendship ignited into a love that—with the outstanding exception of the relationship with Lou—proved the most significant of the poet's life. The tension between Rilke's passionate interest in the woman he called Merline and the solitude he so jealously guarded generated the emotional energy that finally enabled him to resume work on the massive poem cycle that from the first had sung of impossible love.

It was Merline, as well, who helped discover and prepare the place that finally rebirthed the *Elegies*. In the summer of 1921, Rilke had just spent the better part of six months desperately trying—and miserably failing—to make progress on the *Elegies* while housed in Castle Berg am Irchel. His term there expired, the poet found himself yet again seeking a suitable refuge for himself and his work. Scouting in the bucolic Swiss Valais—a landscape that, significantly, reminded Rilke of both Spain and Provence—he and his lover came across an advertisement for a small medieval chateau posted in a barbershop window. Once the Chateau Muzot had finally been secured (friends ultimately purchased it to put at Rilke's disposal), Merline worked indefatigably to make it habitable, cleaning and beautifying the little citadel Rilke would call home for the rest of his life. According to the dedication, the *Duino Elegies* are "the property" of Princess Marie von Thurn und Taxis-Hohenlohe. By rights, though, the finished work should belong every bit as much to Merline, the woman whose long-suffering love finally enabled their completion.

Finishing the *Elegies*, however, required still more than Merline and Muzot. Rilke would not rediscover the poetic source of his *Elegies* until the spirit of another woman—or rather, girl—intervened, inspiring another wholly unexpected work, one that not only paved the way for the *Elegies* but represented an independent, equally remarkable achievement.

Chateau Muzot (left); Rilke and Merline, ca.1923

Sonnets to Orpheus, Rilke's last renowned work, may well be regarded as the culmination of his whole poetic opus. The book's dedication, "geschrieben als ein Grab-Mal für Wera Ouckama Knoop" ("written as a grave-monument for Vera Ouckama Knoop"), acknowledges the personal occasion that triggered its writing. Rilke had known the Knoops casually in Munich, before the war; their daughter, Vera—already at that time a promising young dancer—had been his own daughter Ruth's playmate. In 1919, the nineteen-year-old Vera died of leukemia. Though Rilke learned of Vera's death soon after the fact, it was not until November of 1921—when Ruth announced her engagement—that Rilke communicated his condolences. Subsequently, a warm correspondence sprang up between Rilke and Vera's mother, Gertrude, culminating in the poet receiving from Gertrude on New Year's Day, 1922, sixteen densely written pages recording Vera's own account of the final stages of her illness—its painfully halting yet ultimately inexorable progress.

Vera's pages moved Rilke profoundly. By way of her words, she became a presence to him, a haunting image and source of inspiration. In his letter of thanks to Gertrude, Rilke interprets what he understood as "the two outermost boundaries of her [Vera's] *pure intuition*":

> ...*this*, that suffering is an error, a dull misapprehension arising from the physical that drives its wedge, its stony wedge, into the unity between heaven and earth; *and*, at the other extreme, the oneness of her wide-open heart with the existing and enduring world, this assent to life, this joyous impassioned communing to the very last moment with her native earth—ah, with only the earth? Nay (and this she could not know in these first attacks of breakup and parting)—with the Whole, with much more than the earth. Oh, how, how she loved, how she reached out with the antennae of her heart beyond all that can be grasped or encompassed here.[934]

The meditative stream thus inspired initiated the flood of work that burst Rilke's creative dam. On February 2, 1922, Rilke commenced an extraordinary exercise in "dictation." In a matter of three or four days, he composed or "transcribed"—in order, and without revision—all but one of the twenty-six sonnets that comprise Part I of the *Sonnets to Orpheus*. Then, on February 7, the poet—riding his creative wave—turned back to the half-finished *Elegies*. Tossing off the Seventh, Eighth, and Fifth entire, finishing the Sixth as well as the previously fragmentary Ninth and Tenth Elegies, Rilke completed the whole cycle in roughly a week. By February 15, the fabled *Duino Elegies* existed, at last.

Rilke, naturally, was ecstatic. He did not, however, allow his jubilation to impede the as yet unfinished flow of creative energy. Between February 12 and 15, in addition to the remaining Elegies, he wrote the well-known "Young Workman's Letter" discussed in both the Introduction to this book and Appendix I. Still more importantly, the following week saw him compose—once more out of whole cloth—the twenty-nine sonnets comprising Part II of *Sonnets to Orpheus*. By February 23, that second poem cycle, too, was finished. Rilke's productivity between the February 2 and 23, in Muzot, represented a bout of creative inspiration of astonishing intensity and duration, one virtually unparalleled in the annals of literary history. Predictably, the two great works that issued from it bear a deep—and profoundly complex—relationship to one another.

Given the creation story just rehearsed, it is natural that Rilke would regard the *Duino Elegies* and *Sonnets to Orpheus* as twin works, even a kind of diptych. In his famous letter to the Polish translator of the *Elegies*, the poet wrote:

> Elegies and Sonnets constantly support one another, and I consider it an infinite grace that with the same breath I was permitted to fill both these sails: the little rust-colored sail of the Sonnets and the Elegies' gigantic white canvas.[935]

Not all critics, however, consider *Sonnets* and *Elegies* to be—as Rilke himself phrased it—"of the same birth." Butler (one of the poet's first major interpreters) opines otherwise:

> Although the first sequence of *Sonnets to Orpheus* preceded and heralded the final elegy-crisis, whilst the second followed and concluded it, both sequences belong chronologically and by their inspiration to a later period.[936]

To be sure, the *Sonnets* and the *Elegies* do share profound affinities, especially with respect to thematic content. Both probe the great subjects that constantly characterize Rilke's poetry of soul—Death, Love, Anima, the World of Things, Suffering, Praise, Transformation. Even so (as Butler implies), it would be a grave error to underestimate how fundamentally different the two works actually are. Edward Snow aptly writes:

> Once all the similarities are enumerated, what remains most remarkable about the *Sonnets* is how completely other they are from the *Elegies* (even from those only days away from them). Their very exhilaration lies in being so.[937]

Snow continues to maintain that the difference dividing the two works is "less [one] of vision than of stance or demeanor." While recognizing the fundamental continuity underlying Rilke's oeuvre, we may nonetheless ask if the divergences Snow alludes to do not add up to—if not an entirely novel poetic vision—a whole new stage of Rilke's poetic soul-making.

Signal distinctions between the *Elegies* and *Sonnets* appear at the outset. Compare, for instance, the beginning lines of each:

> Who, if I cried out, would hear me then among the angelic
> orders? And even if one suddenly
> took me to heart: I'd be consumed by the strength
> of his more powerful being.
>
> A tree rose up. O pure transcendence!
> O Orpheus sings! O tall tree in the ear!
> And everything hushed.[938]

With respect to most every basic poetical perspective—voice, tone, theme, image, rhythm and form, grammar and rhetoric, phonetic sound, even[939]—one can hardly imagine two more dramatically divergent openings. The *Elegies* issue forth as the despairing cry of a first person—the authorial I—whose voice rolls onward in "the mighty current" that bears the poem. This poetic voice immediately identifies its distinctly human source and subject to be a form of consciousness alienated from both the divine realm (identified with the angel) and "the interpreted world" of objective things—the tree, for instance, on the slope, seen, perhaps, every day. The drama of the poem unfolds as the poem's author and speaker seeks to overcome his existential isolation by way of the transformative power of his own visionary calling. In the course of the poem, the poetic self (representing the archetypal human being) redefines or reconstitutes itself as a medial agent of transformation capable of bringing spiritual and earthly realms into creative relation, finding its own redemptive purpose and station in so doing. In the aforementioned letter on the *Elegies* (his most extensive and explicit discussion of their meaning), Rilke asserts, "We are, let it be emphasized again, in the sense of the Elegies, we are the transformers of the earth..."[940]

The same letter sheds light on the *Sonnets*, as well. It continues, parenthetically (and did not Rilke tend to regard the *Sonnets* as a kind of parenthesis to the *Elegies*?): "The Sonnets show particular instances of this activity, which here appears placed under the name and protection of a dead girl..."[941] Yet, if the *Sonnets* do reveal us as "transformers of the earth," it is only after "we" human beings ourselves have been transformed. For the *Sonnets* effectively *begin* where the *Elegies* leave off, and the poetic voice that authorizes the opening of the lighter cycle is *not* readily recognizably "ours"—a human voice—at all.

Look at the first line of the sonnet. No "I" speaks the opening of the poem; nor is its point of departure any manifestly human subject. In the beginning, instead, we are given the simple declarative record of a poetic event ("A tree rose up") followed by a series of apostrophes which link that event to the poem's chief subject and poetic source—no patently human being, but the divine mythic figure of Orpheus.

In order to best construe the opening lines of the sonnet (and, indeed, the whole poem and the cycle that follows its lead), it will prove most helpful to recall another of the *Sonnets*' historical sources of inspiration, another image that—together with that of Vera—fueled Rilke's imagination and kindled his creative fire. On an excursion with Rilke to Sion, Baladine Klossowska purchased a postcard reproduction of a drawing by the Renaissance artist Cima da Conegliano. Upon the couple's return to Muzot, Baladine tacked the image above Rilke's writing desk at Muzot, where it remained, for his meditation, months after she herself had departed. When Rilke began his sonnet cycle in February 1922, it was still there.

The drawing presents an archetypal image of Orpheus.[942] It depicts him playing a lyre or viol and singing while sitting up against a tree which rises (and branches, sheltering the singer) directly above Orpheus' tilted head, almost as if the tree were an extension of his figure. As Orpheus sings, animals emerge from the surrounding forest, attentively gathering around to listen to the divine music.

The first poem of *Sonnets to Orpheus* manifests the influence of the drawing upon Rilke's cycle. A classic instance of ekphrastic poetry, the entire poem reads as a poetic rendition of the visual work of art. To begin with, the relative positions of the tree and the figure in the painting make it plausible to "see" the tree rising up out of the aural center of Orpheus' intense musical concentration. Thus Rilke's first sentence and the string of exclamations following upon it ("A tree rose up. O pure transcendence! / O Orpheus sings! O tall tree in the ear!"). The rest of Rilke's poem reads naturally as a poetic version of da Conegliano's portrayal of the effect of Orpheus' song upon the animals.

In chapter 14, we sought to show how the *Elegies* may be understood as a poetic expansion of an originating archetypal image—one captured in El Greco's *View of Toledo*. The same may well be supposed (perhaps with less argument) of *Sonnets to Orpheus*. But how different the mood of the two images! El Greco's dark stormy sky swirls above a proto-expressionist landscape fraught with tumultuous (e)motion; heaven and earth clash and converge in a play of intersecting lines of force which the picture itself seems barely able to contain.

Da Conegliano's *Orpheus*, on the other hand (despite Orpheus' own somewhat pained facial expression), presents an image of peace, a magical soothing of naturally wild animal energies drawn—as if by a magnet—to the Orphic source of the song. Indeed, in the midst of the music, a divine silence reigns, ushering in some new, unheard of beginning.

> And everything hushed. Yet in that quiet cadence
> New transformations were beginning to appear...

As the archetypal scene itself makes clear, the serene mood prevailing in Rilke's *Sonnets*—so different from the *Sturm und Drang* of the *Elegies*—flows from the unique character of the Orphic voice that sings (in) the poem. The *Sonnets*' opening lines metaphorically identify that Orphic music with a motion of *transcendence* figured—initially—as the rising of a tree. The (often maligned) line "O tall tree in the ear" emphasizes that the act of transcendence inheres in the (f)act of song itself; that the sudden event of the tree's rising—*and indeed all the imag(in)ed action that follows in the poem*—transpires *in* and *through* the medium of poetic voice and song. In fact, even while ekphrastic, Rilke's poetic utterance refuses to figure itself as subservient or secondary to any visual imagination *but instead reclaims the mythic events to which the drawing itself refers as an issue of poetic song.* As befits the mythic figure of Orpheus itself, the poem's initiating speech acts identify myth with lyric poetry, representing each as the origin and essential nature of the other.

The poem enunciates and performs this truth in its first four short, quickly brushed sentences, the very tempo and rising rhythm of which contrasts so markedly with the long, heavily falling lines that roll out Rilke's *Elegies*. It is natural, too, that three of these sentences are apostrophes, for (as their "meaningless" signature "O" reveals) apostrophes register the power of pure voice and, in so doing, stand as rhetorical figures of the poetic *vocation* whose archetypal origin is the mythic figure of Orpheus. Consequently, the *Sonnets* do not—like the *Elegies*—originally strike a personal note. Attaining the peak of his lyrical genius, Rilke—in taking down "the strange dictation" that birthed the *Sonnets*—no longer speaks in so intimately personal an idiom, but sounds a purely mythic register.

From the first, we, as readers of (or, better, listeners to) the *Sonnets to Orpheus*, enter a scene dramatically different from the one we are made party to at the opening of the *Duino Elegies*. Rather than indwelling the agonized consciousness of a human subject cut off from heaven and from earth, we find ourselves introduced—as if by magic—into a mythopoetic realm. With the master poet's first strokes, we are invited into an entirely imaginal reality conjured by pellucid voice and transparent image, a realm, moreover, where divine and earthly, spiritual and natural realities intersect; a world far removed from the familiar experience of our own human subjectivity navigating swirls of thought and emotion amidst essentially foreign material and spiritual things. Indeed, in the poetic space of this "new beginning," the existential question of who and what we are—the pressing question that storms center stage as the *Elegies* open and never surrenders that privileged position—does not put in even a token appearance.

It does not remain so, entirely. Still, even when human figures (the speaker himself; you and I) enter the scene, they do not do so as primary authors of all that is going on, but rather as supporting actors playing in a mythopoetic space defined "once and for all" by Orpheus. Or rather, by Orpheus and his archetypal consort; the feminine presence suggested by the girl, Vera, but ultimately, inevitably, named Eurydice.

Very well, but what does this all finally mean? How are we to make sense of the critical difference between the two great works—the *Elegies* and *Sonnets*—that crown Rilke's career; how account for that difference, and how comprehend its deeper significance? To do so, we shall turn once more to the theoretical discourse that—seeing itself in the mirror of poetry and myth—construes these sister domains in terms of the logos of the soul: namely, archetypal psychology.

Perhaps it all comes down, once more, to psychology and religion, the spiritual premises that lie behind the poetry, molding the form of its soul, and the soul of its form. Speaking of form, let us glance once more at the *Elegies* and *Sonnets*—not, now, at the first lines of each, but (quickly, as if to gain a first impression) at the sculptural gestalt of the whole. Here, too, the contrast is immense and telling. The "tragender Strom" of the somber *Elegies*—the mighty river-current that bears the heavy cargo of the human self—gives way to a sparkling brook flash-dancing playfully down a meandering series of small translucent reflecting pools. The massive, monumental *ten*—the number of commandments Moses brought down from the mountain—simplifies into a duality spilling out into multiplicity: *two* groups of twenty-some-odd sonnets adding up to a more or less indefinite number, a long beaded sequence that—while not exactly unending—does not mathematically or esoterically figure any form of completion.

Nor is the reference to Moses here accidental. We have seen, in chapter 14, that Moses and Mohammed were both very much on Rilke's mind in Spain when the archetypal lineaments of the *Elegies* took shape in his mind. Moses and Mohammed—two great prophets of monotheism; two great messengers of the One God whose essence lay in a transcendent power so complete His true name could not be uttered, nor His aspect lawfully imaged. The spiritual burden Moses had to carry to promote this God and defend his ways to a people desiring, by nature and custom, to see divinity manifest in many things (including the "graven images" smashed as idols) is well known. Yet one image, at least, has been sanctioned and hallowed and passed down through time's long corridors: western man himself has been (re)made in the image of the One God. So it is (as Freud recognized in one of his latest works[943]) that Moses' ancient spiritual burden is carried, still, today; borne, for better or for worse, by the human ego. The weight of that burden—its beauty and its terror—remains inscribed in our psychology, in the language of consciousness, and is present whenever we say, simply, "I"—as Rilke (donning the mantle of the prophet) says "I" at the beginning of his *Elegies*, lamenting the fact that the transcendent God and his angels seem to have abandoned him and his world, leaving his singular human being as an image without origin, an empty reflection, a mere shadow and idol of itself.

There is, however, another tradition; a tradition that recognizes innumerable faces of divine presence pictured in diverse images of many Gods. It is not exactly a religious tradition—in the sense usually understood by that term—in part because the dominant monotheistic stream has shaped our very notion of "religion," and in part because (as Hillman points out) the Greeks themselves did not have a proper "theology" or even a word for "religion" per se. The Greeks did, however, have (even before their famed and noble philosophy) *mythology,* a rich body of poetic lore that spoke of divine forces—*theoi*, or Gods—of which there were many. It is this polytheistic tradition Hillman champions in his many books and views as the root and foundation of archetypal psychology. It is to this tradition as well that Rilke turns in addressing his Sonnets to Orpheus.

To be sure, on any conscious level, Rilke could never be called a "polytheist." Despite his lifelong wrestling match with Christianity, the poet, when speaking the language of religion, most often addressed "God" in a manner thoroughly conditioned by monotheistic tradition. This is true in his early, Russian-influenced *Book of Hours* and its prose companion, *Tales of God*, as well as in much of *Malte* (which draws, in significant measure, on that same Russian stream). As late as "The Young Workmen's Letter"—the signal prose work born with the late *Elegies* and the *Sonnets* in that fateful February—Rilke treats religious matters in a manner unquestionably framed by monotheistic presumption and vocabulary.

In that letter, Rilke is still struggling to wrench his mind loose from the Christian prescriptions he first confronted—violently—in his *Visions of Christ* twenty-five years earlier. As in the crucial gestation period for the *Elegies*, he does so in good measure, not by turning away from monotheism, but by recourse to his own imaginations of Jewish and Islamic spirituality. Rilke's workman—a thin mask for his own deep convictions—affirms: "When I say: God, that is a great conviction in me, not something learnt" before boldly lashing out at the spiritual barriers erected between man and God in the name of Christ: "But now at last leave him out of the question. Do not always force us back into the labour and sorrow that it cost him to 'redeem' us, as you put it. Let us, at last enter into the state of redemption." The workman continues:

> Otherwise the situation of the Old Testament is certainly better, it is full of pointers toward God, wherever you open it, and when one is heavy, one falls right into the middle of God there. And once I tried reading the Koran...it too is a mighty pointer, and God stands as the end towards which it points, in his eternal rising, in an East without end.[944]

Later, in the same letter, Rilke explicitly heralds the founding principle of monotheism:

> One should endeavour to see in every power claiming a right over us all power, the whole of power, power in essence, the power of God. One should say to oneself, there is only *one* power.[945]

Despite such arguments, however, Rilke—as this book repeatedly reveals—can in no wise be identified as an adherent to any traditional form of monotheistic religion. From his adolescent break with his native Catholicism onward, his central commitment to his poetic vocation required him to mold his religious feelings into forms that subordinated any orthodox concept of "God" to the internal demands of his own individual soul's creative art. His early *Visions of Christ* announced the lifelong struggle, and his early liaison with Lou empowered him to rethink religion in a manner reformed by her profound *psychological* intelligence. For all its native religiosity, Rilke's *Book of Hours* is, by any orthodox measure, a heretical text, and the deeply interior, subjective, and soulful *Elegies*—despite their huge debt to religious scripture—center upon the transformative role of the poetic human being, not worship of any (one) God.

And yet, and yet...the psychology of these great works remains profoundly conditioned by the monotheistic religions that feed the spirituality expressed in them. Both speak from the center of an "I," a prophetic self or literary persona, whose self-conscious self-concern bears the stamp of the monotheistic vision that ultimately grounds the psychology of the modern self qua ego, or ego qua self. ("Since the religion in our culture has been monotheistic," writes Hillman, "our psychologies are monotheistic."[946]) For all the archetypal dissemination deeply at work in the discourse of the *Elegies*, the heroic ego (as the Sixth Elegy testifies) still stands—though bent and bowed—at its center, even as it is the voice of an agonizingly self-preoccupied human "I" that so dramatically opens the poem.

I do not levy these charges pejoratively. Even if it were to be desired, no one steps lightly out of history's shoes, let alone one's own skin. *The Book of Hours* and the *Elegies* work to transform Rilke's cultural heritage—including its dominant monotheism—and help recast its spiritual language in such a fashion as to rejuvenate and open it to soul.

Still, something else is going on, as well, especially in many of Rilke's *New Poems*—a less subjectively centered work which carefully attends innumerable things of the world and begins (both volumes, in fact) with ekphrastic poems about Apollo, Orpheus' mythic father. Nor can we speak of "an agonizingly self-preoccupied human being" at the start or finish of Rilke's *Sonnets*. This is so, in some measure, because Rilke's Orpheus—the "God" to whom the *Sonnets* are addressed—is not derivative of a Judeo-Christian or Muslim deity, but belongs to that other spiritual tradition not so readily recognizable as "religion"—the mythological polytheism of the Greeks. Consequently, the *psychology* that underlies the poetics of Rilke's *Sonnets* possesses a different point of departure than that informing the *Elegies*. This is so even if we regard the psychologizing accomplished in the *Elegies* as the indispensable prerequisite to and preparation for the unique kind of soul-making enacted in the *Sonnets*. From the outset, the psychology of the *Sonnets* is less centered on the empirical human self, and is even more purely an *archetypal psychology* that puts soul at the center, envisioning the heart of the human psyche to lie in its original relation—not to "God"—but the gods.

Not that Rilke populates the *Sonnets* with hymns to a host of pagan deities. Though Apollo gains passing mention, Orpheus remains the sole central deific figure. Even so, in no wise can the *Sonnets* (unlike, for instance, *The Book of Hours*) be made to conform to an essentially monotheistic universe of thought derived from Judeo-Christian or Islamic models. Rilke himself refers to Orpheus as "*a* God" (I, 3), and directly addresses him as (the) "singing God," (I, 2) or "divine one" (I, 26), but *never* as (the one) "God." The resonances of that singular and exclusive name would be wholly incommensurate with the tenor of the poetic world of the *Sonnets*. Orpheus, to be sure, reigns supreme in his province ("We shouldn't take / pains over other names. Once and for all / It is Orpheus, when it sings"—I, 5) but his *particular* power of song is not absolute sovereignty, not "the whole of power, power in essence, the power of God." One can feel the poetic effect of that all-important difference in every line.

Correspondingly, the psychology at work in the *Sonnets* is not determined by the conceptual delineations derived from monotheistic religion which (as we've emphasized) have tended to stamp our very idea of religion, setting it apart—for instance—from "psychology," separating the logic of the one God (theology) from the logos of the soul. Hillman, on the other hand, defines some of the fundamental features of a *polytheistic psychology* rooted in Greek mythology in the following terms:

> Polytheistic thinking shifts all our habitual categories and divisions. These are no longer between transcendent God and secular world, between theology and psychology, divine and human. Rather, polytheistic distinctions are among the Gods as modes of psychological existence operating always and everywhere. There is no place without Gods and no activity that does not enact them.[947]

We begin here to see more clearly the way a polytheistic vision cleaves us away from the world of *Elegies*, ushering us into that of the *Sonnets*. The *Elegies* open by wrestling with the very divisions Hillman names: the terrible cleft between the divine (the angel) and the human being, between some transcendent God or his numinous representatives and the mundane reality of a despiritualized world. Hillman's description of the Gods as "modes of psychological existence operating always and everywhere," on the other hand, begins to lay a foundation for a deeper understanding of the nature of the Orphic God of the *Sonnets*, one substantially furthered by a companion passage that begins with a further elucidation of the relation between psychology and religion:

> The difference between religion and psychology lies not in our description of the Gods but in our action regarding them. Religion and psychology have care for the same ultimates, but religion approaches Gods with ritual, prayer, sacrifice, worship, creed. Gods are *believed* in and approached with religious methods. In archetypal psychology Gods are *imagined*. They are approached through psychological methods of personifying, pathologizing, and psychologizing. They are formulated ambiguously, as metaphors for modes of experience and as numinous borderline persons. They are cosmic perspectives in which the soul participates. They are the lords of its realms of being, the patterns for its mimesis. The soul cannot be, except in one of their patterns.[948]

Most every sentence of this passage illuminates a critical dimension of Rilke's relation to his "singing God," Orpheus, "lord" of the realm of nature and lyric song, the "numinous borderline person" at home in the (non)dual realms of life and death who provides "the cosmic perspectives" our author's individual poetic soul (and, ideally, ours as well) participates in, the ground of his very being.

Hillman makes clear, too, that a polytheistic psychology does *not* entail literalistic belief in many Gods. No psychological perspective is gained—no soul-making space expanded—by retaining a traditional notion of and relation to deity while simply fracturing and pluralizing that relation. Rilke, too, rejects overly external, literalized forms of belief and worship in the *Sonnets*. Rather—echoing a theme already sounded in the *Elegies*—the poet affirms that the domain of sacred relation remains *interior* to the imaginal domain and faculty of the soul itself. In the very first sonnet, the poet implies that the "temple" wherein Orpheus' divine music may be received and honored is no outward sanctuary, but the soul-space opened by the most inward of our senses: hearing. The third sonnet sounds a similar theme, albeit more bluntly: "At the crossroads of two / heartpaths, there is no temple to Apollo."

Rilke's fifth sonnet, however, does highlight another significant contrast between the *Sonnets* and *Elegies* with respect to the abode—or rather, the *abiding*—of the God(s), one traceable to the different psychologies underlying the two "twin" works. The romantic poet Friedrich Hölderlin exercised enormous influence upon the *Elegies*. Tonally and thematically, Hölderlin's Odes and Hymns figure as the *Elegies*' closest literary ancestors.[949] The *Elegies* open in the space of what Hölderlin called the *dürftige Zeit*—a "needy" or "lacking" time, a historical period or moment marked by the felt absence of divine presence. If, however, according to the tenets of polytheistic psychology, the archetypal power of the Gods indwells the soul so that "there is no place without Gods and no activity that does not enact them," the idea of (to employ Owen Barfield's term) a "disgodded world" or *dürftige Zeit* marked by the departure of the God(s) loses a certain quotient of force and intelligibility. Hillman, in fact, begins one late essay by raising doubts about the logic informing Hölderlin's classic notion:

> The question is: Have the gods truly fled? Is this a *dürftige Zeit?* Even should this indeed be a time of need, a time of impoverished

soul, does it necessarily follow that therefore the gods have fled? Can they leave the world at all?[950]

Rilke, in the beginning of his fifth sonnet, supplies his own sort of answer:

Raise no memorial. Only let the roses
bloom each year for his sake.
For it is Orpheus. His metamorphoses
in this thing and that.

Orpheus, Rilke intimates, should hardly be memorialized with a gravestone, because Orpheus lives on in all things; since the rose's (and all of nature's) transformation *is* Orpheus, it naturally follows that Orpheus *is*. Accordingly, the poetic universe of the *Sonnets* is not marked by divine *absence*, but rather by divine *presence*: the ubiquity of Orphic divinity in the soul and in the world. The angel of the *Elegies* never surrenders his transcendent numinosity, remaining, even in the most affirmative passages of the *Elegies*, at a significant distance from the speaker and his earthly world; the Orphic divinity, on the other hand, remains immanent in all things and in the poetic soul that sings their changes. This dramatic difference underlies what may well be the most patent contrast between the *Elegies* and the *Sonnets*. The former are primarily poems of lament keyed to the dominant of sorrow, whereas the *Sonnets* (for the most part) pour forth as songs of joy.

By the way, the title and topic of that Hillman essay calling into question the idea of the *dürftige Zeit?* It is "Orpheus."

But let us return, for a moment, to the longer Hillman quotation cited earlier, and his statement that in traditional religion "Gods are *believed* in" while in archetypal psychology "Gods are *imagined*." Even at his most religious, the poet Rilke had always aggressively pushed his spirituality away from the pole of doctrinal belief towards active imagination. *The Book of Hours* represents a concerted and radical effort to reimagine a relation to God—or divinity—true to the creative prerogatives of the individual soul. The same can be said of the *Elegies*, though Rilke's own soul history necessitated a very different treatment of the theme at the later date.

Both works, however, do struggle heroically with the difficult psychological legacy bequeathed by the monotheistic religiosity Rilke—even as a child—had taken to heart.[951] We can well speculate, however, that the *Sonnets* owe much of their beauty and levity to their quite different, quintessentially mythopoetic point of spiritual departure. The inner transformations achieved through Rilke's other works no doubt made possible the novel platform; still, it may be imagined that the soul-perspective finally achieved accorded more naturally with the poet's intrinsically poetic soul and its calling. Discussing Rilke's late turn to Orpheus, Butler writes:

> Here, in the transparent radiance of Greek symbolism, was to be found the apotheosis of art as a cosmic, creative, transforming force, which Rilke had tried to achieve in the God of *The Book of Hours* and the angels of *Duino Elegies*.... The functions and the destiny of Orpheus were clearly a mythical counterpart of Rilke's, and therefore of all poets and of poetry itself. Almost at the end of his poetical career Rilke ceased to strive after esoteric symbolism and surrendered to the power of the greatest poetical mythology the world has known. Orthodox Russia, the Bible, the Apocrypha and the Koran had hitherto supplied Rilke with his mythical framework at the expense of violent ambiguities. His aesthetic religion accorded better with Orpheus.[952]

Well said. We need merely add that what is here called Rilke's "aesthetic religion" can only be understood when simultaneously comprehended as his (mytho)poetic psychology.

We have argued that certain defining differences between the *Elegies* and *Sonnets* flow, in good measure, from the divergent spiritual traditions informing these works (religious monotheism on the one hand, and Greek mythological polytheism on the other) and the distinct psychologies drawn from those traditions. To comprehend more fully exactly *why* and *how* this is so, we must refocus our attention upon a crucial correlative difference: namely, that between (the idea of) *Man* and (the idea of) *Soul*. It is this critical difference that Hillman concentrates upon in the fourth and final chapter of *Revisioning Psychology* named, fittingly, "Dehumanizing or Soul-making." In accordance with the schema underlying the argument of this book, it is to this chapter we shall turn in order to construe the unique soul-initiative at the heart of the fourth great work of Rilke's maturity, his *Sonnets to Orpheus*.

Hillman introduces the fundamental issue as follows:

> Now the crucial emphasis is upon the distinction between psyche and the human. This does not, however, imply a division between the human and psyche, separating actual man from actual soul....
>
> However, of these notions, psyche and human, psyche is the more embracing, for there is nothing of man that soul does not contain, affect, influence or define. Soul enters into all of man and is in everything human....
>
> But the statement that soul enters into everything human cannot be reversed. Human does not enter into all of soul, nor is everything psychological human. Man exists in the midst of psyche; it is not the other way around. Therefore soul is not confined by man, and there is much of psyche that extends beyond the nature of man. The soul has inhuman reaches.[953]

The difference between man (or the human being) and soul finds clear expression in the initial sonnet to Orpheus, effectively opening the space of the speaker's relation to the Orphic God. We've argued that the first sonnet—unlike the beginning of the *Elegies*—hardly revolves around the human personality of its voice, but, sounding a mythopoetic register, focuses its lyric force upon conjuring the divine figure of Orpheus, invoking the archetypal power of his song and evoking the imaginal world that issues forth in and through it.

It would, however, be dead wrong to suppose that the human character of the speaker does not register at all in the first poems of the cycle. Even while singing of Orpheus, the poem's speaker does not wholly identify his own (human) being with that of Orpheus, the God whom he addresses as an other—"du"—in the first poem's last line. While the *Sonnets* do not, like the *Elegies*, begin with the author decrying the distance between his own human being and divine being, that difference itself remains inscribed in the very generic form of the poem—Sonnets *to* Orpheus—and remains, too, a generative force in it, especially towards the beginning. The third poem takes this difference as its point of departure:

> A God can do it. But how—tell me—shall
> a man follow through the narrow lyre?
> His sense is cleft.

and elaborates the theme in the cycle's signal moment of ontological (re)definition:

Song is Being. Simple, for a God.
But when will we *be*. And when will he

spend the earth and stars on our being?

To be sure, a trace of the angst that infuses the *Elegies* echoes in this poem—but it is only a trace, for the distance between the divine and the human appears much less absolute in the *Sonnets*. The *Elegies* famously open on a note of anguish as the author despairs of any audience among the angelic orders, lamenting that no member of the divine hierarchy appears disposed to hear his all too human cry. In the *Sonnets*, however, the speaker opens by celebrating Orpheus' presence, and (throughout the early poems) appears on rather intimate terms with the God whom he addresses directly, employing the familiar (rather than impersonal and formal) form of "you" (*du*). The energy of the poetic discourse, moreover—rather than repeatedly dwelling upon the inaccessible nature of the God—consistently strives (in accord with Hillman's definition of archetypal psychology) to *imagine* the essence of Orpheus' divine being, and to re-envision the world from that perspective. The momentum of the poetic address generically constituting Rilke's *Sonnets to Orpheus* persistently tends, not to *erase* the difference between human and divine being, but to *bridge* it; not to deny the God's inhuman reach, but to employ the vessel of poetic voice as a means of entry into the God's archetypally mythopoetic world.

Very well, but how does this discourse about man and god reflect upon the difference between man and soul? To see this, we must ask still more exactly *how* Rilke's sonnets achieve the ends just described. The *Sonnets* do not bring their human speaker into the neighborhood of divine power (as does, to some degree, *The Book of Hours*) by inflating man, and willfully expanding the power and province of the "I," *but rather by opening "man" up to the power that participates in both the human and divine realms, enabling true converse between them: namely, soul.* Hillman—drawing upon neo-Platonic roots of archetypal psychology—writes: "Even if psyche refers to an individual soul here and now lived by a human being, it always refers equally to a universal principle, a world soul or objective psyche distinct from its individuality in humans."[954] Consequently, it is soul that mediates between the human individual and the universal or archetypal realm of divine beings, powers, and ideas. If "man exists in the midst of psyche," and the archetypal power of the God(s), too, indwells the soul, then it follows that man does indeed have access to the Gods—not through the unbroken center of his own egoity—but in and through the currency of "his" multifaceted soul.

True, the distinction between human self and soul is not always easy to make or maintain, especially given the legacy of a psychology that tends to identify the soul with the self of man. Hillman notes that the very term "psychology" originated with Melanchthon, an associate of Luther, and "makes its appearance together with the new terms of the Reformation: self-regard, self-love, self-conceit, self-destruction."[955] Rilke, however, draws the distinction between self and soul quite clearly and decisively near the opening of his cycle. In fact, doing so—if it is not the poet's very *first* order of business—counts as his *second*.

In the first sonnet, Rilke introduces the Orphic God, calling little attention to himself. In the second sonnet, the speaker does present himself, repeatedly employing (as he does not once do in the first sonnet) forms of the first person: *my, me; myself, I*. He does not, however, foreground or delve into the ground of his own independent human personality but rather introduces himself in connection with an imaginal figure quite distinct from his own being. Indeed, it is "her" advent that opens the poem, preceding and preparing all mention the speaker makes of his own self:

> And it was almost a girl who emerged from
> the consonant pleasure of song and lyre
> and shone clear through her shady spring attire
> and made her bed within my ear's deep drum.

This figure—*like* a girl, but not, after all, wholly human—is, of course, an anima image, a figure not of the speaker of the poem, the man himself, but of his soul.

Or, at least, the soul that may *appear* to be his, insofar as it is *in* him, in his hearing (just as Orpheus' "temple"—the place wherein his music may be received—is in the animals' hearing). Yet, as Hillman details, this inherence does not, literally speaking, identify soul and human being, does not make soul "his":

> That the soul is experienced as my "own" and "within" refers to the privacy and interiority of psychic life. It does not imply a literal ownership or literal interiority. The sense of "in-ness" refers neither to location nor to physical containment. It is not a spatial idea,

> but an imaginal metaphor for the soul's nonvisible and nonliteral inherence, the imaginal psychic quality within all events.[956]

Rilke—or his poetic persona—knows this. The girl-like figure issues forth from the region of divine song, takes up dwelling in the poet's organ of inner receptivity (the ear), and—unpredictably—may readily retreat and even vanish from the sphere of his human consciousness:

> Whither is she sinking out of me?. . . . A girl almost. . . .

So at the end of the poem—as well as its beginning—we are in the domain of a familiar mythic topos of soul:

> The sense of in-ness is fundamental to all psychologizing. The soul draws us through the labyrinth of literalisms ever inward, realizing itself through retreat. The retreating nymph is a perennial anima image in myth.[957]

So it is that—just as Rilke forged a new connection with the Orphic myth through his encounter with the spirit of Vera Ouckama Knoop—the speaker of the poem maintains his relation to the power and province of the Orphic song through a feminine soul figure, one who appears throughout the cycle as a nymph, a dancing girl modeled on Vera herself, or Eurydice. For Rilke, at least, we may well say: no Orpheus without Eurydice, no poetic God without personified (and personifying) soul.

The *Sonnets* provide no end of evidence of this imaginative truth. To begin with, the dual world of the Orphic deity—the ready passage between the worlds of life and death so central to his archetypal identity—depends, in Rilke's poem as well as the Ovidian myth, upon Orpheus' relation to a feminine soul figure. Addressing Orpheus, the last tercet of the second poem opens:

> Where is her death? O, will you yet invent
> this theme, before your song consumes itself?

The singing of Rilke's Orphic song, the *event* of the poem in time, unfolds in a mythopoetic space opened by soul qua anima's inherent relation to death, and so—among other things—represents Rilke's last and greatest variation on the theme of Death and the Maiden.

It is, however, not only the relationship to the underworld that is opened by the soul. In the imaginal domain of Rilke's Orphic myth, underworld and overworld cannot be divided, and the soul, in "her" unconscious sleep, mediates the poetic speaker's relationship, not just to the realm of the dead, but to all things of the living world as well, the *whole* world. The second poem tells us that girl-like figure "made a bed inside my ear..."

> And slept in me. And her sleep was everything....
>
> She slept the world.

So it is, too, that the *Sonnets'* superb treatment of things (reminiscent of the *New Poems*) and the crucial thematic of their inherent transience likewise finds itself under the auspices of an Orphic deity who—if he has not *literally* brought Eurydice back from the dead—has remained united with the soul's dark knowledge:

> Be forever dead in Eurydice—in praise of things
> ascend, singing, back in the pure relation...

That soul-character, moreover, remains intrinsic to the poet's very being:

> Be—and know at the same time the condition of not-Being...[958]

"To be or not to be"—this, then, is *not* the question, for the poet of the soul must know what it means to be *and* not be—both, at once.

This soul, we must reemphasize, is *not* exclusively human, and its illimitable poetic reach in fact depends upon its transcendence of human egoity and subjective self-reference. Hillman:

> Should we dehumanize psyche, we would no longer speak so possessively and with such clinging subjectivism, about *my* soul, *my own* feelings, emotions, afflictions, dreams.... The psyche displays itself throughout all being. Present and past, ideas and things, as well as humans, provide images and shrines of persons. The world is as much the home of soul as is my breast and its emotions. Soul-making becomes more possible as it becomes less singly focused upon the human; as we extend our vision beyond the human we will find soul more widely and richly, and we will rediscover it, too, as the interiority of the emptied, soulless objective world.[959]

This passage speaks volumes about the psychology underlying the remarkable art of Rilke's *Sonnets* and may well be read as a kind of gloss on the passage from the *Elegies* to the *Sonnets*. The *Elegies*, we may imagine, plumb the depths of the subjective human psyche so profoundly that the alchemical soul work accomplished in them allowed Rilke, finally, to "come out the other side" in his *Sonnets*. The human solution sought in the *Elegies* suddenly transforms—like a substance at a boiling point—into something quite different: a poem issuing less from the soul of a human person(ality) than from the soul of the world, or (perhaps more accurately) an inspiration finally arriving at the confluence of these terms.

It is, indeed, just this transcendence of the thoughts and emotions comprising the personal strata of the human psyche that the poet—speaking, fittingly, a purely symbolic language—heralds at the opening of the *Sonnets to Orpheus*. For the tree that rises in the first line is no "ordinary" tree, but akin to the philosophic tree illustrated in the sixth plate of the alchemical series *Splendor Solis*. Henderson and Sherwood comment:

> Here the emphasis is upon growth as the central symbol, represented by a tree with golden roots and gold-highlighted branches and leaves.... From a psychological point of view, this plate refers to the growth that has come from the labor of working-through, preparing the way for *an encounter with the unconscious which goes deeper than the personal complexes and issues derived from childhood*. The tree has a golden crown around the base of its trunk, rather than at the part of the tree we call its crown, signifying that this is the tree of the philosophers.[960]

Orpheus, in da Conegliano's image, sits and plays—just there, at the base of the trunk, in the magic circle defining the philosophic tree.

Given that privileged position, it is perhaps not surprising that another passage from Henderson and Sherwood explicitly identifies the symbolism of this alchemical plate with the Jungian version of the archetypal idea Rilke first associates with Orpheus: *transcendence*. The symbolic elements of the plate

> represent receptivity to what flows from below, permitting the contents of the unconscious to be transferred to consciousness effectively. It is like the transcendent function—"the cooperation of conscious reasoning with the data of the unconscious... progressively unit[ing] the opposites"—that allows nature to change human life.[961]

This passage articulates a (psychological) idea of transcendence not simply identified with a movement up and away, and in so doing sheds light upon Rilke's image of Orpheus. The continuation of the passage, moreover, may be understood to illumine still further the essential difference between the *Sonnets* and the *Elegies:*

> In contrast, the intellectual recognition of a union of opposites doesn't reconcile them, but it can be a transition of an unconscious idea into consciousness. A symbol, on the other hand, can emerge as a meaningful image and pattern of behavior that *does* reconcile what was experienced previously as irreconcilable from either a rational or from an emotional point of view.[962]

Rilke's great "diptych" sets the practical poetic consequences of these difficult theoretical distinctions in sharp relief in a way that depends and expands upon the critical difference between man and soul. Rilke's *Elegies* devote no end of intellectual attention to the tensions bred of various opposites. At the same time, anyone reading the poem will readily acknowledge that it is saturated by human emotion: grief and pain, despair and triumph, travail and joy run like an electric charge through the cycle from beginning to end, powering its "mighty current." Almost as if the *Elegies* had, in fact, *discharged* it, no such fraught feeling sounds in the more serene sonnets *the initiating mythopoetic scene of which dramatizes a quieting of soul emotion, and entrance into another, more purely archetypal domain.* In the "clear, released" imaginal wood of the *Sonnets*, human thought and emotion is no longer central in character, no longer the driving force running the show, but rather appears (as does "Lament" itself in Sonnet I, 7) in the form of clarified, personified image-symbols in the lucid pool of Orphic song.

Nor does Rilke neglect to thematize, quite explicitly, the crucial dynamic Hillman finally identifies with soul-making itself: "dehumanization." Arguing against "Modern Humanism's Psychology," Hillman critiques the idea—central to many modern psychologies but harking back to Romanticism and even, ultimately, to Augustine—that (personal) feeling provides the door to the heart of the soul. Correlatively, he expounds "the insufficiency of love" and, too, "the egoism of forgiveness." On the face of it, Hillman's discourse may seem rather mean-spirited, if not positively grinch-like; yet he does not fail to make clear the archetypal gist of his aim:

> [O]ur notions of man tend to encroach upon psyche. The soul and its afflictions, its emotions, feelings, and varieties of love are all certainly essential to the human condition. But they are all archetypally conditioned. We cannot come to terms with them merely as human, merely as personal, without falling into humanistic sentimentalities, moralisms, and egocentricities. Then soul-making becomes making better human connections, while the real issue of feeling—discriminating among and connecting to archetypes—is ignored.[963]

Hillman's critique is Rilke's as well. It is integral to his *Sonnets*' psychological platform, and the poet accordingly lends it lucid expression near the beginning of the cycle. The third sonnet—after questioning when we humans will finally attain the kind of authentic being inherent in Orphic song—ends:

> This is not it, youth—that you love, even if
> your voice poured hymns from your mouth. Sing
>
> and forget that you sang out: it will end.
> True singing demands a wind less stiff.
> A breath about nothing. A wafting in the God. A wind.

For Rilke, too, the mere feeling of personal love and its expression does not ultimately suffice for poetic truth, does not connect the poet's voice with divine breath. The next sonnet continues in a similar vein:

> O you tender ones, step now and then
> into the breath that pays you no mind;
> let it part upon your cheeks—behind
> you, quivering, it rejoins itself again.

Rilke's point, like Hillman's, is not to deny the reality of love, but to direct attention toward its impersonal and archetypal sources—toward no particular human connection, but toward daimonic powers like those of Psyche and of Eros. In relation to the motif of (impossible) love, this is, of course, no new theme for Rilke, yet the *Sonnets* speak of the matter in a less emotionally weighted manner than do the *Elegies*. While the

Elegies rather stridently herald "the great lovers," the decidedly lighter touch of the *Sonnets* moves to conduct us into the very realm Psyche herself comes to inhabit *after* successful completion of her fourth and last labor—the imaginal domain of the Gods, the mythic sphere where Love and Soul finally meet and unite again.

But that is a theme for our concluding chapters. To move toward the end of this one, we must remember again that the archetypal psychology we are exploring here—the archetypal psychology I am claiming as Rilke's as well as Hillman's—originates in Greek polytheistic mythological culture. "The human in this Greek view of man," writes Hillman, "depends not upon personal relationships but on relationships with archetypal powers which have their inhuman aspects." Hillman, however, lays claims to a more recent ancestry as well, a more proximate historical source which—yet again—Rilke's *Sonnets to Orpheus* tangibly share.

For it was not only Orpheus and Greek mythology that inspired Rilke's *Sonnets*, but, as well, another culture that drew deeply upon Greek genius even while lending it a more modern aspect—the same period, in fact, that lent Rilke's sonnets their classic poetic form.

> Here, where the psychology of soul-making reaches out to the polytheistic imagination, the major themes of this book now gather to a head. The place of their gathering is the Renaissance.[964]

So Hillman introduces the last truly major theme in his *Revisioning Psychology*. He quickly tells us, too, just why the topic of the Renaissance is so central to his book's revisionary project: "I believe," he writes (italicizing for emphasis), "that *were we better able to understand the psychology of the Renaissance, we might find both base and inspiration for a renaissance of psychology.*"[965]

At first blush, Hillman's choice of historical source may seem odd. He dedicates his fourth and final chapter, after all, to "dehumanizing" psychology. Does not the Renaissance—that harbinger of "humanism"—stand for just the opposite gesture, and in so doing usher in a new era centered upon the genius and power of man?

Hillman begs to differ with that popular conception. While readily admitting that in the Renaissance "we found ourselves...at the heart of humanism," Hillman points out that our notion of "humanism" originally derives from the Renaissance *humanitas*. In its more restricted meaning, *humanitas* implied, simply, the study of classical works—humane literature that had been largely ignored on account of the theological biases of the medieval church. In Hillman's view, however, a distinct and to some degree covert *psychological* imperative underlay the love of classical poetry, moral essay, biography, and philosophy characteristic of the period:

> Overtly, they [the Italian humanists] were studying rhetoric, style, and the material of language. But from the very beginning in Petrarch the inner content of the materials was the mythical persons and ideas from a pre-Christian polytheistic world.[966]

The strong pagan and mythopoetic undercurrent of humanist study naturally coincides with the specifically *imaginative* initiative Hillman sees as the true heart of Renaissance *humanitas*:

> Renaissance humanitas began among readers and writers as a *care for the contents of the intellectual imagination*. This humanitas was in fact...an exploration and discipline of the imaginal, whether through science, magic, study, love, art or voyages. It sought the development of the imaginative mind and its power of imaginative understanding, in contradistinction to both the theological mind of Church philosophy and the feeling heart of mendicant and monastic church orders.[967]

This "care for the contents of the intellectual imagination" qualifies, moreover, as "care of soul" focused upon the archetypal power of words and images, rather than upon personal feelings and human relations or capacities per se. ("Renaissance 'care of soul,'" writes Hillman, "looked less to social context and human experience for its models and insights into soul than to the archetypes of the imagination disguised in the antique texts."[968]) In Hillman's view, therefore, it is the being of *soul—not* that of man—that founds and grounds Renaissance *humanitas*.

Hillman anchors his position by elaborating his image of the era's inaugurating figure—Petrarch. Remarking that "Petrarch has been considered the first modern man, which perhaps means the first psychological man," Hillman notes Petrarch's preoccupation with "an imaginal world represented by the fantasy of antiquity," contending that "these two—soul and antiquity—were his primary concerns." Distinguishing Petrarch's characteristic imaginative soul-making from any anthropocentric view of his putative "humanism," Hillman remarks:

> Even his meticulous scholarship and passion for style were for the sake of soul. Right expression and right psyche were one: "Speech can have no dignity unless the soul has dignity." His interest in man followed from his interest in soul. Psyche, not "humanism," came first.[969]

Fortunately, Hillman refuses to rest the weight of his argument upon general formulations alone and centers his discussion of Petrarch and the era he inaugurated on a specific historic event. Petrarch's ascent of Mt. Ventoux in April 1336 has long been regarded as a pivotal moment in western intellectual history, but the very terms in which Hillman introduces his discussion of the event betray his unorthodox interpretation of its underlying significance:

> The muddle of psyche and human which it is the express aim of this chapter to relieve begins at that symbolic moment when the Renaissance itself "begins," Petrarch's descent from Mont Ventoux.[970]

Hillman recounts the famous episode as follows:

> At the top of the mountain, with the exhilarating view of French Provence, the Alps, and the Mediterranean spread before him, he had opened his tiny pocket copy of Augustine's *Confessions*. Turning at random to book X, 8, he read: "And men go abroad to admire the heights of mountains, the mighty billows of the sea, the broad tide of rivers, the compass of the ocean, and the circuits of the stars, and pass themselves by.... "
>
> Petrarch was stunned at the coincidence between Augustine's words and the time and place they were read. His emotion both announced the revelation of his personal vocation and heralded the new attitude of the Renaissance.... Petrarch draws this crucial conclusion from the Mt. Ventoux event: "Nothing is admirable but the soul" (*nichil preter animum esse mirabile*).[971]

For Hillman, Petrarch's climb—and, still more importantly, his "turning inward" while *descending* Mt. Ventoux—did mark the inception of the Renaissance. It also functions as the historic point of departure of what he terms "the humanistic fallacy":

> Commentators and translators interpret the "soul" and the "self" in [Petrarch's] writing as "man"; to them the event on Mt. Ventoux signifies the return from God's world or nature to man.[972]

Hillman, naturally, takes violent issue with this reading of the event, and turns to Petrarch's own Augustinian source to substantiate his own, quite different interpretation of its epochal significance:

> If one looks again at the passage Petrarch was reading which so stunned him, one finds that Augustine was discussing *memoria*. Book X, 8 of the *Confessions* is important to the art of memory. It is about the soul's imaginative faculty.
>
> > Great is this force of memory [imagination] excessive great. O my God: a large and boundless chamber! who ever sounded the bottom thereof? yet is this a power of mine, and belongs unto my nature, nor do I myself comprehend all that I am. Therefore is the mind too strait to contain itself.
>
> These sentences immediately precede the passage Petrarch opened on the mountain. In them Augustine is wrestling with the classical problems, beginning with Heraclitus, concerning the measureless depth of the soul, the place, size, ownership, and origin of the images of *memoria* (the archetypal unconscious, if you prefer). It was the wonder of this train of thought that struck Petrarch, the wonder of the interior personality, which is both inside man and yet far greater than man.... The revelation on Mont Ventoux opened Petrarch's eyes to the complexity and mystery of the man-psyche relationship and moved him to write of the marvel of the *soul*, not the marvel of man.... Renaissance psychology begins with a revelation of the independent reality of soul.... *It is not the return from nature to man that starts the Renaissance going, but the return to soul.*[973]

Thus the premier importance of Petrarch and the Renaissance to Hillman: both are precursors of the soul-centered perspective that inaugurates archetypal psychology. Let us see how matters stand in this regard for Rilke.

No less than Hillman's archetypal psychology, Rilke's *Sonnets to Orpheus* may well be considered an essentially Renaissance inspiration. We have already seen that a Renaissance image—da Conegliano's painting *Orpheus*—supplies the ekphrastic source of Rilke's cycle. Despite the signal importance of that visual point of departure, however, da Conegliano's painting hardly represents the sole, or even chief, Renaissance influence upon Rilke's sonnets.

Rilke, we should recall, was himself no stranger to the field of Renaissance studies. On assignment from Lou, he had traveled to Florence in 1898 and been deeply affected by Renaissance art (especially Michelangelo). As we discussed in chapter 3, the self-conscious engagement with questions of art, psychology, and religion inspired by that journey—pursued in close connection with Lou—proved a watershed in the poet's intellectual and creative career.

Nor did the interests kindled by that excursion expire over the course of the years.[974] Just before the beginning of the war, Rilke (who had not long before finished a translation of the French Renaissance poet Louise Labé's sonnets) began translating Michelangelo's sonnets. In the difficult years during and immediately after the war, those translations constituted, in Rilke's own words, "the most regular part of my occupation."[975] Rilke, in fact, was hard at work on those sonnet translations in the Chateau Muzot in the winter of 1921, completing the project little more than a month before the creative storm that produced his own *Sonnets to Orpheus*.

No doubt Rilke's work on the Michelangelo sonnets helped motivate Rilke's own—rather more experimental—compositions in that same form. "To modify the sonnet," he later wrote to Katharina Kippenberg,

> to raise it, to carry it so to speak while running without destroying it, was in this case a peculiar test and task which, by the way, I hardly had to decide. It was posed that way and bore the solution within it.[976]

Insofar as the sonnet—and, too, the sonnet cycle—qualifies as a Renaissance kind, the genius of the period pours into the Rilkean vessel by virtue of the shaping power of poetic form.

In the next chapter, we will explore some of the contours of that formal influence; for the moment, however, we turn our attention to a different, albeit intimately related, subject.

The author of the sonnet form employed by both Michelangelo and Rilke is none other than that bright herald of the Renaissance, Francesco Petrarcha himself. Yet Petrarch's influence upon Rilke's sonnets does not consist solely in providing the cast for their generic mold, hugely important as that in itself may be. The Italian poet and humanist had been of first importance to Rilke for over a decade,[977] and certain famous passages of Petrarch's own meditative prose proved instrumental in framing Rilke's archetypally psychological theme, engendering the soul animating his sonnet form. The relevant text here is (what else?) Petrarch's famous account of his climb of Mont Ventoux, that symbolic origin of the Renaissance itself.

Rilke had long been intimate with the letter (written to Dionisio da Borgo San Sepolcro) in which Petrarch records and comments upon his Ventoux event, including the reading of Augustine that serves as the focal point of the whole episode. Rilke first read it in a French translation (the first!) by Victor Develay[978] acquired in Avignon in the fall of 1909, and "the little book" clearly meant a great deal to him. In 1910, he made a gift of it to Rodin, but the book was back with him the following year. In May of 1911, in a letter to Lili Schalk, Rilke reflected upon his own recently completed Egyptian voyage in light of Petrarch's historic experience:

> So I really was in Algiers, in Tunis, finally in Egypt, but it would have served me right if everywhere before the greatest external objects I had opened St. Augustine to the passage that strikes home to Petrarch when, up there on Mont Ventoux, opening with curiosity the familiar little book, he finds nothing but the reproach of turning his eyes from himself to mountains, oceans and distances.[979]

Rilke's critical involvement with Petrarch's meditations did not stop at passing mention in personal correspondence. In fact Rilke—despite his less than superior Latin—produced a draft translation of Petrarch's letter while living in Paris.[980] Unfortunately, that work counts as one of the minor casualties of the First World War. When Rilke's Paris property was confiscated some time after the outbreak of war, the draft of his Petrarch translation was lost to the poet and to history as well.

That unhappy fact, however, did not put an end to Rilke's engagement with Petrarch's letter but merely suspended the matter—left it hanging in air—for the poet was by no means finished with the subject

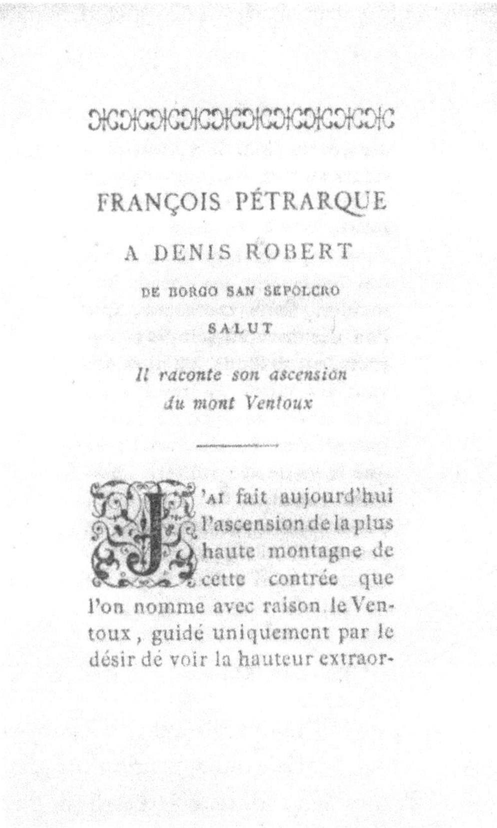

FRANÇOIS PÉTRARQUE

A DENIS ROBERT

DE BORGO SAN SEPOLCRO

SALUT

Il raconte son ascension du mont Ventoux

J'AI fait aujourd'hui l'ascension de la plus haute montagne de cette contrée que l'on nomme avec raison le Ventoux, guidé uniquement par le désir de voir la hauteur extraor-

Develay's Petrarch translation

altogether. At the beginning of 1922, just after finishing his translations of Michelangelo's (Petrarchan) sonnets, Rilke—no doubt energized by that Renaissance-related project—resolved to resume work on the long-lost Petrarch translation. On January 6, he wrote (in French) to his friend Jean Strohl:

> Among the items of business that I lost in Paris there was a small piece of work that I would not like to give up on entirely. It was a letter (in Latin) by Petrarch, in which he describes his ascent of Mont Ventoux. . . . the bold enterprise, rare for his time, rather than providing him the opportunity for a broader view, reveals a new interior horizon [*un nouvel horizon interieur*]. But to bring this

> translation, of which a first draft once existed, to a satisfactory conclusion, I would need, alas, a whole apparatus.[981]

Rilke accordingly goes on to request not only the Latin letter itself, but a French translation of it, as well as Latin-German dictionary.

Rilke did indeed receive these materials from Strohl and almost certainly spent time with them. On February 7, however, he wrote Strohl that he had had to give up on the Petrarch translation because other, more urgent work had intervened. That letter continues:

> I'm sending you my little manuscript, still warm, which I ask you to send back to me someday, but not in any hurry, after you have read it at leisure with Madame Strohl.... all the same, the whole thing could represent a kind of "tomb."[982]

This "little manuscript"—indeed "still warm"—was Part I of Rilke's *Sonnets to Orpheus*. The poet's Petrarch translation had not been so much abandoned as transcendently transformed.

Against the background of Hillman's thought, we can well imagine the general terms of Petrarch's historic influence upon the soul of Rilke's *Sonnets*. According to Hillman, after all, it was Petrarch ("the first modern man, which perhaps means the first psychological man") who inaugurated an era devoted not so much to God, or even man, but to *soul*, and to the inner vision that defines the psyche's imaginal world. Rilke himself lends credence to this view in his letter to Strohl, speaking of Petrarch's adventure as "this bold undertaking, rare for his time... [which] reveals a new inner horizon." That horizon is one Rilke (in the spirit, perhaps, of the great Renaissance voyages of discovery) spent no end of time exploring, and indeed made his own.

So much for the broader view. If, however, we wish to gain a more intimate sense of intellectual converse between our two writers and see revealed, in poetic detail, the light of one mind shining—transfigured—through the words of another, we must look still more closely at our chosen texts. Before doing so, however, we must prepare the interpretive ground by revisiting our critical point of departure.

So far, we have accepted without real question Hillman's strong and highly original reading of Petrarch's momentous experience on Mont

Ventoux. In his *Cosmos and Psyche*, Richard Tarnas devotes several pages to the complex and highly provocative topic. Tarnas, an author generally friendly to Hillman's archetypal angle, grants Hillman's unorthodox views qualified acceptance while at the same time—speaking from the perspective of the objective cultural historian—registering crucial critical caveats.

Hillman champions Petrarch as the herald of a profoundly imaginative sense of soul, one that breaks decisively from the more traditionally religious path—stemming in large part from Augustine himself—that subordinates soul to the moral prerogatives of the spirit. Tarnas does not altogether disagree with Hillman on this score, but rightly points out that—if one reads the Petrarch's Ventoux letter more fully—crucial passages of it lend, at best, equivocal support for Hilllman's view. Petrarch:

> How many times, think you, did I turn back that day, to glance at the summit of the mountain which seemed scarcely a cubit high compared with the range of human contemplation—when it is not immersed in the foul mire of earth? With every downward step I asked myself this: If we are ready to endure so much sweat and labour in order that we may bring our bodies a little nearer heaven, how can a soul struggling toward God, up the steeps of human pride and human destiny, fear any cross or prison or sting of fortune?...How earnestly should we strive, not to stand on mountaintops, but to trample beneath us those appetites which spring from earthly impulses.[983]

Petrarch, Tarnas observes, has hardly thrown off the yoke of medieval religious morality entirely. On the contrary, he in fact "portrays the event above all as a powerful metaphor for the arduous spiritual ascent to God, and...depicts his reading of Augustine's words as...calling him back to that most important commitment." Tarnas—sensitive to the profound ambiguity of the Ventoux event—offers this balanced conclusion:

> It is certainly true that the impulse and will to make the ascent at all and the sharply polarized nature of the inner dialogue he conducts with himself as he climbs the mountains and later reflects on the event suggest that Petrarch is indeed, in spite of himself, beginning to break from the powerful hold of the Augustinian medieval spirit while simultaneously assimilating it. But his own account makes clear just how immense was the struggle to do so.

> We should also note that the Latin word Petrarch uses that Hillman and others translate as "soul" is not *anima* but *animus*. This can also be translated as "spirit," or as the "soul" in the Christian spiritual sense rather than as the more psychological and imaginative "soul" developed by Hillman and archetypal psychology.[984]

Pursuant to this last point, Tarnas questions Hillman's construction of a "humanistic fallacy" initiated (in Hillman's view) by Renaissance scholars' supposed misinterpretation of Petrarch's notion of soul:

> The ambiguous conflation of "soul" and "self" with "man" does not begin with Renaissance scholarship but is in an important sense central to the birth of the modern self in the Renaissance, visible in Pico and Ficino and in the larger ethos of the age.[985]

Tarnas's commentary makes clear that—so far as a reading of Petrarch is concerned—Hillman's perspective, while possessing its own validity, cannot be considered the only side of the story. Even so, what remains most important to us here is not, in the last analysis, Petrarch and his reading of Augustine, but another, later link in the historic chain: namely, Rilke's reception of both Petrarch and Augustine.

Rilke, in fact, inscribed his reading of the whole Ventoux matter—not only in his letter to Strohl—but far more importantly, in the text of the "Petrarch translation" he did finish—his *Sonnets to Orpheus*. Not only does most every aspect of the form and content of his *Sonnets* in some wise reflect the essential terms of Rilke's Petrarch reception; our poet cryptically encodes his reading of the Ventoux dialogue in one of the very first poems of the cycle. Let us then look yet again—and still more closely—at the poem that introduces the soul of Rilke's *Sonnets*.

> And it was almost a girl who emerged from
> the consonant pleasure of song and lyre
> and shone clear through her shady spring attire
> and made her bed within my ear's deep drum.
>
> And slept in me. And her sleep was everything.
> The trees I always marveled at, those
> palpable distances, the deeply felt meadows
> and every wonder that concerned my own being.
>
> She slept the world....

We focus now on the second stanza, especially its last line. To best hear the special resonance we are after, however, we must provide a missing link—supply the few sentences that connect the Augustine passage Petrarch read atop Mont Ventoux and the Augustine passage Hillman quotes in order to substantiate his own interpretation of the event. I recite the whole passage (though in a different translation than that quoted by Hillman), italicizing the most crucial sentence:

> The power of memory is prodigious, my God. It is a vast immeasurable sanctuary. Who can plumb its depths? And yet it is a faculty of my soul. Although it is part of my nature, I cannot understand all that I am. This means, then, that the mind is too narrow to contain itself entirely. But where is that part of it which it does not itself contain? Is it somewhere outside itself and not within it? How, then, can it be part of it, if it is not contained in it?
>
> *I am lost in wonder when I consider this problem.* It bewilders me. Yet men go out and gaze in astonishment at high mountains, the huge waves of the sea, the broad reaches of rivers, the ocean that encircles the world, or the stars in their courses. But they pay no attention to themselves.[986]

Perhaps you, reader, already see—or rather hear—what I am driving at. Read against the background of Augustine's text, the last sentence of Rilke's second stanza ("and every wonder that concerned my own being") gives the game away. It indubitably echoes Augustine, resonating most especially with the line "I am lost in wonder when I consider this problem"—the problem, that is, concerning himself and his soul.

Unfortunately, if you are reading Rilke in English, you are unlikely to hear this echo at all. Most English translations of Rilke's line render this resonance largely—if not entirely—inaudible. The German reads:

Und jedes Staunen, das mich selbst betraf.

As so often in Rilke, the line admits of two meanings. On one level, the line can be read merely to denote something like "every instance of wonder I have experienced in my life" as in Snow's translation: "and an entire life's astonishments." In this reading, the sense of wonder can stem from anything and everything. On another level, however, the lines can be read to mean "every wonder pertaining to or concerning myself; every marvel emanating from the wonder of my own being." While Rilke undoubtedly meant both meanings to be in play, the doubly reflexive intention encoded in the words *mich* and *selbst* (me, (my)self), gently but forcefully emphasizes this second reading—the reading most translations obscure or elide, and the one that makes Rilke's German positively ring with Augustinian overtones.

We should recall that Rilke, after all, had just been studying Petrarch's Ventoux letter with an eye toward venturing a translation. Rilke, moreover, had been an inveterate reader of Augustine throughout his life and knew the *Confessions* intimately. The language of Rilke's sonnet assuredly stems from his own internal dialogue with the Petrarchan and Augustinian texts.

Very well, but how are we to interpret Rilke's reading of the Ventoux event given the allusive language of his sonnet? As we have already discussed in some detail, Rilke's poem does register the critical distinction between soul and the self of man so central to Hillman's reading of the Renaissance. Tarnas's just caution about the *general* validity of Hillman's revisionary history does not affect this poetic truth at all. After first *metaphorically* (*not* literally) locating the figure of soul within himself (in his ear, organ of inwardness), Rilke turns around and places everything—*including all wondering reflections on the nature of the self of the kind Augustine rehearses—**within*** that girl-like figure of soul and its constitutive relation to the archetypal unconscious (this latter symbolized by the state of sleep). *The whole world of the* Sonnets*—the poetic universe explored in the entire cycle—unfolds in the imaginal space we enter into through that portal of the soul qua anima which transcends and encompasses the narrower ego or self of man.* Both the seemingly objective world of nature (e.g., trees and meadows) and the more subjective world of the human mind—the mind of man and his questions—appear *within* the "new inner horizon" of the soul—a soul that, moreover, manifests in its intrinsic and intimate relationship to—not God qua Augustine's Almighty—but the singing God, the archetypal power of poetry and myth, Orpheus.

What is the intellectual-historical upshot of all this? It means that as far as Rilke is concerned, Hillman's reading of Petrarch and the Renaissance is dead on. Even if Hillman's is not the only Petrarch, or the only Renaissance, it *is* Rilke's. Conversely, Rilke effectively makes good Hillman's archetypally psychological line of interpretation. The poetics of the *Sonnets* do effect a definite break with any humanism that would place an essentially unpsychological view of man, human reason, and the self-conscious power of mind at the center of the cosmos. Coincidently—finishing or at least carrying forward the job Petrarch started—Rilke breaks with the medieval world of God and its pervasive Augustinianism, that mountainous spiritual matter the poet had been working through virtually the whole of his creative life.

With respect to this latter point, we should emphasize that Rilke's sonnet *reframes* the terms of the Ventoux dialogue, effectively using the psychological depth implicit in Augustine's *Confessions* to overturn the spiritual thrust that dominates the saint's own moral theology. We may here recall the passage from St. Paul's epistles that triggered Augustine's own momentous conversion experience: "Not in reveling and drunkenness, not in lust and wantonness, not in quarrels and rivalries. Rather arm yourselves with the Lord Jesus Christ; spend no more thought on nature and nature's appetites." Tarnas, commenting on the epochal character of both Augustine's and Petrarch's linked synchronistic experiences, writes:

> Augustine's emotion in the garden of Milan both announced the revelation of his personal vocation and heralded the new attitude of the Christian epoch being born. A thousand years later, Augustine's own words randomly encountered provided a strikingly similar catalyzing force for Petrarch on Mont Ventoux. This time the synchronistic epiphany unfolded in a new direction and with different consequences—one revelation in the garden, pointing to Christianity and the Middle Ages, the other on the mountain, pointing to the Renaissance and modernity.[987]

Still—as Tarnas himself makes clear—Petrarch himself remained internally torn, and his talk of "trampling beneath us those appetites that spring from earthly influences" patently echoes the Augustinian doctrine of moral aversion. We too are still struggling to break free from the suffocating aspects of Augustinian Christianity and still trying to comprehend and realize the authentic soul-spiritual ground of the Renaissance Petrarch inaugurated. Rilke's *Sonnets to Orpheus*, and the revisioning of Augustine, Petrarch, and the Ventoux moment inscribed in his text, should be placed alongside those great ancestral *tolle lege* ("pick up and read") moments, and read for the (distinctly un-Nietzschean) joyful wisdom they contain. In contrast with Petrarch himself, little trace of Augustine's aversion to the world can be found in the cycle of *Sonnets* that invoke girl-like anima energies while turning the sensually rich experience of eating oranges into ripe poetic occasion (I, 15), or pleasurably celebrating the spontaneous joy of the earth in spring (I, 21). In Rilke's *Sonnets*, a new, very different ethos reigns, one that is (as Hillman says) "demoralized," but by no means *immoral*; "dehumanized," but not in the direction of incivility or bestiality—rather inclining towards a freer and fuller reception of the imaginative spirit of life, *anima mundi*. An ethos and poetics, that is, of soul and its constant remaking; a breath—not of the stale air of old prescriptive codes and pieties—but of the winds of healing song; a true Renaissance spirit where, even in the midst of divine silence,

> ...new beginning, beckoning, and change transpires.[988]

Hillman's psychology of the Renaissance—the inspiration for his proposed renaissance of psychology—emerges as a tightly woven fabric of closely interrelated initiatives and motifs. It is a psychology centered (not on man made in the image of the one God but) on soul, privileging imaginative truth above all, unfolding insight in the sphere of imaginal figures it views as eminently real. Among the most important of these are figures of and from the past, furnishing a "fantasy" of history (including ancient and Renaissance history) that provides depth to psyche's thought. Inevitably, *anima* plays a leading role. Her intrinsic relation to death (mythically imaged by Persephone's, or Eurydice's, descent into the underworld, the realm of Hades-Pluto) infuses and paradoxically vivifies the psyche's relation to life and the things of this world and invests Psyche heavily in games of love and the endless interests of beauty. Revealing fond regard for the myriad facets of being (Proteus' innumerable forms, Fortuna's spinning wheel of fate), the Renaissance soul expresses that regard in devoted attention to the fine art of speech, the poetry and rhetoric that conjure the imaginal world in which it dwells. Soul, Imagination, Anima, History, Death, Love and Beauty, Logos as the mythopoetic speech of the soul, regard for the Many as well as the One—these are the pillars of Hillman's invisible Renaissance temple.

These are, too, the founding terms of Rilke's poetry. It had been so from the beginning, and yet never more transparently, purely, and consummately than in the poet's crowning work, his *Sonnets to Orpheus*. In the next chapter, we will delve more deeply into the poetic details of Rilke's *Sonnets* and their "Renaissance connections." To bring this one to a close, however, let us turn briefly to the last signal motif Hillman discusses in his *Revisioning Psychology*, one consonant with the matters of religious history we have foregrounded in this chapter.

The psychology that has dominated our culture, Hillman argues, derives from a not-so-distant episode of our monotheistical religious history: the Reformation.

> So psychology has been obsessed by one overvalued idea: man—an ideology arising from the Reformational hero... battling his way through binary choices, responsible, committed, progressing toward light, casting soul and darkness from him.... [Psychology] has been looking at soul in the ego's mirror, never seeing psyche, always seeing man. And this man has been monotheistic Reformational man, enemy of images.[989]

Hillman adds a geographical dimension to his cultural soul-history, positing oppositions between "Reformation and Renaissance, transalpine and cisalpine, between Hebraic monotheistic consciousness and Hellenic polytheistic consciousness." Contending that depth psychology has been born and bred in northern climes—those European domains (most especially, Germany) north of the Alps—he writes:

> What we have come to call "Western" consciousness is in truth northern consciousness. And we falsify the psychological situation by imagining the basic opposition in the soul to be between East and West.... The other pairing in our souls is that of North and South, light and shadow, conscious and unconscious, a vertical division between what is above and what is below, a reflection in imaginal geography of our cultural history.
>
> Venturing South is a journey for explorers.... Venturing South may mean departing from all we have come to consider "psychology."[990]

In his sonnet cycle, Rilke himself makes (or completes) just such a Renaissance voyage, styling himself vassal and vessel of an Orphic God whose poetic mission harks—geographically, imaginally—from that mythic South:

> Praising, that's it! Appointed to praise
> he emerged like ore from the deep mine's

deafness. His heart—o ephemeral press
of one of humankind's unending wines.

His voice never failed him—turning to dust—
when the divine image thrust open his mouth.
All turns to vineyard held in his trust,
grapes ripened in his feeling South.[991]

Hillman, meanwhile, carries his psychological crusade on towards its conclusion:

> I have drawn so much attention to the Renaissance in order to offer a background adequate to the forces threatening our individual psychic welfare and our civilization.... Northern man... has long been cursed by the singleness of vision of monotheistic consciousness.... As happened during the Renaissance, we are discovering that concealed in the shadow are the old Gods. To recognize these imaginal powers and to find precise, intelligent, and cultural ways of providing for them—"or not to be—that is the question."[992]

In his *Sonnets to Orpheus*, Rilke found(s) just such a way. Only thus can the last words of the poem issue forth from its soul-center, and the poet (writing as one who does *not* come in his own name) affirm in answer to that question:

"I am."

CHAPTER 19

FOUNTAIN-MOUTH

"Marsilio Ficino," Andrea Ferrucci
(Cathedral of Florence, Santa Maria del Fiore)

In the fourth and final chapter of his *Revisioning Psychology*, James Hillman probes the cultural impulses that triggered the Renaissance, that epochal movement that supplies archetypal psychology with its imaginal root and ground. Hillman accents one major impetus:

> How was the Renaissance possible? It was possible because the new life experienced in northern Italy during the fifteenth century

> had its source in the rediscovery of the imaginal psyche; the discoveries about man, nature, art, and thought arise from the rebirth of soul as formulated by Neoplatonic philosophy.[993]

As Hillman emphasizes, one man in particular played an extraordinary role in catalyzing this development. If Petrarca figures as the herald of the Renaissance, Marsilio Ficino may well be regarded as its intellectual standard-bearer. Cosimo de' Medici chose Ficino to lead the influential Platonic Academy, and the latter's translation of ancient authors—including Plato and Neoplatonic philosophers—helped furnish the philosophic foundations of Renaissance thought. The lynchpin of Ficino's own teachings, the central idea taken over from his ancient sources, was that of soul:

> Renaissance Neoplatonism is mainly the work of one man: Marsilio Ficino.... To make Ficino the only source of *quattrocento* rebirth goes too far, but there is no doubt that he was the formulator of its central idea. This was soul, and for Ficino the soul "was all things together... the center of the universe, the middle term in all things".... "Ficinian philosophizing is in essence only an invitation *to see* with the eyes of the soul, the soul of things... an incentive to plumb the depths of one's own soul so that the whole world may become clearer in the inner light."[994]

Ficino's renown rests primarily upon his achievements as a translator and philosopher. Hillman, however, casts the soulful Florentine in a rather different role as well. Noting, especially, Ficino's work elaborating the archetypal powers personified by the planets, Hillman argues that "Ficino was writing, not philosophy as has always been supposed, but archetypal psychology." In accordance with this perspective, Hillman names Marsilio Ficino, "Doctor of Soul," as one of the preeminent progenitors of his own psychological Renaissance.

"So that the whole world may become clearer in the inner light." That phrase, prompted by reflections on Ficinian philosophizing, recalls the lucent world of Rilke's *Sonnets to Orpheus*, echoing the transformation announced in the first poem of cycle ("Creatures of calm thronged out of the clear / freed forest"). The echo signifies more than one might at first suppose, for a deep connection allies the figure of Marsilio Ficino and the archetypal God of Song. Noel Cobb writes:

> In his circle Marsilio Ficino was celebrated as an embodiment of Orpheus. The poet Naldo Naldi even traces Orpheus's soul from Homer to Ficino, saying that after the death of Ennius the soul of Orpheus had to wait sixteen hundred years for its next incarnation.[995]

Not only were *The Hymns of Orpheus* and *Orpheus among the Argonauts* among the very first texts Ficino translated, but Marsilio himself (in addition to his many other accomplishments) was a devoted musician, one who chose as his chief instrument the lyre—indeed, one adorned with a picture of Orpheus among the animals. Ficino, in fact (and can one imagine a more perfect image of Orpheus?), would often sing the Orphic hymns he himself had translated to the tuneful accompaniment of his lyre. ("Come, and bring your Orphic lyre with you," wrote Cosimo de Medici to Ficino.[996]) Traveling through Florence, the Bishop Campano was fortunate enough to witness one such performance: "It was as if curly-headed Apollo took up the lyre of Marsilio and fell victim to his own song....His eyes catch fire...and he discovers music which he never learnt."[997] Campano's last phrase may well call up, too, images of another Orphic singer, another "doctor of soul" receiving the "strange dictation" we know as the *Sonnets to Orpheus*.

Given the historic role Hillman ascribes to Ficino, the Florentine's musical character suggests a deep connection between *the philosophical and psychological origins of the Renaissance*, the *archetypal psychology* that builds on that foundation, *and Orphic myth*. Indeed, the major archetypal motifs that collectively comprise Hillman's (neo-)Renaissance psychology (anima, underworld, the transformative power of poetic language, to name a few) find clear imaginative expression in the myth of Orpheus. So much so that when Cobb, reflecting upon archetypal psychology in light of its own method of mythic epistrophe, asks "who is behind archetypal psychology," his answer (notably taking the Psyche-Eros myth as its point of departure) unfolds thus:

> Archetypal psychology, apart from its character as a polytheistic psychology and a theophanic psychology, is also an *aesthetic psychology*. And the mythic person within it must be an artist, even a poet. Now if we ask ourselves, what mythic figure is not

> only an artist, but an artist whose art is dedicated to the Gods, polytheistically, in their particularity, an artist who embodies the imagination and who is associated with the anima and the underworld and who sings of the beauty of Psyche, we must conclude that the mythic person for whom we have been searching is Orpheus.[998]

Given this archetypal perspective, it is logical that the founding tenets of Hillman's revisioning of his field find brilliantly imaginative expression in the poem cycle Rilke addresses to Orpheus, legendary wellspring of lyric poetry *and* archetypal psychology. So it is that the two streams we have been following all along reveal themselves united at the mythic source.

We have, in the course of this book, elaborated in some detail the foundations of Hillman's psychology. Hillman's construction of the psychology of the Renaissance reiterates those fundamental bases. It is a psychology that (à la Ficino) puts the soul at the center of heaven and earth, envisioning all things past and present *animated* by creative imagination; a *pathologizing* psychology that sees Hades, Lord of Death, at the core of the soul qua anima's spiritual life, binding underworld and overworld and secretly authoring all rebirth or *renascence*; a *poetic* psychology that recognizes "a special relation between soul and word...giving soul to language and finding language for soul" and seeing the ever-transforming truth of image, myth, and metaphor as the undying essence of the world; a psychology, too, born of love and beauty and the delicate dialectic of soul and spirit, or Psyche and Eros; an *archetypal psychology*, finally, that follows the method of epistrophe, striving to see all things in the light of transpersonal deific powers. We have seen these archetypal motifs, as well, embodied in Rilke's life and (still more clearly) his poetic opus, enacted again and again, and in constantly evolving forms. It is only logical that these mythemes—*but most of all the last*—come to heightened expression in the poet's crowning accomplishment, the transcendently clarified distillate of his life's work, the sonnet cycle addressed to the mysterious archetypal source of his own poetic and psychological being, Orpheus.

In the last chapter, we began the critical work of reading the *Sonnets*, highlighting the initiating image of the God and the accompanying figure of soul inscribed in the opening poems. Let us, then, continue reading roughly where we left off, focusing upon how the mythic image of Orpheus (his divine presence ever implied, if not always explicit) deepens and condenses the expression of Rilke and Hillman's privileged mythemes. In so doing, we quickly find ourselves looking into the ubiquitous world of the dead.

> Raise no memorial. Only let the roses
> bloom each year for his sake.
> For it is Orpheus. His metamorphoses
> in this thing and that.

As we have observed already, Rilke's *Sonnets* imagine Orpheus as a living and present deity, not one past and gone, but one whose endless song indwells the here and now—most especially the evanescent, ever-changing forms of earthly nature. Yet while Orpheus may be a God of Nature, this fifth sonnet lets us know that his province does not remain restricted to the living or visible kingdom of the world.

> Is it not already much if at times
> he overstays for a few days the bowl of roses?
>
> O how he must vanish, so you might see!
> Even if he feared that he might disappear.
> When his words surpass all that's here
>
> he's already There, beyond your company.
> The lyre's lattice does not restrain his hands.
> And he oversteps, as his heart commands.

Physical nature verges eternally upon another world, the unseen ground of all its visible transformations. Mere human beings do not readily pass between these realms, but (as the next poem affirms) Orpheus is another matter:

> Is he of this world? No, his widespread
> nature stemmed from above and below.
> He who knows the roots of the willow
> can better bend the branches overhead.

As you go to bed, leave on the table
no bread, and no milk; it draws the dead.
But he, the conjurer, let him be led
under the mildness of your eyelid, able

to mix their shades into everything seen;
may the spell of earthsmoke and rue
be clear as day to him, and as true.

In the best known (Ovidian) version of the Orphic myth, Orpheus descends into Hades in his attempt to retrieve his lost wife. In one of his earliest and most famous "new poems," "Orpheus. Eurydice. Hermes," Rilke depicts an all too human, callow, and distinctly proprietary Orpheus who (in accordance with the popular legend) loses his bride a second time by looking back at her before exiting the underworld. The Orphic God of Rilke's *Sonnets*, however—if not another story altogether—represents a decidedly different version of this one.

"Orpheus. Eurydice. Hermes" is an ekphrastic poem based upon a famous fourth-century BCE stone relief. Rilke's sixth sonnet ("Is he of this world?") begins with a quasi-ekphrastic allusion to another ancient artifact, a fifth-century BCE Delphic fresco painting by Polygnotos. According to the Roman author Pausanias' detailed description, the painting depicts Orpheus leaning against a willow among the dead in the underworld. Guthrie remarks:

> In the description which Pausanias gives of the underworld scenes painted by Polygnotos, there is no mention of Eurydice being present to explain the situation.... It may be that in the eyes of some, his followers, Orpheus had an established position there, as it were in his own right...without the necessity of any conjugal errand to account for his presence.[999]

As we've discussed, the "Death and the Maiden" motif remains enormously important in Rilke's *Sonnets*, not in the least in the inspiration offered by the anima figure of Vera Ouckama Knoop. Yet—even if we do not go so far as to suppose an Orpheus who does not require a Eurydice-figure to explain his relation to the nether realms—the Orphic god of the *Sonnets* is a far cry from the poor, torn human figure exiled from the sphere of Hades' and Eurydice's dark knowledge in Rilke's earlier poem. He is, at the least, "forever dead in Eurydice"—an initiate in the wisdom of the underworld, his archetypal being rooted (like the sorrowful willow) in the realm below even while rising up into the world of visible, living nature.

When thinking of archetypal images of the Renaissance, Hades and his dark domain may well not come quickly to mind. In Hillman's opinion, however, they should:

> [W]e misapprehend the Renaissance by seeing it as a turbulent tribute to Gods of love, light, life, and nature. I believe the God of the Renaissance and of *all psychological renascences* to be Hades, archetypal principle of the deepest aspect of the soul.[1000]

Hillman elaborates:

> Greek mythology shows the wholly psychological perspective of Hades by stating that he has no temples on the surface of the earth and that he receives no libations. It is as if the Hades perspective is concerned only with soul, with what happens "after life," that is, the reflections and images and shadowy afterthoughts lying apart from and below life. Death here is the point of view "beyond" and "below" life's concerns...[1001]

...or, as Rilke puts it, Orpheus, like his words, "passes beyond all that's here." He is part, not only of the world of the blooming rose, but of the death-force already working its changes in the fading and drooping petals. If Orpheus cannot be wholly identified with Hades, it is not because he lacks knowledge of the underworld but because the Singing God knows Death and Life and (like Hermes) the constant passage between; he is a denizen not of one or the other domain but, as Rilke phrases it in I, 9, the *dual* or *double* realm (*Doppelbereich*), the *whole* that encompasses both. Shades—we may say—of the angel.

Still, while above and below may form one dual reality, it is the underworld that remains most closely associated with reflections and images, shades and shadows, the soul's essentially (non-physical) *imaginal* reality.

> The richness of Hades-Pluto psychologically refers to the wealth that is discovered through recognizing the interior deeps of the imagination. For the underworld was mythologically conceived as a place where there are only psychic images. From the Hades perspective *we are our images*.[1002]

So it is that the last tercet of I, 6 concludes by introducing another of the cycle's chief themes: the *reality* of image, and (correlatively) the soul's essentially imaginal reality.

> Nothing, in him, makes true image seem mean;
> be it from chamber, be it from tomb
> let him praise vase, ring, and silver heirloom.

Rilke's sonnet cycle returns to the issue of the image again and again, weaving poetic statements of the soul's imaginal (or metaphoric, or figurative) essence throughout its whole texture. In Part I, Sonnet 9 issues the cryptic Orphic command "know the image"; 11, musing on the symbol of a starry constellation, concludes with an exhortation "to believe in the figure" because "that suffices"; the next poem (12) reaffirms, "For truly we live our lives in figures"; and I, 20 makes a sacred, ritual offering to the poet's God in the form of no liturgical prayer, but a single image of a white horse. The theme figures no less prominently in Part II, and receives concentrated treatment in a set of poems toward the beginning of that part. Before returning to our more or less orderly reading of Part I, let us make something of a digression to look more closely at the opening sequence of Part II, paying particular (though not exclusive) attention to the soul of the images—and the images of soul—contained therein.

An Excursion on Soul and its Image in Rilke's Sonnets, Part II

As befits Orphic speech, an aura of mystery surrounds Rilke's *Sonnets*. While the sonnet sequence may be considered generally more accessible than the dense and intellectually complex *Elegies*, the underlying meaning of its small poems may nonetheless ultimately seem still more elusive, as if their sense were at once *there* and *not there*, like an image trembling in a pool—a *self*-image, perhaps, at once readily recognizable and uncannily unfamiliar, beckoning from the inscrutable depths of some *other* realm. This quality flows, in good measure, from the degree to which Rilke's art immerses itself in the milieu of the *purely imaginal* that is, too, the element of *pure soul*—that liminal, transitional domain the poet made the special province of his opus.

Not surprisingly, the *Sonnets* themselves are full of poetic effects conveying the primacy of the soul's imaginal reality. In the last chapter, we witnessed how the first poems of the cycle work to usher us into a different dimension, a mythic world not detached from but rather underlying things themselves. In accordance with a general pattern that persists throughout the sequence, corresponding poems in Part II echo those poetic initiatives, albeit with a somewhat different slant.

The *Sonnets* open by announcing a purely poetic event: "A tree rose up. O Orpheus sings!" The debut poem of Part II does likewise, but here—as perhaps behooves a second section—the gesture is less manifestly mythical and more philosophically *reflexive.* The poet explicitly addresses the "world-space" (*Weltraum*) entered into in the living rhythm of his writing, the *breath* of his own being-in-song:

> Breathe, invisible poem!
> World-space continually in pure
> interchange with our own being. Counterweight
> in which I rhythmically occur.

The poem ends by addressing the envelope of the poet's speech, the native element of his poetic word:

> Do you know me, Air, full of space I once won?
> You, once smooth rind,
> swell and leaf of my Word.

Like the first poem of Part I of the cycle, this sonnet forcefully distinguishes the poetic universe of the *Sonnets* from that of the *Elegies.* If the poet does say "I" in this poem, it is not because the second part of the cycle strikes a more personal note than the first, but rather because the bridge between the authorial voice and archetypal perspective of the Orphic God has already been built and traveled. In the more massive *Elegies*, air most often figured as the element the human being was perpetually *falling out* of—like migratory birds exhausted in flight, or circus performers whose leaps, bounds, and balancing acts always end—quickly—in coming back down to earth. In the *Sonnets*, by contrast, the poetic voice finds itself entirely at home in this element, for the speaker is frequently not so much a recognizably human subject as the motion and force of pure breath, a manifestly spiritual being kin to the cosmic nature of Orphic deity. In this connection, it is worth noting that *Atmen*—the German word for breath, and the first word of Part II—is distantly related to the ancient Indian word for (not the ego, but) the true Self: *atman.*

Still—even while it may be the most immediate and intimate vessel of the poetic word—air cannot in and of itself act as a sufficient container of its force, one that might adequately embody and personify its creative effects. Consequently—echoing, again, the pattern established in Part I—the second poem of Part II segues from logos to psyche. Evoking the capacity of the soul qua anima to contain Orphic inspiration, poetic *reflexion* transforms into mirror *reflection* as the poet deliberately begins to explore the peculiar ontology of the *image*.

> Just as the Master will sometimes leave
> his true mark on the page that's near
> by chance; so will mirrors often receive
> the singularly sacred smile (so clear!)
>
> of girls, as they test the morning alone
> or dress in candle-lit shawls.
> And later, in the breathing of their known
> faces, only a reflection falls.

Plato's divided line, following common sense, construes corporeal fact as the source of any (potentially deceptive) specular image, and accordingly awards it a distinctly higher degree of reality. Rilke's poetic logic, however, reverses the order of things, putting the mirror(ed) image first, temporally, ontologically, and valuatively. It is a mirror—not the physical body—that mimes the inwardly reflective nature of the girls and so manages to capture and contain within its transparent depths the invisible soul-essence they in themselves are.

The next sonnet carries this image-theme onward. It opens by stating, flat out, the as yet unresolved mystery inherent in the nature of the true mirror-image, the interstitial, threshold reality that—like Alice's looking-glass, perhaps—falls between the cracks of our usual notions of space-time:

> Mirrors: no one yet has spoken the rhyme
> revealing what you, in essence, are.
>
> You, interstices of time
> filled with nothing, it seems—holes of sieves.

As this poem illustrates, Rilke's *Sonnets*, no less than his *Elegies*, are replete with metaphysically difficult figures. Fortunately, however, this sonnet ends by returning its mind-bending motif to a seemingly familiar mythological source:

Sometimes paintings fill you full.
Some even seem to go inside you;
others pass by your glassy pond.

But the loveliest will remain until
the unbound Narcissus presses through
those chaste cheeks—there, beyond.

Since Freud, Narcissus has most often been psychologically construed as a symbol of excessive self-love, but another dimension of the mythic figure registers in Rilke's poem. In the original German, the poem ends with the phrase "klare gelöste Narziss"—"clear, released Narcissus." The two adjectives are the identical words the poet employed to describe "the clear, freed wood" in the first poem of the cycle. Their combined force implies release from some sort of psychic bondage and entrance into another, more authentic order of soul-reality. As Rilke's poem *and* Hillman's unorthodox reading of Narcissus imply, this latter may well be the reality of the archetypal imagination itself:

> Is Narcissus the patron saint of imagination? His love was wholly given to and fulfilled by the reflected image that took him to the underworld. . . . as if it were enough for the psyche to see its own reflection by means of images, as if it were enough to imagine in poetic form its physical body and needs, its love, and its own self.[1003]

The *Sonnets* thus reveal themselves as very significantly invested in questions pertaining to the self, but—as we saw in the handling of the Augustine allusion in "And it was almost a girl"—Rilke consistently reinterprets classical problems of self as issues of the soul and, correlatively, does so in a manner uniquely responsive to the psyche's way of *imagining* things.

The fourth poem of Part II carries Rilke's poetic train of thought on to a kind of logical conclusion, evoking the capacity—born of the force of psyche's love and desire—to engender a purely imaginal reality, a creature with no prototype in the sensible order of things:

O this is the creature that does not exist.
They didn't know that, and, regardless, loved
it—its walk, its neck, and the white-gloved
gaze lifting lightly as the morning mist.

True, it *was*n't. But because they loved, it became
a pure creature. They always left it room.

And in that clear, preserved space, it came
and simply raised its head, not asking whom

or if it was. They didn't nourish it with corn
but only with the chance that it might be.
And they gave such strength to the creature

it sprouted a horn upon its head. One horn.
To a virgin it came—white, perfectly—
and was in the silver mirror and in her.

This sonnet brings leading motifs from the preceding poems together: *mirror*, *image*, *anima*, and *animal* all gather together to make its chief poetic argument: *that pure image exists as a living spiritual reality, but only in the mirror of the pure, the virgin soul.* In Christian iconography that soul is Mary, for legend holds her to be the only one pure enough to catch and hold the image of the unicorn (a symbol of spirit) in her being. Rilke's virgin, though, may as well be a medieval Lady, a girl like Vera, or Orpheus' Eurydice, all of which were, for him, archetypal anima images, heart and soul of his poetic opus.

To conclude this excursion on soul and image, let us briefly remark several closely associated motifs.

First, *image* and *animal*. As the word itself implies ("animal" derives from *anima*, soul), the animal realm bears a deep intrinsic relation to the soul, so much so that Hillman devotes an entire volume of the uniform edition of his works[1004] to the theme. Of course, animals play a key role in defining Orpheus' mythic image, and naturally figure prominently in Rilke's *Sonnets*. Celestial and terrestrial horses, a dog (I, 16), and the unicorn all make feature appearances, while fishes, lambs, and crying or singing birds all contribute important cameos. In fact, Noel Cobb begins his exploration of the "Orpheus among the animals" theme by citing (in full) his translation of Rilke's first sonnet. Cobb's gloss on the poem helps make clear how the close relation between *animal* and the *soul* translates into an equally intimate relation between *animal* and *image*, *animal presence* and *imaginal reality*—at least in the poetic world opened by Orphic song:

> Orpheus' relaxed, unafraid stance among the animals, whether facing the king of beasts or a snake in the grass, and *their* calm alertness, ears cocked, listening intently, display a deep communion in soul. Listening, they enter his mythic music, become pure image, pasture in his imaginal meadows....Orpheus opens an imaginative perspective on the animal, saying that when you

> remain quiet and play, images, as animals, will come out of hiding and come close.... [We see] that the animals of poetry are images; the images, animals.[1005]

Second, (mirror) *image* and *death* (again). A close reader might remark that the Part II poems we've read—while thematizing image—do not explicitly connect that topic with the topos of the underworld which connection had (for the moment, anyway) been our ostensible topic. It would, however, be unreasonable to expect that the whole scope of the topic of image would remain imprisoned in its native realm; images, like wild horses, must be free to wander. Even so, if we recall Rilke's treatment of mirrors, Jean Cocteau's *Orphée* (1950) may nonetheless suggest a hidden connection. In the film, Heurtebise tells Orpheus: "I will tell you the secret of secrets. Mirrors are the doors by which Death exits and enters. Don't tell anyone. What is more—look for a lifetime in mirrors and you will see Death at work, like bees in a hive of glass."

Third—speaking of glass yet again—the *real* world of imagination:

> Sing the gardens, my heart, unknown to you yet—as if in glass
> poured gardens, inaccessible, clear.
> Fountains and roses from Ispahan or Shiraz
> blissfully sing of them, praise them, like none other here.

Ispahan, Shiraz—these are locales in Iran; the latter was the birthplace of the superb Sufi poet Hafiz. In chapter 5, we read Rilke's *The Book of Monastic Life* in the light of Ibn Arabi's Sufi teachings, and Ibn Arabi's doctrine of the Creative Imagination remains intensely relevant to our current topic. Preparing his discussion of the Sufi philosophy of Imagination, Corbin opens his prologue with this citation from Alexandre Koyré:

> The notion of the imagination, magical intermediary between thought and being, incarnation of thought in image and presence of the image in being, is a conception of the utmost importance, which plays a leading role in the philosophy of the Renaissance....[1006]

Sufism construes the heart—seat of the soul's desire, the force of its creative yearning, or *himma*—as the primary organ of the imagination.

> Show, my heart, that you never lack them.
> That they're intended for you, their ripening figs.
> That you converse with the breezes rising between the
>   blossoming twigs
> conjuring—almost—a face, a flower, a gem.

Corbin emphasizes, too, "the notion of the image as a body (a magical body, a mental body) in which are incarnated the thought and will of the soul."[1007]

> Avoid the illusion that life might be rent
> by the decision once taken: to be!
> Silken thread, you became part of the weaving.
>
> Whatever image you own inwardly
> (be it a moment of pain, or even deep grieving)
> feel that the whole, the marvelous carpet is meant.

Ibn Arabi (in Corbin's understanding) posits the world of imagination as "an intermediate world, the world of Idea-Images, of archetypal figures, of subtile substances"; a world that is, too, "real and objective, as consistent and subsistent as the intelligible and sensible worlds."[1008] This world—"the clear, freed forest" in the first sonnet, or the gardens—"clear, inaccessible," "as if poured in glass" of II, 20—this world of the *imaginal psyche* or *soul-image* ("whatever image you own inwardly") *is* the world of Rilke's *Sonnets to Orpheus.*

In his *Book of Hours*, the artist-monk endeavors to engender and enter such a world by way of his creative prayer. The authorial voice of the *Sonnets*, on the other hand, conjures it effortlessly and dwells there almost as if (like Orpheus) it were his permanent home: in the mythic soul-space of this work that weds poetry, psychology, and religion, *image* and *prayer* are one. Corbin writes: "The organ of this universe is the active Imagination; it is the place of theophanic vision, the scene on which visionary events and symbolic histories appear in their true reality."[1009] In Sonnet I, 20, Rilke—after offering the image of the hobbled white horse singing on the Russian steppes—writes:

> He sang and heard. Your myth-circle, Sayer
> closed in him.
>
> His image: my prayer.

The poetic image: Hillman repeatedly insists that this is the g(r)ist of archetypal psychology. We've addressed the image of image in Rilke's *Sonnets*, but the topic of image hardly exhausts the full range of the poem's language, the texture and tenor of all the various aspects of its quintessentially poetic speech. As mythology teaches, *voice* and *image* may echo each other, but the two are not quite one and the same.

As we've seen throughout this book, the broader issue of language does attain to definitive importance in Hillman's in psychology: "Psychology," he writes, "ideally means giving soul to language and finding language for soul."[1010] Inevitably, the topic figures centrally, too, in Hillman's construction of Renaissance psychology. "The word is the starting point of Renaissance humanism and of psychotherapy both," he writes. If, on the one hand, the Renaissance originates with "the rediscovery of the imaginal psyche," on the other:

> A mark of imaginal man is the speech of his soul...the range of this speech, its self-generative spontaneity, its precise subtlety and ambiguous suggestion, its capacity, as Hegel said, "to receive and reproduce every modification of the ideational faculty..."[1011]

It is hardly necessary to argue the preeminent importance of language to Rilke. It is, however, worth noting that his *Sonnets*, in particular, embody precisely the qualities Hillman mentions to an almost unparalleled degree. What work reveals greater "self-generative spontaneity" or "ambiguous suggestion" than Rilke's *Sonnets*? In this cycle, the poet's speech achieves a truly Orphic resonance, and it behooves us to look more closely at what both Hillman and Rilke's own poem may have to say about the turns of phrase that help engender that archetypally poetic character, which character (it *turns* out) happens to entertain a singular relation to the origins of Renaissance art and thought.

In the seventh poem of Part I, Rilke's sonnet sequence—still sketching Orpheus' essential lineaments—addresses the province of poetic speech.

> Praising, that's it! As one appointed to praise
> he emerged like ore from the deep mine's
> deafness. His heart—O ephemeral press
> of humankind's unending wine.

The poem associates the transformative power of Orphic voice with what is not only the God's native place of origin, but as well (as Hillman reminds us) the imaginative locale of the Renaissance...

His voice never failed him—flagged in the dust
when the divine image thrust open his mouth.
All turns to vineyard held in his trust;
grapes ripened in his feeling South.

...before tying the theme of poetic language to motifs central to the immediately preceding sonnets, death and the underworld:

Neither the decay in a king's grave bed
nor the shadow old Gods have cast
renders his praising moot.

He is one of the messengers who last,
still reaching bowls of praiseworthy fruit
deep into the doors of the dead.

Fruit is the end-product of the life-process of organic growth; a sweet, nutritive substance that sustains life even while itself being subject to rapid decay. Likening poetic speech to fruit gifted to the underworld, Rilke figures the poetic word—no less than Orpheus himself—as a vehicle of communion between the upper and the lower worlds, the linked realms of the living and the dead.

The subsequent poem (1, 8) intensifies the sonnet cycle's self-conscious understanding of speech as a vehicle of soul. It, too, expresses a special connection to the historical horizon of the Renaissance—not, this time, by mention of the South, but by virtue of the aura of pagan antiquity that pervades the poem. Employing figurative language as a means of entering an imaginal realm wherein the poetic present remains intimately linked to the ancient past, the poem figures the act of praise as a "space" or realm within which *another* archetypal mode of discourse may rightfully come into its own:

Only in the realm of Praise may Lament
linger, nymph of the spring tears have sown,
watching over our falling water, intent
on showing clear upon the self-same stone

that bears the ancient portal and the altar.
See, around her calm shoulders dawns
the feeling she may be the youngest sister
of all the soul-moods still not gone.

Jubilation knows, and Longing will tell why—
only Lament still learns; night after night
her girlish hands reckon the old wrong.

Yet, suddenly—awkward and awry—
she lifts a constellation of our song
into the sky; unclouded, clear, and bright.

In this sonnet, Rilke personifies not distant beloveds, or near objects, or ubiquitous deities, but *specific rhetorical forms of poetic discourse.* For its part, Lament appears in the guise of a rather shy nymph, another girlish type akin to the anima figure introduced in "And it was almost a girl...." Both the *theme* of Rilke's poem and its (self-consciously) *rhetorical form* relate, once more, to what are (for Hillman, at least) defining features of Renaissance art.

"Anima" contends Hillman, "reigned in Renaissance Italy," an assertion he supports by pointing to the innumerable Renaissance paintings of Mary (especially as the young Virgin), Petrarch's Laura and Dante's Beatrice, and Botticelli's pagan deities.[1012] We have already devoted a good deal of time and attention to the vital role anima plays in Rilke's *Sonnets*; what concerns us here is her manifestation in the field of language. "*Rhetoric*," writes Hillman, "played such an important part in Renaissance writing because it *is the speech form of the anima archetype*, the style of words when informed by soul." He elaborates further:

> Not unlike this exposition, the style of Renaissance "philosophers" follows a wandering course...This is a style attempting to be precise in distinguishing among the faces of the soul, all the while appealing to that many-sided soul by speaking in figurative language to the emotions, senses, and fantasy, working its persuasion through artfulness....This has all been called rhetoric.[1013]

Rilke's *Sonnets*, too, exhibit an intensely rhetorical style. True, all writing retains a rhetorical dimension. Even so, most expository forms of discourse generally endeavor to employ grammar as a tool of clear and logical exposition while minimizing meanings dependent upon evident rhetorical device. Poetry, on the other hand, by its very nature, relies most heavily on linguistic tropes. Even in the realm of poetic discourse, however, degrees of "rhetorical saturation" differ greatly. A good deal of modern poetry, for instance, inclines toward a "plain" style that deliberately tends to flatten out the rhetorical surface. Rilke's *Sonnets*, on the other hand, tip toward the opposite pole; replete with apostrophe, direct and indirect address, myth and metaphor, personification, allusion, riddle, etc., it would be difficult to imagine a work much more steeped in patently *poetic* rhetoric than Rilke's sonnets. While this does not mean that Rilke's *Sonnets* are "flowery" in any clichéd fashion, it does imply—in accord with Hillman's psychological definition of rhetoric—an extraordinary accent upon how the soul qua anima informs and shapes speech, and vice versa.

Sonnet I, 8 ("Only in the realm of Praise") epitomizes this kind of *archetypally poetic* (and so, *Orphic*) consciousness. The poem personifies Lament, Jubilation, and Longing, directly and deliberately imputing (distinct moods of) soul to different rhetoric types. This naturally confers psychological character to specific rhetorical kinds—figuratively *ensouls* language—even while self-consciously seeking rhetorical forms that may serve as adequate vessels for the archetypal energies speaking in and through the sonnets themselves. Hillman writes: "There is a special relation between soul and word, between psyche and logos, and . . . their union is our field, psychology."[1014] That field, however, is also the "imaginal pasture" of poetry, particularly poetry as archetypally psychological and rhetorically self-aware as Rilke's.

I do not, however, mean to impute a kind of clever, reflexive "self-consciousness" to Rilke's "language" itself, the kind of critical gesture which, for a time, became something of a fad among disciples of Paul de Man. In the hands of a purely academic theoretician like de Man, such a move does not invite recognition of the living unity of psyche and logos but rather inclines to deny the reality of both soul and the living word in the name of Baron Intellection and his indentured servant, a senseless page named Language. Nothing could be further from the truth of Hillman's own sense of rhetoric or the general intention of his "dehumanizing" of psychology, the aim of which remains not the repression of psyche, but a mode of *soul-making* that ultimately realizes *psyche's original relation to the archetypal power of the Gods*, a recognition ultimately achieved in and through her incarnation of the Word that is logos, mythos, and eros all in one.

Defining his neo-Renaissance psychology's own rhetorical goals, Hillman quotes Plato asserting that one "should exert oneself not for the sake of speaking to and dealing with his fellow men, but that he may be able to speak what is pleasing to the gods."[1015] Rilke's *Sonnets to Orpheus*, directly addressed (and implicitly dedicated) to the God of Song, embody that intention from beginning to end. How, the poet asks in Sonnet I, 3, can a man follow him (Orpheus) through the portal of divine speech or song? Love songs steeped in the passing passion of youth will not sound tones like to those plucked on the immortal lyre, for "true singing demands a different breath ... A wafting *in the God*."

Rilke provides another, similar image of this transpersonal goal in the last tercet of Sonnet I, 8—one that, moreover, figures the poetic and psychological step accomplished in moving from the language of the *Elegies* to that of the *Sonnets*. The personified figure of Lament "lifts a constellation of our song / into the sky (or heavens)—unclouded by her own breath." Remarking upon the raising of the figure of the Orphic lyre into the heavenly constellation Lyra, Cobb notes, "Reverting the lyre to a constellation in the heavens is another way of indicating its archetypal nature."[1016] Similarly, Rilke's concluding image symbolizes a "lifting up" of the elegiac form of Lament, transforming it from a rhetorical mode expressive of human emotion and personality into one that might embody a more purely archetypal octave of intelligence—or (phrased otherwise) one capable of speaking "what is pleasing to the Gods."

Rilke's *Sonnets* allude to the Gods several times. One poem in particular—lamenting modern ways as too industriously straightforward—overtly encourage reconnection with the world of the ancient polytheistic imagination. The twenty-fourth sonnet opens:

> Shall we reject our ancient friendship with the great
> unwooing Gods, because the steel-hard trap
> we forge doesn't recognize their state—
> or suddenly seek them out upon a map?
>
> These most powerful friends, who take the dead
> from us, touch nowhere on our rigid rounds.
> Banquet and bath are banished from our grounds
> and their messengers—we're long since way ahead
>
> of their slow bidding.

Significantly, the poem concludes by identifying ancient forms of imaginations with the "wandering" way of things Hillman associates with a distinctly rhetorical style:

Still more alone, yet more
dependent on another whom we do not know
we no longer lay out our paths in lovely meanders

but trace straight lines. The fires we once bore
burn only in boilers, lifting hammers that grow
ever larger. But we—we lose strength, like swimmers.

Rilke's own sonnet sequence—while far from disorderly—itself indubitably follows a wandering course, delivering its Orphic messages in a rhetorically rich style suited not to streamline human understanding, but to conjure remembrance of the archetypal *theo-phanic*[1017] imagination.

To be sure, the meandering course of Rilke's *Sonnets* retains its own poetic source of order—a logic more *recursive* and *echoic* than linear. Here, for instance, is Sonnet I, 9:

Only he who can raise
his lyre among shadows
returns the unending praise
intuiting what he knows.

Only one who with the dead
ate of their poppy
will hear what's softly said
and keep fairest copy.

Even when the reflecting pool
blurs, and is dumb:
Know the image.

In the domain of the dual
voices first becomes
mild, eternal.

Lyric tone, poetic speech and praise; the dead and (Hades') underworld; shadow, reflection, and image; doubleness and the voice of true knowing: Rilke's ninth sonnet integrates many of the themes introduced in the prior poems, producing a cryptic yet clear poetic distillate of what, Orphically speaking, has gone before. In fact, Sonnet I, 9 may tentatively be regarded as the "end" of the first loose "group" of sonnets, a series that lays out the premises of Orphic speech and wisdom.

There is, of course, more to come; still, essential bases have been covered, and the figure of the Orphic God himself recedes into the background for a time before emerging, again, in the last third or so of this first part. Meanwhile, the next sonnet (1, 10) sounds a somewhat new tone as the poetic "I," having assimilated itself to the tenets of Orphic vision, comes more into its own, playing itself off against a wide array of different objects and subjects. This (self-)reflective vis-à-vis suggests that it may be an appropriate moment to look into a dimension of Rilke's rhetoric we have so far have touched upon only tangentially. No discussion of the rhetoric of Rilke's *Sonnets*—even if it be, perforce, quite cursory—can neglect mention of the generic form that houses the soul of the work. Let us, then—abandoning the pretense of sequential treatment—embark upon an unsystematic meditation on the sonnet querying the form's relation to the Orphic source of Rilke's poetic inspiration, or: why *sonnets* to Orpheus?

We have remarked before that—in contrast to the cycle's debut poem—the first poem of Part II does say "I."

> Breathe, invisible poem!
> World-space continually in pure
> interchange with our own being. Counterweight
> in which I rhythmically occur.
>
> Lone wave, whose
> slowly gathering sea I am...

The way the author identifies himself here—while hardly accenting his human personality—does set his elementally poetic character in strong relief. If we credit William Sharp's sense of the sonnet, moreover, the (self-)defining metaphor opening the poem's second quatrain pertains less to poetry in general than it does to the peculiar nature of Rilke's chosen form:

> For the concise expression of an isolated poetic thought—an intellectual or sensuous "wave" keenly felt, emotionally and rhythmically—the Sonnet would seem to be the best medium, the means apparently prescribed by certain radical laws of melody and harmony, in other words, of nature: even as the swallow's wing is the

> best for rapid volant wheel and shift, as the heron's for mounting by wide gyrations, as that of the kite or the albatross for sustained suspension.[1018]

Sonnet—from the Italian *sonnetto*—means "small song." In German—in addition to the usual, borrowed form Rilke employs in his title—the form has also been called a *Klanggedicht*: a poem that *sounds* or *rings*. In II 13, the key German word echoes in another one of Rilke's Sonnets' pivotal moments of self-definition:

> *Hier, unter Schwindenden, sei, im Reiche der Neige,*
> *sei ein klingendes Glas, das sich im* ***Klang*** *schon zerschlug.*
>
> Here, in the realm of decline, amid what's vanishing
> be a ringing glass that shatters even as it rings.

Rilke's famous figure (borrowed, by Donald Prater, to serve as the title of his biography of the poet, *The Ringing Glass*) foregrounds the two chief qualities inherent in the name of the sonnet form: *musical sound*, and (relative) *brevity*. Given that these are chief qualities of lyric poetry per se, what better form to employ in addressing Orpheus, endeavoring to speak to—and from—the mythic origin of poetry itself?

Still, some significant caveats require mention here. While definitively associated with the quality of sound, the sonnet is not a purely lyric form. Despite its name, the sonnet is seldom if ever sung,[1019] and its "music" remains essentially verbal, pitched to the peculiar phonic quality of spoken language. Correlatively, though a short form, the fourteen lines of the sonnet do, as Sharp contends, provide sufficient space and time to develop—concisely!—a given thought, and so mold it as a form capable of containing significant intellectual substance. One can well imagine that such capacity—naturally greatly expanded in a long sonnet sequence—would prove essential to any work effectively taking the *Duino Elegies* (not to mention the whole course of Rilke's intellectual career) as preparation and point d'appui.

In particular, the dual nature of the sonnet structure—the opening octave (composed of two quatrains) set off by the famous *volta* or turn from the closing sextet (in the Petrarchan form, composed of two tercets)—invites internal complication. In his *Forms of English Poetry*, C. F. Johnson asserts:

> The sonnet is well adapted to the presentation of two related thoughts, whether the relation be that of contrast or of parallelism, but it is so short that the body of thought must be *very condensed and striking, lucidly presented and yet of far-reaching suggestiveness.*[1020]

These are qualities, I would suggest, amply in evidence in Rilke's *Sonnets to Orpheus*, poems clear as if poured in glass, and often figuring the cosmic (read, archetypal) significance of what is *contained*, right *here*. The transcendent gesture of Rilke's *Sonnets*—while aiming at archetypal significance—does not thereby imply displacement of interest to some place *other* than the earth, as Sonnet II, 20 makes clear:

> Between the stars, how far; and yet, how much greater
> the distance we learn from all that is here.
> One, for instance, a child.... and another, his neighbor—
> how inconceivably far is their near.

The peculiar *beauty* of the sonnet, moreover, inheres in good measure in the *balanced* resolution of the (potentially competing) lines of force bred of the *duality* intrinsic to the form:

> Sonnet beauty depends on symmetry and asymmetry both.... In this it resembles things of organic beauty.... It involves the principle of balanced yet dissimilar masses, of formality and freedom, like a tree which has developed under the rigorous law of its growth and yet is shaped by the chance of wind and sunshine into something individual.[1021]

"A tree rose up..."—so begin Rilke's Sonnets. In the last chapter, we reflected upon the scene that opens the cycle: the mythic image of Orpheus under a tree, calming the wild animals with his music, drawing them toward the silence at its center. While it would be hard to imagine a like stilling achieved by the thundering *Elegies*—that monumental poem unfolding in long, weighty scrolls of thought—something of the magic *harmony* and *soul-serenity* imparted by Orpheus evidently inheres in the delicately balanced rhythmic and phonic structure of the sonnet itself. "The sonnet form" writes Johnson, "could not have endured the test of time for so many years did it not embody some of the underlying principles of beauty."[1022]

As David Young aptly observes, moreover, the thematic and formal structure of Rilke's sonnet *sequence* effectively magnifies the *unity in duality* inherent in the individual sonnet itself. The *Sonnets* possess an essentially dual subject—the Orphic God and the Eurydice-Vera soul figure—a pairing reflected in the first two and last two sonnets of each of the cycle's two parts.[1023] Unity in duality inheres, again, in that very (unusual) two-part structure of the whole sequence. After remarking both the *Sonnets*' dual subject and two-part structure, Young (turning his attention back to the individual sonnet) proceeds to interpret the larger significance of the two-in-oneness that inheres on so many levels of Rilke's cycle:

> The sonnet traditionally goes in one direction and then "turns".... Like the human mind itself, "hesitating between," everything divides, threatening to remain separate.... Out of the nettle of duality, however, Rilke plucks the flower of unity, finding ways, again and again, of closing the fissured self, healing the god/man and spirit/matter splits, so that the entire sequence becomes a giant demonstration of the rhythms of dividing and uniting, wounding and healing, rhythms that the poet feels must characterize experience.[1024]

Given the understanding so far conveyed in this book, those rhythms may be recognized as intrinsic to what is essentially "the *middle* term in all things," whose nature and function it is to connect the poles of the cosmos (spirit and matter, heaven and earth, subject and object, god and man)—namely, *soul.*

Cobb, in amplifying Rilke's initiating image of Orpheus, speaks of the "deep communion in soul" effected in and through his music. While Cobb's remark refers specifically to Orpheus' relation to the animals, the idea of a "communion in soul" he evokes may well qualify as another general attribute of the sonnet form. As we've implied already, the fourteen-line sonnet does not—like the far more compressed haiku—incline toward a Zen-like simplicity, but represents an intensely reflective form that tends, in its inherent duality, to open out to embrace an other—whether that "other" be person, idea, God, object, or all of the above.

Rilke's *Sonnets*—both inheriting and extending the established sonnet traditions—are, in fact, full of direct address to all orders of being (*Singing God.... O you tender ones.... I greet you, sarcophagi.... You, my friend, are all alone.... But you—so swiftly departed....*) A form of poetic relation well suited to address and redress, the sonnet naturally weds affect and intellect, internal reflection and intersubjectivity. Indeed, its historic record as *an incomparable vehicle of (impossible) love* reveals the sonnet's underlying relation to the psyche-eros mytheme, revealing it as an archetypally *psychological* genre, one peculiarly adapted to the expression of the soul-images that compose thought of the heart.

In his discourse on the Renaissance, Hillman notes the "obsessive preoccupation with love and beauty" that marks the period. Hillman rejects the tendency to regard this inclination as "a rash of frivolous poeticizing," instead encouraging us to

> regard these events from the perspective of the soul-making that takes place through the intercourse of anima and eros.... [These obsessions are] inherent in the movement of soul, the activity of anima, which seeks eros. For the corollary reason, for an eros with soul, for a psychological eroticism which has been correctly called platonic, we may turn to these writings and paintings.[1025]

While the sonnet was invented in medieval Italy, it was, after all, Petrarch—that herald of the Renaissance—who first established the lasting lineaments of the form. Petrarch's acquaintance with his Laura was fleeting, the "dark lady" of Shakespeare's immortal sonnets quite possibly purely fictive. Impossible love thus weaves in the work of the two poets who originated the major sonnet forms. Such momentous precedent qualifies the sonnet as, essentially, a Renaissance form, one instrumental to the "rebirth of the imaginal psyche" inaugurated by that epochal movement, and revivified in Rilke's own heterodox version of the historic genre.

In our discussion of form, we have so far concentrated on the sonnet per se. Let us continue by devoting some more deliberate attention to the longer, overall form of Rilke's *Sonnets to Orpheus*.

> Perhaps the Renaissance's most popular figure from myth was Proteus. His ceaselessly changing image that could take on any shape or nature represented the multiple and ambiguous form of the soul.... the Protean idea could keep the soul's many *daimones* in inherent relation.[1026]

The arrangement of multiple sonnets in a *sequence* incarnates the principle of *unity in diversity* that counts as yet another signature concern of both Neoplatonic philosophy and Renaissance psychology. It qualifies, too, as yet another index of the latter's central concern with the soul that is—as Plotinus teaches—inherently one *and* many. David Young observes that the sonnet sequence "occupies a sort of middle ground between the long poem and the loose collection of individual lyrics." As such, Young opines, it represents "something of a risk, but it also creates . . . a potential advantage since it combines diversity with unity."[1027]

Young proceeds to reflect upon how the traditional sonnet sequence—building upon Petrarchan precedent—most often centers upon an unfulfilled love relationship. As in the myth of Psyche and Eros, the difficulty or impossibility of consummating the relationship opens "a window on the infinite," encouraging reflection upon a wide-ranging array of "topics, moods, occasions and ideas." Young understands Rilke as both inheriting and transforming this tradition:

> He does not center his poem on love for a particular person, but writes instead a kind of extended love-poem to the world, celebrating such diverse love-objects as mirrors, dogs, fruit, ancient sarcophagi, roses, a strip of cloth, unicorns, breathing and childhood. Thus the expansiveness and diversity of the traditional sequence are extended.[1028]

Young quickly adds an important qualification: one crucial to understanding the underlying unity of the diverse sonnets: "[T]his sequence of sonnets does have two recurrent figures . . . addressed frequently enough to raise the possibility that the entire poem is devoted to either or both of them." As Rilke's title (addressing Orpheus) and dedication (remembering a young dancer) suggestion, this is more than a mere "possibility."

Generically speaking, Rilke's *Sonnets to Orpheus* display closest kinship with—not *Malte* or the *Elegies*—but *New Poems*, another long, two-part collection of individual poems, many of which are sonnets. The *New Poems*, moreover, tend (as the *Dinggedichte* show) to face out toward the objective world while *Malte* and the *Elegies* remain, generally speaking, more subjective in focus and intent. The synthetic *Sonnets*—while retaining and elevating the inner soul-perspective gained in *Malte* and the *Elegies—simultaneously* turn attentively back to the world of things opened in the *New Poems*. In fact, a number of the sonnets in Rilke's cycle treat of subjects similar or identical to those addressed in the *New Poems*; sarcophagi, unicorns, and fountains represent a few of the clearest, most objective instances.

Even so, while the objects addressed may be more or less the same, the poetic world they inhabit has been profoundly transformed. The two volumes of *New Poems*—while exhibiting their own forms of coherence—lack the Orphic voice and vision that binds the sheaf of sonnets together. Nor are the individual pieces—while magnificent in their own right—animated by the same soul-mood as the sonnets. We can register some significant differences by setting comparable poems from the two volumes side by side.

In chapter 8, we read Rilke's "Roman Fountain," exhibiting it as an instance of how Rilke adapted Rodin's sculptural aesthetics (especially the art of "modeling") to his own poetic medium. The poem (the whole of which may be found in chapter 8) begins:

> Two basins, one rising from the other
> in the middle of an old marble pool,
> and from the one above, water gently bending
> to water, which below stands waiting...

The *Sonnets to Orpheus*, too, include a fountain poem. Sonnet II, 15 reads:

> O fountain-mouth, you whose gift is always going,
> inexhaustibly speaking one pure sound—
> you, marble mask before the flowing
> face of water. And in the far background
>
> the aqueducts' descent. From faraway hills,
> passing by graves in the Apennines,
> they bring their Saying to you, which then falls
> over the blackened aging of your chin
>
> into the basin waiting down below.
> This is the prone and sleeping ear,
> the marble-ear, in which you always speak.
>
> Earth's ear. So that she's talking here
> to herself alone. Slip a pitcher in the creek
> and it seems to her you interrupt her flow.

The "new poem" remains unrelentingly descriptive—albeit very poetically so. As we discussed in chapter 8, most every clause shapes the imaginative surface of the depicted thing in a new light. At the same time, the voice that speaks "Roman Fountain" remains rhetorically quite flat. Maintaining a kind of even monotone, the speaker remains wholly out of the picture, and no trope of voice (e.g., direct address) has any place at all in the poem.

The Orphic sonnet, on the other hand, displays less intensive concern with the physiognomic details of the thing itself. It is not so much *the visual image of the thing* that grabs and holds the poet's attention as it is its character as *a (metaphoric) vehicle of poetic voice*. This sonnet, in fact, begins with the archetypal figure of poetic vocation—apostrophic exclamation—and sees the fountain itself as, not so much a series of visual transitions, an animated modeling of corporeal surface, as a mouth, an organ of speech, of poetic Saying (*Sagen*) that flows from "far away" (from mountains slopes, from graves) to concentrate in the fountain's ceaseless water-song, an endless, self-contained circle of speaking and hearing that becomes—not only the fountain's—but the oral (and aural) life of the whole earth, the living pulse of its poetic heart.

In Plotinus, the fountain figures as a favorite image of the highest divinity—the One or the Good—constantly flowing out of its own center, and (at the outer periphery of its contemplative vision) flooding the sense world with images of its being even while incessantly returning back into itself in unending cycles of *emanation* and *epistrophe*. A poetic universe as capacious as the one sketched in the sonnets cannot stand on sand; if the biblical God did not vouch for Rilke's version of the creation, some other source of intelligence had to fill that void. Rilke generally avoided the genre of philosophy, and did not (so far as I know) study Neoplatonism per se. Even so, the fountain had long been one of his favorite figures—he chose Vogeler's image of a fountain for the cover of *The Book of Images*, and found deep joy in the small fountain that adorned the Chateau Muzot's own garden. It should therefore not be surprising that the principles of creative motion, life, and being that inform his Orphic vision—animating and ordering the world of his sonnets—reveal a deep affinity with the Neoplatonic philosophy that helped birth the Renaissance.

Far from being any kind of accident, this confluence flows from a common source: the profound attention both Rilke's poetry and Neoplatonic philosophy devote to the soul and (what Plotinus calls) its "double-act." Itself (like Rilke's fountain) an image of the One, the soul perpetually pours forth its creative life into the *many* manifest forms of nature, while at the same time another, complementary act constantly moves to return all things to their supernatural source, the *archetypal* origin of being (*Nous*) that serves as the ground of all true knowing. "Wer sich als Quelle ergiesst, den erkennet die Erkennung," Rilke writes in Sonnet II, 12: "Whoever pours him or herself forth as a spring, is recognized by Knowing"

> ...and she leads him, enchanted, through creation's fair paths
> that often end in beginning, and with ending, begin.

While it would be worthwhile to delve more deeply into the metaphysical dimension of Rilke's sonnets in relation to Plotinian doctrine, we cannot compass such a project here—one that, in any event, could all too easily occlude critical attention to the central poetic and psychological dimension of Rilke's work. Let us, instead, pursue our comparison of the *New Poems* and the *Sonnets* by looking at another pair of poems with virtually identical subjects. In so doing, we may open up exploration of the crucial theme announced in the first phrase of Sonnet II, 12: "Wolle die Wandlung"—"will the transformation."

First, this "new poem":

Roman Sarcophagi

But what is there to hinder our believing
(the way we're set down here, and scattered about)
that, for a short while only, thirst and hate
and gross confusion dwell in our receiving

as once in well-adorned sarcophagi
by rings and glasses, by godly figurines
garbed in slowly self-consuming skeins
a slowly dissolved something would lie

until swallowed by the reserved mouths
that never speak. (Where exists the brain
that might serve them, even as they lie?)

Then the ancient aqueducts' stony troughs
steered into them the everlasting rain
that runs in them, waving to the sky.[1029]

By comparison, Sonnet I, 10 reads:

> You, who have stayed in my heart always,
> I greet you, sarcophagi that have lain so long,
> whom the cheerful waters of Roman days
> flow through like a wandering song.
>
> Or those so open, like the deeply calm
> eye of a happily awakening shepherd,
> —full of stillness and blooming bee balm—
> from which delighted butterflies rose and fluttered;
>
> all we can wrest from the realm of doubt
> I greet—the mouths that open with strange power
> having known what it means to keep shut.
>
> Do we know it, friends—or do we not, perchance?
> Both help form the hesitant hour
> in the human countenance.

In this tenth sonnet, Rilke effectively condenses the characteristics of Orphic voice and vision evoked in the prior nine sonnets into (the multifaceted image of) one symbolic object. Given this astonishing feat, it is perhaps not surprising that this poem effectively *begins* where the "new poem" leaves off. The earlier poem opens by likening human beings to Roman sarcophagi insofar as we are vessels that—"for a short while only"—house temporal stuff (emotions that pass, bodies that decay), while the poem's conclusion celebrates the sarcophagi as containers of a purer, more lasting substance. It is this "eternal water" that the sarcophagi in the Orphic sonnet contain *from the start*—this *water of life* that is at once undying and yet—like the poet's own song—ever wandering, ever changing course.

Both poems compare the sarcophagi to mouths in the closing sestet. Even so, the characterization of that figure in the two poems establishes a marked contrast—one that echoes the thematic difference we discovered in reading the fountain poems. In the sculptural, rhetorically less adventuresome "new poem," the sarcophagi are "unknown mouths" that—while swallowing up purely temporal contents—"never speak." In the Orphic sonnet, the poet—in a characteristic gesture made, too, in the first line of the poem—*greets* "die wiedergeöffneten Munde" —"the mouths opened once again / after having known what silence means." The poet's greeting indicates identification: the voice of the *Sonnets* recognizes death as a vessel of new poetic life and affirms what the "new poem" cannot (at least not with the same authority): its mission of *speaking (out) from that primordial knowledge-source.*

Bearer of a "wandering song," the Orphic voice of the *Sonnets* moves freely through the world, kaleidoscopically reflecting the hidden imaginal reality inhering in all visible and invisible appearances, ringing nature *and* psyche's constant changes. In the course of that poetic peregrination, the boundaries that divide existence into distinct metaphysical categories: subject and object, spirit and matter, thought and emotion, you and I, God and the human being, are—provocatively and metaphorically—crossed and recrossed *out* as all is absorbed in the meandering, ever-changing stream of *soul* that constantly translates everything into everything else—in I, 10 for instance, *water* into *song*; *sarcophagi* (in and of themselves figures of *death*) into *open eyes* (which in turn transform into a *well of stillness*, the *soil of sweetness*, and the *cocoon of flight*)—or *mouths*; mouths into *ciphers of certainty*; certainties into *questions* that mold *the features of the human face*, which in turn mirror a *historical moment.* In comparison with this acrobatic poetic reach, the art of the *New Poems*—agile enough in its own right—appears rather more limited and self-contained. No wonder: it did not appear under the sign of the Orphic God, who, as the personification of (among other things) the principle of *metamorphosis*, is perfectly Protean in nature.

We have seen, in chapter 8, that Rilke builds the art of his *New Poems* upon a sculptural model borrowed from Rodin. The *Sonnets to Orpheus*, on the other hand, take another *sister* art as exemplary point of departure. The *Sonnets*, after all, are dedicated to the soul of a young dancer, and, in addition to the few (very important) poems that explicitly figure her art form, the whole cycle remains infused with a dance-like art of movement, an attention not so much to the images conjured by working poetic surfaces and planes as to the (invisible) paths of thought traced by the continual transformations of figurative and rhetorical form. In his own comparison of the opening of the *Sonnets* and the *Elegies*, Snow writes:

> [In the first sonnet] the ego and exposed subjectivity of the *Elegies* are absent. The poem proceeds more like choreography: an

abrupt statement that *posits* with the force of a speech act ("A tree arose"), then transforms at once into invocation and apostrophe ("O pure transcendence!"), modulates back seamlessly into hushed, perfectly paced narration ("And all was silent") before becoming in its very last line direct address ("you built temples for them in their hearing").[1030]

Rilke did not consciously study the art of dance as he did (inspired by Rodin) the art of sculpture. He did, however, possess his own haunting image of Vera, and his imagination of her preferred art form was enhanced by his reading of Paul Valéry, whose "Dance and the Soul" profoundly influenced Rilke's *Sonnets*. Written in the form of a Platonic dialogue (!), "Dance and the Soul" features Socrates, Phaedrus, and Eryximachus witnessing a dance performance by a young woman (girl), Athikte, and—thoroughly enraptured by what they see—discoursing upon the event. The following passage may offer some indication of the tenor of the writing, and, too, its deep relevance for Rilke:

> Socrates: She is wholly in her shut eyes, alone with her soul, in the bosom of deepest attention. She is feeling herself become an event....
> Phaedrus: Delicious moment...This silence is a contradiction....How can one help calling out. "Silence!"
> Socrates: Moment of absolute virginity. And then, moment when something is about to break in our souls, in our waiting, in our company...Something break...And yet it is like a welding too.[1031]

Some of Rilke's lines may even sound echoes of Valéry. Valéry (qua Eryximachus): "I care for nothing so much as for what is on the point of occurring," Rilke: "...the spirit... / loves, in the figure's swing, nothing more than the pivotal turn." Eryximachus: "She has become wholly dance and is wholly consecrated to movement"; and Rilke: "Dancer: O you translation / of all vanishing into movement," or, translated more poetically,

> Dancer: o you transposition
> of transience into the flow of your form: how you offered it there!

And the swirl at the end; this tree made of motion,
did it not fully capture the far-flung year?

Did not—so your just finished swinging would whirl round
    it—the crown
suddenly bloom with stillness? And over, above,
wasn't it sun, wasn't it summer up there pouring down
the immeasurable warmth of your love?

But it bore, too, your tree of ecstasy.
Are not these its tranquil fruit: the striped urn
growing ripe, and the vase—ripening still more fully?

And in the drawing: the dark stroke of your brow
swiftly sketched on the face of its turn:
can we not see it, even now?

For all the dynamism Rodin manages to incorporate in his hardly stationary statues, *movement* and the *continual metamorphosis* of form remain far more patently the very element of dance, and the inspiration of that art contributes essentially to the soul of the *Sonnets*. Just as—in the second sonnet—the anima figure "sleeps the world," here, a whole universe of (both "figurative" and "literal") things—a tree, the year and its seasons of sun and warmth; a pitcher, an urn, a painting—are conjured by the dance of the soul.

At the same time, Orpheus and Vera-cum-Eurydice, logos (or speech) and psyche, song and dance, are one. In the fifth sonnet, Orpheus "comes and goes." In the penultimate sonnet of Part II, the young dancer does, too:

You come and go. You, still almost a child, fill
out, for a moment, the dance-figure
into a pure constellation of the dance wherein we will
fleetingly transcend the sure

dumb order of nature.

This is another moment of "pure transcendence," another "lifting up" of things to the level of archetypal intelligence. But the magical dance begins *only* when the Orphic music starts. It is initiated by, and wholly attuned to, the voice of song:

For she'd stirred herself
to listen only then, when Orpheus sang...

You still knew the place where the lyre
lifted, resounding—the unheard-of center.

In his *Sonnets*, Rilke consummates the immense soul-spiritual journey commenced near the beginning of his poetic career. In the endless wave of this cycle's poetic breath, he transmits a voice and vision not riven by the dualisms that split the traditional western world view into incommensurate opposites of Heaven and Earth, Spirit and Matter, Eternity and Time, Life and Death, the One God and the multiplex Mortal World of nature and humankind. He does so not by repudiating duality altogether, but by plumbing the depths of that medial, imaginal in-between soul world where "the lyre lifted, resounding," that "unheard-of center" where Orpheus and Eurydice, logos and psyche, wor(l)d and soul are one.

In so doing, moreover, Rilke offers a fresh draught of the Renaissance spirit; delivers a poem that—even now—fosters "the rediscovery of the imaginal psyche" and "rebirth of soul." If the soul of Orpheus had to wait sixteen hundred years before incarnating in the person of Marsilio Ficino, the interregnum preparing the *next* poetic embodiment did not last nearly so long.

Chapter 20

ARE WE NOW THE HEARERS

If Rilke crowned his poetic career with an Orphic inspiration, how does the soul-making accomplished in and through his *Sonnets* fit into the Psyche-Eros narrative, the mythic plot that has guided our wandering course through Rilke's soul-history all along? How indeed, do the imaginal voices of these two founding myths sound together in the concluding movement of Rilke's poetic opus? Before seeking to weave these story lines together, we (after long intermission) return to Psyche's own saga to find out just how her unusually "heroic" tale ends.

The fourth and last labor Venus assigns to Psyche appears the most dangerously impossible of all. "Take this casket," the goddess commands,

> and straightaway descend to the world below and the ghastly halls of Orcus himself. There present the casket to Proserpine and say, "Venus begs of thee to send her a small portion of thy beauty, such at least as may suffice for the space of one brief day..."[1032]

This awful charge pushes Psyche's toward suicide yet again. Psyche goes "to a certain high tower that she might throw herself headlong from," thinking this the quickest and most honorable way to journey to the underworld. The tower, however, has other ideas, and exclaims:

> Why poor wretch, seekest thou to slay thyself by casting thyself headlong down? And why rashly dost thou faint before this task, the last of all thy perils? For if once the breath be severed from thy body, thou wilt assuredly go to the depths of Tartarus, but thou shalt in no wise have power to return thence.[1033]

The "far-seeing tower" then proceeds to "perform its task of prophecy," providing Psyche with detailed instructions as to how she may successfully fulfill Venus' request. She must go to a certain deserted place where she will find a dark cavern that leads to the underworld; avoid a host of snares designed to foil her on her way down, and—once having received the box of beauty from Persephone—must "above all, beware...not to open or look within the casket." Naturally, Psyche follows all the tower's instructions—except this last most pressing injunction.

Having emerged from the underworld and set foot on the earth once more, Psyche—eternally yearning for reunion with Eros—cannot resist the temptation to anoint herself with the divine beauty she imagines may draw her lover to her once more. Accordingly, Psyche opens the box, "but there was no beauty therein, nor anything at all save a hellish and truly Stygian sleep" which immediately rushes out and overcomes her.

Nonetheless, Psyche does achieve her ultimate aim—though not in the manner intended. Upon seeing what has befallen Psyche, Eros (whose wound, meanwhile, has finally healed) rushes to the side of his unconscious beloved, wipes the deathly sleep off her, and locks it back in the casket. Gently chiding her, Eros bids Psyche to bring the casket to Venus, adding the comforting assurance that he "will see to the rest."

After this, the tale proceeds quickly to its joyous conclusion. After sending Psyche off to Venus, Eros immediately flies to Jove and pleads for aid in his suit. Jove (after asking a small favor from Eros in return!) promptly sends Mercury to call all the Gods to a marriage feast. Telling the gathered guests it is high time "to set some curb upon the wild passions of his youthful prime," Jove announces Eros' marriage to Psyche, taking special pains to assuage Venus' qualms:

> "And you, my daughter, be not downcast, and have no fear your son's marriage with a mortal will shame your lofty rank and lineage...." Then straightway he bade Mercury catch up Psyche and bring her to heaven. This done, he offered her a goblet of ambrosia and said: "Psyche, drink of this and be immortal. Then Amor shall never leave your arms, but your marriage shall endure forever."[1034]

After describing the rich trappings of the nuptials—including music offered by the Muses and by Pan, Apollo singing to the accompaniment of his lyre, and Venus dancing "with steps that kept time to the sweet music"—Apuleius' tale ends with these words: "Thus did Psyche with all solemnity become Amor's bride, and soon a daughter was born to them: in the language of mortals she is called Pleasure."

The symbolism of Psyche's three initial labors bears little obvious relation to the Rilke poems (or novel) we have associated with them. Ants sorting seeds, reeds advising how to avoid the violence of solar rams, eagles scooping water from mountainous waterfalls: it requires no little interpretive labor to connect these motifs with (respectively) *New Poems*, *The Notebooks of Malte Laurids Brigge*, and the *Duino Elegies*. In the case of *Sonnets to Orpheus*—the last of Rilke's tetralogy of great mature works—the situation initially appears somewhat different. The *Sonnets to Orpheus* do transparently involve entering into Hades ("Where is her death? O will you reinvent this theme / before your song consumes itself," the poet asks of Orpheus) and, correlatively, some kind of attempt to return to the world of the living bearing the immortal beauty that comes from knowledge of death. Surely, this evident congruence may be expected to simplify our interpretive task?

Appearances, however, often prove deceptive, and the present instance proves to be a case in point. Upon closer examination, the deeper connection between Psyche's fourth labor and Rilke's *Sonnets* remains anything but clear—we are seeking, remember, not merely thematic resonance, but poetic *enactment* of symbolic content. If Rilke's *Sonnets* indeed *perform* the actions defining Psyche's last labor, where are the signboards of the crucial scenes? Where Psyche's initial anguish; where the farseeing, prophetic tower; where the dramatic action of Psyche's descent; where her (potentially fateful) disobedience, and Eros' final rescue?

I would submit that images of these motives cannot in fact readily be found in the *Sonnets*; not, however, because they do not compose an important part of Rilke's poetic text, but because Rilke covers this symbolic ground already in *Malte* and—still more centrally—the *Elegies*. Correlatively, *while essential elements of the* Sonnets *do symbolically reflect the prior accomplishment of Pyche's fourth labor, the tone and theme of the cycle itself may better be associated with three mythic events which conclude and succeed that labor: namely, Eros' rescue of Psyche from the sleep of death, Psyche's apotheosis and marriage in Heaven with Eros, and—finally—the birth of Pleasure.* Before turning to these events and their connection with Rilke's *Sonnets*, we will take time to address the prior issue of the imagery of the fourth labor itself and—despite any "backtracking" this may entail—its mythic inscription in the text of Rilke's oeuvre.

It would, after all, be too neat if we could unproblematically identify each of Rilke's four great mature works, in order, with each of four Psyche's labors. It does not reduce the value of our interpretive scheme if we decline to apply it dogmatically and recognize that the soul-making work of Rilke's imagination—while indeed following a broad mythic plot-line—cannot be rigidly compartmentalized.

In the present context in particular, we should recognize that elements of Psyche's fourth labor enter into Rilke's work already in Paris, if not before. Psyche's horror at the imminent prospect of death and—at the same time—her fateful attraction to it; the magnetic draw generated by the knowledge that she cannot truly know love without first knowing death—this certainly qualifies as one of the chief psychic forces driving the writing of *Malte* and the *Elegies*. Both works, too, stage a descent into the underworld, though the markedly divergent styling of those descents reflects defining differences between them.

Malte's agonizing descent into psychic darkness can hardly be deemed conscious, controlled or willed in any way. The young, unstable Dane's encounter with death threatens to undo him utterly; it is by no means certain that Malte will manage to return from the nether spheres of the psyche alive, or with his conscious faculties intact. In the *Elegies*, on the other hand, a much surer hand guides the speaker's underworldly episodes even as the elder Lament in the Tenth Elegy leads the dead youth calmly, and with wisdom, through her domain. Final success may remain in question, but the poetic speaker's imaginal action remains deliberate, proceeding as if instructed by ultimate ends. Metaphorically speaking, we might suggest that the figure of Malte echoes Psyche's state when she is first ordered to enter the underworld and filled with uncontrollable dread at the prospect of her own imminent death, while the poetic action of the *Elegies* mirrors Psyche on her underworld journey *after* being wisely instructed by the "far-seeing tower."

The tower itself, in fact, qualifies as a symbol of singular significance. Neumann, in his commentary on the myth, aptly remarks that, in contrast with the creatures that come to Psyche's aid in her other labors (the ants, the reed, and the eagle), the tower is a *human* construction, an emblem not of natural or divine wisdom, but of culture.

> The tower is an edifice, something erected by human hands, a product of man's collective spiritual labor; thus it is a symbol of human culture and of the human consciousness and is therefore designated as a far-seeing tower.[1035]

This significantly strengthens the symbolic association between this fourth labor and Rilke's *Elegies*, for we have seen how the nature and problem of human consciousness per se qualifies as spiritual source and center of Rilke's elegy cycle even while that consciousness strives to reconnect with the transcendent power of the angel. Nor do the *Elegies* lack passages explicitly evoking both the form and function of that signpost of human culture, "the far-seeing tower." In the Seventh Elegy, Rilke writes:

> For to humans even what comes next lies far away.
> This ought not to baffle us but strengthen our defense
> of a still recognized form.—This once *stood* amidst men,
> stood amidst Fate, the destroyer, stood
> amidst Not-Knowing-Whither, as if it were alive there,
> and arched stars closer from the safeguarded heavens.[1036]

This could well describe, on the one hand, Psyche's existential situation after receiving Venus' final, fateful assignment, and on the other, the saving "task of prophecy" performed by the "far-seeing" tower.[1037] Indeed, after sketching an architectural imagination of the "form" alluded to above ("Pillars, pylons, the Sphinx, the striving thrust / of the cathedral spire, grey, out of the decaying or alien city"), the poet continues celebrating the spiritual potential of human culture in a passage that evokes the imagery of the myth still more explicitly:

> But one tower was great, was it not? O Angel, it was—
> even next to you. Chartres was great—,and music
> rose still higher, soared beyond us. But even
> just one woman in love, alone, at night, at her window . . .
> didn't she reach to your knee—?[1038]

The resonance with the Psyche-Eros story is startling: the first symbol Rilke cites is indeed a tower, and the last—like Psyche—a woman lover plunged in the dark night of her yearning.

In this context, we may mention as well that in El Greco's *View of Toledo*—the painting we likened to the scene of Psyche's third labor, and proposed as an archetypal image of the *Elegies*—church towers stand prominently near the center of the picture. Given that all the human figures in the painting are minuscule to the point of invisibility, these architectural forms—riding the dynamically charged horizon line dividing the heavens and the earth—represent the place of human consciousness in the natural and spiritual landscape.

In his commentary, Neumann remarks another important and distinctive feature of Psyche's fourth labor:

> The first three problems... are solved by "helpers," that is, by inner powers of Psyche's unconscious. But in this last task Psyche herself must do what is asked of her.[1039]

Neumann's next sentence highlights the coincidence of this feature with the character of the tower itself. "Hitherto her helpers belonged to the plant and animal world; this time she is sustained by the tower, as symbol of human culture." These twin symbolic facts—the cultural character of the tower,[1040] and Psyche's own agency—tie into the long story of Rilke's writing of the *Elegies*.

As we saw in chapter 14, even before the initial inspiration that birthed the *Elegies*, Rilke quite deliberately prepared the next step on his spiritual path. Once the *Elegies* were begun, Rilke very consciously undertook the task of completing what he himself recognized as a prophetic mission—one analogous to the symbolic tower's "task of prophecy." In this respect, the *Elegies* are a product of consciously formulated intent and human will—far more so, at any rate, than the *Sonnets*, which appeared out of the blue, and were finished before Rilke had any real idea of what he was doing or (more accurately) what was manifesting through the vessel of his art. Despite the coincidence of their completion in February 1922, the two works feature markedly divergent "creation stories," and mode of composition thus counts as yet another regard in which they cut dramatically different figures: on the one hand, willed intent, a sense of prophetic mission, and a decade of travail; on the other, spontaneous genesis beginning and ending in virtually the same breath.

This contrast may be understood to parallel a decisive transition in the myth itself, one that leads us, at last, toward the mythic landscape of Rilke's *Sonnets to Orpheus.*

As indicated earlier, three events in the Psyche-Eros story form the mythic backdrop of Rilke's *Sonnets*: first, Eros' rescue of Psyche wrapped in a deathlike slumber; second, Psyche's assumption into the sphere of the Gods and the celebration of her marriage in heaven; and—finally—the birth of Pleasure. All of these mythic moments reflect the above-mentioned genetic difference between the *Elegies* and *Sonnets*, for (in marked contrast to Psyche's last labor) none of these can be identified as acts achieved by—or even at all accessible to—human will or conscious intent. Instead, they are all transparently divine interventions, acts of the Gods—even the last, for the birth of the divine child Pleasure is no natural matter, but another moment of spiritual consecration.

Herein lies another—and indeed perhaps the clearest—signature of the underlying archetypal difference between the *Elegies* and the *Sonnets. The telling stylistic contrasts that so dramatically distinguish these "twin" works do not so much reflect differences between two of Psyche's four labors; rather, they stem from the more fundamental distinction between, on the one hand, the whole phase of the myth centered upon Psyche's labors (when the action centers almost exclusively upon Psyche and her doings), and, on the other, the final stage ushered in by Eros' spectacular reappearance.* In the myth's climactic dénouement, the Gods hold sway, and the whole action of the myth is returned to the scene of its divine sources, sweeping the no longer merely human Psyche up in its triumphant epistrophe.

Can we, then—looking beyond the generic difference between the *Elegies* and *Sonnets*—find specific inscriptions of the three climactic events in the text of Rilke's life-work?

Turning, first, to the moment that prepares the myth's finale—Eros' rescue of Psyche—we may recognize its *transitional* character: it both concludes the stage of Psyche's labors and initiates all that follows. Interpreting this event requires—even before Eros enters the scene—construing the act that prepares his entrance: Psyche's opening of Persephone's casket. As the tale tells us, contrary to Psyche's hope for the casket, "there was no beauty therein, nor anything at all save a hellish and truly Stygian sleep." Overcome, Psyche falls even where she stands. There, "she lay motionless, no better than a sleeping corpse."

Rilke himself, in fact, was no stranger to "that thick cloud of slumber," the nothingness that hid beneath the lid of supposed beauty. On one level, we may say that there had long been the danger that an all too virginal aesthetics of death might freeze Rilke's soul-life, that his fascination with sleeping beauty might overpower him and render him insensible or unresponsive to life's changing currents. Rilke, after all, was repeatedly saved from psychic and artistic stagnation by the revivifying power of love. Even if his affairs did not always prove happy or evidently fruitful, they did stir his soul with hope and endless aspiration for union with the (mythical) beloved, an idealized aim that recurrently reawakened his sleeping soul. The poet's love for Merline provides the most signal instance of this dynamic in the latter phase of his life. The energy engendered by this love played a crucial role in enabling Rilke to raise himself—or his *Elegies*—out of their six-year slumber even as Rilke (*too* self-consciously and deliberately, perhaps) sought to drape himself in the mantle of the prophet, and draw divine inspiration toward himself once again.

Of course, it was not Merline alone who "saved" the *Elegies*, though it *was* she who tacked the image of da Conegliano's painting above Rilke's writing desk and so acted as an emissary of the God. Eros, after all, may be anagrammatically found in *Or*(ph)*e*(u)*s*, the archetypal poet whose song was inspired by Love, and, if Merline alone did not "save" the *Elegies*, the spirit-wind that blew in Orpheus did. In the *Elegies*, Rilke's human, all too human psyche had indeed essayed a (more than) symbolic plunge into the underworld, and yet (even after the "hellish" pall of war lifted) remained unable, despite all efforts of conscious will, to revive the work and bring it to completion—as if the "Stygian sleep" contained in the *Duino Elegies* had indeed wrapped the voice that bore it in an impenetrable shroud. That psychological impasse remained unbroken *until* the moment of the poetic God's spontaneous intervention—until the breath of life, the spirit-wind that conceived and dictated the *Sonnets to Orpheus,* resuscitated the innermost soul of Rilke's creative work.

Then, too—if we were to look at things the other way around—there was Vera, the young woman whose soul-life the dark fumes of death threatened to consume. Vera's diaries attest that the power of love—while not preventing her physical death—revivified her soul at the last. While Rilke played no role in the concluding scenes of Vera's own life, his pen did take part in the immortal gesture of love's saving inspiration in its storied aftermath.

We should, then, not be too particular in searching for images of Eros' coming in Rilke's *Sonnets*, for it is nowhere and everywhere there, the very air the *Sonnets* breathe and exude, "the breath... about nothing, the wafting in the God, the wind" that inspires its lines. And if (as the poet declares in I, 2) the soul of the *Sonnets* never really wakes—she does not need to, for hers is no Stygian slumber, but a dream song sung by the God, a shadow dance moving to the sound of love's voice.

So it is, as well, with the *second* main event: Psyche's assumption and marriage. The whole poem bears witness to the *hieros gamos*, the divine syzygy, the sacred marriage of soul and spirit. This lives not only in the constant pairing of poems focused upon Orpheus and his feminine consort, but, too, in the very voice of the poem—its swift and constantly changing poetic motion tempered by the slow work of recursion and the reflective form of the sonnet (and sonnet sequence) itself. As for the figure of Psyche's assumption, this act of "pure transcendence"—the lifting of a constellation of our voice into the heavens—qualifies as the work's defining gesture and is woven into the very fabric of the poem. Symbolically speaking, it figures the *positive* dimension of Hillman's "dehumanization"; it connotes nothing other than the raising of human psychology up to the level of archetypal verity, divinization of the imagination of the soul.

Finally, Pleasure, too, dwells in every measure of the poem. Above all, Rilke's work breathes joy; his *Sonnets to Orpheus* is a poem of consummation and of celebration.

> Lucky Earth! On holiday now, play
> with the children. We want to catch you
> happy Earth. And the most joyful may.[1041]

Hillman, too, has much to say of this last, most pleasurable issue:

> If the tale ends with the birth of this child, then it is no mere incident. The goal of *voluptas* affirms that the process of development modeled upon the union of eros and psyche is not Stoic, not a way of denial and control, of work and will. It is not at all a way of ego development in the usual sense of ego as reality opposed to pleasure.... On the authority of Plotinus, *voluptas* of the senses is the model for the soul's joy.[1042]

No Augustinian asceticism here, to be sure. And Plotinus brings us back, too, to our Renaissance theme:

> Ficino and the Neoplatonic Academy insisted that *voluptas* and joy were more important than cognition and were even a manner of insighting.... For the Neoplatonists *voluptas* was generally both sensual voluptuousness and a transcendent bliss beyond the senses. We might call it *psychic sensuality*, the physical delight in the opus of soul-making, the psyche so infused with eros that its movements.... yield a voluptuous enjoyment.[1043]

I, 15

Wait... that tastes good... already it's flown.
... a little music... light steppings and hummings—:
Girls, you warm things, girls, in silent rings,
dance the taste of the fruit you have known!

Dance the orange. Who can forget how,
drowned in itself, it still seemed to rue
its own sweetness. You possess it now,
deliciously converted into you.

Dance the Orange. The warmer land within—
fling it out of you, so its ripeness streams
in the breezes of your homeland! Aglow, reveal

scent after scent! Recreate your kin-
ship with the chaste rind's reluctant gleam,
with the juice inside the joy-filled peel!

So Rilke's soul-itinerary does follow the Psyche-Eros story through to its conclusion, and—in his *Sonnets*—arrives at an end not in the least bitter, but of the essence of the true sweetness of the soul.

In chapter 16, we discussed at some length the Hillmanian rubric of "dehumanization," and noted signs of that soul-making process at work in the *Sonnets*. Identifying Psyche's fourth labor primarily with the soul work accomplished in *Malte* and the *Elegies* rather than the *Sonnets*—while it does wobble our interpretive scheme somewhat—does not contradict that earlier analysis. Nonetheless, the critical revisions proposed in this chapter do raise a somewhat thornier interpretive question. Associating *Malte* and the *Elegies* with Psyche's fourth labor does imply "dehumanizing" processes going forward in those works; at the same time, we have repeatedly heralded the *Elegies*, at least, as a poem devoted to plumbing the meaning of human being per se. The complexity inherent in this apparent contradiction suggests that, before finally turning to the pending question of the relation of Orphic myth to Apuleius' tale, we should revisit and reexamine the whole rubric of "dehumanization" and inquire anew what exactly Hillman might mean by this (on one level, quite unappealing) term.

Our reading of Rilke's oeuvre in connection with the Psyche-Eros story helps clarify certain aspects of this mode of soul-making, especially if we add consideration of the dangers and traps Psyche faces on her journey to the underworld. In addition to the most conventional motifs (coins for Charon for passage over the river of the dead; cakes to appease Cerberus at the threshold of Hades' realm), Psyche must also refuse to help a lame donkey-driver pick up twigs from his load, ignore the appeal of a floating corpse to be taken aboard the ferry, and deny the request of old women weaving a web to lend them the aid of her hands.

Neumann understands these images in relation to the archetypal theme of the individuation of the feminine self. That goal, Neumann claims, can be undercut by the tendency to honor "relatedness" at the expense of one's own ultimate aims. "This is the difficult task that confronts every feminine psyche on its way to individuation: it must suspend the claim of what is close at hand for the sake of a distant abstract goal."[1044] The prophetic tower, counseling Psyche to ignore the supplicants, teaches Psyche that (in Neumann's words) "Pity is not lawful." It is not so, because the various pleas for her aid (so the tower tells her) are not genuine, but "snares," Venus' own "crafty designs against thee." In this instance, Venus stands for (not only Eros' mother, but) the great matriarchal principle that resists Psyche's spiritual individuation in the name of *collective* social and instinctual norms and the common welfare.

The tower's lesson is one Rilke learned well, and he continues to be severely judged for what many see as morally indefensible repudiations of many of the more usual norms of human relationship. Yet the point is not moral attack or defense on a case-by-case (lover-by-lover, friend-by-friend, relative-by-relative) basis, but to comprehend the archetypal dynamics of "dehumanization" and its essential role in the art of soul-making.

When Hillman writes of dehumanization he does so in the context of his ongoing critique of those strains of psychology that regard human feeling and relationship per se as the beginning and end of psychology, failing to see or duly honor the archetypal background that lends the human universe a true transpersonal dimension. In this all too human world, we may have Psyche, but have lost her Cosmos. The soul stunts for lack of imaginal space, suffocates in the absence of spiritual air, and dies for lack of divine love. Rilke, on the other hand, understood protection of individual spiritual space as a condition of his vocation and made zealous defense of it into something akin to a personal credo. Though he did not always live up to his own standards in this regard, his efforts to free himself from temporal enmeshments, undue claims upon his attention, and the demands of passing emotion finds ample inscription in his life and work.

Figuratively speaking, Malte's Paris is full of floating corpses. In Rilke's novel, the Parisian streets assume the aspect of an above-ground underworld, and Malte's phobic relation to the sick, the dying, and the poor—his intense fear about being seen as one of the them, and so subsumed into an essentially faceless collectivity devoid of any individual (and individuating) sense of purpose—mirrors this motif in the myth. In the *Elegies*, that individual sense of purpose is too strong to be threatened from such a poor quarter, but love continues to make claims of emotional connection that threaten the independence essential to the poet's spiritual progress:

> Isn't it time...that we tenderly loosed ourselves
> from the loved one, and, unsteadily, survived:
> the way the arrow, suddenly all vector, survives the string
> to be more than itself?[1045]

Malte and (especially) the *Elegies* thus exhibit the poet driving forward a process of "dehumanizing" (*as well as* those of "pathologizing" and "psychologizing"). The *Sonnets*, consistently enough, reflect an end-state of that process. With respect to the vagaries of love, they issue forth from a place that is "ahead of all parting." (II, 13) As far as pity is concerned, the poet—describing a pigeon hunt in the limestone caves of the Karst (II, 11)—writes:

Let every breath of pity be far from those who watch....
In the spirit that is clear
what happens to us is pure.

Just as in the myth, the accomplishment of Psyche's last labor brings her—literally—to the threshold of her reunion with Eros, the alchemical process of "dehumanization" prepares the soul for the marriage with spirit that consummates its endless striving.

Even so, we should exercise great caution in employing the rubric of "dehumanization." For if it is clear that the term refers, ultimately, to the aim of reconnecting the human soul with its divine archetypal origins—the movement mythically figured by Psyche's assumption into heaven, her finding her place among the Gods—*it must be equally evident that this represents anything but a* ***premature*** *form of transcendence that might entail, not a fulfillment of Psyche's ideal aim, but either repression or inflation of her individuality, or (most likely) both.* Psyche's heavenly assumption is premised upon all that has gone before; most proximately, the accomplishment of her labors. The myth itself tells us that the attempt to unite with transcendent spirit *before* all that imaginative labor precipitates Love's flight and the soul's consequent despair. While perhaps a vital and inevitable moment of the soul's journey, Psyche's earlier wild seizure of Eros cannot be confused with their ultimate, divinely consecrated union.

The trajectory of Rilke's life-work makes this all-important truth perfectly clear. The astonishing accomplishment of the *Sonnets*, Rilke's transmission of Orphic voice and vision, depends radically upon the labor involved in all Rilke's prior soul work, *including* the intensely self-reflective imagination of personal history pursued in *Malte* and the relentless probing of patently human thought and emotion—the plumbing of the depths of human consciousness per se—essayed in the *Elegies*. The logic of soul-making cannot involve a shirking of human psychology, but rather entails delving so deeply into the archetypal nature of the human soul and its inherent spiritual aspirations that one emerges—if graced by the Gods—truly *transformed*.

Nor, of course, can the ideal aim—Psyche's apotheosis and union with Love—imply transformation into something wholly "inhuman." Instead, it entails attainment of a *new* humanity that realizes the seed of divinity inherent in the human soul—the theophanic power of the heart, the soul's creative imagination. For the secret of the universe—some version of which has been treasured by spiritual streams from the Vedas to Emerson and beyond—is that the *archetypal* human being is coincident with the whole creation; that Anthropos and Cosmos[1046] are one.

Why, then, one may well ask, employ the rhetoric of "dehumanization" at all? As Hillman himself acknowledges, one could as well speak of a kind of "rehumanization" (realization of the archetypally human) instead. Why, too, the great emphasis placed upon distinguishing between "the human" and "the soul" when—in the myth of Psyche and Eros—the two appear archetypally one and the same?

Hillman could have chosen a somewhat different rubric; his choice of words was, however, no doubt in part strategic. On the one hand, the Psyche-Eros story itself reveals that the truly human—the divinity intrinsic in the soul's imagination—can only be realized by letting go of one-sidedly personal and empirical notions of the human and opening Psyche to the wisdom of the cosmos in *all* its diverse (animal and vegetable, mineral and transcendentally spiritual) forms. Only so may Psyche's labors even begin. On the other hand, the West's grandest ideas of the human being have often (though by no means always) tended to identify the true human being with the idea of *man*—man as the spirit of divine reason, or creative logos, made in the image of God—neglecting or subordinating dynamics peculiar to the idea of *woman*, the specifically feminine (and archetypally *psychological*) character of the soul.

In confronting the rubric of "the human," then, a destructive split or schism marks a good deal of the most relevant intellectual history. On one side, we have humanistic psychologies (often in thrall to the Great Mother) that may actually repress Psyche by denying her union with the transcendent and vivifying spirit of archetypal ideation; on the other, religious and philosophical inspirations that entertain ideas of man's cosmic reach and intelligence, but lack sufficient regard for the soul-making processes that chart the distinctly feminine psyche's path to participation in the cosmos, the archetypally *psychological* and *intrinsically poetic* itinerary of Psyche's labors of love ultimately necessary for the embodiment of spirit. That is to say, *archetypal principles of the masculine and feminine, man and woman, spirit and soul, have often been split off from each other (rather than being truly united) in forming the very idea of "the human."* This reveals, again, the peculiar genius and healing power of the myth of Psyche and Eros, for the story—unlike so many classically heroic mythologies—traces the spiritual path of the archetypal human being qua (feminine) soul, and vice versa.

One of Rilke's early letters—one sign of his own endeavor to honor the feminine dimension of the soul—resonates with this last point:

> The girl and the woman, in their new, individual unfolding, will only in passing be imitators of male behavior and misbehavior and repeaters of male professions.... This humanity of woman, carried in her womb through all her suffering and humiliation, will come to light when she has stripped off the conventions of mere femaleness in the transformations of her outward status.... Someday there will be girls and women whose name will no longer mean the mere opposite of the male, but something in itself.... This advance will transform the love experience... change it from the ground up.[1047]

Rilke's remarks could be heard as smugly condescending; they could also be heard as presciently adumbrating many signal developments over the last hundred years. Whatever their merit on the sociological level, however, these words do point to an archetypal shift in the very conception of humanity—one essentially commensurate with the soul-making enterprise that underlies archetypal psychology, whether that individuating enterprise be construed as "dehumanizing" or "rehumanizing" or both.

We have spoken of the human being and the soul, but should also recall a third, intimately related term, remembering, as well, that Psyche is born of the earth. Her assumption into heaven at the end of the story does not in any wise belie or alter her earthly origin, nor can that mythical heaven be literalized into the notion of some transcendent realm set off in a dualistic opposition to the earth. For his part, Rilke throws the full weight of his poetic soul-making, the invaluable currency of his spiritual career, against the dualisms he assailed in his *Visions of Christ*—against, that is, the schizoid Augustinian notion that (as Charles Wright puts it) "We live in two landscapes... / One that's eternal and divine, and one that's just the back yard." The whole thrust of Rilke's poetry aims to open up the excluded middle, the transitional, inherently imaginal domain of love and the soul, the *metaxy* that translates between timeless ideas of spirit and the mutable sphere of material forms. Accordingly, the species of transcendence finally achieved in Rilke's poetry (and mythically figured by Psyche's assumption into heaven) by no means entails a leaving behind of the earth, or a going elsewhere—this the texts of the *Elegies* and the

Sonnets make abundantly clear, again and again, in explicit statement as well as poetic image. Indeed, paradoxically, the "pure transcendence" celebrated in the *Sonnets* introduces, simultaneously, a poetic philosophy of immanence, one dedicated to actualizing the presence of spirit here and now by way of the ministry of the creative imagination, realizing the cosmic unity of heaven and earth in and through the marriage of the embodied (and embodying) soul and the eternal spirit, the *hieros gamos* of Psyche and Love.

Very well, but what, then, of the God to whom the *Sonnets* are addressed? What of Orpheus, and his love? For the poetic God's own story—in marked contrast to the tale of Psyche and Eros—seems to come to anything but a happy ending. How is Orpheus' evidently tragic end accommodated in Rilke's joyous sonnets? More broadly, how, finally, are our two central myths interwoven in the work that culminates Rilke's soul-history?

We may begin by noting that the story of Orpheus and the tale of Psyche and Eros do share a good deal of mythic ground. Indeed, we may well imagine that Orpheus and Eurydice can play such climactic roles in Rilke's own archetypal psychology in part because their saga echoes that of Psyche and Eros—or vice versa—in so many respects, Both tales center on love between a masculine spirit and a feminine soul, its loss, and a (seemingly impossible) quest to regain that love which culminates in a journey down and into the underworld. In both stories, too, success in that venture appears to hinge upon a pivotal moment transpiring either just before or just after reemergence upon the earth, a moment that tests the ability of one or the other character to respect the edicts of the underworld. Can Psyche resist opening the box of beauty? Can Orpheus restrain himself from glancing back? In both instances, too, the answer (no!) is the same.

Here, however, the common ground between the myths appears to end, for the consequences of this failure appear drastically different in the two myths. Eros easily remedies the (potentially lethal) effects of Psyche's hasty decision, and the two quickly proceed to consummate the *hieros gamos*—the sacred marriage—in heaven. No such intervention rescues Orpheus from his dire fate: having once looked back at Eurydice, he seems to lose her forever. Rather than resurrecting his bride and marriage, Orpheus ends up wandering in despair—sounding tones of lament upon the lyre—until torn to shreds by maenads. It would be difficult, it seems, to imagine more radically disparate conclusions.

If Rilke's last great work reveals him remaking the poetic self in the image of Orpheus, does this dramatic divergence imply that the inner plot of his soul history does not, after all, follow the lines of the Psyche-Eros myth to its glorious conclusion?

No. The endings of the two myths—while certainly different—might be less diametrically opposed than it would at first appear, and may in fact rather complete than negate each other in the text of Rilke's *Sonnets*. In its effective integration of the two myths, Rilke's poetry of soul in fact achieves a fuller imagination of the whole world, and of the ultimate unity of life and death.

First of all, we should observe that Rilke's cycle indeed appears to subscribe to the traditional, Ovidian ending of the Orpheus story, including as it does poems registering the tragic aftermath of Orpheus' loss. The last sonnet of Part I (I, 26) records Orpheus' dismemberment by the maenads; Sonnet II, 26 closes by referring to the concluding image of the classic Orpheus story: the God's severed head, as well as his lyre, floating down the river. These narrative allusions, however, by no means necessarily prove that Rilke's Orpheus has been entirely unsuccessful in his quest to rescue his union with Eurydice. The mythic plot, after all, cannot be read too literally. Symbolically understood, the Orpheus myth represents the poet's attempt to descend into the underworld in order to regain the soul he has lost there and, consequently, his effort to return soul to the world. The Ovidian version of the story depicts Orpheus succeeding in the first phase of the endeavor, yet forfeiting his prize by virtue of his subsequent failure. Rilke's *Sonnets*, however, may well be read as indicating a different outcome.

By this I do not mean to imply that Rilke's *Sonnets* (like Monteverdi's opera) propose a dramatically different narrative. I mean rather that, if understood from an archetypally psychological perspective, the events of the traditional story (including Orpheus' death and dismemberment) may well be construed as commensurate with—and even integral to—ultimate completion of the Orphic mission of restoring soul to the world.

Cobb offers this view of Orpheus' violent death:

> In his dismemberment Orpheus becomes Dionysos—the Loosener (as Dionysos was known) being loosened from himself. He is Dionysos suffering a psychic death, a death into psyche. Orpheus is thus a true psychopomp, for *he* conducts *himself* to the underworld. The dismembered Orpheus is an image of initiation into the

> experience of the imaginal ego—psyche sparkles in every piece/place of our depths.[1048]

In accord with Cobb's perspective, Rilke's Orpheus—although he may, earlier, have looked back—was not thereby definitively sundered from Eurydice forever. "Be forever dead in Eurydice" chants the voice of the *Sonnets*, and we have already maintained that Rilke's Orpheus unites, in poetic truth, with the soul of his beloved in the tone and texture of the poem. And if this (re)marriage does not seem to be made in heaven, but in the realm of the dead—is this really, in the last analysis, such an irreconcilable difference? After all, Zeus and Hades are brothers: we are not speaking here of a Christian heaven and hell, but two inherently kindred, timeless archetypal realms which—although not one and the same—may nonetheless be more apposite than opposite.

If Rilke's poetry aims at a form of "transcendence" that does not split spirit wholly off from matter, or divide the realm of eternal life from the domain of time and change, it reveals, too, that the key to the realization of this cosmic harmony lies hidden in the dark house of Hades. It is by passing through death's door that earthly things are released into the sphere of transformation, that imaginal domain of the soul's creative metamorphoses. Rilke's oeuvre, especially from his Parisian period (and most particularly *Malte*) onward, unfolds his poetic elaboration of the truth symbolized by Psyche's last labor: *that transformation of the fear of death into knowledge of it is the ultimate threshold of love.* In this respect, Psyche held eternally in Eros' arms, and Orpheus, "forever dead in Eurydice"—at home in Hades' halls—are flip sides of one immortal coin.

Another aspect of Orpheus' descent and dismemberment, moreover, brings the power of the myth to bear, not only upon linked imaginations of heaven and the underworld, but still more directly upon the sphere in between eternal life and death; namely, the realm of the earth. While we have repeatedly addressed initiation into the underworld depths of soul in this and prior chapters, the Dionysian aspect of Orpheus' fate encompasses another crucial dimension as well: namely, the poetic ensouling of the multifaceted world itself. Rilke's Sonnet I, 26 concludes:

> Finally, mad for vengeance, they tore you apart
> yet your voice echoes on in birds and in trees
> in lions and stones. There you sing yet.

O you lost God. You unending spur!
Only because you were scattered by enmities
are we now the hearers and a mouth of Nature.

Cobb's comment on this dimension of the myth includes a crucial quote from Hillman:

> Viewing *anima mundi* as the scattered fragments of Dionysos gives to each thing a touch of ecstatic divinity; viewing *anima mundi* as the scattered fragments of Orpheus reveals these same things as poetry. "Psyche as the *anima mundi*, the Neoplatonic soul of the world, is already there with the world itself, so that a second task of psychology"—beyond that of providing soul with an adequate account of itself—is "to hear psyche speaking through all the things of the world, thereby recovering the world as a place of soul."[1049]

"To hear psyche speaking through all the things of the world, thereby recovering the world as a place of soul." Do not Rilke's *Sonnets*—even while speaking from "the imaginal ego" of the Orphic I—do just this? Indeed, can one imagine a more accurate or concise abstract of Rilke's *Sonnets to Orpheus*? And do not the *Sonnets* themselves, in their entirety, thus stand as powerful evidence of the accomplishment of Orpheus' poetic mission?

As the passages from Cobb and Hillman imply, just as Rilke's poetry and archetypal psychology share an Orphic source, so too do the ultimate destination of these two paths of soul-making meet at their end—this end that is also a beginning. "Archetypal Psychology," writes Cobb, "is Orphic in that its primary rhetoric is myth and its primary intention the recovery of soul in speech through image work." It is also

> passionately concerned with the return of soul to the world. . . . [Hillman imagines] the *anima mundi* as crucial for contemporary psychology, imagining it "as that particular soul-spark, that seminal image, which offers itself through each thing in its visible form. . . . " This is Eurydice returned to the world, not as a "personality," but as the soul of the world, glowing in each event as the physiognomy of the world itself.[1050]

It is the lines of that face that Rilke's *Sonnets*—living up to the great sonnet tradition—so lovingly trace. The *Sonnets*, to be sure, open a window on inner precincts of thought and emotion, affect and intellect, but they also give us, in full glow, the radiant gist of fruits, sarcophagi and fountains, stars, horses, flowers, park statues, children and their playthings, birds and human cries, mirrors, clouds, heraldic coats of arms, dogs, dancers, beggars, gardens, the dead of winter and the earth in early spring—in short, all manner of visible as well as invisible things. In so doing, Rilke's Orphic voice fulfills the prophetic intent announced already in the *Elegies:*

> Earth, isn't that what you want: to arise
> in us *invisibly*? Isn't it your dream
> to be invisible someday? Earth! Invisible!
> What, if not transformation, is your urgent charge?
> Earth, my darling, I will![1051]

Perhaps the end of Orpheus' story is not, after all, merely tragic, but rather integral to the therapeutically redemptive mission of poetic song.

> Suffering we do not comprehend.
> and Love's as yet unlearned;
> where Death takes us at life's end
>
> is shrouded in veils.
> Only the song over the land
> hallows and heals.

In the course of this book, we have set out to explore what Rilke himself called the "basic postulates," or "essential premises" of the world view that informed his poetic vision from his *Visions of Christ* and *The Book of Hours* to the *Elegies* and the *Sonnets*. The essential bases have been covered, the defining arcs of thought and image traced, again and again. To summarize, we may merely emphasize once more that Rilke's *Weltanschauung* embodies itself in his literary oeuvre. The sequence of works enacting the archetypally psychological and poetical processes of personifying, pathologizing, psychologizing, and dehumanizing unfold the poet's soul-history, and bear him on towards his ultimate spiritual aim: the individuation of being that ultimately proves (as Rilke himself readily acknowledged) much larger than "Rilke" himself, the realization of a voice and vision auguring world-transformation. To venture further metaphysical synopsis at this point risks betraying the soul of the work, the angel of this book. The flowers of wisdom are plucked in meandering the wandering paths that stray through field and forest; attempting to pave the way to a more straightforward conceptual understanding could too easily end up burying Rilke's roses in a heap of intellectual rubble.

So let us close with one last poetic moment, a last mythic image of Orpheus that seals this book binding poetry and archetypal psychology together.

Rilke, from Sonnet II, 26:

> Array the criers,
> singing God! Let them wake a resounding
> current bearing the head and the lyre.

Cobb:

> For the Greeks the head was the beginning, the source of generation. The seed of life was in the head. The head was packed with seed, like a pomegranate. It was the seat of the soul.... What more wonderful source could there be for archetypal psychology to be "returned to"? Imagination as a singing head![1052]

We have remarked that—while the myth of Psyche and Eros comes to a most fortunate end concluding with the birth of Pleasure—the myth of Orpheus evidently ends in tragic disassociation. At the same time, Rilke's *Sonnets*, while not obviously altering the story, do not sound a tragic chord, but resonate with the joy consonant with Pleasure's entry into the world. The Orpheus myth's final image—the image of the lyre and the singing head—may help further reconcile these apparently contrary poetic facts.

We've indicated already that the separation of Orpheus and Eurydice cannot be taken too literally; that Rilke in fact reimagines Orpheus reunited with his bride in the knowledge of death that brings eternal life:

> Be forever dead in Eurydice—in praise of things
> ascend, singing, back in the pure relation.

Even so, we cannot too cavalierly turn one ending into the other, the sad into the happy, endless loss into eternal fulfillment. As Rilke's lines imply, the life Orpheus regains persists as an essentially poetic one, and poetry, no less than the soul itself, remains perpetually marked by emptiness as well as fullness. That is of the very being of soul, and, too—as Russell Hoban's fictional Eurydice-figure declares—of the imaginative enterprise called art:

> Art is a celebration of loss, of beauty passing...not to be held. Now that I'm lost, you will perceive me fully and you will find me in your song; now that underworld is closed to you the memory of the good dark will be with you always in your song. Now you are empty like the tortoise-shell, like the world-child betrayed, and your song will be filled with what is lost to you.[1053]

So the two endings are neither simply different nor simply the same but both at once, just as eternal joy and eternal sadness are two modes of the soul's endless song, each requiring the other for the beauty of its being, even as—in the soul's own image—presence and absence are inextricably and endlessly intertwined.

Similarly, Orpheus, in his dismemberment and his death, is—like Eurydice—lost to himself, and given to us. More delicate, less invincible, than the great God Eros, Orpheus—like Osiris, like Christ—is broken, and scattered, and so surrendered to the earth itself, and to all the many creatures and things of the earth, including ourselves. Yet even in his dissemination, the unity of his being endures—inviolate—in the head and the lyre, in the spiritual essence of the unstoppable mouth of song. It was Rilke's vocation and mission to hear that voice, and, singing, pass it on. Now—as the poet tells us—it is ours.

Remember. The soul of the world is listening, even as we speak.

AFTERWORD

Rilke's grave in Raron

After completing the *Duino Elegies* and *Sonnets to Orpheus*, Rilke continued to live at Chateau Muzot, the little castle that had incubated his poetic consummation. The poet struggled with the sense (expressed to the Kippenbergs upon their last visit to him) that he had completed his life's work; even so, the tail end of his life proved hardly uneventful. The story of Rilke's last years includes a deepening engagement with the French language—indeed, a kind of second career as a

French poet (one that excited intense and unsettling controversy in certain German circles); loud acclaim *and* dispraise upon the publication of the *Sonnets* and *Elegies*; the writing of no few important German poems (most notably, perhaps, *Correspondence in Verse with Erika Mitterer* and—a scant six months before his death—"Elegy to Marina Tsvetayeva-Efron"); complex and absorbing relationships with new as well as old loves; political instability; and—above all—the intermittent yet ever more pitched battle with the physical and psychological manifestations of the little-known illness—leukemia—that would finally cause the poet's death on December 29, 1926.

By his own stipulation, Rilke was buried in a small churchyard in Raron, a Swiss village very near Muzot. His gravestone—standing alone on one side of the small church—commands an impressive view of the Rhone valley. On it are inscribed these words:

Rose, oh reiner Widerspruch, Lust
Niemandes Schlaf zu sein unter soviel
Lidern.

Rose, oh pure contradiction, the joy
of being no one's sleep under so many
lids.

In German, the last word is a homonym for *Liedern*—Song.

APPENDIX 1

WRIGHT, HASS, RILKE: MODERN POETRY IN SEARCH OF SOUL

"Each line should be a station of the cross."[1054] This injunction indicates just how profoundly the Christian past haunts the work of Charles Wright. By force of deep cultural habit, many of Wright's poems reinscribe Constantinople's splitting in two of the universe and manifest its tragic effects. Tragic because—absent the rejuvenating mediation of the soul—the traditional locus of spirit (heaven) inevitably recedes from view, becoming more and more inaccessible and illusory, and its opposite—bodily life on earth—concomitantly emptied of grace. "I look up at the black bulge of the sky and its belt of stars.... And know that what I have asked for cannot be granted,"[1055] writes Wright. Such is the dark horizon of modernity; we live under a canopy of tinsel.

This is an intolerable situation. Modern poetry, including Wright's, often tries to redeem this state of affairs by investing earth with the lost gleam of heaven, but—without a conscious concept of soul that might radically transform the underlying dualism—such a "secular epiphanic aesthetic"[1056] tends to prove frangible, for it is not, at root, metaphysically tenable. "The smoke of transience / blows through everything seen,"[1057] writes Rilke, who knew and felt this keenly—mortal life is too obviously subject to limitation, evanescence, and degradation to be able to bear, in and of itself, the valences of eternality and ultimacy that have always been the prerogative of spirit. In Wright's "Indian Summer II"—a poem that explicitly and programmatically affirms the traditional dualistic universe of spirit and matter even while displaying its egregious consequences—the faint glimmer of redemption offered at the end seems little more than a poetic sleight of hand.

Indian Summer II

As leaves fall from the trees, the body falls from the soul.
As memory signs transcendence, scales fall from the heart.
As sunlight winds back on its dark spool,
November's a burn and an ache.

A turkey buzzard logs on to the late evening sky.
Residual blood in the oak's veins.
Sunday. Recycling tubs like flower bins at the curb.

Elsewhere, buried up to her armpits,
someone is being stoned to death.
Elsewhere, transcendence searches for us.
Elsewhere, this same story is being retold by someone else.

The heavenly way has been lost,
no use to look at the sky.
Still, the stars, autumnal stars, start to flash and transverberate.
The body falls from the soul, and the soul takes off,
a wandering, moral drug.

This is an end without a story.
This is a little bracelet of flame around your wrist.
This is the serpent in the Garden,
her yellow hair, her yellow hair.

We live in two landscapes, as Augustine might have said,
One that's eternal and divine,
and one that's just the back yard,
Dead leaves and dead grass in November, purple in spring.[1058]

This in many ways beautiful and powerful poem, far from challenging the soul's historic erasure, reenacts it, and does so all the more dramatically for the soul's signal presence at its outset. The poem begins with an image of the soul's release from the body after death and then immediately gestures toward the traditional spiritual reward: the assumption of the soul into heaven. But the motion of transcendence is quickly aborted; while sunlight may withdraw to its celestial source, the soul cannot, but instead is led downward through a train of ever more earthbound imagery (the buzzard in the November sky, the sap in the veins of the oak) to land with a thud on the street curb alongside recycling tubs put out on Sunday. Unfortunately, this humble residence is as good as it gets for the soul in this poem; the rest is yet further downhill.

Transported suddenly "elsewhere" (the poem's style is persistently paratactic, jumping often unpredictably from one complete sentence to another), the reader is confronted with an image of terrible transgression: the stoning of a woman. Is this the human soul's own doing? Presumably—for who or what else could be held responsible?—and perhaps it is the endless, senseless repetition of "this same story" (the intransigence of the death penalty in the United States, Iran, and elsewhere, for instance?) that precludes the fallen soul from rising, puts it out of reach of the spiritual world which nonetheless still "searches for us." In any event, it is clear that—contrary to memory's initial indication—"The heavenly way has been lost." The transcendent realm of spirit can no longer be attained, even while the flashing stars continue to advertise its inaccessible presence.

Where does this leave the soul? If capable of vice, is soul also granted the possibility of virtue; granted the agent power to amend its fallenness and errancy, to search intently for the lost way, or explore some new track out of the no-man's-land, the limbo, in which it seems to finds itself? Not in this poetic universe. After summoning the soul (and in exactly the same words as in the first line) for its last undisguised appearance, the poetic voice summarily condemns it as a kind of vagrant delusion—"a wandering, moral drug"—and, apparently, banishes it from its world of concern.

The poet does so, however, at his own peril, for the harsh sentence leaves him—leaves us—without the capacity to carry the story on to a next stage, or alternative conclusion; without the power, that is, to *change* anything at all. For the soul, in truth, is not the author of shibboleth, but of authentic moral imagination; the capacity to address injustice and redress psychic wounds. That, after all, is the very basis of psychology qua therapy: the psyche, through the help of another, may revisit and revise its story, and so heal itself. With the soul off wandering in delusion elsewhere, there is no storytelling; there is—as the poet himself acknowledges—only an "end without a story": dead body, banished soul, distant spirit. Incapable of narrative reaction, we are set out alongside tree and rock vainly waiting for Godot. As the poem says over and over, we have been here, and may stay here, forever.

But the curtain is not quite ready to come down on so bleak a scenario. In its last five lines, the poem strives to reach a more satisfying conclusion, and in so doing unwittingly reveals yet more about the treatment of the soul hidden in the tradition it reinscribes. The middle line of the penultimate stanza is cryptic, but not undecipherable. Since the wrist is a place of both power and adornment, the bracelet of flame seems a token of the (never wholly lost) spiritual heritage of humanity, an image of the potential union of spirit and body, inspiration and will, or perhaps the burning *impossibility* of the same. Neither is the banished soul truly absent from the stanza: it returns, unnamed, in the guise of the feminine figures lurking behind the stanza's last line—a line that may reveal something of why spiritual tradition so often damns the soul. Here the poem covertly associates soul, qua woman or anima, with evil both at its mythical source (the serpent in Eden) and at its world-historical acme. The phrase "her yellow hair, her yellow hair" echoes similar ones ("your golden hair, Marguerite") in Paul Celan's famous "Deathfugue," and so evokes the horrific events of the Holocaust. What is going on here?

It is possible to suppose that the soul, in its feminine susceptibility, lies at the root of all evil, in which case it might indeed be most politic to suppress it entirely; exile it, and subsequently pretend it never even really existed in the first place. This is exactly what the clerics of Constantinople did in their edict, and Wright's poem follows suit. Blithely leaving all trace of the Holocaust behind, the poem's last stanza restates, in poetic terms, the dogma propounded at Constantinople: declaims what is not a priori metaphysical truth, but the effect of the soul's effacement, as if it were eternal verity. Declaims it as if—despite all that has gone before, and is still going on—we might be safely at home in that world, taken in by poetic conviction.

Whatever its intent, "Indian Summer II" actually dramatizes the lethal consequences of the suppression of soul its language enacts. With soul absent offstage, the universe becomes static; nothing really moves, and history itself becomes a series of endless repetitions, frozen in place. Without psychological culture, we surrender ourselves to unconscious forces, which—as in the case of Nazi Germany—can be devastatingly dehumanizing. Without a conscious connection with the soul, humanity itself is lost.

For in the larger scheme of things it is the soul that holds our place, and represents the heart of the mystery of human being. A bipolar universe composed of a divine heaven and dead earth holds no place for anything in between, including the specifically *human*. Wright's poem does purport to speak to and for us human beings. The last stanza begins: "We live in two landscapes...," but the body of the poem belies this declaration by conveying clearly enough that, in fact, we can neither reach heaven nor rest content with mere earth. In the landscape of the poem, "we" human beings live neither here nor there, but nowhere. We are homeless. Or, more precisely, we are off wandering in the middle of nowhere—spiritual orphans adrift in the universe, lost souls.[1059]

If Robert Hass did not read "Meditation at Lagunitas" (one of his most widely admired poems) as part of his Berkeley talk,[1060] he should have. This poem, which employs many of the key terms of his address ("luminous," "wonder," "numinous"), takes Hass's own critical discussion a step further. In so doing, moreover, it charts a poetic course that reverses the spiritual direction taken by Wright's "Indian Summer II." The discursive action of both poems revolves around a hidden center: the shunning or embracing of the soul.

Meditation at Lagunitas

All the new thinking is about loss.
In this it resembles all the old thinking.
The idea, for example, that each particular erases
the luminous clarity of a general idea. That the clown-
faced woodpecker probing the dead sculpted trunk
of that black birch is, by his presence,
some tragic falling off from a first world
of undivided light. Or the other notion that,
because there is in this world no one thing
to which the bramble of *blackberry* corresponds,
a word is elegy to what it signifies.
We talked about it late last night and in the voice
of my friend, there was a thin wire of grief, a tone
almost querulous. After a while I understood that,
talking this way, everything dissolves: *justice,*
pine, hair, woman, you and *I*. There was a woman
I made love to and I remembered how, holding

her small shoulders in my hands sometimes,
I felt a violent wonder at her presence
like a thirst for salt, for my childhood river
with its island willows, silly music from the pleasure boat,
muddy places where we caught the little orange-silver fish
called *pumpkinseed*. It hardly had to do with her.
Longing, we say, because desire is full
of endless distances. I must have been the same to her.
But I remember so much, the way her hands dismantled bread,
the thing her father said that hurt her, what
she dreamed. There are moments when the body is as numinous
as words, days that are the good flesh continuing.
Such tenderness, those afternoons and evenings,
saying *blackberry, blackberry, blackberry.*[1061]

"Meditation at Lagunitas" effectively begins where "Indian Summer II" leaves off. The poem opens by elucidating—albeit in a more philosophical vein than Wright's—the "tragic" effects of thinking and living in a dualistic universe in which the terms of spirit ("the luminous clarity of a general idea") and matter ("each particular") are mutually exclusive and reciprocally negating: "the clown-faced woodpecker...is, by his presence / some tragic falling off from a first world / of undivided light." This bipolar structure of exclusion afflicts language as well: the true essence of a thing is set over and against the word which can never truly re-present it (recall Hass's critical mention of "the thing itself which cannot be named") so that, inevitably, "a word is elegy to what is signifies." Reflecting upon the sense of loss and (finally) utter deprivation the human mind suffers when it allows itself to be controlled by these dualisms, the speaker of the poem moves toward quiet catastrophe: "After a while I understood that, / talking this way, everything dissolves: *justice, / pine, hair, woman, you* and *I*." This pivotal sentence resounds with Rilkean overtones, though in negative form. It figures as a counterstatement to one of the defining moments of Rilke's great *Duino* cycle, enunciated in the penultimate Elegy:

Are we perhaps *here* simply to say: *house,*
bridge, fountain, gate, jug, fruit tree, window,—
at most: *column, tower*...but to *speak*, you understand,
oh, to speak *so*...as to exceed the things' own innermost hope
of being.

If Rilke's is a statement of poetic mission that guarantees human meaning, the end to which Hass apparently comes in the dead center of his poem augurs the negation of both; conjures the desolate emptiness that is present, as well, at the center of "Indian Summer II's" dualistic universe.

In general, Hass's style in "Lagunitas" contrasts sharply with Wright's. While "Indian Summer II" makes frequent and often enigmatic imaginative leaps, Hass's "Lagunitas" moves fluidly through a continuous stream of meditation—until it arrives at the crucial moment that the whole poem hinges upon, formally as well as thematically. The half-line that initiates the poem's second half—"There was a woman / I made love to..."—marks a rather sudden departure, and initiates a dramatic shift in scene as well as mode of consciousness that entirely alters the face of things, the flavor and texture of the world. What effects so revolutionary a change? While the logic of first half is controlled by the *spirit* of rationalism, it is at this point that the *soul* makes its decisive entrance. In Hass's poem, though—instead of bearing the burden of humanity's fall—the intervention of the soul carries the promise of redemption.

> ...*pine, hair, woman, you* and *I*. There was a woman
> I made love to and I remember how, holding
> her small shoulders in my hands sometimes,
> I felt a violent wonder at her presence
> like a thirst for salt...

Once again, the soul makes its appearance in the archetypal guise of woman qua anima. Lost in speculation that brings him to the edge of an abyss of meaningless, the poet turns to the memory of something that stops him from going over; to a figure who brings in her train the recollection of a radically different kind of world. In the image of the poet uniting with the woman in love and then—literally, physically—holding on to her, we see a symbol of man on the brink reaching out, in spirit and body, to the soul, and holding on for dear life. And what is it that the soul has to offer?

The intervention of anima and the wonder it brings (recall that Hass identified "wonder" as one of the keys to spirituality in his Berkeley talk) opens the door to a realm unavailable to the mind mercilessly torn between the poles of spirit and matter. The presence of the soul opens the place between idea and fact, between "the thing itself" and the body of the word—the world of memory and imagination, image and dream that is the world of psyche. Given the long history of its spiritual suppression (of which Hass provides an abstract in the first part of the poem) and the starvation that entails, it is no wonder that the hunger for sustenance from that realm—"soul-food" we might say—is "violent" in its strength.

Once soul is embraced, and the connection with the anima opens the floodgates to the unconscious, one can feel (almost physically) the images and memories pouring in:

> ...a thirst for salt...my childhood river
> with its island willows, silly music from the pleasure boat,
> muddy places where we caught the little orange-silver fish
> called *pumpkinseed*.

No longer imprisoned by the dictates of a binary logic, the poet's imagination is free to wander this realm where word is image, and the image *is* the "thing in itself": an *essentially poetic imaginal reality*. The word *pumpkinseed*, for instance—no longer bound to be the mere shadow of one "real" thing so that its utterance brings loss and desiccation—may instead ring gorgeously in eye and ear, a poetic image that immerses the mind in a flood of evocative analogies and correspondences. And that the principal locus of memory here should be not some mountaintop but "muddy places" in a river is also archetypally appropriate. As the very title of Hillman's "Peaks and Vales" indicates, the dimension of the soul is depth, its phenomenological geography associated not with the stark snowfields of spirit, but with the teeming waters of life.

The poem's next half-line ("It hardly had to do with her") explicitly acknowledges that it is truly *soul* that is the agent power here, the *archetypal* power of the speaker's anima rather than any particular human relationship. Acknowledged, too, is the central truth that the soul, even while overflowing with images, is nonetheless never completely filled by them. It is in the essential nature of spirit to indeed be full in and of itself, essentially self-present and sufficing, while matter (as any Buddhist or physicist knows) is ghosted by emptiness. Soul, however—as precisely that which constantly translates between spirit and matter—moves, too, between the poles of fullness and emptiness, self-presence and absence, being and non-being or nothingness. In and of itself, it is never wholly one or the other—neither full nor empty—but just this *movement between*. Affectively, we experience this movement as the (e)motive force of *longing* or *desire*, the archetypal nature and power of which transcends any given subject or object. "It hardly had to do with her. Longing, we say, because desire is full / of endless distances." These lines are quintessentially Rilkean. That they may be so readily recognized as such shows the degree to which Rilke's work has taken out a virtual patent on this most basic dynamic of the soul, so much so that the search for soul on the part of many moderns often includes—as in the case of Hass himself—"Looking for Rilke."[1062]

While the soul may never be wholly full in and of itself, it nonetheless can (as the conclusion of Hass's "Meditation" reveals) experience fulfillment. How? By accomplishing its own authentic nature and task: connecting the otherwise divided and mutually repelling poles of the universe, filling the canyon between spirit and matter with a river of creative life. For the bridging act of the soul does not merely connect two distant sides statically; it is, inherently, a dynamically *imaginative* act that changes what it touches; transforms the nature and matter of the world. It is this transformative act of the creative imagination —which relates us, as soul, to numinous realities (some might say, the divine)—that defines the soul's ultimate spiritual function and reveals, too, the ground of what (following Jung) might be called its native religious instinct.

> But I remember so much, the way her hands dismantled bread,
> the thing her father said that hurt her, what
> she dreamed. There are moments when the body is as numinous
> as words, days that are the good flesh continuing.
> Such tenderness, those afternoons and evenings,
> saying *blackberry, blackberry, blackberry.*

Even while the concluding lines of "Lagunitas" unmistakably indicate the archetypically *psychological* dimension the poem has encompassed ("the thing her father said that hurt her, what / she dreamed"), they are simultaneously laden with rich religious echoes, most signally in the image of the woman dismantling—or breaking—bread. In its Catholic context, the ritual of communion is understood to effect a transubstantiation, transforming matter (the body and blood) by virtue of its actual union with spirit (Christ). At the climax of Hass's poem, the poetic act of the soul effects a similar transformation: the body becomes "numinous" (the very word that stood for spirit in Hass's Berkeley talk), as do the "words" that are vehicle of all that transpires. The poetic magic undertaken under the auspices of the muse/anima integrates what without it is a schizoid world in the process of falling apart, for the creative act unites spirit, soul, and body in a harmonious continuum that imbues the world with substance, life, and meaning. The world is no longer remote stars and dead leaves—with naught but emptiness where we must stand, between—but "days that are the good flesh continuing." And the word "blackberry" no longer rings hollow. Rather, its incantation conjures a world of felt connection, a meaning-full communion of spirit and body in and through the soul. By the end of the poem, word has become Word. If it were not much too Catholic an expression, one might say that—by virtue of its own act—here, now, for the moment, at least—the poet's soul has been saved.

The kind of communion figured at the end of Hass's "Meditation at Lagunitas" is notoriously precarious. For the most part, the human soul, beset with all the intransigent conflicts that constitute its paradoxical nature, is neither pure nor mature enough to unify material and spiritual life in a seamless, effortlessly and endlessly transforming whole. It is one thing to conjure the vision of a unity of spirit, soul, and body in a moment of lyric epiphany; it is another to image this as a more or less permanent state of being not disrupted by (but rather inclusive of) the defining exigencies of mortal life: loss, sorrow, suffering, death. Nonetheless, such an integral state of being remains Rilke's ultimate object: it is the ideal figured by the Orpheus of Rilke's late *Sonnets*, and the silent center of the contemporaneous "The Young Workman's Letter," which puts an exclamation point to Rilke's decades-long struggle with Christianity:

> I cannot conceive that the *cross* should *remain*, which was, after all, only a cross-roads. It certainly should not be stamped on us on all occasions like a brand-mark.

The contrast between Wright's sentence ("Each line should be a station of the cross") and this salvo could hardly be more stark.

Rilke's letter continues:

> For is the situation not *this*: he intended simply to provide the loftier tree, on which we could ripen better. He, on the cross, is

this new tree in God, and we were to be warm, happy fruit, at the top of it.

We should not always talk of what was *formerly*, but the *afterwards* should have begun. This tree, it seems to me, should have become so one with us, or we with it, and by it, that we should not need to occupy ourselves continually with it, but simply and quietly with God.... [1063]

"The Young Workman's Letter" lays bare Rilke's main contentions with popular Christianity. He vehemently rejects the figure of Christ as mediator between the individual soul and God, or spirit, regarding such intercession as superfluous and obstructive. He just as aggressively repudiates the traditional dualistic splitting of the universe into a spiritual heaven and a purely material earth, a dichotomy that inevitably defines the latter to be essentially devoid of intrinsic value. Does Rilke, in the "Letter," propose a specific antidote, suggest means of moving towards the "afterwards" he so yearns for?

The rhetorical structure of Rilke's "Letter" bears an intriguing resemblance to that of Hass's "Lagunitas." Both begin, in their own very different idioms, by describing a situation—the universe according to Constantinople—and evoking its ill effects. Then, at a central juncture, both texts pivot, performing a sudden rhetorical turn that initiates entrance into an altogether different reality. After acknowledging that the Church itself has included elements that contravene its own doctrine (for instance, its sanctification of St. Francis, who cherished "the obvious friendliness and cheerfulness of the earth"), Rilke's "young workman" continues:

I mean, we do not know what will come of the great teachings, we must only allow them to stream forth and follow their course, and not be alarmed when they suddenly pour into the disrupted parts of life, rolling through indiscernible beds underground.

I worked in Marseilles once for some months. It was an important time for me, I owe a lot to it. Chance brought me into contact with a young painter who remained my friend until his death. He had lung trouble and had just come back from Tunis. We were a lot together, and...were able to arrange to spend a few days in Avignon. I have never forgotten them. Partly because of the town itself, its buildings and its surroundings, but also because my

> friend, in those days of uninterrupted and somehow more intimate intercourse, told me many things, particularly about his *inner* life, with that eloquence which, it seems, is peculiar to such sufferers at certain times. Everything he said had a strangely prophetic force; through all that he poured out...one saw, so to say, the bottom, the stones on the bottom...I mean by that, something more than merely what is in us,—Nature herself, her oldest and hardest core....Furthermore, he had an unexpected and happy love affair.[1064]

Though Hass's lyric poem and Rilke's letter are generically very different, the crucial *volte* in both works bear a marked formal resemblance to one another. In each instance, a train of discursive logic suddenly gives way to narrative recollection ("There was a woman I made love to"; "I worked in Marseilles once... "). The recollection evokes profoundly cherished memories and images of a specific place, time, and person connected, in both cases, with what lives at the (river) bottom of things, and with love, desire, absence and loss; joy, sorrow, and inward revelation. In Rilke as well as Hass, the way toward that "afterwards," a new world not rent and emptied by traditional schisms, begins with a turn toward the soul.

"The Young Workman's Letter" is a late composition, but the subject of the soul and its longings defines Rilke's work virtually from the outset, so much so that it should surprise no one if we declare Rilke a poet of the soul. Even his detractors might readily concede this point: when J. D. McClatchy complains about Rilke's "buzzwords," "soul" and "longing" head the list. We have said a good deal about the nature of the soul, but to understand more fully what it is, and why Rilke may be considered a preeminent poet of soul, we should see what James Hillman himself may have to say on this subject which is—truth to tell—immeasurable; vast as the human being him- or herself.

"The definition of man is the definition of his soul." Hillman places this quotation—like a sign above the Academy gate—as a motto or epigraph at the opening of his book *Myth of Analysis*. If Hillman did not fervently believe the statement, he would never have inscribed it there. Still, some irony attaches to its privileged placement, for Hillman generally recoils from the very act of definition, regarding it as a tool ill fitted to the task of approaching a subject so deep as the soul. Nonetheless, while eschewing rigid formulation, Hillman has indicated what he regards as some of the soul's most essential characteristics:

> [T]he word [soul] refers to that unknown component which makes meaning possible, turns events into experiences, is communicated in love, and has a religious concern. These four qualifications I had already put forth some years ago; I had begun to use the term freely, usually interchangeably with psyche (from Greek) and anima (from Latin). Now I am adding three necessary modifications. First, "soul" refers to the *deepening* of events into experiences; second, the significance soul makes possible, whether in love or in religious concern, derives from its special *relation with death*. And third, by "soul" I mean the imaginative possibility in our natures, the experiencing through reflective speculation, dream, image, and *fantasy*—that mode which recognizes all realities as primarily symbolic or metaphorical.[1065]

True to the Aristotelian motto, the issues that Hillman identifies with the soul qualify as the great existential determinants of the mystery of human being. In our discussion of Wright and Hass, we have touched these bases already; within the context of lyric scenarios implicating death, religion, and love, articulated soul as "the imaginative possibility of our natures" and disclosed it as the principal agency transforming outward event into inward experience, generating existential meaning. Few writers, however, have probed *the whole interrelated nexus of all these fundamental motifs* as consistently and intensely as Rilke. Who, for instance, has understood more thoroughly that "the significance soul makes possible, whether in love or in religious concern, derives from its special relation with death"? Consequently, Rilke's oeuvre possesses a range, depth, and dimension matched by few other modern poets. A truly Orphic poet, Rilke plumbs the alpha and omega of human being.

Moreover, Rilke's responses to the great questions remain tuned to the harmonics of the soul itself—that is to say, they are at one and the same time *poetic* and *archetypally psychological* in character. Steadfastly refusing to divert his river of insight into traditional religious or philosophic channels, Rilke, like Hillman, puts the soul at the center, and keeps it there for the duration of his long creative career. Rilke's poetic opus consequently enacts a reflective unfolding of the soul's own nature, the metamorphoses by and through which it knows—and makes—itself. His is an art—and (if you will) a religion—of soul-making.

Appendix II

A SYNOPSIS OF APULEIUS' TALE OF EROS AND PSYCHE

This appendix is provided to facilitate comprehension of the foregoing soul history. It is a bare-bones synopsis that lacks the artful development, nuance, and inimitable flavor of the original. The author strongly recommends that those interested obtain and read the full text of the story.

Psyche, the youngest of three daughters born to a king and a queen, is of such ravishing beauty that people worship her as if she were a Goddess. Not only does this infuriate Venus—who commands her son Eros (or Amor) to avenge the wrong—it isolates and severely depresses Psyche, for no man dares approach to woo her. Distressed at Psyche's plight, the king and queen seek counsel from an oracle, but Apollo's answer causes still greater woe. The oracle declares that Psyche, arrayed in funeral robes that double as her bridal train, shall be set upon a high crag to await a groom so terrible that even Jove fears him. Grieved to the marrow by the dreadful edict, the king and queen nonetheless lead the whole city in conducting the appointed rite. At last, they leave Psyche to her fate, the dark destiny she nonetheless welcomes with preternatural calm.

Contrary to expectations, no awful monster comes to claim Psyche. Instead, the West Wind gently spirits her off the crag and sets her down near a dwelling so palatial and gorgeously appointed she recognizes it as the abode of some God. Psyche soon gathers courage and enters; servants whom she can hear but not see address her as their mistress and minister to her needs. Finally, she retires to the bedchamber, and there, in the dark of the night, her unknown husband-lover comes and makes her his own. Psyche continues to dwell in the temple for a long while, receiving nightly visits from the husband whom she comes to cherish even though his identity remains shrouded in mystery.

Meanwhile, Psyche's sisters (who long ago married kings in distant lands) hear of Psyche's end and voyage home to mourn her and allay their parents' grief. Psyche's husband warns her of impending danger, but when she learns of her sisters' return and their distress, she implores him to permit her to assuage their sorrow. Against his better judgment, her husband finally gives in to her passionate appeal, but warns her in no uncertain terms that, if she allows her sisters to persuade her into prying into his identity, she will lose all that is hers, including himself. She assures him that she loves him as she loves life itself, but prevails upon him to permit the West Wind to bring her sisters to her.

Psyche's sisters soon visit the crag where she was once abandoned to her fate. The West Wind brings them safely to her door; Psyche allays her sisters' fears and shares with them the wealth and blessings of her estate. Obedient to her husband's command, she deflects all questions as to his identity and sends them on their way laden with gifts.

Naturally, Psyche's most unhappily married sisters are consumed with jealousy. They return to their distant homes plotting how to avenge the terrible wrong implicit in the contrast between Psyche's bliss and their own comparatively poor and dismal circumstances.

Soon thereafter Psyche's husband informs her yet again, and in still stronger terms, of the peril her sisters represent. At the same time, he tells her that she will soon bear a child. If she keeps his secret intact, it will be born a God, but if she fails to do so, the child will be mortal. Psyche is thrilled at this news, but—availing herself of all her feminine powers of persuasion—again prevails upon her husband to permit a visit from her sisters. They come once more, feign pleasure at Psyche's imminent motherhood, and ply her with questions about her husband. Spinning a different tale than she did during the first visit, Psyche puts her sisters off again and sends them away with more gifts.

The sisters' rage and jealousy boils over. They gather that Psyche really has no idea who her husband is and employ this red thread in the weaving of a sinister plot. Returning the next day, they persuade the innocent Psyche (who remains dreadfully impressed by her husband's insistence that she must *never* seek to look upon him) that her mystery husband is in fact a huge and venomous serpent that has recently been seen frequenting the area, a monster only waiting for Psyche's child to be born before devouring both mother and child. When the terrified Psyche asks for counsel, her sisters advise her to conceal an oil lamp and a sharpened razor in her bedchamber. When her husband lies in deep slumber beside her, she should illumine his hideous form with the lamp and use the razor to slice off his head, thus assuring her own safety and rich fortune.

Psyche's fear lends her the necessary strength to pursue this plan. Yet when she lights the lamp, it is no monster, but the beautiful God of love she finds asleep on her couch. Distraught, Psyche attempts to bury the blade in her own heart, but the knife—refusing to commit such a deed—slips from her grasp. Psyche sinks into dumb admiration of the sleeping God until, goaded by curiosity, she takes an arrow from her husband's quiver. Accidentally pricking her finger with its point, she falls still more passionately in love with Love and throws herself upon his sleeping form.

While she is kissing him, however, the lamp sputters and casts a drop of burning oil upon Eros' shoulder. Eros leaps up, sees his secret betrayed, and, wrenching himself from Psyche's grasp, flies up without a word. Psyche catches hold of his leg and clings to him until her strength fails and she falls back to earth.

Eros flies to a nearby cypress and upbraids her. He first reveals how he had disobeyed his mother's orders and, instead of making her fall in love with some vile creature, pricked himself with his own arrows and fallen in love with her. Then he tells Psyche that her sisters will pay dearly for their maliciousness, but her own punishment will be nothing more than his departure. Sorely wounded, Eros finally soars off into the heavens.

The grief-stricken Psyche follows Eros' flight; when she can no longer see him, she throws herself into a nearby river. The river, however, will no more be guilty of Psyche's life than the knife, and brings her safely to rest upon its bank. The God Pan finds her there and, discerning the cause of her distress, gently counsels her to desist from thoughts of self-slaughter, and to seek remedy for her ills by searching out Love himself. Though she makes no reply, Psyche understands the wisdom of Pan's words and sets off on her quest for Eros.

After much wandering, Psyche finds herself near the home of one of her sisters. Visiting her, Psyche relates her discovery of her husband's identity, but then—cunningly twisting the tale—says that he turned away from her in anger, and expressed his intent to marry her sister instead. Filled with guilty lust, Psyche's sister rushes to the crag and leaps off. The wind, however, does not answer to her command, and she is dashed to pieces on the rocks. After Psyche wanders into her second sister's city, a like sequence of events leads to her death as well.

Meanwhile, Eros has retreated to his mother's (empty) chamber, suffering from the grievous burn dealt by the lamp. A white sea bird informs his absent mother of all that has transpired, including Eros' own betrayal of his mother's command and his infatuation with Psyche. This naturally excites Venus' wrath. She hurries home to her chamber and proceeds to excoriate her errant and ailing son, and resolves to seek the aid of her foe, Sobriety, to constrain and punish him. On her way to find Sobriety, she meets Ceres and Juno, imploring them to seek out and punish Psyche and scorn Eros. Ceres and Juno, though, chide Venus for her rather hypocritical ire.

Psyche, suffering miserably, continues to search in vain desperation for Eros. Happening upon one of Ceres' temples, she is putting the ill-kept place in order when Ceres herself appears. The Goddess asks Psyche if she knows that Venus is seeking to wreak vengeance upon her, whereupon Psyche casts herself to the ground and begs refuge and protection from Ceres. Ceres, however, declares that, as much as pity moves her, she cannot cross her kinswoman, and bids Psyche be on her way without further ado.

The unexpected rebuff worsens Psyche's desperate state. Still, she soon happens upon Juno's temple, and prays for protection from the Goddess of marriage and protector of pregnant women. Juno herself appears, but her response echoes Ceres'. As much as she would like to offer Psyche refuge, she cannot gainsay Venus' wishes or contravene the law that prohibits harboring another's runaway slaves.

This second rejection crushes Psyche. Resigning herself to the inevitable, she resolves to submit herself willingly to Venus' jealous wrath. Though she expects the confrontation to end in her own destruction, she comforts herself with the thought that she may yet find Eros in his mother's house.

Venus meanwhile has taken to the skies and asked Jove for the services of the herald Mercury. She orders the swift God to publish and distribute a bill offering a reward for Psyche's discovery: seven kisses from Venus' own lips and one "more honeyed than the rest" from her sweet tongue. This destroys Psyche's last shred of hope. Already on her way to Venus, she is soon apprehended by Habit (one of Venus' servants) and dragged by her hair into the presence of the dread goddess.

With the help of her handmaidens Trouble and Sorrow, Venus cruelly abuses Psyche both physically and verbally, declaring her de facto marriage to her son illegitimate and asserting that the child in Psyche's womb will be born a bastard—if she allows Psyche to bear it at all. So saying, Venus ironically essays to make trial of Psyche's worth, and sets her the first of four labors.

After the host of ants help Psyche separate all the spilled seed (see the discussion of the first task in chapter 11), Venus attributes Psyche's success to the clandestine help of her divine lover, even though Eros remains a convalescent confined under close watch in his mother's house. She sets Psyche a second labor: the gathering of the gold wool from the solar rams. Thinking the task impossible, Psyche intends to cast herself from a cliff near the river, but is saved by the slender green reed who gives her the counsel she requires in order to complete the task (see the discussion of the second labor in chapter 13). Upon her return, Venus once more chalks up her success to Eros' invisible intervention, and immediately sets her another seemingly impossible task: collection of water from a stream near the summit of a high crag. Psyche ascends the peak, thinking that, if all else fails, there she will surely be able to make an end of it all. Jove's eagle intervenes and helps Psyche complete this, her third labor (see discussion in chapter 14). Venus' wrath is hardly ameliorated, and she promptly assigns Psyche her fourth and most terrible task, entailing a descent into the underworld to obtain a portion of Proserpine's beauty. Psyche believes that the true end of this mission is her own death and destruction, but the tower from which she intends to throw herself breaks into speech and provides the guidance necessary for her to complete her fourth labor. This task is discussed in chapter 20, but as its description there is not wholly continuous, I give an unbroken summary of its details here.

Near the city of Lacedaemon, Psyche seeks the vent of Dis and enters it, treading the path she will find there straight to the palace of Orcus, the underworld. She takes a cake of barley in each hand and two coins in her mouth. When she meets the driver of a lame ass bearing wood, he asks her to pick up a few fallen twigs, but (following the tower's instructions) Psyche ignores him and passes on in silence. When she reaches the river of the dead, she gives Charon the ferryman a single coin which he must take with own hand from her mouth. She encounters a rotting corpse on the river who prays to be taken into the boat, but she may not pity him; nor may she aid the old weaving women she encounters on the other side of the river. She uses one cake to allay the hunger of the hound with three heads (Cerberus) who guards Proserpine's halls, and refuses Proserpine's offer of a soft seat and a rich meal. Sitting on the ground, she asks for coarse bread before divulging the reason for her visit. Taking the portion of beauty Proserpine gives her, she retraces her steps, using her last cake for Cerberus and the second coin for Charon.

After reentry into the day world, Psyche ignores the tower's strict admonition and opens the box. She is immediately overcome by a slumber. Fortunately, Eros, whose wound has finally healed, rushes to her aid and wipes the sleep from her eyes. Psyche delivers the box to Venus while Eros flies off to Jove to ask him to countenance his marriage to Psyche. Jove agrees, and a great wedding feast is held; Jove mollifies Venus by bidding Mercury bring Psyche up to heaven and offering her the cup of ambrosia that makes her immortal and her union with Eros eternal. Eros and Psyche wed, and soon thereafter their child, Pleasure, is born.

NOTES

Translations are the author's unless otherwise indicated. *The following abbreviations are employed for texts repeatedly cited:*

AN Edward Edinger, *Anatomy of the Psyche* (Peru, IL: Open Court Publishing, 1985)

AP *Amor and Psyche: A Commentary on the Tale by Apuleius*, Erich Neumann (Bollingen/Princeton: Princeton University Press, 1956/1971)

APN *Anima: An Anatomy of a Personified Notion*, James Hillman (Woodstock, CT: Spring Publications, 1985)

CI *Creative Imagination in the Sufism of Ibn Arabi*, Henry Corbin (Princeton: Princeton University Press, 1969)

DE *Duino Elegies*, by Rainer Maria Rilke, trans. Edward Snow (New York: North Point Press, 2000)

DU *The Dream and the Underworld*, James Hillman (New York: Harper and Row, 1979)

DYP *Diaries of a Young Poet*, Rainer Maria Rilke, trans. Edward Snow and Michael Winkler (New York: W. W. Norton, 1998)

GN *Letters of Rainer Maria Rilke 1910–1926*, trans. Jane Bannard Greene and M. D. Herter Norton (New York and London: W. W. Norton, 1972)

GNI *Letters of Rainer Maria Rilke 1892–1910*, trans. Jane Bannard Greene and M. D. Herter Norton (New York and London: W. W. Norton, 1945)

HF *Healing Fiction*, James Hillman (Woodstock, CT: Spring Publications, 1983)

LP *Life of a Poet*, Ralph Freedman (New York: Farrar, Straus and Giroux, 1996)

MA *The Myth of Analysis*, James Hillman (New York: HarperCollins, 1992)

MLB *The Notebooks of Malte Laurids Brigge*, Rainer Maria Rilke, trans. M. D. Herter Norton (New York, W. W. Norton, 1949)

NP *New Poems*, Rainer Maria Rilke, trans. and ed. Edward Snow (Berkeley: North Point Press, 1984)

OV *Oedipus Variations*, James Hillman and Karl Kerényi (Woodstock, CT: Spring Publications, 1995)

PP *Puer Papers*, ed. James Hillman (Dallas: Spring Publications, 1989)

PR *The Poetry of Rainer Maria Rilke*, trans. Edward Snow (New York: North Point Press, 2009)

RBH *Rilke's Book of Hours: Love Poems to God*, Rainer Maria Rilke, trans. Anita Barrows and Joanna Macy (New York: Riverhead Books, 1996)

RP *Revisioning Psychology*, James Hillman (New York: HarperCollins, 1975)

SW *Sämtliche Werke*, Rainer Maria Rilke (Frankfurt am Main: Insel Verlag, 1955), V 1–6

TH *The Thought of the Heart and the Soul of the World*, James Hillman (Dallas: Spring Publications, 1982)

VC *Visions of Christ*, Rainer Maria Rilke, trans. Aaron Kramer, ed. Siegfried Mandel (Boulder: University of Colorado Press, 1967)

WSR *Where Silence Reigns—Selected Prose*, Rainer Maria Rilke, trans. G. Craig Houston (New York, New Directions, 1978)

INTRODUCTION

1. I refer to *Rilke's Book of Hours: Love Poems to God*, translated by Anita Barrows and Joanna Macy (New York: Riverhead Books, 1996). This translation is no longer quite so "new," though the book was republished in a new anniversary edition in 2005. Prospective readers should know that Barrows and Macy's translation of *The Book of Hours*—while excellent—is abridged and heavily edited. Susan Ranson's still more recent *Rainer Maria Rilke's The Book of Hours* (Rochester: Camden House, 2008) provides a more scholarly but poetically less compelling translation of the entire work.

2 J. D. McClatchy, "Antagonisms: Rainer Maria Rilke," *Poetry* 185 (October 2004), 43.

3 Ibid.

4 Robert Hass, "Raiding the Inarticulate: A Talk on Poetry and Spirituality," *Poetry Flash* 293 (Summer/Fall 2004), 9.

5 Ibid., 10.

6 "Far too much…" is from the original version of the Tenth Duino Elegy (*The Selected Poetry of Rainer Maria Rilke*, trans. and ed. Stephen Mitchell; New York: Vintage International, 1989); "when the longing…" is from the First Elegy (*Duino Elegies*, trans. J. B. Leishman and Stephen Spender; New York/London: W. W. Norton, 1939); and "Who, if I cried…" is the author's translation of the opening of the First Duino Elegy.

7 Rilke to Nanny Wunderly-Volkart, Muzot, 18 February 1922, in *Briefe an Nanny Wunderly-Volk* (Frankfurt am Main: Insel Verlag, 1977), I, 676.

8 James Hillman, "Peaks and Vales: The Soul/Spirit Distinction as Basis for the Difference between Psychotherapy and Spiritual Discipline," in PP, 54.

9 In his talk, Hass amplifies his basic ideas by way of a reading of the Dickinson poem beginning "There's a certain Slant of light /Winter Afternoons—" and

proceeds to record, with great subtlety, the soul's response to the presence or absence of that classic image of spirit. Hass reads the poem with acute sensitivity, yet his failure to distinguish between (the more objective) attributes of spirit and those (more subjectively inflected ones) of soul rather riddles his own conclusion:

> But the bravery of what it says...that the choice is between a kind of pain and a kind of deadness, and she would choose the pain any day, is something like one of the things that I mean by spirituality in poetry and the presence of the numinous. *Numinous in this case really being some inarticulate feeling* that rose up in her with that quality of light which of course is the old image of the relationship to the divine. (Hass, "Raiding the Inarticulate," p. 12; italics mine)

10 RP, 168.

11 Rilke, "The Young Workman's Letter" in WSR, 69.

12 Ibid. Anyone who doubts that "The Young Workman's Letter" was truly of one birth, conceptually as well as temporally, with the great late poems may wish to contemplate the echo of this passage sounded in the second sonnet (Part II): "Ah, the Earth—who knows her losses?"

13 For a further discussion of "The Young Workman's Letter" in relation to both the nature of soul and currents in contemporary poetry, see Appendix I, "Wright, Hass, Rilke: Modern Poetry in Search of Soul."

14 RP, xvii.

15 C. G. Jung, *The Collected Works*, trans. R. F. C. Hull, Bollingen Series XX (Princeton: Princeton University Press, 1953 ff.), vol. 6, paragraph 743.

16 Sonnet I, 9, SW I, 736.

17 James Hillman, *The Soul's Code* (New York: Random House, 1996). See chapter 1: "In a Nutshell: The Acorn Theory and the Redemption of Psychology."

18 M. H. Abrams, *Natural Supernaturalism: Tradition and Revolution in Romantic Literature* (New York: W. W. Norton, 1973).

19 Keats to George and Georgiana Keats, 21 April 21 1819: "Call the world if you Please 'The vale of Soul-making' Then you will find out the use of the world." Keats continues to draw a distinction equivalent to that between soul and spirit and to sketch a "religious" position deeply consonant with Rilke's:

> I say *'Soul making'* Soul as distinguished from an Intelligence—There may be intelligences or sparks of the divinity in millions—but they are not Souls till they acquire identities, till each one is personally itself....How then are these sparks which are God to have identity given to them—so as ever to possess a bliss peculiar to each ones individual existence? How, but by the medium of a world like this? This point I sincerely wish to consider because I think it a grander system of

salvation than the chrysteain religion—or rather it is a system of Spirit-creation.

(John Keats, *Selected Poems and Letters*, ed. Douglas Bush; Boston, Houghton Mifflin: 1959, 288)

20 Goethe's classic "novel of education" was first published in 1795–6; Novalis's was published posthumously in 1802.

21 See for instance Zweig's remarks in "Abschied von Rilke," in *Rainer Maria Rilke und Stefan Zweig: Briefe und Dokumente* (Frankfurt am Main: Insel, 1987), 121–122.

22 Frank Wood, *Rainer Maria Rilke: The Ring of Forms* (Minneapolis: University of Minnesota Press, 1958), 11.

23 To Witold von Hulewicz, 13 November 1925, GN, 372.

Chapter 1

24 Hofmannsthal to Hans Carossa, 29 January 1908, in *Hugo von Hofmannsthal–Hans Carossa, Briefwechsel 1907–1929*, in *Die neue Rundschau* 71, vol. 3 (1960), 385.

25 Robert Hass, *Twentieth Century Pleasures: Prose on Poetry* (Hopewell, NJ: Ecco Press, 1984), 235.

26 Cited in Wolfgang Leppmann, *Rilke, A Life* (New York: Fromm International, 1984), 3.

27 LP, 14.

28 Donald Prater, *A Ringing Glass* (Oxford: Clarendon Press, 1986), 4.

29 VC, 12.

30 Ibid.

31 LP, 16–17.

32 Ibid., 22.

33 "Empor," SW III, 91.

34 James Rolleston, *Rilke in Transition* (New Haven/London: Yale University Press, 1970), 16.

35 Leppmann, *Rilke*, 40.

36 LP, 35.

37 Ibid., 47.

38 Peter Demetz, *René Rilkes Prager Jahre* (Dusseldorf: Eugen Diederichs Verlag, 1953), 126.

39 "Vom Lugaus," SW I, 13.

40 SW III, 34.

41 "Volkweise," SW I, 39.

42 *Zwei Prager Geschichte*, SW IV, 97.

43 "Königslied," SW I, 73.

44 James Hillman, *Archetypal Psychology: A Brief Account* (Dallas: Spring Publications, 1983), 26–27.

45 Robert Fuerst, *Phases of Rilke* (New York: Haskell House, 1974), 10.

46 SW I, 75.

47 Ibid.

48 Hillman, *Archetypal Psychology*, 23.

49 SW I, 81–82.

50 Ibid., 77–78.

51 Mandel, introduction to VC, 15.

52 Ibid.

53 SW, III, 489.

54 Translation by Kramer, VC, 15.

Chapter 2

55 VC, 3.

56 As his correspondence shows, the poet regarded his *Visions of Christ* as a work of great importance, not only at the time of his composition but much later as well (see also chapter 15). Though the poet

intended to publish the work, grave misgivings about its reception ultimately discouraged him from doing so. This decision is no doubt partly responsible for the relatively scant attention accorded the work to date.

57 Karl Eugene Webb, *Rainer Maria Rilke and Jugendstil* (Chapel Hill: University of North Carolina Press, 1978), 3–4.

58 Cf. VC, 17.

59 This and all subsequent translations from VC by Aaron Kramer. As subsequent poetic passages can be easily located in the separately numbered Visions, I give no further page references. The original German text of "Christus / Elf Visionen" may be found in SW III, 127–170.

60 Rilke had already written about Rabbi Löw in his *Offering to the Lares*.

61 Notably, J. B. Leishman; cf. Mandel, VC, 38.

62 Mandel, VC, 40.

63 As discussed in chapters 15–17, Rilke's *Duino Elegies* carry forward just this kind of imaginative revisioning of Christ's archetypal legacy—without any explicit reference to the Passion at all. As noted in chapter 15, both Rilke and Lou Salomé recognized the deep ties between Rilke's *Visions* and the world view informing his *Elegies*.

64 Rilke, "The Young Workman's Letter" in WSR, 68. See also the discussion in Appendix I, "Wright, Hass, Rilke."

65 SW I, 84.

66 Mandel, VC, 9.

67 Stephen Mitchell, trans., *Letters to a Young Poet*, by Rainer Maria Rilke (New York: Vintage Books, 1986), 25.

68 Rilke, "The Young Workman's Letter" in WSR, 75.

69 MA, 17.

70 Ibid.

71 Ibid., 70.

72 Ibid., 65–66.

73 SW I, 88.

74 PP, 66.

75 Ibid., 65.

76 Ibid., 23.

77 Ibid., 25–26.

78 Ibid., 68.

79 Ibid.

80 Ibid.

81 SW II, 158.

Chapter 3

82 To Witold von Hulewicz, 13 November 1925, GN, 372.

83 Author's translation. SW I, 256.

84 To Phia Rilke, 7 October 1897, cited in Donald Prater, *A Ringing Glass* (Oxford: Clarendon, 1986), 39.

85 Sophie von Kühn, Novalis's betrothed, died in her early teens and thereafter functioned as muse and love-ideal in the poet's imagination. Charlotte von Stein was Goethe's mature and deeply intelligent confidante for many years.

86 MA, 27.

87 Lou Andreas-Salomé, *Looking Back*, trans. Breon Mitchell (New York: Paragon House, 1990), 85.

88 MA, 58.

89 The fifth vision, "The Night," had been written in December; the dating for the sixth is not so certain, but it was most likely written right around his first meeting with Lou

in April or May of 1897, and the two last visions of the first series in the following summer and fall.
90 SW I, 101.
91 Ibid., 107.
92 Ibid., 103.
93 DYP, 4. The translation as well as the date and positioning in the diary are taken here from Snow. In *Sämtliche Werke* (SW III, 611), the poem is dated April 23.
94 This as well as the two following poems (translated by the author): SW III, 608–610.
95 SW III, 609.
96 Ibid., 610–611.
97 DYP, 20. This and all the following prose excerpts are in Edward Snow's translation.
98 Ibid., 18.
99 F. W. van Heerikhuizen, *Rainer Maria Rilke: His Life and Work* (London: Routledge and Kegan Paul, 1951), 94.
100 DYP, 19.
101 DYP, 14. Prior citations are from pages 15 and 17.
102 SW V, 360–361.
103 Ibid., 370–371. Prior citations are from pages 361 and 370.
104 Lou Andreas-Salomé, "Grundformen der Kunst," *Pan*, November 1898 – April 1899, 177–178.
105 LP, 79.
106 Lou Andreas-Salomé, "Der Realismus in der Religion," *Die Freie Bühne*, 1891, 1005.
107 Indeed, Lou felt she knew her Kant better than her professional philosopher friends, Nietzsche and Rée.
108 Andreas-Salomé, "Der Realismus in der Religion," 1004. Prior citations from the same page.
109 Ibid., 1005.
110 Ibid.
111 Ibid., 1006.
112 Ibid., 1005.
113 Ibid., 1026.
114 Ibid.
115 Lou Andreas-Salomé, "Jesus der Jude," *Neue Deutsche Rundschau*, 1896, 343.
116 Ibid.
117 Andreas-Salomé, "Der Realismus in der Religion," 1027.
118 Ibid., 1009.
119 Ibid., 1028.
120 Ibid.
121 Ibid., 1029.
122 Ibid.
123 Andreas-Salomé, "Jesus der Jude," 381.
124 Lou Andreas-Salomé, "Gottesschöpfung" in *Die Freie Bühne*, 1893, 70.
125 M. D. Herter Norton, trans., *Tales of God*, by Rainer Maria Rilke (New York: W. W, Norton, 1963), 9.
126 DYP, 24–25.
127 Ibid. 26–27. All the immediately following citations are from page 27.
128 VC, 32.
129 Ibid., 47.
130 SW V, 427.
131 SW III, 203.
132 Ibid., 263.
133 To Frieda von Bülow, May–June 1899, in GN I, 31.
134 W. L. Graf, *Rainer Maria Rilke: Creative Anguish of a Modern Poet* (Princeton: Princeton University Press, 1956), 91.
135 cited in Patricia Brodsky, *Russia in the Works of Rainer Maria Rilke* (Detroit: Wayne State University Press, 1984), epigraph on page 5.

136 To Leopold von Schlözer, January 1920, in GN, 214.
137 Anna Tavis, *Rilke's Russia* (Evanston, IL: Northwestern University Press, 1994), chapter 1.
138 Angela Livingstone, *Lou Andreas-Salomé* (London: Gordon Fraser, 1984), 225.
139 Brodsky, *Russia in the Works of Rainer Maria Rilke*. Citations in this paragraph all from pages 15–16.
140 Lou Andreas-Salomé, "Russische Dichtung und Kulture," *Cosmopolis*, August–September 1897, 572.
141 Maximilian Harden in V. Dudkin and K. Azadovskij, "Neoromantizm, Legenda o 'russkoj duse,'" cited in Brodsky, 16.
142 Nina Hoffmann, *Th. M. Dostojewsky*, cited in Brodsky, 22. Following citations also from Hoffmann and cited in Brodsky, 21–22.
143 Diary entry of 2 December 1899, cited in Brodsky, 21.
144 Andreas-Salomé, "Russische Dichtung und Kulture," 574.
145 Ibid., 575.
146 Ibid., 576.
147 Lou Andreas-Salomé, "Leo Tolstoi, unser Zeitgenosse," *Neue Deutsche Rundschau*, 1899. Translated and included as an appendix in Tavis, *Rilke's Russia*, 142.
148 Ibid.
149 Lou Andreas-Salomé, "Russische Philosophie and semitischer Geist," *Die Zeit*, 15 January 1898.
150 Lou Andreas-Salomé, "Das Russische Heiligenbild und sein Dichter," *Vossische Zeitung* (Sonntagsbeilage) 2, 1 January 1898.
151 Andreas-Salomé, "Leo Tolstoi," 142.
152 Andreas-Salomé, "Das Russische Heiligenbild."
153 van Heerikhuizen, *Rainer Maria Rilke*, 97.
154 SW V, 494.
155 Rilke, *Geschichten der Lieben Gott*, cited in Brodsky, 22.
156 "Russische Kunst," SW V, 494.
157 Cited in Brodsky, 20.
158 "Russische Kunst," SW V, 495.
159 Ibid., 497.
160 Ibid.
161 Andreas-Salomé, "Der Realismus in der Religion," 1029–1030.

Chapter 4

162 E. M. Butler, *Rainer Maria Rilke* (New York and London: MacMillan and Cambridge University Press, 1941). For instance, page 70: "Rilke's seemingly religious monk was worshipping at the shrine of art, and seeking a God that never was on sea or land."
163 The gist of Rilke's spiritual initiative has sometimes been lost on his critics, especially earlier ones. In his *Ring of Forms*, for instance, Frank Wood echoes Butler's complaint:

> No one today regards Rilke, as was formerly the case, as a mystic in the traditional sense of the term. His concern is not with the divinities of either Eastern or Western churches, but with his own inspiration. Instead of the humble passage from human to divine modes of experience, as with Eckhart or St. John of the Cross,

> *The Book of Hours* presents a merging of divine and human merely as a function of creative power...a view of poetry is projected under a religious guise; religiosity is here the product of artistic consciousness; the divinity a catalyst in a solution of many lofty, if somewhat specialized images...

This litany of half-truths discloses a maddening intellectual complacency. Rilke *was* vitally concerned with the divinities of both the Eastern and Western churches; the problem was, of course, that this divinity had lost life and credibility for him, and he was (is) hardly alone in that estrangement. Wood, moreover, speaks confidently of "art" and "religion" as fixed categories—as if we knew, without the least reflection, not only the familiar activities associated with these terms (painting a picture, going to church), but the *essence* of the underlying spiritual activities they signify, and as if these activities were obviously neatly separable. Many before and after Rilke have, like him, construed human creativity as inimitably bound to the deepest religious instinct.

The kind of intellectual inattention evident in Wood's passage derives, in large part, from conventions of thought that lack any component of *psychological* reflection; that *fail even to begin to interrogate the nature of religion, art, and creativity from the standpoint of the (individual) soul.* That is exactly what Rilke had been doing for years, most especially—under Lou's tutelage—in the years leading up to his *Book of Hours.*

164 From *The Book of Monastic Life*, SW I, 259.

165 Richard Tarnas, *Cosmos and Psyche* (New York: Viking, 2006), 17.

166 Ibid., 16–17.

167 Ibid., 23.

168 Ibid.

169 Ibid.

170 The term is Owen Barfield's. For a fascinating discussion that complements Tarnas's, see Barfield, *Saving the Appearances* (Hanover, NH: Wesleyan University Press, 1965).

171 F. W. van Heerikhuizen, *Rainer Maria Rilke: His Life and Work* (London: Routledge and Kegan Paul, 1951), 22. The whole of Heerikhuizen's first chapter is relevant to the theme.

172 SW I, 253.

173 Samuel Taylor Coleridge, *Biographia Literaria* (Princeton: Princeton University Press, 1983), 304.

174 SW I, 253.

175 RBH. Barrows and Macy number the poems in the *The Book of Hours.* Thus the sixtieth poem in the first of the three books is designated I, 60; the first poem of the second book II, 1; etc. No like numbering will be found in the *Sämtliche Werke*, so references to that text provide volume and page number only.

176 Robert Bly, trans., *Selected Poems of Rainer Maria Rilke* (New York: Harper and Row, 1981), 15.

177 SW I, 293.

178 RBH, I, 60.

179 SW I, 254.

180 Rilke's first draft of *The Book of Monastic Life*, called *Gebete*, includes a long letter poem omitted from the version finally published in 1905 (SW III, 360). In this letter, Rilke's monk declares himself a proponent of the Stoglav style. See Patricia Brodsky, *Russia in the Works of Rainer Maria Rilke* (Detroit: Wayne State University Press, 1984), 69:

> The Stoglav...is a church council of 1551 which called for strict adherence to traditional forms of painting....The Stoglav declared that "in nothing will the painters follow their own fancy." In 1658, another Stoglav council put it even more bluntly: "He who shall paint an icon out of his imagination shall suffer endless torment."

Still, as Brodsky notes, even in this version Rilke's monk reveals inner conflict; that Rilke omitted the piece from the 1905 version signals the poet's own deep ambivalence about these crucial matters of freedom in representation.

181 RBH, I, 4.

182 Ibid., I, 5.

183 SW I, 255–256.

184 "Indian Summer II," the Charles Wright poem discussed in Appendix I, provides a particularly relevant instance of Augustine's authority and influence.

185 TH, 27.

186 Ibid.

187 SW I, 263.

188 RBH, I, 39.

189 In 1910, in Tunis, Rilke wrote to his mother, "One must recall how on just this ground early Christianity sent down its deep roots, Carthage or the region around Carthage is the home of the holy Augustine!" *Rilke's Weihnachtsbriefe an die Mutter* (Frankfurt: Insel Verlag, 1996) 39.

190 TH, 29.

191 Ibid., 28–29.

192 Ibid., 30.

193 Augustine, *Confessions*, trans. R. S. Pine-Coffin (New York: Penguin Books, 1961), 21 (Bk. I, 1).

194 Ibid., 23 (Bk. I, 4).

195 Ibid., 284 (Bk. XII, 7).

196 Ibid., 256–7 (Bk. XI, 4).

197 Ibid., 21 (Bk. I, 1).

198 PP, "Peaks and Vales," 55.

199 One might compare, for instance, Augustine's moralizing on his theft of pears as a youth in Book II of the *Confessions* with Wordsworth's account of this unauthorized borrowing of a boat in the first book of *The Prelude*. In the latter, the cliffs themselves take on a kind of life that exceeds the bounds of the author's immediate comprehension or ethical compass. No merely dead objects serving as ciphers in a prescripted morality play, the things comprising Wordsworth's world of nature interpenetrate the soul of the poet, mixing moral life with animate mystery and incompletely understood symbolic meaning:

> ...the huge cliff
> Rose up between me and the stars, and still
> With measured motion, like a living thing
> Strode after me...
> ...and after I had seen

That spectacle, for many days
my brain
Worked with a dim and
undetermined sense
Of unknown modes of being.
(l. 410–420)

This is quite different from Augustine's prosaic description of the pear tree, the theft, and his settled moral conclusion, which deliberately erases (the significance of) the pears themselves: "The evil in me was foul, but I loved it. I loved my own perdition and my own faults, not the things for which I committed wrong, but the wrong itself. My soul was vicious and broke away from your safe-keeping…" (47). In Augustine, the whole world of things—*not* consubstantial with God—is always really beside the point.

200 Augustine, *Confessions*, 82 (Bk. IV, 12).

201 Ibid., 178 (Bk. VIII, 12). The citation is from Romans 13:13, 14.

202 In the long run, of course, my contention that Augustine did not effectively *reimagine* the Christian faith is not entirely true. Augustine's own version of the essence of Christianity—extrapolated from the dramatic spiritual struggle recorded in his *Confessions*—did ultimately gain enormous authority. His views achieved such influence in part because of the imaginative power marshaled by his mythologizing of key concepts such as sin and salvation. Unfortunately, however, Augustine's imagination of faith *did* indeed canonize precisely those tenets distilled in the passage from Paul's epistles—including, effectively, a handing over of the power of the individual soul's own spiritual imagination to a canonical system of belief. Consequently, it may be said that Augustine used the power of imagination (and of course, his agile intellect and strong will) to promote a doctrinal understanding fundamentally inimical to the soul and its own power of creative imagination. He did so in large part because he persistently imagined (as cited in note 24 above) that "My soul was vicious…"

In time, of course, Augustine himself became the foremost framer of Church doctrine—deciding what is and is not spiritually acceptable or true according to the faith. The gist of the authoritarianism that plagues the history of the church—so tragically evident in unrelenting persecutions of heresy—is inscribed in the structure and character of Augustine's own conversion experience. That event reveals *the easy cooperation between personal feeling and dogmatism* that continues to fuel the phenomenon of "born again-ism" and various forms of evangelical (not to say fundamentalist) belief. Augustine's is the classic archetype of the familiar narrative "I was a sinner, found belief in Jesus Christ, and now (feel I) am saved." Part of the problem is that the faculty of feeling readily attaches a given value and meaning to certain experiences and "sticks" there; imagination, on the other hand, requires constant transformation.

It is significant, too, that the episode of Augustine's conversion coincided with his surrender of his hopes for marriage and intimate relations with women. Immediately after his conversion, he tells his devout mother of what has happened and, addressing the Lord, declares, "You converted me to yourself, so that I no longer desired a wife or placed any hope in this world but stood firmly upon the rule of faith." Predictably enough, his *spiritual* victory entails, not only aversion to the world, but a marginalizing of vital relationship with the (feminine) soul, source of temptation. The shelving of eros is simultaneously a putting down and away of psyche; consequently, Christianity's highly spiritualized conceptions of love tend to be un- or antipsychological or (as Hillman states) antisoul. In practice, however, I expect *agape* has a better chance of thriving when it is not premised upon the suppression of eros.

203 PP, "Peaks and Vales," 56.

204 Cited in George Galavaris, "The Icon God's Birthmark in Rilke's *Prayers*" (Athens: European Cultural Center of Delphi, Offprint, 1987), 266.

205 Ibid., 267.

206 RBH, I, 60.

207 Patricia Brodsky, *Russia in the Works of Rainer Maria Rilke* (Detroit: Wayne State University Press, 1984), 57.

208 SW III, 657–658.

209 LP, 101.

210 SW V, 496.

211 August Stahl, "...und es war die Znamenskaia, Rilke und die Kunst der Ikonenmaler," *Blätter der Rilke-Gesellschaft,* 7–8 (1980–81), 89.

212 Ibid.

213 Ibid.

214 TH, 28.

215 Ibid.

216 Stahl, "...und es war die Znamenskaia," 90.

217 RBH, I, 12, modified by the author.

218 Ibid., I, 60.

Chapter 5

219 TH, 35.

220 Ibid., 36.

221 Henry Corbin, *Creative Imagination in the Sufism of Ibn Arabi* (Princeton: Princeton University Press, 1969). Hereafter abbreviated CI.

222 Lou Andreas-Salomé, "Jesus der Jude," *Neue Deutsche Rundschau*, 1896, 344.

223 Ibid.

224 Ibid., 345.

225 SW I, 255–256.

226 RBH, I, 5.

227 DU, 24–25.

228 SW I, 276.

229 To Witold von Hulewicz, 13 November 1925, in GN 375.

230 CI, 180.

231 Ibid., 184.

232 Ibid., 113.

233 Ibid., 108.

234 Ibid., 185.

235 Ibid. The preceding sentence is also vitally relevant: "The theosophist avoids from the outset the theological opposition between *Ens increatum* and an *ens creatum* drawn from nothingness, an opposition which makes it doubtful whether the relationship between the

Summum Ens and the *nothingness* from which He causes creatures to arise has ever been truly defined." Also:

> There is no place in Ibn Arabi's thinking for a creation *ex nihilo*.... The existentiation of a thing which had no existence before, a creative operation which took place once and for all and is now complete is for him a theoretical and practical absurdity. *Creation* as the "rule of being" is the pre-eternal and continuous movement by which being is manifested at *every instant* in a new cloak. (200)

Emerson held a similar vision of "the perpetual revelation." Finally, another passage explicitly relates ideas of creation to the ontological and valuative status of imagination. After elucidating the Sufi notion of the authentic imaginal world, Corbin writes:

> In general we note that the degree of reality thus imputed to the Image and the creativity imputed to the Imagination correspond to a notion of creation unrelated to the official theological doctrine, the doctrine of *creation ex nihilo*, which has become so much a part of our habits that we tend to regard it as the only authentic idea of creation. We might even go so far as to ask whether there is not a necessary correlation between this idea of a *creatio ex nihilo* and the degradation of the ontologically creative Imagination and whether, in consequence, the degeneration of the Imagination into a fantasy productive only of the imaginary and the unreal is not the hallmark of our laicized world for which the foundations were laid by the preceding religious world, which precisely was dominated by this characteristic idea of the Creation. (182)

This is, in effect, Tarnas's argument, elaborated in connection with Augustine in the prior chapter of this book.

236 Ibid., 186–187.

237 Cf. CI, 186: "The initial theophanic operation by which the Divine Being reveals Himself, 'shows Himself' to Himself, by differentiating Himself in his hidden being...this operation is conceived as being the creative Active Imagination, the theophanic Imagination. Primordial Cloud, absolute or theophanic Imagination, and existentiating Compassion are equivalent notions."

238 Ibid., 3–4.

239 Ibid., 188.

240 Ibid., 182.

241 RBH, I, 45.

242 Ibid., I, 21.

243 Ibid., I, 22.

244 CI, 188.

245 SW I, 283.

246 RBH, I, 51.

247 Augustine, *Confessions*, trans. R. S. Pine-Coffin (New York: Penguin Books, 1961), 23 (Bk. I, 4).

248 SW I, 261.

249 RBH, I, 16.

250 Lou Andreas-Salomé, "Der Realismus in der Religion," *Die Freie Bühne*, 1891, 1082.

251 RBH, I, 14.
252 CI, 222.
253 Cf. C. G. Jung, *Memories, Dreams, Reflections* (New York: Vintage Books, 1965), 256: "Man is indispensable for the completion of creation...he himself is the second creator of the world, who alone has given to the world its objective existence—without which, unheard, unseen, silently eating, giving birth, dying, heads nodding through hundreds of millions of years, it would have gone on in the profoundest night of non-being down to its unknown end. Human consciousness created objective existence and meaning..."
254 CI, 236.
255 Ibid., 198.
256 Ibid., 224.
257 Ibid., 191.
258 Ibid., 196.
259 RBH, I, 13.
260 Ibid., I, 55.
261 CI, 211.
262 Ibid., 197.
263 Ibid. It should be emphasized that the reality of any general version of "the God created in the faiths" is not the end point of gnostic vision. Any more general or collectivized version of deity may be further individualized, which process, however, does not necessarily negate the reality of "the God created in the faiths," but may further define and intensify it. Thus Corbin speaks of "the profound difference between the Imagination of 'the God created in the faiths' and the 'theophanic vision' dispensed to the heart in the course of the 'confidential psalm' between Lover and Beloved." (268) Similarly, the God of *The Book of the Monastic Life* is manifestly Judeo-Christian in origin and hardly conceivable except against that religious background; at the same time, this God is the unique and singular product of Rilke's highly individualized spiritual imagination.
264 RBH, I, 36.
265 CI, 258.
266 Ibid., 271.
267 Ibid., 248.
268 SW I, 268.
269 CI, 267.
270 RBH.
271 Ibid.
272 Ibid., I, 17.
273 CI, 251.
274 RBH.
275 Ibid.
276 SW I, 288.
277 RBH, I, 44.
278 Ibid., I, 61.
279 Ibid.
280 SW I, 293.
281 RBH, I, 55, modified by the author.
282 CI, 214.
283 SW I, 300.
284 Ibid., 301.
285 Ibid.
286 CI, 155.
287 Ibid., 147.
288 Ibid., 146.
289 Ibid., 251.
290 RBH.
291 Ibid., 56.
292 Cited in CI, 272.
293 Ibid.
294 Ibid., 55.
295 Ibid., 61.
296 Ibid., 270.
297 Ibid., 250.
298 Ibid., 270.
299 Ibid., 268.

300 Relatedly, both Psyche and the Jesus of Rilke's *Visions* were the subject of false, idolatrous worship, and consequently (though in different ways) were given to death.

301 RBH, I, 35.

302 Ibid., II, 7.

Chapter 6

303 SW III, 688. Author's translation; Snow's translation in DYP, 152.

304 A letter from St. Petersburg, 31 July 1900.

305 DYP, 147.

306 Cited in APN, 18.

307 APN, 23.

308 Ibid., 19.

309 Christopher Bamford, "Deserts and Gardens," in *An Endless Trace* (New Paltz, NY: Codhill Press, 2003).

310 DYP, 163.

311 H. F. Ellenberger, *The Discovery of the Unconscious* (New York: Basic Books, 1970), 199–201. Cited in APN, 43.

312 APN, 25.

313 Rainer Maria Rilke, *In und nach Worpswede, Gedichte Mit Bildern von Heinrich Vogeler* (Frankfurt: Insel Verlag, 2000).

314 Ibid., 11.

315 Ibid., 13.

316 DYP, 159 (Snow). The German reads: "Das was er mußte / in Dunkelheit: / das Unbewußte / soll nichtmehr sein." SW III, 692.

317 Cited in APN, 128.

318 Cited in APN, 64.

319 APN, 25.

320 Ibid., 87.

321 Ibid., 39.

322 DYP, 173–174.

323 SW I, 375.

324 Ibid., 374.

325 APN, 69.

326 Eric Torgersen, *Dear Friend: Rainer Maria Rilke and Paula Modersohn-Becker* (Evanston, IL: Northwestern University Press, 1998).

327 DYP, 156.

328 Rilke, *In und nach Worpswede*, 17. Author's translation; Snow's translation in DYP, 175.

329 APN, 69.

330 Ibid., 37.

331 DYP, 220.

332 Rilke, *In und nach Worpswede*, 16.

333 Edward Snow, trans., *The Book of Images*, by Rainer Maria Rilke (New York: North Point Press, 1991), xiv.

334 Rilke, *In und nach Worpswede*, 31.

335 SW III, 699. Author's translation. Snow's translation in DYP, 194.

336 Cited in APN, 68.

337 F. W. Van Heerikhuizen, *Rainer Maria Rilke: His Life and Work* (London, Routledge and Kegan Paul, 1951), 130.

338 SW I, 402.

339 Cf. Snow, trans., *The Book of Images*, 185–203.

340 DYP, 141.

341 Ibid., 175–176.

342 A sentence from Emerson's *The Conduct of Life*—one Rilke knew well—highlights the connection between the just-cited diary passage and the archetypal idea of the hero: "The Hero is he who is immovably centered."

343 APN, 87, 89.

344 DYP, 162–163.

345 From the Introduction to Rilke's *Worpswede* (Frankfurt: Insel Verlag, 1987), cited in WSR, 6–7.
346 Rilke, *In und nach Worpswede*, 97.
347 APN, 39.
348 Ibid., 47.
349 Cf. Ellenberger, *The Discovery of the Unconscious*, and APN, 43.
350 From Rilke's Worpswede monograph, SW V, 88.
351 DYP, 158.
352 Ibid., 157.
353 Rilke, *In und nach Worpswede*, 28.
354 Ibid., 34.
355 Ibid., 46.
356 SW IV, 672.
357 All citations from APN, 45.
358 SW I, 402.

Chapter 7

359 DYP, 200.
360 Heinrich Petzet, *Das Bildnis des Dichters* (Frankfurt am Main: Insel Verlag, 1983). Cited in Eric Torgersen, *Dear Friend: Rainer Maria Rilke and Paula Modersohn-Becker* (Evanston, IL: Northwestern University Press, 1998), 78.
361 SW I, 405–406.
362 SW I, 396.
363 DYP, 235.
364 SW I, 397.
365 Ibid., 236.
366 Diary entry, 20 January 1901??, cited in LP, 138. Also *Rainer Maria Rilke and Lou Andreas-Salome, The Correspondence* (London and New York: W. W. Norton, 2006), 39.
367 DYP, 267.
368 C. G. Jung, *The Psychology of Transference* (Princeton: Princeton University Press/Bollingen Series, 1954/69/74), 95.
369 Ibid., 98.
370 DYP, 267–268.
371 Jung, *The Psychology of Transference*, 95.
372 Ibid., 96–98.
373 DYP, 268.
374 AN, 148.
375 Cited in ibid., 149.
376 SW I, 401.
377 Cited in Jung, *The Psychology of Transference*, 109.
378 Ibid.
379 “Ritter, Welt und Heide” in *In und nach Worpswede, Gedichte Mit Bildern von Heinrich Vogeler* (Frankfurt: Insel Verlag, 2000), 34–35.
380 PR, 101, 103.
381 “Der Kahn” in *In und nach Worpswede*, 37–38.
382 AN, 152.
383 DYP, 245.
384 Sonnet II, 13 ends in a complex arithmetical metaphor involving the “counting” of being and non-being.
385 Torgersen, *Dear Fnend*, 93.
386 James Hillman, *Suicide and the Soul* (Putnam, CT: Spring Publications, 1965/97), 61.
387 Ibid., 60 and 68, respectively.
388 Ibid., 70.
389 Ibid.
390 Ibid., 63.
391 To Paula Becker, 5 November 1900, in GN I, 50–51.
392 SW I, 469–476.
393 DYP, 270–271.
394 Jung, *The Psychology of Transference*, 95.
395 DYP, 274.

396 LP, 137.
397 AN, 165.
398 All citations (including Jung) from ibid., 166–167.
399 DYP, 276.

CHAPTER 8

400 C. G. Jung, *The Psychology of Transference* (Princeton: Princeton University Press, 1966) 100.
401 APN, 23.
402 DYP, 191–193.
403 One of Lou's diary entries included in *Rainer Maria Rilke and Lou Andreas-Salome, The Correspondence*, trans. Edward Snow and Michael Winkler (London and New York: W. W. Norton, 2006), 39.
404 Ibid., 42.
405 LP, 140.
406 Cited in Eric Torgersen, *Dear Friend: Rainer Maria Rilke and Paula Modersohn-Becker* (Evanston: Northwestern University Press, 1998), 111.
407 Ibid., 112.
408 RBH, II, 3.
409 Ibid., II, 1.
410 Ibid., II, 2.
411 Ibid., I, 55.
412 Ibid., I, 3.
413 Jung, *The Psychology of Transference*, 102.
414 Cf. Joseph L. Henderson and Dyane N. Sherwood, *Transformation of the Psyche: The Symbolic Alchemy of the Splendor Solis* (Hove and New York: Brunner-Routledge, 2003).
415 AN, 151.
416 RBH, II, 4.
417 Ibid., 25.
418 Ibid., II, 5.
419 Ibid., II, 6.
420 AN, 175, 179.
421 Jung, *The Psychology of Transference*, 102–103.
422 SW I, 313.
423 To Phia Rilke, cited in LP, 153.
424 Ibid., 314.
425 RBH, II, 10.
426 PP, 27.
427 SW I, 322.
428 RBH, II, 27.
429 Ibid.
430 James Hillman, *Loose Ends* (Dallas: Spring Publications, 1975), 53.
431 Ibid., 58.
432 RBH, II, 19.
433 SW I, 323.
434 In the close confines of his very small house, for instance, little Ruth's noisemaking continually disturbed Rilke's attempts to work.
435 "Puer Wounds and Ulysses' Scar" in PP, 101.
436 RBH, II, 22.
437 Ibid., II, 34.
438 "Puer Wounds and Ulysses' Scar" in PP, 109.
439 Ibid., 111.

CHAPTER 9

440 LP, 162–163.
441 PR, 87.
442 Ibid., 83.
443 Ibid. 81.
444 SW I, 392–393.
445 "The Neighbor" forms an interesting contrast with another, still earlier poem as well. In the most famous lyric in *Offering to the Lares*, the speaker—wherever he may travel—hears echoes of folk

melodies from his native Bohemia, sweet strains recalling a treasured homeland that, though perhaps physically distant, is always imaginatively present, and always spiritually sustaining. Here, the inescapable violin sings of having no home in this world.

446 SW I, 393–394.

447 PR, 75.

448 Ibid., 71.

449 SW I, 343.

450 RBH, III, 2. Here I provide the last line, which Barrows and Macy omit.

451 Ibid., III, 4.

452 Ibid., III, 13.

453 Ibid., III, 4.

454 SW I, 348–349. Barrows and Macy do not include these lines.

455 SW I, 346–347. Again, in their version, Barrows and Macy cut much of this material.

456 RBH, III, 6.

457 Ibid., III, 7.

458 SW I, 347. Lines not included in Barrows and Macy's version of III, 7.

459 Plato, *Phaedo*, 67e in *The Collected Dialogues*, ed. Hamilton and Cairns (Princeton: Princeton University Press, 1961).

460 James Hillman, *Suicide and the Soul* (Putnam, CT: Spring Publications, 1965/97), 64. In general, Hillman's position in this book is entirely consonant with the (Jacobsen-influenced) ideas Rilke expresses in *The Book of Poverty and Death* and, later, *Malte*. For example, Hillman writes: "Each event in my life makes its contribution to my death, and I build my death as I go along day by day.... Life matures, develops, and aims at death. Death is its very purpose. We live in order to die. Life and Death are contained within each other, complete each other, are understandable only in terms of each other." (59) Hillman, indeed, may well have had Rilke in mind in framing the argument he presents in this section of his book, for in it he quotes the pivotal lines from *The Book of Poverty of Death*: "O Lord, give each man his own death..." (62)

461 SW I, 351.

462 RBH, III, 12.

463 C. G. Jung, *Mysterium Coniunctionis*, CW 14, par. 670ff. Cited in AN, 171.

464 RBH, III, 18.

465 Ibid., III, 28.

466 AN, 167.

467 SW I, 356.

468 Edward Snow, trans., *The Book of Images*, by Rainer Maria Rilke (New York: North Point Press, 1991), 17.

469 AP, 79–80.

470 AN, 150.

471 SW IV, 678.

472 Ibid., 679–80.

473 Ibid., 680.

474 Ibid., 681.

475 AP, 80. Italics mine.

476 SW IV, 687.

477 AP, 81–82. Italics mine.

Chapter 10

478 SW I, 405.

479 Ibid., 505.

480 Robert Hass, "Looking for Rilke" in *Twentieth Century Pleasures* (Hopewell, NJ; Ecco Press, 1984).

481 The well-known 1990 film (starring Robert De Niro and Robin Williams) based on the book by Oliver Sacks.

482 NP, xiii. This 1984 edition of Snow's translations, along with its companion volume (*New Poems: The Other Part*) published in 1987, includes *all* of Rilke's "new poems" and so is a fitting context for Snow's apt remark. A later, one-volume edition is *not* complete; the very much smaller selection in Snow's *The Poetry of Rainer Maria Rilke* (see reference below) omits many poems vital to the present discussion and renders invisible much of the "context" Snow alludes to in his 1984 remark. Snow did, however, rework his translations, and when a newer translation of a given poem is available in *The Poetry of Rainer Maria Rilke* I generally cite that later version.

483 SW I, 481.

484 NP, 7.

485 PR, 133.

486 NP, 11.

487 Ibid., 19.

488 Ibid., 35.

489 SW I, 491–2.

490 SW I, 492–494.

491 Dan Brown, *The Da Vinci Code* (New York: Doubleday, 2003).

492 NP, 43.

493 PR, 197.

494 Ibid., 202–203.

495 Ibid., 209.

496 Ibid., 169.

497 Ibid., 213.

498 NP, 139. I've stayed with Snow's earlier version here.

499 Ibid., 31.

500 Rilke, *Auguste Rodin (First Part)* in WSR, 112–113.

501 Ibid., 95.

502 11 September 1902, in GN I, 88.

503 To be sure, this concept and commitment was old as well as new, a further refinement and empowerment of the poetic vision already articulated in *The Book of Hours*.

504 AP, 28.

505 Ibid., 97–98.

506 WSR, 93. In connection with motifs of Nature and Art, it is interesting too that Neumann's riff on Apuleius' description of Pan evokes deep resonances with the mythic figure of Orpheus. "It is no accident that (Pan) has Echo in his arms, the unattainable beloved, who transforms herself into music for him..." (AP, 97) Pan, after all, can be *both* old and eternally young in love. Like him, the Orpheus/Eurydice figure of Rilke's *Sonnets* embodies a successful fusion of senex and puer.

507 WSR, 93.

508 Ibid., 95.

509 LP, 169.

510 WSR, 91–92.

511 Ibid., 94.

512 By contrast, the loose liturgical flow surging through *The Book of Hours* produced poetic objects that feel far less spatially or temporally discrete.

513 This and the following phrases from WSR, 95.

514 SW I, 529.

515 RBH, I, 60.

516 WSR, 101.

517 Ibid., 125.

518 Ibid., 108.

Chapter 11

519 AP, 41–42.
520 Ibid.
521 Ibid., 95.
522 PR, 197.
523 Ibid., 203.
524 AP, 95.
525 SW I, 366.
526 NP, 57.
527 PR, 159.
528 SW I, 512.
529 AP, 96.
530 RP, 1.
531 Ibid., 3.
532 Ibid., 29.
533 Ibid., 26–27.
534 Cited in RP, 14.
535 Ibid., 13.
536 Ibid., 12.
537 PR, 217.
538 NP, 135.
539 Ibid., 16.
540 RP, 16–17
541 Ibid.
542 This and following from WSR, 95.
543 RP, 1.
544 NP, 87.
545 Ibid., xi.
546 Ibid., 75.
547 PR, 217.
548 WSR, 131.
549 RP, 23.
550 NP, 77.
551 RP, 3.
552 Ibid., 31.
553 Ibid.
554 Ibid.
555 NP, xi.
556 PR, 219.
557 RP, 14.
558 SW I, 557.

Chapter 12

559 HF, 53. The time in question birthed Jung's *The Red Book (Liber Novus)*, and the publication of that work in 2009 spectacularly confirms its preeminent importance in Jung's life-work.
560 RP, 98–99.
561 Ibid., 3.
562 MLB, 13.
563 RP, 58.
564 Ibid., 70.
565 Ibid., 57.
566 Ibid., 107.
567 Ibid., 78. (Italics mine.)
568 Ibid., xvi.
569 To Clara, 31 August 1902, cited in MLB, 219.
570 MLB, 16.
571 Ibid., 26.
572 Ibid., 26–27.
573 Ibid., 28–30.
574 RP, 75.
575 Ibid., 26. (Italics mine.)
576 MLB, 14.
577 Ibid.
578 RP, xvi.
579 Cf. Hillman: "Pathologizing forces the soul to a consciousness of itself as different from the ego and its life—a consciousness that obeys its own laws of metaphorical enactment in intimate relation with death." (RP, 89)
580 MLB, 14–15.
581 Ibid., 16.
582 RP, 74.
583 Ibid., 55.
584 Ibid., 70.
585 MLB, 17–18.
586 Ibid., 18.
587 Ibid., 22–23.
588 RP, 110.
589 MLB, 85.

590 C. G. Jung, *Memories, Dreams, Reflections* (New York: Vintage, 1965), 21–23.
591 All citations in this paragraph from MLB, 86.
592 MLB, 105.
593 Ibid., 108.
594 Ibid., 87.
595 Ibid., 96.
596 Ibid., 137.
597 Ibid.
598 RP, 69.
599 This and the citations in the following paragraph: MLB, 32.
600 MLB, 35.
601 Ibid., 37–38.
602 Ibid., 31.
603 Ibid., 130.
604 HF, 46.
605 RP, 92.
606 DU, 53–54.
607 Ibid., 54.
608 MLB, 61.
609 Ibid., 48–49.
610 Citations from DU, 18–19.
611 MLB, 51.
612 Ibid.
613 Cf. Hillman: "The deepening and interiorizing that goes on through pathologizing lends neurosis an extraordinary feeling of significance, that through it we are elected, separated from merely ordinary people. This appraisal, deriving itself from neurosis, is of course neurotic...But the sense of significance points beyond neurosis....The feeling of election through the complex is above all a psychic statement which says that a pathologized awareness is fundamental to the sense of individuality. It tells of a difference, not between kinds of people, but between styles of consciousness, natural and psychic, literal and imaginal. Having forced the reality of the imaginal upon one, pathologizing leaves one marked by its imprint. A piece of the person has been struck by the Gods and drawn into a myth and now cannot let go of its mad requirements..." (RP, 111–112)
614 Ibid., 67.
615 Ibid., 78.
616 Ibid.
617 Ibid., 122.

Chapter 13

618 GN, 45.
619 For a handy edition of the classic text cf. Sigmund Freud, *Dora: An Analysis of a Case of Hysteria* with an introduction by Philip Rieff (New York: MacMillan, 1963).
620 HF, 40.
621 Ibid., 41.
622 Ibid., 11.
623 Hillman, "Oedipus Revisited," in OV, 130.
624 Ibid.
625 Ibid., 135–136.
626 Sophocles, *Oedipus Rex* (l.58–61), in Grene and Lattimore, *Greek Tragedies Volume I* (Chicago: University of Chicago Press, 160), 113.
627 OV, 139–140.
628 MLB, 109. All immediately following citations likewise.
629 Ibid.
630 Ibid., 111.
631 Ibid., 175.
632 Ibid., 119.
633 Ibid., 185.
634 MA, 92–93.
635 Ibid., 95.

636 MLB, 198. Following citation likewise.
637 Ibid., 176.
638 MA, 95.
639 AP, 43.
640 Ibid.
641 Ibid., 99.
642 MLB, 145.
643 Cited in OV, 141.
644 Sophocles, *Oedipus Rex*, l. 339–347.
645 OV, 113.
646 http://en.wikipedia.org/wiki/Seven_deadly_sins#Pride. In Dante's *Inferno*, for instance, a satanic Lucifer presides over the ninth and lowest circle of hell—Lucifer, whose name means "light-bearer," and whose primordial sin consisted in seeking to place himself above God. ("How art thou fallen from heaven, O Lucifer, son of morning!... For thou hast said in thine heart, I will ascend into heaven, I will exalt my throne above the stars of God... Yet thou shalt be brought down to hell, to the sides of the pit." Isaiah 14:12–15)
647 AP, 100–101.
648 Sophocles, *Oedipus at Colonus* (l. 5–6), in Grene and Lattimore, *Greek Tragedies Volume 3*.
649 *Oedipus at Colonus* (l. 1612–1617), translated by Moebius, as cited in OV, 154.
650 MLB, 26, 119, 215, respectively.
651 HF, 18.
652 Ibid., 23.
653 Cf., for instance, the early passage in which Malte records his walk through the Tuileries: "Where the sun fell all was hung with the mist as with a grey curtain of light. Grey in the grey, the statues sunned themselves in the not yet unshrouded gardens. Single flowers in the long parterres stood up and said: 'Red,' with a frightened voice. Then a very tall, slim man came round the corner from the Champs-Élysées; he carried a crutch, but no longer thrust under his shoulder, he held it in front of him lightly, and from time to time set it down firm and loud like a herald's staff." (24) Or the next entry, beginning, "How much such a little moon can do..." (25)
654 MLB, 117.
655 MA, 171.
656 Ibid., 173.
657 MA, 173.
658 Ibid., 184.
659 Ibid., 175.
660 MLB, 191.
661 Ibid., 183.
662 Ibid., 184.
663 MA, 259.
664 Ibid., 262.
665 Though we will not probe the subject here, Dionysius' relation to madness (and Hillman's discussion of it in his essay) is also powerfully relevant to Malte's psychology.
666 HF, 36–37.
667 MLB, 194.
668 HF, 40.
669 MA, 263. (Italics mine.)
670 MLB, 187.
671 MA, 95.
672 AP, 101.
673 MLB, 175.
674 Ibid., 203.
675 Cited in OV, 98.
676 MLB, 201.

CHAPTER 14

677 Cited in Donald Prater, *A Ringing Glass* (Oxford, Clarendon Press, 1986), 175.

678 Ibid.

679 GN, 17.

680 Ibid., 32.

681 To Mimi Romanelli, May 11, 1910. Cited in Prater, *A Ringing Glass*, 177.

682 See chapter 15 for a fuller discussion of Rilke's relationship with Magda von Hattingberg.

683 SW I, 638.

684 Cited in Karl J. Kuschel, "'Gott von Mohammed her fühlen' Rilke's Islam-Erfahrung und ihre Bedeutung für den religionstheologische Diskurs der Zukunft," *Blätter der Rilke-Gesellschaft*, 24 (2002), 87.

685 To Clara Rilke, 26 November 1910, in GN, 19, 20.

686 GN, 21.

687 To Karl and Elisabeth von der Heydt, 25 February 1911, cited in Kuschel, "Gott von Mohammed her," 73.

688 SW I, 667.

689 To Witold von Hulewicz, 13 November 1925, in GN, 375.

690 Kuschel, "Gott von Mohammed her," 88, 89.

691 To Princess Marie, 17 December 1912, in GN, 76.

692 Jaime Ferreiro Alemparte, "Das Marien-Leben von Rainer Maria Rilke im Lichte der hagiographischen spanisch-deutschen Quelle. P. Ribadeneira; J. Hornig: Der Flos Sanctorum / Die Triumphierende Tugend," *Blätter der Rilke-Gesellschaft*, 22 (1999), 49–68. Further source information in the paragraph also from Alemparte.

693 To Princess Marie, 17 December 1912, in *Rainer Maria Rilke und Marie von Thurn und Taxis, Briefwechsel* (Zurich, 1951) I, 245.

694 *Rainer Maria Rilke Lou Andreas-Salomé Briefwechsel* (Frankfurt, 1975), 276.

695 GN, 70.

696 Ibid., 72.

697 See Appendix I.

698 SW I, 685.

699 To Lotte Hepner, 8 November 1915, in GN 146–7.

700 *Rainer Maria Rilke und Marie von Thurn und Taxis, Briefwechsel* I, 172.

701 Anna L. G. Künkler, "Rilke auf dem Weg zur Vollendungen der Duineser Elegien," *Blätter der Rilke-Gesellschaft*, 22 (1999), 12.

702 Cited in Kuschel, "Gott von Mohammed her," 74.

703 Ibid.

704 SW I, 688.

705 To Ellen Delp, 27 October 1915, in GN, 144, 145. (Italics mine.)

706 SW I, 685.

707 Ibid., 689.

708 This and immediately following citations: AP, 44–46.

709 Ibid., 103.

710 Ibid.

711 Ibid.

712 SW I, 689.

713 Ibid., 693.

714 AP, 104.

715 SW I, 703, 705.

716 *Letters Summer 1926, Pasternak Tsvetayeva Rilke* (New York: Harcourt Brace, 1985), 87.

717 Helmut Naumann, "Rilke und Toledo," *Blätter der Rilke-Gesellschaft*, 18 (1991), 114.

718 Ibid.
719 Ibid.
720 Ibid., 115.
721 GN, 81.
722 To Lou, 12 December 1912, cited in Kuschel, "Gott von Mohammed her," 78.
723 Ibid., 75.
724 Naumann, "Rilke und Toledo," 114.
725 GN, 70.
726 To Ellen Delp, 27 October 1915, in GN, 146.
727 Indeed Ibn Arabi's concept of the angel—while steeped in the profound complexity characteristic of his thought—does resonate with Rilke's own. Corbin:

> This two-dimensional structure of a being seems to depend on the notion of an eternal hexeity which is the archetype of each individual being in the sensible world, his latent individuation in the world of Mystery, which Ibn Arabi also termed the Spirit, that is, the "Angel," of that being.... To know one's eternal hexeity, one's own archetypal essence, is to know one's "Angel," that is to say, one's eternal individuality as it results from the revelation of the Divine Being revealing Himself to Himself. In "returning to his Lord" a man constitutes the eternal pair of the servant and his Lord, who is the Divine Essence not in its generality but individualized... Consequently, to deny this individuation that takes place in the world of Mystery is to deny the archetypal or theophanic dimension specific to each earthly being, to deny one's "Angel."(CI, 210)

This resonance indicates that the underlying affinity connecting Rilke and Sufi esotericism sketched in chapter 5 remains invisibly in force in the later phase of Rilke's career.
728 SW II, 48–49.
729 Naumann, "Rilke und Toledo," 121.
730 Ibid.
731 *El Greco*, National Gallery Company Limited (London 2003), 200.
732 Cited in Künkler, "Rilke auf dem Weg," 17.
733 SW II, 46–7.
734 To Princess Marie, 13 November 1912, in GN, 72.
735 SW II, 43–44.

Chapter 15

736 GN, 372.
737 In 1911, Clara (as a result, in part, of her ongoing psychoanalysis) requested a divorce. Rilke agreed—and, though the proceedings ran into what turned out to be insurmountable legal barriers, the fact and symbol of the attempt itself remain significant.
738 Rilke's notion of "the unknown (or future) beloved" who would, in the near future, appear derived from a séance Rilke participated in not long before his Spanish journey. The poet had long dabbled in spiritualism and lent the notion of the "unknown beloved" special credence because it answered so closely to his own inner yearnings.

739 SW II, 79.
740 Cited in LP, 374. As Freedman notes, the language of this passage recalls the concluding stanza of the Third Elegy: "And you yourself, how could you know—stirred / primordial times in your lover."
741 *Rainer Maria Rilke and Lou Andreas-Salomé: The Correspondence*, trans. Edward Snow and Michael Winkler (New York and London: W. W. Norton, 2006), 237.
742 SW II, 83.
743 GN, 124.
744 Rilke, after all, had virtually no patriotic attachment to either Germany or Austria, while his connections with both Russia and France were deep and durable.
745 To Anna, Baroness von Münchhausen, 29 August 1914, in GN, 118.
746 To Lou, 9 September 1914, in GN, 120.
747 GN, 133.
748 Snow and Winkler, *Rainer Maria Rilke and Lou Andreas-Salomé*, 278.
749 GN, 124.
750 Ibid., 139.
751 To Karl and Elisabeth von der Heydt, 6 November 1914, in GN, 125. (Italics mine.)
752 LP, 366.
753 Ibid., 213. The letter dates from July 24, 1913.
754 Carl Jung, *Aion*, 2nd ed. (Princeton: Princeton University Press, 1969), 36–37.
755 "The kingdom of God cometh not with observation: neither shall they say, Lo here! or lo there! for it is within and everywhere." (Luke 17:20)
756 VC, 16.
757 11 February 1922, in GN, 291.
758 RP, 3.
759 RP, 129.
760 Ibid., 115.
761 Ibid., 118.
762 Ibid., 117.
763 Ibid.
764 SW II, 689.
765 Ibid., 142.
766 Ibid., 129–130.
767 Ibid.
768 Plato, *Republic* Bk. VI (507b) in *The Collected Dialogues* (Princeton: Princeton University Press, 1961), 742.
769 Ibid., 508b, 743.
770 Genesis 1:7.
771 Good translation of the Greek terms—no less than construction of their meanings—is notoriously difficult.
772 SW I, 711.
773 RP, 132.
774 Ibid.
775 Compare Bollnow: "And if for Plato the experienced world of visible and audible things is only a mirroring of eternal ideas, Rilke looks at this process, so to speak, the other way around: the realm of the invisible is the realm of ideas—but this is not looked upon as if it were there before the appearances of the visible world and served as the original imaged by that world; rather, the reverse is true: the ideas are first distilled out of the visible world; must first be produced and won through the deed of spiritually mastering that world. This is therefore a kind of reverse Platonism." Otto Friedrich Bollnow, "Rilke: The Transformation of the Visible," in Ulrich Fülleborn and

Manfred Engel, *Rilke's Duineser Elegien, Band 2* (Frankfurt Am Main, Suhrkamp Taschenbuch, 2010), 113.

776 SW I, 736.

777 A term coined by the French philosopher Jacques Derrida characterizing, if you will, the "top-down" orientation so dominant in western intellectual history. See, for instance, Jacques Derrida, *Of Grammatology* (Baltimore: Johns Hopkins University Press, 1974).

778 AP, 3.

779 Kinship with another Christian motif—that of the Incarnation—emerges here. Christ may be the only begotten son of the Father, and so native to heavenly realms, but his incarnation in a mortal body unites his destiny with that of the earth. Christ's life and passion play out upon the earth, and ultimately are supposed to *transform* it into "a (new heaven and a) new earth," though many versions of the Christian myth tend to emphasize an otherworldly orientation wherein attainment of a heavenly state implies leaving the earth behind.

Chapter 16

780 To Countess Margot Sizzo, 6 January 1923, GN 314.

781 From "On the Young Poet," SW VI, 1046.

782 DE, 45.

783 Ibid., 63.

784 Edouard Schuré, *The Great Initiates* (Blauvelt, NY: Rudolf Steiner Publications, 1961), 132.

785 See Rudolf Steiner, *The Gospel of St. John* (Hudson, NY: Anthroposophic Press, 1962), especially chapters 11 and 12. Steiner introduces the basic ideas of purification and illumination in connection with "pre-Christian initiation," but they remain foundational to his more complex development of "Christian initiation" as well.

786 In his book *Son of Man*, Andrew Harvey supplies a more comprehensive "map" of initiatory process modeled on the spiritual accomplishment of the Christ. The first two of Harvey's four stages—"purgation" and "illumination"—coincide with those mentioned by Steiner. As the next three chapters of this book reveal, Harvey's third and fourth stages—"union" and "birthing"—are likewise fully and dramatically enacted in Rilke's *Elegies*. See Andrew Harvey, *Son of Man* (New York: Jeremy P. Tarcher/Putnam, 1998), Part Two.

787 Rilke's *Duino Elegies* is doubtless one of the most influential poems of the twentieth century. Many important recent works in English—Galway Kinnell's *Book of Nightmares*, Mark Doty's *My Alexandria*, Larry Levis's ten late elegies (not yet published as a whole)—take the *Elegies* as a point of formal and spiritual departure, and this is just one indication of the poem's rich legacy. Rilke's sway is by no means limited to literature: Wim Wenders' landmark film *Wings of Desire* (originally *Himmel über Berlin*) likewise owes an enormous debt to the *Elegies*.

788 Theodore Ziolkowski, *The Classical German Elegy*

1795–1950 (Princeton: Princeton University Press, 1980), 99–100. (Italics mine.)

789 Kathleen Komar, *Transcending Angels* (Lincoln and London: University of Nebraska Press, 1987), 21.

790 Brian P. Copenhaver, ed., *Hermetica* (Cambridge: Cambridge University Press, 1992), 37.

791 T. S. Eliot, *The Waste Land*, lines 1–2; 12; 69–70; 111; 128.

792 RP, 136.

793 Eliot, *The Waste Land*, l. 19–22.

794 DE, 5.

795 Ibid., 7.

796 Ibid., 139.

797 Ibid., 148.

798 GN, 46.

799 DE, 5, 7.

800 Ibid., 7.

801 Ibid., 9.

802 Ibid.

803 J. B. Leishman and Stephen Spender, trans., *Duino Elegies*, by Rainer Maria Rilke (New York: W. W. Norton, 1963), 94.

804 Manfred Koch, "Rilke und Hölderlin—Hermeneutik des Leids," *Blätter der Rilke-Gesellschaft*, 22 (1999), 98.

805 Northrop Frye, *The Great Code: The Bible and Literature* (San Diego, New York, London: Harcourt, Inc., 1982), 31.

806 Joseph Campbell, *The Hero With a Thousand Faces* (London: Sphere Books Ltd, 1975), 13.

807 Komar, *Transcending Angels*, 21.

808 AP, 45.

809 RP, 141.

810 Komar, *Transcending Angels*, 200–204; Elaine E. Boney, "Structural Patterns in Rilke's *Duineser Elegien*," *Modern Austrian Literature*, 15, 3 (1982), 71–91.

811 As Hillman indicates, these fundamental concerns may well be regarded not so much as impossible obstacles, or even problems demanding final solutions, as perennial sources of the soul's psychologizing: "The psyche seems more interested in the movement of its ideas than in the resolution of problems.... Psyche's obstinate problems...are the unchanging ground to which psychologizing returns ever again, like Antaios, to draw its strength....the problems we call our own—what it is to be truly human, how to love, why to live, and what is emotion, value, justice, change, body, God, soul, and madness in our lives...bring us to psychologize, to go deeper into caring for soul....the purpose of these eternal psychological problems? To provide the base of soul-making." RP, 148–149.

812 DE, 11.

813 Ibid., 13.

814 Ibid., 11.

815 Ibid., 11, 13.

816 Ibid., 15.

817 Ibid., 17.

818 Ibid., 21.

819 Ibid.

820 Ibid., 23.

821 Ibid., 25.

822 Ibid., 136.

823 Ibid., 137.

824 DE, 27.

825 Ibid.

826 Nor did Rilke write the *Elegies* in the order of the finished sequence. Indeed, the Fifth was the last to be composed.

827 Ibid., 29.
828 Ibid.

Chapter 17

829 DE, 37.
830 AN, 117. It is crucial to recognize at the outset that "*sublimatio* has nothing to do with the Freudian theory of sublimation." (Ibid., 118) Edinger continues to quote Jung on this point: "Sublimatio is part of the royal art where the true gold is made. Of this Freud knows nothing, worse still, he barricades all the paths that could lead to the true sublimatio. This is just about the opposite of what Freud understands by sublimation..." (Ibid.)
831 In the prior chapter, we mentioned the El Greco painting historically called *Assumption of the Virgin* as one of the works that informed Rilke's conception of the angel that presides over his *Elegies*. As Edinger notes, imagery of the Assumption qualifies as a classic *sublimatio* motif. El Greco's *View of Toledo* also includes strong *sublimatio* elements (a mountain, church towers reaching up into impressive heavens), though less classically and unequivocally so. And of course Rilke's angel in and of itself is a consummate image of the sublime.
832 AN, 125.
833 DE, 7.
834 Ibid., 11.
835 Ibid., 25.
836 AN, 117.
837 Ibid., 118.
838 Ibid., 125.
839 Cited in Ibid., 125.
840 DE, 9.
841 See Otto Friedrich Bollnow, "Rilke: The Transformation of the Visible" in Fülleborn and Engel, *Rilke's Duineser Elegien, Band 2* (Frankfurt Am Main: Suhrkamp Taschenbuch, 2010), chapter 15, note 33.
842 Ibid., 122–123.
843 Ibid., 121–122.
844 Shocked horror does enter Rilke's language towards the end of the First Elegy, when the poet speaks of the "ershrockenem Raum" ("shocked or horrified space") that resulted from Linos' death. In line with the rebirth motif, it is that space that the music of Orpheus comes to fill.
845 DE, 5.
846 Ibid., 41.
847 Ibid., 63.
848 Ibid., 55.
849 AN, 123.
850 DE, 59.
851 SW I, 758–9.
852 Ibid., 43. (Seventh Elegy)
853 Kathleen L. Komar, "Rethinking Rilke's *Duineser Elegien* at the End of the Millenium," in Erika and Michael Metzger, eds., *A Companion to the Works of Rainer Maria Rilke* (Rochester, NY: Camden House, 2001), 197–199. See also Komar's *Transcending Angels: Rainer Maria Rilke's Duino Elegies* (Lincoln and London: University of Nebraska Press, 1987).
854 Komar's interpretation, in fact, remains caught in the very classic dualism Rilke—in his *Elegies* and indeed all his work since his *Visions of Christ*—seeks to overcome. Setting heaven off *against*

earth, the transcendent spiritual world of the angel off *against* the physical world of things, Komar understands the early Elegies as striving for wholesale union with the former—indulging a "futile" craving for transcendence which the poet finally repudiates in favor of dedication to earthly existence in the Seventh. This formulation, however, entirely elides (once again!) the *independent reality of the whole soul realm* that ***mediates*** (shades of "Evening" and the *New Poems*) stone and star, the cosmic poles of spirit and matter. It is precisely the soul consciousness that abides in and moves ceaselessly through that intermediary realm that Rilke explores in the *Elegies*. The heart of the poem unfolds in the form of transformations of consciousness within that capacious soul-space which—like Plato's line and Hermes' cosmological strata—encompasses grades or strata of activity extending from physical sensation and mythic imaginations up to subtle movement in and through the realm of ideas and intuitive connections with spiritual beings.

855 DE 40/41 (German/English).

856 I refer to an important passage in the Fourth Elegy wherein a soul form of cyclic, seasonal transformation grounds the human capacity to mediate "the above" (the invisible, superconscious realm of angels) and "the below" (the externalized unconscious realm of mechanically moved puppets):

> Angel and puppet: then at last
> there's a play.
> Then there comes together what
> we always divide
> by our very existence. Then there
> first arises
> from our own inner seasons the
> whole cycle
> of transformation. Then the angel
> plays
> over and above us.

857 DE, 41.

858 Ibid.

859 Elsie Weigand, "Rilke and Eliot: The Articulation of the Mystic Experience," *Germanic Review* 30 (October 1955), 199.

860 Ibid., 200.

861 DE, 43.

862 See chapters 6 and 7.

863 DE, 43. Snow translates *herrlich* as "magic" ("*Life* here is magic"), but this seems too restrained. I would prefer "glorious."

864 Ibid.

865 Ibid.

866 Ibid.

867 Ibid. 45.

868 Ibid.

869 SW II, 93. The cited stanzas are the last of an untitled five-stanza poem. The translation is by Leishman and Spender.

870 Brian P. Copenhaver, trans., *Hermetica* (Cambridge: Cambridge University Press, 1992), 38.

871 Ibid., 41.

872 DE, 45.

873 Ibid.

874 RBH, II, 34.

875 PP, 111.

876 The German *Schicksal* does not distinguish between "destiny" and "fate." Snow chooses the former here, but I would prefer "fate," reserving "destiny" for less

negative, fixed determinations of the soul's horizon of possibility.

877 DE, 45, 47.

878 Ibid., 49, 51.

879 It is hard to agree with Boney that the Eighth Elegy can be grouped with the Sixth, Seventh, and Ninth as essentially *positive* in character.

880 DE, 53.

881 Ibid., 55.

882 Ibid., 53.

883 Ibid.

884 Ibid., 55.

885 Ibid.

886 A version of the tale by Dan Lindholm may be found in *Christmas Roses: Legends for Advent* (Hudson, NY: Anthroposophic Press, 1991), 7.

887 DE, 57.

888 Ibid.

889 Anonymous, *Meditations on the Tarot* (Rockport, MA: Element Inc., 1985).

890 Ibid.

891 SW II, 174.

892 This translation is my own. Snow's (p. 55) is similar, but uses "superabundant" instead of "supernumerary." I wanted the resonances of the more literal translation.

893 AN, 142.

894 DE, 15.

895 Ibid.

896 All citations in this paragraph are from DE 37.

897 The author's own translation.

898 DE, 65.

899 The *circulatio* may be considered to shape not only the poem's imagery but its underlying rhythm as well. Though Rilke's meter permutes the elegiac distich traditionally characteristic of the classical German elegy, that metric nonetheless remains the cycle's rhythmic point of departure. In the mind of one of founding practitioners of the form, the distich itself embodies the *circulatio*. Schiller offered this famous distich on the distich:

> Im Hexameter steigt des
> Springquells silberne Saüle.
> Im Pentameter drauf fällt sie
> melodisch herab.

> In the hexameter rises the
> fountain's silvery column.
> In the pentameter aye falling in
> melody back.
> (translation by Coleridge)

900 AN, 143.

901 Cited in ibid.

902 Cited in ibid., 142.

903 Just as Rilke's angel does find resonance with the Sufi idea of the same, the world view enunciated in the *Elegies* may well be regarded as commensurate with the Sufistic *theophanic* vision elaborated in connection with *The Book of Hours* in chapter 5. In the Ninth Elegy, the poet aspires not *only* to sing the things of the world but to show them to the angel, emissary of the divine. The gesture remains profoundly related to the primordial function of the creative imagination as elucidated earlier: the heart of the gnostic, or word of the poet, serves as the eye of God, enabling the Divine to comprehend the beauty of the creation by virtue of that reflective mirroring. Reciprocally, the Divine's involvement in the creative process remains essential. Throughout the cycle he inspired, Rilke's angel continues to vouch for the reality of the spiritual world, and his initial

distance recedes in the course of the cycle's transformative soul work. The Ninth Elegy imagines the angel's prospective astonishment at the "things" shown to him by the poet, while the triumphant climax trumpeted at the beginning of the Tenth remains contingent upon angelic assent and, implicitly, participation.

904 In the last decade or two, esotericism has emerged as a major field of academic endeavor, an exploration of a "third current" of western culture identified with neither institutionalized religion (though historically suppressed by it) nor mainstream science. In one essay, Antoine Faivre—a pioneering authority of the field—identified "the four fundamental elements by which a work, an author, or a current qualify as pertaining to what I propose to call 'esotericism.'" Those four elements are ***(1) The idea of correspondence*** ("the ancient idea of the microcosm and the macrocosm"); ***(2) Living Nature*** ("*Magia*... refers to the knowledge of the network of sympathies...that weave together Nature and Man"); ***(3) Imaginations and mediations*** ("Imagination is considered here as an organ of the soul, permitting access to different levels of reality"); ***(4) The experience of transmutation*** ("the belief that people, and...parts of nature...may undergo a modification of their very being"). All of these elements are fundamental to the vision informing the *Duino Elegies* and indeed Rilke's entire opus, which (despite Rilke's own marginal knowledge of esoteric currents) may thus be considered a major and original work within the esoteric tradition. See Faivre's essay "Renaissance Hermeticism and Western Esotericism" in van den Broek and Hanegraff, *Gnosis and Hermeticism: From Antiquity to Modern Times* (Albany: State University of New York Press, 1998). Arthur Versluis' *Magic and Mysticism* and Jocelyn Godwin's *The Golden Thread* offer two accessible introductions to the field. Another significant contribution—Christopher Bamford's *The Endless Trace: The Passionate Pursuit of Wisdom in the West* (New Paltz, NY: Codhill Press, 2003)—fittingly takes its title from Rilke himself.

905 AN, 144.

906 For variation and emphasis, I have cited Leishman and Spender's (New York: Norton, 1939/67; p. 73) translation here.

907 Virgil, *The Aeneid*, translated by Robert Fitzgerald (New York: Random House, 1981, 12.

908 Ibid. (Leishman and Spender)

909 DE, 65.

910 Northrop Frye, *The Great Code* (San Diego: Harcourt, Inc., 1982), 216.

911 Cited in LP, 537. A letter Tsvetaeva wrote to Rilke later that year is yet more unequivocal: "You are not the poet I love most. 'Most' already implies comparison. You are poetry itself." Cited in Robert Hass, *Twentieth Century Pleasures* (Hopewell, NJ: Ecco Press, 1984), 230.

912 Frye, *The Great Code*, 220.

913 Ibid.

914 Ibid.

915 Ibid., 6.
916 Ibid., 7, 8.
917 Ibid., 13.
918 Kathleen Komar, *Transcending Angels: Rainer Maria Rilke's Duino Elegies* (Lincoln and London: University of Nebraska Press, 1987), 203.
919 Ibid.
920 Frye, *The Great Code*, 23.
921 Komar, *Transcending Angels*, 204.
922 Frye, *The Great Code*, 27.
923 Hass, *Twentieth Century Pleasures*, 230.
924 Frye, *The Great Code*, 28–29.
925 The preceding string of citations from the *Elegies* are all from Leishman and Spender's translation.
926 Frye, *The Great Code*, 29.
927 Ibid., 212.
928 DE, 25.
929 Frye, *The Great Code*, 213, 216.
930 Ibid., 214.
931 Hass, *Pleasures*, 231.
932 LP, 537. See also *Rainer Maria Rilke–Marina Zvetajewa–Boris Pasternak: Briefwechsel* (Frankfurt: Insel, 1983)
933 Frye, *The Great Code*, 29.

Chapter 18

934 GN, 284.
935 Ibid., 372.
936 E. M. Butler, *Rainer Maria Rilke* (New York: MacMillan, 1941), 340.
937 Edward Snow, trans., *Sonnets to Orpheus*, by Rainer Maria Rilke (New York: North Point Press/Farrar, Straus and Giroux, 2004), xii.
938 Author's own translations. All the translations of the *Sonnets to Orpheus* in this and the following chapters are the author's own. The original German for the text may be found in SW I, 731–771. As the numbering of the sonnets makes finding them a simple matter, I dispense with further footnoting of them.
939 Though one cannot hear this quite so well in English as in German, the opening of the *Elegies* is densely consonantal, featuring "v" and "ng," sounds, while the corresponding sonnet, with its multiple apostrophes, sings more freely in the realm of vowel sounds. This distinction in phonic texture remains in force through these two cycles of poems.
940 GN, 376.
941 To Witold von Huleciwz, 13 November 1925, in GN, 376.
942 The image is reproduced at the beginning of Part IV of this book.
943 Cf. Sigmund Freud, *Moses and Monotheism* (New York: Vintage, 1939).
944 WSR, 68.
945 Ibid., 73–74.
946 RP, 168.
947 Ibid.
948 Ibid., 169.
949 A new authoritative edition of Hölderlin's works, edited by Rilke's young friend Norbert von Hellingrath, was published in 1914. Rilke (who heard Hellingrath lecture on Hölderlin) steeped himself in it. Tragically, Norbert von Hellingrath was killed in the war in 1916.
950 Hillman, "Orpheus," in *Mythic Figures* (Uniform Edition of

the Writings of James Hillman, Volume 6.1) (Putnam, CT: Spring Publications, 2007), 296.

951 Cf. Part I of this book, especially chapters 2 and 4.

952 Butler, *Rainer Maria Rilke*, 345.

953 RP, 173.

954 Ibid.

955 Ibid., 172.

956 Ibid., 173.

957 Ibid., 174.

958 II, 13.

959 Ibid., 181.

960 Joseph Henderson and Dyane Sherwood, *Transformation of the Psyche* (Hove and New York: Brunner-Rutledge, 2003), 67. (Italics mine.)

961 Ibid., 71.

962 Ibid.

963 RP, 189.

964 Ibid., 193.

965 Ibid., 194.

966 Ibid.

967 Ibid., 194–195.

968 Ibid., 195.

969 Ibid.

970 Ibid.

971 Ibid., 195–196.

972 Ibid., 196.

973 Ibid., 196–197.

974 For contemporary discussions illuminating Rilke's enduring involvement with the Renaissance see Curdin Ebneter, ed., *Rilke: Les jours d'Italie / Die italienische Tage* (Sierre: Fondation Rainer Maria Rilke, 2009).

975 Rilke to Gräfin Aline Dietrichstein, 12 September 1916, in *Rainer Maria Rilke: Briefe aus den Jahren 1914 bis 1926* (Leipzig: Insel Verlag, 1937), 109.

976 To Katharina Kippenberg, 23 February 1924, cited in LP, 482.

977 For a fuller discussion of Rilke's relation to Petrarch see Erich Unglaub, "Wallfahrten zum Mont Ventoux und zu Petrarch's Grab," in Ebneter, *Rilke: Les jours d'Italie / Die italienische Tage*, 245–268. Notes 980 and 988 below introduce some of Unglaub's chief evidence and insights.

978 Victor Develay, trans., *Petrarque: L'Ascension du Mont Ventoux* (Paris: Develay, 1880). According to Unglaub, this obscure work remained unidentified for many years. See Unglaub for more particulars on its publication history.

979 GN, 25.

980 Not only did Rilke make a stab at translating Petrarch; inspired by Petrarch's engagement with Augustine, Rilke tried his hand at translating Augustine as well, though his inferior Latin impeded the effort. Nor did these attempts at translation exhaust Rilke's involvement with Petrarch and his work. In fall 1912, Rilke made a pilgrimage to Petrarch's grave in the company of Marie Taxis, and thereafter the two (the Princess's Italian was better than Rilke's) often read Petrarch's *Canzoniere* together. Indeed, in 1919, Rilke published translations of two Petrarch sonnets. Still, perhaps the substantive significance of Rilke's longstanding engagement with Petrarch is best documented in the passage from Rilke's 1912 essay "On the Young Poet" (see note 988 below). For all these details, see Unglaub, "Pilgrimage to Mont Ventoux," in Ebneter, *Rilke: Les jours d'Italie / Die italienische Tage*.

981 Cited in Ingebor Schnack, *Rilke Chronik* (Frankfurt am Main: Insel Verlag, 1996), 774. Translation from the French by the author and by Dan Bellm.

982 Ibid., 780.

983 Cited in Richard Tarnas, *Cosmos and Psyche* (New York: Viking, 2006), 496.

984 Ibid.

985 Ibid., 495.

986 Augustine, *Confessions*, trans. R. S. Pine-Coffin (New York: Penguin Books, 1961), X, 8; p. 216.

987 Tarnas, *Cosmos and Psyche*, 53.

988 Sonnet I, 1. I encountered Erich Unglaub's illuminating essay "Wallfahrten zum Mont Ventoux und zu Petrarca's Grab" ("Pilgrimage to Mount Ventoux and Petrarch's Grave") too late absorb its full insight into my main text, but Unglaub's evidence and argument do nothing to contradict and much to bolster my own. Most interesting, perhaps, is Unglaub's discussion of the Petrarch-related passage that appears in Rilke's essay "Über den jungen Dichter" ("On the Young Poet"). The relevant Rilke passage reads:

> The poet, with increasing insight into his limitlesss tasks, will undoubtedly attach himself to what is greatest.... But if it lay before him, openly revealed, in its assured, disregardful glory,—would he not then, like Petrarch, be compelled, at the sight of the countless vistas seen from the mountain he had climbed, to flee back to the ravines of his own soul, which are of inexpressibly greater concern to him, although he will never explore their depths, than that foreign region which might, at need, be explored?
>
> Alarmed within by the distant thunder of the god, bewildered from without by an irresistable excess of appearances, the object of such violent treatment has only just room to stand on the narrow space between two worlds, until suddenly a neutral little event inundates his monstrous condition with innocence. This is the moment which places the great poem in the scales, in the one tray of which there rests his heart, overburdened with infinite responsibilities ["sein meteorisches Herz"], the great poem producing the sublimely tranquillized balance. (WSR, 61)

Unglaub's analysis interprets the passage in a manner roughly commensurate with the chief conclusions of my own treatment of Rilke and Petrarch:

> Petrarch's situation on Mount Ventoux is reproduced from Rilke's own point of view... Rilke's new reading of the Ventoux letter concerns itself exclusively with a poetological theme, not a religious one.... The "conversion" initiated by recourse to Augustine's book leads away from Christian "conversion" toward a Rilkean "turning" ["Wendung"], that is, toward

> a poetic and artistic task. Rilke connects this important secularizing move that transforms the role of art from that of a servant to religion to an ultimate end qua life-mission ("Art as the Task of Life") with the Ventoux letter. (Unglaub, 252–255)

Relatedly, though still more compellingly, Unglaub's discussion foregrounds the importance of Petrarch's letter to the conception of *not only the* Sonnets, *but the* Elegies *as well*. Unglaub dates the "Young Poet" essay from February 1912; Rilke's *Collected Works* gives the probable date of its composition as summer of the 1913. In either case, the time period coincides with that of that of the inception of the *Elegies*. The passage itself resonantly echoes certain lines in the *Elegies* as well as the conclusion of "Spanish Trilogy I" (cf. the "weighing" motif at the prose passage's end, with its reference—lost in translation—to a "meteoric heart."). Even as the angel and the landscape of Toledo were inspiring Rilke's *Elegies*, Petrarch's Ventoux letter, too, provided intellectual historical backdrop and foil for the poet's conception of his great task. In the imaginative geography of Rilke's soul history, a direct line (previously unrecognized by this author) connects the topoi of Duino and Toledo (as well as Muzot) with Ventoux. (Unglaub, "Wallfahrten zum Mont Ventoux," in Ebneter, *Rilke: Les jours d'Italie / Die italienische Tage*).

989 RP, 222.
990 Ibid., 223.
991 I, 7.
992 Ibid., 225.

CHAPTER 19

993 RP, 200.
994 Ibid., 201.
995 Noel Cobb, *Archetypal Imagination* (Hudson, NY: Lindisfarne Press, 1992), 245.
996 Cited in Ibid., 245.
997 Arnoldo della Torre, *Storia dell' Accademia Platonica* (Firenze: Tip. G. Carnescchi, 1902), 791. Quoted from Campano, *Epistolario*, ed. Mencken (Leipzig, 1707).
998 Ibid., 236.
999 W. K. C. Guthrie, *Orpheus and Greek Religion* (Princeton: Princeton University Press, 1952), 30.
1000 RP, 206.
1001 Ibid., 207.
1002 Ibid.
1003 DU, 119–121.
1004 James Hillman, *Animal Presences*, vol. 6 of The Uniform Edition of the Writings of James Hillman (Putnam, CT: Spring Publications, 2008).
1005 Cobb, *Archetypal Imagination*, 237.
1006 Cited in CI, 179.
1007 Ibid.
1008 CI, 4.
1009 Ibid.
1010 RP, 216.
1011 Ibid., 217.
1012 Ibid., 210.
1013 Ibid., 213.
1014 Ibid., 208.
1015 *Phaedrus* 273e, cited in RP, 216.

1016 Cobb, *Archetypal Imagination*, 241.

1017 Phanes is a god of light, of showing forth. "Theo-phany" accordingly indicates a showing forth or revelation of the divine.

1018 William Sharp, ed., *Sonnets of This Century* (New York and London: White and Allen, 1887); beginning of Sharp's introduction, "The Sonnet: Its Characteristics and History."

1019 Indeed, the sonnet plays an important role in the establishment of poetic literature *not* integrally dependent upon oral and musical tradition.

1020 From C. F. Johnson, *Forms of English Poetry* (New York: American Books Co., 1904). (Italics mine.)

1021 Ibid.

1022 Ibid.

1023 That is, the first and last sonnets of both parts center upon Orpheus (Part I) or the speaker's own masculine voice (Part II), while the second and penultimate sonnets of each part focus upon feminine counterparts evocative of Eurydice or Vera. In each case, the adjacent sonnets are indeed effectively pairs.

1024 David Young, trans., *Sonnets to Orpheus*, by Rainer Maria Rilke (Hanover: Wesleyan University Press, 1987), x.

1025 RP, 211.

1026 Ibid., 203.

1027 Young, *Sonnets*, viii.

1028 Ibid.

1029 SW I, 509.

1030 Edward Snow, trans., *Sonnets to Orpheus*, by Rainer Maria Rilke (New York: North Point Press, 2004), xii.

1031 Paul Valéry, "Dance and the Soul," in *Selected Writings of Paul Valéry* (New York: New Directions, 1950), 189.

Chapter 20

1032 AP, 46.

1033 Ibid., 47.

1034 Ibid., 52.

1035 Ibid., 111.

1036 DE, 45.

1037 Snow's phrase "as if it were alive there" seems to me poorly chosen in the above Rilke passage. The German, "wie seiend," makes no reference to organic life, and could be better translated "as if truly existent (or existing)." This is more commensurate with the architectural character of Rilke's description and, as well, the symbolic tower we are discussing.

1038 DE, 45.

1039 Ibid., 110.

1040 Nor is it out of place to recall the *Elegies'* place of inception, *towering* Duino Castle, even today a symbol of cultural accomplishment.

1041 I, 21.

1042 MA, 103.

1043 Ibid., 104.

1044 AP, 113.

1045 DE, 7.

1046 In fact, the use of the term "anthropos" in this context is unhappy, as the term may be considered no more (and no less) gender neutral than "man." Perhaps it would be better to speak (as does Richard Tarnas) of "Psyche and Cosmos," just as Rudolf Steiner's "anthroposophy" ("wisdom of man or the human being") has recently spawned a kindred stream called "psychosophy"—"wisdom of the soul." As my further remarks in the text indicate, the Hillmanian distinction between "man" and "soul" is still working itself out in history.

1047 Rilke to Franz Kappus, 14 May 1904, in *Letters to Young Poet*, trans. Stephen Mitchell (New York: Vintage, 1986), 76.

1048 Cobb, *Imagination*, 253.

1049 Ibid.

1050 Ibid., 259–260.

1051 DE, 57.

1052 Ibid., 254.

1053 Russell Hoban, *The Medusa Frequency* (London: Jonathan Cape, 1987), 119.

APPENDIX

1054 Charles Wright, "Improvisations on Form and Measure" in *Halflife: Improvisations and Interviews* (Ann Arbor: University of Michigan Press, 1988), 5.

1055 Charles Wright, "Noon" in *China Trace* (Hanover: Wesleyan University Press, 1977), 53.

1056 Edward Hirsch, "The Visionary Poetics of Philip Levine and Charles Wright" in Jay Parini, ed., *The Columbia History of American Poetry* (New York: Columbia University Press, 1993), 795.

1057 *Sonnets to Orpheus*, II, 27.

1058 Charles Wright, *Negative Blue: Selected Later Poems* (New York: Farrar, Straus and Giroux, 2000), 136.

1059 Although I think it fair to say that "Indian Summer II" manifests tendencies latent in much of Wright's work, I do not intend my reading of this one poem to stand as a summary judgment of his work as a whole. Wright is one of the most original, accomplished, and spiritually compelling of contemporary American poets, and the astonishing fertililty of his imagination perpetually cuts against the grain of the metaphysical proclivities I focus upon in this poem. I would claim, though, that Wright's readers do feel the heat of this very friction almost constantly. Wright lives up to the mantra cited as the first sentence of this appendix to a remarkable degree.

1060 See the discussion in the introduction to this book.

1061 Robert Hass, *The Apple Trees at Olema* (New York: Ecco Press, 2010), 79.

1062 Cf. "Looking for Rilke" in Robert Hass, *Twentieth Century Pleasures* (Hopewell, NJ: Ecco Press, 1984).

1063 Rainer Maria Rilke, "The Young Workman's Letter" in WSR, 68.

1064 Ibid. 70.

1065 RP, xvi.

SOURCES AND PERMISSIONS

Excerpts from the ***Metamorphoses or Golden Ass of Apuleius of Madura,*** translated by H. E. Butler (1910); by permission of Oxford University Press.

From ***Rilke's Book of Hours: Love Poems to God*** by Rainer Maria Rilke, translated by Anita Barrows and Joanna Macy, copyright © 1996 by Anita Barrows and Joanna Macy; used by permission of Riverhead Books, an imprint of Penguin Group (USA), Inc.

From ***Visions of Christ,*** by Rainer Maria Rilke, edited by Siegfried Mandel and translated by Aaron Kramer; copyright © 1967 by University of Colorado Press; used by permission of Laura Kramer. Further information about the work of Aaron Kramer is available at www.aaronkramer.com.

From Henry Corbin, ***Creative Imagination in the Sufism of Ibn Arabi,*** copyright © 1969 Princeton University Press, 1997, renewed PUP; reprinted by permission of Princeton University Press.

Excerpts from ***The Poetry of Rilke: Bilingual Edition,*** translated by Edward Snow; translation copyright © 2009 by Edward Snow; reprinted by permission of North Point Press, a division of Farrar, Straus and Giroux.

Excerpts from ***Duino Elegies*** by Rainer Maria Rilke, translated by Edward Snow; translation copyright © 2000 by Edward Snow; reprinted by permission of North Point Press, a division of Farrar, Straus, and Giroux.

From ***Where Silence Reigns: Selected Prose*** by Rainer Maria Rilke, translated by G. Craig Houston; copyright © 1978 by New Directions Publishing; reprinted by permission of New Directions Publishing.

From ***Letters of Rainer Maria Rilke: 1910–1926,*** by Jane Bannard Greene and M. D. Herter Norton; copyright 1947, 1948 by W. W. Norton & Company, renewed © 1975 by M. D. Herter Norton; used by permission of W. W. Norton & Company.

From ***Diaries of a Young Poet,*** by Rainer Maria Rilke, edited by Ruth Sieber-Rilke and Carl Sieber, translated by Edward Snow and Michael Winkler; copyright © 1942 by Insel Verlag 1997 by Edward Snow and Michael Winkler; used by permission of W. W. Norton & Company.

From ***The Notebooks of Malte Laurids Brigge*** by Rainer Maria Rilke, translated by M. D. Herter Norton; copyright © 1949 by W. W. Norton & Company, renewed © 1977 by M. D. Herter Norton Crena de Iongh; used by permission of W. W. Norton & Company, Inc.

Excerpts from ***The Great Code,*** copyright © 1982, 1981 by Northrop Frye; reprinted by permission of Houghton Mifflin Publishing Company.

"Indian Summer II" from ***Negative Blue: Selected Later Poems,*** by Charles Wright; copyright © 2000 by Charles Wright; reprinted by permission of Farrar, Straus and Giroux, LLC.

"Meditation at Lagunitas" from ***Praise,*** by Robert Hass, copyright © 1979 by Robert Hass; reprinted by permission of HarperCollins Publishers.

ILLUSTRATION CREDITS

Schweizerische Nationalbibliothek: cover, 481 top

Ludwig von Hofmann Nachlaß: 1, 305

Fondation Rilke: 8, 330–32, 615

Deutsches Literaturarchive: 60, 63, 97, 480, 481 bottom, 586 bottom

Barkenhoff-Stiftung/Heinrich Vogeler Museum: 186, 188, 192, 196–98, 221, 251, 279

Art Resource, New York in conjunction with:

Tretyakov Gallery, Moscow: 137

Adoc-photos: 330

Uffizi Gallery, Florence, Italy: 442

Metropolitan Museum of Art, New York: 466

Los Angeles County Museum of Art: 306

Galleria Sabauda, Turin, Italy: 584

Duomo, Florence, Italy: 625

Daniel Joseph Polikoff: 324, 408, 586 top, 681

The following images are used with permission of the Artists Rights Society [(c) 2011 Artists Rights Society (ARS), New York / VG Bild-Kunst, Bonn]:

Ludwig von Hofmann, *Parzival II* and *Kissing Pair* (1, 305)

Heinrich Vogeler, *Singing Women; Death and Age; On the Edge of the Moor* (186, 188, 221)

INDEX OF RILKE'S WORKS

Numbers in bold face indicate citations from the work. Titles in bold face indicate poems given in their entirety. Italicized numbers indicate discussions in the endnotes.

INDEX OF NAMES

ABOUT THE AUTHOR

Poet, translator, and independent scholar Daniel Joseph Polikoff received his Ph.D. in Comparative Literature from Cornell University and his Diploma in Waldorf Education from Rudolf Steiner College. In addition to work in numerous literary journals and anthologies, he has published two books of poetry (*Dragon Ship* and *The Hands of Stars*), as well as *Parzival/Gawain: Two Plays,* his edited translation of a dramatic version of the Grail legend.

Dr. Polikoff has taught literature in Waldorf schools and shared his passion for Rilke in a wide variety of venues, including the Festival of Archetypal Psychology at Notre Dame (where the idea for *In the Image of Orpheus* was born), the San Francisco Jung Society, and seminars in literary circles. He resides with his wife Monika and two children in the San Francisco Bay area.

www.ingramcontent.com/pod-product-compliance
Lightning Source LLC
LaVergne TN
LVHW051051220926
848485LV00001BA/70
* 9 7 8 1 6 3 0 5 1 0 6 2 6 *